Social Work
Research Methods

Sara Miller McCune founded SAGE Publishing in 1965 to support the dissemination of usable knowledge and educate a global community. SAGE publishes more than 1000 journals and over 800 new books each year, spanning a wide range of subject areas. Our growing selection of library products includes archives, data, case studies and video. SAGE remains majority owned by our founder and after her lifetime will become owned by a charitable trust that secures the company's continued independence.

Los Angeles | London | New Delhi | Singapore | Washington DC | Melbourne

Social Work Research Methods

Learning by Doing

Reginald O. York
University of North Carolina, Wilmington

Los Angeles | London | New Delhi
Singapore | Washington DC | Melbourne

FOR INFORMATION:

SAGE Publications, Inc.
2455 Teller Road
Thousand Oaks, California 91320
E-mail: order@sagepub.com

SAGE Publications Ltd.
1 Oliver's Yard
55 City Road
London, EC1Y 1SP
United Kingdom

SAGE Publications India Pvt. Ltd.
B 1/I 1 Mohan Cooperative Industrial Area
Mathura Road, New Delhi 110 044
India

SAGE Publications Asia-Pacific Pte. Ltd.
18 Cross Street #10-10/11/12
China Square Central
Singapore 048423

Printed in the United States of America

Library of Congress Cataloging-in-Publication Data

Names: York, Reginald O.

Title: Social work research methods : learning by doing / Reginald O. York, University of North Carolina, Wilmington.

Description: Los Angeles : SAGE, [2020] | Includes bibliographical references and index.

Identifiers: LCCN 2018043453 | ISBN 9781506387192 (pbk. : alk. paper)

Subjects: LCSH: Social service—Research—Methodology.

Classification: LCC HV11 .Y574 2020 | DDC 361.3072/1—dc23 LC record available at https://lccn.loc.gov/2018043453

Acquisitions Editor: Joshua Perigo
Editorial Assistant: Sarah Dillard
Content Development
Editor: Alissa Nance
Production Editor: Myleen Medina
Copy Editor: QuADS Prepress Pvt. Ltd.
Typesetter: Hurix Digital
Proofreader: Rae-Ann Goodwin
Indexer: Teddy Diggs
Cover Designer: Janet Kiesel
Marketing Manager: Jenna Retana

This book is printed on acid-free paper.

SUSTAINABLE FORESTRY INITIATIVE

Certified Chain of Custody
At Least 10% Certified Forest Content
www.sfiprogram.org
SFI-01028

19 20 21 22 23 10 9 8 7 6 5 4 3 2 1

BRIEF CONTENTS

DETAILED CONTENTS

Chapter 3 • Ethics and Cultural Competence in Social Work Research

Chapter 9 • Conducting Qualitative Research That Explores the Unknown   227

PART 3 • CONDUCTING EACH PHASE OF SOCIAL WORK RESEARCH 289

DESCRIPTION OF CHAPTERS

PART 1: THE FUNDAMENTALS OF SCIENCE AND SOCIAL WORK RESEARCH

The purpose of this part is for the reader to acquire an appreciation of science as a way of knowing and as a guide to practice. It will illustrate how the scientific process works when the focus is social work practice and research. The theme of learning by doing influences the use of examples and the engagement of readers in step-by-step exercises, some of which entails the process of collecting and analyzing data in the pursuit of a research question.

Chapter 1: Science, Research, and Social Work Practice

This chapter reviews the nature of science and how it differs from other ways of investigating our world, especially pseudoscience. Also reviewed are the connections of science with logic and critical thinking, the nature of evidence-based practice, and the process of investigation that leads the scientist to conclusions. This presentation highlights how science contributes to social work practice. A major part of this chapter shows how science is connected to various common-sense sayings, which are illustrated through the examination of the question of whether people are affected by the full moon. Readers begin their journey of learning by doing through an exercise in which they ask others to answer the question about the full moon. At the completion of this chapter, the readers have a better sense of the nature, and process, of science and how it differs from other ways of knowing.

Chapter 2: Purposes and Processes of Social Work Research

This chapter provides an overview of how social work research can be characterized and described, so the researcher will know where he or she is when engaged in various research endeavors. Research is characterized with regard to scope, general approach to measurement, and the purpose of the study. It is further described with regard to four processes you go through when you are conducting a research study. On completion of this chapter, the reader will know how to characterize research in these ways and identify key issues to address in each category. Readers continue their journey of learning by doing through exercises where they conceive of studies that might be undertaken with regard to both specific interventions and broad social work programs.

Chapter 3: Ethics and Cultural Competence in Social Work Research

This chapter focuses both on ethics in the use of human subjects in research and on cultural competence in research. The reader will learn about the major issues in the ethical use of human subjects in research, such as privacy, harm, coercion, and justice. In later chapters, the reader will be asked to collect data for research studies. Information from this chapter will be essential in the assurance of ethical practice in research. The nature of cultural competence is discussed with regard to social work research methods. The importance of cultural competence is discussed with regard to each of the major phases of the research process. For example, the determination of the purpose of the research study should include reference to the implications of this endeavor to cultural issues. Measurement should attend to the possibility that different cultural groups may be more likely to volunteer to participate under certain circumstances. Also, the cultural meanings of concepts included in measurement tools should be addressed. Finally, sampling should consider ways to ensure appropriate representation of different cultural groups.

Chapter 4: Evidence-Based Practice

This chapter provides an overview of evidence-based practice and examines how the evidence-based practitioner goes from one step to another. Also included is a review of issues and criticisms of this perspective. Students will engage in an exercise that applies evidence-based practice to a practice of interest to themselves.

PART 2: CONDUCTING DIFFERENT TYPES OF SOCIAL WORK RESEARCH

The purpose of this part is to understand the different types of social work research and to gain greater motivation to engage in it. The theme of learning by doing is furthered by the use of research exercises that illustrate how social work research works. Some of these studies call on the reader to analyze their own data. This part starts with a discussion of the social survey, the main vehicle used to collect data for social work research.

Chapter 5: Conducting Research That Employs Social Surveys

In this chapter, the reader reviews the basic form for the collection of data for social work research—the social survey. Several forms of the social survey are examined (questionnaires, interviews, online, etc.) with specific tips for best use. A major emphasis is a set of guidelines for developing the instrument for the survey when the evaluation of practice is the purpose of the study.

Chapter 6: Conducting Research That Describes People

The nature and phases of descriptive research are the key themes of this chapter, which begins with a summary of how descriptive, explanatory, evaluative, and exploratory research are similar and different. Qualitative and quantitative description are distinguished, and the reader sees how the quantitative study illustrates how to describe people through statistics such as the mean, median, mode, and standard deviation. The level of measurement of the variable is presented as a necessity for selecting the proper descriptive statistic. The learning-by-doing exercise in this chapter calls on readers to undertake a descriptive study of the traits of the good work manager. They collect and analyze data on this theme to see (a) what traits are most valued and (b) whether the study subjects exhibit a sex-role stereotype about what it takes to be a good work manager. They employ statistical tests in the examination of the data using Internet sites. Thus, in this chapter the reader implements the research process in brief form, from A to Z, with help on the nature of the issue and the measurement tools to be employed.

Chapter 7: Conducting Research That Explains Things

The reader reviews how explanatory research examines the relationship between variables, which requires the use of inferential statistics. The development of the knowledge base that justifies the study hypothesis is one theme, and the role of theory is a part of this examination. The reader is taken through the four phases of research regarding a study of the relationships between stressors, stress, and social support (as a stress buffer). Critical concepts such as the study hypothesis and the dependent and independent variables are examined. The Pearson correlation coefficient is the statistic employed in the examination of the empirical relationships between these variables. The reader is taken through the entire research process, including the collection and analysis of their own data, using the Internet. The goal of this chapter is for the reader to acquire an understanding of critical concepts in explanatory research and inferential statistics for testing the hypothesis.

Chapter 8: Conducting Research That Evaluates Services

Because the evaluation of practice could be argued as being the most important use of research methods for the social worker, the evaluative research study is given a lot of emphasis in this text. The key themes include the analysis of the behavior being treated, the comprehensive description of the intervention being used, and the research design employed. A review of the system of evaluation (input, process, output, and outcome) provides a framework for understanding the various things that may be evaluated in human services, and places outcome evaluation, the key theme of this chapter, into perspective. The reader is taken through the steps in evaluative research with regard to an example of the treatment of depression in a mental health facility. A set of practice exercises are given, one for each phase of the evaluation process.

Chapter 9: Conducting Qualitative Research That Explores the Unknown

In this chapter, the reader examines exploratory research that is appropriate for a subject where little is known. Qualitative and quantitative research are compared. The flexibility of qualitative research is presented as having a natural connection with exploratory studies, but not an exclusive one, given the various forms of qualitative research. The goal of this chapter is for the reader to gain an understanding of the nature of qualitative research as well as an understanding of key concepts and methods in studies of this type. Information from this chapter will be used in a later chapter where the reader engages in the analysis of a set of qualitative data.

Chapter 10: Conducting Program Evaluations

The evaluation of an entire program (e.g., the Child Welfare Program of Hampton County) is the focus of this chapter. The program evaluation is contrasted with the more specific evaluation of an intervention (e.g., the evaluation of this support group service for these victims of violence), the latter being the focus of much of this book. The systems concepts of input, process, output, and outcome serve as the guides for this presentation. Readers learn about the examination of client need, the review of service quality, the calculation of service outputs, and the examination of client outcome.

PART 3: CONDUCTING EACH PHASE OF SOCIAL WORK RESEARCH

The purpose of this part is to acquaint readers with knowledge about the phases of social work research and skills in the development of each. Readers will gain an enhanced appreciation of research by engaging in the design of their own study with one component included in each of the chapters in this section. Emphasis will be given to evaluative research.

Chapter 11: Developing Your Knowledge Base and Your Intervention

This chapter reviews how knowledge serves as a guide for research methods, and how to describe the intervention in evaluative research in a comprehensive manner. Among the concepts reviewed for the knowledge base are theory, observation, conceptual clarity, documentation, and organization. Tips for presenting the literature review are examined. Readers are given an exercise on the development of the knowledge base for a study they will conduct using the knowledge addressed in this section of the book. The readers learn how to describe the intervention in evaluative research with regard to objectives, structure, model, and personnel. Also examined are the themes of evidence for the intervention and treatment fidelity, the extent that the planned intervention was actually carried out in the study. Readers engage in exercises with regard to both the development of a knowledge base and the description of their own interventions.

Chapter 12: Drawing Your Study Sample

Drawing a study sample from a study population addresses the issue of the generalization of study results. In this chapter, the reader views this theme with regard to various methods of drawing a study sample (e.g., random sample, convenience sample, purposive sample) with special emphasis on generalization from a random sample or one that is not random. A unique idea in this book is the theme of logical generalization when you do not have a random sample. Logical generalization has a special place in social work research because social work students and practitioners normally do not have the opportunity to draw a random sample when engaged in the evaluation of practice. But they want to engage in generalization even if it is logical rather than based on scientific knowledge of sampling distributions.

Chapter 13: Measuring Your Study Variables

Perhaps the first task in measurement is to determine the suitability of measuring variables in a quantitative or qualitative manner. After a review of this question, the reader will be taken through a series of tasks related to quantitative measurement. The reader examines concepts such as measurement error, reliability, and validity and examines tools for addressing these issues such as the alpha coefficient. Also discussed are tips for finding a measurement tool and tips for developing your own measure. A concept given more emphasis in this book than others is that of practical significance. The reader sees how a study result can be of statistical significance without being of practical significance. Perhaps the conclusion in this situation would be that the trivial gain for the clients in this study is not explained by chance, but it is only trivial, so we did not achieve what we expected.

Chapter 14: Selecting a Research Design for a Group Evaluation Study

This chapter focuses on the choice of a research design when you are working with a group of clients who are receiving a common intervention and are being measured by a common instrument. The choice of a research design begins with a review of those things most likely to explain client growth independent of treatment. Readers are encouraged to realistically think of such explanations (i.e., threats to internal validity) that should be of special concern and to select an appropriate research design that controls for this influence. The reader reviews the group research designs (e.g., one-group pretest–posttest design, comparison group design) that are most likely to be employed by frontline socials workers in the evaluation of practice. These group research designs are presented according to the threats to internal validity that are addressed by the design.

Chapter 15: Selecting a Research Design for a Single Client

The choice of a research design for the evaluation of service for a single client is the focus of this chapter, which builds on the knowledge about the function of the design presented in the previous chapter. The reader examines the single-subject designs most likely to be employed by frontline social workers in the evaluation of practice, organized according to the threats to internal validity that are addressed by the design. A unique design described here is the limited AB design, where the researcher is only able to measure the client once before treatment begins, and then several times during the treatment period. This design is feasible for most social workers, whereas the traditional AB single design is not.

Chapter 16: Analyzing Data and Drawing Conclusions

In this chapter, the reader examines the basic concepts with regard to the analysis of descriptive data, explanatory data, and evaluative data. Various descriptive statistics are described with regard to data, such as the frequency, the mean, the median, and so forth. Inferential statistics are examined with regard to the testing of the hypothesis in research, including the one-sample t test, the paired t test, the independent t test, the chi-square test, and the binomial test. An example is given of data analysis using an Internet website.

Chapter 17: Analyzing Qualitative Data

This chapter provides an opportunity for the reader to engage in the analysis of qualitative data gathered from a survey. One protocol for content analysis of qualitative data is employed in this data analysis exercise, so the reader can get an experience in the analysis of qualitative data using only one of many forms that could be used to do so. The protocol includes reference to levels of coding, bracketing, enumeration, saturation, and credibility assessment.

PREFACE

This book is designed to help students of the human service professions to gain the ability to use research to inform practice and to conduct their own research, with an emphasis on the evaluation of practice. It is written for the beginning and intermediate students in social work research. It begins with no assumption of knowledge of research methods and takes the readers beyond the basic level of understanding to a level of competence in the execution of the various tasks of the research study.

When students complete this book, they will know how to inform their practice by reviewing the research of others. They will know, for example, how to determine the extent to which a social work intervention has been shown to be effective in the treatment of a given target behavior.

On completion of this book, readers will also know how to evaluate their own practice. There are a number of research questions that are relevant to this endeavor. For example, was their support group intervention effective in the improvement of the self-esteem of the at-risk youth in the group? Was their cognitive–behavioral therapy effective in the reduction of the depression for a group of adults they served? Did their homeless clients find a home faster than the homeless people in their shelter who did not have the special strengths-based case management services that they implemented?

LEARNING BY DOING

The key distinction of this text is the theme of learning by doing, which refers to putting knowledge into practice. My decades of teaching social work research at more than one university has taught me to agree with Confucius. He said that what you are told, you will forget; what you are shown, you will remember; but what you do, you will understand.

There are several features of this book that execute this major theme. For example, each chapter begins with a vignette that illustrates the basic content of the chapter. The vignette explains how one social worker made use of the knowledge that is addressed in the chapter.

Another feature is that priority is given to themes of practical use, such as the steps in the use of systematic reviews of evidence, where to find published tools for measuring client progress, and how to use the Internet for the analysis of data. In many of these instances, students are guided through a step-by-step process that makes the task very clear.

The most important mechanism for executing the learning-by-doing theme, however, is that each chapter has a practice exercise that calls on the reader to apply the knowledge gained from the chapter. One of these exercises asks the reader to conduct a study of the relationship between stress, social support, and life satisfaction using data from members of the research class. The class completes the survey and each student analyzes the data using a convenient Internet website. They report the results and offer their conclusions. Another practice exercise calls on students to report their assessment of how well a familiar agency evaluates need, service process, and client outcome.

Many of the current research texts on the market offer myriad concepts with little step-by-step guidance on how this understanding can be applied. These texts make the improper assumption that students can apply their abstract understanding of concepts without any step-by-step guidance on the research task. For example, they will be taught about measurement reliability and validity but will not be given guidance on how to select a good published measurement scale for their study. They may be taught about the nature of the systematic review of evidence but not be given instructions on how to examine a given systematic review. These other texts will teach students about the nature of statistical tests but will not give them step-by-step guidance on analyzing their data using the Internet. In other words, the assumption of these alternative texts is that students will figure things out for themselves, in their own unique ways, just how to apply what they have learned. This is a faulty assumption in my opinion, based on my experience as a research teacher in social work.

THE USER-FRIENDLY APPROACH

This book is designed to be user-friendly, which means it has special features that will help students understand the meaning of concepts and retain their learnings. For example, each chapter places emphasis on essential concepts and techniques rather than on esoteric knowledge. While technical terms are presented, more common phrases are used to help students to remember the meaning of them.

One of the features of this text is that each chapter ends with a review section that contains discussion questions, a list of key learnings, a chapter quiz, and a chapter glossary. These items help the students review the content of the chapter and focus on key themes.

The discussion questions help the students reflect on critical concepts in the chapter. Their answers can be a good vehicle for class discussion. The listing of key learnings should help the students review critical concepts and make note of which concepts are more important than others. When students take the chapter quiz, they can see whether they need further review of the content. The chapter glossary is a convenient tool for review of definitions of concepts and the determination of concepts that are most critical for understanding.

In addition, there is an emphasis on how the parts of the research process fits together. For example, the sampling procedures helps the researcher draw conclusions about the generalization of study results; the definition of the target behavior helps the researcher select the proper tool for measurement; the selection of a research design helps in the drawing of conclusions about the extent that the treatment should be credited with causing the clients' improvement. These mechanisms help the student understand both the *what* and the *why* of research procedures.

Learning is also facilitated through the use of terms that are easier to remember. For example, the reader is repeatedly reminded that the concept of threats to internal validity refers to alternative explanations of client outcome. Students are not as likely to remember what is meant by "threats to internal validity" without this help. Wherever possible, this text employs user-friendly language such as "credibility" as an overall category for the concepts of reliability and validity.

One chapter in this book presents the connections between common sayings in everyday life and research ideas. One example is "Don't put the cart before the horse!" In other words, be sure to execute the research process in proper order. Another is "Two heads are better than one." This saying is relevant to the establishment of the credibility of measurement tools when they are subject to comparisons to other tools. If both tools are correlated, you have evidence of two heads being better than one.

A final feature of this book that facilitates learning is the repetition of concepts in different contexts with later versions being more complex than earlier discussions. This should help the students always be able to see the forest for the trees. Students are introduced to concepts in simple fashion in the early chapters and are given more depth of knowledge in later chapters. For example, the student will have learned basic lessons about sampling in the early chapters before they encounter this theme at a higher level in a later chapter. They will already understand how the research design addresses the issue of causation in evaluative research before they reach the chapter that discusses myriad different research designs. They will understand the concept of chance in the very first chapter of this text, but will return to it later when they examine data statistically.

ORGANIZATION OF THIS BOOK

There are three major goals of this book. The first goal is to equip students with competence in the application of research tasks that are congruent with the nature of scientific inquiry. For example, you are not supposed to conduct research to prove a point; instead, you conduct it to discover the truth. Most important, you learn to appreciate the contribution of science to your understanding of social reality, with special attention to evidence with regard to social work practice. Furthermore, the social worker must undertake research with attention to ethics in the use of human subjects in research.

The second goal is to give students the ability to conduct the tasks of various types of research. For example, a social worker as researcher may conduct a study to describe a study sample (descriptive research) or to explain phenomena by examining the relationships between variables (explanatory research). They may evaluate a service (evaluative research) or explore the unknown (exploratory research). With regard to each type of research, the student goes through each of the four phases of the research process at a basic level.

The third goal is to equip students with the skills necessary for conducting the major phases of the research process at the intermediate level. This is accomplished by giving more details and tools for the research tasks. First, students learn how to engage in the development of a knowledge on which their research is founded. Developing the methods for finding the answer to their research questions is a second phase of research. They learn how to analyze data as they undertake the third phase of research. Then they review how to draw conclusions, the final phase of this process.

These three goals serve as the guides for the three parts of this book. In the first part, the student reviews the fundamentals of science that help them achieve the first goal. The second part acquaints students with the necessary tasks in the development of the methods for conducting the research study. In the third part, the student learns how to analyze data while the final section focuses on the conclusions that should be drawn based on the data analyzed. These three sections are described below.

Part 1: The Fundamentals of Science and Social Work Practice

In Chapter 1, students face challenges in the demonstration of the spirit of scientific inquiry. They learn, for example, that research is a process of discovery rather than justification. The scientific researcher does not cherry-pick information to prove a point. Instead, the researcher examines information in a systematic and objective manner and lets the data drive the conclusions. The practice exercise for this chapter calls on the student to engage in a dialogue with someone about whether the full moon affects unusual behavior, with contributions from research on this theme. The objective is to learn how people do or do not embrace science as a way of knowing.

The student learns about the four phases of social work research in Chapter 2. Also included in these lessons of this chapter is how research can be classified into four ways based on the general purpose of the study (description, explanation, evaluation, or exploration). In the practice exercise of this chapter, students demonstrate competence in conceptualizing the four phases of research work with regard to a study they might undertake on the evaluation of their practice.

In Chapter 3, students learn how to apply the key principles of research ethics and cultural competence with regard to a research study they would like to undertake. For example, how will the issue of privacy be accommodated? Also, how will cultural competence be addressed in each phase of the research process?

Chapter 4 focuses on evidence-based practice. Students learn the nature of evidence-based practice and how to find evidence for their own research pursuits. The practice exercise for this chapter asks the students to review a specific systematic review of evidence and answer a set of questions about what was learned from the review.

Part 2: Conducting Different Types of Social Work Research

The second part of this book gives students competence in conducting various types of research, including the use of convenient Internet websites for the analysis of data of various kinds. In Chapter 5, they examine the use of the social survey with an exercise on the design of a client satisfaction survey for a familiar agency. The content of Chapter 6 shows how to conduct descriptive research with emphasis on the definition and measurement of variables, and the employment of descriptive statistics. The exercise in this chapter asks students to collect and examine data on the characteristics of the good work manager, with lessons on sex-role stereotypes. They are given step-by-step instructions on how to statistically analyze data using an Internet site.

Chapter 7 gives the student competence in conducting explanatory research where the relationships between variables are examined. This chapter introduces the student to inferential statistics. The exercise for this chapter calls on students to collect and examine data on the relationships between stress, social support, and life satisfaction. They submit that data for statistical analysis using an Internet site. In Chapter 8, students learn how to conduct evaluative research. The content of this chapter focuses on the identification of target behavior, the selection of the intervention, the measurement of client progress, the analysis of data, and conclusions. Further lessons on inferential statistics are included. The exercise for this chapter requires the student to examine data given to them from a study of the treatment of depression for a hypothetical mental health agency. An Internet website is employed. Chapter 9 provides students with concepts and skills of qualitative research. After a review of general concepts in qualitative research methods, students engage in a research practice exercise in content analysis. Program evaluation is the theme of Chapter 10. In this chapter, students learn about how agencies evaluate client need, service process, and client outcome in their comprehensive assessment of their programs. The exercise asks them to report on how a familiar agency addresses some aspect of the service system evaluation.

When students complete this section, they will be prepared to conduct basic research studies, including the statistical analysis of data. In other words, the mystery of research will have been substantially resolved and the students will be prepared to take action. But they will need additional lessons to take the step of competence at the intermediate level. That is the goal of the third part of this book.

Part 3: Conducting Each Phase of Social Work Research

In the third part of this book, the student examines each of the four major phases of social work research in more depth. Developing the knowledge base and the intervention is the theme of Chapter 11. The intervention part of this chapter, of course, relates to the evaluative type of study, which is the emphasis in this book. One of the practice exercises for this chapter asks students to undertake a preliminary review of the literature with regard to an evaluative study they would like to undertake. They report the procedures they employed in their search of the literature and summarize their findings in simple terms. Another exercise calls on the students to describe the intervention they would like to evaluate with regard to objectives, structure, model, and personnel.

Study methodology is the theme of Chapters 12 through 15. In Chapter 12, students review sampling as the tool for understanding study generalization. Different types of samples are described, and the student examines the distinction between scientific generalization (when you have a random sample) and logical generalization (when you do not have a random sample). Procedures for selecting a study sample from a study population are described, based on the type of sampling method employed. In the practice exercise, students describe how a random sample could be selected for a study they have designed. Various concepts such as sampling interval are included in this exercise.

Measurement is the theme of Chapter 13. Following the review of essential concepts in measurement (e.g., measurement error, reliability, validity), students examine how to select a published measurement scale or how to develop one themselves. One of the practice exercises in this chapter requires the student to find a tool for measuring alcoholism for a hypothetical set of clients and to explain what amount of gain on this scale would constitute practical significance.

In Chapter 14, students examine how to select a group research design with emphasis on the threats to internal validity that are addressed by various designs. The practice exercise calls on the study to discuss which threats are of special importance in a set of hypothetical studies in their decision of the research design that would be optimal with regard to both practicality and threats to internal validity.

Chapter 15 focuses on the single-subject research design. Various single-subject designs are discussed, including the limited AB design, a unique feature of this book. The practice exercise for this chapter is similar to the one for Chapter 14 except that it deals with the selection of a single-subject research design.

Chapters 16 and 17 focus on the analysis of data, both quantitative and qualitative. In Chapter 16, students review concepts related to the analysis of quantitative data and the drawing of conclusions from study results. Students review basic concepts in data analysis (e.g., correlation, effect size, levels of measurement) and are guided through a process of selecting a statistic for a given study. For example, they may find that the paired *t* test is appropriate if you have a set of matched pretest and posttest scores for a single group of clients. After they find the statistic, they are given instructions on how to use an Internet website to examine their data. They use these websites to examine hypothetical data in the practice exercise for this chapter.

Qualitative data analysis is the theme of Chapter 17. Both narrative analysis and content analysis are described along with examples of each. Coding in content analysis is a major emphasis of this chapter and is the focus of the practice exercise at the end of this chapter.

NEW IDEAS IN THIS BOOK

There are several ideas in this book that may be unfamiliar to those who have read other texts on social work research methods. These new ideas are motivated by my attempt to present content that is of practical value to the social worker. They address various tasks in social work research in a way that enhances comprehensiveness of application.

One of these new ideas deals with the theme of the generalization of study findings based on the method of sampling employed. Most texts suggest that you must have a random sample to generalize your findings. My new idea is that there are two bases for generalization: scientific and logical. You can generalize your findings on a *scientific* basis if you have a random sample. If you do not have a random sample, you can generalize your findings on a *logical* basis if you can show that your study sample and your study population are similar on variables important to the study. My rationale for using the word *scientific* for the first form of generalization is that you have a scientific basis for estimating sampling error when you employ a random sample.

Admittedly, scientific generalization is superior to the logical alternative. But I believe that we should engage in practical alternatives when we have a study that is less than perfect. In other words, we should not simply say that we cannot generalize our findings because we do not have a random sample. Instead, we should say we cannot scientifically generalize our findings but we may be able to generalize on a logical basis.

Another idea is that we should carefully determine what causes of client improvement (other than the intervention) should be of special concern in a given situation before we decide on the research design that is warranted. We should decide if a given alternative cause of client improvement (e.g., normal growth over time) is likely to occur in our specific evaluative study. If it is likely, we should make special efforts to use a research design that controls for that cause. In all situations, we should use the best research design that is feasible. However, if there are no alternative causes of client improvement that seem likely, we do not need to apologize for the fact that our chosen research design fails to control for them. We should report that our design does not control for these alternative causes but that we do not have reason to believe that these causes are likely to be important in our particular situation.

A third idea that you will not likely find in other social work research texts is the use of what I call the *limited AB* single-subject research design. This is a single-subject design where there is only one baseline recording of target behavior before the treatment begins, accompanied by several measurements during the treatment period. Most texts will describe the AB single-subject design, where you have repeated measurements during both the baseline and treatment periods, but these texts do not describe the limited AB design. This idea is promoted by practicality: Most social work students do not find it feasible to measure a target behavior for a single client several times before treatment begins. The social worker typically begins to offer service in the first or second encounters with the client. They may have the opportunity to measure client behavior at the end of an assessment session that takes place before they begin the service that is being evaluated, but they are not likely to be able to measure this behavior each week for several weeks before service begins. There is a statistical measure that can be used in this situation when the client's behavior is measured as a score (the one-sample t test). Many of the students in my research courses have employed this evaluative research design, but few have employed the traditional AB single-subject design.

A fourth distinction of this book is the use of the Internet to analyze data in a simple application. There are several practice exercises where the student analyzes data using an Internet website. They are given step-by-step instructions that they will find to be rather simple. They will be able to compose a study hypothesis, enter their data, and report whether the data supported the study hypothesis. They can also report on the study conclusions that are supported by the data analysis. This simple application of data analysis has the effect of reducing the technical mystery of statistics often encountered by social work students.

SUMMARY

When students have completed the content of this book, they will be able to enhance their practice with the use of published research studies. They will know the extent to which the practices they choose are based on evidence. In addition, students will be able to evaluate their own practice through their own research. This means they will be able to evaluate whether their practice achieves the intended objectives using data they have collected and analyzed statistically.

In this text, students will encounter knowledge about social work research methods that is user-friendly, practical, and applied to specific tasks in the completion of research studies. They will end this experience with an enhanced appreciation of science, an understanding of the research process, knowledge of critical concepts in research, and the ability to complete an entire research study on their own.

Emphasis is placed on the application of knowledge of essential concepts, with special attention given to the evaluation of practice. The interdependence of research tasks is illustrated in several ways, such as, for example, the fact that a good definition of target behavior will guide the selection of the appropriate measurement tool. The mystery of statistics will be substantially reduced by the student's experience with the analysis of data using a convenient Internet website using simple instructions.

This content of this text is grounded in my several decades of experience teaching research methods at more than one university and by my experience as the author of four other research texts. I have observed the experiences of more than a thousand social work students in the pursuit of knowledge about research methods. My students have taught me a lot about how best to present knowledge about this topic. I am in indebted to them for their contributions.

ACKNOWLEDGMENTS

SAGE Publishing gratefully acknowledges the following reviewers for their kind assistance:

Kathleen Boland, Cedar Crest College

J. Mark Dyke, Associate Professor, New Mexico Highlands University

Dione Moultrie King, University of Alabama at Birmingham

Claudia L. Moreno, PhD, LMSW, Dominican College of Blauvelt

Julie Schroeder, Jackson State University

ABOUT THE AUTHOR

Reginald O. York, PhD, is a professor in the School of Social Work at the University of North Carolina Wilmington, where he has taught since 2005. Previously, he served on the social work faculties of East Carolina University and the University of North Carolina Chapel Hill. He is the author of *Human Service Planning* (1982), *Building Basic Competencies in Social Work Research* (1997), *Conducting Social Work Research* (1998), *Evaluating Human Services* (2009), and *Statistics for Human Service Evaluation* (2017). Prior to his entry into academia, he served as a foster care social worker, a child protective services supervisor, and the director of two human service organizations. His research interests include evidence-based practice, social work education, and human service management.

THE FUNDAMENTALS OF SCIENCE AND SOCIAL WORK RESEARCH

When you complete the content and exercises in this section of the book, you will have achieved an enhanced appreciation of science as a guide for social work. This means that you will be more likely to examine scientific evidence in the pursuit of knowledge to guide practice. You will be less likely to accept someone's claim that the full moon makes people act differently without a comprehensive examination of this question using the principles and processes of science.

On completion of this section, you will also be more familiar with the phases of the social work research process. You will be less likely to put the cart before the horse because you will know that there is a rationale for the sequence of activities in the research process. In addition, you will understand how research can be usefully categorized according to the purpose of the study. For example, you will know that you must employ descriptive statistics if your study is descriptive in nature and inferential statistics if your study is explanatory in nature.

An appreciation of the ethics in the use of human subjects in research will be another outcome of this section for you. You will know the basic ways to ensure

PART ONE

that you have appropriately demonstrated this appreciation in your research tasks. Furthermore, you will know more about how to incorporate culture competence in the tasks of research. Finally, you will be familiar with the nature of evidence-based practice in social work. This also means that you will have a better appreciation of what evidence can do for you in enhancing the effectiveness of your practice.

SCIENCE, RESEARCH, AND SOCIAL WORK PRACTICE

Susan is a social work intern at a family counseling agency, where she engages in intake interviews of persons seeking the help of the counseling center. Her agency supervisor has been helpful in her efforts to improve her interviewing skills. But she realizes that being a professional social worker goes beyond intake interviewing skills. It entails knowledge of practice, social policy, and social justice. She has examined how science is different from other ways of gathering information to help with decisions. For example, she recently heard a fellow social worker say, "Things were really crazy last night at the emergency room of the hospital; it must be because there was a full moon." When Susan questioned this social worker, she responded, "Well, I have seen this with my very own eyes; whenever there is a full moon, things get really crazy in the emergency room." Susan realized that this social worker had witnessed "crazy" behavior when the moon was full, but what about when the moon was not full? Had this social worker ever made a note of behavior when the moon was full and when the moon was not full and compared the number of crazy incidents? Susan realized that she would be more convinced of the effect of the full moon if her colleague had seen a greater incidence of "crazy" behavior when the moon was full than when it was not. That would be using science as a way of knowing. But this was not what this social worker had done. She had only witnessed behavior during the full moon.

Susan also made a few notes about the scientific way of investigating behavior during the full moon. For example, what does this fellow social worker mean by the word "crazy"? Was she referring to the number of admissions to the emergency room, the number of patients who engaged in aggressive behaviors, or what? How would we measure these things? And, of course, Susan would need data both when the moon was full and when it was not. In other words, Susan would need to employ methods consistent with the spirit of scientific inquiry, which seeks to discover rather than to justify, through methods of inquiry that are objective and comprehensive. Susan is aware that anecdotal evidence (evidence from a single example) is not good evidence. You can offer proof of just about any weird theory with a single example. You must go beyond a single example to engage in the scientific process of investigation.

Susan might start a process of scientific research by reviewing the literature on the subject of the full moon and unusual behavior. If her question is well answered by the current literature, she would decide that she does not need to reinvent the wheel by doing another study. If not, she would define the concept of unusual behavior, find a method of measuring it, collect data on this behavior when the moon was full and when it was not, analyze the data to see if unusual behavior was more prevalent when the moon was full than when it was not, and draw conclusions consistent with the results. That would exemplify the scientific method of inquiry.

INTRODUCTION

In this chapter, you will examine the nature of inquiry, with an emphasis on science as a guide for social work practice and research. You will see how science is different from other means of inquiry that you employ on a regular basis. In this regard, you will see how science and critical thinking are founded on similar principles and how certain commonsense phrases are related to various steps in the research process. In contrast to science, you will view mechanisms of inquiry that are flawed, with a special emphasis on pseudoscience as different from science. In essence, you will see how scientific research can contribute to the improvement of your practice decisions, even though it is not the only useful means for doing so.

In this chapter, you will implement certain learnings about the scientific method in the examination of current research on whether people's behavior is influenced by the full moon. Do people act more strange during the full moon than at other times? You will see that common perceptions can be incorrect and how science can help you avoid such errors. You may have a perception about social work practice that is supported by scientific research, or it may be refuted by it. In either case, it is the intent of this chapter that you acquire an appreciation for how science can improve decision making.

You will acquire several competencies from this chapter. At the end of this chapter, you will be able to do the following:

1. Distinguish between science as a way of learning from other means like experience, common sense, tradition, and so forth

2. Explain how scientific research can contribute to social work practice

3. Distinguish between science and pseudoscience

4. Identify the aspects of inquiry that make the process scientific

5. Report on how certain commonsense phrases and science can be used to report on research that addresses the question "Do people act differently when there is a full moon?"

6. Explain how common sense, critical thinking, and the scientific method are connected

7. Identify the steps in the process of scientific research

HOW DO WE KNOW WHAT WE KNOW?

How did you come to your opinion about whether the full moon affects behavior? How about another opinion? Do you believe that giving clients homework to undertake between therapy sessions is effective? What about the view that long-term treatment for depression is justified when compared with short-term treatment because it is more cost-effective?

We come to our opinions in a variety of ways. Sometimes we believe something because it has been handed down to us from a source of authority, like our parents. Other times we come to hold a belief because it makes sense to us. Maybe we believe in a way of doing something because this is the way we have always done it. These are three of many ways by which we come to our opinions.

None of these ways is supported by science, which requires the systematic collection and analysis of data. We could ask ourselves if we have beliefs about social work practice based on scientific evidence. Do we know of scientific studies that show that a certain service is effective with regard to a certain outcome? Many human service agencies advertise that they use evidence-based practices. This means that their practices are supported by evidence. In other words, their services are supported by science. They don't just ask for the opinions of staff and leave it at that. They subject their practice questions to scientific inquiry.

It Makes Sense to Me

Much of what we come to believe is supported by our own logical examination of the information we encounter in our daily lives. We ask ourselves if it makes sense to us. If we believe that homework was helpful to our learning in high school, then maybe we will believe that it makes sense for our clients to have homework between therapy sessions.

Sometimes we are convinced of a certain practice in social work because we were convinced of the logic of a service activity by someone. Perhaps it makes sense that we should involve the parents in the treatment of children because (a) we can learn more about the causes of the child's behavior, (b) we can convey some knowledge to the parents that will help them improve the behavior of the child, and (c) the parents must be involved in the improvement of the child's behavior for the service activities to work.

This basis for forming opinions is not founded on science, although any of them could be subjected to scientific inquiry. Instead, they are based on a particular logic that we embrace. But what if this logic is flawed? For many years, it was popularly believed in psychology that schizophrenia was caused by a form of parenting where the father was distant and the mother was controlling. This was the dominant belief among psychologists for a period of time, even though this theory was not supported by science. Finally, there were enough scientific studies to disclaim this idea and conclude that the brain of the schizophrenic is different. In other words, schizophrenics are the way they are because of genetics, not parenting.

Many new programs or services are sold on the basis that their practices make sense as a treatment for a given condition. But they do not become listed as evidence-based practices until they have been subjected to a sufficient amount of scientific studies. An example of a service that proved to make things worse was a program called Scared Straight. The idea of this program was that if at-risk youth were required to visit a prison where prisoners would tell them how bad prison life was, they would be scared enough to avoid a life of crime. This made a lot of sense to a lot of people, some of them important enough to ensure a good deal of funding for this program for a period of time before it was subjected to scientific study.

As you will see in a later part of this chapter, the evidence on the outcomes from this program suggested that at-risk youth who encountered this program were more likely to engage in criminal behavior than those who did not. So it was worse than being ineffective; it was making things worse.

It Is the Way We Have Done It

Social workers take jobs in agencies where they are taught how to deliver certain services. Their orientation program will include the collected opinions of staff and supervisors about how best to implement the service. Often social workers do not question these practices, nor do they subject them to scientific inquiry.

Should you, as a social worker, engage in practices that have been found to be effective and not to harm clients? Of course, you should! In fact, it is a requirement set forth in the Code of Ethics of the National Association of Social Workers (NASW). At a minimum, you should review the literature with regard to service practices for this purpose.

Several decades ago, there were far fewer publications revealing evidence about social work practices. With the enormous number of such studies today, there is no excuse for a social worker to ignore all this evidence. And if there is little evidence, it seems that you would have an ethical obligation to engage in the scientific study of your practices. You will learn how to do this in this book.

It Is Evidence-Based Practice

For a practice to be evidence based, it must have been subjected to various studies that revealed that it was effective with regard to a given outcome. For example, cognitive–behavioral therapy has been subjected to many studies that revealed it was effective in the treatment of depression.

Many human service agencies advertise that their services are evidence based. The social worker in these agencies should inquire into the basis for this statement. Can it be found on a legitimate list of evidence-based practices (some may refer to this as empirically supported practices)? Is there a list of publications that provide the evidence?

There is a chapter in this book that deals with this theme. For now, let's be aware of what it means to have evidence as support for a service decision. It means that the evidence in support of this practice is greater than the evidence not in support of it, to lead a reasonable social worker to conclude that it is evidence based.

AVOIDING ERRORS IN DECISION MAKING

There are several common errors in decision making when we avoid the **spirit of scientific inquiry** and the methods that support it. Among these errors to be discussed here are (a) incomplete information, (b) illogical reasoning, and (c) personal investment. Sometimes we make decisions without all the information we need. At other times we fall into the trap of a common method of illogical reasoning (i.e., a rationale that is not logical). Finally, we sometimes come to an opinion based on what will satisfy our ego investment in a situation (e.g., what will make us look better or gain more power).

Incomplete Information

A popular form of incomplete information is the **cherry-picking** of information to prove a point. This refers to the search behavior of only reporting the facts that support a given position and intentionally suppressing known facts that refute it.

Suppose you reviewed 12 studies on the effectiveness of a given form of therapy in the reduction of postpartum depression and found that only 2 studies show effectiveness but the other 10 fail to show that clients were better off because of this form of therapy. Which one of these are you most likely to report to others?

1. Would you report only on the two studies that showed effectiveness and declare this form of therapy to be an evidence-based therapy for the treatment of postpartum depression?

2. Would you report on all studies and conclude that the evidence, taken as a whole, fails to support the classification of this form of therapy as evidence based in the treatment of postpartum depression?

3. Would you report on all studies and conclude that this shows that this form of therapy is evidence based in the treatment of postpartum depression?

4. Would you report only on the 10 studies that failed to reveal success and conclude there is no evidence that supports this form of therapy for postpartum depression?

The social worker, as a **social scientist**, would select Option 2 above. There were far more studies with negative findings than positive ones. Unfortunately, some social workers, not embracing the spirit of scientific inquiry, would select Option 1, especially if the social worker has a personal investment in this form of therapy. Perhaps this is a form of therapy this social worker has been suggesting, and this revelation will be embarrassing.

Personal Investment

The personal investment in a given outcome was illustrated in the previous sentence. If you have been advocating for a certain action, you do not want to find evidence that suggests that it is a bad idea. If a certain kind of evidence has the potential to lead to the loss of your job, you will not want to embrace it.

A good issue to understand with someone is whether the information would normally be good news to that person or the kind that would not. In other words, what does this person need to believe?

Illogical Reasoning

Illogical reasoning refers to arguments that are not logical. It is not logical, for example, for you to say that the reason I am grumpy today is because of what I will have for breakfast tomorrow. This is not logical because it is not possible for a cause of something (my grumpiness) to come after it. It must come before. If I am grumpy right after breakfast today, you might logically say that one reason for it might be my breakfast. But not what I am going to have for breakfast tomorrow.

One form of illogical reasoning is the **false dichotomy**—the claim that there are only two options in an argument when, in fact, there are more. Consider this conversation the author once had with a friend. The friend asked, "Do you believe in doing a lot of testing of elementary school students?" I replied, "Yes, I do." The friend responded, "Don't you believe in instilling a love of learning?" The tone of voice suggested that this friend did not think that you could believe in testing and also believe in instilling a love of learning. He was presenting only two options as being possible when there were more.

According to this false dichotomy, if you believe in testing you must not believe in instilling a love of learning. But there are four alternatives here, not just two. You could possibly (1) believe in testing and not believe in instilling a love of learning, (2) not believe in testing but believe in instilling a love of learning, (3) not believe in testing and also not believe in instilling a love of learning, and (4) believe in testing and also believe in instilling a love of learning. By the way, my position is the last one: I believe in both. I do not think that you fail to believe in instilling a love of learning if you believe in testing.

My friend had entered this conversation with a perception that entailed incomplete information. There were four alternatives rather than two. This is the false dichotomy, which is a false claim that there are only two options (yes/no) when, in fact, there are more options logically in the argument.

There are other forms of illogical reasoning and other ways we make mistakes in decision making when we avoid the spirit of scientific inquiry. The next section will begin our review of this spirit and show how it helps with practice decisions.

SCIENCE AS A WAY OF KNOWING

A social scientist is someone who applies the principles and methods of science to learn more about social phenomena. This might include being able to describe the students in a club with enough clarity to draw some basic conclusions about what the members are like. It might include examining whether there is a relationship between variables (e.g., Do people who regularly exercise have fewer illnesses than those who do not?). It might include the examination of whether a social program is effective (e.g., Is there a lower rate of absenteeism in schools that employ the strengths model of schooling than in schools that do not?). Science employs certain methods of inquiry that are different from other ways of searching for meaning. These methods are designed to reduce human error in observation.

What Do You Already Know?

In this section are a few situations that will illustrate various aspects of the use of science to inform decisions. You will review each and decide if there is a problem.

Let's examine the following situation:

A group of researchers started their study process with the purpose of determining the extent to which clients treated for depression have shown improvement in their levels of depression. They collected scores on a depression scale for a group of clients in treatment for depression. They collected these scores both before and after a service was provided that was designed to reduce depression. These scores showed improvement from the first to the last measurement. They were subjected to statistical analysis and were found to be statistically significant. The researchers concluded that these clients had experienced improvement with regard to depression, but they were not clear about the population to whom these results could be generalized because these clients had not been selected on a random basis from a larger population.

Do you see any problems with this situation? It is a summary you may have read from your search of the literature with regard to evidence about the treatment of a condition like depression. There are no major flaws here. The process started with a purpose, data were collected consistent with that purpose, and conclusions were drawn that were consistent with the data analyzed.

You saw a reference to statistical analysis, which will be discussed many times in this book, but you are not expected to fully understand it at present. But you surely have seen references to statistical analysis of data and concepts such as "**statistical significance**." These clients showed improvement, and the level of their improvement cannot be easily explained by **chance** (because the data were found to be statistically significant). If your data can be explained by chance, you cannot conclude that they can be taken seriously.

A reference was made to the **generalization of data results**, another concept that will be discussed many times in the chapters of this book. It was noted that the clients had not been selected at random, a basis for scientific generalization. It is likely that you have seen numerous references to random samples in your review of the literature. That is the superior form of sampling and strengthens the extent to which you can generalize your findings to persons who were not in your study.

Now, let's examine another situation.

A group of researchers had the purpose of determining if after-school tutoring was effective in the improvement of grades for middle school students. Grades were compared for the period of time before tutoring was offered and measured again after tutoring was completed. The results showed that the average student improved but that statistical significance was not achieved (i.e., these results can too easily be explained by chance). These researchers concluded that tutoring is an effective way to improve grades for middle school students.

Do you see a problem with this situation? You need an appreciation of the theme of chance to grasp the lesson provided here. These researchers treated the data seriously in their conclusions even though the data failed to be statistically significant. The proper conclusion would be that the study failed to find an improvement in grades. What they discovered was chance. If chance can explain your data, you cannot take them seriously with regard to your study conclusions.

What do you think of the following situation?

Some fellow students conduct a study of students in one social work research class and find that the majority of them are identified with the Democratic Party. They conclude that there are more people in this university who identify as Democratic than Republican.

The problem here is easy to identify. You cannot generalize from a small sample of people in one class in a university to the entire university. The issue of generalization is discussed with regard to the nature of the sample that you employ. A small class of students in one specific place is not a random sample. And you would need a much larger sample than this to generalize to the entire university.

Now examine this situation.

Paul is a social work research student who starts the process of conducting research by deciding that he would like to conduct interviews of his fellow students. He has not yet decided on the purpose of his study.

What is the problem here? Well, Paul has put the cart before the horse. He has decided on the methods he will use to conduct his study before he decides on the purpose of the study. The purpose should come first. Why? Different purposes suggest different types of methods to be used. You need to know the purpose before you can make decisions on your methods. Interviews serve some purposes better than others.

Finally, let's examine this situation.

Paula is an individual and family counselor who has been trained in New Beginnings Therapy (hypothetical). Paula has used this treatment for the past 3 months when the objective was to reduce stress. She believes that it has been effective with some clients but has not collected evidence on the outcomes with her clients. She examined the literature on evidence regarding the effectiveness of this approach to counseling. She found 1 study that revealed that New Beginnings Therapy was effective in the reduction of stress, and she found 23 studies that showed that it is not effective in this regard. Paula concluded that this therapy is effective because she found a study that showed that it is.

Is there a problem here? Is it okay to use only 1 study that shows a certain outcome and ignore 23 studies that show an opposite outcome? No, not if you are being scientific. Science is comprehensive. You use all the evidence that you can find, not just the ones that support your predetermined conclusion. Perhaps Paula could report on all the evidence and conclude that she will conduct her own study given the fact that there is more evidence against this approach to therapy than evidence that supports it. Perhaps she will find it to be effective with the types of clients she serves. The lack of sound evidence should encourage Paula to measure client outcome with her individual clients or to search for other methods of treatment.

The Nature of Science

According to the Science Council, **science** is defined as "the pursuit and application of knowledge and understanding of the natural and social world following a systematic methodology based on evidence" (http://sciencecouncil.org/about-us/our-definition-of-science). According to Wikipedia, science is "a systematic enterprise that builds and organizes knowledge in the form of testable explanations and propositions about the universe" (https://en.wikipedia.org/wiki/Science). It is not about hunches, or untested opinions, or something you were told.

Science is based on a special method of inquiry that includes clarity of the research question, a systematic method of investigation, the objective collection and analysis of data, and the drawing of conclusions that are logical based on the results of your data analysis. It is not the cherry-picking of facts to support an opinion, nor is it an incomplete inquiry with many critical avenues untouched by the inquiry. Instead, it is open and comprehensive.

Scientific research is a means of gaining relevant knowledge through the use of the scientific methods. The scientific method is orderly and strives for the achievement of objectivity. An inquiry that is designed to prove a point is not an example of research that fits the spirit of scientific inquiry. A study that is incomplete or illogical also fails to meet the standards of the scientific method.

Sometimes our observations from day to day are a good guide for action. Sometimes, however, our observations are in error. A typical error is a failure to see the evidence that contradicts an opinion that we have embraced. The scientific method is designed to reduce human error in observation. It moves in a logical sequence of steps. For example, we must have a clear idea of what we want to find out before we select a method for our inquiry. We should be clear about the nature of our target population before we select people for our study. Before we can draw conclusions about our research question, we must collect and analyze data. If we are abiding by the spirit of scientific inquiry, we will use study methods that provide us with the opportunity to find that our previous expectations about reality are not supported, as well as the opportunity to find support for our expectations.

Research methods can be used to test certain assumptions you have acquired in your work or questions that you have developed. When your perceptions are supported by your research efforts, you can have more confidence in their accuracy, and perhaps, you will learn something in this process that will refine your understanding. When your expectations are not supported by your research results, you can be stimulated to further growth by your efforts to rethink the problem under study. As you continue in this growth and the validation of practice principles and methods, you will be in a better position to meet the challenges of accountability in social work, which have been increasing in recent decades.

The spirit of scientific inquiry suggests certain behaviors. First, you would not state the purpose of your study as proving that your expectation is correct. You do not study the effectiveness of your tutoring program in improving the grades of your clients for the purpose of proving that the program is effective. You conduct it for the purpose of finding out whether it is effective.

Second, your examination of information should be objective and comprehensive. You should not cherry-pick information so that you only consider data that support your expectations and you systematically ignore data that fail to do so.

Third, you follow a logical set of procedures when you conduct scientific research. This means that you do not start the process by deciding on the questions you want to put on the questionnaire. Instead, you start the process by deciding on the purpose of your study.

Fourth, your conclusions should be consistent with the data you analyzed. You should keep your opinions out of the conclusions that you draw from a scientific study. If your data were found not to be statistically significant, then you have data that can be explained by chance, so you cannot take them seriously with regard to the study conclusions. Your statement should say that you failed to find improvement in anxiety in your clients or you failed to find that those who engage in regular aerobic exercise had less stress than others. This may seem counterintuitive, because you did find that scores were higher at the end of treatment than before treatment. But if these differences were not found to be statistically significant, you cannot rely on them to do a good job of predicting what you would find if you repeated this study with another sample of people drawn from the same study population.

Suppose you undertook a study of the relationship between various sources of social support and social functioning (school grades, health behaviors, etc.) for a sample of adolescent mothers. You measured support with regard to four sources: partners, mothers, fathers, and grandmothers. Suppose you found that those with high support from partners had better outcomes. Suppose further that you found the same relationship between support from mothers and outcomes for the adolescent subjects. What should be your conclusions? Should you include the variable of grandmother support as a key element of a service plan for this population? See Figure 1.1 for a graphic display. If you failed to find that grandmother support was related to social functioning for this population, why would you conclude that this be included in a service plan? It does not make sense.

Fifth, the scientist assumes that people sometimes err in making observations. The questionnaire may not accurately measure what it was intended to measure. For this reason, methods are used in science to test the accuracy of a measurement tool. Furthermore, we continue to conduct research on a given theme to see if the results are consistent with what was found previously.

FIGURE 1.1 ■ Consistency: What's Wrong With This Picture?

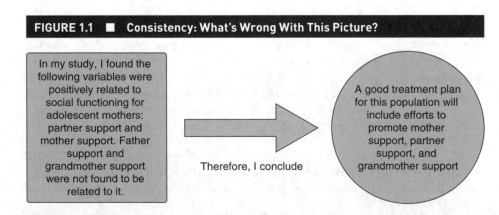

In my study, I found the following variables were positively related to social functioning for adolescent mothers: partner support and mother support. Father support and grandmother support were not found to be related to it.

Therefore, I conclude

A good treatment plan for this population will include efforts to promote mother support, partner support, and grandmother support

SCIENCE AND CRITICAL THINKING

According to two of the prominent authors of work on this subject, **critical thinking** is a "process in which the thinker improves the quality of his or her thinking by skillfully taking charge of the structure inherent in thinking and imposing intellectual standards upon them" (Paul & Elder, 2004, p. 1). The focus is on the structure of thinking rather than the conclusions that you draw about life. There is no liberal or conservative bias in critical thinking; so if you want a structure that supports your bias, you will not find it in critical thinking.

You probably have already concluded that there is an inherent compatibility between the concept of critical thinking and the concept of science. According to Eileen Gambrill (2015),

> Critical thinking and science go hand in hand. In both, there is an openness—even an eagerness—to learn by discovering that one has been wrong, a desire to accurately understand, present, and learn from other viewpoints, a deep curiosity about the world, and a willingness to say "I was wrong." (p. xvi)

Steps in the Scientific Research Process

Several comments have been offered on the process of scientific research. Here we will examine four simple steps in this process: (1) the determination of the research question and the knowledge base that supports your inquiry, (2) the determination of the methods to be used to find a sample of study participants and to measure the study variables, (3) collection and analysis of data, and (4) the drawing of conclusions.

The first logical step is to determine the basic research question to be pursued. In other words, you are determining the purpose of your study. Let's say your purpose is to determine if your tutoring service is having the intended effect of improving the grades of your at-risk students in your tutoring program. The second logical step is to select your study methods. In the tutoring example, you have your current clients as your study subjects. You will measure their grades to answer your research question. You will compare the grades of these clients at the end of the tutoring program with their grades at the beginning. The third step is the collection and analysis of data. In your example, let's suppose the grades at the end of the program were statistically significantly better than the grades at the beginning. Your final step is to draw conclusions. With your data, you can conclude that the tutoring program was effective in the improvement of the grades of your clients.

Summary of What Makes It Scientific

We have reviewed the nature of science with regard to both its spirit and its processes. Several principles have emerged, such as the following:

1. If it is scientific, it is an investigation into the natural world, not the supernatural.

   This places emphasis on things that can be observed (measured). The Salem witch trials were an illustration of a supernatural investigation based on an unintelligent examination of things that could not be observed in the natural world.

2. If it is scientific, it starts with knowledge that has emerged from the work of other scientists, not the idiosyncratic curiosities of an individual.

While we are all at liberty to examine idiosyncratic curiosities, we would not usually refer to this as scientific because it fails to be based on the existing knowledge. It leaves you vulnerable to the mistake of reinventing the wheel.

3. If it is scientific, it employs systematic procedures, not haphazard ones.

In scientific inquiry, we do not put the cart before the horse. We do not, for example, decide that we want to conduct a study using interviews of social work research students before we decide on the research purpose. We do not just "go with the gut" about how to conduct a research study.

4. If it is scientific, it has objective methods of inquiry rather than biased ones.

If we undertake a study to prove a point, we are not adhering to the spirit of scientific inquiry, no matter how important we believe the point is and how much the world will be better off if all believed it. Such endeavors may be found in political maneuvers or other methods of data collection, but it is not based on the scientific process, which is objective.

5. If it is scientific, it employs methods of measurement that reduce human error in observation (**measurement error**).

People sometimes err in making observations, like responding to a questionnaire in a way that is not totally honest. Science uses multiple ways of observation (two heads are better than one) to reduce the effect of human error.

6. If it is scientific, it has an analysis of data that appreciates the idea of chance as one of the possible explanations.

Scientific analysis of data tests for the likelihood that chance is an appropriate explanation for what has been tested. If we appreciate what chance means, we will avoid drawing conclusions based on nonsignificant data.

7. If it is scientific, it presents conclusions that are restricted to the results of the data analysis.

The scientist avoids the temptation to offer opinions as study conclusions when these opinions are outside the bounds of the data analyzed. The scientist also avoids drawing conclusions that go beyond (exaggerate) the study results, keeping in mind the limitations of the study methods. Consequently, the scientist presents conclusions from a study that are tentative in nature, not given as the final answer to a question.

SOCIAL WORK PRACTICE AND SCIENCE

Social work practice is aided by science in many ways. When we assess our client's behavior, we can review scientific studies on the nature of this behavior and gain a better understanding of it. When we consider the methods we will use to help our clients, we can examine evidence about the different approaches that have been undertaken for the achievement of the objective our client is pursuing. We can examine whether certain interventions are better than others with a given client population. And we can do much more with science as a guide to social work practice.

Social work can be defined in many ways. One such way was presented in the *Dictionary of Social Work* (Barker, 2003). This definition indicated that social workers improve the capacity of individuals for problem solving and coping, and help those in need to find resources. It also emphasizes the interaction of the individual and the environment. Social workers, according to this definition, work with individuals, families, and communities.

This definition is quite broad and encompasses the large number of tasks and functions that are part of the social worker's job. Clinical social work is one type of work in this profession. A definition from the NASW (2005) refers to clinical social work as being related to the application of social work theory and methods to the diagnosis, treatment, and prevention of psychosocial dysfunction, including behavioral and mental disorders.

Clinical social work, therefore, is related to work with individuals and small groups with regard to problems we typically classify as related to mental health. Social workers are employed in a variety of settings, but the greatest number serve in direct practice roles. Those who serve in different roles are spread out among many functions, like education, supervision, administration, planning, and so forth. Because of these facts, this book will put more emphasis on research methods for direct practice.

Alison Miley (2016), a student in a Master of Social Work program, undertook a study of the effectiveness of a caregiver support intervention in the reduction of caregiver burnout for the caregivers of dependent elderly individuals. A review of the literature assisted this student in defining caregiver burnout as a state of physical and emotional exhaustion that affects the attitude of the caregiver with regard to the caregiver service. The effect of burnout is a reduction in the quality of care and the termination of the caregiver service.

Miley (2016) also learned from the literature that social support reduces much of the stress associated with the provision of caregiver service. It also improves morale and life satisfaction and enhances feelings of self-confidence and self-esteem. Thus, a support group experience was designed for a group of caregivers served by the agency. This support group was offered monthly for 2 hours. It not only provided a support group experience but also provided for the caregiver to have some time off from the caregiver service.

Miley (2016) designed an evaluation of this support group intervention by administering a scale that measured burnout. This scale was to be administered before the service began and at the end of 6 months of service. She noted from the literature that this scale had been tested and was found to be reliable. Her next step in this process would be to collect and analyze these scores to see if the one taken at the end of the service was significantly better than the one taken at the beginning.

As is evident from the example given above, science can inform various aspects of social work practice. Practice, with this group of clients, was informed by science with regard to the definition and analysis of the client's target behavior, the search for an effective treatment, and how to measure success. After Miley collects data, she will need to be careful to allow her data to inform her conclusions.

The above example is of direct social work practice. If you are engaged in a program evaluation, there are many avenues you could take. You could examine whether the clients in your program have the characteristics that the program is supposed to serve. If the target population consists of people in poverty, you could collect data on the proportion of the clients in this program who live below the poverty line. You could examine the standards employed in this program as compared with official standards of good practice, such as the credentials of the staff who provide the service. You could examine the efficiency of certain services compared with that of similar agencies. What, for example, is the cost per client served by this agency as compared with other agencies? And, of course, you could examine outcomes for this program, such as the recidivism rate for confirmed cases of child neglect or the gain in feelings of support among those in the support group for victims of violence.

COMMON SENSE AND THE SCIENTIFIC METHOD

There are commonsense sayings that we can relate to scientific inquiry. They are offered below to show that science and common sense often have much in common, even though they originated in different ways. These similarities were presented in a previous text by the same author (York, 1997) and will be summarized here. Most of these statements come from commonsense sayings you may have heard.

Don't Reinvent the Wheel!

In the history of human inquiry, there has been an enormous amount of social research that has been undertaken. When we develop a research question, we usually find that there is a great deal of guidance that can come from an examination of the literature. Often, we will find a suitable answer to our question from this review and will not find it necessary to undertake a new study of the subject. Even when we do not find a suitable answer to our question, we will find much guidance from the literature on those aspects of the question that have been left more unanswered, and we can find assistance with the conceptualization of our study and the measurement of social phenomena required to answer our question.

It is not reasonable for us to expect a novice researcher to acquire an exhaustive review of the literature on a given subject. You will find a wide range of knowledge in places that are not well known or easily accessed. However, we can expect a novice researcher to delve into the most available and best known literature on the subject of inquiry, so that he or she can avoid repeating the mistakes of early work on the subject or failing to contribute anything of substance about the topic.

You will find that there is normally a wide array of research on any given subject. You will also find that there is usually a good deal of research that needs to be added. Often what is needed is the use of a different type of person as the study subject or a different way of conceptualizing or measuring the phenomena under inquiry. Thus, we are not likely to encounter a situation in which the research we wish to undertake is substantially redundant. The greater reason for examining the previous literature is to help us avoid the mistakes of the past. We might find that the way we wish to undertake our study has been done many years ago but has been found wanting in its ability to provide a good means of addressing our research question. Later research will be found to have corrected for these mistakes in research methods.

Don't Put the Cart Before the Horse!

The research process follows the same basic path as good problem solving and critical thinking. If you are engaged in good problem solving, you will start with the identification of the problem and the objectives to be achieved by solving it. You will then identify methods for solving the problem. Following implementation of the solution, you will evaluate the results. One of the common pitfalls in basic human problem solving is for us to state the problem in terms of only one solution. In doing so, we are starting with a solution rather than with the identification of the human condition to be addressed.

Social research begins with the formulation of the problem resulting in the articulation of the research question. After the research question has been clearly identified, we determine the methods to be used in the pursuit of the answer to our question. One of the mistakes commonly made by the novice researcher is to begin a process of inquiry with a research instrument. It is not uncommon for a student of research to review a set of research instruments that measure certain psychological conditions and become especially interested in the use of a certain instrument in some kind of research.

The process of research conceptualized in this book starts with problem formulation and moves logically to research methodology, then to data collection and analysis, and ending with conclusions. Obviously, we should not start with conclusions about the research question. We have covered this mistake in our examination of the purposes of scientific inquiry (discovery rather than justification). Likewise, it is not logical to start with data and formulate a research question that fits the data. (However, it is legitimate to use an exploration of data as a springboard for focusing a set of questions that guide the investigation of the literature.) Furthermore, as mentioned above, we should not start the process with the selection of study methods. We need to know our research question before we can select the optimal means of measurement of our variables.

Let's go over the critical steps in the social research process. First, we decide on the purpose of our study. Do we want to describe the members of a class of students in a university program, so that we will know the distribution of these people by age, gender, race, and so forth? Or do we want to examine whether males and females are different with regard to satisfaction with life? Or do we want to know if after-school tutoring helps at-risk children improve their grades? The first of these examples is about descriptive research—our attempt to describe people. The one about gender and life satisfaction is sometimes referred to as explanatory research because we wish to explain whether there is a relationship between variables, which would help us explain the variables. The one about tutoring is evaluative in nature because we are examining if a service program is effective with regard to the objectives it is seeking to achieve.

Two Heads Are Better Than One!

Because objective reality is so difficult to discover in the field of human behavior, we must rely on a method of inquiry that reduces human error in observation. One such method is to ask for more than one observation of a given phenomenon in order to become confident that we have a true picture of it. In research, we assume that reality is more likely to be discovered the more we find different people perceiving things in the same light. We know, of course, that it is possible that one person who is in the minority has the true picture while those in the majority are incorrect. But in view of the fact that we have so little truly "hard" evidence of reality about human behavior, we make the assumption that our best bet is to go with the consensus of many people rather than the unsupported opinion of one person. And we have many methods that have been developed to test the dependability of a given method of measuring our subjects of study. Thus, we could say that this principle serves as one of the assumptions of scientific inquiry.

Some Things Happen Just by Chance!

The fact that I had eggs for breakfast this morning does not necessarily mean that I prefer eggs over cereal for breakfast in general. It could be that I have eggs half the time and cereal half the time and I just happened to have had eggs this morning. If you observed me at breakfast several times and noted that I had eggs each and every time, you would have more reliable evidence that I prefer eggs for breakfast. The more observations you make, the more confident you would be in your conclusion that I prefer eggs for breakfast.

We are referring to a thing called "probability." Let's discuss this concept in a general way. Logic would suggest that there is a 50% chance of getting a heads on a given flip of a coin because there are only two possibilities—heads and tails. But let's suppose that someone said that there was one coin in a set of coins that was rigged to land on heads more often than on tails because of the distribution of the weight of the coin. You pick out one coin, and you want to know if this is the one that is rigged. Let's suppose that your first flip was heads and the second was also heads. Are you convinced you have the rigged coin? Probably not because you have only flipped it 2 times and we know that two heads in a row can happen just by chance. What if you have flipped this coin 10 times and it came out heads every time? Now you have more reason to believe that you have the rigged coin. A similar result after 20 flips would be even better. If you do not have the rigged coin, you would not likely have very many flips in a row that were similar. The more flips you have that are similar, the better are your chances that you have found the rigged coin. Determining how many flips you need to be confident is a matter for statistics. If you knew how to use a statistical test known as the binomial test, you could see that 5 flips in a row with only heads appearing would be so unusual that you would be safe to bet that you have found the rigged coin.

Now let us put the same lesson to use with a more practical example. Suppose that you wanted to know whether males and females differ in their satisfaction with instruction in research courses. Are females higher or lower than males in their level of satisfaction? You could ask a given group of students if they are generally satisfied with their research instruction, with the options of YES or NO. You could then compare the proportion of females who answered YES with the proportion of males who answered YES. What if you found that 63% of females were satisfied and that 65% of males were satisfied? Does that mean you can conclude that there is truly a difference between males and females? If so, would you be prepared to bet a large sum of money that a new study of this subject would result in males having a higher level of satisfaction? I doubt that you would, because you would realize that this small a difference between males and females could be easily explained by chance. If you had found that 60% of females were satisfied as compared with only 40% of males, you would be more likely to see this difference as noteworthy. However, such a difference with a sample of only 10 students would likely make you wonder if you should take these results seriously. Results with a sample of 100 students would be much more impressive.

You examine the theme of probability in scientific research with the use of statistics. A **statistical test** applied to your data will tell you the likelihood that these data could have occurred by chance. If you fail to achieve statistical significance with your data, you cannot rule out chance as a likely explanation of them. Thus, you cannot take them seriously in your conclusions. Suppose you found that students had a slightly higher score on knowledge of scientific research at the end of a lesson than before the lesson began but your data failed to be statistically significant. Under these circumstances, you should conclude that you failed to find that your students improved in research knowledge. You should not conclude that they had a slight improvement. Why? Because your data can be explained by chance, and you should not take them seriously. If you had found your data to be statistically significant, then you could conclude that you found that your students had achieved a slight gain in knowledge.

Limitations of Common Sense

There is much wisdom in common sense, but there are pitfalls as well. Common sense is not a form of knowledge based on scientific inquiry. It is used here to show the connections between ideas we may embrace and the nature of science. There are many commonsense phrases from past times that may have been refuted by science; so we no longer embrace them.

PSEUDOSCIENCE AS AN ALTERNATIVE TO SCIENCE

Pseudoscience presents the appearance of science but lacks a scientific basis (Thyer & Pignotti, 2015). An assertion of an idea based on pseudoscience may provide tables and charts that are behind the idea presented, but these tables and charts have not been validated by scientific studies. Another characteristic of pseudoscience is the reliance only on anecdotal evidence to support the idea or theory. Anecdotal evidence is the use of single examples that fit one's theory. But anecdotal evidence is quite weak and is not considered to be a legitimate basis for scientific inquiry. You can find an example to prove just about any point you make. Science is based on the systematic review of many facts, not just a few examples.

Another characteristic of claims based on pseudoscience is a tendency to cherry-pick facts to fit the theory rather than make an objective examination of all facts relevant to the theory. One of the red flags of pseudoscience is a profound claim of effectiveness. You have heard the statement "If something seems to be too good to be true, it probably is not true." Solutions based on pseudoscience often claim greatness in the absence of scientific evidence of any effectiveness at all.

Advocates of approaches that are in the category of pseudoscience usually are not inclined to engage in serious scientific work to test the approach, and these people will work hard to make excuses when evidence is produced that refutes the theory. The approach of science is to put the burden of proof on the researcher, to prove that an assertion is correct. The approach of the advocate for pseudoscience is to reverse the burden of proof and claim that the new approach should be considered correct until science clearly proves that it is not.

A good source on this topic is the book *Science and Pseudoscience* by Thyer and Pignotti (2015). You can see in this book a discussion of many treatment approaches that fall into the category of pseudoscience. For example, you will find information on Reiki assessment, thought field therapy, neurolinguistics programming, holding therapy for children, and militaristic boot camps for youth. There are many more. These are just a few examples.

If you see a model of practice that has met the criteria for being pseudoscience, you do not necessarily have evidence that this practice is effective or that it is not effective. Instead, you have information suggesting that there is a lack of evidence of its effectiveness. You also have information suggesting that the basis for the claim of success is not consistent with a scientific basis for decision making. It may be effective but without evidence to prove it. It may be ineffective. In fact, it may even be harmful. We will not know unless we have full evidence.

There have been treatments that have been found, through scientific evidence, to be harmful. An example is the Scared Straight approach to the prevention of delinquency. This program exposes at-risk youth to the perils of prison life by taking them to prison for the day and having them listen to the messages of the prisoners about how bad prison life is. The assumption of this program is that this exposure will scare these youth sufficiently to cause them to avoid a life of crime. The results, however, have shown that it makes things worse. Here is the plain language summary of a review of many studies of this program:

> Programs such as "Scared Straight" involve organized visits to prison facilities by juvenile delinquents or children at risk for becoming delinquent. The programs are designed to deter participants from future offending by providing firsthand observations of prison life and interaction with adult inmates. This review, which is an update of one published in 2002, includes nine studies that involved 946 teenagers, almost all males. The studies were conducted in different parts of the USA and involved young people of different races whose average age ranged from 15 to 17 years. Results indicate that not only do these programs fail to deter crime, but they actually lead to more offending behavior. The intervention increases the odds of offending by between 1.6 to 1 and 1.7 to 1. Government officials permitting this program need to adopt rigorous evaluation efforts to ensure that they are not causing more harm to the very citizens they pledge to protect. (Petrosino, Turpin-Petrosino, Hollis-Peel, & Lavenberg, 2013)

In Figure 1.2, you can see a graphic depiction of how pseudoscience sometimes convinces people of the credibility of a practice that does not deserve it.

What should you do if you see a claim about a practice that might be based on pseudoscience? You should find evidence with regard to the approach that you see advocated. A quick review of literature databases can reveal if there is such evidence and what the evidence shows. If you fail to find evidence, this should not be interpreted to mean that a given service is not effective. But if there is no evidence, why should you embrace it in view of the fact there are likely many alternatives that have been subjected to scientific testing? And, of course, if there have been a lot of studies with consistent negative findings, you should see this as clear evidence that this is not a good approach to service.

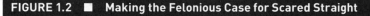

FIGURE 1.2 ■ Making the Felonious Case for Scared Straight

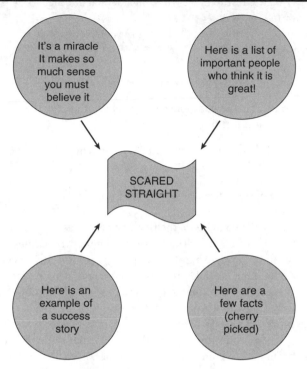

Keep in mind that science relies on relevant facts, objectively reviewed, on a carefully articulated question. You can review evidence about a particular question through a review of literature databases that will show you articles that have examined the particular question scientifically.

APPLYING THE BASIC PRINCIPLES OF SCIENCE: DOES THE FULL MOON MAKE US DIFFERENT?

Let's employ our learning about these principles with regard to a research question. This is an example that was presented in another text (York, 1997). We will use one that is simple and may even be fun. Have you ever heard someone say "It must be the full moon" when they witness strange behavior? When this author asked whether the full moon affects the behavior of mental health clients, he often received an affirmative response from social workers and others. Many people are convinced that the full moon has such an effect.

Let's suppose that we have decided to conduct a study to see if this proposition is true. We will go through the research process to examine it. We will examine the knowledge base currently available to decide where to go from there. If the question has already been well answered by existing research, we will conclude that another study is not necessary; so we will stop our inquiry there.

What is the purpose of our study? Which is the better way to state our purpose given the spirit of scientific inquiry?

1. To prove that the full moon causes unusual behavior

2. To demonstrate that there is more strange behavior during the full moon than when the moon is not full

3. To determine if there is more strange behavior during the full moon than when the moon is not full

4. To prove that the full moon is not related to unusual behavior

What is your choice? If you choose the first one or the last one, you will clearly find yourself outside the bounds of the spirit of scientific inquiry. Remember that science is a method of finding out rather than a method of proving a point. If you choose the second one, you will make the same mistake. If your purpose is to demonstrate that something is true, you are not speaking according to the spirit of scientific inquiry. So this leaves the third option, which is consistent with the spirit of scientific inquiry.

If we seek to prove a point, we will naturally fall into various traps that will hamper our pursuit of knowledge about the subject. Remember that research is a process of discovery, not justification. We should engage in a process of inquiry that is designed to provide an objective appraisal of our research subject. The reduction of the potential of human bias is key to accomplishing this. So our first principle of science is as follows: *Scientific research is a process of finding out, not a process of justification.*

Another principle that undergirds the scientific method is that *you should not reinvent the wheel*. This means that you should start your inquiry with a review of what is already known about your research question. In our review of the question about the full moon and strange behavior, we found that there have been a great number of studies undertaken.

So do we need to engage in another one? Maybe but only if the existing research has left some point of the debate uncovered. If you search enough, you will usually find a special aspect of your inquiry that has not yet been fully investigated. The main point here is not to discourage the continued pursuit of a theme but to find what is already known, so that you can couch your inquiry in a manner that is more likely to add to our existing knowledge base.

There have been numerous studies on this question. One such study was conducted on attempted suicides (Mathew, Lindsay, Shanmjganatan, & Eapen, 1991). The records of the Accident and Emergency Department of a large urban hospital were examined to determine if the rate of suicide attempts that came to the attention of this hospital was different during the full moon and at other times. The number of suicides attempted for each day of 1 month were recorded. The full moon fell on Day 15. On that day, a total of 19 suicide attempts were recorded. The largest number of suicide attempts (23) were recorded on Days 3 and 17, one of which was close to the full moon, but the other was at a great distance from it. The number of attempts on the day of the full moon was slightly higher than the average for the entire month, but the difference was determined to be nonsignificant (statistically). When we examine this question, we might also want to compare the 3 days when the moon was at its fullest with the 3 days when it was the least full. If the full moon causes suicide, we would expect the 3 days of the full moon to have a significantly higher suicide rate. For the data from this study, the average number of suicide attempts during the full moon period was 18 as compared with 17 for the new moon period (the 3 days during which the moon is the least full). You would probably conclude that this difference was not significant; therefore, the rate of suicides close to the full moon was not different from the rate when the moon was the least full.

So what do you think? Are you yet convinced that the full moon does not affect behavior, or do you believe that there is a need for further review of the literature?

I hope you said that there is a need for further review of the literature. Why? This is only one study that addressed only one type of behavior (suicide). Maybe the full moon affects mental health in some way other than suicide.

So let's assume that you said there is a need for further review of the research on this theme. In one such study, a set of researchers examined the records of a psychiatric hospital to determine if dangerous behavior of patients was more prevalent during the full moon than at other times. Dangerous behavior was defined as "erratic behavior which was assessed by qualified mental health professionals as dangerous to self or others to the extent that isolation (seclusion) or restraints were necessary to prevent harm to self or others" (Durm, Terry, & Hammonds, 1986, p. 988). Data for 3 years (1982, 1983, and 1984) were collected. The average number of such incidents of dangerous behavior was actually higher (13.17 per day) during the period when the moon was not full than it was during the period of the full moon (11.61 per day). So these data clearly did not support the idea that the full moon makes people different.

Well, where are you now? Are you ready to conclude that the full moon does not affect behavior? Or are you prepared to review additional studies? I would be inclined to review additional studies because there are so many other aspects of behavior that might be influenced by the full moon.

If you wish for further review, there is a special type of research that could be quite useful. It is a type of research that combines the data from many studies to see the answer to the research question. Such was the case in an article by Byrnes and Kelly (1992). They reviewed 12 studies that examined the relationship between the full moon and things such as crisis calls to police stations, poison centers, and crisis intervention centers. Their conclusion from this review was that "there is no evidence whatsoever for the contention that calls of a more emotional or 'out-of-control' nature occur more often at the full moon" (p. 779).

Now maybe you are more convinced that there is little evidence of a relationship between human behavior and the full moon. But if you are a tenacious reviewer of the literature, you might go another step and see if there are other reviews of the literature that combined various studies about the full moon. Another review of many studies was undertaken by Rotten and Kelly (1985). A total of 37 published studies were included in their review. They also concluded that there was little evidence to support the theory that the full moon affects people's behavior.

This pattern of findings of nonsignificant differences between behaviors during the full moon and other periods is found in a review of other sources. But one study was found that claimed to have found a relationship between the full moon and behavior.

That study was conducted by Hicks-Casey and Potter (1991). They found that there was more aggressive acting-out misbehavior in a sample of 20 developmentally delayed women during the full moon than at other times. However, the analysis of their data was challenged by Flynn (1991) as having major flaws. And even if you believed that this was a sound study, you should recognize that it is only one study of only 20 people. Perhaps now the score is 1 for the full moon and about 50 against it. Where do you now make your bet about the next study to be undertaken on this theme?

Do we still want to conduct a study of the effect of the full moon on behavior? Our review of the existing literature would suggest that this question has been substantially answered already. Do we want to spend our time reinventing the wheel? We would not, however, be reinventing the wheel if we found a new angle on this topic, such as a type of behavior not yet examined. But, generally speaking, it seems that the evidence clearly fails to support the conclusion that the full moon affects behavior.

Are you convinced? Maybe you are of the opinion that you have seen strange behavior during the full moon yourself, so you don't need help from research studies. Let's examine that opinion by considering the nature of the data that would be included in a review of our question. Let's suppose that we have conducted a study in which we measured people during both the full moon and the new moon (when the moon is least full) and have also measured whether the individuals in our study have exhibited unusual behavior. Exhibit 1.1 reflects hypothetical data that illustrate how this would be examined.

The hypothetical data in Exhibit 1.1 show that the proportion of people with unusual behavior during the full moon was 25%, and this is the same as the proportion of people who demonstrated unusual behavior during the new moon. This would suggest that unusual behavior occurs at the same rate during the full moon and when the moon is not full. Note that it was the proportions rather than the numbers that were the critical facts to review here.

If Jim says that he has seen unusual behavior during the full moon and does not review other data, he is restricting his inquiry to only one cell in this table—the one that reflects unusual behavior during the full moon. He has not examined the number (and proportion) of people who did not exhibit unusual behavior when the moon was full, and more important, he has not compared the behavior during the full moon with behavior when the moon was least full. So he has engaged in an inquiry that is incomplete, something that is not characteristic of the scientific method (or critical thinking).

A third principle that undergirds the scientific method of inquiry suggests that *two heads are better than one*. If we believe this statement, we will want to assess the

EXHIBIT 1.1
HYPOTHETICAL DATA ON THE FULL MOON AND UNUSUAL BEHAVIOR

	Full Moon	New Moon	Total
Number with unusual behavior	25 (25%)	50 (25%)	75
Number who did not exhibit unusual behavior	75 (75%)	150 (75%)	225
Total	100 (100%)	200 (100%)	300

dependability of our method of measuring strange behavior. If we believe that two heads are better than one, we would seek evidence of different kinds. If hospital records are not accurate, a review of them would not provide an accurate answer to our question. But if we examine both hospital records and police records, we are in a better position. If fact, the more "heads" we examine, the better. We could also review school records or something else. If we find a consistent pattern, we would feel more comfortable drawing a conclusion. Our review of the evidence regarding the full moon considered a good number of sources of data, not just one. So we adhered to the saying that two heads are better than one.

The fourth principle is that *things sometimes happen just by chance*. What if we found that the proportion of the 217 patients in a mental hospital who were observed to act more strange than usual was 37% during the full moon and 31% when the moon was not full? Could this difference be something that we could write off to chance? If so, we would not conclude that there was a relationship between the full moon and this kind of behavior. This means that we would be unlikely to bet our money on the discovery of a relationship between the full moon and strange behavior if we had the opportunity to repeat this study.

What if we found that 68% of these 217 patients acted more strange than usual during the full moon while only 24% did so when the moon was not full? In this case, we would be less likely to write off these differences to chance. We would be more likely to conclude that we had found a legitimate relationship between the full moon and strange behavior. There are ways to estimate the likelihood that a given set of results would occur by chance. This is the task of statistics. Ruling out chance as a good explanation of our data is based on things like proportions that reveal the strength of the relationship, as noted above, but it is also determined by the number of people from whom you drew the data (i.e., the sample size). In our example, we might be more cautious in our conclusions if the number of people in our data from the mental hospital had been 17 rather than 217. We would normally be more cautious the less the number of people in our study.

The final principle that undergirds the scientific approach is that *we should be cautious in drawing conclusions when we are wearing the research hat*. For example, we should be very careful to ensure that our study conclusions are consistent with the data we have analyzed. If we had applied a statistical measure to our data and found that the likelihood that our results would occur by chance was high, we would be reluctant to conclude that we had found a legitimate relationship between the variables in our study (e.g., the full moon and strange behavior). In addition, we should be cautious in concluding that our one study has found the final proof of an assertion. We should consider our data to be incomplete to some extent, and we should invite others to continue the research.

When we examine the literature, we will find that different researchers have found different methods for studying our research question. The results are not always consistent. Thus, we should treat the results of any one study with caution. The more studies we find with consistent results, the more confident (and less cautious) we are entitled to be.

We have examined common sense and science though our examination of the literature on whether people act differently when the moon is full. Our literature review has lead us to the conclusion that we do not need to collect and analyze new data on this question because it has been fully reviewed already. To do another study would make us vulnerable to the criticism that we are trying to reinvent the wheel.

Chapter Practice Exercises

Why Do Some People Think the Full Moon Affects Human Behavior?

In this section is a practice exercise where you apply what you have learned. You will be asked to conduct a discussion with a person about his or her opinions about the relationship between the full moon and human behaviors. You will explore their appreciation for science as a way of learning. You will do the same for a second and a third person, and you will report your findings to others.

Competencies Demonstrated by This Practice Exercise

1. The ability to identify differences between the use of science as a way of knowing and other alternatives for guidance in coming to conclusions

2. The ability to identify sources of resistance to using science as a way of knowing

3. The ability to identify some mechanisms that can improve one's appreciation of science as a way of knowing

4. The ability to identify how science can help with important decisions

5. The ability to identify some of the limitations of science as a way of knowing

Activities for This Practice Exercise

In this chapter, you examined evidence about the effect of the full moon on human behavior. You are asked to select someone for a discussion of this theme. The steps are given below.

1. Make a copy of Exhibit 1.2 to share with people with whom you will conduct a discussion about the effect of the full moon.

2. Select your first person for this dialogue. This cannot be a classmate who knows about this exercise. It must be someone who does not know about the evidence with regard to the full moon and human behavior. Engage in the following discussion:

a. Ask, "Do you believe that people act differently during the full moon than at other times?"

b. Classify this person's answer as (i) I believe it, (ii) I am not sure, or (iii) I do not believe it.

c. Ask the person why he or she believes that the full moon affects behavior or does not affect it (or is not sure). Make notes about the answer. Use direct quotes from what is said to the extent this is feasible. The title of your page of notes for this first person should be the category the person is in (i.e., I believe it, I am not sure, or I do not believe it).

d. Share the information from Exhibit 1.2 with this person. Ask for his or her response, and make notes about it, with particular reference to the extent that this person appreciates science as a way of knowing and why he or she does so or does not.

e. Repeat these procedures (Steps a–d) for a second person, and make notes as directed. Do the same for a third person.

What You Will Report From This Practice Exercise

Prepare a brief report on your exercise experience, with a focus on how the participants demonstrated an appreciation (or lack of appreciation) for science. How many of your three respondents had each of the three possible categories of belief about this question? What were the key reasons why they held their views? Was it because others had told them this or because they had witnessed it or what? How were they influenced by the review of Exhibit 1.2?

EXHIBIT 1.2

A BRIEF REVIEW OF THE LITERATURE ON THE FULL MOON AND UNUSUAL BEHAVIOR

In a research textbook by York (1997), a brief review of the literature on the full moon and behavior was undertaken. York employed a library database to find scientific studies on this question. He decided to review the first five articles he could find that reported scientific studies of behavior during the full moon and when the moon was not full. He used search words such as *full moon* and reviewed the first five articles that reported a scientific study of the relationship between the full moon and behavior. He did not engage in the selective review of only those studies with a certain result, such as a finding that there was a relationship between the full moon and human behavior. He realized that such a procedure would not be consistent with the nature of scientific inquiry. Here are the results of the first five sources he found.

1. Mathew et al. (1991) reviewed suicide attempts reported to a hospital. He found that the suicide attempts during the full moon were slightly more than on other days of the month but the amount of difference was not statistically significant (i.e., it could easily be explained by chance).

2. A study by Durm et al. (1986) found that the incidence of dangerous behaviors exhibited by patients in a psychiatric hospital was actually higher when the moon was not full than when it was but this difference was not statistically significant.

3. A pair of researchers reviewed 12 studies that examined the relationship between the full moon and things such as crisis calls to police stations, poison centers, and crisis intervention centers. Their conclusion from this review was that "there is no evidence whatsoever for the contention that calls of a more emotional or 'out-of-control' nature occur more often at the full moon" (Byrnes & Kelly, 1992, p. 779).

4. Another review of many studies was undertaken by Rotten and Kelly (1985). A total of 37 published studies were included in their review. They concluded that there was little evidence to support the theory that the full moon affects people's behavior.

5. A study was conducted by Hicks-Casey and Potter (1991). They found that there were more aggressive acting-out misbehaviors in a sample of 20 developmentally delayed women during the full moon than at other times. This was the only study with results suggesting that there was a relationship between the full moon and unusual behavior.

York (2018) reviewed these findings and concluded that the evidence clearly showed that the full moon was not related to unusual behavior. A total of 51 studies, from the five articles, had been found that failed to show a relationship between the full moon and unusual behaviors. Only 1 study was found that showed this relationship. The evidence was so overwhelming that York felt that he did not need to engage in further review of the literature unless he was undertaking a study of his own regarding this question. This was enough evidence for him for the time being.

CHAPTER REVIEW

Chapter Key Learnings

In this chapter, you have reviewed the nature of science and social work research, which is founded on it. You have examined alternatives to science, with special emphasis on pseudoscience. You should now be more wary of false claims. You have been encouraged to use science to help with practice decisions. Connections between critical thinking and science have also been examined in this chapter.

You have reviewed how the social scientist is unique. After this chapter, you are more likely to recognize that social work research is designed to further existing knowledge. You will recognize that it relies on a systematic process of inquiry, including the collection and analysis of data. You will be aware of the fact that science provides a fair playing field for opposite claims of reality. Armed with these learnings, you will see that science should be used as a guide for social work practice.

Among the specific learnings from this chapter are the following:

1. Science is a method of inquiry that has the purpose of discovery, not justification. You do not engage in scientific research to prove a point. Instead, you do it to find out the truth.

2. Science is systematic, objective, and comprehensive.

3. Science relies on objective measurement, leading to data from which conclusions are drawn.

4. Science is designed to reduce human error in decision making, as evidenced by a reduction in decision regret.

5. Science is founded on common principles with critical thinking, which emphasizes each of the critical aspects of scientific inquiry, including the purpose of reducing decision error.

6. Science as a basis for knowledge is different from experience, authority, or tradition, each of which may be useful for the social worker but are based on methods that are different from the methods of scientific study.

7. Science is distinctively different from pseudoscience as a way of discovery because pseudoscience, unlike science, tends to rely on unsubstantiated claims, anecdotal evidence, authority, and cherry-picking of facts to support a preconceived conclusion.

8. Science, as a method of inquiry, can be viewed in light of some commonsense phrases such as the following:

    a.   Don't put the cart before the horse!

    b.   Two heads are better than one!

    c.   Some things happen just by chance!

    d.   Don't reinvent the wheel!

Chapter Discussion Questions

1. Suppose someone said to you, "My 20 years of practice experience is my scientific evidence." What do you think of this statement?

2. Under what circumstances have you engaged in service activities (or treatment approaches) for which you had no scientific evidence of effectiveness. Did you think about evidence in this regard? Did you seek evidence by asking others or going to the literature?

3. What is one of the signs that an assertion about practice may be based on pseudoscience?

4. Suppose you found that your clients had a measured gain of 20% on an anxiety scale between the beginning and end of treatment but the differences between the pretest and posttest were not found to be statistically significant. Would you conclude that your clients had a modest gain with regard to anxiety? Explain.

5. What do you think about the question of whether the full moon is associated with unusual behavior?

6. What kinds of professional decisions do you believe are most in need of assistance from scientific studies?

7. Suppose you are using a practice method that has little evidence of its effectiveness with the target population on whom you are using it. Do you believe that the burden on you to evaluate your practice (with data) is greater because of this lack of evidence?

Chapter Test

1. A researcher has decided that he wants to conduct a research study of the people in his fishing club, using interviews of each member of the club. He has not decided on a purpose or general research question that he should pursue with this group of people. He asks others for advice on what research question or issue he should pursue in this study. What is the error in this situation, in reference to the various phrases that connect common sense with *science*?
   a. Don't put the cart before the horse
   b. Two heads are better than one
   c. Don't throw the baby out with the bathwater
   d. Some things happen just by chance

2. Suppose you have decided to get feedback from your clients. What step would logically come first in the research process?
   a. Selecting the questions to put on the questionnaire
   b. Selecting the sample of persons to receive the questionnaire

   c. Determining the purpose of the study and the general question to be answered
   d. Selecting the statistical measures to employ in the analysis of the data

3. Which of the following statements of the purpose of a research study is consistent with the spirit of scientific inquiry?
   a. To demonstrate that dialectical behavioral therapy is effective in the treatment of persons with borderline personality disorder
   b. To challenge the criticism that human services are not worth the cost
   c. Both of the above
   d. None of the above

4. Which of the following is demonstrated by the above quiz question?
   a. Don't put the cart before the house!
   b. Don't reinvent the wheel!
   c. Scientific research is a process of discovery, not a justification
   d. Two heads are better than one

5. Suppose you have decided to conduct a study of whether the full moon makes people act strange, or different. Many people have asserted that the full moon makes people "crazy" or "strange" or "weird" and so forth because they have witnessed such behavior during the full moon. Is this information sufficient to draw a scientific conclusion about the effect of the full moon?

   a. Yes, because the perceptions of people of the behavior of others should be considered trustworthy; otherwise, there would be no way to do scientific studies of social behavior

   b. Yes, because this information provides a clear connection between this kind of behavior and the presence of the full moon; if people act this way during the full moon, it is logical to assert that the full moon has an effect

   c. No, because you would need to employ only instruments published in books to measure your variables

   d. No, because you need also to analyze information about the presence of this behavior when the moon is full and when it is not full as well as the absence of this behavior when the moon is full and when it is not full

6. Suppose you conducted a study with the purpose of determining if those who regularly engage in aerobic exercise have less stress than others. You collect data on exercise and stress for a group of people and find that those who exercise have less stress but the difference in stress scores between those who did and did not exercise was not statistically significant. What commonsense phrase is related to this situation?

   a. Don't reinvent the wheel

   b. Some things happen just by chance

   c. Don't put the cart before the horse

   d. You can't make a silk purse out of a sow's ear

7. A researcher gave a questionnaire to those who attended his dinner party and found that the eight men at the party had an average salary that was higher than the average salary for the 13 women in attendance. These differences were found to be statistically significant. What would be the appropriate conclusion?

   a. Salaries for men are higher than for women

   b. Salaries for men are higher than for women in the city where this party took place

   c. Of those who attended this party, salaries for men were found to be higher than for women

   d. Of those who attended this party, there were not enough people to draw any conclusions

8. A police officer investigated an auto accident and needed to decide who was at fault. There were three people on the street who were witnesses. The officer interviewed all these three people. What basic saying in common sense does this situation illustrate?

   a. Some things happen just by chance

   b. Two heads are better than one

   c. Don't put the cart before the horse

   d. Don't throw the baby out with the bathwater

9. Are there any steps you take before you draw conclusions in a scientific study?

   a. Yes, you develop the basic research question

   b. Yes, you develop the research methods (who will be in the study, how the variables will be measured, etc.)

   c. Yes, you do both of the above

   d. No, you draw your conclusions from the literature review you conducted

10. A researcher has decided to conduct a study of whether people act differently during the full moon than at other times. She has decided to compare the number of disciplinary incidents in school during the full moon and the new moon (when the moon is least full). A fellow researcher has reported that dozens of many similar studies have been done and almost all show that there is no difference in behavior during the full moon. When this fellow researcher suggests that it does not make sense to do such a study, what is the saying that is most appropriate for this?

    a. Don't reinvent the wheel
    b. Two heads are better than one
    c. Some things happen just by chance
    d. Don't put the cart before the horse

ANSWERS: 1 = a; 2 = c; 3 = d; 4 = c; 5 = d; 6 = b; 7 = c; 8 = b; 9 = c; 10 = a

Chapter Glossary

Chance. A possibility. The absence of any cause of events (actualities) that can be predicted. In scientific inquiry, you typically have a theory being tested by systematically collected data, but you realize that data can occur by chance, so you test to see if your data can too easily be explained by chance to be taken seriously with regard to the research question being examined.

Cherry-picking. A biased selection and presentation of facts to support an opinion.

Critical thinking. Disciplined thinking that favors rationality, open-mindedness, and systematically analyzed evidence, and requires an idea (theory, proposal, opinion, etc.) to be effectively subjected to criticism.

False dichotomy. Asserting a claim based on the faulty assumption that there are only two alternatives when there are actually more.

Generalization of data results. The likelihood that these results would be repeated in another study using the same methods as in the current study.

Measurement error. The difference between a measurement and reality.

Pseudoscience. A process that relies on methods that are not scientific but is portrayed in a manner that seems scientific.

Science. A process that relies on a carefully articulated question, the systematic collection of data on an objective basis, the analysis of the data, and the drawing of conclusions consistent with the data.

Social scientist. Someone who applies the principles and methods of science to learn more about social phenomena.

Spirit of scientific inquiry. An atmosphere that adheres to the principles of science.

Statistical significance. A finding that suggests that chance is not a good explanation of the data results.

Statistical test. A mathematical formula that determines the likelihood that a set of data would occur (or be explained by) chance.

2

PURPOSES AND PROCESSES OF SOCIAL WORK RESEARCH

Jennifer is a social worker who serves on the research committee of a human service agency, where she works with Paula, among others. It is the responsibility of this committee to undertake research studies that can assist the agency in better achieving its mission and meeting the challenges of accountability. Paula is rather preoccupied with a simple device she has found that measures the body's level of stress. She wants to use this device in a study. Jennifer asked Paula what kind of study she wanted to undertake. Paula was not sure, but she really wanted to use this device. Jennifer asked, "Do you want to describe our clients or evaluate the outcome of a service or determine what is related to client no-shows or what?" Paula was not sure.

Jennifer discussed with Paula the fact that you should start the process of a research study not by deciding on how to measure something but, instead, with the determination of the purpose of the study. Some studies describe people. Some studies explain things by examining the relationship between variables (e.g., age might be related to client no-shows). Some studies evaluate services. Your purpose might be to describe, to explain, or to evaluate. Then you need the specific research question (e.g., Are younger clients more likely to fail to show up for appointments?). After you determine the research question, according to Jennifer, you should review the literature to see how it can guide your process of inquiry. Then you determine who will be your study subjects and how you will measure the relevant variables in your study.

The collection and analysis of data is the next step, followed by the drawing of conclusions relevant to the study results. That is the way it should go, according to Jennifer.

INTRODUCTION

This chapter will guide you through the various purposes of social work research as well as the processes you will undertake when you seek to use research to answer your questions. Do you want to describe people, explain things, evaluate services, or explore unknown territory? Your purpose will guide the decisions about your study methods. For example, are the students in your college liberal or conservative? Anyone who reviewed your study of this question would be interested in how you defined and measured your key variable. What indicates that you are liberal? What shows that you are conservative? There are many ways these terms can be defined and many ways they can be measured. What were the choices of the researcher in this instance? Because your intent is to describe people with precision, your approach to measurement is perhaps more important than it might be in some other studies.

In Chapter 1, you examined the saying "Don't put the cart before the horse!" The relevance of this saying to research is that you must follow a sequence of steps to be systematic as required by scientific inquiry. You do not decide on measurement before you have decided on the purpose of your study.

The major goal of this chapter is to help you understand the various ways in which you can characterize research so that you can heighten your awareness of the myriad concepts you need to understand in order to know where you are in a given type of research and what your essential tasks and issues are. As a social worker, for example, you need to understand the essential tasks in the evaluation of client outcome. Evaluation of client outcome is one of the four types of research when it is organized by purpose.

The basic competencies you will achieve from this chapter are as follows:

- You will better understand how to classify research by purpose, with a focus on the differences and similarities between research that is descriptive, explanatory, evaluative, or exploratory.

- You will know the differences between a program evaluation and an evaluation of an intervention and what is entailed in each.

- You will be able to distinguish between qualitative and quantitative types of measurement.

- You will be able to portray the research process from the articulation of the research question to the drawing of conclusions from your study.

The first of the above themes is the classification of studies by purpose. How would you characterize the purpose of a study you would like to undertake? Is the purpose focused on describing people, explaining things, or evaluating the outcomes of your service? These are three of the general purposes of research. Each purpose is a little different with regard to the tools you use to conduct it. This is why one of the themes of this chapter is the classification of social work research studies according to the general purpose of the study.

Another way to characterize social work research is the scope of the study. Some studies will focus on the evaluation of a broad program that has several services, while some studies will focus on a specific intervention (service) that is one part of the general program. The focus of these two types of studies is different in the scope of the data analyzed.

A third way to characterize social work research is according to the general approach to measurement. Some studies (or parts of studies) measure variables in a quantitative fashion, such as a score on a scale. Other studies measure things in a qualitative manner. Qualitative data are in the form of words from interviews or statements in a questionnaire. The analysis of these two forms of data is substantially different.

A final manner of classification of social work research is based on the steps you go through when you undertake such a study. The starting point, of course, is the purpose of the study. You don't want to put the cart before the horse!

In this chapter, you will get an overview of how social work research can be characterized and described. This guidance should help you know where you are when engaged in various research endeavors. The first theme to be examined is the characterization of social work research according to the general purpose of the study.

FOUR PURPOSES OF SOCIAL WORK RESEARCH

Among the various ways we could characterize social work research is its purpose. What is the purpose of the study? One purpose is to describe people. We will call that **descriptive research**. Another is to explain things. **Explanatory research** is the label for this type. In this research, you attempt to explain things by looking at the relationship between two (or more) variables. **Evaluative research** has the purpose of evaluating broad programs or specific interventions. **Exploratory research** is the fourth type of research when we characterize it by purpose. This type of research examines phenomena that are not well known.

The Descriptive Study

Descriptive research simply describes people (or things) one variable at a time. What, for example, is the average age of persons receiving a Master of Social Work degree at your favorite university? What is the proportion of clients in your agency who have a preschool-age child? What is the average family income of your clients? These are all descriptive questions. They do not attempt to explain. They just describe. Variables will be described one at a time. You may have eight different variables you wish to describe, but you will analyze them one at a time. So if you are posed with the question of how many variables are in your descriptive analysis, the answer is always one when it comes to the analysis of your data.

A descriptive study should pay special attention to measurement because the purpose is to accurately describe people. While accurate measurement is critical to all types of research, it is especially important in the descriptive study. If you are trying to characterize the conservatism of your fellow students, it is critical that you clearly define what is meant by conservatism before you seek a tool to measure it.

The Explanatory Study

The purpose of explanatory research, on the other hand, is to explain things by examining the relationship between variables. Are people who are regular exercisers less likely to have recent minor illnesses? This question requires the measurement of two variables: (1) whether the individual engages in regular exercise and (2) whether the individual has experienced recent minor illness. It also requires the examination of the relationship between these two variables. You would examine the data to see if the proportion of exercisers who experienced recent minor illness is lower than the proportion of those with recent minor illness who do not engage in regular exercise. And you would engage in the statistical analysis of data to see if the degree of differences between the two groups can easily be explained by **chance**. When you examine data for an explanatory study, you will always have two or more variables in your analysis of data.

A key issue for the explanatory study is the conceptual framework or theory, which provides guidance on the selection of the variables to be measured and your expectations of what you will find from your data. A **theory** is an attempt to explain. It can often be a display in a chart that shows the expected relationships between things. For example, you might find a graphic that shows that stressors cause stress but stress can be reduced by more social support.

The conceptual framework shows a connection between the knowledge base gathered from the literature review and the methods used to find the answer to the research question. Why would you expect to find that people who exercise are less likely to have minor illnesses? Why would you expect to find that people with more social support have less stress? Why would you expect to find that parents with more knowledge about child development will be less likely to be abusive parents? These are among the questions on which your knowledge base will provide guidance.

The Evaluative Study

The purpose of evaluative research is to evaluate programs or interventions with regard to various measures of success. In this book, we will focus on the evaluation of interventions. An intervention is a specific service to an individual or a small group (e.g., therapy for Mr. Smith, support group for caregivers of handicapped individuals, etc.). This requires the measurement of client outcome. Did our clients have lower depression scores at the end of treatment than before treatment? Did our clients have higher grades during the semester of our special intervention than in the semester prior to it? Were our homeless clients more likely to find a home within 6 months compared with the national average for homeless people?

A key issue for the evaluative study is causation. If you find that your clients have improved during the course of the treatment, what do you conclude is the cause of this improvement? Is it the treatment? Could it be something else? The study methods you employ will help answer this question.

The Exploratory Study

The purpose of exploratory research is to examine concepts or themes that are not well known. Suppose you are interested in the theme of adolescent moral values, especially with regard to stages of decline. How does an adolescent typically move from one stage of morals to a lower one? The literature database PsycINFO has approximately 4 million articles, so it seems like a good way to examine how much is known about a subject like this. A review of this database in May 2016 with the words "moral decline" resulted in only six articles, but none of these articles addressed the theme of stages of moral decline. Perhaps we now know that this theme has not been researched very much. If we continue our search of the vast literature that is available, we will likely find something on this theme, but our examination of this large database shows that there is not a vast amount of literature on it. So perhaps an explanatory or exploratory study is needed.

A key issue for the exploratory study is whether the methods employed capture the essence of the theme you are pursuing. Exploratory studies will be connected with qualitative measurement in this book, not because you must use qualitative methods but because there is a natural fit between exploratory research and qualitative measurement. The exploratory study attempts to go into themes on which there is little existing knowledge. Qualitative measurement is more flexible than quantitative measurement. It seems logical that flexible measurement would be suitable for finding more information when little information is readily available.

Evaluating Programs and Interventions

There are two major ways we characterize an evaluative research study with regard to scope. The scope of some evaluative studies is broad, and they could be labeled as program evaluations. The scope of other evaluative studies is narrower, and they will be labeled as evaluations of interventions. More detail on this distinction will be offered in a later chapter. In this chapter, you will be given an introduction to this distinction.

A **program evaluation** may entail the examination of various aspects of a program. An example could be the child abuse treatment and prevention program, which has services designed to review complaints of child abuse and take necessary legal action, services designed to offer treatment for abused children or abusive caregivers, and services designed to prevent child abuse in the community. This evaluation might examine the effectiveness of the intake service in the initial assessment of complaints of child abuse, the extent to which good standards of service are being implemented, or the degree to which repeat offenses of child abuse have gone down in the past year. Each of these could be viewed as an evaluation of success.

An **intervention evaluation** is more narrow. An example could be your evaluation of your parent education intervention for a group of 11 parents confirmed for child abuse. You want to measure the extent to which they have increased their knowledge of good parenting practices. Another example could be your evaluation of the effectiveness of your treatment for a single abused child for the improvement of self-esteem. For each evaluation of an intervention, you have a designated client or group of clients, and you will measure each client on the same outcome measures.

You might say that your evaluation of your practice as an individual social worker is an evaluation of an intervention, while your participation in the evaluation of a major program is an example of a program evaluation. In the latter case, the outcomes are not significantly due to your own practice. This book places emphasis on the evaluation of your practice as a social worker, so we will focus more on the evaluation of interventions.

The Program Evaluation

When you participate in a program evaluation, you may examine any aspect of the service system. The service system will show all the parts of a program that contribute to success in one way or another. We can view some of the aspects of the system as follows:

1. A depressed woman asks your agency for therapy.

2. This woman is eligible for your service because she is a resident of your county and this is the only eligibility criterion that is employed for this service.

3. The client receives cognitive–behavioral therapy.

4. The therapist is a licensed clinical social worker, so she is qualified to offer the service.

5. The therapy is in the form of eight 1-hour treatment sessions.

6. The client's level of depression is reduced by 35%.

7. The estimated cost of this therapy is $800 ($100 per hour of therapy).

In a later chapter, you will see the above in the systems terminology of input, process, output, and outcome. You will also see that efficiency is determined by the cost per output (e.g., an hour of therapy). For now, you will review the complexity of the aspects of service that could be the subject of a program evaluation.

Let's suppose you are evaluating the system for the Hampton Behavioral Health Practice. Each of the clients treated for depression by this agency is given a pretest for depression using a given depression scale where higher scores represent higher depression. This scale has the score of 20 as the cut point for a level of depression that indicates that treatment is needed. Let's suppose that you examined the mean pretest depression score for the clients of this agency and found that it was below 20. This suggests that the typical depressed client did not have a level of depression that suggested a need for therapy. These data are contrary to the major goal of the agency, which focuses on the rehabilitation of persons who are severely depressed. You have evaluated one aspect of the service system for this agency and learned that it is not doing a good job of reaching the intended target **population**.

You may learn from a program evaluation that a given agency is not adhering to the standards of good service with regard to things such as the credentials of the staff or the size of caseloads. Adherence to established protocols for the delivery of service is another possible theme for a part of a program evaluation. For example, the Rape Crisis Program of your hospital may have a list of seven things that must be done for each victim of rape who is served. You might examine the cases for this service to see if all these elements of service were offered. What percentage of clients had all the elements provided?

The most critical aspect of an evaluation of a service system is the measurement of client outcome. Did the clients get better? Is the level of depression lower? Are the school grades higher? Is the recidivism rate for delinquency lower? Here you can see some conceptual overlap between the program evaluation and the evaluation of an intervention. You might want to characterize a program evaluation as having, among its many components, data on various interventions.

The Intervention Evaluation

For the part of this book that deals with evaluation research, the evaluation of an intervention is the priority. An intervention is a set of activities designed to achieve an objective with a client or group of clients. The focus is on outcomes. Did this group of 18 discharged hospital patients adhere to the discharge plan at a level higher than that for patients of other hospitals? Were the treatment scores for Ms. Jones for self-esteem higher in the treatment period than in the baseline period (i.e., before the treatment started). Did this group of eight at-risk middle school students have higher grades during the semester of the intervention than in the prior semester?

QUANTITATIVE AND QUALITATIVE MEASUREMENT

There are two major types of measurement in social work research—quantitative and qualitative. With **quantitative measurement**, you measure each variable either as a category (e.g., male or female) or as a number (e.g., age measured in years, score on the anxiety scale, etc.). When you measure your variables in a qualitative manner, on the other hand, you will normally have words to examine. This would be the case if you have responses to an open-ended question on a survey. For example, you may confront the following question on a questionnaire: "In your own words, how would you describe your feelings about being a parent?" In this case, you put down words on the page. These words will be examined in a qualitative study. Sometimes you make notes from your observations of an environment you are studying. In this case, you are also analyzing words, the words you wrote down.

For quantitative measurement, the researcher decides how to categorize things and wishes for the study subject to respond according to these categories. As a study subject, you may be asked to select one of the following categories that best reflect your opinion about a theme: *strongly agree, agree, undecided, disagree,* or *strongly disagree*. With **qualitative measurement**, the study subject has the flexibility to determine the words that will characterize his or her thoughts on the theme of the question being posed. Because of this flexibility, the qualitative method of measurement is more often found in exploratory studies.

While you can measure your phenomenon of interest either qualitatively or quantitatively with regard to any of the four types of research, we will use examples in this book of qualitative measurement (i.e., words) for the exploratory research study, and we will examine the other three types with examples of quantitative research (i.e., categories or numbers). The rationale for this decision is that you are more likely to find quantitative measurement in descriptive, explanatory, and evaluative studies and qualitative measurement is more likely to be found in exploratory studies.

Among the various definitions of qualitative research is the one below from the University of Southern California Libraries Research Guides (n.d.):

> The word qualitative implies an emphasis on the qualities of entities and on processes and meanings that are not experimentally examined or measured [if measured at all] in terms of quantity, amount, intensity, or frequency. Qualitative researchers stress the socially constructed nature of reality, the intimate relationship between the researcher and what is studied, and the situational constraints that shape inquiry. Such researchers emphasize the value-laden nature of inquiry. They seek answers to questions that stress how social experience is created and given meaning. In contrast, quantitative studies emphasize the measurement and analysis of causal relationships between variables, not processes. Qualitative forms of inquiry are considered by many social and behavioral scientists to be as much a perspective on how to approach investigating a research problem as it is a method.

The qualitative study is more suitable for situations where little is known, so you are not in a good position to develop a study hypothesis and measure variables in a quantitative manner. If there are few theories that guide your understanding of the phenomenon of interest, you will likely choose a qualitative method of measurement. If you are seeking to understand social processes rather than describe or explain reality, you are more likely to select the qualitative method.

The quantitative method of measurement, on the other hand, is more suitable for the testing of a theory or hypothesis, or the careful description of a phenomenon in concrete terms. It is more likely to be used in an evaluative study, which has the purpose of determining if a social work intervention has had the intended effect on the client's target behavior. In such situations, you will normally have an idea about how to measure variables in a quantitative manner.

THE RESEARCH PROCESS

There are four steps in the research process that will be discussed in various examples throughout this book. The first entails the development of the research question and the knowledge base that will guide various aspects of the study. The second step is the development of the study methods with regard to themes such as sampling, measurement, and so forth. The third step entails the collection and analysis of data, while the final step engages the researcher in the presentation of the study conclusions.

Step 1: Developing the Research Question and Knowledge Base

The research study starts with a particular interest. You may want to know what causes client no-shows for appointments. Perhaps you want to know if women have better outcomes than men. Maybe your question is whether the clients of your program are satisfied with their services or have achieved the objectives of the intervention.

Here are some research questions you could examine:

1. Do those who engage in regular aerobic exercise have less of a tendency to experience minor illnesses (e.g., colds, flu) than those who do not?

2. What traits of a good work manager are viewed as more valuable than other traits?

3. Do those with higher scores for stressors have higher scores for stress?

4. Do those with higher scores for social support have lower scores for stress?

5. Do the clients of the New Horizons Program have lower scores for depression at the end of the treatment than before?

Can you characterize each of the above questions with regard to purpose? In other words, which ones are descriptive, explanatory, evaluative, or exploratory? Before you go further, give it a try. Select a label for each of these questions.

What about the first question? Is it descriptive? If so, it is a question that attempts only to describe one variable, even though it may have several variables that are to be described, such as age, income, race, or gender. You will notice that two variables are identified—exercise and illness. Does this question attempt to describe exercise by itself or examine the relationship of this variable with the other variable? Well, it requires the examination of the relationship between exercise and illness, so it is an explanatory study question. You cannot answer this question by reporting that 40% of your study subjects say that they engage in aerobic exercise. You must compare this rate with the rate for those who do not exercise.

What about the second question? Is it a descriptive question? Even though it lists traits, it is attempting to find out the rate at which the study subjects value a particular trait, so it is a descriptive study. The results may show that 34% favor Trait 1, 55% favor Trait 2, and so forth. It attempts to describe each trait one by one, not to examine the relationship between the traits and another variable.

Is the third question descriptive? It lists two variables (stressors and stress) and seeks to see if there is a relationship between the two in an attempt to examine whether one of these variables explains the other. So it is an explanatory research question. The same is true for the fourth question. It examines the relationship between stress and social support.

What about the last question? Is it descriptive, explanatory, evaluative, or exploratory? This study will examine two sets of scores (pretest and posttest) for the purpose of determining if an intervention has improved depression in the clients. This makes it an evaluative study. Whenever your intent is to evaluate an intervention, you are engaged in evaluative research.

The knowledge base for a research study has several functions. One is to define critical variables so that measurement is facilitated. Another function is to examine the relevant literature that will guide the analysis of the behavior or the theme of the research question. This clarification can assist with the identification of the variables to be measured. It can also assist with the identification of theories that suggest what kinds of relationships we would expect to find between the variables.

Step 2: Determining the Study Methods

Your study methods indicate how you will examine your research question in your study. From whom will you collect data? How will you measure your study variables? What is your study design? These are all about the *how* of your study.

You will decide on the study population that is relevant to your study. This might be as broad as anybody or as narrow as persons with a certain type of eating disorder. If you are examining a very broad question, such as whether those who exercise are better off regarding health, you have a broad study population, because this question is relevant to everyone. But if you are evaluating a treatment program for those suffering from bulimia, you will have a small study population.

You will select a group of people from that study population from whom you will collect data. This is your study **sample**. The method you use to select the sample from the population determines how well you can generalize your study findings from the sample to your population. This will be discussed in more detail in a later chapter. To generalize means that you would expect similar results from another sample of people from the same population. So what you found in your study is relevant to other people in your study population.

You will select a means of measuring each of the variables in your study. This might be a scale for measuring self-esteem, school records on school absences, or agency records on whether a client followed the suggestions on the discharge plan.

If you are conducting an evaluative study, you will determine the research design. This design instructs you on the procedures for the collection of your data on client outcome. One design, for example, calls on you to measure a group of clients once before treatment begins and once at the end of treatment. This design measures client progress.

Step 3: Collecting and Analyzing Data

You will collect data according to the relevant protocol. The term *data* refers to the discrete information that you have, such as the age of each client, the depression score for each client, and so forth. You must have data for each variable in your study. You cannot have a research question that contains age as a variable unless you collect data on age for each study subject.

Your data collection procedure may mean giving a questionnaire to a group of people at one point in time. It might entail the administration of a tool more than once to the same group of people. In this book, you will have exercises where you will collect data from a group of people (perhaps the members of your class) at one point in time. The instrument used will have items designed to measure each of the variables in your study. One of the variables may designate the group the respondent is in, so that two groups can be compared.

You will select a statistic for each of your research questions. Some of these statistics will be descriptive in nature, such as a frequency or a mean. Some will be explanatory in nature because the statistic helps you determine if there is a relationship between two variables that cannot be explained by chance (i.e., the data are statistically significant). Later in this book, guidance is provided on how to find the appropriate statistic and how to employ it in the examination of your data.

One of the issues you will encounter in both explanatory and evaluative research is whether your data can be explained by chance. **Statistical significance** refers to the likelihood that a given set of data would occur by chance. You will see much on this theme later. If your data can be explained by chance, you cannot logically conclude that the data are meaningful. For example, if you find that your clients' posttest scores for anxiety are better than their pretest scores but you find that the data failed to be statistically significant, you cannot logically declare that you found that the clients gained with regard to reduced anxiety. You cannot do this because you found data that can be explained by chance, so the next time you do the same study, you are just as likely to find that they did not gain as to find that they did. Your data must do better than being the result of chance to be taken seriously.

Step 4: Drawing Conclusions

Based on your data findings, you draw conclusions about your research question. Is this the place for you to offer your opinions about the research question? No! Your conclusions should stick to the data you analyzed. It does not matter how strong your opinion is or how much experience you have had with it. The research study is about the collection and analysis of data in a certain manner using certain measures of certain variables. Your conclusions must adhere to the data analyzed. However, you may offer suggestions regarding future research or your opinion about the strengths and limitations of your research methods. But your opinions on the research question of your study should be kept apart from the study conclusions.

To summarize this presentation on the process of social work research, let's take an example from evaluative research. The target behavior is depression because you have a group of 11 clients who have entered your special program for the treatment of depression. The research question is whether these 11 clients will have lower depression at the end of the treatment than before. Your method of measurement is the Beck Depression Inventory, a highly tested tool for measuring depression. Your intervention is cognitive–behavioral therapy, which has more positive evidence for the treatment of depression than any other treatment method. The outcome is that the mean score for these 11 clients at the end of the treatment is 40% higher than their scores before the treatment began. These differences between the scores before and after treatment were found to be statistically significant. This means that the gain cannot be easily explained by chance and, therefore, can be taken seriously. You draw the conclusion that cognitive–behavioral therapy was effective in the reduction of depression for this group of 11 clients. However, you are not in a position to generalize these findings to depressed people who were not in your study, because you did not employ a random sample. Instead, you used a convenience sample. You used this type of sample because your primary concern was to find out whether your treatment was effective with this group of clients.

The research process is illustrated in Figure 2.1. In this presentation, a group of at-risk middle school students were randomly divided into two subgroups: one subgroup would get tutoring during the first grading period and the other subgroup would get tutoring in the second grading period. To test the effectiveness of this tutoring intervention, the grades of these two groups would be compared for the first grading period. It would be expected, of course, that the first subgroup (who had the tutoring) would have higher grades during this first grading period than the second subgroup (who did not have tutoring in this grading period). In this example, the tutored group had grades that were 34% higher than the nontutored group.

FIGURE 2.1   ■   The Research Process

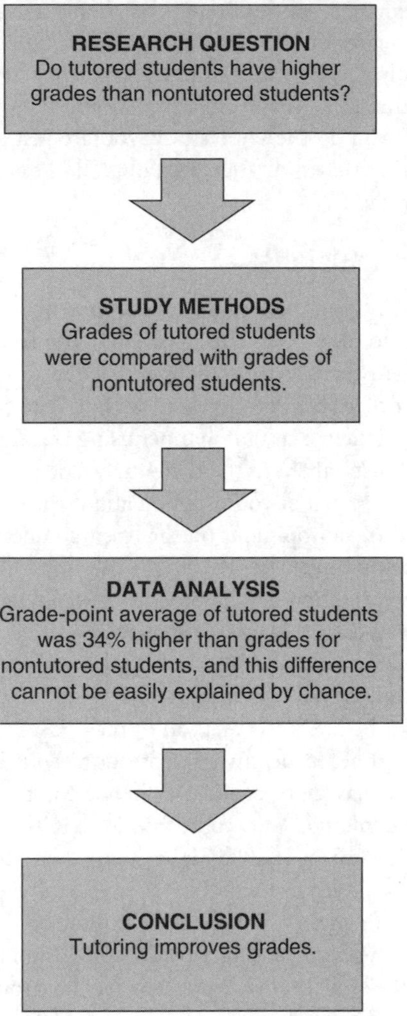

RESEARCH QUESTION
Do tutored students have higher
grades than nontutored students?

STUDY METHODS
Grades of tutored students
were compared with grades of
nontutored students.

DATA ANALYSIS
Grade-point average of tutored students
was 34% higher than grades for
nontutored students, and this difference
cannot be easily explained by chance.

CONCLUSION
Tutoring improves grades.

Chapter Practice Exercises

For this chapter, there are two practice exercises. In the first exercise, you will examine a selected aspect of program evaluation for a familiar human service agency. The second exercise calls on you to provide a brief report on certain aspects of an evaluative study you might undertake in a familiar agency.

Practice Exercise 1: Evaluating a Human Service Program

Here are a few parts of the service system that could serve as the focus of one part of a program evaluation. You should select one of these questions and see what you can find in the information available to you at your agency for this program.

1. This program should be serving people in the target population. Important characteristics of this population might include poverty, having young children, being pregnant, being at risk for delinquency, facing death or dying, having marital problems, and so forth.
   a. How would you characterize the target population?
   b. Does this agency seem to be serving this population? Do you have any data that confirm it? Do you have informed opinions of staff that would support this conclusion?

2. Services should be accessible to those in need. In other words, prospective clients should be able to take advantage of what your agency offers. For example, employed persons may have a difficult time going to your agency before 5:00 p.m. If so, does your agency have service hours after 5:00 p.m.? Certain persons may have transportation problems. Does your agency facilitate transportation in any way?

3. Clients should be appropriately screened at intake to ensure that services are being used by those most in need. What does your agency do to ensure this? Is there any evidence available to you that would suggest that this is true?

4. The program should be documenting outcomes for the program (e.g., higher grades in school, lower depression, higher employment, fewer acts of delinquency, improved marital relations, etc.). Does the agency collect data to evaluate client outcomes?

5. Clients should be appropriately terminated from a service when the need has been met. What does the agency do to ensure that this happens?

6. Services should have an impact on indicators of need, such as rate of child abuse, rate of

delinquency, and so forth. Does the agency have data on this?

Competencies Demonstrated by Practice Exercise 1

1. The ability to distinguish between a human service program and a human service intervention

2. The ability to collect information on one important program evaluation question for a given human service program

3. The ability to identify what a given human service agency needs to do to improve its program evaluation information

Activities for Practice Exercise 1

1. Select a human service organization and a human service program within that agency for your analysis.

2. Select one of the six statements given above to serve as the focus of your report.

3. Investigate what the selected agency does with regard to your question about program evaluation.

4. Prepare a report on what you found regarding your selected question for your selected program.

What You Will Report From Practice Exercise 1

1. The name of your agency and the name of your human service program

   Examples:
   a. Parker Middle School is the agency, and school social work is the program.
   b. The Harper County Department of Human Services is the agency, and child protective services is the program.
   c. Oak Hill Behavioral Health is the agency, and adult therapy services is the program.

2. A brief description of your selected program with regard to (a) basic goals and (b) services

    Examples:

    a. The social work services program at Parker Middle School has the goal of improving the ability of at-risk students to perform in school at the level of their abilities. It provides a school social worker who works with individual at-risk students and their families in a variety of ways.

    b. The child protective services program of Harper County Department of Human Services has the goal of preventing child abuse and neglect. It provides an array of social work services including investigation of complaints of child neglect and abuse, provision of case management services to client families, and referral of clients to needed services.

    c. The adult mental health program of Oak Hill Behavioral Health provides psychotherapy to adults for the purpose of improving their mental health and promoting their self-sufficiency.

3. The question you have selected for your analysis

4. What you found with regard to your question

5. What you would recommend for the agency to improve its program evaluation information

Practice Exercise 2: Evaluating an Intervention

You will select a group of clients with a common target behavior and answer a set of questions to report on some selected information that would guide the evaluation of a human service intervention designed to address this target behavior.

Competencies Demonstrated by Practice Exercise 2

1. The ability to identify a target behavior that is treated by a given intervention that will be evaluated

2. The ability to identify a human service intervention that will be evaluated with regard to outcomes for the target behavior that is being treated

3. The ability to identify an outcome objective that fits the evaluation of a given intervention for a given target behavior

4. The ability to identify a piece of data that would be relevant to a given outcome objective in the evaluation of a given human service intervention

Activities for Practice Exercise 2

1. Identify a human service intervention (service) that you would like to evaluate. Be prepared to describe the activities of this intervention.

    Examples: (a) A support group for victims of rape, (b) tutoring services for at-risk middle school students, and (c) therapy for persons who are depressed.

2. Identify the target behavior that is addressed by the above human service intervention.

    Examples: (a) Feelings of social support, (b) grades in school, and (c) depression.

3. Identify an outcome objective for the above intervention with regard to the above target behavior.

    Examples: (a) To enhance feelings of social support, (b) to improve grades in school, and (c) to reduce depression.

4. Identify a piece of data (information) that could be used to evaluate whether the above intervention has been effective with regard to the achievement of the above outcome objective.

   Examples: (a) Improvement in scores on a social support scale from the beginning of the service period to the end, (b) grades in school for the grade term of the period of the service compared with the grades in school for the previous grade term, and (c) improvement in scores on a scale of depression taken both before and after the therapy was given.

What You Will Report From Practice Exercise 2

1. A brief description of your selected human service intervention

2. A brief description of your selected target behavior

3. The outcome objective that should be evaluated

4. The piece of data that could be used to measure the effectiveness of the selected intervention with regard to the selected target behavior

CHAPTER REVIEW

Chapter Key Learnings

1. Human service research can be categorized in several ways. Three of these ways that were examined in this chapter were purpose, scope, and basic approach to measurement.

2. Human service research can be classified with regard to purpose. One purpose is description, where precise measurement is critical. Another purpose is explanation, where two or more variables are measured and compared to test whether one explains the other. A third purpose is evaluation, where client outcome is measured. A final purpose is exploration, which makes good use of qualitative measurement because it is an examination of a phenomenon that is not well known.

3. A manner of characterizing evaluative research is its scope. This type of research can be classified as program evaluation or intervention evaluation. Program evaluation is broader in scope and may include several intervention evaluations; the latter is given greater emphasis in this book.

4. The general type of measurement is a third way to characterize human service research. When you measure variables in a quantitative manner, you will give each study subject either a category to fit into or a number that indicates the numerical value it represents on a concept to be measured. When you measure variables in a qualitative way, you ask the study subjects to give you words to analyze.

5. When you engage in program evaluations, you may ask questions such as the following: (a) Were appropriate clients offered service? (b) Were good standards of service implemented? (c) Did the clients achieve the objectives of the service?

6. The evaluation of the intervention tends to focus on client outcome for a single client or a group of clients.

7. The research process was presented as having four basic phases: (1) articulation of the research question and the knowledge base that guides it, (2) determination of the methods that will be used to select a study sample and measure the study variables, (3) collection and analysis of data, and (4) drawing the study conclusions.

8. The nature of scientific inquiry necessitates the systematic examination of human phenomena through a step-by-step process where each phase naturally leads to the next. You do not, for example, decide how you are going to measure the study variables before you articulate the study question and examine an appropriate knowledge base.

9. From the knowledge base, you can better understand the phenomena of your study through theories or conceptual frameworks. From this understanding, you will be in a better position to measure your study variables and to predict your study results.

10. From the report on your study methods, we can learn about the extent to which the results of the study can be generalized to a population of people who were not in the study. We can also learn about the confidence we can have that you have measured your study variables accurately.

11. If you are conducting an evaluative study, you will determine the research design. This design instructs you on the procedures for the collection of your data on client outcome. It helps you answer the following question: Did the treatment cause the measured client gain? Some designs do a better job of answering this question than others.

12. A critical issue in data analysis is statistical significance, which addresses the issue of chance. If your data can easily be explained by chance, you cannot rely on them to give you the truth.

Chapter Discussion Questions

1. Present three research questions below, one that is descriptive, one that is explanatory, and one that is evaluative.
   a. Descriptive research question
   b. Explanatory research question
   c. Evaluative research question

2. What general purpose for research (descriptive, explanatory, evaluative, or exploratory) do you find most suited to your own interests or professional development?

3. What is the form of qualitative data? What about quantitative data?

   a. Qualitative data
   b. Quantitative data

4. What is a research question that is in the category of a program evaluation? What is a research question that is in the category of the evaluation of an intervention?
   a. Program evaluation
   b. Evaluation of an intervention

5. What is the general category (descriptive, explanatory, or evaluative) of research that is the focus of most of the data that your agency collects and reports?

Chapter Test

1. Suppose you collect data on the following variables for your current clients: age, gender, marital status. You report such data as the mean age, the proportion who are male and female, and the proportion who are in each of several categories of marital status. What is the category of research that you are conducting?

   a. Explanatory research
   b. Exploratory research
   c. Evaluative research
   d. Descriptive research

2. Suppose you collect data on the scores for anxiety for your nine clients who are being treated for anxiety with a special intervention. You collect data on their anxiety scores once before the treatment begins and once at the end of the treatment period. You report whether the anxiety scores improved and whether these data are statistically significant. What type of research are your undertaking?

   a. Explanatory research
   b. Exploratory research
   c. Evaluative research
   d. Descriptive research

3. Suppose you collect data on a group of 24 students in your class with regard to two variables: (a) whether the study subject engages in regular aerobic exercise and (b) whether the study subject has experienced minor illnesses in the past 6 months. You are expecting that those who exercise are less likely to have experienced minor illnesses recently. You test this expectation with your data. What type of research are you undertaking?

   a. Explanatory research
   b. Exploratory research

   c. Evaluative research
   d. Descriptive research

4. If an improvement in scores on depression for your clients can be explained by chance, which of the following does this mean?

   a. You can conclude that your intervention caused the client's improvement
   b. You can generalize your findings to the study population
   c. Both of the above
   d. None of the above

5. A theory is

   a. An attempt to explain
   b. A truth
   c. An expression
   d. A conclusion

6. Which of the following statements is/are true?

   a. A program evaluation has a broader scope than an evaluation of an intervention
   b. A program evaluation may include evaluations of various interventions
   c. Both of the above
   d. None of the above

7. Qualitative research measures concepts with regard to

   a. Numbers
   b. Categories
   c. Words
   d. None of the above

8. Statistical significance provides information with regard to

   a. Causation
   b. Chance
   c. Generalization
   d. Consideration

ANSWERS: 1 = d; 2 = c; 3 = a; 4 = d; 5 = a; 6 = c; 7 = c; 8 = b

Chapter Glossary

Chance. A possibility that is not predicted.

Descriptive research. Research that has the purpose of describing people (or things).

Evaluative research. Research that has the purpose of determining the success of an intervention or program.

Explanatory research. Research that has the purpose of explaining things by examining the relationship between two or more variables.

Exploratory research. Research that has the purpose of examining things that are not yet well known.

Intervention evaluation. The assessment of the success of a social work intervention (service) for an individual or a group of clients with a common treatment objective.

Population. The people from whom your study sample was drawn.

Program evaluation. An assessment of the success of a program with regard to various components of the program.

Qualitative measurement. Research that measures concepts with words rather than numbers or predetermined categories.

Quantitative measurement. Research that measures concepts numerically (e.g., age or score on the depression scale) or by predetermined categories (e.g., gender, race, etc.).

Sample. The people from whom you collect your data for your study.

Statistical significance. The likelihood that this set of data would occur by chance, rather than having meaning with regard to causation.

Theory. An attempt to explain, usually by portraying the relationships between concepts.

3

ETHICS AND CULTURAL COMPETENCE IN SOCIAL WORK RESEARCH

Paul is a social work student who is an intern in a community center, where he provides services to persons who have recently been released from prison. He has decided to conduct a study that includes both his current clients and a group of persons who are presently in prison. His supervisor informed him that he would have to have this proposal reviewed by the institutional review board (IRB) of his university. When he consulted this board, he learned that prisoners are viewed as a vulnerable population for research requiring special attention. He would need to be sure to implement certain safeguards, including the necessity that the outcome of this research be beneficial to people who are prisoners. He should not, for example, ask prisoners to be subjects for a research study that is not especially relevant to being a prisoner because this population is not likely to benefit from it. Prisoners are vulnerable to feeling compelled to participate, so the benefit of the study must be to this population.

Voluntary participation, Paul has learned, is just one of many issues in the use of human subjects in research. This issue is especially important when the study subjects are members of vulnerable populations. He recognized that the theme of vulnerable population is one that ties together the subjects of ethics and cultural competence in research. The most important functions of social work, Paul believes, are services and advocacy for vulnerable populations. In this regard, knowledge of culture is essential. It is also essential that the social work researcher appreciates the various ethical considerations in the use of human subjects in research.

Paul also learned that the IRB monitors research projects for the protection of human subjects. In his university, researchers must submit reports to this board when human subjects are being asked to participate in a research project. The IRB must approve the project before it is being implemented.

INTRODUCTION

This chapter has two major sections, one focusing on ethics and one on cultural competence. These are two themes that you will consider when you conduct social work research. Ethics provide rules of behavior based on moral values. For example, you should not conduct research that would potentially harm the study participants or invade their **privacy**. And you should not engage in behaviors designed to coerce people into participating in your study. When you complete this chapter, you should have fundamental competence in the consideration of ethical principles for your research study and be prepared to deal with the organizational body that must review your research protocol for ethical concerns.

Cultural competence refers to competence that recognizes the influence of culture with regard to practice. For social work research, this means including culture in the review of literature about the behaviors being researched, recognizing cultural influences on the target behaviors in selecting a study sample, and analyzing data in a way that includes relevant cultural variables. This type of competence informs the research process in a way that makes it more meaningful for our understanding of the cultural influences on behavior.

This chapter addresses the themes of ethics in the use of human subjects in research and cultural competence in research. On the completion of this chapter, you will be able to do the following:

1. Define the concept of ethics in the use of human subjects in research

2. Identify several ethical issues in the use of human subjects in research with special focus on (a) protection from harm, (b) protecting privacy, (c) obtaining voluntary consent, (d) avoiding deception, and (e) weighing the risks and benefits of actions that might avoid certain protections

3. Explain several ethical principles that support the expectations related to the issues in the use of human subjects in research

4. Identify the nature of the IRB in the monitoring of social work research that employs human subjects

5. Report on some of the violations of human rights that led to the use of IRBs

6. Identify how cultural competence is relevant to social work research

7. Explain how cultural competence is related to various types of research

8. Identify several strategies for culturally competent evaluation

9. Report on the question of the extent to which social workers have been found to be culturally competent in survey research

10. Discuss one approach to rethinking cultural competence

A concept that binds ethics and cultural competence is the **vulnerable population**. People in a vulnerable population are viewed as vulnerable because they are likely to view their participation in research to be necessary because of the population in which they reside. For example, prisoners may feel that they cannot say no to the invitation to participate. Children are not viewed as being in a position to give **informed consent** because they are too young for this task. The **institutional review board** (IRB) of the University of Virginia lists several groups as being vulnerable populations. These groups include prisoners, children, cognitively impaired individuals, minorities, economically disadvantaged persons, terminally ill patients, students, and employees (Institutional Review Board for Health Sciences Research, University of Virginia, 2017).

This review board explained the inclusion of members of minority groups as follows:

In addition to requiring the equitable selection of women as research subjects, Federal regulations require the equitable selection of minorities as research subjects. The inclusion of minorities in research is important both to ensure that they receive an equal share of the benefits of the research and to ensure that they do not bear a disproportionate burden. (Institutional Review Board for Health Sciences Research, University of Virginia, 2017)

As you can see, there are two themes addressed: (1) the sufficient inclusion to the benefits of research and (2) the avoidance of excessive burden.

SECTION A: ETHICS IN THE USE OF HUMAN SUBJECTS IN RESEARCH

Human subjects research is "research involving a living individual about whom an investigator (whether professional or student) conducting research obtains data through intervention or interaction with the individual, or identifiable private information" (National Institutes of Health, n.d.). The typical human subjects research that you will undertake (as a social worker or a social work student) will entail a survey of individuals where questions are asked about the variables in the study. The variables may be descriptive (gender, age, etc.) or related to study hypotheses (depression, attitudes about agency service, etc.). This means that you will be collecting data from a living individual; thus, it qualifies as being research with human subjects. If you collect identifiable private information from living persons through records, you will also be conducting research involving human subjects according to this definition from the federal government. If the data are not identifiable (e.g., the names of the persons are not attached to the data), your study does not qualify as the use of human subjects for research. If the names are with the information, however, your study qualifies for this designation, even if you do not plan to report the names of the persons with their information. If it is available to you as a researcher, your study is classified as using human subjects for research.

There are four main themes in this presentation of **ethics** in human service research: (1) the code of ethics as a guide, (2) the key ethical principles social workers should implement, (3) some special challenges the social worker faces in doing ethical research, and (4) the IRB as a monitor of the use of human subjects in research. You will review each of these themes in this chapter.

The Code of Ethics as a Guide for the Professional Social Worker

The Code of Ethics of the National Association of Social Worker (NASW) provides a guide for ethical practice. Section 5.02 of that code deals with the ethical use of human subjects in research. This part of the code is presented in Exhibit 3.1.

EXHIBIT 3.1

SECTION 5.02 OF THE NASW CODE OF ETHICS

a. Social workers should monitor and evaluate policies, the implementation of programs, and practice interventions.

b. Social workers should promote and facilitate evaluation and research to contribute to the development of knowledge.

c. Social workers should critically examine and keep current with emerging knowledge relevant to social work and fully use evaluation and research evidence in their professional practice.

d. Social workers engaged in evaluation or research should carefully consider possible consequences and should follow the guidelines developed for the protection of evaluation and research participants. Appropriate institutional review boards should be consulted.

e. Social workers engaged in evaluation or research should obtain voluntary and written informed consent from participants, when appropriate, without any implied or actual deprivation or penalty for refusal to participate, without undue inducement to participate, and with due regard for participants' well-being, privacy, and dignity. Informed consent should include information about the nature, extent, and duration of the participation requested and disclosure of the risks and benefits of participation in the research.

f. When evaluation or research participants are incapable of giving informed consent, social workers should provide an appropriate explanation to the participants, obtain the participants' assent to the extent they are able, and obtain written consent from an appropriate proxy.

g. Social workers should never design or conduct evaluation or research that does not use consent procedures, such as certain forms of naturalistic observation and archival research, unless rigorous and responsible review of the research has found it to be justified because of its prospective scientific, educational, or applied value and unless equally effective alternative procedures that do not involve waiver of consent are not feasible.

h. Social workers should inform participants of their right to withdraw from evaluation and research at any time without penalty.

i. Social workers should take appropriate steps to ensure that participants in evaluation and research have access to appropriate supportive services.

j. Social workers engaged in evaluation or research should protect participants from unwarranted physical or mental distress, harm, danger, or deprivation.

k. Social workers engaged in the evaluation of services should discuss collected information only for professional purposes and only with people professionally concerned with this information.

l. Social workers engaged in evaluation or research should ensure the anonymity or confidentiality of participants and of the data obtained from them. Social workers should inform participants of any limits of confidentiality, the measures that will be taken to ensure confidentiality, and when any records containing research data will be destroyed.

m. Social workers who report evaluation and research results should protect participants' confidentiality by omitting identifying information unless proper consent has been obtained authorizing disclosure.

n. Social workers should report evaluation and research findings accurately. They should not fabricate or falsify results and should take steps to correct any errors later found in published data using standard publication methods.

o. Social workers engaged in evaluation or research should be alert to and avoid conflicts of interest and dual relationships with participants, should inform participants when a real or potential conflict of interest arises, and should take steps to resolve the issue in a manner that makes participants' interests primary.

p. Social workers should educate themselves, their students, and their colleagues about responsible research practices. (NASW, 2016)

Source: Copyrighted material reprinted from the National Association of Social Workers, Inc.

The first theme noted in the above list is the expectation that social workers will engage in research that contributes to the knowledge base of the profession and the enhancement of practice. Thus, you do not have the option of avoiding all efforts at research to make sure you avoid ethical problems. You are expected to contribute. You are also expected to understand the principles and policies that guide the assurance of ethical research practice.

The most profound requirement enumerated in Exhibit 3.1 is that research participants must be protected from any harm that might come from the research experience. This is seldom an issue in human service research because the participants are typically asked only to supply information. Medical experiments that put people into hypnosis or administer drugs or give electric shocks are in an entirely different arena on this issue.

In evaluation research, confidentiality is one of the issues. Persons who are asked to participate in research are normally informed that their responses will be treated confidentially. Often this is guaranteed by asking for an anonymous response. This procedure assures the protection of privacy.

Another issue is **voluntary participation in research**. In social work research, you will almost always find that participation is voluntary. This means that you should not ask people to provide data for your study in a way that might be perceived as coercive. This also means that an agency does not conduct studies where the clients are made to feel that their eligibility for continued service depends on their participation in your study. You have reviewed the concept of vulnerable population. This concept helps us understand the importance of voluntary participation and the fact that some people are vulnerable to not understanding this right.

Honesty is another ethical theme. You should not be deceitful with clients in either your practice actions or your use of human subjects in research. This includes the accurate reporting of research findings. Social work research is not a process of justification; it is a process of discovery. You will encounter this theme many times in this book.

The Code of Ethics warns against the dangers of engaging in actions that constitute a conflict of interest. You should not ask the clients to participate in a study simply because you will make money from it. There must be a better reason.

Finally, the Code of Ethics enumerates the ethical responsibility of using knowledge to guide practice. A major part of that knowledge comes from research. For you to ignore evidence about your intended social work practices would be a violation of the Code of Ethics.

Major Principles About Protection of Human Subjects in Research

There are several major principles that the IRB will employ to evaluate a given proposal to determine if it should be approved. The Collaborative Institutional Training Initiative provides online courses on the use of human subjects in research. In this training is information about the history of IRB reviews of proposals for the use of human subjects for research. According to the Collaborative Institutional Training Initiative (n.d.), the National Commission for the Protection of Human Subjects in Biomedical and Behavioral Research met in 1979 and prepared the Belmont Report. This report identifies three basic principles that underlie all human subject research:

1. Respect for persons

2. Beneficence

3. Justice

The principle of **respect** deals with autonomy and self-determination. People should be allowed to choose for themselves the risk they wish to undertake. Study subjects have full autonomy when they can understand the risks involved and have the freedom to volunteer without coercion.

The principle of **beneficence** requires that we minimize harm and maximize benefits. Risk assessment is a key theme. The principle of **justice** requires us to design research that does not unduly target its risks to certain groups of people and fails to treat different types of people equally or fairly. If you plan to collect data from people in prisons, you can expect the IRB to give your proposal a full review because of the vulnerable nature of the prison experience. If your study is about prison life, you will probably be okay with that because the class of people who are the participants is the same as the class of people who will benefit from the results.

Informed Consent and Privacy

For most research studies, informed consent is required. This means that the study subjects have given their consent, and they were clearly informed about the risks and were truly given the opportunity to refrain from participation without coercion. In this process, information about risk should be complete. There are a few exceptions where consent is not required, but these situations rarely refer to human service evaluation studies, so they will not be discussed here.

A key issue is the subject's ability to give informed consent. Research using children as research subjects often requires full review because children are not in a position to give fully informed consent. Research involving persons of limited literacy or intellectual ability requires more care in the assurance of this consent.

Not only must subjects give their consent, but they must also be given the opportunity to withdraw from participation at any time they desire. In this regard, the subject must be notified that there will be no penalty for withdrawal, such as losing service benefits.

Privacy refers to our ability to control access to information about ourselves. **Confidentiality (for research subjects)** refers to implied or explicit contracts among individuals about the sharing of information one person may have about another. To the extent feasible, privacy should be protected by the researchers.

There is a distinction between private behavior and public behavior. Public behavior can be observed for research purposes without the need for formal review of research proposals, whereas private behavior cannot. Private behavior is that behavior that one would normally expect to be private. This would include a conversation between two people alone on a park bench where there clearly is no one within hearing distance. The use of an electronic device for hearing conversations from someone 30 yards away could be interpreted as a violation of privacy because it would be reasonable for these individuals to believe that their conversation was private. However, the behavior of a group of people playing football in a park would be considered public behavior.

Risks and Benefits

A risk is a disadvantage to the study subject, while a benefit is an advantage to either the study subject or society in general. Risk normally refers to privacy or harm to participants. Examples of the latter are procedures that place study subjects under stress or risky procedures like administration of drugs. Asking a client to complete a scale designed to measure target behavior normally holds no risk of harm from the procedures, so the issue of invasion of privacy is usually the only theme to be addressed in a typical study of human services.

When there are risks, you must review the balance of risks with benefits. Sometimes the risk is only held by the study subject, and the benefit is to society in general. In this case, you will determine if the benefit warrants the risk. This is not an easy question to answer.

An issue you should consider when facing risks is whether you have available procedures that are less risky. Even if you could cogently argue that the benefits of this study will outweigh the risks, you will be expected to employ a less risky procedure that will achieve equal benefits. Whatever the risks, they should always be minimized to the extent feasible.

Justice

Justice refers to whether certain vulnerable populations are being singled out for unusual burden from the study procedures being undertaken. This is not likely to be an issue for human service research for the day-to-day practitioner because you are dealing with clients who have asked for service. If you were conducting a different kind of study with a national sample of persons from low-income communities, the question would be raised as to whether your study purpose necessitates that data be drawn only from this type of population. It might seem unfair to target governmental housing projects simply because it is well known that persons in these homes feel that they must answer anyone's questions because their housing is being subsidized. If your study is about people in subsidized housing, this would be okay. But if it is about a general topic that has nothing specific to do with subsidized housing or poverty, your IRB might raise a question about using only such communities for your study subjects.

Challenges for the Social Work Researcher

There are a number of challenges facing you as a social work researcher in the implementation of the ethical principles for the use of human subjects in research. This includes adhering to all the principles discussed above. There are several questions you will confront, some of which are discussed in this section of the chapter.

Obtaining Informed Consent

Informed consent refers to the consent of the study subject to participate in your study. It is your duty to provide the necessary information to assure that the consent to participate is informed. You can obtain guidance on this theme from the IRB of your institution. The essential elements of informed consent are displayed in Exhibit 3.2, along with an explanation and an example for each element. These elements were taken from a document from the University of Michigan (Research Ethics and Compliance, 2018).

The social work researcher has a special challenge in obtaining consent for children or those who are mentally limited. Children are often considered not to have this competence to give informed consent, so a parent or guardian often has to sign for the consent. But what about adults who are impaired in some way. There is no clear rule for how to do this, but it is a major challenge in some situations.

Protecting Privacy

Protecting privacy means the study subject remains anonymous regarding the data you employ. You do not report, for example, the depression score of Jane Dougherty or the age of Paul Samuels. No one really does this in social work research, partly because it has no benefits to research and also because of the obvious fact that it provides an ethical problem.

An aid in the protection of the privacy of the study subject is to obtain your information from the subject anonymously. In this way, you do not know the identity of the subject, so you have no opportunity to violate his or her privacy. The other avenue is to assure confidentiality. This means that you will not divulge the identity of the study subject with the data associated with his or her answers to the questions. In either case, you

EXHIBIT 3.2
ELEMENTS OF INFORMED CONSENT

Element	Explanation	Example
Title of the project	The title should appear at the beginning of the statement	A study of the treatment of anxiety
Name of researcher and organization	Names of all researchers, along with the name of the faculty advisor if the researcher is a student	Paulette Jones, University of North Carolina Wilmington. Reginald York, faculty advisor
Invitation to participate	Circumstances of the invitation	You are being invited to participate in this study because you are a current client of Paulette Jones at the Hampton Behavior Health Center
Description of the subject involvement	How will the study subject participate? Will this person be completing a survey, being interviewed, or what?	You will be asked to complete a scale to measure anxiety one time before service begins and one time again at the end of the service period
Benefits	What types of people will benefit from this study?	People who are seeking help with anxiety will benefit from the results of this study because they will help us know how to be more successful in this regard
Risks	Indicate the risks involved, and if there are risks, how they will be handled	There are no known risks for participating in this study because the information obtained is anonymous and the topic is not sensitive
Compensation	Indicate if the study subject will be compensated financially	You will not receive money for participating in this study
Confidentiality	Indicate how confidentiality will be assured	Because your data are given anonymously, your identity cannot be revealed in any publication that comes from this study
Voluntary participation	Indicate if the participation is voluntary, and the subject may withdraw at any time	Your participation in this study is voluntary, and you may withdraw at any time
Contact information	To whom may the subject report to secure more information?	If you have questions about your participation in this study, you may contact Dr. Reginald York, the student's advisor
Consent statement or signature	Indicate if the study subject has been asked to sign a consent form	Your completion of the scales used in this study indicates your consent for the information to be used in any publication that might be presented

Source: The "Element" and "Explanation" are taken from Research Ethics and Compliance (2018).

will report to the study subject this information when you are working on the informed consent issue.

The social work student may need to match the clients' pretest scores with their posttest scores for the analysis of data. This can be done anonymously by using a set of questions where the study subject answers questions, not known to the researcher, that provides an anonymous identification number. See, for example, the following set of questions:

_____ ← What is the first letter in your father's middle name? [If unknown, enter X]

_____ ← What is the number of letters in your mother's maiden name? [If unknown, enter 9]

_____ ← What is the first letter in your mother's maiden name? [If unknown, enter X]

_____ ← What is the last digit in your social security number? [If unknown, enter 9]

If you ask the participant to answer these questions on your questionnaire and you must administer the same questionnaire two times, you will be able to match this person's pretest score with his or her posttest score, but you will not know the identity of this person. You can imagine other questions that might be used to achieve the same.

Weighing the Risks and Benefits

It is easy to make the mistake of assuming that you are not permitted, under any circumstances, to create any risk to the human subject of research. Can you, for example, have someone fake a heart attack on a busy city street so that you can observe the behavior of people on the street who observe this behavior? Maybe you want to know how many will help, or how they react emotionally. Can you do this? The answer depends on the level of the risk and the level of the benefits of the study. If the study is viewed by your IRB as having no benefits, the board is likely to deny your proposal. If they view it as having a lot of benefits, they may approve on the basis that the benefits outweigh the risks. How likely are people on the street to have a major problem when they observe such behavior? The question here is not whether it is possible that someone may be damaged by this action but whether it is probable that people will be damaged by it. In the final analysis, it is the judgment of the IRB that will determine the outcome of the request to undertake this study. There is no formula that will guide them, only their judgment.

Risks and benefits must be addressed as an issue when you have the opportunity to deny service to a group of potential clients for a given service in order to use this group as your control group in your research study. Suppose that you have 40 persons who have asked for your special tutoring program for at-risk middle school students, and you are considering the option of randomly selecting 20 of these students to be your experimental group and randomly selecting the other 20 to be your control group. You will give your tutoring program to those in the experimental group but not to those in the control group. You will measure the students in each group to determine if the experimental group had better gains in functioning than the control group.

Is this ethical? The answer lies in the examination of risks and benefits. If you only have the resources to provide your tutoring to 20 students for the current service period, the ethical challenge is reduced. If you can only serve 20, you could select your 20 at random and use the others as the control group. If you have the resources to provide tutoring to the 20 in your control group at a later time period, the burden is further diminished. If you have the capacity, however, to serve all but will only serve 20 for the sake of research, the burden on you to justify this decision on the basis of benefit is great. You will need to make the case that this is a situation where the benefit is so great as to offset the harm to those who have been denied this service for the sake of research. Social workers seldom make such claims because of the duty to serve those in need.

The typical response of the social worker in this situation is to provide the service to all prospective clients and measure their gain during the treatment period as a measure of success. The use of the control group is a superior research design as we will review in future chapters, so you may consider the option of the control group if you have the capacity to serve those in the control group at a later time. You should be cautious, however, of selecting those for the experimental group on the basis of level of need and using the others as our comparison group because you have made the two groups unequal by your selection process. This makes the use of the comparison group questionable from the research standpoint.

Reamer (2010) offers more guidance on the above challenges related to risk, privacy, and informed consent. He admonishes social work researchers to be mindful of risks, sensitive to privacy, and diligent in obtaining informed consent. He offers many suggestions on how to pursue each of these issues.

The Institutional Review Board

The institutional review board (IRB) in major institutions monitors the protection of human subjects in research. The protection of the rights of human subjects in research is the purpose of this review mechanism. This form of monitoring emerged from early examples of the violation of human rights by researchers. In this section, you will review some of these examples before you examine the nature and procedures of the typical IRB.

Violations of Human Rights That Led to Ethical Review Boards

A concern for ethics in research emerge historically from a number of incidents of unethical behavior. One of the earliest examples in this country was the Tuskegee syphilis study that included a 40-year study of the effects of syphilis on the body of a group of poor African American men from Alabama in the 1930s (Reamer, 2010). These men were not given the standard treatment for syphilis so that the researchers could study the nature of the progression of the disease when untreated. They were also deceived about the nature of the experiment. Some, of course, died from the disease. Another example given by Reamer (2010) was an experiment (the Willowbrook study) where a group of retarded children were deliberately infected with hepatitis so that the trajectory of the disease when left untreated could be studied.

According to Reamer (2010), the first prominent regulation to prevent these abuses was enacted in the United States in 1966 when the surgeon general issued a directive that the Public Health Service would not fund research unless the procedures for the research would ensure that certain ethical principles were enacted. Documentation of these procedures were required. In social work, the Code of Ethics has become more specific with regard to principles related to ethical conduct in the use of human subjects in research.

The Kinds of Research That Are Reviewed

Not all forms of collection and analysis of data are classified as being subject to review by the IRB. A key is whether the data are for research that will be made public because it has the purpose of contributing to our collected knowledge about the theme of the study or if its purpose is for nonpublic uses such as the improvement of your practice with a given group of clients. If the report of the research has no public intent, it is not normally subjected to IRB review because it is not classified as research in the nomenclature of the IRB. As an example, the collection of depression scores for a single client for the purpose of improving service would not normally be subject to review unless you plan to make these data public, like through a publication or a public presentation of some kind.

Research using existing data from records normally does not require formal review. An exception would be for data where the individual can be identified with his or her data. If there was no way for the researcher to identify the data for a given subject, the study normally would not be subject to review.

If you collect data from human subjects (surveys, interviews, etc.) on a research topic where the results will be made public, you will normally be expected to engage in the procedures required by your IRB. It does not matter if the data are obtained anonymously or if confidentiality is assured. If you collect data from human subjects for the purpose of advancing knowledge, and if you plan to make these data public, then you must complete the forms used by your IRB. The members of the IRB will review your information to see the level of review that is necessary.

The IRB Review Process

For some situations, the procedures for IRB review will be simple; for others, it will be more complex. The greater the danger that ethical rights will be violated, the more complex will be the process you will encounter.

The IRB typically has several levels of review. Some proposals for studies will be exempted from full review because of the limited nature of the study procedures. For example, if you are conducting a social survey of adults where the questions posed are not the ones that could put study subjects at risk of harm or violation of privacy, you may find that your IRB has an expedited review process whereby your report is not presented to the full board for review. This normally takes less time. The full review, of course, takes much more time because the entire board must review your proposal, and the board will normally have regular meetings where it reviews as many proposals as time permits.

Advice for the Social Work Researcher

The social work researcher must, of course, abide by the principles enumerated in this part of the chapter. This means achieving voluntary participation from nonvulnerable populations, protecting privacy, and causing no harm by your research procedures.

Your interaction with your IRB will be less complicated if certain things are present in your research situation. If you are engaging in a study where the results are not being made public (publication, poster presentation, newsletter, etc.), you are in a situation where some IRBs will not consider your work to be subject to review by the board because it is not designed for the achievement of general knowledge.

If you intend to make your research results public, you are likely to be expected to provide some form of report to your IRB. You will be in better shape if you can collect your data anonymously, use a harmless questionnaire or scale, and obtain the voluntary participation of adults who are not in a place like a prison where people are considered especially vulnerable. Failure to achieve any of these elements of research will make your interaction with your IRB more complicated.

SECTION B: CULTURAL COMPETENCE IN SOCIAL WORK RESEARCH

In this section, you will examine the nature of cultural competence and understand why you should be attentive to this subject. The second theme is the influence of cultural competence on how you conduct research, including a reference both to the types of research and to the research process. The third theme is a set of recommendations for strategies for culturally competent research. The final topic is how we might rethink the concept of cultural competence.

The Nature of Cultural Competence

Cultural competence refers to your ability to take culture into consideration in your practice. This requires sufficient knowledge of culture to engage in practice that is well informed. It also requires sufficient self-awareness to avoid the interference of your own life experiences with regard to culture. Being aware of the similarities and differences between your culture and that of others is a critical part of this self-awareness.

Culture has a major influence on all aspects of social work practice. The National Association of Social Workers has articulated 10 standards related to cultural competence among social workers. These are as follows: (1) ethics and values, (2) self-awareness, (3) cross-cultural knowledge, (4) cross-cultural skills, (5) service delivery, (6) empowerment and advocacy, (7) diverse workforce, (8) professional education, (9) language and communication, and (10) leadership. There are suggestions within each of these 10 categories. For example, embracing culture as essential to effective practice is one of the values enumerated for the first item of this list. The standard about self-awareness suggests that social workers must demonstrate an appreciation of their own cultures as well as the cultures of others. In addition, social workers must develop both knowledge and skills related to cultural competence.

Cultural Competence Among Types of Research

You have viewed purpose as a guide for classifying research studies. Descriptive studies, for example, are designed only to describe people, while explanatory studies attempt to explain by the examination of relationships among variables. Exploratory studies review relatively unknown themes where research and theory are not well developed. Moreover, evaluative studies examine the success of social work programs and interventions.

When we undertake exploratory studies, we start with little information on the details of the phenomenon under investigation. We should always consider culture as a theme in these studies because of the widespread influence of culture on human behavior. To what extent have we developed a research methodology that is suitable for the inclusion of culture as a theme? Will we examine things that will reveal this?

When we conduct descriptive studies, we must construct measurement tools that are sensitive to cultural differences. An advantage of the descriptive study is that it is easily undertaken by way of a social survey with a large sample. Therefore, measurement sensitivity and sampling are concerns with regard to cultural sensitivity. A key purpose of descriptive research is to obtain an accurate portrayal of the people being described. Culture will surely be a key theme for such studies.

The explanatory research study deals with **causation**. With these studies, you examine relationships among variables because you have reason to believe that one of these variables explains the other one. In other words, you are dealing with the issue of causation. Does being in a certain culture, for example, cause a person to have a lower salary?

A caution with these studies, however, is that a simple relationship between two variables is not itself a complete portrayal of causation. It is one of the three features of causation. You also must address the possibility that other variables may do a better job of explaining the key variable or serve as an intervening variable between the two identified. A third feature of causation is that the cause should precede the effect in time order. Therefore, a complete portrayal of causation would be one that showed that there was a relationship between the cause and the effect, that this cause is not explained by other variables, and that a change in this cause comes before a change in this effect.

The evaluative research study seeks to examine the success of a program or an intervention. Did the grades of the at-risk middle school students improve after the clients received the special after-school program? When you are examining a single client, you need to be sensitive to the cultural influences on this client's behavior. When you are examining an entire program, you should be concerned with the distribution of people in your sample concerning culture.

Cultural Competence and the Research Process

In social work research, cultural competence means knowing how cultural factors have meaning for different aspects of the research process. This begins with the research question. Does it adequately reflect culture? People from a certain culture may have perceptions that differ, and they may accept a given type of service in a different way. If you are evaluating a program, you should ask if there is evidence that this program is effective with people of different cultures. You can also examine whether it is logical to assert that it would be effective with people of this culture, given what you know about this culture.

Cultural competence is reflected in the selection of your study sample. Is there adequate representation of persons of different cultures? If not, you will have a problem with the generalization of your findings to people of various cultures. In other words, you should not assume that your results will likely be achieved with members of the missing cultures.

Measurement of study variables is another task where culture is important. What tools will you use for this task? How bound are the words on your tools to a specific culture? Different words may have different meanings for people based on their culture.

When you analyze your data, you can examine cultural variables to see if people of different cultures were different regarding the variables in your study. Perhaps people of a certain culture did not achieve a significant gain in anxiety when given your treatment program, but people of other cultures did achieve a significant gain. Without this analysis, you would not know of this differential effect of your treatment.

Sometimes you will have immigrants in your caseload. A variable to include in your analysis is the length of time an immigrant has lived in this country. Those who have recently arrived may be different from those with many years of experience here.

Strategies for Culturally Competent Evaluation

According to the Office of Minority Health in the U.S. Department of Health and Human Services, culture and language may influence several aspects of the services system and the people who are served. One of these is the belief systems people have about health, healing, and wellness. What tells us we are healing? What is wellness? These are beliefs that may differ with regard to culture. Another aspect is how we perceive illness and disease and their causes. To what extent are causes potentially influenced by medical care? A third way in which culture may influence the system are the attitudes of patients toward health care providers. Are these attitudes positive, leading patients to have hope that health care will make a difference. A fourth influence of culture is on the providers who deliver the service, and their own particular values can compromise access to patients from cultures different from that of the providers (Centers for Disease Control and Prevention, 2014).

The Centers for Disease Control and Prevention has offered a set of practice strategies for culturally competent evaluation. These strategies are listed in six categories: (1) engage stakeholders, (2) describe the program, (3) focus on the evaluation design, (4) gather credible evidence, (5) justify conclusions, and (6) ensure use and lessons learned.

A strategy for engaging the stakeholders is to access cultural awareness. This means knowing ourselves and those who are different. Can we, for example, interact genuinely? In this regard, it is important to recognize multiple identities. A given culture does not totally define a given person. What are the different identities that help us understand someone?

Clarifying the nature of the program is a second strategy. In this regard, we need to clarify the stakeholders' perception of the program. Can we highlight community strengths? Can we use models that resonate with the community?

After completing the program description, the evaluator needs to focus on the evaluation design. This is Step 3. What kind of information do the stakeholders trust? Do they understand the importance of some aspects of the evaluation design that are highly technical? Can these things be explained? Are they important to the stakeholders?

Step 4 is to gather credible information. What counts as credible evidence to the stakeholders? Perhaps the opinions of certain actors are more credible than scientific evidence. In this step, it is important to employ measurement tools that stakeholders understand and consider valid. Are these tools culturally appropriate?

Step 5 is to justify conclusions. This requires the engagement of the stakeholders in the determination of how data will be presented so that it has meaning to them. The technical experts and the stakeholders need to collaborate on this endeavor. This process needs to involve diverse stakeholders in the interpretation of the data.

The final step is to ensure the use of evaluation findings and to share lessons learned. Stakeholders will not use evaluation results that they do not understand or do not find to be useful to what they need to know. In this regard, you need to ensure that recommendations emanate from an inclusive process. You should involve various types of stakeholders in the determination of the recommendations that are warranted from the evaluation results.

Are Social Workers Culturally Competent?

While there are numerous sources of literature on what cultural competence means, why it is important, and how we can demonstrate it in our agencies, there is very little literature regarding the measurement of it. A question that arises for social work is whether social workers are culturally competent. The following paragraphs report on one such study.

Hall (2009) conducted a dissertation that focused on predictors of cultural competence among Masters of Social Work (MSW) students. While she found a number of studies showing that training in cultural competence achieves its learning objectives, she failed to find studies that answered the question of whether social workers (or students) are culturally competent at a reasonable level. This dissertation reported the results of a study of cultural competence among MSW students and recent graduates of MSW programs. A national sample of 186 persons participated. It was found that MSW students and recent graduates had high scores on cultural competence as measured by the Multicultural Competence Inventory. Students in various stages of matriculation (foundation year, advanced year, and recent graduates) were found to have similar levels of cultural competence. One might conclude from this discovery that schools of social work recruit people with high cultural competence.

Another discovery by Hall (2009) was that the personal characteristics of the MSW students were not related to the scores for cultural competence. Educational variables also failed to be related to this competence. One might conclude from the data that persons who enter social work education program tend to possess a high level of cultural competence and that this characteristic tends to be rather uniform, among different types of people.

Rethinking Cultural Competence

Reflecting on the evolution of our attention to the idea of cultural competence, Kirmayer (2012) offered the following observation:

> In actual practice, cultural competence in the US has been largely approached through sensitization of clinicians to the social predicaments of these ethnoracial blocs or through efforts at ethnic matching of patient and practitioner. The cultural competence literature tends to treat culture as a matter of group membership (whether self-assigned or ascribed). This assumes that members of a group share certain cultural "traits," values, beliefs and attitudes that strongly influence or determine clinically relevant behaviour. Unfortunately, this approach tends to reify and essentialize cultures as consisting of more or less fixed sets of characteristics that can be described independently of any individual's life history or social context—hence the plethora of textbooks with chapters on specific ethnocultural groups. This is an old-fashioned view, now largely abandoned by anthropology. (p. 155)

Contemporary anthropology, according to Kirmayer (2012), emphasizes that culture is not a fixed characteristic of people, either as individuals or as groups. It is an ongoing process of sharing and using knowledge that depends on variables in communities that interface between ethnocultural communities and institutions of the larger society, like the health care system. As a result, cultures are constantly undergoing change. Yet cultural processes remain central to the health promotion and health delivery system.

This requires a different approach to cultural competence that includes respect for the identity of individuals and communities with attention to the politicized nature of individuals and interactions with collectives, both local and global. This cultural identity must be understood with regard to multiple networks of communities and the larger society.

Chapter Practice Exercises

There are two practice exercises for this chapter. The first exercise calls on you to discuss issues of ethics in your own research study. The second exercise asks you to discuss issues in cultural competence. For each exercise, you will imagine a research study that you might undertake, and you will reflect on selected issues with regard to that study. At the end of the first exercise, you will have demonstrated competence in recognizing ways to ensure that you are adhering to key ethical issues in the use of human subjects in research. At the end of the second exercise, you will have demonstrated competence in the inclusion of issues in cultural competence in various tasks in the research process.

Practice Exercise 1: Ethics for Your Study

In this exercise, you will think of a research study that you might undertake. With regard to various tasks in the research process, you will be asked to consider several ethical issues in the use of human subjects in research.

Competencies Demonstrated by Practice Exercise 1

1.   The ability to recognize what ethical issues in research are most likely to be problematic with regard to a given research study

2.   The ability to recognize how to address the ethical issue of potential harm that may be caused to human subjects by a research study

3.   The ability to recognize how to address the ethical issue of privacy in a research study

4.   The ability to recognize how to address the ethical issue of voluntary participation in a research study

5.   The ability to recognize how to address the ethical issue of justice in a research study

Activities for Practice Exercise 1

1.   You will briefly describe a research study that you would like to undertake. This study can be descriptive, explanatory, evaluative, or exploratory. Indicate which of these types of study you will undertake, the research question you will pursue, the study sample you would employ, and the tools you might use to measure the study variables.

Example 1: I will conduct an evaluative study. The research question is as follows: Is a social support group experience effective in the reduction of the level of anxiety experienced by victims of rape? The study subjects will be rape victims currently being served by the Family Services Center of Oak Hill. These clients will be asked to complete an anxiety scale both at the beginning of the group experience and again at the end of the experience.

Example 2: I will conduct a descriptive study of the needs of the current clients of the Hampton Behavioral Health Center. I will ask a sample of current clients to indicate which of a series of our current services they find most helpful and what new services they would like for us to offer. For each question, they will be given a list of services they can check. They will also be given an open-ended question that asks how we can better serve them. In addition, the variables of race, gender, and income level will be measured in this study.

Example 3: I will conduct an explanatory study of the causes of depression for adult females being serviced by the Hampton Behavioral Health Center. The study subjects will be asked to complete a survey that measures their depression and asks questions that identify potential causes of depression such as (a) whether they are currently having family difficulties, (b) whether they are having financial problems, (c) whether they are in good physical health, and (d) whether they have recently been the victim of assault of any kind

2. Describe how you would recruit and employ human subjects in this research study.

    Example: The current clients of the tutoring class at Rondale Middle School will be asked to participate in this study. The nature of the study will be explained, and they will be given the instructions on how to participate. Because they are minors, their parents will be asked to give consent to this participation.

3. Is there any reason for people to believe that participating in this study will cause harm? If

so, indicate how you will address this issue so as to prevent harm.

Example 1: These clients will be asked to respond to an anxiety scale. This is the only research activity that calls for their participation. I am not aware of any type of harm that would normally come from such an experience.

Example 2: These study subjects will be asked to respond to a questionnaire that asks whether they have been sexually abused by a parent and to reflect on this experience in several ways. It seems logical to expect that some people will be emotionally upset by this experience.

4. How will you protect the privacy of these study subjects?

    Example 1: These clients will be asked to respond to the anxiety scale anonymously.

    Example 2: These clients will be asked to discuss their experiences as a victim of sexual abuse by a parent. Given the possibility that study subjects will be emotionally upset by this experience, a social worker will be present to offer assistance.

5. How will you ensure voluntary participation?

    Example 1: These clients will be informed that their participation in this study is voluntary. They will be told that they can turn in a blank copy of the anxiety scale in the envelope being distributed for their completed forms so that their participation will not be known.

    Example 2: The behavior of study subjects will be observed while a person fakes a heart attack on a busy street in a city. Their participation cannot be voluntary because the intent of the study is to describe behaviors of people who witness people in crises on a street in a city. If they know that the heart attack is fake, they will not behave in their typical ways to a real crisis. Because some people may be upset by this experience, a social worker will be present to offer help.

6. Do you have any reason to believe that the issue of justice should be scrutinized for this study?

   Example: The types of people who will benefit from the results of this study are the same as the study participants (victims of rape who are being treated for anxiety); therefore, justice is not an issue that requires special scrutiny for this study.

What You Will Report From Practice Exercise 1

Your report for Practice Exercise 1 will be your answers to the six questions given in the description of activities presented above.

Practice Exercise 2: Demonstrating Cultural Competence for Your Research Study

In this exercise, you are asked to reflect on issues of cultural competence with regard to the study you would like to undertake. It can be the same study as you described in Exercise 1 or it can be different.

Competencies Demonstrated by Practice Exercise 2

1. The ability to demonstrate cultural competence in the determination of a research question

2. The ability to demonstrate cultural competence in the development of research methods

3. The ability to demonstrate cultural competence in the analysis of data

4. The ability to demonstrate cultural competence in the drawing of conclusions for a research study

Activities for Practice Exercise 2

1. You will briefly describe the research study you would like to undertake.

2. With regard to your proposed study, reflect on the theme of cultural competence with regard to the development of the research question. How will you address this theme? In other words, how will cultural competence be demonstrated by you with regard to the development of your research question?

   Example: In my study of the expressed needs of the clients of the Hampton Behavioral Health Center, I will collect data on race, gender, and income to see if the needs of our clients are different among categories of these variables.

3. With regard to your study, your will reflect on how you will demonstrate cultural competence with regard to the methods you might employ in the determination of how variables will be measured and how you will select study participants.

   Example: In my study of the expressed needs of the clients of our agency, I will compare the respondents to my survey with our agency data with regard to race and gender to see if the different groups are represented in our study sample at the same rate as they exist in our agency. If 30% of our study respondents are African American but only 10% of our study respondents are from this group, I will be concerned about the extent to which our African American clients are appropriately represented in our study sample.

4. With regard to your study, reflect on how you will demonstrate cultural competence when you analyze data.

   Example: In my study of the needs of the current clients of my agency, I will analyze data on the relationship between variables such as race and gender and the expressed needs of our clients.

5. With regard to your study, reflect on how you will demonstrate cultural competence when you draw conclusions.

   Example: In my study of the expressed needs of our current clients, I will draw conclusions that are based partly on the results of my analysis of data on the representativeness of racial groups in our study sample. If a group is not appropriately represented, I will make a note of this fact in the study conclusions. This would suggest that our data are not appropriately representative of this group and that other

means should be employed to obtain information from this group.

What You Will Report From Practice Exercise 2

Your report for Practice Exercise 2 will follow the questions posed in the presentation of the activities of this exercise. In other words, you will report a description of your proposed study along with your ideas on how you will demonstrate cultural competence with regard to (a) the selection of your research question, (b) the research methods you will employ with regard to tasks such as drawing your study sample and measuring study variables, (c) the analysis of your data, and (d) the drawing of your conclusions.

CHAPTER REVIEW

Chapter Key Learnings

1. Ethics provide rules of behavior based on moral values. It does not depend on research for validation because it is more like philosophy than it is about science. Ethics are monitored by professional organizations through mechanisms such as the code of ethics.

2. Cultural competence refers to competence that recognizes the influence of culture with regard to practice. In social work research, this means incorporating knowledge about culture into the design and execution of the research study.

3. A concept that binds ethics and cultural competence is the vulnerable population. People in a vulnerable population are viewed

as vulnerable because they are likely to view their participation in research to be necessary because of the population in which they reside, and thereby, they may feel compelled to participate.

4. Human subjects research is research involving a living individual about whom an investigator (whether professional or student) conducting research obtains data through intervention or interaction with the individual or identifiable private information.

5. The Code of Ethics of the NASW provides a guide for ethical practice.

6. Social workers should not undertake research that has serious potential of causing harm to the study subjects unless

the benefits of the research clearly outweigh the harm.

7. Social work researchers should obtain informed consent from study subjects before undertaking the activities of the research project.

8. The social work researchers should engage in actions that protect the privacy of the human subjects of research. This entails protecting the identity of the subject in research reports. This protection is best maintained when the data are collected anonymously.

9. The principle of respect deals with autonomy and self-determination. People should be allowed to choose for themselves the risk they will undertake. Study subjects have full autonomy when they can understand the risks involved and have the freedom to volunteer without coercion.

10. The principle of beneficence requires that the social work researcher minimize harm and maximize benefits. If the researcher can find a less harmful way to conduct the needed research, then that way must be used instead of the more harmful ways.

11. The principle of justice requires us to design research that does not unduly target its risks to certain groups of people and fails to treat different types of people equally or fairly.

12. The IRB in major institutions monitors the protection of human subjects in research. This body reviews research proposals from researchers, including students, to ensure that the rights of human subjects in research are protected.

13. The NASW has articulated 10 standards related to cultural competence among social workers. These 10 standards include ethics and values. These standards require the social work researcher to understand his or her own culture and to apply knowledge of other cultures in their practices.

14. The methodology of the social work research study should include culture as a theme when appropriate, including measurement tools that are culturally sensitive.

15. In social work research, cultural competence means knowing how cultural factors have meaning for different aspects of the research process. For example, does the research question adequately reflect culture? Was culture considered in the definition of variables and the analysis of data? Was it considered in the conclusions that were drawn?

16. A rare study on cultural competence among social workers revealed a high level of competence among them.

Chapter Discussion Questions

1. Do you believe that there is a need for the existence of the IRB for human service research? What is likely to happen, and how often do you believe it will happen, if there were not an IRB to review proposals for the use of human subjects in research that relates to human services? For example, how many of your fellow students do you believe would violate ethical principles if they did not have to submit their ideas for IRB review?

2. What do you believe are the legitimate interests of the IRB and what are not their legitimate interests. For example, is it legitimate for this body to review your plan for the administration of a scale to a group of your clients when you are conducting a study whose results will be made public? Is it legitimate for this body to evaluate the overall quality of your study methods? What about the importance of the subject you plan to study?

3. Which of the principles of ethics in research do you believe you need to understand better?

4. Which of the principles of ethics in research do you believe will be the greatest challenge for you when you conduct research?

5. Can you think of a situation where your agency may expect you to engage in behaviors you find questionable from the standpoint of ethics in the use of human subjects in research?

Chapter Test on Ethics

1. Which of the following situations is/are considered research on human subjects and typically requires full review by the IRB or its equivalent in your agency?
   a. You ask one client to respond to a depression scale on a weekly basis for several weeks of treatment, and you expect to employ these measurements for clinical purposes but you do not expect to include this information in a report
   b. You conduct an anonymous client satisfaction survey where the data will be used only on an internal basis for program improvement, and you do not expect to include this information in a report to be distributed for general understanding of the nature of the treatment and/or target behavior
   c. Both of the above
   d. None of the above

2. Which of the following situations is/are considered research on human subjects and requires either expedited or full review by the IRB or its equivalent in your agency?
   a. You are examining whether the support model of treatment will reduce caregiver burnout for those caring for relatives suffering from seriously debilitating illnesses. You will administer a stress scale to a group of persons before and after the treatment and will use the data in a public report on the effectiveness of this treatment model for caregiver burnout
   b. You are testing whether a new drug will reduce depression for those suffering from AIDS by administering this new drug during a treatment period when you will also regularly conduct blood tests. The results will be made public
   c. Both of the above
   d. None of the above

3. Which of the following statements is/are true?
   a. Children are not considered capable of giving informed consent to engage in research as human subjects
   b. Studies employing existing databases normally do not require full review by the IRB if individual names of persons are not listed in the database
   c. Both of the above
   d. None of the above

4. Which of the following statements is/are true?
   a. Under no circumstances may you conduct research using human subjects without the written consent of the person who provides the information for the study
   b. If you wanted to conduct a study of social norms that are prevalent in public housing projects, you would not be able to collect data only using people from public housing projects because of the issue of justice
   c. Both of the above
   d. None of the above

5. Which of the following statements is/are true?
   a. Sometimes the IRB will approve a study proposal that entails notable risk to study subjects because the benefits to society outweigh the risks to the individual study subject
   b. If a study procedure is available to the researcher that is less risky than the one planned, the IRB will usually require its employment in the study
   c. Both of the above
   d. None of the above

6. Suppose a researcher has proposed to conduct a study on the natural responses to stressful encounters by faking a heart attack on a busy street corner while another researcher observes the behavior of people who react, not knowing the apparent heart attack is a fake. The observer will make notes about the behaviors of the bystanders but will not know their identities. Which issue in research ethics would be most problematic for this study? (Note: The question is not whether this study is so problematic that it is unlikely to be approved by the IRB. The question focuses your attention on the issue most likely to present questions for closer review.)
   a. Confidentiality
   b. Voluntary participation
   c. Harm
   d. Justice

7. Suppose a researcher wishes to conduct a study on the validity of astrology, by gaining information on each study subject's astrological sign (Leo, Vergo, etc.) and asking questions to the individual to determine if the information from astrology accurately predicts the answers the individual gives to questions about his or her personality. This study will be conducted in eight prisons, some for males and some for females. A total of 1,200 prisoners will be asked to volunteer for this study. The data will be collected anonymously. Which issue in research ethics would be most problematic for this study?
   a. Confidentiality
   b. Voluntary participation
   c. Harm
   d. Justice

8. Which of the following statements is/are true?
   a. It is usually better to collect data in an anonymous manner than to collect it by identifying information on the measurement tool
   b. It is usually necessary to get parental permission for data that are to be collected from children
   c. Both of the above
   d. None of the above

ANSWERS: 1 = d; 2 = c; 3 = c; 4 = d; 5 = c; 6 = b; 7 = d; 8 = c

Chapter Test on Cultural Competence

1. Cultural competence refers to which of the following:
   a. A liberal ideology
   b. A commitment to social justice
   c. The ability to understand and work effectively with people of different cultures
   d. A conservative ideology

2. Which of the following is/are essential parts of cultural competence?
   a. Knowledge of different cultures
   b. Self-awareness with regard to culture
   c. Both of the above
   d. None of the above

3. For which type of study is culture an important consideration?
   a. Descriptive study
   b. Explanatory study
   c. Evaluative study
   d. All of the above

4. Which of the following statements is/are true?
   a. If you find out that there is a relationship between two variables, you have proven that one of these variables is the cause of the other
   b. When you examine causation, you need to consider the time order of changes in variables, for example, a change in the cause should be followed by a change in the effect
   c. Both of the above
   d. None of the above

5. Which of the following are parts of the research process for which culture is an important consideration?
   a. The drawing of the sample
   b. The measurement of variables
   c. Both of the above
   d. None of the above

6. Which of the following is/are true?
   a. Much research has revealed that MSW students are seriously lacking in cultural competence
   b. Some research has shown that characteristics of MSW students are highly related to cultural competence
   c. Both of the above
   d. None of the above

ANSWERS: 1 = c; 2 = c; 3 = d; 4 = b; 5 = c; 6 = d

Chapter Glossary

Beneficence. The ethical principle that requires that we minimize harm and maximize benefits when engaging in the use of human subjects in research.

Causation. The influence of one variable on the other, as evidenced by three realities: there was found to be a relationship between the cause and the effect, the effect is not explained by other variables, and a change in this cause comes before a change in this effect.

Confidentiality (for research subjects). The practice of not reporting the identity of an individual who participated in a research study along with the information derived from that individual.

Cultural competence. Knowledge, values, and skills that recognize the influence of culture with regard to practice.

Ethics. Rules of behavior based on moral values.

Informed consent. The practice of ensuring that study subjects have given their consent and that they were clearly informed about risks.

Institutional review board. A body of people whose job is to review proposals for conducting research with the objective of protecting human subjects in research from harm, invasion of privacy, and/or coercion.

Justice. An ethical principle that requires us to design research that does not unduly target its risks to certain groups of people and fails

to treat different types of people equably or fairly.

Privacy. Our ability to control access to information about ourselves.

Respect. An ethical principle that deals with autonomy and self-determination, so that potential research subjects are allowed to choose for themselves the risk that they will undertake.

Voluntary participation in research. Avoiding the coercion of people to participate in a research study, so that each participant is engaging in the research study on a voluntary basis.

Vulnerable population. A group of people who are vulnerable to feeling pressured to participate in a research study because of their social status, such as being in prison, living in a public housing project, or being a member of a minority group.

4

EVIDENCE-BASED PRACTICE

Janice is a social worker in a program for at-risk middle school students where various services are in place, such as tutoring and support groups in addition to individual and family counseling. A fellow social worker, Bethany, has suggested the addition of equine-assisted therapy for this program. Bethany had seen this service in action and was convinced of its effectiveness. She had seen a good outcome with an autistic child with whom she had worked in an agency where she was previously employed. Equine-assisted therapy is a treatment approach that employs horses in the therapeutic process, sometimes in the form of riding and sometimes in the form of other activities such as grooming.

Janice has had some training in evidence-based practice, the idea that you should examine research studies on the effectiveness of a given treatment for a given behavior before deciding on what services to offer. She is aware that the systematic review of evidence is the best source because it includes a review of all the evidence that can be found on a given theme, not just the "cherry-picked" sources that support one's preconceived conclusions.

Her first step was to examine the National Registry of Evidence-Based Practices (from the Substance Abuse and Mental Health Services Administration) to see if equine-assisted therapy was listed. She found that it was not. Next, she examined two different sources for systematic reviews of evidence: (1) the Cochrane Collaboration and (2) the Campbell Collaboration. She found no systematic reviews of evidence of equine-assisted therapy on either of these sites. She also reviewed the American Psychological Association website for evidence about this treatment. Again, she did not find equine-assisted therapy listed as an evidence-based treatment. She concluded, from this review of four major sources of evidence, that this treatment approach is not well known or well researched. She continued her search for a systematic review of evidence.

Following her failure to find evidence from the first four major sources, Janice sought evidence from a major electronic literature database from her library. She found many articles that described equine-assisted therapy but only a few studies of its effectiveness. Many of the latter articles were related to autism, which is not her clients' target behavior. As she continued her search, she entered the words "equine-assisted therapy" into the Wikipedia website and found a very thorough article that reported a systematic review that concluded that this treatment is not evidence based for mental health behaviors. There was some weak evidence reported in this article, but there were more questions about it than positive conclusions. The authors of this systematic review concluded that equine-assisted therapy should not be used instead of mental health treatments that were evidence based. Janice concluded that equine-assisted therapy should not be added to the array of services that her program delivers. She is open to the examination of further evidence, perhaps even to the experimental use of it within a research study. But for now, she will not recommend it as an ongoing service for her agency.

INTRODUCTION

Human service agencies are expected to use practices that are backed by **evidence**. Many actually advertise this fact. This means they consider scientific evidence when making practice decisions. If they totally ignore evidence, they cannot honestly refer to their practices as evidence based. The standard for what constitutes an **evidence-based practice** (EBP) will vary somewhat with sources of expertise. You are challenged to establish a standard for yourself using the information in this chapter. You already know that cherry-picking of evidence to suit your opinion is not an option for the social worker who appreciates the spirit of scientific inquiry. Instead, you need to review evidence in a systematic and objective manner. Your guide for this task will be addressed in this chapter.

A critical question for the social worker is, "What contributes to good client outcome?" There is a myriad of evidence on this question, particularly for clinical social work practice. EBP tends to focus on a given type of intervention. Is this intervention effective in the reduction of anxiety for victims of rape? Does this type of tutoring work better than normal tutoring in the improvement of grades for at-risk middle school males?

Your intervention will have components that distinguish it from others. For example, it may call on you to focus on the client's dysfunctional thoughts, to employ structured homework of a certain kind, or to focus on the client's strengths rather than problems or weaknesses. Research evidence suggests that some interventions are effective, some are not effective, and some have been insufficiently studied to determine if they are evidence based. It is the duty of the evidence-based practitioner to know the status of the evidence related to the interventions they employ.

There are factors that contribute to client outcome that are not related to the specifics of the intervention you are using. They are called **common factors** because they improve client outcome regardless of the intervention you have selected. They are common to all interventions that are effective.

There is a good deal of research on the common factors. Many reveal the contribution of the common factor on client outcome with the use of the **effect size**, a concept that will be reviewed later in this book. For the time being, you should know that an effect size is the amount of difference a common factor makes with regard to proportions of a standard deviation of change. An effect size of 1.0 means the effect was equivalent to 1 standard deviation of change in client outcome. An effect size of 1.0 is considered to be large in the view of the human service statisticians. Effect sizes smaller than 1.0 are typical for human service research and effect sizes as low as 0.20 are sometimes considered noteworthy.

One of these common factors is the therapeutic relationship, sometimes called the alliance between the client and the social worker. To what extent does this client and this social worker have a good helping relationship? Is it healthy? Is it affectionate? Is it characterized by trust? Horvath, Del Re, Fluckinger, and Symonds (2011) found that a good alliance was related to good client outcome (effect size = 0.57).

A second common factor is the demonstration of empathy. Elliot, Bohart, Watson, and Greenberg (2011) found that empathy has an impressive effect on client outcome (effect size = 0.63). Social workers who demonstrate better empathy can expect better client outcomes.

Another common factor is goal congruence between the social worker and the client. Tryon and Winograd (2011) found that social workers who have strong goal congruence with the client on what is to be accomplished by service have better client outcomes (effect size = 0.72).

Positive regard of the client on the part of the social worker is another of the common factors. According to Farber and Doolin (2011), social workers who do a better job of demonstrating positive regard have better client outcomes. In their review, the effect size of this common factor was 0.56.

If you have all these commons factors with your client, you will likely have positive client outcomes regardless of your chosen intervention. The common factors are likely to be more important than the specific ingredients of your chosen treatment (see the information on the dodo bird verdict given later in this chapter). But your choice of a superior intervention will elevate your treatment to the optimal level. Most of this chapter will be focused on how to find the evidence for the various interventions that you may consider, much like the experience of Janice in the vignette that started this chapter.

At the completion of this chapter, you will be able to do the following:

1. Explain the nature of evidence and what distinguishes it from other guides for practice.

2. Define the concept of EBP.

3. Identify levels of evidence with emphasis on the systematic review as the highest level.

4. Use Internet sources for finding evidence.

5. Employ the steps in EBP.

6. Discuss one of the major controversies with regard to EBP.

THE NATURE OF EVIDENCE AND EVIDENCE-BASED PRACTICE

Some definitions of evidence suggest that it refers to any information presented on behalf of an assertion. In the scientific world, however, evidence refers to systematic collection and analysis of data using the principles and practices of scientific inquiry. Your intuition may be a good guide for your practice, but it is not evidence. Your practice experience may be a good guide, but it is also not evidence. If you have systematically examined several publications that report scientific studies of the outcomes of the practice in which you are engaged, you will be using evidence.

EBP is social work practice that employs the judicious use of the best available evidence, along with the considerations of client preferences and therapist expertise, in making practice decisions. Therefore, evidence is only one of the ingredients. This process does not suggest that the clinician tally the votes on evidence for various treatments and choose the treatment with the highest score. Instead, this process says that the clinician and client will jointly decide on the goals of treatment, and the chosen practice will be the one that is best according to several factors. It is certainly possible that the chosen practice deemed best for a particular client is one that is not at the top of the list of votes according to the evidence.

EBP is a process for making practice decisions with evidence in mind, not as the only thing, but as one of the items that influences practice decisions. There is a distinction between EBP as a process and the idea of evidence-based interventions. The **evidence-based intervention (or program)** is one that has suitable supporting evidence for a particular target behavior. Suitable evidence means that there are multiple studies showing its effectiveness and that this evidence clearly outweighs the evidence that fails to support the intervention for this target behavior.

Finding evidence-based interventions is only one of the steps in the process of EBP. Other considerations include careful attention to the characteristics of the client and the skills of the social worker. A given evidence-based practice may not work best with your clients and with your skills as a practitioner.

The elements of practitioner expertise, client preferences, and best evidence are portrayed in Figure 4.1. You can see that these three elements come together to depict EBP. Evidence, therefore, is one of the three elements of EBP.

The EBP movement has generated a number of new ideas about how to examine the evidence. You may have heard the term *cherry-picking*. This means restricting your inquiry to evidence that supports your preconceived ideas about what works. This term, of course, is contrary to the idea of EBP, because the latter works according to the principles of critical thinking and the spirit of scientific inquiry. This means you would engage in a comprehensive examination of the evidence in an objective manner.

FIGURE 4.1 ■ Evidence-Based Practice

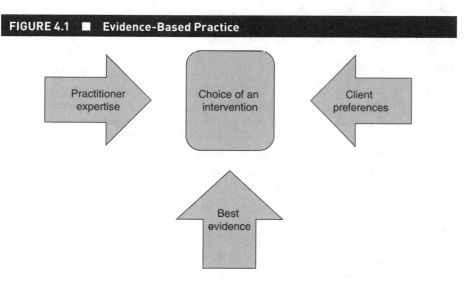

The results of scientific studies are quite varied and inconsistent. Some studies may show that cognitive–behavioral therapy (CBT) is superior to psychodynamic therapy in the treatment of depression, and other studies may show no difference in outcome between these two treatments for depression. It would be rare for you to find that only one **bona fide treatment** for a target behavior has credible evidence to support it. You may find that a given treatment for a given target behavior has many supportive studies, while certain other treatments for the same target behavior have only a few studies of supportive evidence.

The best approach, according to the spirit of scientific inquiry and critical thinking, is to examine the evidence according to certain conditions determined prior to the search of the literature. This means that you would have to do the following:

1. Decide on the nature of the target behavior you wish to treat.

2. Determine the sources of evidence to be reviewed.

3. Decide on the keywords that would be used in your search.

4. Search the evidence sources.

5. Draw conclusions about what treatments are evidence based.

You will notice that the above list calls on you to determine the nature of your inquiry before you search the literature. The spirit of scientific inquiry would require you to give fair treatment to all sources of evidence whether they tell you what you want to know or not.

When Janice was examining evidence with regard to equine-assisted therapy (see the vignette at the beginning of this chapter), she used "equine-assisted" in some searches and "equine-assisted therapy" in other searches. The literature sources she examined were the Cochrane Collaboration, the Campbell Collaboration, the American Psychological

Association (APA), and a major literature database from her library. She also did a Google search and found a useful article in Wikipedia.

Levels of Evidence

There are four levels of evidence that will be discussed here: (1) the **single research study**, (2) the **traditional review of the research literature**, (3) the **meta-analysis**, and (4) the **systematic review**. Excluded from this list are articles that do not report evidence. This might include articles on the opinions of experts or practitioners or articles that provide information on the nature of a given practice. In this review of evidence, the focus is on evaluative studies, not on ones that are descriptive, exploratory, or explanatory. You will be examining studies of outcomes when clients have been given a service.

The Single Article on Evidence

The single research study of evidence is a study of a specific sample of people (e.g., women with postpartum depression), who have been given a certain treatment (e.g., CBT), and have been given a certain method of measurement (e.g., the Beck Depression Scale). The data from the tool will have to be subjected to statistical analysis to determine if behavior improved and if chance is a good explanation of the results. This source can serve as one piece of evidence, but it is limited because the literature is replete with articles showing contrary evidence with regard to a given research question.

The results of published studies can be a guide to what new interventions you should consider employing with a given group of clients. These results can also serve as a basis for presenting your intervention as being evidence based if the summary of evidence qualifies it for this designation. You will find many articles in the literature that report on a single study that tested an intervention for a given target behavior with one sample of clients. This is the first level of scientific evidence to consider. It is useful, but could be limited by the fact that it is only one piece of evidence and may not perfectly fit your practice situation. The single study is also vulnerable to being misused by people who wish to engage in cherry-picking of evidence to prove a point. If you have a colleague who has been arguing with you about what is most effective for a given practice objective, you should be wary of a single piece of evidence that this person shares with you. You should ask, "What do the other studies of this practice tell us?"

Traditional Literature Review of Evidence

The second level of evidence is the traditional literature review that examines evidence. It is a review of selected articles of evidence that have been secured by the authors of the work, where the protocol for the selection of articles for review is not enumerated.

You might find an article that reports on a number of studies of a given intervention for a given target behavior. The summary of this source should provide useful guidance. This form of evidence has the advantage of including a number of studies on a given theme rather than just one study. But we must consider the fact that the research literature varies a great deal on the conclusions that should be drawn from studies on a given theme; thus, the review of a single article can be rather misleading. The traditional literature review of the evidence takes us to a higher level.

The traditional literature review, however, can represent the biased review of the literature by the author of the article. It certainly is better to review an article that reports on a dozen research studies that show the effectiveness of a given intervention rather than a single study on it. Now you have the evidence from a dozen articles rather than one. This should be adequate to provide guidance for practice because this intervention has been shown to be effective by several research articles. But you may not be informed by such a review of the limitations of this intervention or whether it is better than other interventions. That agenda will be better served by the next level of evidence—the meta-analysis.

Meta-Analysis

The meta-analysis combines the results of a number of studies of a common theme. It is more than the author's summary of the evidence. It uses a specific scientific technique for combining the results into a specific metric (the effect size) for drawing conclusions about the research question.

The meta-analysis begins with the establishment of a protocol for searching the literature. The protocol includes the selection of the electronic literature databases to review, the keywords that will be used to search these databases for articles, and the criteria that will be used to select the studies for the meta-analysis from all the articles that appear in the review. Some meta-analyses will include only studies that used a randomized controlled trial as the research design. This is the design that includes the random assignment of people to the treatment group and the control group with the treatment group getting the treatment. The protocol has the function of reducing the bias of the researcher. You cannot cherry-pick articles when you are following a protocol.

An example of a meta-analysis was the report by Payne and Marcus (2008). They reviewed articles on the effectiveness of group psychotherapy for older adult clients. Four electronic databases were selected: PsycINFO, Medline, Academic Search Premier, and Dissertations Abstracts. The search terms were *geriatric, older adult, elderly, aging,* and *gerontology*. These initial terms were combined with the terms *group psychotherapy, group therapy, group dynamics, psychotherapy,* and *support groups*. To be included, the studies had to have measurements of client gain and be testing group psychotherapy. A total of 44 studies were found in this search that together included 1,381 clients. The authors of this meta-analysis concluded that group psychotherapy was generally effective in the treatment of a variety of target behaviors. The effect sizes of the various studies included in this analysis ranged from 0.24 to 0.42, indicating a modest effect of group psychotherapy on the conditions being treated.

Systematic Review

Like the meta-analysis, the systematic review employs a protocol for searching the evidence literature. The difference is that a systematic review may include one or more meta-analyses and does not normally include the computation of an overall effect size for all studies included.

According to the Campbell Collaboration (www.campbellcollaboration.org), the purpose of the systematic review is to sum up the best available research on a research question. This is done by synthesizing the results of various studies through a rigorous protocol for the collection and analysis of results. A key theme of the systematic review is transparency. When you read one of these reviews, you will be given a great deal of information on just how the included studies in the review got to be there and how they were analyzed. Studies in a review are screened for quality. Peer review is a key part of the process.

A systematic review is not a report prepared by a single person. It usually starts with a team of researchers who get continued peer review from others on the process whereby the research reports will be examined. For these reasons, the systematic review is the highest quality of scientific inquiry normally available to the human service professional.

It also tends to employ a more comprehensive protocol for searching the literature. For example, it usually includes "gray literature," or the literature that has been recorded somewhere but not published in a journal. Another feature of the systematic review is that the authors of the review have the assistance of the professional staff of the collaborative that will publish the paper. These are people who review the protocol for the systematic review and make suggestions.

There are two major collaborations of interest to the evidence-based social worker: (1) the Cochrane Collaboration, with a focus on medical research (including mental health), and (2) the Campbell Collaboration, with a focus on social science research. Of particular interest is that each of these collaborations publish reviews that are considered of the highest validity. In addition, they are presented in a format that is helpful for those who just want a summary as well as those who wish to examine the methodology in detail. At the end of the review, you will find a simple summary of the findings and conclusions that do not require sophisticated understanding of statistics and research concepts.

These four levels of evidence are portrayed in Figure 4.2. In this figure, you can see that these types of evidence start with the single research article, the lowest level of evidence. The second level is the traditional literature review. The third and fourth levels of evidence are the meta-analysis and the systematic review. These four types of evidence vary in the extent of their systematic use of scientific evidence and the likelihood that they will present you with objective evidence, not just the cherry-picked studies that are used to prove a point.

Places to Find Evidence on the Internet

There are numerous sources of evidence that you can find on the Internet in addition to the Cochrane Collaboration and the Campbell Collaboration mentioned above. These sources include the APA and the Substance Abuse and Mental Health Services Administration (SAMHSA) of the federal government. Another one is the California Evidence-Based Clearinghouse for Child Welfare.

Some of these sources will provide a rating system that shows the level of evidence that supports a given treatment. You will need to review the criteria each gives for their system to decide whether a given treatment should be considered evidence based.

A division of the APA provides information on evidence with regard to a great number of treatments. You can access this organization through the Internet (www.apa.org).

FIGURE 4.2 ■ Levels of Evidence

			Systematic review
		Meta-analysis	
	Traditional literature review of evidence		
Results of a single evaluation research article			

The link for reviewing evidence regarding treatments will give you a page that lists many treatments for many conditions (http://www.div12.org/psychological-treatments). When you reach this link, you can click on *cognitive therapy for the treatment of depression*. This action will give you a review of what CBT is and a statement that the research support is strong (rather than modest or controversial). This should be an indicator that CBT is an evidence-supported treatment for depression. If you click on *family-based treatments for anorexia nervosa*, you will also get the message that the research support is strong. If you click on a treatment and find that the evidence is labeled *modest*, you have a treatment for which there is evidence of effectiveness but that evidence is from only a few studies, whereas the *strong* support designation is for treatments that have stronger support from the evidence.

The SAMHSA provides a wide array of information on evidence for treatments. One link will direct you to the web page for evidence-based treatments for mental health (https://www.samhsa.gov/ebp-web-guide/mental-health-treatment). Another link will get you to a national registry of evidence-based treatments and programs (https://www.samhsa.gov/nrepp).

The California Evidence-Based Clearinghouse for Child Welfare provides, among other things, a list of many human service programs and interventions that have been used in child welfare. One example on this list is the Adolescent Parenting Program (APP). If you click on this program option under the list of programs, you will get the following description:

> *APP* provides support to first-time pregnant and parenting teens through intensive home visiting and peer group education. Each *APP* serves a caseload of 15–25 teens that may enter the program at any time during their pregnancy or after their child's birth. Participants in the program receive monthly home visits using either the Partners for a Healthy Baby or Parents as Teachers home-visiting curriculum, along with 24 hours of prescriptive group education with their peers. Supporting adolescent parents to prevent a repeat pregnancy, complete their high school education, acquire job skills, and improve their parenting skills helps them become self-sufficient and better able to support themselves and their families. It also establishes a strong, stable foundation upon which their child will be raised. By investing in teen parents today, *APP* strives to protect the future of two generations—the young parents themselves and their babies. (California Evidence-Based Clearinghouse for Child Welfare, n.d.)

The level of the scientific evidence supporting APP is given as a 3 on a 5-point scale, meaning that the research is promising but not at one of the higher levels. From Exhibit 4.1, you can see the five levels of evidence that supports the programs enumerated on that list of programs along with a rating of NR (not able to be rated) if the agency was not able to give a rating because of insufficient information. As you can see, the first three levels on this scale indicate that the program has evidence to support. The fourth level indicates that the evidence fails to support it, and the fifth level suggests that there are some concerns about the possibility of difficulties from the program. So you should be cautious in using a program listed with a 4 and should avoid ones with the rating of 5. Surely, there will be programs on this list that have evidence behind them that would suit your clientele, so it is not likely you will be thrust into a situation where you will find a program with a rating of 4 or 5 to be worthy of your clients.

Exhibit 4.2 provides summaries of several searches of evidence from the Cochrane Collaboration. Each provides a conclusion and a plain language summary.

EXHIBIT 4.1

FIVE RATING LEVELS OF THE EVIDENCE-SUPPORTING PROGRAMS

Listed for the California Evidence-Based Clearinghouse for Child Welfare

Rating of 1: Well-supported by research evidence
Rating of 2: Supported by research evidence

Rating of 3: Promising research evidence
Rating of 4: Evidence fails to demonstrate effectiveness
Rating of 5: Concerning practice
NR: Not able to be rated

EXHIBIT 4.2

SUMMARIES OF EVIDENCE FOR SELECTED TARGET BEHAVIORS

Cochrane Collaboration

The following is a set of summaries and conclusions for systematic reviews from the Cochrane Collaboration. The Cochrane systematic reviews are very complicated with an array of research methods and statistical analysis of data. At the end is an author's conclusions and a plain language summary, each of which should be useful for the social work student and practitioner.

Treating Obesity in Children

Oude Luttikuis, H., Baur, L, Jansen, H., Shrewsbury, V. A., O'Malley, C., Stolk, R. P., & Summerbell, C. D. (2009). Interventions for treating obesity in children. *Cochrane atabase of Systematic Reviews*, (1), CD001872. doi:10.1002/14651858. CD001872.pub2

Authors' conclusions

While there is limited quality data to recommend one treatment program to be favoured over another, this review shows that combined behavioural lifestyle interventions compared to standard care or self-help can produce a significant and clinically meaningful reduction in overweight in children and adolescents. In obese adolescents, consideration should be given to the use of either orlistat or sibutramine, as an adjunct to lifestyle interventions, although this approach needs to be carefully weighed up against the potential for adverse effects. Furthermore, high quality research that considers psychosocial determinants for behaviour change, strategies to improve clinician-family interaction, and cost-effective programs for primary and community care is required.

Plain language summary

Childhood obesity affects both the physical and psychosocial health of children and may put them at risk of ill health as adults. More information is needed about the best way to treat obesity in children and adolescents. In this review, 64 studies were examined including 54 studies on lifestyle treatments (with a focus on diet, physical activity or behaviour change) and 10 studies on drug treatment to help overweight and obese children and their families with weight control. No surgical treatment studies were suitable to include in this review. This review showed that lifestyle programs can reduce the level of overweight in child and adolescent obesity 6 and 12 months after the beginning of the program. In moderate to severely obese adolescents, a reduction in overweight was found when either the drug orlistat, or the drug sibutramine were given in addition to a lifestyle program, although a range of adverse effects was also noted. Information on the long-term outcome of obesity treatment in children and adolescents was limited and needs to be examined in some high quality studies.

Psychosocial and Psychological Interventions for Treating Postpartum Depression

Dennis, C.-L., & Hodnett, E. D. (2007). Psychosocial and psychological interventions for treating postpartum depression. *Cochrane Database of Systematic Reviews*, 2007 (4), CD006166. doi:10.1002/14651858.CD006116.pub2.

Authors' conclusions

Although the methodological quality of the majority of trials was, in general, not strong, the meta-analysis results suggest that psychosocial and psychological interventions are an effective treatment option for women suffering from postpartum depression. The long-term effectiveness remains unclear.

Plain language summary

Postpartum depression affects approximately 13% of all new mothers. Many women desire to try treatment options other than medication. Results from nine trials involving 956 women found that both psychosocial (e.g., peer support, non-directive counselling) and psychological (e.g., cognitive behavioural therapy and interpersonal psychotherapy) interventions appear to be effective in reducing symptoms of postpartum depression. The long-term benefits are unknown. Larger trials evaluating psychosocial and psychological treatments for postpartum depression are needed to provide clear conclusions about specific intervention benefits.

Psychotherapeutic Treatments for Older Depressed People

Wilson, K., Mottram, P. G., & Vassilas, C. (2008). Psychotherapeutic treatments for older depressed people. *Cochrane Database of Systematic Reviews*, (1), CD004853. doi:10.1002/14651858.CD004853.pub2

Authors' conclusions

Only a small number of studies and patients were included in the meta-analysis. If taken on their own merit, the findings do not provide strong support for psychotherapeutic treatments in the management of depression in older people. However, the findings do reflect those of a larger meta-analysis that included patients with broader age ranges, suggesting that CBT may be of potential benefit.

Plain language summary

Depression is a common problem facing older people and is often associated with loneliness, physical illness and pain. The condition can last for some years and causes considerable distress and illness. A significant majority of depressed elders do not receive treatment because of difficulty in recognition of the condition. Not only can it present with lowered mood but may also present with physical problems including sleep disturbance, loss of appetite, loss of interest, anxiety and lack of energy. Psychotherapy is recognised as a treatment for mild depression. In this review we included seven small trials, involving a total of 153 participants, that examined psychotherapeutic treatments for depression in older people. Five trials compared a form of cognitive behavioural therapy (CBT) against control conditions, and the findings showed that CBT was more effective than control. Two individual trials compared CBT against psychodynamic therapy, with no significant difference in effectiveness indicated between the two approaches. Our review shows that there is relatively little research in this field and care must be taken in generalising what evidence there is to clinical populations.

Advice for the Social Worker

You have seen a hierarchy of evidence starting with the single article and ending with the systematic review. You have reviewed web sources that list programs and interventions according to the level of evidence that has been found to support them. Perhaps these web sources of listed programs could be the first step for the social work researcher when encountering a situation where evidence is needed. You may remember that Janice, in the initial vignette that began this chapter, found an answer to her question through an entry on Wikipedia. She found a reference to a systematic review she had been seeking.

You have seen that the systematic review is the highest level of evidence. You should look there before going to lower levels of evidence. If you find little guidance there, you should consult the literature for meta-analyses. The next avenue will be the traditional literature review on evidence. Finally, if all else fails to generate sufficient evidence for your purposes, you can seek articles that report single studies that are of interest to your research question. But you should be careful not to engage in the cherry-picking of evidence to support your preconceived conclusion. A review that contains only one source would be too limited, unless you have engaged in a protocol-driven review that generates only one article.

STEPS IN THE PROCESS OF EVIDENCE-BASED PRACTICE

A major leader in the development of EBP is Sackett who is from the field of medicine (see Sackett, Straus, Richardson, Rosenberg, & Hayes, 2000). His work has influenced the themes of EBP in social work. Among the contributions of Sackett is the suggestion of the steps in the process of conducting EBP. The steps enumerated in this section are similar to those of Sackett but modified to better fit the situation in social work. These include developing the evidence-based research question, finding evidence, critically reviewing that evidence in light of client preferences and practitioner expertise, implementing the intervention, and reviewing the results. These steps are best suited to the evaluation of an intervention rather than a program, but EBP can also be employed in program administration.

Sometimes the social worker has the opportunity to choose the intervention for a given set of clients with whom he or she works. This is often the case when there is only one client being the focus of the treatment. This situation is ideal for the process of EBP. In some instances, however, the social worker (or social work intern) is a part of an intervention that has been designed for the agency for the treatment of a given target behavior. In this situation, the social worker can simply review the evidence the agency has put together to support the treatment. If this evidence is not present, it would be necessary for an evidence-based practitioner to examine the evidence to see if the chosen treatment is supported. If the social worker engages in this activity and finds little evidence for the chosen treatment, it would be recommended that this literature be shared with the supervisor in the agency.

Step 1: Articulate the Evidence-Based Research Question

When you engage in the process of EBP, you will first engage in an assessment of the target behavior of the individual or group being served. From that assessment will emerge a goal of treatment and a research question regarding evidence for practice in this situation.

A social work student (Roberts, 2016) was faced with the task of assisting an experienced clinical social worker in conducting group therapy for veterans who were diagnosed with post-traumatic stress disorder (PTSD). The target behavior had been presented to her as behaviors associated with PTSD, a target behavior for those who have experienced a major trauma. For veterans, this would usually involve being engaged in military combat. The behaviors associated with PTSD include the emotional reexperiencing of the traumatic event, avoidance of what is associated with the trauma, anxiety, and so forth.

Roberts was engaged in a clinical situation where the treatment had been chosen by the agency and was based on evidence according to the representatives of the agency. When this student was not satisfied with the information given to her about evidence, she decided to assume that she had the power to change the treatment and to engage in the process of EBP. She would share her discovery of evidence with the agency.

The treatment chosen by the agency was a version of exposure therapy. Roberts's question for the review of evidence was, "Is exposure therapy effective in the reduction of symptoms of PTSD?"

Richardson (2016) is another social work student who was pursuing EBP in her internship. Her target behavior was anxiety among high school students whose performance in school was being affected by it. Because CBT had been suggested by her supervisor, she decided to focus attention on this treatment modality. Her research question became, "Is CBT effective in the treatment of anxiety among adolescents?" A more comprehensive question would have been, "What treatments are effective for anxiety among adolescents?" In the latter case, she could have compared the evidence on CBT with other treatments. However, her review of the evidence for CBT revealed that it was believed to be the treatment most effective in this situation.

Step 2: Search for Evidence

The next step is the systematic search for evidence in the pursuit of the research question. Your research question might be, "Is the caregiver support group effective in the reduction of caregiver burden for caregivers of handicapped individuals?" If you entered the keyword "caregiver support group" into the library of the Campbell Collaboration, you might not get any listing of a systematic review. In that situation, you would need to review the literature for evidence using established literature databases.

Roberts (2016) began her review of the evidence literature by determining the electronic databases she would review and the keywords she would employ. When her first search solicited a large number of sources, she narrowed the scope by using more keywords that generated a reasonable number of articles to review. She further narrowed the scope with a number of criteria for inclusion (e.g., the publication had to be within the past 8 years). From the review of this literature, she discovered support for exposure therapy for the treatment of PTSD. One example was the work of Cusack et al. (2016) who conducted a meta-analysis of 64 different studies of the outcomes of therapy for PTSD. Prolonged exposure therapy and CBT were found to be effective in this meta-analysis. Other evidence from the literature was also presented. The conclusion was that exposure therapy had a good deal of evidence that was supportive in its use as a treatment for PTSD.

Richardson (2016) used one of the psychological databases to find evidence on the effectiveness of CBT in the treatment of anxiety among adolescents. She used the keywords *anxiety, adolescent, treatment*, and *evaluative study* and received more than a thousand references. She started a review of these articles until a pattern emerged, which suggested that she need not do any further review. She discovered a lot of support for CBT in her situation and little evidence that it was not effective. Richardson concluded that CBT was supported by evidence. Given the fact that she had been trained in CBT, she felt no need for further review of the evidence.

In neither of the above illustrations did the student engage in a comprehensive review of the evidence in support of the question of what was the treatment with the most evidence. Instead, the question was whether a given treatment was supported by evidence. When this question was answered, the review of the evidence was terminated. If there had been no treatment modality that had been suggested, the review would have been different and the research question would have been different. In neither of these illustrations did the student start the process with a review of either the Campbell Collaboration or the Cochrane Collaboration, two sources of systematic reviews of evidence. If they had done so, they may have found evidence of other treatments for their target behavior.

Step 3: Decide on the Chosen Treatment Based on Evidence, Client Preferences, and Practitioner Expertise

If you, as a social worker, are lacking in competence in the delivery of a given evidence-based intervention, it will be necessary for you either to obtain the competence or to refer the client to a social worker who has the necessary skills. In many situations, however, you will find that more than one treatment has supportive evidence. Your competence will help determine the evidence-based treatment to employ.

Another consideration is the preferences of the client. The social worker can share the evidence with the client and see if there is a preference for one of the evidence-based interventions. A clinical social worker may have questions about a given treatment based on knowledge of the client with regard to themes such as level of education, ability to deal with abstract concepts, and so forth.

The choice for both Roberts (2016) and Richardson (2016) was obvious from the search of the literature. For Roberts, it was exposure therapy. For Richardson, it was CBT. Each had been supported by evidence and each had agency support.

Figure 4.1 depicts the relationship of practitioner expertise, client preferences, and evidence. As shown, the choice of an intervention is dependent on each of these factors. It is not just the evidence, the practitioner, or the client. The three factors must come together for the choice of the intervention to be an example of EBP.

Step 4: Implement the Treatment and Evaluate the Outcome

Your next step is to employ the intervention and measure client outcome. Implementation, of course, requires a good knowledge of the techniques for the treatment you are implementing. Experience with this intervention is also of critical importance.

A critical question is whether you implemented the treatment according to the recognized protocols for this approach. If client homework is a part of the treatment protocol, a question would be whether you employed client homework in your treatment. If the discussion of thought processes is a part of the treatment protocol, a question would be whether you employed this in your treatment process.

You will want to see if the treatment is effective. The measurement of client outcome is suggested. This book provides the guidance you need for evaluating outcome. This might include a group research study if you are implementing your treatment with a group of clients, or it might include a single client evaluation. Perhaps you will measure the treatment objective of reducing anxiety with an anxiety scale administered at both the beginning and the end of the treatment period. Maybe you will measure depression for a single client one time before treatment began and five times during the treatment period. Each of these examples requires that you measure the client outcome objectives.

Step 5: Draw Conclusions

Having implemented a given treatment for a given target behavior, you are in a position to draw conclusions about the effectiveness of this treatment for this type of client in the achievement of the intended outcomes. Perhaps you will conclude that it did work very well, and you will examine the things you believe were most instrumental to success. If you conclude that it did not work very well, you will analyze the reasons why. You may focus on certain characteristics of the clients that seem to have rendered this treatment less effective. Maybe some of your clients seemed to have done well but a majority did not. What can you conclude by examining the differences between these two groups?

CRITICAL APPRAISAL OF EVIDENCE-BASED PRACTICE

In the future, it is unlikely that social work agencies that ignore evidence will thrive. However, EBP is not without its controversies and misconceptions. One of the criticisms is that it promotes a cookie-cutter approach to practice that does not adequately provide the social worker with sufficient flexibility to employ creative techniques in practice. Perhaps there is a practice that is better for a given client but does not have the evidence of another approach, so the social worker is encouraged to use a treatment (the one with more evidence) that is not ideal for this particular client. However, if you examine the definition of EBP, you will see that there is flexibility with regard to the treatment approach to undertake. Most target behaviors addressed by social work practice have supporting evidence for more than one treatment. Therefore, the practitioner has flexibility to select the one that is most appropriate for the given client. The limitation would be that the evidence-based social worker would avoid treatments that have no credible evidence that supports it. If the treatment is so new that there are no good quality studies of it, the evidence-based practitioner would be encouraged to use this treatment only as an experiment and to evaluate client outcomes.

Social workers could get so obsessed with a particular treatment protocol that opportunities for creativity are ignored. It is the position of this book that social work is both an art and a science. The science is promoted by endeavors such as EBP. The art is promoted by experience and the individual creativity of the social worker. The social worker should make optimal use of both art and science.

The Dodo Bird Verdict

A controversy in the literature is the idea that bona fide treatments are equal in effectiveness, so your focus should be on making sure that the common factors are well attended and the bona fide treatment you employ is one for which you have skills and the client approves. A bona fide treatment, according to Wampold and Imel (2015), is one based on sound psychological principles. All bona fide treatments familiar to this author are the ones with supporting evidence, so the distinction between a bona fide treatment and an evidence-based one is not useful.

The common factors are things that influence client outcome that are common to all bona fide treatments. Included among these common factors are the therapeutic relationship, empathy, warmth, positive regard, and the cultivation of hope. Another common factor is goal congruence between the social worker and the client. The extent that the practitioner believes in the chosen treatment is an additional common factor. The more you believe in your intervention, the more effective you will be. According to the **dodo bird verdict**, the common factors determine client outcome, not the differences in the specific ingredients of various approaches to treatment (e.g., CBT vs. psychodynamic therapy).

According to the dodo bird verdict, it does not really matter if your bona fide treatment is CBT, psychodynamic therapy, or dialectical behavioral therapy. Each treatment is assumed to be equally effective for your client. A very impressive review of the evidence that supports the dodo bird verdict can be found in the work of Wampold and Imel (2015).

The controversy regarding the dodo bird verdict lies in the review of evidence. Some of it supports this verdict, and some of it does not. From this body of evidence, some writers have concluded that the dodo bird verdict is true, and some have questioned it. In Exhibit 4.3, you can review the case for the dodo bird verdict. In Exhibit 4.4, you will see evidence against it. In a nutshell, it seems that the evidence for the influence of the common factors is stronger than that for the argument that one bona fide treatment is better than another. However, there is sufficient evidence of the superiority of certain treatments for certain behaviors to refute the dodo bird verdict. The evidence that is contrary to the dodo bird verdict clearly justifies the continuance of research on what therapies are more effective than others in the treatment of certain behaviors. The ideal approach of the evidence-based social worker is to focus both on the common factors and on the evidence of what works best.

EXHIBIT 4.3
THE CASE FOR THE DODO BIRD VERDICT

The most salient case for the dodo bird verdict has been made by Wampold (2001) and by Wampold and Imel (2015). Here are a few of the claims by these works based on a comprehensive review of the evidence:

1. The common factors are clearly related to client outcome. For example, your clients will have a better chance for improvement if you (a) have a good therapeutic relationship, (b) have goal congruence, (c) demonstrate empathy, and (d) demonstrate positive regard.

2. In addition to the common factors, you should employ your work in a healing environment and you must be skilled in the techniques you employ. The techniques you employ provide necessary structure to the helping process. Therefore, the effective therapeutic process is not a helter-skelter experience of demonstrating the common factors; it is also structured in a way that has meaning both to the therapist and to the client.

3. When two bona fide treatments have been compared in scientific studies, the outcome usually is that the two treatments are found to be equally effective. Exceptions to this claim are so rare as to fail to demonstrate difference between treatments at a significant level.

4. Some studies have compared therapists who did a good job of adhering to the practice techniques required by the chosen model of therapy with those who did not. If the model of therapy makes a difference, you would expect to find a positive relationship between adherence to the model and client outcome. This has not been found to be true in scientific studies. The therapists who better adhered to the model did not have better outcomes.

5. Research has found that therapists who have stronger allegiance to the chosen treatment method have better client outcomes. This finding is true regardless of the chosen treatment selected. In other words, it is allegiance, not treatment techniques, that makes a difference. If you really believe in your treatment approach, you are more likely to have good client outcomes, regardless of the approach you take.

6. When a major component of a treatment model has been dropped, it has been found that client outcome is not reduced. If the treatment model is important, you would think that dropping a major component of it would make a difference. But it doesn't!

EXHIBIT 4.4
THE CASE AGAINST THE DODO BIRD VERDICT

A variety of authors have submitted research that refutes the dodo bird verdict. These studies have been discussed in the literature by those authors who support the verdict. And the debate goes on. Here are a few of the notes from the opposition:

1. There is evidence that some treatments work better than others for given behaviors. For example, Tolin (2010) found that CBT was superior to psychodynamic therapy in the treatment of depression. Many others have found a form of treatment for a given behavior to be superior to other treatments. Among these are the following: Svartbert, Tore, and Stiles (1991); Siev and Chambless (2007, 2009); Watson, O'Hara, and Stuart (2008).

2. Much of the published research in support of the dodo bird verdict has biases in the way in which the data are analyzed. For example,

Wampold has been accused of several flaws: (a) using a measure of effect size that favors the reduction of the size of the effect that supports the claim of no difference between treatments, (b) using a procedure for excluding studies from the analysis that fail to support the dodo bird verdict, (c) focusing on indirect measures of outcome when the indirect measures support the verdict but the direct measures do not. In other words, Wampold has been accused of failing on the tenets of critical thinking in the examination of this issue (see Howard, Krause, Sanders, & Kopta, 1997; York, 2015).

3. Sometimes the evidence on behalf of the superiority of one treatment over another is small, and the proponents of the dodo bird verdict tend to dismiss this small difference as failing to refute the verdict. But a small advantage of a given treatment suggests

(*Continued*)

(Continued)

that it is better. A small advantage should not be treated as no advantage at all—a tendency of some of the proponents of the dodo bird verdict.

4. One source of evidence of the superiority of a given treatment is the extent of the effect sizes of studies that support the superior treatment. While this is not ideal, there have been scholars who are witness to this difference. In this regard, CBT is often cited as having higher effect sizes.

There is enough evidence of the effectiveness of most bona fide treatments that you might be safe to assume that your choice of it, rather than another bona fide treatment, is correct. Remember that a bona fide treatment is one that works under sound psychological principles and has been used extensively for a good period of time. It is one that has been well accepted in clinical social work. New treatments with little evidence would not qualify as bona fide.

You should keep in mind, however, that you will not be a fully grown evidence-based social worker unless you become familiar with good evidence about any treatment that you employ. Furthermore, treatments with insufficient evidence to be classified as evidence based, will only be employed as an experiment where you will conduct an evaluative study of client outcome.

Most important, you must avoid using a treatment that has been found to cause harm. Such a treatment would not be classified as bona fide, as that term is used in this book. But a harmful treatment (or one with no evidence of effectiveness) might be portrayed as scientific. Don't be fooled by the techniques of pseudoscience (see Chapter 1).

It is the position of the author of this book that the social worker should not only be strong on the common factors but should also consider the evidence for specific treatments. Each will contribute to client outcome. It is not advisable to consider evidence that supports the common factors as evidence that diminishes the importance of specific treatments. Rubin and Babbie (2014) referred to this error in analysis as the false dichotomy (p. 45). It is not just one or the other that matters: It is both.

Chapter Practice Exercises

There are two practice exercises that will give you some experience with the review of information from sources of the systematic review of evidence. These exercises ask you to employ the Campbell Collaboration for this purpose. In Practice Exercise 1, you will be guided through an examination of a specific systematic review of evidence regarding parent training programs. You will be asked to examine this review and draw conclusions about what it says about the effectiveness of parent training in the improvement of parenting skills.

Competencies Demonstrated by These Practice Exercises

1. The ability to articulate a research question aided by a systematic review of evidence on human services that address a given target behavior

2. The ability to find evidence on a systematic review website with keywords that relate to a chosen research question

3. The ability to review basic information from a systematic review and draw appropriate conclusions from the review

Practice Exercise 1: Examining a Systematic Review on Maternal Psychosocial Health

In this exercise, you are pretending to be a social worker who is seeking evidence regarding parent training programs for the improvement of maternal psychosocial health. Your agency is considering such a program for women who are at risk for problems with parenting. You will gain access to a designated systematic review, examine that review, and draw conclusions about the research question.

Activities for Practice Exercise 1

1. Review the research questions for this analysis. They are as follows:

   a. Are parent training programs generally effective in the improvement of the psychosocial health of parents in the short term (e.g., at the end of the training program)?

   b. Are parent training programs generally effective in the improvement of psychosocial health of parents in the long term (e.g., 2 years after the training program)?

   c. Is there one approach or model of parent training that is superior to others in the improvement of psychosocial health of parents?

2. Review the information on the following systematic review:

   Barlow, J., Smailagic, N., Huband, N., & Bennett, C. (2012). Group-based parent train-ing programmes for improving parental

psychosocial health. Campbell Systematic Review.

   a. Access the Campbell Collaboration website campbellcollaboration.org. You may do so by inserting this Internet address or just insert the words "Campbell Collaboration" into your web browser, then find campbellcollaboration .org from there.

   b. On the first Internet page, you will see several options in boxes. Select "The Campbell Library."

   c. From the first page of "The Campbell Library," you will see a set of boxes into which you can insert words to help you find the review you are seeking. In the box "Keyword," enter the words "psychosocial health." You will see the number of entries in this category. You should scroll down until you see the above-named review by Barlow and others. Select this review.

   d. You will see several options, such as Review, Plain Language Summary, and Previous Version. Select "Review" from these options. You will then be on the title page of the entire review, which will contain an enormous amount of information about the review that is being reported. Go to "Abstract" on page 9 and review this information. It will provide a summary of the information that you will need for this exercise. (If you are curious about certain specific details, you can search the entire review for further information.)

3. Answer the following questions from your examination of the abstract of the systematic review by Barlow et al. (2012).

   a. What are some of the variables that are included in the concept of psychosocial health? (*Example:* Is anxiety included?)

b. What is one reason that psychosocial health is important? (*Example:* Is psychosocial health related to child health?)

c. Did this systematic review follow a specific protocol for the collection of evidence, or did the authors go about just finding articles where they could. What is one thing done by the authors that supports your answer to this question? (*Example:* Did the authors share with one another all the articles they could find with the method they individually selected, or did they follow a given protocol for finding studies through the Internet using electronic literature databases?)

d. How many different studies were included in this systematic review?

e. How many study participants were included in this systematic review?

f. Were the training services included in this review group-based services or individually based services? In other words, was this training given in the traditional group setting or offered to individuals one by one?

g. What psychosocial variables (e.g., alcoholism, social support) were included in this systematic review?

h. What variables were found to be improved in these studies right after the training was completed?

i. What variables were found to be improved in these studies in 6 months following treatment?

j. What variables were found to be improved in these studies 2 years after treatment?

k. Were any types of training found to be more successful than other types?

l. How can these results be best employed by agencies that include services designed to improve the psychosocial health of parents? (*Example:* Does this review of evidence support the use of group-based training for the improvement of psychosocial health of parents? Are there limitations on this type of training as depicted in this evidence?

What You Will Report From Practice Exercise 1

Your report for Practice Exercise 1 will be your answers to the questions (a–l) for Item 3 above. For example, your first theme will be your answer to question "a" under Item 3, which deals with the concept of psychosocial health. You will report your answers in complete sentences. For example, if your answer to question "d" is 31, you might say "The number of different studies included in this review was 31."

Practice Exercise 2: Finding a Systematic Review for Your Proposed Study

In this exercise, you will develop a research question related to evidence in social work practice. You will employ the steps for the use of the Campbell Collaboration given in Practice Exercise 1 for your search for an appropriate systematic review. You will examine that review as you did in Practice Exercise 1 and provide a report similar to the one you developed for that practice exercise. Your report should include information on the following:

1. Your research question. If you fail to find a systematic review for your research question, you will need to change your research question. The purpose of this exercise is to learn how to find a systematic review using the Campbell Collaboration.

2. A brief report on the process you employed for your initial search.

   a. What keywords did you employ?

   b. How many different reviews did you find from this initial search?

      i. If you found no reviews, did you change the keywords you employed or change your research question?

      ii. If you found more than one review from the initial search, how did you select a single review for analysis from all that were identified?

      iii. What is the reference information for the review you selected?

3. A brief report on what you found from your systematic review.

   a. What is the target behavior that was examined?

   b. What is the service (intervention, program) that was examined?

   c. How many studies and how many study subjects were included in the review?

   d. What were the chief findings of the review with regard to what services were effective with regard to what target behaviors?

CHAPTER REVIEW

Chapter Key Learnings

1. Evidence refers to the systematic collection and analysis of data using the principles and practices of scientific inquiry. Your intuition may be a good guide for your practice, but it is not evidence.

2. A bona fide practice is one that is based on sound psychological principles and has been widely accepted among professionals for an extended period of time. They tend to be evidence based. Recent fads in practice are outside the boundary of bona fide practice. These practices are not among those that appear in the normal debates about the evidence with regard to social work practices.

3. EBP is the judicious use of the best available scientific evidence, along with considerations of client preferences and practitioner skills, in decisions about treatment. It does not refer only to the consideration of evidence, but failure to consider evidence is clearly outside its bounds. The intervention with the most evidence of effectiveness may or may not be the best choice for a given social worker in a given client situation because there may be EBPs that are more compatible with the given client and the skills of the given social worker.

4. Among the factors common to all effective interventions are the therapeutic relationship of the social worker and the client (Is there trust and affection?), the demonstration of empathy by the social worker, goal congruence between the client and the social worker, and the extent that the social worker demonstrates positive regard for the client.

5. Research has shown that common factors have a positive relationship with client outcome.

6. An EBP is one that has a noteworthy amount of research showing it is effective with regard to a certain client outcome, and little research showing it is not effective. For example, CBT has a great deal of research showing that it is effective in the reduction of depression and anxiety for clients.

7. There is a great deal of research demonstrating that certain interventions are effective with regard to certain outcomes. There is some evidence that shows that one bona fide practice is more effective than another, but this research pales in comparison with the evidence regarding the positive effects of the common factors. Therefore, it is much easier to find an evidence-based practice for a given client behavior than to find the one practice that is clearly superior to all others.

8. Some research has shown that certain bona fide treatments are more effective regarding certain client outcomes than other bona fide treatments. But proponents of the concept of practice-based evidence claim that this evidence is so sparse as to be unworthy of our attention, and that we should focus on the common factors, the preferences of the client, and the skills of the practitioner. In this view, it is best for the client to have a situation that is good with regard to common factors than to be given the practice with the most evidence. The position articulated in this book is that the evidence-based social worker should consider both the common factors and the research on EBPs. It is not one or the other that is important: It is both.

9. The process of EBP starts with the determination of the goals of treatment between the social worker and the client. It moves to the search for evidence on the best practices with regard to the treatment goals. The social worker normally shares the evidence with the client, and the two come to conclusions about what type of treatment to undertake. Finally, the evidence-based social worker will collect data with regard to the outcomes of the treatment and will change the treatment approach if warranted.

10. There are several levels of evidence for the social worker to consider. At the highest level is the systematic review of evidence. Failing to find sufficient information from this fourth level of evidence, the practitioner will seek information from meta-analyses, the third level of evidence. If this is not sufficient, the social worker can consider the traditional review of evidence, which is presented as the second level of evidence. The lowest level of evidence is the single research study on client outcome. Evidence-based practitioners are cautioned not to rely solely on a single research study as the basis for declaring a given practice as evidence based. Literature that offers opinions or descriptions of given practices are not considered to be evidence.

11. There are a good number of sources of evidence. Among these are the Campbell Collaboration, the Cochrane Collaboration, the APA, the California Evidence-Based Clearinghouse for Child Welfare, and SAMHSA of the federal government. In the latter, you can find a registry of EBPs.

12. The *dodo bird verdict* is a phrase coined to portray the argument that the common factors are related to client outcome but the differences between treatments are not. In other words, the common factors are important, but it does not matter which bona fide treatment you employ as a social worker. It is the argument of the author of this book that they both are important.

Chapter Discussion Questions

1. In your opinion, what role should evidence play in social work practice decisions? Is it a necessary part of the decision process? Is it more or less important than other things?

2. What is the one thing you cannot do if you are an evidence-based practitioner?

3. What should you do if you find more than one treatment with evidence but you find more evidence for one of these treatments than another?

4. What would you say to someone who said "My 20 years of clinical social work experience is my evidence?"

5. What level of evidence should be the first one for you to encounter when you are seeking evidence regarding a given treatment for a given target behavior? Why?

6. What is an evidence-based research question you would like to pursue?

7. What is the final step in the process of using EBP?

8. What is the main lesson you have taken from the debate about the importance of common factors and differences in evidence between different treatments?

Chapter Test

1. Scientific evidence refers to
   a. Any information presented on behalf of an assertion
   b. Information that is statistically significant at the $p < .001$ level
   c. The systematic collection and analysis of data using the principles and practices of scientific inquiry
   d. All of the above are suitable definitions

2. Which of the following are characteristics of the process of EBP?
   a. The examination of scientific evidence
   b. Consideration for the preferences of the client
   c. Consideration of the skills of the practitioner
   d. All of the above

3. An evidence-based intervention is one that
   a. Has some credible evidence that supports its use with a given target behavior

   b. Has more evidence than any other intervention
   c. Has been found to be superior to at least one other intervention
   d. Has little evidence in its support

4. Which of the following statements is/are true?
   a. Cherry-picking of evidence in support of a conclusion is a good thing for the evidence-based practitioner
   b. The search for evidence should begin with a protocol of the steps to use in the search
   c. Both of the above
   d. None of the above

5. Which of the following is considered the highest level of evidence?
   a. The single research article that reports evidence about a given treatment and a given target behavior

b. The systematic review

c. The meta-analysis

d. The traditional literature review

6. Which of the following are sources of evidence on the Internet?

   a. The APA

   b. The federal government, through entities such as SAMHSA

   c. Both of the above

   d. None of the above.

7. Which of the following statements is/are true?

   a. Some of the sources of evidence on the Internet (e.g., SAMHSA, APA, California Evidence-Based Clearinghouse for Child Welfare) give ratings for individual treatments or programs based on the extent that evidence has been established, from a low point where there is little or no evidence to a high point where the evidence is strong

   b. When you find a systematic review on either the Cochrane Collaboration or the Campbell Collaboration, you will find it very difficult to discern what was found because they present complicated statements about research methodologies and statistics but do not have brief statements of conclusions or brief summaries of the review that would help those untrained in statistics

   c. Both of the above

   d. None of the above

8. Which of the following would be legitimate evidence-based research questions?

   a. What are the opinions of our most experienced clinical social workers on the effectiveness of psychodynamic therapy in the treatment of depression?

   b. Does the evidence show that psychodynamic therapy is an effective treatment for depression?

   c. Both of the above

   d. None of the above

9. Which of the following statements is/are true?

   a. The common factors in therapy (e.g., the therapeutic relationship) have been found to be far less important in determining client outcome than the difference between the specific ingredients of different bona fide treatments.

   b. Some meta-analyses support the theory that some bona fide therapies are better than others and some meta-analysis support the theory that there is no differences between bona fide therapies.

   c. Both of the above.

   d. None of the above.

10. Which of the following statements is/are true?

    a. The dodo bird verdict suggests that all bona fide treatments for a given target behavior are equivalent in outcome

    b. The dodo bird verdict provides strong support for EBP

    c. Both of the above

    d. None of the above

ANSWERS: 1 = c; 2 = d; 3 = a; 4 = b; 5 = b; 6 = c; 7 = a; 8 = b; 9 = b; 10 = a

Chapter Glossary

Bona fide treatment. A well-recognized treatment that is based on sound psychological principles.

Common factors. Those variables that affect treatment outcome and are common to all bona fide treatments, such as the quality of the therapeutic relationship between the practitioners and the client.

Dodo bird verdict. The assertion that all bona fide treatments are equal in achieving client outcome.

Effect size. The outcome of a given treatment measured with regard to standard deviations of gain for one study of evidence, or standard deviations of difference between gains of different studies.

Evidence. Data that have been systematically collected and analyzed according to the principles and practices of scientific inquiry.

Evidence-based intervention (or program). An intervention or program that has credible evidence in support of it for a particular target behavior.

Evidence-based practice. Practice that employs the judicious use of the best available evidence, along with considerations of client preferences and therapist expertise, in making practice decisions.

Meta-analysis. A review of the evidence on a selected theme using a specific protocol for searching the literature and combining the results of all selected results into a common metric, the effect size.

Single research study. An evaluative study of a specific sample of people (e.g., women with postpartum depression), who have been given a certain treatment (e.g., cognitive–behavioral therapy) and have been given a certain method of measurement (e.g., the Beck Depression Scale) that has measured success.

Systematic review. A comprehensive review of evidence designed to sum up the best available research on a research question, through a rigorous protocol for the collection and analysis of results.

Traditional review of the research literature. A review of selected articles of evidence that have been secured by the authors of the work, where the protocol for the selection of articles for review is not enumerated.

CONDUCTING DIFFERENT TYPES OF SOCIAL WORK RESEARCH

PART TWO

This section of the book will give you fundamental competence in conducting various types of social work research. You will be able to employ social survey methods with regard to research that describes people, research that explains things, research that evaluates services, and research that explores unknown conceptual territory. You will also have an understanding of how program evaluations are different from the evaluation of a single social work intervention. In other words, you will be able to conduct various types of research from the first phase of the research process (developing the research question) to the last one (drawing conclusions).

This means you will have basic skills in conducting research, skills that will be enhanced when you examine each phase of the research process one by one in the final section of this book. You will, of course, encounter the various tasks of research (e.g., measuring study variables) when you engage in each type of research. This will give you an opportunity to achieve a basic understanding of these tasks before you examine them in depth in the last section of this book. One of the lessons I have learned in teaching research for several decades is that students are better served if they can have repeated opportunities to see the forest before they encounter a close examination of the trees. For example, it is best for students to first understand the concepts of reliability and validity in a general way before they are called on to engage in the specific examination of the internal consistency of the items on a scale.

On completion of this section of the book, you will be able to conduct research studies of four kinds—descriptive, explanatory, evaluative, and exploratory. You will not have the skills to demonstrate a mastery of the skills necessary for each type of research, but you will be able to conduct research at a basic level. In other words, you will be able to conduct a research study for a beginning research course but not one of an intermediate or advanced nature.

5

CONDUCTING RESEARCH THAT EMPLOYS SOCIAL SURVEYS

Joan was given the job of determining the level of satisfaction of the clients of the Women's Center, where she is a social worker, and finding recommendations on how the services of this agency could be improved. The agency's administrative team wants to know if the agency has a level of client satisfaction that is at least equal to that of other human service agencies. They also want to get recommendations about how their services can be improved.

Joan realized that personal interviews with a sample of clients would do the job, but this is not a very efficient way of finding the information she needs. It would take many hours of staff time to conduct these interviews, and they could not afford to include many clients in this study. She needed a general report on the clients of this agency, so a mailed survey of clients was undertaken. She reviewed the records and found that there were 78 persons whose cases had been closed in the past 3 months, and she decided to conduct a mailed survey of all these individuals. If this number had been in the thousands, she would have selected a random sample of them because of the cost of the survey—considering both the mail costs and staff time in the collection and analysis of data.

A major task, of course, is to compose the questions for the questionnaire. Joan designed a questionnaire that sought information on how well the clients felt they had been treated, whether they would return to the agency if services were needed again, whether they would recommend the agency to others in need, and whether the service had helped meet their needs. In addition, she asked for recommendations on how to improve the services of the agency. She wanted to keep her questionnaire simple to improve the response rate. She composed the items on the questionnaire keeping in mind that the items should be clear, concise, and relevant to the information she needed to generate. The question about recommendations was open-ended because she did not have a template of recommendations that she could use for a quantitative response.

Joan considered the question of what to expect from the survey. She had designed the questionnaire so that the items had the options (a) agree, (b) undecided, and (c) disagree. She had stated each item in the positive direction so that a response of "agree" to an item would be considered positive, while responses of "undecided" or "disagree" would not.

She wondered what level of positive response would be good news. If half the clients gave a positive response, would she view this as good news or bad news? What about 75% or 85%? She reviewed the literature on client satisfaction surveys and found that they tended to be uniformly positive, meaning that clients tended to be positive regardless of the type of agency or type of service. A positive response rate of 75% was considered typical. Consequently, Joan decided that a positive rate higher than 75% would be the expectation. She believed that her agency was better than most.

INTRODUCTION

You have been asked on many occasions to answer questions on a social survey. Perhaps it was a questionnaire that was mailed to you or a questionnaire sent to you over the Internet. The survey had a major purpose for the sender, and you were but one of many people who were asked to participate. Perhaps you responded to some of these surveys and ignored the others.

Maybe you have wondered about how to conduct a survey yourself. What things should you consider as you go through this process? What study purposes and research questions are well addressed by the social survey as the mechanism of collecting data? What are tips for constructing the questionnaire or getting a good rate of participation from the study sample? These are among the questions examined in this chapter.

On completion of this chapter, you will be able to undertake a social survey. In that pursuit, you will be able to do the following:

1. Describe the nature of the social survey

   a. Define the concept of the social survey

b. Explain why you would employ a social survey

c. Identify the conditions that suggest that a social survey is appropriate

2. Identify several types of social surveys and the circumstances that make each one appropriate in a given situation

3. Conduct each step in the survey research process

4. Define the study variables for your own study and compose the questionnaire to measure each one

5. Describe several tips for getting a good participation rate from your study sample

6. Discuss the advantages and disadvantages of using a survey to conduct your research study

THE NATURE OF THE SOCIAL SURVEY

A **social survey** is a purposeful inquiry into a social subject for a designated sample of people by a researcher using a recording instrument, typically a questionnaire. If you make free-form notes from your observations about what you see in a given social context, you are not engaged in survey research, partly because you do not have a tool like a questionnaire for recording the observations. When you make clinical notes, you are not engaged in survey research. If you collect school grades from the school of your clients, you are not employing survey research. Instead, you are employing public documents to gain the data you need.

However, if you decide to employ the Beck Depression Inventory in order to measure the depression level of a set of clients, you are engaged in survey research. Your purpose is to measure depression because it is one of your treatment objectives. You have a tool, the Beck Depression Inventory, which you will use to measure the depression level of your clients who constitute your study sample. If you administer a client satisfaction questionnaire to the clients served by your program, you are employing a social survey. If you mail out a questionnaire about attitudes toward work to the employees of your agency, you are also employing a social survey. In each case, you have a questionnaire to be completed by all the people in your study sample.

Why should you employ a social survey? For one thing, it is an efficient way to measure study variables. Asking a client to spend 5 minutes responding to a depression scale is lot less time-consuming than conducting an interview, or observing a behavior on a busy street. A second advantage is transparency. When you employ a standard scale for measuring client behavior, those who read your report will understand how you measured the variables of interest in your study. When you employ your own questionnaire about attitudes, you can display your questionnaire in your report and the reader has the opportunity to scrutinize it for validity.

A third advantage of the survey is generalizability. You can easily administer a questionnaire to a large sample of people, supporting the generalization of study results to a large population. Furthermore, you can use variables that characterize the study sample in ways in which the data can be analyzed for differences among types of people.

When is the social survey a good tool for measurement? The survey is an instrument for a description of a social phenomenon. That phenomenon may be a psychological condition like anxiety, a set of opinions about political issues, or the level of satisfaction for a group of people with regard to a given service. Therefore, the survey is highly useful for the descriptive research study.

When you evaluate services, you must describe the client's conditions in such a way as to measure growth about the service objectives. This means that the evaluative study employs descriptive tools.

The explanatory study also must describe variables. It will examine the relationships among variables as the chief target of analysis. It starts with description.

TYPES OF SOCIAL SURVEYS

The type of social survey you are most likely to employ as a social worker is the **face-to-face self-administered questionnaire**. This is a questionnaire completed by the study respondent when face-to-face with the researcher. When you employ a social survey in evaluative research, you will typically ask the client to respond to a tool that measures the target behavior under treatment. The client responds to the questionnaire, typically, before treatment and again at the end of treatment. You will compute the amount of gain by comparing the pretest and posttest scores.

The **mailed survey** is a form of the self-administered survey because it is completed by the study subject but is not administered face-to-face. In this situation, you develop a questionnaire, select a sample of people for mailing, secure the addresses of these people, mail out the questionnaire, and analyze the results for those who reply.

The **phone interview survey** is a third type of social survey. In this alternative, you select a study sample, such as a **random sample** of all the clients of your agency whose cases have been closed in the past year. Then you secure the phone numbers of these people. Next, you compose a set of questions for inquiry. Finally, you phone these people and record their answers to your questions. These questions may be closed-ended or open-ended. If they are open-ended, the researcher must be careful to record the answers in a way that captures what the respondent is saying. This is not the time for you to interpret the meaning of the answer; it is time for you to record the response as closely as possible to what is being said.

The **online survey** is a fourth option. Typically, you send your questionnaire to your study sample members by email. A good vehicle for this survey is a survey website such as **SurveyMonkey**, where you compose the questionnaire through this mechanism and email the survey link to your sample members. The respondents go to this website and provide their answers, which are conveniently compiled by the website for use by the researcher.

The **face-to-face interview survey** is a fifth vehicle for conducting the social survey. If you have a questionnaire with specific questions to be given to all study subjects and you use the interview to get the answers, you will be using the interview for conducting a survey. The more concrete the questions, the more your study will resemble the use of the survey method for conducting a study using the interview.

The researcher needs to be attentive to ethics in the use of human subjects in research, as discussed in a previous chapter. Participation in your survey should cause no harm, nor should the respondent's privacy be invaded. The ethics of voluntary participation is not as much of a concern with the mailed or online survey because it is easy for the prospective study subject to avoid responding. When you give the instrument to a set of clients, ethical issues are more important. You need to consider ethical issues such as potential harm, privacy, and voluntary participation.

The Face-to-Face Self-Administered Survey

When you employ the face-to-face self-administered survey, you ask the respondents to answer your questions while you are present. Perhaps you will administer an anxiety scale for a set of clients and collect their responses.

A major advantage of the face-to-face self-administered survey is that the participation rate is much higher when the measurement tool is given in person by the researcher to a captive audience, such as the clients in your caseload or the students in your class. It is also more efficient than the interview, because it should take much less time to complete. However, it is more likely than the interview to have incomplete data. It is much easier for a respondent to avoid answering a given question if it is self-administered than if it is being asked in an interview.

The Mailed Survey

The mailed survey uses a questionnaire much like the self-administered option. The difference is that it gets to the respondent by mail rather than being administered in person or over the phone. A key issue with the mailed survey is the response rate. It is quite easy for the potential respondent to fail to respond. If fact, you should not be surprised to have fewer than 20% of your sample members to return the questionnaire on the first mailing. Mailed reminders is a normal part of the mailed survey process. A 50% response rate is considered very good in this case.

When you employ the mailed survey, you should employ an introductory letter along with an addressed, stamped envelope for the return of the questionnaire. A key objective is to reduce the amount of trouble the respondent must endure in order to be a participant. A key issue here is how long it will take to complete it. It is helpful to create a survey instrument that will take only about 10 minutes to complete and that you mention this in the cover letter, which also should be brief. The more the respondent is invested in the theme of the study, the more likely he or she will respond to a questionnaire that takes longer. For example, a survey of former clients will tend to have a higher response rate than a general survey from a polling organization. Former clients have a major connection with the agency and are likely to have a personal investment in contributing to it.

The cover letter should explain the purpose and importance of the study in a way that will motivate participation. You should describe your sponsoring organization in a way that establishes credibility. The respondent will be more motivated to the extent that the study seems to be adding something of importance to our knowledge. Assuring the anonymity of the responses is another item to mention.

The first step is to mail out your questionnaire to your potential study sample. If the response rate is satisfactory (e.g., 50%), you have completed this step in the process and you are now ready to analyze the data. If your response rate is not satisfactory, you should send out a reminder letter about 2 weeks after mailing the questionnaire. Failing to obtain a satisfactory response rate from this step, you should mail another reminder along with another copy of the questionnaire about 2 weeks after sending out the first reminder letter. You will probably find that these procedures will improve the response rate significantly.

The Phone Interview

When you employ the phone interview, you select your sample by way of phone numbers. If you are surveying clients, you can get the numbers from the records. If you are surveying the general population, you can select the numbers from the phone book, preferably at random. You will need a method for substituting additional numbers when you find a given number is not in service. This may include going to the next number in the book.

An advantage of the phone interview is that of better participation. A sample member is more likely to throw the mailed survey into the trash than to say no to a person on the phone. A good participation rate will accompany a telephone interviewer with the skills to get the needed participation.

A key challenge is to get cell phone numbers because an increasing number of people have cell phones only. They have abandoned the landline. If this is not possible, this situation should be reported so that the reader of your study will know about this limitation.

The Face-to-Face Interview

With this option, the interviewer selects people from a list and gains access to them in person. This will typically entail a phone call to introduce the respondent to the study and the scheduling of the interview.

The interview can be of several forms with regard to structure. It can be highly structured, whereby the interviewer is highly restricted in what can be said or asked of the interviewee. The questions will be rather specific, and the interviewer simply asks the questions and records the response, sometimes on a questionnaire that might look a lot like the questionnaire for the self-administered survey. For the highly structured interview, it is critical that the questions be posed in the same manner to all study subjects. The interviewer should not spend time discussing the nature of the study, other than the general purpose, which will be given to all participants. Discussing the nature of the study in detail might give the interviewee some ideas about what would be the socially desirable responses. The interviewer should stick to the questions posed on the questionnaire and provide them in the correct sequence. The interviewer should not suggest answers when asked by the interviewee. If the interviewee asks, "Don't you think this is a good response," the interviewer might reply, "The important thing is whether this is your response." Moreover, the interviewer should not disagree with the interviewee in words or expressions.

The interview can be semistructured, where there will be a set of open-ended questions, which are asked of the interviewer. A sample of such questions would be the following:

1. What does stress mean to you?

2. How do you experience stress?

3. What are the three things you are most likely to do when you are under stress?

4. What have you found to be the best way to reduce your stress?

The **semistructured interview** generates information that is qualitative in nature because the data are words rather than numbers or placement into discrete predetermined categories (e.g., *strongly agree*, *agree*, *undecided*, *disagree*, and *strongly disagree*). It is useful for the interviewer to engage the interviewee in the validation of the notes taken. For example, the interviewee might say, "So you are saying that stress means being agitated about something—is that correct?"

The highly unstructured interview would be one where a very general question is posed and the interviewee responds to that general question. This is not the kind of study that we normally classify as a survey, because there is insufficient structure to the interaction between the interviewee and the interviewer. In Exhibit 5.1, you can find a set of 10 tips for improving the research interview when you are engaged in an exploratory study with semistructured questions.

EXHIBIT 5.1
TIPS FOR IMPROVING THE RESEARCH INTERVIEW

The information in this exhibit is paraphrased from "Tipsheet: Qualitative Interviews" (Clifford, n.d.). These tips are for the survey in exploratory research that will employ open-ended questions.

1. Use less structured interviews early in the process of understanding the social phenomenon under study. Use more structured interviews as you gain theoretical knowledge that allows you to identify details that need more understanding.

2. Questions should be designed to elicit an individual's experiences and understanding. The question "Can you tell me about the last time you voted in a general election, from the time you got to the polling site until you left?" will generate more focus than the question "What do you find it to be like when you go to vote?"

3. Avoid questions that are too specific, especially those that could result in a response of "yes' or "no."

4. Avoid biasing responses. Do not share your hypothesis or use emotional language in your questions that suggest what a socially desirable response would be like.

5. Follow-up questions should be used to encourage expansion of idea deemed most relevant to the research question (e.g., "What do you mean by . . ." or "Can you tell me more about . . .").

6. If the question causes discomfort or confusion, rephrase it.

7. Summarize key ideas and themes you have recorded from the interview to the person being interviewed and ask if you have a proper understanding of what was said.

8. Create a comfortable environment for the interview that is free from distractions.

9. Generate trust early in the interview with information about the nature of the study and themes such as confidentiality, information on shared experiences between the interviewer and the interviewee, or mutual acquaintances.

10. The order of questions should start with the least threatening or emotional questions and end with a question that allows the interviewee to add any additional information.

The Online Survey

A major advantage of the online survey is efficiency. It is very inexpensive to send a questionnaire to a list of people through their email addresses. In fact, the email mechanism does not cost at all. In addition, you can use a survey software such as Survey Monkey to compile the data for you. This software has a simple option that does not cost at all, and the more elaborate options are not very expensive.

With Survey Monkey, you access the software, select the type of survey to be employed (one option is the agree–disagree format), compose the questions for the survey, make a copy of the web link to this particular survey, and send that link to the study sample. Of course, you have a carefully prepared introduction to the survey using the lessons you know about the mailed survey. The task of constructing a questionnaire is addressed later in this chapter.

There are many suggestions for the online survey that are similar to the mailed survey (see Exhibit 5.2). For example, the survey should take a short amount of time (15 minutes or less), should be easy to read on the screen, and should be introduced in a way that motivates participation. With regard to the latter, think of the kinds of people in your sample with regard to motivators for this group.

Like the mailed survey, you should send out reminders after the initial message. You can include the link to the survey in your reminder message. Some survey software will

---

EXHIBIT 5.2
TIPS FOR IMPROVING THE ONLINE SURVEY

1. Clearly define the purpose of your online survey.

   What difference will the results make with regard to things that are important? Clarity should help with motivation to participate.

2. Keep the survey short and focused.

   Shorter surveys have higher response rates and lower rates of failure to complete them.

3. Keep the questions simple.

   Questions should get to the point and avoid jargon and acronyms.

4. Use closed-ended questions whenever possible.

   Give respondents specific categories for responses, rather than open-ended questions.

5. Keep rating scale questions consistent throughout the survey.

   If you use a 5-point rating scale for certain questions, make sure to use the same 5-point scale for other questions that are similar. Moving from 5 points on some questions to 7 points on others may be confusing.

6. Order the questions in a way that is logical.

   Make sure your survey flows in a logical order. Begin with items that are not controversial and will motivate participation. Use broader based questions at the beginning before more specific ones. Ask for demographic information at the end.

7. Pretest your survey.

   Get a group of people to complete the survey who are not in your study and ask them for their impressions. Compute the results to see if there is anything unusual about the responses that will influence the design of the survey.

8. Consider your audience when sending survey invitations.

Surveys of people at work should be sent during the week rather than during the weekend. However, in general, there is no difference in quality between weekend mailings and weekday ones.

9. Consider sending several reminders.

This should improve response rates.

10. Consider offering an incentive.

Survey Monkey has found that incentives boost response rates by 50% on average.

Source: Ten Tips to Improve Your Online Survey, Survey Monkey Blog (Johnson, 2012).

allow you to use a password for access to this survey. This will be necessary if you have any reason to believe that people would respond to the survey more than once, in order to "stuff the ballot box." This is rather unlikely.

WHEN TO USE EACH TYPE OF SURVEY

There are advantages and disadvantages of each type of survey. The face-to-face self-administered survey is efficient and has a high response rate, but it is vulnerable to incompleteness. It is often a convenient tool because you have a captive audience, like the clients in your caseload or the students in your class. The mailed survey is efficient but typically has a low participation rate. The phone interview is not efficient but has a high participation rate and provides for some opportunity to secure a rich content if it employs open-ended questions. The face-to-face interview is the least efficient of the survey types but has the highest potential for generating rich content. Both interview options have an advantage of securing data that are more complete because respondents are less likely to leave a question unanswered. The online survey is the most efficient of all types, but it has some of the disadvantages of the mailed survey concerning participation.

The major issue, therefore, is the relative importance of these advantages and disadvantages for your particular study. As you have seen in other chapters, the qualitative study tends to be highly appropriate for exploratory studies. The use of open-ended questions can generate a richer kind of content for analysis. This type of study would likely employ a phone interview or a face-to-face interview. If each of these options is too expensive, the use of open-ended questions in the survey would make sense. The mailed or online survey would be appropriate for the descriptive study because you can obtain a high number of participants and employ descriptive questions that are not subject to interpretation. The evaluative study will most often employ the face-to-face self-administered survey for reasons mentioned above. In this case, you normally need to measure growth, so the administration of the questionnaire more than once is usually needed. The explanatory study can employ any of these survey options with the issues of efficiency and participation playing a key role in the determination of the appropriate one for use in your study.

Here is a summary:

- If you are conducting evaluative research, the face-to-face self-administered survey is likely to be your choice.

- If you are conducting a qualitative study, one of the two forms of the interview is usually going to be your best option.

- If you are conducting a descriptive study for a large population, you will likely need to employ the mailed or online survey.

- If you are conducting an explanatory study, your choice will depend on your need for efficiency or the sample that is appropriate and convenient.

CONDUCTING YOUR OWN SOCIAL SURVEY

When you conduct a study using survey methods, you will engage in a process that begins with the determination of the purpose of the study, as noted in previous chapters. You do *not* start the process by thinking of the questions you want to put on your questionnaire. Don't put the cart before the horse! Your purpose should guide the next step, which will guide the one that follows that step. These steps are enumerated below.

Step 1: Clarifying the Purpose of Your Study and the Variables That Are to Be Measured

The first step in this process is to clarify the purpose of your study. If your purpose is to describe the characteristics of your fellow social work students regarding family circumstances, you will identify the variables to be included in your questionnaire. These variables might be marital status, whether one or both parents are alive, whether the student is a parent, the number of siblings of the student, and so forth. Each of these characteristics should be identified, and they must agree with the purpose of the study. For example, the variable of political party affiliation does not fit into the category of family characteristics, so this would not be identified as a variable in your study. However, there may be some general characteristics that fit, such as age, race, and ethnicity. You may want to know if the characteristics of students are related to one of these general variables.

You should avoid the temptation of starting this process by thinking of the questions to put on the questionnaire, without clarifying your purpose and variables with precision. Why? You are likely to put some questions on your questionnaire that are not needed and that will make the questionnaire too long. Perhaps you will fail to identify some critical variables if you fail to clarify the study purpose at the beginning.

If your purpose is to examine the relationship between client characteristics and the tendency to fail to show up for an appointment, you will be conducting an explanatory study because you have a reason to believe that client characteristics explain (cause) the no-show phenomenon. You will have the no-show variable to measure as well as a variety of client characteristics. Do you believe that this phenomenon (no-show) is related to family income, employment status, type of service received, or diagnosis? If so, you will have four causal variables to measure along with the no-show variable. Now you have five variables to measure.

Step 2: Securing a Study Sample From Your Designated Study Population

If you wish to know the political opinions of social work students, you will need to define the study population. Are you interested in social work students throughout the United States, or just those at your university? If the latter, you will need to secure the names of all such students and select a sample from that list. If it is a small list, you can send your questionnaire to all of them. The study sample consists of those from whom you collected data. The study population consists of the larger group of people from which the study sample was selected.

A later chapter addresses the various dimensions of sampling. A key issue is whether you drew the sample on a random basis from the designated study population. If so, your study results can be generalized on a scientific basis because sampling error can be computed. If you did not select the people in your sample randomly, you can generalize on a logical basis. With logical generalization, you will use information you know about both the population and the sample to determine if they are similar on relevant variables. If you are familiar with the population and have no reason to believe the population is different from the sample regarding your variables measure, you can present this opinion along with information on how you came to this conclusion.

Step 3: Measuring Each Study Variable

You will develop the items you will use to measure each variable in your study. You will put each of these items on the questionnaire that your study subjects will complete. You may employ standardized scales (e.g., the Beck Depression Inventory) or develop your own items.

You can find hundreds of standardized scales and questionnaires from the literature and online sources that may be of assistance whether you are employing a standardized one or developing the items for the questionnaire yourself. An advantage of the standardized scale is that it has been constructed by an expert on the theme of the scale and has likely been tested for reliability and validity. When this alternative does not adequately measure your variable, you can compose your own tool for measurement.

Step 4: Distributing the Questionnaire and Analyzing Data

A critical issue for the distribution of the questionnaire is the response rate, the proportion of people who reply to the questionnaire. In Exhibit 5.3, you can see a set of tips for increasing the response rate of your mailed survey.

Step 5: Drawing Conclusions and Reporting Your Results

Your conclusions for your study must be consistent with your findings and be free of opinions that appear as though they might be the results of your study. It should start with a statement of the research question and your basic findings. If you studied the relationship between social support and drug abuse and found that social support is significantly higher for those who recovered from drug abuse, you should report this finding at the onset of your conclusions section. If your data failed to achieve statistical significance, you should not conclude that you found a relationship between your variables.

EXHIBIT 5.3

TIPS FOR IMPROVING QUESTIONNAIRE RESPONSE RATES

Personalize all mailings by doing the following:

- Using agency letterhead on high-quality paper (for the cover letter)

- Signing cover letters individually in blue ink

- Handwriting addresses on mailing and return envelopes

- Personalizing the mailing address on the envelope and the salutation in a cover letter rather than using a generic approach (i.e., Dear Colleague, . . .)

- Avoiding traditionally busy periods such as holidays, districtwide testing days, and summer breaks

- Contact potential participants four times by doing the following:

- Sending personalizing prenotification or postcard 1 week prior to mailing the questionnaire asking people to participate. You should indicate when they will receive the questionnaire and explain its purpose

- Sending the questionnaire along with a cover letter and a hand-addressed postage-paid return envelope by first-class mail. Like the prenotification letter, the cover letter should explain the importance of the questionnaire, state that the responses are confidential (if they are), explain how the results will be used, and who should answer the questions

- Sending a reminder postcard by first-class mail 1 week after mailing the questionnaire to thank the participants for their responses

or to encourage them to respond if they have not done so

- Sending a replacement questionnaire to participants who have not responded (with a dated follow-up letter and a hand-addressed postage-paid return envelope) about 3 weeks after the initial questionnaire mailing

Create a participation-friendly questionnaire by doing the following:

- Limiting the number of questions to what you really need to know and by asking about topics that are relevant to the participants

- Providing clear and easy-to-follow instructions that make the questionnaire simple and complete

- Using clear and simple language at or below the reading level of your participants. Avoid using abbreviations and technical jargon

- Ending the questionnaire with a "thank you" and restating the due date and how to return the questionnaire

- Folding the questionnaire forms into a booklet, rather than stapling the pages together

- Using lightly shaded background colors, preferably light blue or green with white answer spaces to help participants quickly and clearly determine where to write their answers

- Providing adequate space for participants to answer each question completely

Source: Increasing Questionnaire Response Rates (U.S. Department of Health and Human Services, Centers for Disease Control and Prevention, 2010).

Don't say that social support is related to age in the conclusions section of your study unless this was one of your findings. It does not matter that social support and age have been found to be related in published studies. You could mention this in your knowledge base part of your report but not in the conclusions. If you mention this fact in your conclusions, you should do so only as a mechanism for reporting that you did not find the same thing as other studies.

The overall report of your study should follow the format for the reporting of research findings from various types of studies. This means you state the purpose of your study, the knowledge base that is relevant, the study methods used (the sample, the means of measurement, etc.), the collection and analysis of data, and the conclusions. When you report the findings of a mailed or online survey, you should be attentive to the issue of response rate. What did you do to encourage participation and what participation rate did you achieve? If you are aware of any variables that are likely to be related to the response rate, this should also be reported.

COMPOSING YOUR OWN QUESTIONNAIRE

In some situations, you will need to compose your own questionnaire. When you come to this point in your study process, you will have decided on the purpose of your study and the variables to be measured. Your next step will be to decide on the form of the items to be used to measure each variable. You may have different forms for different variables because of the nature of the variable. An opinion is different from a piece of knowledge.

Deciding on the Form of the Items on the Questionnaire

Once you have identified your variables, you need to examine each one to determine the form that items on the questionnaire should take. If you are asking for opinions, you are likely to compose items with the response format of (1) *strongly disagree*, (2) *disagree*, (3) *undecided*, (4) *agree*, and (5) *strongly agree*. Do not use this agree–disagree format if your intent is to measure knowledge. The latter would be better measured by items that look like they belong on a test, such as multiple choice questions or true/false items. Opinions and knowledge are distinctly different things.

Some variables are measured in a very simple way, such as response categories of *yes* or *no*. You could employ a survey questionnaire that asked if the respondent had experienced minor illnesses during the past 6 months, with categories of *yes* and *no*. They were also asked if they regularly engaged in aerobic exercise with the same options for response. These variables could have been measured in more complicated ways, but the exercise that employed them needed only to have some simple measurements, so the *yes* and *no* options seemed appropriate.

Scales that measure psychological functioning typically have a number of items, each of which has similar categories of response, and scores are computed by assigning values to each option. An example is the Hare Self-Esteem Scale (Hare, 1985), which is designed to measure self-esteem in school-age children. One of the items on this scale is as follows: "I have at least as many friends as other people my age." The response categories are (1) *strongly disagree*, (2) *disagree*, (3) *agree*, and (4) *strongly agree*. Some items on this scale are positive like the above example, and some are negative like this one: "I am not as popular as other people my age." If the item is positive, the *strongly agree* option is given 4 points in the computation of the overall score for self-esteem, the *agree* option is given 3 points, the *disagree* alternative is given 2 points, and the *strongly disagree* option is given 1 point. If the item is negative, the scores are reversed (e.g., *strongly agree* now gets 1 point instead of 4). This is an example of a scale to measure psychological functioning with several items that are used to compute a score.

Perhaps you will want to conduct a survey of client satisfaction. You might employ a standard form for this task such as the Client Satisfaction Questionnaire (CSQ-8) by Larsen, Atkisson, Hargreaves, and Nguyen (1979). This scale has eight items where the respondent gives one of four ratings for each: *poor, fair, good,* and *excellent.* One item of this scale is as follows: "How would you rate the quality of service you have received?" Another item asks, "If a friend were in need of similar help, would you recommend our program to him or her?" You may find a scale like this will do the job for you. If not, you should review such examples to give yourself ideas of how to compose your own items for your questionnaire.

Constructing the Questions

Your first task in the composing of the items for your questionnaire is to clarify the variable to be measured. Are you measuring attitudes, political opinions, psychological conditions, knowledge, or what? You have seen from the previous section that the meaning of the variable will determine the best form that items on a questionnaire should take.

One of the exhibits in the chapter on measurement in this text provides tips for composing the items on a questionnaire. You should review this chapter before composing your questionnaire. Among the tips are ones that suggest simplicity and clarity. The questions should be free of professional jargon and acronyms. You can test this out by giving your instrument to a group of people before your conduct your study and asking them a set of questions about how they interpreted the questions. Keep in mind the education level of the respondents and be sure to use terms that the lowest group can understand.

ADVANTAGES AND DISADVANTAGES OF THE SURVEY

The social survey is very good in producing data in large quantities. Some forms of the survey are very efficient in producing data because their costs are low. The survey can improve the credibility of your agency policies because we value data of this sort. When the survey produces data from random samples of people, it facilitates the generalization of results from the sample to the study population. The survey is especially useful for the descriptive study where you wish to describe a large number of people with some precision.

Credibility of surveys are enhanced by the standardized manner of responses by those who participate. Everyone responds to the same question asked in the same format, so we are not left with unanswered questions in our minds about what the respondents are trying to say.

The mailed or online survey can reach people in locations that are remote from the researcher. They also facilitate an impression of objectivity on the part of those who read the results because of the uniformity of questions and recording mechanisms. People often review survey results with a feeling that the results are credible.

The disadvantages of the survey are related to this theme of uniformity, which reduces the flexibility of responses. Flexibility, which is more apparent in interviews with open-ended questions, promotes a rich content that goes beyond what the researcher could think of asking. A major disadvantage of the survey is the low response rate that comes with this mechanism for many people who attempt it. The question that arises is, "What is the difference between those 30% who responded to the survey and the 70% who did not?"

Chapter Practice Exercises

In this practice exercise, you will be asked to complete some of the tasks in conducting a client satisfaction survey. First, you will select a human service agency where a client satisfaction survey would be helpful. Then you will engage in several activities such as the articulation of the general purpose of the survey, developing some of the items that will be on the questionnaire, and identifying the type of survey that would be the best in this situation.

Competencies Demonstrated by This Practice Exercise

1. The ability to identify the research question that might be posed in a client satisfaction survey

2. The ability to identify the variables that must be measured in a survey given the research questions that have been posed

3. The ability to construct items for a questionnaire that will appropriately measure an identified variable

4. The ability to justify the selection of a specific vehicle for the distribution of survey questionnaires

Activities for This Practice Exercise

1. List all the specific questions that might be pursued in this survey.

   The basic purpose of your survey is to determine the level of satisfaction expressed by the clients of this agency. This can be articulated by the general research question, "To what extent are the clients of this agency satisfied with the services they received?" This is the general question, but there will be questions of a more specific level.

   One of the questions on a more specific level might be, "To what extent are clients generally satisfied with the services they received?" Another question might be, "Do the clients perceive that their needs were met?" A third question could be "To what extent do the clients perceive that they would recommend this agency to others in need?"

   The agency might be interested in comparing different groups of clients to see if the satisfaction levels are different. The variables identified in this analysis might be gender, age, income level, race, or type of service received. In other words, the staff of this agency might want to know the extent to which there are differences in satisfaction between clients of different services, different ages, different races, or different income levels. If so, you can articulate these special interests as separate research questions such as "Are the clients with lower income levels as satisfied as clients with higher income levels?

2. Identify the variables that will be measured in this survey?

   Example: You might measure the variables of (a) the extent of general satisfaction with the services that clients received or (b) the extent of satisfaction with the degree to which clients would recommend this agency to others in need.

   In another category, you might identify the variables of age, income level, race, and gender. This would add four more variables to your list.

3. Select three of the variables from the above list and construct a questionnaire item that would be used to measure it. Review the information in Exhibit 5.4 that illustrates some of the forms that have been used in published scales of client satisfaction. This can be a useful guide for the construction of your three questionnaire items.

   Example: One item on the questionnaire might be as follows:

To what extent are you satisfied with the types of services that were available to you?

____ Very satisfied   ____ Somewhat satisfied
____ Not satisfied

4. Identify the vehicle that will be used to distribute your questionnaire. Will it be the mailed survey, the telephone survey, the online survey, or a survey that current clients put into the Suggestion Box in the agency lobby? Briefly explain your choice.

What You Will Report From This Practice Exercise

Your report for this exercise will be your responses to each of the four activities described above. You will report your responses in complete sentences rather than as lists or in some other form. For example, one of the sentences of your report in response to Activity 3 might be, "The vehicle I will use for delivering the questionnaire will be the mailed survey."

EXHIBIT 5.4
EXAMPLES OF ITEMS FROM CLIENT SATISFACTION QUESTIONNAIRES

There are many examples of client satisfaction questionnaires. You can find some of them on the Internet. Two of them are (1) the Reid–Gundlach Social Service Satisfaction Scale and (2) the Client Satisfaction Questionnaire. In this exhibit, you will be given some examples of items that were included on each of these scales. Each of these tools can be found in Corcoran and Fischer (1987).

The Reid–Gundlach Social Services Satisfaction Scale is designed to assess the extent of consumer satisfaction with social services. It contains 34 statements that ask for the degree of agreement with the statement using the following five options for reply: (1) strongly agree, (2) agree, (3) undecided, (4) disagree, and (5) strongly disagree. Some of the statements on this questionnaire are as follows:

1. The social worker took my problems very seriously.

2. Overall, the agency has been very helpful to me.

3. The social worker asks a lot of embarrassing questions.

4. The agency is always available when I need it.

5. The social worker sometimes says things I do not understand.

As you can see, some of these statements are positive and some are negative. For positive statements, an answer of strongly agree would be given 5 points, an answer of agree would be given 4 points and so on, with a response of strongly disagree being given only 1 point. Responses to negative statements are reverse-scored as follows: strongly agree = 1 point; agree = 2 points; undecided = 3 points; and strongly disagree = 4 points. This scoring procedure means that all client responses are given higher scores for responses that are more positive.

The Client Satisfaction Questionnaire (CSQ-8) is designed to assess client satisfaction with treatment. It has eight items that ask the following: (1) How would you rate the quality of service you have received? (2) Did you get the kind of service you wanted? (3) To what extent has your program met your needs? (4) If a friend were in need of similar help, would you recommend our program for him or her? (5) How satisfied are you with the amount of help you have received? (6) Have the services you received helped you deal more effectively with your problems? (7) In an overall, general sense, are you satisfied with the service you received? (8) If you were to seek help again, would you come back to our program? Each of these items has a different 4-point scale for response. For example, the response options for Question 1 are *excellent, good, fair,* and *poor.* For Question 2, the options are *No, definitely; No, not really; Yes, generally;* and *Yes, definitely.*

CHAPTER REVIEW

Chapter Key Learnings

1. The social survey is a purposeful inquiry into a social subject for a designated sample of people by a researcher using a recording instrument, typically a questionnaire. Each study participant is asked to respond to a set of questions. The responses are typically given by the respondent, not by the researcher. When you are making direct observations of human behavior on a street corner, you are not conducting a social survey because you do not have an instrument that is being administered to each person uniformly. When you are viewing agency records, you are not conducting a social survey because you have not composed a tool for measuring variables and asked participants to complete it.

2. The social survey has been widely used by social researchers for a variety of study purposes, such as description, explanation, and evaluation. It has the advantages of efficiency, uniformity, and specificity. It has the disadvantage of weak flexibility because items on the questionnaire are asked in a uniform way to each respondent. Thus, participants lack flexibility in the information they give. They typically respond by selecting one option from a list of options, rather than being able to give a response in their own words. However, qualitative items may be placed on the questionnaire that reduces this limitation.

3. There are various types of social surveys, some of which are administered face-to-face, while most are delivered by mail or the Internet. The advantages and disadvantages differ by the type of survey. For example, the mailed survey is efficient but not usually flexible, while the interview is not efficient but has the potential for finding a richer array of information.

4. The steps in the process of employing the social survey are similar to those for other types of social research. It starts with a study purpose and knowledge base, which generates a major research question. Then study methods are developed, which are executed in the data analysis phase of research. The conclusions phase comes last.

5. When you are conducting survey research, you may need to develop the items for your questionnaire rather than using a published tool. There are several tips for good item construction. You should keep the questionnaire short, concise, simple in terminology, consistent in format, and organized in a logical order. It is best to place controversial items and demographic data items at the end of the questionnaire.

6. Reviewing existing instruments for measuring variables should be the first place the social researcher should look in the determination of the items to be included on the survey questionnaire. Existing instruments have typically been developed by experts and tested for reliability and validity. This inquiry is useful for the researcher in planning to use an existing instrument or in developing his or her own. In the latter incidence, the researcher can get ideas on how to word the items on the questionnaire.

7. The response rate to a social survey is a key issue. If you are using a mailed survey, you could send out reminders and an additional copy of the questionnaire to improve this rate.

Chapter Discussion Questions

1. What type of social survey do you believe is most helpful to the typical social worker who wishes to engage in a survey study (e.g., face-to-face self-administered survey, mailed survey, phone survey, face-to-face interview, online survey)? In other words, which type of survey is most likely to be used by most social workers with this need? Explain.

2. Why is the mailed survey considered more efficient than the interview survey?

3. What are two things you could do to improve the response rate of a mailed survey?

4. Why would you employ an interview survey rather than a mailed survey?

Chapter Test

1. Which of the following statements is/are true?
   a. A social survey is a purposeful inquiry into a social subject for a designated sample of people by a researcher using a recording instrument, typically a questionnaire
   b. If you make free-form notes from your observations about what you see in a given social context, you are not engaged in survey research, partly because you do not have a tool like a questionnaire for the recording of observations
   c. Both of the above
   d. None of the above

2. Which of the following is/are advantages of the mailed survey over the interview?
   a. It is more flexible in the content it will report than is the case of the interview
   b. It is efficient
   c. Both of the above
   d. None of the above

3. For which kind of research can the social survey be useful?
   a. Descriptive
   b. Explanatory
   c. Evaluative
   d. All of the above

4. Which of the following should NOT be in the cover letter that accompanies the mailed survey?
   a. The purpose and importance of the study
   b. The sponsoring organization
   c. The study hypothesis
   d. None of the above. In other words, all should be in the cover letter

5. Which of these survey types is most likely to have the best response rate?
   a. The mailed survey
   b. The online survey
   c. The interview survey
   d. None of the above is likely to be better than any of the others with regard to response rate

6. Which of the following has the greater flexibility regarding the content that might be acquired from the study?
   a. The mailed survey
   b. The online survey
   c. The interview survey
   d. None of the above is likely to be better than any of the others with regard to flexibility

7. The online survey that measures variables in a quantitative manner is
   a. A survey that is distributed over the Internet
   b. A survey that is very efficient
   c. A survey that provides questions that are uniform from one respondent to another
   d. All of the above

8. Which of the following statements is/are true?
   a. The interview survey is better than the mailed survey of having fewer questions left unanswered
   b. The mailed survey is better than the interview survey with regard to response rate
   c. Both of the above
   d. None of the above

9. The interview survey is better suited to which type of study?
    a. Descriptive
    b. Explanatory
    c. Evaluative
    d. Exploratory

10. The face-to-face self-administered survey is more likely to be used by what type of research?
    a. Descriptive
    b. Explanatory
    c. Evaluative
    d. Exploratory

Answers: 1 = c; 2 = b; 3 = d; 4 = c; 5 = c; 6 = c; 7 = d; 8 = a; 9 = d; 10 = c

Chapter Glossary

Face-to-face interview survey. A survey conducted face-to-face between the researcher and the respondent.

Face-to-face self-administered questionnaire. A questionnaire completed by the study respondent when face-to-face with the researcher.

Mailed survey. A form of self-administered survey that is completed by the study subject but is not administered face-to-face.

Online survey. A survey where the questionnaire is sent to respondents through the Internet.

Phone interview survey. A type of social survey conducted through a phone call where the respondent answers a set of questions given from a questionnaire administered by the researcher.

Random sample. A study sample that was drawn at random from the persons in the designated study population, meaning that each person in the study population has an equal chance of being selected.

Semistructured interview. An interview where the researcher provides a set of focused open-ended questions to the interviewee.

Social survey. A purposeful inquiry into a social subject for a designated sample of people by a researcher using a recording instrument, typically a questionnaire.

SurveyMonkey. A software program on the Internet that can be used to conduct an online survey.

6

CONDUCTING RESEARCH THAT DESCRIBES PEOPLE

What Are the Traits That Describe the Good Manager?

Harrison is a social worker who manages a grant-funded program designed to prevent delinquency. He needs to develop the structure for the client record that would provide information on age, gender, race, family income, and family structure. He has consulted the literature for examples of descriptive studies where he could get suggestions on how to construct the items to be recorded in agency records.

Gender is easy. It will be recorded as (a) male or (b) female. Age is also easy. It will be recorded as age in years. This is preferable to using categories for age because Harrison does not know the breakdown that will be needed by the funding source, but he does know they will want the average age, which can only be computed when age is recorded in years, not categories. Race is more complicated because there are several alternatives that can be found in various government reports that are descriptive. Harrison knows, however, that the funding source wants a breakdown into four categories: (1) Caucasian, (2) African American, (3) Hispanic, and (4) Other. The funding source is interested in these categories, and he realizes that there will not be a sufficient number of clients in any other category for race to have meaningful data on the variable race. Family income can be recorded as the actual amount of the family's annual income, or in categories of income. Like the variable age, Harrison does not know the breakdown of family income that will be needed in descriptive reports, so he decided to have the actual family income recorded in dollars in the client record. He consulted the literature to get ideas on how to record family structure. Based on his knowledge of the family structures of the clients of his agency and the information needs of the funding source, he decided to record family structure as (a) one biological parent living in the home, (b) both biological parents living in the home, and (c) other.

Harrison has given some thought to how the data from agency records must be reported. When he has a variable that is a score or a number (e.g., age measured in years), he can compute the range and the mean. With a variable measured in categories (e.g., gender), he can report the number and percentage who are in each category.

With this record system, Harrison will be able to report a number of ways to describe the clients of his agency. First, he can report the number and proportion of clients who are male and female. He can also report the number and proportion of clients who are (a) Caucasian, (b) African American, (c) Hispanic, or (d) something else. A third characteristic he can report is the mean age of clients. Finally, he can report the number and proportion of clients who live with (a) one biological parent, (b) both biological parents, or (c) neither biological parent.

INTRODUCTION

This chapter is about research that describes people. Perhaps you have wondered about certain characteristics of your clients, your classmates, or the members of your favorite club. Maybe you have been curious about how males and females are similar or different concerning the initial approach to a relationship. If you have wondered about what characteristics make one work manager better than another, this chapter will be of special interest because this theme is used as an illustration of the nature of descriptive research.

In this chapter, you will learn how to undertake a simple descriptive research study. At the end of this chapter, you will be able to do the following:

1. Explain the nature of descriptive research contrasted with research that is explanatory, evaluative, or exploratory

2. Distinguish between qualitative and quantitative measurement in descriptive research

3. Describe how the study purpose guides study measurement

4. Describe how the descriptive research study can describe human characteristics, attitudes, behaviors, and/or psychological conditions

5. Explain the functions of sampling and measurement in descriptive research with a special focus on the generalization of study results

6. Compose a simple questionnaire that will adequately collect descriptive data for a given study sample

7. Describe the distinction between descriptive statistics and inferential statistics

8. Explain how the level of measurement of a variable influences the descriptive statistics that you will use

9. Describe several common descriptive statistics such as frequency, proportion, mean, and standard deviation

10. Draw appropriate study conclusions based on a set of data that you analyzed

The first part of this chapter is devoted to an examination of the research process when you are engaged in descriptive research. You have reviewed the four major phases of this process in a previous chapter. In this chapter, you will review this process with descriptive research as an example. Following this review, you will be given two practice exercises, one where you are given data from a study of the traits of the good manager and one whereby you are asked to collect your own data from your class or members of another group. In each exercise, you will respond to questions about the entire research process.

PRELIMINARY STEP FOR PRACTICE EXERCISE 2 FOR THIS CHAPTER

Before you review the information in this chapter, you will be asked to select a **sample** of people to complete the questionnaire given in Exhibit 6.1. The reason you should collect your data first is that there is information in this chapter that could make the questionnaire given in Exhibit 6.1 vulnerable to the social desirability bias. If your study participants review this chapter before they take this questionnaire, they may be influenced to mark their answers to the questions in this tool with a bias in favor of what they consider to be the socially desirable response to the question. Therefore, you should give this questionnaire now rather than later.

You will see a further explanation of the role of this questionnaire later in this chapter, when you undertake the practice exercise. Now, let's turn our attention to a general overview of the nature of descriptive research.

EXHIBIT 6.1
QUESTIONNAIRE ON THE TRAITS OF THE GOOD MANAGER

Instructions: You are being asked to respond to this questionnaire as a research project for a group of students. Your participation is voluntary, and your information will be anonymous because you are asked not to put your name on this questionnaire.

You are asked to review the list of traits below and select eight that you believe best describe the good manager. By manager we mean a person who is employed in a management position. Indicate your choice by drawing a circle around each of the eight traits you select. Be sure to select exactly eight traits, because your responses cannot be used in this study unless you do so.

1. Helpful	9. Creative
2. Ambitious	10. Analytic
3. Aware of the feelings of others	11. Sophisticated
4. Consistent	12. Competitive
5. Modest	13. Intuitive
6. Well-informed	14. Self-confident
7. Humanitarian values	15. Cheerful
8. Objective	16. Aggressive

TYPES OF SOCIAL WORK RESEARCH

We can characterize social work research in many ways. In this book, you will see two themes for characterizing it—purpose and measurement. Social work research can be characterized as having the purpose of describing, explaining, evaluating, and/or exploring. It can also be characterized according to whether the approach to measurement is qualitative or quantitative. You saw an examination of these themes in a previous chapter, so we will only review them briefly here.

Four Purposes of Social Work Research

Among the various ways by which we could characterize social work research, one is purpose. What is the purpose of the study? You reviewed four purposes of social research in Chapter 2. As you saw, one purpose is to describe people. We call that descriptive research. Another is to explain things. **Explanatory research** is the label for this type. In this research, you attempt to explain things by looking at the relationship between two (or more) variables. **Evaluative research** has the purpose of evaluating broad programs or specific interventions. Exploratory research is the fourth type of research when we characterize it by purpose. This type of research examines phenomena that are not well known.

Descriptive research simply describes people (or things) one variable at a time. What, for example, is the average age of persons receiving a Master of Social Work degree in our university? What is the proportion of our clients who have a preschool-age client? What is the average family income of our clients? These are all descriptive questions. They do not attempt to explain. They just describe.

If what you wanted to describe was a **population** concerning something that is complicated and difficult to define, you will have a special challenge with both definition and measurement. Suppose, for example, that you wanted to describe the students in your university regarding whether they were politically conservative or liberal. The definition of political conservatism would be a special challenge. What does this term mean? You can probably imagine several people coming up with several different definitions of the concept. Moreover, you already know that the measurement of a variable must be guided by your definition of the concept it measures. In your report of such a study, you would be careful to provide your definition of conservatism and liberalism as well as your means of measuring this theme.

Quantitative and Qualitative Measurement

There are two major types of measurement in social work research: (1) quantitative and (2) qualitative. In quantitative measurement, you measure each variable either as categories (e.g., male or female) or as numbers (e.g., age measured in years, score on the anxiety scale, etc.). When you measure your variables in a qualitative manner, you will have words to examine. This would be the case if you have responses to an open-ended question on a survey (e.g., In your own words, how would you describe your feelings about being a parent?).

While you can measure your phenomenon of interest either qualitatively or quantitatively with regard to any of the four types of research, we will use examples in this book of qualitative measurement (i.e., words) for the exploratory research study and we will examine the other three types with examples of quantitative research (i.e., categories or numbers). The rationale for this decision is that you are more likely to find quantitative measurement in descriptive, explanatory, and evaluative studies, and qualitative measurement is more likely to be found in exploratory studies.

Descriptive research often uses quantitative measurement because the purpose of the study is to describe people (or things) with precision. How many families are there in the caseloads who have preschool-age children and might make use of a new preschool program? What is the proportion of the families that are single parent and, thereby, might be more likely than others to be in need of one of the services? What is the range of ages for the clients? What is their mean age? These are just some of the questions we might want answered in quantitative measurement.

Purposes and Measurement

In Exhibit 6.2, you can see information on measurement for each of the four types of research. For the descriptive study, the purpose is to describe a group of people, one variable at a time. For example, you might be interested in knowing several characteristics of your fellow students if you are in school. What percentage are male and female? What is the average age? What is the age of the youngest student and the oldest student? How many live with their parents? How many have both parents still alive?

EXHIBIT 6.2
TYPES OF RESEARCH AND MEASUREMENT

	Type of Study			
	Descriptive	**Explanatory**	**Evaluative**	**Exploratory**
Purpose of the study	Describe a group of people, one variable at a time	Examine the relationship between two (or more) variables to see if one explains the other	Evaluate the effectiveness of a service	Examine themes that are not well known
Do you predict the results before you collect data?	Not usually	Yes	Yes	No
What kind of data do you normally have?	Quantitative data on each individual in the study sample on each of the variables that describe them	Quantitative data for each study subject on each of the variables to be compared	Quantitative data on outcome for the service for each study subject, organized by study design	Words (qualitative data) that express ideas, feelings, etc.
What are your key issues?	Have the variables been defined clearly? Have the variables been measured accurately?	How much does one variable explain the other? Did the data support the hypothesis?	Does the research design address important explanations of outcome other than the treatment? Did the data support the hypothesis? Was practical significance achieved?	How can study methods ensure credibility of finding?

You may have several variables in your descriptive study, but you will engage in the statistical analysis of these variables one at a time. You are not examining the relationship between variables because you believe that one causes the other (as would be the case for the explanatory study). Instead, you are just describing things. You may examine the average age of a group of people. Then, you might examine the average income of these people. However, you will not examine the relationship between age and income in a descriptive study. That would be the purview of the explanatory study.

The explanatory study, on the other hand, will have more than one variable to examine. You will have a study hypothesis that predicts the outcome, and you will use your data to test this hypothesis. A key distinction of the evaluative study is that you will likely be examining data on service outcome.

Like the descriptive study, you are not likely to have a prediction of your results when you conduct the exploratory study. You are dealing with unknown territory, so how could you predict the results? The credibility of study methods is not as easy to establish when you examine exploratory themes.

THE PHASES OF DESCRIPTIVE RESEARCH

The process of descriptive research follows the basic steps of any social research study. It starts with a research question. In descriptive research, the research question refers to things that need to be described, not things that need to be explained. The second major phase of descriptive research is the question of what research methods you will employ. In other words, how are you going to construct the questionnaire and select study subjects? The third major phase is data analysis. What did your data reveal? The final phase is the drawing of conclusions. What are the most important findings concerning your general study purpose? What trends did your descriptive data reveal?

In the coming sections of this chapter, we will examine each of these phases one by one. Because we are only dealing with quantitative research using survey methods, we will stick to this in our examination of each phase of the research process. We will *not*, for example, examine research questions that are best addressed by interviewing people and making notes from those interviews and drawing conclusions from our notes. We will not address how to collect data from major national archives that are held by the federal government. Instead, we will address descriptive research questions where we will design the survey instruments that produce quantitative data (not qualitative data), select the study subjects, collect data, analyze that data, and draw conclusions. In each of the four phases of research, we will use an example of a study of the traits of the good manager.

Phase 1: The Research Question and Knowledge Base

We begin the process by deciding on our major research question or questions. Our general purpose is to describe. We can describe the general *characteristics* of people, like age, gender, race, salary, marital status, and so forth. We could also describe the *attitudes* (or emotion or opinions) of people regarding topics such as online education versus traditional face-to-face education. What do people prefer? What do people see as the strengths and weaknesses of each? We could describe political attitudes. Are you liberal, conservative, or independent? Do you prefer a strong military? If so, for what purposes should the military be used, and which should they avoid? Should abortion be allowed? If so, under what circumstances? What are the traits of the good manager or supervisor?

Your research question should clearly identify the variables to be described. Which one of these questions is the least clear with regard to identifying what needs to be measured in a study?

1. What are the demographic characteristics of the members of the Hanover Club, such as age, income, marital status, and political party affiliation?

2. Do people know about the full moon?

3. What are the opinions of middle school students about what should be on the menu of the school cafeteria?

Suppose you selected Question 2. What would you measure if you started with this question? Perhaps a better question would be, "To what extent have social workers learned about the research on the effects of the full moon on mental health behaviors like admissions to the mental health services?"

When you pose the descriptive research question, you should make clear what variables you will measure. With Question 1 above, we can see four of the variables that are to be measured, and we can see that similar variables will likely be measured as well. (You can see the expression "such as" as a clue that other variables of a similar nature will be measured.) The third question identifies items for a lunch menu as the variables you will measure. The second question refers to the full moon but otherwise is rather vague.

Before you are ready to measure your study variables, you should have a clear definition of each one. Variables such as gender and age are easy to define. In fact, they usually need no definition. You just present the label. However, depression will be a bigger challenge. What about the concept of political philosophy? That one would be an even bigger challenge.

Phase 2: The Methods to Be Used to Conduct the Study

The construction of the study methods includes the measurement of study variables, the selection of the study sample from the study population, and the determination of how data will be collected. In the practice exercise for this chapter, you will conduct a study of the traits of the good work manager. You have administered a tool to measure perceptions of the good manager (Exhibit 6.1) from a study sample that you chose. That sample might be made up of the students who are in your research class.

You will address several key issues about the quality of the study methods you employ. The theme here is whether you have chosen methods that provide confidence to the readers of your study that you have a credible means of finding an answer to your research question. One mechanism for asserting credibility is by making sure that the methods you adopt for measurement are accurate.

Reliability and Validity in Measurement

When you conduct a descriptive study, you will consider testing your measurement device (e.g., score for depression, attitudes about family planning, opinions about online education, etc.) for credibility. In social research, we test for both reliability and validity as methods for establishing the credibility of our means of measurement. To be reliable, your measurement tool must operate consistently when used at different times. An example of a test for reliability would be for you to give your measurement tool on the first day of the month to a group of people and then give these same people the same tool 1 week later. You would check to see if the responses were consistent from one week to the next. If Janet has a score that is higher than Jim's score on the first day of the month, she should have a score higher than Jim's score a week later too. If the comparison of Janet and Jim were typical of all comparisons of people in the sample, you would have evidence of reliability. These results are consistent. If the pattern shows consistency, you have evidence of reliability.

You could test your measurement tool for validity by comparing it with another tool designed to measure the same thing. You could administer both tools to a single group of people and compute a correlation of the scores of the two tools. If there is a positive correlation between these scores that is statistically significant, you have evidence of the validity of your tool. A positive correlation means that scores on the two scales tend to show a pattern whereby higher scores of one of the scales is associated with higher scores on the other. For example, if the score for Jane is higher on one of these scales than the score for Paul, you are likely to find that the score for Jane will be higher than the score for Paul on the other scale too. You will recall the phrase "Two heads are better than one." The testing of the validity of your measurement tool is an illustration of this common-sense phrase. A lack of correlation between the two scales that are designed to measure the same thing indicates that one or the other of these scales is not accurate or that neither of these scales is accurate. While it is possible for one of these scales to be accurate and the other not to be accurate, you do not know, simply from the lack of correlation of the two, which one is accurate. What you have is evidence that fails to support the accuracy (validity) of either of the two scales.

Sampling

The sample is composed of those who provided data for your study. The study population is the larger group from which you selected your study sample. The key issue addressed by sampling is generalization of the findings. **Generalization of study results** means that you can be confident that another study with the same tools with another sample of people from this population would generate similar results.

If you have a random sample, you will have selected your study participants from a list of all those in the designated study population on a random basis. You could get the list of members of the Scuba Club and draw a random sample of these people. In this case, you would have a random sample of the members of this club (your study population), and you could scientifically generalize your findings from your study sample to this group. However, you could not scientifically generalize these findings to people other than those in the Scuba Club.

There are at least two types of generalization: scientific and logical. Scientific generalization is appropriate if you have a random sample. If you have a random sample, you have selected the members of your study sample from a list of all persons who are in the study population on a random basis. Scientific generalization means that you have the basis for estimating sampling error on a scientific basis. This is true for the random sample, but it is not true for the nonrandom sample.

Logical generalization is based on your argument of relevance between your sample and your study population. It does not have a scientific basis like drawing a random sample using a table of random numbers. There is no formula or standard for determining if a given type of nonrandom sample is suitable for logical generalization. It is a matter of informed opinion. Therefore, the random sample is clearly stronger with regard to generalization. With the random sample, you are clearly in a superior position to bet your money that a repeat of your study with another sample from the study population would have similar results.

Phase 3: Data Collection and Analysis

Your first task in this phase is to distribute the questionnaire used to measure your study variables. Then, you submit these data to analysis using various descriptive statistics. If you examined the question of whether those who exercise are less likely to have recent minor illness, you could employ the Fisher exact test as your statistic. This is one of many statistics that are labeled *inferential statistics*. Descriptive statistics are different. They are used to describe variables one at a time. We will illustrate descriptive statistics in this chapter.

Levels of Measurement

The **level of measurement** is a concept that you need to understand when you are selecting a descriptive statistic for a given variable. There are three levels of measurement that we will discuss here (we will not discuss the ratio level): (1) **nominal level of measurement**, (2) **ordinal level of measurement**, and (3) **interval level of measurement**.

The *nominal* variable is one where study subjects are placed into categories that have no particular order. An example would be gender, which has two categories without an order. Variables that are recorded as Yes or No are similar in that each person is placed into a category. The variable of political party affiliation is another example of a nominal variable whereby each person is placed in a category that has no order.

The *ordinal* variable is one where people are placed into categories, but the categories for such a variable have an order. Look, for example, at the following options for a question that asks for your opinion:

1 = *strongly disagree*

2 = *disagree*

3 = *undecided*

4 = *agree*

5 = *strongly agree*

As you can see, there is a hierarchy such that strongly disagree has the lowest score and strongly agree has the highest score.

The next level of measurement is the *interval* level. The interval level is a number that has numerical value, rather than being a number that simply identifies someone, like an ID number for you in school. Your score on a self-esteem scale would be an example of a variable measured at the interval level. Your age measured in years (not in categories of years) would be another example of an interval variable. Your social security number would NOT be an example of an interval variable. Why? Because a higher number does not represent a higher value on the variable.

There is a reason why we speak of these as *levels* of measurement. That is because an ordinal variable is higher than a nominal one and an interval variable is higher than an ordinal one. Any statistic that is appropriate for a lower level of measurement can be used with a variable that is measured at a higher level, but the reverse is not true. You cannot use a statistic for an ordinal variable if your variable is measured at the nominal level.

Descriptive Statistics and Inferential Statistics

When you conduct a descriptive study, you will employ descriptive statistics, such as the proportion of people in one category or the **mean** age of all participants. Another descriptive statistic would be the **frequency** of people in a given category for a variable. Other descriptive statistics include the range of scores, the **median** score, and the **standard deviation** of scores. These statistics will be described in a later chapter. For the practice exercise in this chapter, you will focus on the proportion of people who fell into a category, like the proportion who selected "objective" as a trait of the good manager.

When you conduct explanatory or evaluative research, you will be testing a hypothesis. When you test a study hypothesis, you will employ inferential statistics, such as the paired *t* test, the chi-square test, or the Pearson correlation. Inferential statistics tell you the extent to which your data can be explained by chance. In the study you conducted on aerobic exercise and recent minor illness, you were testing the hypothesis that those who exercised would be less likely to report recent minor illness. You employed the Fisher exact probability test for this analysis.

Descriptive Statistics and Levels of Measurement

You may want to describe your study sample regarding gender measured at the nominal level, an opinion measured at the ordinal level, or age measured at the interval level. The level of measurement will determine the appropriate descriptive statistic to employ. You can, for example, compute a frequency or proportion (percentage) for a variable measured at any of the three levels. However, you can compute a mean only for variables measured at the interval level. There are several descriptive statistics that are available for your analysis depending on the level of measurement of your variable. These statistics will be enumerated in a later chapter on data analysis. For now, we will simply focus on the frequency and proportion for a variable measured at the nominal level, which is the case for the practice exercise in this chapter.

Phase 4: Drawing Conclusions

Conclusions in descriptive research refer to the general results and what meaning may be derived from them. This section of the research report will often begin with a broad summary of what you found. If the purpose of the study was to establish priorities among a set of characteristics of the good manager, the conclusion might be that the top characteristic was "aware of the feelings of others" or it might have been "well-informed" or something else. You are putting this in your conclusion part of the report on your descriptive study because this was the item most prominent in the minds of your study subjects. You might also report on the next few items that were prominent, and you might report on the characteristic that was the lowest on the list. You might reflect on the fact that the items that were relationship oriented were more valued than the ones that seemed more task oriented. In each case, you are describing rather than explaining or evaluating. That is the nature of descriptive research.

Chapter Practice Exercises

There are two practice exercises for this chapter: (1) a review of data from a descriptive study of the traits of the good work manager that was conducted among social workers in 1986 and (2) a repeat of the 1986 study with data from a contemporary sample of social workers (perhaps the students in your research class). From these exercises, you will see the results of the 1986 study, and you can see if your contemporary sample of study subjects has similar answers to the survey questions of the study.

For each exercise, you will engage in the steps in the research process for a descriptive study. This means you will identify the research question, review a knowledge base regarding that research question, determine the research methods that will be employed in the search for an answer to your research question, examine data based on the chosen methods of research, and draw conclusions about the research question.

At the beginning of this chapter, you were asked to respond to a question about the traits of the good work manager. If you did not do that then, you should do it before you continue with the instructions for this exercise. If you review further information before responding to this questionnaire, data from your survey will not be included in the second practice exercise where you conduct a contemporary study similar to the 1986 one. The reason for this step in the procedures is that research should be independent. In other words, you should answer the questions from the survey independent of what you know about research on this theme that has been undertaken

in the past. We do not want to have data using answers to questions that could be influenced by what study respondents know about prior research on the theme of the study.

Here is a summary of the 1986 research study that serves as the guide for these two practice exercises for this chapter:

A survey of social workers in the state of North Carolina served as the focus of the 1986 study (York, 1987). A random sample of the members of the North Carolina Chapter of the National Association of Social Workers (NASW) constituted the sample for this study. They were given the questionnaire from Exhibit 6.1, where they reviewed a list of 16 characteristics and selected the 8 traits that best described the good work manager. The even-numbered items on that list represented a male stereotype, while the odd-numbered ones revealed a female stereotype. The respondents, of course, were not informed about the gender stereotypes of the items on the list. Scores for male stereotype were computed by assigning one point for each of the male-stereotyped traits selected; thus, scores could range from 0 to 8, with a score of 4 representing a gender-neutral description of the good manager. A score of 4 for male stereotype would mean that the individual selected 4 male-stereotyped traits and 4 female-stereotyped traits. Scores below 4 would represent a female stereotype. The mean sex role stereotype (SRS) score was computed. Because the mean score for these respondents was above 4.0, these data were subjected to statistical analysis to see if it was significantly greater than 4.0.

Competencies Demonstrated by These Practice Exercises

1. The ability to organize a descriptive research study from the development of the research question to the review of a knowledge base, to the determination of research methods to be employed, to the collection and analysis of data, and, finally, to the drawing of conclusions about the research question

2. The ability to analyze data on frequencies, proportions, and means with regard to specific data regarding a specific research question

3. The ability to rank order descriptive data for a research question

4. The ability to compare a mean score with a threshold score in descriptive data analysis

5. The ability to draw appropriate conclusions from the analysis of descriptive data for a descriptive research question

Activities for These Practice Exercises

1. A review of the knowledge base for this study and the research questions that emanated from it

2. A review of the study methods employed in this study, including considerations of (a) the study sample employed, (b) the tool used to measure study variables, and (c) the procedures employed to ensure that the ethical use of human subjects in research is implemented

3. The analysis of the data, with attention to both the research questions being pursued

4. The drawing of conclusions that are consistent with the data that were analyzed

What You Will Report From These Practice Exercises

With regard to each of the practice exercises, you will report on (a) the research question, (b) the research methods employed, (c) the analysis of the data, and (d) the conclusions of the study.

1. Your research questions. There are two questions being pursed here. You will report them. (You are not expected to report on the knowledge base that supported the research questions.)

2. A report on the research methods for the study. This includes the following:
    a. A one-sentence description of the study sample

Examples:
The members of the Lions Club of Richmond, VA, who attended the club meeting in February 2019
The members of a social work research class who attended a class session in February of 2019 and agreed to participate
The social workers of a human service agency who agreed to participate in the study by completing the questionnaire in February 2019
    b. A description of the tool used to measure the study variables

Example:
The Hare Self-Esteem Scale is a 30-item instrument that is designed to measure self-esteem in school-age children. Items on the scale are statements about the self, such as "I have at least as many friends as other people my age." Respondents indicate their level of agreement with each item. Scores can range from a low of 30 to a high of 120, with higher scores representing higher self-esteem.
    c. A description of the procedures employed to ensure that the theme of ethics in the

use of human subjects in research is adequately addressed

Example:

Participation in this study was not believed to cause harm to the members of the Lions Club because it did not ask participants to engage in dangerous actions or reflect on major mental health problems that they have experienced. The issues both of privacy and of voluntary participation were addressed by the fact that these individuals were notified that participation was voluntary and that they were asked not to put their names on the questionnaire they had completed.

3. A report on the data analysis

Example:

The first research question asked was, "What were the traits most favored in the description of the good manager?" The manager trait selected by more respondents than others in the description of the good manager was ___, which was selected by ___% of these study subjects. The second most favored trait was ___, which was selected by ___% of the respondents, while the third most favored trait was ___, which was favored by ___% of these individuals. The least favored trait was ___, which was selected by only ___% of the study respondents, while the next to last item of the list was ___, which was favored by ___% of these study respondents.

The second research question focused on whether these study respondents would favor the male stereotype when describing the good manager. They were asked to select the eight traits that they believed best described the good work manager. The list had 16 traits, one half of which had been found in research to represent a male stereotype (i.e., were perceived as more likely to be exhibited by men

than women), while the other half represented a female-stereotyped trait.

The score for male stereotype was computed by adding all the male items on the list that were among the eight items selected by the respondent; thus, the score could range from a low of 0 to a high of 8. A male-stereotyped score of 4 would represent a gender-neutral perception because it would mean that the individual had selected four male-stereotyped items and four female-stereotyped items. The mean male-stereotyped score for these respondents was 4.34. Because this mean was above the gender-neutral score, the question next pursued was whether this mean was above the score of 4 at a statistically significant level. The one-sample t test was employed to find the answer to this question. This analysis failed to show that this mean score of 4.34 was significantly higher than the gender-neutral score of 4.0 ($t = 1.23$; $p > .05$).

4. Your study conclusions. You will report your results in brief, with regard both to the most favored (and the least favored) traits of the work manager and the results of your examination of sex-role stereotypes. You will indicate the implications of these findings for social work.

Practice Exercise 1: Reviewing the Results of a 1986 Study

Each of the major steps of descriptive research are included in this exercise. You will start with the research question and end with your study conclusions. For each of these steps, you will review information from a study conducted by York (1987).

Step 1: Reviewing the Research Questions and Knowledge Base for the 1986 Study

For the 1986 study (and the contemporary one as well), there were two key research questions:

1. Which human traits are favored by social workers in the description of the good work manager?

2. Do social workers favor male-stereotyped traits over female-stereotyped traits in the description of the good work manager?

    Part of the knowledge base that led to the above research questions is presented in Exhibit 6.3. The information presented in this exhibit refers to the issue of sex-role stereotypes regarding the description of the good manager. This knowledge base suggested that certain traits (e.g., competitive) are perceived as more like men than women and certain others as more like women than men. Furthermore, past research had suggested that the traits perceived as more like men than women were favored in the description of the good work manager.

EXHIBIT 6.3

SUMMARY OF A LITERATURE REVIEW

SRSs About Social Work Administration (York, 1987)

For several decades, a growing body of literature has suggested that people favor a male stereotype for what it takes to be a good work manager. If we depict the good manager as being more like a man than a woman, we will discriminate against women when we seek our next manager to fill our job vacancy. While this theme has been addressed in studies of the general population, there is little published research on the extent to which social workers possess a male stereotype for describing the good manager.

In the report of the 1986 study by York, the sex-role stereotype was defined as "a standardized mental picture of gender differences in socially designated behaviors which represents an oversimplified opinion or uncritical judgment" (York, 1987, p. 88). An SRS about management is a standardized mental picture of what it takes to be a good work manager that favors the male over the female.

This issue has inspired a number of research studies on the social desirability of perceived differences between men and women. For example, one study suggested that college students had a higher evaluation of stereotypically male than female traits (Rosenkrantz, Vogel, Bee, Broverman, & Broverman, 1968). A review of various studies drew the following conclusion:

> Women are perceived as relatively less competent, less independent, less objective, and less logical than men; men are perceived as lacking interpersonal sensitivity, warmth, and expressiveness in comparison with women. Moreover, stereotypically masculine traits are more often perceived to be desirable than stereotypically feminine characteristics. (Broverman, Vogel, Broverman, Clarkson, & Rosenkrantz, 1972, p. 75)

The key question in this review is whether sex-role stereotypes are related to our perceptions of the good manager. Two studies by Schein (1973, 1975) suggested that employees of insurance companies showed a preference for the male stereotype when describing what it takes to be a good manager. These results were also found in a study of people from the mailing list of a school of business administration (Massengill & DiMarco, 1979). A study of male managers in a variety of organizations found that females were

(Continued)

(Continued)

perceived as lower in rank than males on skill, work motivation, temperament, and work habits (Rosen & Jerdee, 1978). Brenner and Bromer (1981) found that both male managers and female managers described themselves more in line with the male stereotype than the female stereotype. This finding suggests that women who happen to exhibit more male-stereotyped behaviors are favored for management positions when these jobs are filled.

A question arises as to whether the male-stereotyped traits are better than the female-stereotyped traits in describing the good manager. A variety of studies have suggested that this is not true (see, e.g., Day & Stogdill, 1972; Osborn & Vicars, 1976; Powell, Butterfield, & Mainiero, 1981; Rosenbach, Dailey, & Morgan, 1979). The issue of sex role stereotypes among social work students was examined in a number of studies. Harris and Lucas (1976) found that a sample of social work students did not differ in their perceptions of a healthy male, a healthy female, and a healthy adult. A study by Festinger and Bounds (1977), however, found that a sample of social work students viewed masculine traits as more socially desirable than feminine traits.

A survey by York, Henley, and Gamble (1985) is similar to the study conducted in the 1986. That survey was of social work students rather than employed social workers. That survey, like the 1986 study, employed a tool that listed 16 traits, one half of which were in the category of the male stereotype, while the other half were in the category of the female stereotype. Respondents were asked to select the eight traits that best characterized the good manager. The number of male-stereotyped traits selected represented the respondents score for male preference; therefore, a score of 4 would represent a gender-neutral perception, while scores higher than 4 would represent a male preference. The results revealed a mean score of 4.28. The one-sample t test was used to determine if this mean score was significantly higher than the gender-neutral score of 4.0. The results suggested that it was statistically significant ($p < .05$). Therefore, the conclusion was that these social work students had a sex-role stereotype regarding the description of the good manager.

Step 2: Reviewing the Research Methods for the 1986 Study

The study methods for the 1986 survey entailed the sample selection and the means for measuring study variables. The study sample was selected at random from the membership list of the North Carolina Chapter of the NASW. A questionnaire was mailed to 146 persons from this membership list, and 102 responded, for a response rate of 70%, a rate that is considered very good for a mailed survey.

Two variables were measured in this study. The first was the characteristics of the good work manager. A characteristic is a feature or quality of someone that identifies that person in a meaningful way. You might be described as someone who is intuitive, helpful, or respectful. These would be characteristics. A second variable measured in this study was SRS about management that was defined as a standardized mental picture of what it takes to be a good work manager that favors the male over the female.

The questionnaire given in Exhibit 6.1 was used for the measurement of both the favored traits of the good manager and the SRSs about management. This means that a quantitative method of measurement was employed. If the respondents had been asked to describe the good manager in their own words, we would have a qualitative measurement. Quantitative measurement is more efficient, and it suits the purpose of this study quite well. The purpose is to describe something with precision.

The study subjects were presented a list of 16 traits (characteristics) and were asked to select the 8 traits that best described the good work manager. The number of study subjects who selected a given item represented the score for that trait. This provided the opportunity to rank each of these traits from 1 to 16 with regard to the extent that they were viewed as describing the good manager. The highest ranked trait was the one that had been selected by the greatest proportion of respondents. The lowest ranked trait was the one that was selected by the lowest proportion of respondents.

The second research question was about SRSs. On the tool given in Exhibit 6.1, all even-numbered items represent a male stereotype, while each odd-numbered items support the female stereotype. Respondents were asked to select eight items from this list of 16 traits. The male stereotype score is composed of all male-stereotyped traits selected; thus, a score of 4 would represent a gender-neutral preference, while a score higher than 4 would represent a preference for the male stereotype. A score lower than 4 would represent a preference for the female stereotype.

There are several ethical issues in the use of human subjects in research. Among these are (a) harm, (b) privacy, and (c) voluntary participation. Research using human subjects should adequately address each of these issues. In the 1986 survey, participants were mailed a survey and had the opportunity to decline to participate by simply not sending back the questionnaire. This also ensured that privacy would be maintained. In addition, there was no reason to believe that responding to this questionnaire would cause harm. The participants were not asked to engage in dangerous actions nor were they asked to think about serious mental health issues that they had encountered in life.

Step 3: Reviewing the Data Analysis for the 1986 Study

Of the 146 persons sent a questionnaire in the 1986 study, 102 responded, for a response rate of 70%. Of those who responded, 72% were female, and 92% were Caucasian. A majority (51%) indicated that they were employed in direct-service positions. Almost all (95%) held the Master of Social Work degree. The mean age of these respondents was 41.5, while the mean years of social work experience was 14.5.

There were two search questions for the analysis of the data for the 1986 study:

1. Which traits of the good work manager are more favored than other traits?

2. Does the mean score for the traits of the good manager favor the male stereotype?

The results of the analysis of favored traits for the social work manager are given in Exhibit 6.4. That survey revealed that *well-informed* was the most favored trait (97% of the respondents listed it as one of the eight traits of the good manager). The next three favored traits were (a) aware of the feelings of others, (b) possessing humanitarian values, and (c) being creative. The least favored traits were being (1) modest (2) sophisticated, (3) ambitious, and (4) competitive.

The mean number of male-stereotyped traits selected by this sample of social workers was 4.25, which was above the gender-neutral score of 4.0. Because it favored the male stereotype, statistical analysis of the data was undertaken to see if it was significantly higher than 4.0. The one-sample *t* test was used to compare the male SRS scores of these respondents with the gender-neutral threshold score of 4.0. The results was a *p* value of .01, which exceeded the normal standard for **statistical significance** in social science research (e.g., $p < .05$).

EXHIBIT 6.4

PROPORTIONS OF RESPONDENTS SELECTING EACH OF 16 TRAITS FOR DESCRIBING THE GOOD MANAGER

Percentage Who Selected Each Trait	Rank	Trait	Stereotype
97	1	Well-informed	Male
91	2	Aware of the feelings of others	Female
89	3	Humanitarian values	Female
85	4	Creative	Female
79	5	Objective	Male
76	6	Consistent	Male
69	7	Self-confident	Male
60	8	Analytic	Male
52	9	Intuitive	Female
35	10	Helpful	Female
17	11	Aggressive	Male
15	12	Cheerful	Female
10	13/14	Competitive	Male
10	13/14	Ambitious	Male
3	15	Sophisticated	Female
2	16	Modest	Female

Step 4: Drawing Conclusions for the 1986 Study

The social workers who responded to the questionnaire for the 1986 study perceived the good manager as well-informed, aware of the feelings of others, possessing humanitarian values, and being creative. Following these traits in order were the traits of objective, consistent, and self-confident. Not highly valued in the description of the good manager were traits such as being modest, sophisticated, ambitious, and competitive.

When the male-stereotyped preferences for the description of the good manager were compared with the female-stereotyped ones, the pattern was not very clear at first glance. For example, the top 10 traits listed were evenly split between the male and the female stereotypes. However, when the mean score for the male stereotype was computed, it was found to be higher than the gender-neutral score of 4 at a statistically significant level. Therefore, these respondents exhibited a preference for the male stereotype. Was the score of 4.25 higher than 4.0 at a level that you would consider noteworthy? That is the question of practical significance, which is a matter of informed opinion, so you have to make your choice.

Because this study employed a random sample of the members of the North Carolina Chapter of the NASW, the results of this study can be generalized to this chapter of NASW on a scientific basis. Generalization beyond this chapter of NASW would need to be based on logic.

Step 5: Reporting the Results of the 1986 Study

You will report on the results of the 1986 study using the information given above. You will employ the guide for reporting that was given in the introductory section of the practice exercise instructions.

Practice Exercise 2: Conducting Your Own Study of the Traits of the Good Manager

In this part of the practice exercise, you will select a study sample and ask these individuals to complete the instrument given in the 1986 study (Exhibit 6.1). The first step in the research process for your study will be a duplicate of the first stage for the 1986 study. In other words, you will base your study on the knowledge base given for that study. The tool you use to measure study variables will also be a duplicate of the 1986 study. You will, however, have a different study sample and different study results. Thus, you will also have different study conclusions.

Ethics in the Use of Human Subjects in Research

Before you undertake a study using human subjects in research, you should consider the critical ethical issues in this endeavor. These issues have been reviewed in the discussion of the first practice exercise. First, it seems you can safely say that this study will not cause harm to the study subjects. Second, you should collect your data anonymously, so that there will be no opportunity for the invasion of privacy. Third, you will be asking your study subjects to participate on a voluntary basis, so coercion is not an issue. Thus, you should have no reason to believe that an institutional review board would raise ethical concerns about the study you are about to conduct. Because this study is a class exercise and you do not plan to publish the results, you are not likely to be required to submit your study for review by the institutional review board.

Your Study Sample

You will select a study sample from a study population. You sample might be the students in your research class. This would be a sample perhaps most convenient to you. You will designate your study population and draw conclusions about the generalization of your study findings based on the nature of your sample selection procedure.

Data Analysis for Your Study

You will compute the results so that you can report them in a table like Exhibit 6.4, where the results of the 1986 study were presented. A tool you might find helpful for the computation of the basic results is presented in Exhibit 6.5. Your job is to insert a mark in the cells of that exhibit to indicate each person's response. The 16 traits are listed in the columns, and the numbers of the respondents are listed in the rows. For example, if the first respondent that you recorded selected

Trait 1 as one of the eight traits selected, you would insert an X in the first column in the first row of Exhibit 6.5. That row would have a total of 8 marks. If you have a respondent who failed to select eight traits, you should drop this person from your study.

The even-numbered traits are the male-stereotyped ones, so the score for SRS is computed for each respondent by summing the number of X marks in the even-numbered traits (they are shaded). These scores can range from a low of 0 to a high of 8.

Which Traits Are Most Favored?

Your first task is to determine which traits had the highest scores and which had the lowest scores. The score can be derived from the

EXHIBIT 6.5

TRAIT FREQUENCIES AND SEX-ROLE STEREOTYPE (SRS) SCORES FOR CURRENT RESPONDENTS

| Persons | \multicolumn{16}{c|}{Traits} | SRS |
	1	2	3	4	5	6	7	8	9	10	11	12	13	14	15	16	
1																	
2																	
3																	
4																	
5																	
6																	
7																	
8																	
9																	
10																	
11																	
12																	
13																	

14															
15															
16															
17															
18															
19															
20															
21															
22															
23															
24															
25															
26															
27															
28															
29															
30															
31															
32															
33															
34															
35															
Total															

Note: Traits numbered above: 1 = helpful; 2 = ambitious; 3 = aware of the feelings of others; 4 = consistent; 5 = modest; 6 = well-informed; 7 = humanitarian values; 8 = objective; 9 = creative; 10 = analytic; 11 = sophisticated; 12 = competitive; 13 = intuitive; 14 = self-confident; 15 = cheerful; 16 = aggressive. Individual respondents are in the rows and traits are in the columns.

proportion of study subjects who selected the trait. You can compute this score for each of the 16 traits by dividing the number of participant votes by the total number of people in your study. For example, if you had 12 persons who selected the first trait (helpful) and you had 23 total respondents in your study, you would divide 12 by 23 and get a fraction of 0.5217, which could be rounded to 0.52. If you multiply this fraction by 100, you get the percentage equivalent of this fraction. Therefore, 52% of these study subjects selected Trait Number 1 as one of the traits of the good manager. After you have computed the percentage of people who selected each item, you can rank order these 16 traits from 1 to 16 based on the percentage of people who listed each one. Enter these data in Exhibit 6.6.

Did Your Respondents Have a Male Stereotype?

Each even-numbered item on the trait scale was one that has been found to be associated with a male stereotype, while each of the odd-numbered items represents a female stereotype. There were eight male-stereotyped traits and eight female-stereotyped traits on the scale to which respondents were asked to select the eight that best described the good manager. The

EXHIBIT 6.6
RANKS OF TRAITS OF THE GOOD MANAGER BY THE SUBJECTS IN THE CURRENT STUDY

Rank	Trait Number	Trait
1		
2		
3		
4		
5		
6		
7		
8		
9		
10		

11		
12		
13		
14		
15		
16		

score for SRS was computed by summing the number of male-stereotyped traits selected by the study participant. This score can range from 0 (if no male-stereotyped traits had been selected) to a high of 8 (if all traits selected were male-stereotyped ones). A score of 4 would represent a preference for neither the male stereotype nor the female stereotype. The SRS score for each study subject is presented in Exhibit 6.5.

Your job is to determine if your study subjects expressed a preference for the male stereotype. You must first compute the mean for the male SRS. If this mean is not above 4.0, you have data that suggest that your study subjects do not express a male stereotype. If the score is above 4.0, you will examine your data statistically to determine if they are significantly above 4.0.

To determine if your mean SRS score is significantly above 4.0, you can enter your data on SRS scores into the chart on GraphPad (Exhibit 6.7). The one-sample t test is demonstrated in this exhibit. This test is appropriate if you are comparing an array of scores with a single score. In your case, you will compare all the SRS scores with the single score of 4, the gender-neutral score. In this exhibit, you will be given step-by-step instructions. The key piece of data from that analysis is the value of p. Remember that you will only test for statistical significance if your mean SRS score is above 4.0.

If you find a preference for the male stereotype that is statistically significant, you can examine the practical significance question: Is this difference noteworthy in your opinion? It is possible to have statistical significance but not practical significance, but it would be hard to argue the opposite position (i.e., practical significance in the absence of statistical significance). Practical significance is a matter of informed opinion. It is based more on logic than on science.

Conclusions for Your Study

You will draw conclusions from your analysis of data. What, for example, were the traits of the good manager that were viewed by your study subjects as most favorable? What were the traits that were viewed as least favorable? Did the data on favored traits from your current study differ from the results of the 1986 study? Can contemporary administrators make use of these results in personnel decisions?

EXHIBIT 6.7
USING GRAPHPAD FOR THE ONE-SAMPLE T TEST

Here are the step-by-step procedures for using GraphPad on the Internet to determine the value of *p* when you have a set of scores to be compared with a single threshold score. You will do this using the one-sample *t* test.

1. Go to the link GraphPad (http://graphpad.com/quickcalcs).

2. You will see the following heading on the new screen: **Choose the kind of calculator you want to use.**

   a. You will see a dot in *Categorical data* because this is the default. Change this to *Continuous data* by marking the dot in the circle next to it.

   b. Click *Continue*.

3. You will see the following heading: **Analyze continuous data.**

   a. Select *One sample t test* by clicking on the circle next to this choice.

   b. Click *Continue*.

4. You will see the following heading: **One sample *t* test**

   a. Leave Step 1 at the default specification [Enter up to 50 rows] assuming that you do not have more than 50 scores to enter. If you do, you should change this option to the number of scores in your analysis.

   b. Step 2 is where you enter your data (the male preference scores). Enter each of your scores.

   c. Step 3 is where you enter the hypothetical mean value. For you, this is 4.

   d. Step 4 says *View the results*. This gives you the option to calculate the value of *p*. Click *Calculate now*.

5. You will see the following heading on this new screen: **One sample *t* test results.**

   a. The first line of information will give you the value of *p*. You will examine this to see if it is less than .05.

Did your study subjects express a preference for the male stereotype when describing the good manager? Is this similar or different from the results of the 1986 study? What are the implications of these findings for human service administration?

Reporting Your Results

You will report the results of your study using the instructions given at the beginning of the instructions for the practice exercises. For example, your report will begin with the statement of the research questions.

CHAPTER REVIEW

Chapter Key Learnings

1. Descriptive research has the purpose of describing people or things. This type of research is often needed in reports given to funding sources. It helps us understand how well our services are being delivered to the target populations we should be serving. If we have data on the characteristics of our clients, we will have data on variables that could be employed in explanatory studies related to service outcomes. For example, we could examine whether gender is related to client outcome.

2. For descriptive research, the definition of the variables is a key issue. What is measured should be the same as your definition of the variable. Some variables, like political philosophy, will be much more difficult to define than others, like age or gender.

3. Descriptive research often uses quantitative measurement, instead of qualitative measurement, because the purpose of the study is to describe people (or things) with precision. Quantitative measurement is usually more useful for describing people with regard to variables such as family structure, age, race, and gender.

4. Unlike explanatory or evaluative research, you do not normally have a prediction of the results of your study when you engage in descriptive research. For example, when you ask people to select the traits of the good manager, you are seeking to describe the good manager rather than to test a theory about it. When you record the characteristics of your clients with regard to race, age, and gender, you are not predicting the results; you are merely recording them.

5. The major phases of descriptive research are similar to other types of research. The descriptive study starts with a research question such as "What are the characteristics of our clients?" It moves from there to a determination of the methods that will be employed to find the answer to the research question.

6. There are three levels of measurement of special interest to the descriptive researcher in social work: (1) nominal, (2) ordinal, and (3) interval. If you place study participants into a category without an order, such as gender or political party affiliation, you will have a variable that is measured at the nominal level. With the ordinal level of measurement, you place people into categories that have an order, such as *strongly agree*, *agree*, *disagree*, and *strongly disagree*. A variable measured at the interval level is one where you give each study participant a number that has numerical value, such as age measured in years or a score on a depression scale. These levels of measurement form a hierarchy with nominal at the bottom, ordinal in the middle, and interval at the top. A variable that is measured at a higher level can employ any statistic that is appropriate for a variable measured at a lower level.

7. Among the descriptive statistics used in descriptive research are frequency, proportion, mean, and range. Inferential statistics, on the other hand, are used for testing a study hypothesis. It is the inferential statistic that will give you the value of p, which indicates the number of times in 100 that your data would occur by chance.

8. The conclusions section of a descriptive study will simply summarize the descriptions of the study sample. It might also examine the implications of these findings, such as the characteristics of the good manager that were most favored by this study sample were the ones that focused more on relationships than on tasks.

Chapter Discussion Questions

1. Is it more useful to categorize social work research studies by purpose than by some other criteria (e.g., type of measurement, or study design employed)?

2. Why is the qualitative form of measurement more likely to be present in the exploratory type of study than the other types of studies (descriptive, explanatory, or evaluative)?

3. Why do you categorize the number of variables in the analysis of data in a descriptive study as one? Do you do the same for the explanatory type of study?

4. Why do you have a study hypothesis in the explanatory type of study but not the in the descriptive type of study?

5. Suppose that a fellow student says to you, "I want to conduct a study using the telephone interview—I did a telephone interview study in a previous course and it was interesting." Then you might ask, "What is your research question, or purpose of your study," and he says, "I have not yet decided." What advice do you have for this person?

6. To establish the credibility of your tool for measuring a study variable, you can turn your attention to the testing of the reliability and the validity of the tool. What does reliability mean? What does validity mean? Why can you have reliability without having validity but cannot have validity without having reliability?

7. Describe a method you could employ that would demonstrate a random sample for your study. What steps would you take?

8. Did you respond to Exhibit 6.5 and select the eight traits that you thought best described the good work manager? If so, how were your choices different from the average of that of the others in your study?

Chapter Test

1. Suppose that someone reported on a study with the following summary: This study had the purpose of describing people who are victims of domestic violence. It found that victims of family violence were found in various social classes, races, and sections of the nation. It was concluded that family violence is not restricted to social class, race, or geography. Information from what phase of the research process is missing from this description?
   a. The research question or study purpose
   b. The study methodology
   c. The study results
   d. The study conclusions

2. Which of the following statements of study purpose is/are consistent with the spirit of scientific inquiry?
   a. The purpose of this study is to describe first-grade students of Central Elementary School with regard to social class, race, and gender
   b. The purpose of this study is to provide evidence of the need for more teachers for the school system
   c. Both of the above
   d. None of the above

3. Suppose that you have 15 men in your study sample and no women. You have people with various ages, such as 34, 23, 31, 56, and 67 years. You have 23 people who say they are affiliated with the Democratic Party, 34 who say they are affiliated with the Republican Party, and 7 who say they are affiliated with neither of these two parties. Which of the following are potential variables in your study?
   a. Gender
   b. Age
   c. Both of the above
   d. None of the above

4. Suppose that you ask a group of people to participate in your study by completing a questionnaire on a voluntary basis. Your study has little possibility of causing harm to study subjects. You ask your study subjects to put their names on your questionnaire. What theme in research ethics are you in most danger of violating?
   a. Harm
   b. Privacy
   c. Coercion
   d. Justice

5. What is the key thing that helps you with drawing conclusions for your study?
   a. The study sample employed
   b. The methods you used to measure study variables
   c. The results of the data analysis
   d. What you expected to find when you started the study

6. You can report the frequency for variables measured at what level?
   a. Nominal
   b. Ordinal
   c. Interval
   d. All of the above

7. You can report the proportion for variables measured at what level?
   a. Nominal
   b. Ordinal
   c. Interval
   d. All of the above

8. You can report the mean for measures measured at what level?
   a. Nominal
   b. Ordinal
   c. Interval
   d. All of the above

9. You are going to measure the improvement of clients in a support group service by measuring their level of perceived social support once before service began and once again at the end of the support group service experience. What type of research is this?
   a. Descriptive
   b. Explanatory
   c. Evaluative
   d. Exploratory

10. You will measure each of your study subjects with regard to both age and income because you believe that those who are older will report higher income. You will compute a correlation between these two variables to determine if this is true for your study sample. What kind of research is this?
    a. Descriptive
    b. Explanatory
    c. Evaluative
    d. Exploratory

11. If you claim to be able to generalize your study findings on a scientific basis, what is necessary?
    a. You must be using an experimental research design
    b. You must be using a random sample from the study population
    c. You must be using a set of well-studied tools for measuring your study variables
    d. None of the above

12. Which of the following statements is/are true?
    a. An interval variable is at a higher level of measurement than an ordinal variable
    b. Any statistic that is appropriate for an ordinal variable can also be applied to an interval variable
    c. Both of the above
    d. None of the above

ANSWERS: 1 = b; 2 = a; 3 = b; 4 = b; 5 = c; 6 = d; 7 = d; 8 = c; 9 = c; 10 = b; 11 = b; 12 = c

Chapter Glossary

Descriptive research. Research that is used to describe people (or things) one variable at a time, such as the mean age of students in a class or the proportion who are female.

Evaluative research. Research that is used to evaluate a service. You would be undertaking an evaluative study if you measured the grades of at-risk middle school students both before and after your special tutoring program and compared these two sets of grades to see if the tutoring program might be having the effect of improving grades.

Explanatory research. Research that has the purpose of explaining things by examining the relationship between two variables where one is believed to be the cause of the other.

Frequency. The incidence of something, such as the number of females and the number of males in a study sample.

Generalization of study results. The application of the study results to the study population. If you have a random sample, you can generalize your results to the study population on a scientific basis (because you have the mechanism of estimating sampling error). This means that you would probably be safe to bet your money that another study drawn the same way from the same population would generate very similar results to those of your study.

Interval level of measurement. A level of measurement in which the variable is measured as a score or in another way that has numerical meaning, like age measured in years. This is the highest level of measurement that is discussed in this book (the ratio level is not discussed here).

Level of measurement. The hierarchy of measurement that has four levels from low to high. Three of these levels are nominal, ordinal, and interval, in that order. The ratio level is not discussed in this book because it is not useful to the examples used. Level of measurement is related to the proper statistic to employ in the examination of your data.

Mean. The average, which is calculated by summing the frequencies for a variable and dividing by the total number of values (people) in the calculation.

Median. The midpoint in an array of data laid out in numerical order. For example, the frequencies for age might be 12, 15, 16, 19, 27, 28, and 31 years. These values are ordered from low to high, so you look at the middle age to determine the median. In the case of the above ages, the mean age would be 19 years.

Nominal level of measurement. A variable that is measured in categories that have no order, such as political party affiliation. This is the lowest level of measurement.

Ordinal level of measurement. A variable that is measured in categories that have an order, such as *strongly agree, agree, undecided, disagree, and strongly disagree.* In this case, each option is higher than the next.

Population. The study population is the group from which the study sample was selected. Each person in the sample must be a member of the designated study population.

Sample. The people who are in your study. In other words, you have measured each of the people in the study sample.

Standard deviation. A measure of how much the values for a variable vary from one another. Suppose that the ages of the participants for Study A were 19, 28, 29, 36, 54, and 66 years and the ages of participants for Study B were 23, 24, 23, 25, 26, 21, and 21 years. You will notice that the ages for Study A are more different from one another, so the standard deviation for age for Study A would be higher than that for Study B.

Statistical significance. The achievement of a given standard for the likelihood that your study results can be explained by chance. The p value determines statistical significance. It represents the proportion of times your results would occur by chance. The normal standard in the social sciences is a p value of less than .05 ($p < .05$). If your p value is less than .05, you have achieved statistical significance, which means that you have adequately ruled out chance as the explanation for your data. This means that you can take your data as being meaningful.

CONDUCTING RESEARCH THAT EXPLAINS THINGS

What Explains Life Satisfaction?

Jason is a clinical social worker who provides therapy at a behavioral health center. Clients served by his agency are typically depressed or anxious or facing a family crisis. He wanted to know if male clients served by his agency were more likely than female clients to no-show (e.g., fail to show up for a therapy session). He had this question because it seems to him that his male clients are more likely to do this. He also found that other therapists had the opinion that males are more likely to no-show. He decided to review the agency records in order to find the answer to his question, because he wanted to know if he should address this issue more with male clients than with female ones by doing something to prevent it. Because he wants to know if gender explains the no-show phenomenon, he realizes that he will be conducting an explanatory research study. He will examine the relationship between gender and failing to show up for an appointment.

Jason started with his research question: Do male clients have a greater tendency than female clients to fail to show up for therapy appointments? His next step was to determine his research methods for finding the answer to his question. He decided that his study sample would consist of all clients whose cases had been closed in the past 3 months. His data would be the number and proportion of persons in each gender who had failed to show up for at least one appointment and the number and proportion who had not.

Data analysis was his third step. He found that there was a total of 113 people whose cases had been closed in the past 3 months, of whom 48 were male and 65 were female. These 113 people constituted his study sample. Of the 48 males, 17 had at least one failure to show for an appointment and 31 had not. Of the 65 females, 16 had at least one failure to show and 49 had not. He calculated the proportion of males who had no-showed at least once and found this to be 35%. The proportion of females with at least one no-show was 25%. These data showed that males had a higher tendency to fail to show up for appointments, but the differences between males and females did not seem very noteworthy to him. He realized that he should address the issue of chance as an explanation of these data. He wanted to be able to predict future tendencies for no-shows and realized that chance will help him with this goal. If the data can be explained by chance, he cannot rely on it for advice for the future. He used a simple Internet website to determine the value of p with regard to his data. This value tells you the number of times in 100 that your data would occur by chance. If it is less than 5 times in 100, the conventional wisdom of social researchers is that the data cannot be easily explained by chance, so it can be taken seriously. If it is greater than 5 times in 100, it can too easily be explained by chance, according to this standard. The results of his data analysis yielded a p value of 0.15, which did not meet the standard for statistical significance ($p < .05$), so he realized that the data failed to show a meaningful difference between men and women with regard to failure to show up for an appointment. If he repeated this analysis for the next set of clients, he would not be wise to bet a lot of money that he would find that males had the greater tendency than females to no-show. The proportions with a no-show were too close to make such a bet.

In the final step in the research process, Jason concluded that he had failed to find a meaningful relationship between gender and a tendency to fail to show up for an appointment. If he decided on a no-show prevention project, he would have no reason to focus more on men than on women.

INTRODUCTION

In this chapter, you will review how explanatory research examines the relationship between variables because one variable is expected to explain the other. We might think that males receive higher salaries than females. This means that we believe that gender explains salary. We might think that people who exercise are less likely than others to be stressed, so we think that exercise explains stress. Perhaps we have reason to believe that older people are more likely to go the polls and vote. These are all questions that pose a relationship between variables.

A descriptive study, on the other hand, simply describes things one variable at a time, such as the average age of the students in a college course, or the percentage of Hispanics who are unemployed, or the number of families served by an agency who have a pre-school-age child. Each type of study serves a different purpose. The descriptive study describes, and the explanatory study explains. This chapter is about explanatory research.

In this chapter, you will examine key concepts in explanatory research. You will put your new knowledge to use in the collection and analysis of data regarding the relationship between stressors and stress. Your study will also examine the relationship between social support and stress. You will learn how to use an Internet site to employ the Pearson correlation coefficient for the examination of your study hypotheses.

At the end of this chapter, you will be able to do the following:

1. Describe the critical function of each of the four phases of explanatory research and the key tasks that are associated with each phase.

2. Identify the tasks that are associated with each phase of explanatory research.

3. Distinguish between a study variable and a study constant.

4. Describe three levels of measurement (nominal, ordinal, and interval) in social research and how this distinction among variables influences the choice of a statistic for analysis.

5. Describe the distinction between the positive relationship and the negative relationship in explanatory research.

6. Distinguish between descriptive statistics and inferential statistics.

7. Articulate a study hypothesis for an explanatory research study in a proper format.

8. Describe the two pieces of data that determine if a study hypothesis is supported.

9. Describe the connection between random sampling and scientific generalization (as contrasted with logical generalization).

10. Describe how reliability and validity are demonstrated with regard to measurement tools.

11. Employ the statistical analysis of explanatory data in an example using an Internet site.

12. Discuss the connection between data structure and the selection of a statistical measure.

13. Describe how a statistical test can illustrate the empirical relationship between two variables measured at the interval level.

14. Collect data in such a way as to facilitate the statistical analysis of it.

15. Draw conclusions that are consistent with the data analyzed.

In your pursuit of knowledge, you will examine each of the four major phases of research as they are typically undertaken for the explanatory research study. This will be followed by your use of each of these phases with regard to the study to be undertaken on the relationships between stressors, stress, and social support. Your practice exercise will call on you to report the results of your study.

THE FOUR MAJOR PHASES OF EXPLANATORY RESEARCH

This chapter is about the explanatory type of study. It follows the same four phases as other types of research: (1) developing the knowledge base that undergirds the general research purpose (or question), (2) study methods, (3) data analysis, and (4) conclusions. This means that you start with a study purpose (supported by the literature), move to the development of study methods, collect and analyze data, and, finally, draw conclusions about the data. Remember from previous instruction, you do not want to *Put the cart before the horse!* In other words, you do not want to get ahead of yourself by deciding that you wish to conduct a telephone survey before you decide on the purpose of your study. The methods logically follow the determination of the study purpose because certain methods better serve certain purposes.

In this major section of the chapter, you will review the phases of **explanatory research** with an example of the examination of the relationship between stressors and stress as well as the relationship between stress and social support. We will examine the basic research questions, which will be followed by a review of the study methods that logically fit the questions. We examine how to collect and analyze data, and we finish this major section with a discussion of the study conclusions. The second major section of this chapter will take you through this process with specific tasks related to the study of stressors, stress, and social support.

Phase 1: Developing the Research Question and Knowledge Base for the Explanatory Study

The explanatory study process begins with a particular study interest that leads you to develop a study purpose. You may be an elementary school teacher interested in knowing if a certain type of tutoring will be more likely to improve the grades of at-risk students than the traditional type of tutoring. You may be a personal health trainer wanting to know if exercise reduces illness or improves self-esteem. You might be a person who is simply curious about a research question.

A part of this first phase of explanatory research is a review of the knowledge base about the theme. In this regard, you will review the literature. This review will help in defining the study variables and developing the study **hypothesis for a research study**.

If your literature review suggests that stressors cause stress, you would have guidance on the development of a study in which data would be collected on the variables of stressors and stress. This review will help you define the key terms such as *stressors*, *stress*, and *social support*. This definition will guide your determination of how to measure your study variables.

You remember that one of the common-sense phrases is, "Don't reinvent the wheel." If your question has already been well answered with existing literature, maybe this is where you can stop your process. This probably will not be true, because you may have an interest in knowing the answer to your question with regard to a special group of people familiar to yourself, like the students in your college course.

Another function of the review of the literature is to shape your conceptualization of themes and to understand the direction of your research that would be of most benefit. Perhaps you are interested in data that show that males receive higher salaries than females, and that males are more likely to be in management positions, and that managers make more money than those they manage. Therefore, the question that might emerge is whether position level explains the relationship between gender and salary. Do males receive higher salaries only because they are in higher positions? One study conducted by this author found that this was not true. It revealed that annual salaries of male managers were higher than annual salaries of female managers (York, Henley, & Gamble, 1987). Thus, males did not receive higher salaries simply because they were inclined to be in management positions.

The literature review entails the examination of the existing knowledge about your study purpose. This examination reveals unanswered questions from which you can make a choice for your own study. The research question leads logically to the development of a research methodology, which provides details on the way in which you will undertake your study. Data are collected and analyzed, and conclusions are reached about the research question.

Among the themes of special importance to the knowledge base for an explanatory study are (a) theory and (b) the nature of the empirical relationship. These themes will be the focus of the next two sections of this chapter.

Theory in Explanatory Research

A theory is an attempt to explain. It can be formal or informal. A formal theory is published and well recognized. An example is cognitive–behavioral theory, which explains behavior by reference to cognitions. You may be depressed because you have engaged in dysfunctional thinking about your life events. Formal theories are often supported by scientific evidence.

An informal theory is any attempt to explain something, no matter how wise or informed. Some people have the theory that the full moon affects certain kinds of human behaviors. The scientific studies, taken as a whole, have not supported this theory, but the theory exists in some people's minds. You may have developed a theory that your treatment of a child with ADHD (attention-deficit/hyperactivity disorder) will be more effective if you include the parents in most of the treatment sessions. This theory may have been tested in scientific studies, so it would be wise for you to search the literature. The key point here is that a theory is an attempt to explain.

The theory has a critical role in explanatory research. It can guide your inquiry process, from the research question you may pose, to the determination of the variables to be measured, to the articulation of the study hypothesis. "Do you have any theories about the relationships among the variables of stressors, stress, and social support?" In other words, "Do you expect that one of these variables might explain another one?" "Do stressors cause stress?" "Does social support alleviate stress?" These are the key questions you will examine in the practice exercise for this chapter. Each question is based on a theory. You will subject these theories to a scientific study.

The Nature of the Empirical Relationship

When you articulate an explanatory research question, you examine a relationship between the variables. An empirical relationship is a relationship between variables that is demonstrated by research data, rather than your opinion. If there is a relationship between two variables, there is a pattern in the data that reveals it. You would expect the proportion of senior citizens with serious health problems to be higher than that of younger citizens. That is the pattern you would expect to find if you analyzed the data regarding these two variables. In other words, you would analyze the data to see if the proportion of senior citizens with serious illnesses was greater than the proportion of younger people with serious illnesses. You might expect that students with higher scores for self-esteem would have higher school grades. You could examine the data on these two variables to see if there is a significant correlation between them.

Positive and Negative Relationships

Some variables are measured in the form of scores (e.g., scores on the Beck Depression Inventory) or numbers (e.g., age as measured in years). If you measured two variables as scores on a scale, you can examine whether the relationship between them is negative or positive. When there is a **positive relationship** between two such variables, higher values on one of the variables are associated with higher values on the other variable. Suppose, for example, that you asked a group of people to complete a stress scale where higher scores indicated higher stress, and you asked them to indicate the number of times in the past year they had experienced a minor illness. You would expect to find a positive relationship between these variables because you would expect that those higher on stress would also be higher on minor illnesses. You would likely expect to find a positive relationship between self-esteem and grades in school or between depression and the number of days absent from work. The greater you possess one of these conditions, the greater you are expected to possess the other one.

When there is a **negative relationship** between two variables, higher values on one of these variables would be associated with lower values on the other variable. You would expect to find a negative relationship between depression and grades in school. In other words, the *more* depressed you are, the *lower* would be your grades.

When you measure either of your variables as a set of categories rather than as a score, you would normally not speak of the relationship between them as being either positive or negative. Instead, you would report the proportions of people in various categories as a depiction of the relationship between the variables. Suppose, for example, that you expected that people who regularly engage in aerobic exercise would be less likely to have experienced recent minor illnesses. You could collect data on these two variables. You would ask each person if he or she engaged in regular aerobic exercise, and you would also ask them if he or she had or had not experienced minor illnesses in the past 6 months. If the proportion of exercisers with recent minor illnesses were found to be lower than that of the nonexercisers, you would have data that supported your expectation.

Phase 2: Developing the Study Methods for the Explanatory Study

The second major phase of explanatory research is the development of the study methods to be used in order to find the answer to your research question. This entails the selection of a group of people to provide data for your study (your study sample) from a given population of people (your study population). It also entails the selection of tools for measuring your study variables, the articulation of your study hypothesis, and the selection of a statistic for testing your hypothesis.

Sampling in Explanatory Research

From previous instruction in this book, you know that the purpose for the careful examination of the nature of the study sample and study population is to determine the extent to which you should believe that your data are relevant to people not in your study sample. If you have a random sample of the members of your chapter of the National Association of Social Workers (NASW), you can scientifically generalize your study findings to the members of this chapter of NASW. This means that you would likely feel okay about betting your money that you would find the same results (generally) if you conducted another study of another random sample of people from your chapter of NASW. If you do not have *a random sample*, you must rely on logic for your generalization. Why would you believe that a convenience sample of members of your research class would be similar or different from the larger population of students from which your sample was drawn? If you have data on your research class and the study population (e.g., all students in your college social work program) that shows similarity on important variables, you could use this information to make the case of **logical generalization of study results**. In other words, you would assert that you can logically generalize your findings to this population.

Measurement in Explanatory Research

In addition to sampling, the study methods phase of the research process entails the development of the tools to measure our study variables. You must select (or develop) tools that are credible. One aspect of credibility is the relevance of your tool to our definition of the appropriate variable. You should not, for example, have items on your scale for measuring knowledge that seem to be a better fit for a scale to measure opinions. Another aspect of credibility is the reliability and validity of your tool.

Reliability and Validity in Measurement

Validity refers to the accuracy of an instrument. How well does it measure the thing it was supposed to measure? Validity is typically tested by computing the correlation between a given tool and a similar instrument that is designed to measure the same thing. If you gave two different scales for measuring self-esteem to a sample of people, you would expect to find a positive correlation that is relatively high (e.g., correlation of .70 or higher). This is evidence of validity.

There are several other techniques for testing for validity. A simple form of validity is face validity, which refers to the question of whether the tool appears (on the face of it) to be valid (accurate) in the eyes of persons who are knowledgeable. If a group of psycho-therapists say that your depression scale truly measures depression, you have evidence of face validity.

Reliability refers to the consistency of the tool. Does the tool work the same way when administered more than one time? For example, would your score on a particular depression scale be about the same this week as next week, assuming that we have no reason to believe that your depression has changed? If so, we can say that the tool passed the test of test–retest reliability. Does the tool have internal consistency? If so, we would find a positive correlation between each of the various items on the scale and each of the other items on the scale. If, on the other hand, we found a negative correlation of Item 5 with most other items, we would have reason to believe that this item does not seem to be measuring the same thing as the other items, and, therefore, weakens the internal consistency of the instrument. This would be evidence against the reliability of the measurement device. A simple technique for testing for internal consistency is sometimes referred to as the split-half method. With this technique, you simply create a new variable that contains all the odd-numbered items on the scale, and you create another new variable that contains all the even-numbered items on the scale. They you compute a correlation between these two variables. If you find a relatively high positive correlation, you have evidence of reliability.

Measurement tools that have been published typically have been tested for reliability and validity. They have also been developed by experts on the subject of the scale. For example, the Beck Depression Inventory was developed by an expert on depression. Beck had engaged in a lot of study of the nature of depression and had experience that was useful in determining what should be on a scale for measuring it. For these reasons, you are advised to first look for a published scale when you must measure a psychosocial variable before taking on the task of developing your own tool.

The Study Hypothesis in Explanatory Research

A task for explanatory research (but not descriptive research) is the statement of the study hypothesis. The hypothesis is your prediction of the study results that reveals the structure of your data analysis. Examples include the following: (1) Older people are more likely than younger people to vote for president. (2) Depression scores will be lower at the end of psychotherapy than before psychotherapy began. (3) People with higher incomes will have higher happiness than people with lower incomes. Each of these hypotheses are concise statements that reveal the variables to be tested and the direction of the relationship.

The study hypothesis is a precise statement, not normal talk in clinical conversations. It should be specific and focused. It should not assert causation. For example, you should *not* state the hypothesis as, "Clients will have more positive feelings of support because of the support group experience." Causation is a complex concept that is not determined solely by data regarding the relationships between the cause and the effect.

Finding a Statistic for Testing the Hypothesis

In the search for a statistic to test our hypothesis, we need to know the data structure. Among the questions to be posed in the determination of the data structure are the number of variables in the analysis and the level of measurement of each variable. In Exhibit 7.1, you can see a few examples of data structure and possible statistics for that structure. You can see, for example, that the chi-square statistic is appropriate if you are examining the relationship between two variables where each is measured at the nominal level. But that is not our situation. Instead, we are examining the relationship between two variables (e.g., stressors and stress), where each is measured at the interval level. As you can see from Exhibit 7.1, we can use the Pearson correlation coefficient to test our hypothesis. There are many more statistics for various structures. Exhibit 7.1 contains only a few examples.

Phase 3: Collection and Analysis of Data for the Explanatory Study

In the third phase of explanatory research, you will collect and analyze data. You will administer the tools to measure study variables to your study subjects. You will also test your study hypothesis by determining not only whether your data revealed the expected relationship between study variables but also whether this relationship was found to be statistically significant. When you begin this phase, you will have a study hypothesis that was articulated in the study methods phase of explanatory research.

The data analysis phase of explanatory research entails the administration of your tools to those in your sample as well as the examination of your data to determine if the

EXHIBIT 7.1
A FEW EXAMPLES OF DATA STRUCTURES AND POSSIBLE STATISTICS

Data Structure	A Possible Statistic
You are examining the relationship between two variables where each is measured at the nominal level	(1). Chi-square (2). Fisher exact test (only if each variable is dichotomous)
You are examining the relationship between two variables measured at the interval level	Pearson correlation coefficient
You are comparing the matched scores (interval level) of one group of persons	Paired t test
You are comparing the scores (interval level) of two groups of people	Independent t test

data confirmed your hypothesis. For you to report that your data confirmed your study hypothesis, you must answer YES to EACH of these two questions:

1. Were your data in the hypothesized direction?

2. Were your data statistically significant?

If your answer to either of these questions is NO, you will say that your data failed to support the study hypothesis.

One of your tasks in this phase of explanatory research is the determination of your standard for statistical significance. In the social sciences, the conventional wisdom is that a p value that is less than .05 is sufficient for determining statistical significance. In other words, if your data would occur by chance less than 5 times in 100, you can say that you have ruled out chance as the explanation of your data. When you rule out chance, you can take your data seriously with regard to your research question. This standard, however, is arbitrary. There is no scientific basis for establishing .05 as the standard rather than .10 or some other value. As you will see in a later chapter, the determination of your standard relies on the extent to which you wish to be conservative in the interpretation of your data.

Phase 4: Drawing Conclusions in Explanatory Research

The fourth major phase of the explanatory study is the drawing of conclusions. Your first task is to reflect on whether the data supported the hypothesis. If it did support the hypothesis, your conclusion would be that you found a relationship between your two study variables. If your variables are measures as scores, you would indicate whether you found a positive or a negative relationship between the two variables. You might, for example, conclude that you found a negative relationship between social support and stress. This means that the higher your social support, the lower is your level of stress.

If your data failed to support your hypothesis, your conclusion would be that you failed to find a relationship between the two variables. This should be your conclusion if your data failed to be statistically significant, even if your data went in the hypothesized direction. Suppose, for example, that you found a negative correlation between social support and stress that is considered to be a weak correlation (e.g., -.23) and your p value is .27. Do you conclude that you found a weak negative relationship between support and stress? You should say NO to this question because your data can too easily be explained by chance. Instead, you conclude that you failed to find a relationship between these two variables.

It is advisable that you start the conclusion section with a statement related to what was found about the research question or study purpose. For example, your first sentence in your conclusions section of your report might be, "This study of 23 social work students found a negative relationship between social support and stress, meaning that those with more support had lower stress."

The conclusions part of the research report should also address the limitations of the study. One source of limitation could be the sample selected. If it is not a random sample, you cannot scientifically generalize your findings. Another limitation can be found in the credibility of the tools used to measure study variables. If your tools have not been tested for reliability and validity, this should be reported. The conclusion section should also discuss the implications of this study for practice (or life).

In the next section of this chapter, you will review an example of an explanatory study. It seeks to add knowledge to what we know about life satisfaction with a focus on both stress and social support. We would expect to find that stress has a negative relationship with life satisfaction. In other words, the more stress you have, the less is your life satisfaction. On the other hand, we would expect to find a positive relationship between social support and life satisfaction because those with more support would likely have more life satisfaction than would those with less support. This example will provide the framework for the practice exercise for this chapter where you will conduct your own study of the relationships between these variables.

AN EXPLANATORY RESEARCH STUDY EXAMPLE: DOES STRESS OR SOCIAL SUPPORT EXPLAIN LIFE SATISFACTION?

In this research example, you will examine the four major phases of explanatory research for a study that was conducted in 2017 about the relationship of stress and life satisfaction as well as the relationship between social support and life satisfaction. This means that you will review the 2017 study of life satisfaction by (1) reviewing the research questions and the knowledge base that informed the study, (2) examining the research methods employed, (3) analyzing the data, and (4) reviewing the conclusions that were drawn by the author of this study.

You will undertake these same steps in the practice exercise for this chapter. That exercise calls on you to employ the same research methods of the 2017 study in your own study of these research questions. However, you will select your own study sample, administer the tools used to measure study variables, collect and analyze data from your study sample, and draw appropriate conclusions from your study results. In other words, the first phase of research for your study will be identical to that of the 2017 study. Your study will also be identical to the 2017 study with regard to the instruments employed to measure study variables. But you will have a different study sample, a different analysis of data, and a different set of conclusions.

Phase 1: The Research Questions and Knowledge Base for the 2017 Study of Life Satisfaction

The 2017 study examined explanations for life satisfaction, with a focus on stress and social support. Logic would suggest that stress and life satisfaction would have a negative relationship. In other words, people who have higher stress would be expected to have lower life satisfaction. Logic would also suggest that we would find a positive relationship between social support and life satisfaction. This means that we would find that people with higher support would have higher life satisfaction.

This is what logic would suggest. A review of the literature, however, can help clarify these expectations. You can see a brief review of the literature about life satisfaction in

Exhibit 7.2. This review suggested that both social support and stress are related to life satisfaction, but it did not clarify whether one of these variables (stress or social support) would do a better job of explaining life satisfaction. Hence, the 2017 study examined whether either of these two variables (stress or support) did a better job than the other variable in the explanation of life satisfaction. The 2017 study examined these questions using a sample of social work students.

There are three research questions examined in the 2017 study as follows:

1. Is there a negative relationship between stress and life satisfaction?

2. Is there a positive relationship between social support and life satisfaction?

EXHIBIT 7.2
A BRIEF OVERVIEW OF LIFE SATISFACTION

Life satisfaction is one's overall assessment of feelings and attitudes toward life at a particular point in time. It refers to how we assess our lives in general, not in relation to a given dimension such as health, work, or family. It is one of several dimensions of well-being. Life satisfaction is about one's overall assessment of how life has gone rather than an immediate feeling, such as happiness. One of the scales for measuring life satisfaction is the Satisfaction with Life Scale (Diener, Emmons, Larsen, & Griffin, 1985). On this scale are five items that are rated by the respondent. These items include reference to your life satisfaction in general, how well things have gone in life for you in general, and whether you would make changes in your life if it were to be done over.

Research on life satisfaction has indicated that it has a negative relationship with psychological disorders such as depression and anxiety (Proctor, Linley, & Maltbe, 2009). In other words, satisfied people are less likely to have psychological disorders.

Many variables have been examined as predictors of life satisfaction. A place to look for explanations of life satisfaction that is not fruitful are demographic characteristics such as race, age, gender, and social class. Apparently, life satisfaction does not differ in a noteworthy fashion based on these characteristics of people. Better explanations for life satisfaction can be found in variables such as social support and related variables such as social connections and social engagement (Brown, Macdonald, & Mitchell, 2015; Lewis, Huebner, Malone, & Valios, 2011; Proctor et al., 2009). Another explanatory variable for life satisfaction is stress. Those who exhibit more stress tend to perceive that they have lived less satisfactory lives (Burger & Robin, 2017).

There are a number of other variables that have been studied as predictors of life satisfaction, but social support and stress are among the most noteworthy ones. A question that arises is whether these variables do a good job of explaining life satisfaction for any given group of people. In the study reviewed in the practice exercise in this chapter, the study sample was a group of undergraduate social work students. "Does support do a good job of explaining life satisfaction or a moderate job of doing so?" The same question could be posed regarding the variable of stress. A third question could be whether one of these variables does a better job than the other in the explanation of life satisfaction. For example, "Is the correlation of social support and life satisfaction stronger than the correlation of life satisfaction and stress?"

3. Is the strength of the relationship between stress and life satisfaction stronger, or weaker, than the strength of the relationship between social support and life satisfaction?

A brief review of the knowledge base for this study is presented in Exhibit 7.2.

Phase 2: Research Methods for the 2017 Study of Life Satisfaction

The study methods for the 2017 study of life satisfaction contain information on the study sample, the means used to measure study variables, and the study hypotheses.

Study Sample

A group of 39 social work students were administered the tools used to measure stress, social support, and life satisfaction. These study subjects were enrolled in two undergraduate classes in a School of Social Work in the Fall Semester of 2017. These 39 students were the ones who attended a given class in this course, which enlisted a total of 55 students. Students who did not participate were not present in class on the day the data were collected. All who were in attendance agreed to participate.

Ethics in the Use of Human Subjects in Research

Three variables were measured on the questionnaire given to the study respondents: (1) life satisfaction, (2) stress, and (3) social support. The questionnaire started with the following instructions:

You are asked to participate in a study that will be used for research exercises and may be published at some time in the future. Your participation is voluntary and anonymous. If you wish not to participate, you can turn in a blank form when they are collected. Do not place your name on this questionnaire so that your responses will remain anonymous.

These instructions addressed the ethical issues of voluntary participation and privacy. The issue of harm was not relevant, given the nature of the study. In other words, there was no logical reason to believe that study participants would be harmed by completing a questionnaire that measured the three variables in this study. Likewise, justice was not an issue because the recipients of the results of this study would be the participants themselves, because the data were employed in a learning exercise for these students.

Measurement of Study Variables

Measurement begins with the identification of the variables to be included in the study. The 2017 study included the variables of life satisfaction, stress, and social support. The next step is the definition of the variables to be measured. With definitions in hand, you are in a position to find, or construct, the tools to measure your designated variables.

The Measurement of Life Satisfaction

Life satisfaction was defined as the extent to which a person's perceptions are positive about his or her life experience as a whole, rather than specific aspects of life such as health, work, family, and so forth. It is different from happiness, which is related to feelings and moods at the present rather than a reflection on life as a whole. Life satisfaction was measured by the tool given in Exhibit 7.3. It has five items for which respondents were asked to rate their perceptions on a 5-point scale, with higher values representing a more positive perception of life. Therefore, one's score could range from a low of 5 to a high of 25, with scores above 15 representing a positive perception of one's life.

The Measurement of Stress

For the 2017 study, stress was defined as a state of psychological tension exemplified by emotions such as *tense*, *uneasy*, and *nervous* and which is considered the opposite of concepts such as *restful*, *pleasant*, and *cheerful*. The tool for measuring stress for the

---

EXHIBIT 7.3
LIFE SATISFACTION SCALE USED IN THE 2017 STUDY

Examine each of the statements below about your life, and draw a circle around the phrase that indicates the level of your agreement with that statement. In other words, you will indicate, with each statement, if you (1) *strongly disagree*, (2) *disagree*, (3) *neither agree nor disagree*, (4) *agree*, or (5) *strongly agree*.

Statement	Level of Agreement				
In most ways, my life has been what I have wanted it to be.	(1) Strongly disagree	(2) Disagree	(3) Neither agree nor disagree	(4) Agree	(5) Strongly agree
The circumstances of my life have usually been excellent.	(1) Strongly disagree	(2) Disagree	(3) Neither agree nor disagree	(4) Agree	(5) Strongly agree
I am satisfied with what life has offered me.	(1) Strongly disagree	(2) Disagree	(3) Neither agree nor disagree	(4) Agree	(5) Strongly agree
So far, I have accomplished the important things I have wanted to accomplish in life.	(1) Strongly disagree	(2) Disagree	(3) Neither agree nor disagree	(4) Agree	(5) Strongly agree
If I could live my life over, I would change very little.	(1) Strongly disagree	(2) Disagree	(3) Neither agree nor disagree	(4) Agree	(5) Strongly agree

EXHIBIT 7.4

THE STRESS SCALE FOR THE 2017 STUDY

Please review each of the following terms, and decide if it is a feeling you have experienced in the past few months *hardly ever, some of the* *time, or a great deal of the time.* Circle your response to each word.

Strained	(1) Hardly ever	(2) Some of the time	(3) A great deal of the time
Jolly	(3) Hardly ever	(2) Some of the time	(1) A great deal of the time
Edgy	(1) Hardly ever	(2) Some of the time	(3) A great deal of the time
Composed	(3) Hardly ever	(2) Some of the time	(1) A great deal of the time
Unglued	(1) Hardly ever	(2) Some of the time	(3) A great deal of the time
Satisfied	(3) Hardly ever	(2) Some of the time	(1) A great deal of the time
Pleased	(3) Hardly ever	(2) Some of the time	(1) A great deal of the time
Agitated	(1) Hardly ever	(2) Some of the time	(3) A great deal of the time
Shook-up	(1) Hardly ever	(2) Some of the time	(3) A great deal of the time
Joyful	(3) Hardly ever	(2) Some of the time	(1) A great deal of the time

2017 study is presented in Exhibit 7.4. It has 10 words, some of which indicate stress and some of which indicate the opposite of stress. For those that represent stress, a response of *a great deal of the time* was given 3 points, a response of *some of the time* was given 2 points, and a response of *hardly ever* was given a score of 1 point. Words on this scale that represented the opposite of stress were reverse-scored, so that a reply of *a great deal of the time* got 1 point, a response of *some of the time* got 2 points, and a response of *hardly ever* got 3 points. Therefore, higher scores represented a higher level of stress.

The Measurement of Social Support

For 2017 study, social support was defined as a set of feelings that others care about oneself and are prepared to offer assistance when needed. It prevents the feeling of social isolation. It was measured by the tool given in Exhibit 7.5, which provides higher scores for higher levels of social support. This tool has three items that ask for your satisfaction with the level of support you receive from (1) friends, (2) family, and (3) others. Each item has four response levels: (1) *unsatisfied*, (2) *undecided*, (3) *satisfied*, and (4) *very satisfied*. Scores for each item can range from a low of 1 (for unsatisfied) to a high of 4 (for very satisfied). Therefore, scores on this scale can range from a low of 3 to a high of 12, with scores above 8 representing a positive perception of social support.

EXHIBIT 7.5

SOCIAL SUPPORT SCALE USED IN THE 2017 STUDY

Please indicate below your level of satisfaction with social support by responding to each item below.

(a) How satisfied are you with the extent of support you receive from friends?

___(1) unsatisfied   (2) ___undecided   ___(3) satisfied   ___(4) very satisfied

(b) How satisfied are you with the extent of support you receive from relatives?

___(1) unsatisfied   (2) ___undecided   ___(3) satisfied   ___(4) very satisfied

(c) How satisfied are you with the extent of support you receive from others (i.e., not friends or relatives)?

___(1) unsatisfied   (2) ___undecided   ___(3) satisfied   ___(4) very satisfied

---

Testing the Reliability and Validity of the Measurement Tools

The three measurement tools used in the 2017 study of life satisfaction were designed by the author of this text especially for this study. New tools were designed to simplify the study methods for the sake of the practice exercise employed in this chapter. The new tools were not designed to be published for widespread use as tools for measuring these variables. If they had been so designed, the issue of reliability and validity would have been extensively tested. But these issues were not ignored. In Exhibit 7.6, you can see an explanation of how these tools were tested for reliability and validity in a limited way.

In summary, you have been given a description of the study sample and the measurement tools for the 2017 study of life satisfaction. These tools were administered to this study sample to test the hypotheses related to the relationships between life satisfaction, stress, and social support.

Phase 3: Data Analysis for the 2017 Study of Life Satisfaction

The data analysis phase of explanatory research entails the articulation of the study hypotheses and the testing of the hypotheses with the data that were collected. This requires the collection of data and the selection of a statistic for the testing of each study hypothesis. In addition, certain descriptive data are typically given on the variables that are measured and the characteristics of the study sample.

Descriptive Data Analysis

We will begin with the descriptive data. While the 2017 study of life satisfaction is fundamentally an explanatory study, descriptive analysis of the characteristics of the study sample can be helpful to readers of the study results on the generalization of the study results. You will find that almost all published studies will have descriptive data about the study sample that was employed, whether this study be descriptive, explanatory, evaluative, or exploratory.

EXHIBIT 7.6

TESTING THE RELIABILITY AND VALIDITY OF THE TOOLS FOR THE 2017 STUDY OF LIFE SATISFACTION

Each of the tools for the measurement of variables for the 2017 study of life satisfaction were designed to measure the variables as defined for the study, but they were also patterned after existing tools for measuring each of these variables. The goal was to develop tools that were simpler.

A method employed for the testing of the reliability of each tool was the examination of the internal consistency of each scale. Internal consistency means that the items on the scale are measuring the same thing. We would expect to find a positive correlation between the first item on a given scale and the second item on this scale. The same would be true of our expectations of all other comparisons of items on a given scale. If they are all positively correlated, we would have evidence that the scale is consistent, in that all items are measuring the same thing. Internal consistency can be tested with a formula known as the alpha coefficient, which examines all correlations of items on a given scale. A value for this coefficient of .70 or higher is expected for good evidence of internal consistency. The alpha coefficients for each of these three scales were found to be .70 or above. (For the life satisfaction scale, the alpha was .76; for the stress scale, the alpha was .84; for the support scale, the alpha was .70.)

A method for testing the validity of a scale is to see if it has a positive correlation with another scale designed to measure the same thing. Each of the three scales used in the 2017 study were examined in this way. The stress scale employed here had a correlation of .37 ($p < .05$) with the stress items on the Stress Arousal Checklist (see York, 1997, p. 26). This correlation was statistically significant but was weaker in strength than we would expect to find in such a test. The support scale had a correlation of .76 ($p < .001$) with the Interpersonal Support Evaluation List (Cohen & Hoberman, 1983), while the life satisfaction scale used in the 2017 study had a correlation of .80 ($p < .001$) with the Life Satisfaction Scale (Diener et al., 1985).

These results confirmed the conclusion that the scales used in the 2017 study of life satisfaction have a reasonable amount of credibility. They were found to have items that were internally consistent, meaning that the scales were reliable. They were also found to be positively correlated with published scales designed to measure the same variables; thus, they were valid.

Data were collected on the gender, age, and race of the 39 persons in the study sample. For this group of research students, 83% were female, while 17% were male. Regarding age, 61% were below the age of 30 years, while 39% were 30 years of age or older. For race, 68% were White, 15% were African American, and 17% were in the category of Other for race.

Scores on the scale measuring life satisfaction have a possible range from a low of 5 to a high of 25. The lowest score for life satisfaction given by the 39 students in this study was 9, while the highest score for anyone was 24. The mean score for life satisfaction was 16.48.

Scores on the scale measuring stress for this study can range from a low of 10 to a high of 30. The lowest score for this sample of respondents was 13, while the highest score was 28. The mean score for stress was 18.87.

The scale measuring social support for these study subjects can range from a low of 3 to a high of 12. The lowest score for the students in this study was 3, while the highest score was 12. The mean for social support was 8.64.

This review of descriptive data can reveal the general tendencies of study participants on the variables being measured. For example, you can examine the question of whether these individuals tend to be satisfied with life, to feel a lot of stress, or to perceive they have good social support. If almost all participants were found to have very high life satisfaction, you could conclude that you do not have a measure of life satisfaction that is very good. With little variance among study participants, you do not have a good variable.

Another way in which descriptive data can be helpful in an explanatory study lies in the category of the **generalization of study results**. You know that you can generalize your findings from your study sample to your designated study population on a scientific basis only if you have a random sample. Logical generalization, on the other hand, is an informed opinion. One basis for asserting an informed opinion is by comparing the characteristics of your study sample with what you know about your designated study population. In the 2017 study, descriptive data were collected only on the study sample, so logical generalization was not an option.

Testing the Study Hypotheses

There are three research questions for the 2017 study of life satisfaction. Each of the first two research questions were turned into study hypotheses by reference to what is expected, given the knowledge base that has been presented. The first research question asks if stress has a negative relationship with life satisfaction. This question was turned into the following study hypothesis: There will be a negative relationship between scores on the stress scale and scores on the life satisfaction scale. The second research question was turned into this hypothesis: There will be a positive relationship between scores on the social support scale and scores on the life satisfaction scale.

There was not a knowledge base offered in the 2017 study that would predict the results for the third research question, which asks if either stress or support does a better job of explaining life satisfaction. In this situation, the study simply examined the results of the testing of the first two hypotheses, and a conclusion was drawn about whether the strength of one correlation was notably higher than the strength of the other correlation. The basis for this conclusion was logical, rather than scientific. However, there are more scientific means for examining this question, but the statistics for that analysis are not feasible for this chapter, so we will examine the third question only from a logical standpoint.

The Statistical Tests for Examining the Hypotheses in the 2017 Study of Life Satisfaction

There were two hypotheses tested in the 2017 study of life satisfaction. When you seek to find a statistic for testing a study hypothesis, you must know the structure of the data. You need to know the level of measurement of each variable and the form of the administration of the scales. For each of our study hypotheses, there were two variables where each was measured at the interval level (i.e., scores). Thus, the same statistical test was employed for the testing of each of these two study hypotheses.

The Pearson Correlation Coefficient

An appropriate statistic for the testing of the hypotheses for the 2017 study of life satisfaction was the Pearson correlation coefficient (see Exhibit 7.1). The Pearson correlation coefficient is appropriate for the testing of the hypothesis for the examination of the relationship between two variables when each variable is measured at the interval level (i.e., a score). This was the situation with each of the two hypotheses; thus, a correlation coefficient was computed for the relationship between stress and life satisfaction in one of the statistical analyses, and a correlation coefficient was also computed for the relationship between social support and life satisfaction in the other analysis.

The examination of the third research question was simply a logical comparison of the correlation coefficients of the testing of the hypotheses regarding the first two research questions. The third research question was whether stress did a better job of explaining life satisfaction than did social support (or vice versa). If the correlation coefficient for stress and life satisfaction was stronger than the correlation coefficient for social support and life satisfaction, we could answer in the affirmative to this question. However, if the correlation coefficient between stress and life satisfaction was weaker (i.e., lower) than the correlation coefficient between social support and life satisfaction, we would have support for the conclusion that it is support rather than stress that does the better job of explaining life satisfaction. If the correlation coefficients for each of these two analyses were rather similar, it would be logical to conclude that neither of these variables (stress or support) does a better job of explaining life satisfaction than the other. In practical terms, it was believed that two correlation coefficients that are less than 25% different would be considered not different on a noteworthy basis. This decision is a matter of opinion. Whether the noteworthy difference should be 25% or 35% or some other percent is not as much of a scientific decision as a logical one. It is legitimate for your opinion to differ from this opinion. There are statistical tests that are available for a scientific examination of this third research question, but they are technically beyond the scope of this chapter. Instead, you will only have the strength of each correlation as the data for your opinion.

You can see an explanation of Pearson correlation coefficient in Exhibit 7.7. You can also see an explanation for the fact that correlation does not alone mean causation in the explanation given in Exhibit 7.8. Without correlation, you do not have a case for causation. With correlation, you have one argument for causation, but your argument is not complete until you review the other conditions for causation. The data in the 2017 study only provide information for the examination of one of these conditions for causation (i.e., the relationship between the two variables).

Data on the Relationships of Stress, Social Support, and Life Satisfaction

The scores for each of the three variables in the 2017 study for each of the 39 persons in the study are displayed in Exhibit 7.9. You can see the scores for this group on life satisfaction, stress, and social support. The variables are listed in the columns, and the persons are listed in the rows. For example, the scores for the first person are given in the first row (with scores of 13, 22, and 8 for satisfaction, stress, and support, respectively).

The scores in Exhibit 7.9 were entered into a statistical database using SPSS to examine each of the two hypotheses for the 2017 study of life satisfaction. The relationship between stress and life satisfaction was examined with the correlation coefficient.

EXHIBIT 7.7
THE PEARSON CORRELATION COEFFICIENT

The Pearson correlation coefficient is a statistic for examining the relationship between two variables where each is measured at the interval level (e.g., a score on a scale). The value of the coefficient can range from a low of 0 to a high of 1.0. A correlation coefficient of 0 means there is no relationship at all between the two variables. A correlation coefficient of 1.0 means there is a perfect relationship between the two variable.

The coefficients can be either positive or negative. If the correlation is negative, you will find a negative sign in front of the value of the coefficient (e.g., -.22). This means that you have found that higher scores on one of the two variables are associated with lower scores on the other variable. You might expect, for example, to find a negative correlation between numerical grades in school (0–100) and scores on a depression scale because you expect that those with higher depression will have lower grades in school.

If you have a positive correlation, you will not find a sign in front of the correlation coefficient (e.g., .34). This correlation means that higher values of one of the two variables are associated with higher values on the other. For example, you would expect to find a positive correlation between numerical grades in school and scores on a self-esteem scale because those higher on self-esteem would be expected to be higher on grades.

Higher values of the coefficient indicate stronger relationships. Coefficients that are above .70 are considered to indicate a very strong relationship between the two variables. Coefficients between .50 and .70 are considered to represent a strong relationship between the two variables, while coefficients between .30 and .50 are considered moderate. Coefficients between .1 and .3 are considered weak, while coefficients of .1 or lower are considered very weak.

EXHIBIT 7.8
CORRELATION AND CAUSATION

You examine the correlation between two variables because you think that one might explain the other. In other words, you think that one variable may be the cause of the other. Does depression cause people to have worse grades in school? If you find a correlation between depression scores and grades in school, you have evidence on one of the three conditions for causation. The other two conditions for causation are time order and the elimination of alternative causes. If a change in depression is followed by a change in school grades, you would have evidence for depression as a cause of grades. This is the time–order condition. If you find that other variables are not causes of grades, you have a better argument for depression as the cause. This is the alternative

cause condition. A full examination of causation would entail the examination of evidence on all three conditions. If there is not a correlation between depression and grades, however, you have evidence that depression does not cause grades. The same could be said for the other two conditions for causation.

Therefore, correlation is one of the conditions for determining causation. Without it, you do not have evidence for causation. But correlation does not equal causation. You need further information to fully examine the causation issue. In explanatory research, we often have data on only one of the three conditions for causation; thus, a full examination of this issue requires further inquiry.

EXHIBIT 7.9
SCORES FOR LIFE SATISFACTION, STRESS, AND SOCIAL SUPPORT FOR THE 2017 STUDY

Person	Life Satisfaction Score	Stress Score	Social Support Score
1	13	22	8
2	19	14	11
3	15	16	7
4	24	13	12
5	21	17	10
6	16	21	8
7	13	22	12
8	17	23	9
9	13	21	8
10	18	16	6
11	20	22	8
12	17	22	9
13	11	20	8
14	20	22	11
15	17	13	6
16	18	18	9
17	10	25	7
18	12	22	5
19	17	16	8
20	23	13	11
21	15	17	3
22	18	17	9
23	12	20	7
24	14	14	10
25	13	17	10
26	9	28	7
27	10	26	6
28	16	15	9
29	20	17	12
30	18	17	9

(Continued)

EXHIBIT 7.9 (Continued)

Person	Life Satisfaction Score	Stress Score	Social Support Score
31	12	20	8
32	15	15	7
33	19	20	10
34	20	14	10
35	23	20	10
36	20	25	8
37	20	17	9
38	18	18	11
39	17	21	9

The value of this correlation coefficient was found to be negative. It was −.49 ($p < .01$). The negative value of this correlation coefficient revealed that those with higher stress scores had lower scores for life satisfaction. The p value, of course, represents the level of statistical significance that was achieved. This p value means that these data would occur by chance less than 1 time in 100.

The correlation coefficient between life satisfaction and social support was found to be .54 ($p < .001$). The positive value of this coefficient was revealed by the lack of a minus sign in front of it. This positive coefficient indicated that those higher on social support were higher on life satisfaction.

We can examine, logically, whether one of these two variables (stress or social support) does a better job of explaining life satisfaction. The correlation coefficients indicate the strength of the relationship. A higher correlation would indicate a stronger relationship. In our case, the values of the two correlation coefficients were rather similar (.49 and .54). There are statistical tests for determining if this difference is statistically significant, but these tests are beyond the scope of the research lessons in this exercise. Furthermore, the similarity of these coefficients would suggest that such an analysis is not warranted.

Phase 4: Conclusions for the 2017 Study of Life Satisfaction

What are the appropriate conclusions for the 2017 study of life satisfaction? Your conclusions should focus primarily on your data with regard to your major research questions. "Did the data reveal that those higher on social support were more satisfied with life?" "Was this relationship found to be statistically significant?" "Was this correlation noteworthy from a practical viewpoint?" In other words, "Was the relationship strong enough to attract our attention if we are interested in knowing what explains life satisfaction?" "Did the data suggest that those who were higher on stress were lower on life satisfaction?" "Was this correlation statistically significant?" "Was the strength of this relationship noteworthy?" These are some of the questions you will answer in the first practice exercise for this chapter.

Chapter Practice Exercises

There are two practice exercises for this chapter. In the first exercise, you will summarize the results of the 2017 study of life satisfaction. In the second exercise, you will conduct your own study of life satisfaction using the same tools employed in the 2017 study.

Practice Exercise 1: Reporting on the 2017 Study of Life Satisfaction

In this practice exercise, you will be asked a set of questions about the 2017 study of life satisfaction that was described in the previous section. Your answer to these questions will reveal your preparation for conducting your own study of this theme, which will be the focus of Practice Exercise 2. Your job for Practice Exercise 1 is to prepare a report that answers each of the following questions. In your report, provide the specific question and the answer to that question in each case.

1. What are the three research questions examined in the 2017 study of life satisfaction?

2. What is one thing you can report from the literature review that supports one of the study hypotheses for this study? In other words, what was reported there that would suggest that we would find the results that are displayed in one of the two hypotheses for this study?

3. Identify the study sample used in this study.

Examples: The members of the Oak Ridge Swimmers Club who attended a meeting in November 2019; the members of a social work research class who attended a class where the questionnaire was administered in March 2019.

4. Describe the study population.

Examples: Members of the Oak Ridge Swimmers Club; students in the School of Social Work where the questionnaire was administered; students in Schools of Social Work in the United States.

5. Can the results of this study be scientifically generalized to this population? Explain why or why not.

6. What information might you analyze to determine if the results of this study could be generalized to the study population on a logical basis?

7. Identify one of the variables measured in this study and provide the definition of it.

8. Describe how the variable identified in the previous question was measured for this study.

Example: Respondents were measured on marital satisfaction with a set of 10 positive statements about the marriage, to which they selected either Yes or No and received 1 point for each response of Yes; thus, scores could range from a low of 0 to a high of 10.

9. In your opinion, did the tool for measuring the above variable fit well with the definition of the variable as presented in the description? Briefly explain.

10. Were either of the study variables tested for reliability? Were either of them tested for validity? (Answer each of these questions as Yes or No)

11. What was one of the two hypotheses that were tested in this study?

12. What statistical test was used to test the hypothesis identified in the previous question?

13. Did the data support this first hypothesis? Explain your answer with regard to the facts from the statistical analysis of the data (i.e., the value of the correlation coefficient and the value of p).

14. What was the second hypothesis that was tested in this study?

15. Did the data support this second hypothesis? Explain with regard to the facts.

16. Did the results suggest that support did a better job of explaining life satisfaction than did stress? Explain with data.

17. What were your conclusions for this study?

Practice Exercise 2: Conducting Your Own Study of Life Satisfaction

Your task in this exercise is to collect and analyze your own data using the same variables as those in the previous exercises. What will be new will be information on your study sample, your study population, your analysis of data, and your study conclusions.

Step 1: Select a Study Sample From a Designated Study Population

Your first step is to select a study sample. This might be the students in your research class or the members of a social group that is convenient. If you are ambitious, you could select a random sample of people from a designated population by securing the membership list of that population and drawing a sample of people from it on a random basis.

At the completion of this task, you will identify (a) your study population (e.g., all the students in the social work program at your university), (b) your study sample (e.g., the 17 members of a research class who were present in class on the day the questionnaire was administered), and (c)

the label of the type of sample you are using (e.g., a random sample, a convenience sample, etc.).

From the above information, you will be able to discuss the issue of generalization. Can you generalize on a scientific basis? What about a logical basis?

Step 2: Administer the Questionnaire

You will employ the questionnaire contained in the appendix to this chapter. It asks questions about the characteristics of the study subjects as well as their perceptions of life satisfaction, stress, and social support. The items measuring the key variables in your study are taken from Exhibits 7.3, 7.4, and 7.5. The first instruction for your survey is as follows:

You are asked to participate in a study that will be used for research exercises for social work students. You will be asked to answer a set of questions about yourself, your life satisfaction, your stress, and your perceptions of social support. Your participation is voluntary and anonymous. If you wish not to participate, you can turn in a blank form when they are collected. Do not place your name on this questionnaire so that your response will remain anonymous.

The above statement covers the key ethical issues in the use of human subjects in research as noted previously. Because this survey is only being used for an educational exercise, it will not normally be required that it be subjected to the review by an institutional review board for the use of human subjects in research.

Step 3: Record the Scores on the Three Variables for Each Respondent

You will compute the score for each of your three variables. From this procedure, you will have a score for life satisfaction, stress, and social support for each of the persons in your study sample. In addition, you will have data on age, race, and gender. Here are the specific instructions:

Life satisfaction: Record the number next to each answer, and sum these values for the total score for life satisfaction. There are five items, each of which can receive a score from 1 to 5. If the response is *strongly disagree*, you would give 1 point to the score, but if it is *disagree*, you would give 2 points to it, and so forth. The total possible score for a given person is 25 (5 x 5 = 25), while the lowest possible score is 5 (5 x 1 = 5).

Stress: Record the number next to each item, and sum these values for the total score. There are 10 items, each of which can have a score of 1, 2, or 3; thus, the total possible score for stress would be 30 (10 x 3 = 30), while the lowest possible score would be 10 (10 x 1 = 10). You will note that the numbers next to the options are not the same for each option because some of these options are words that indicate stress and some are words that indicate the opposite of stress. In this way, you are not required to do your own reverse scoring. The reverse scoring has been incorporated into the numbers assigned to the words.

Social support: Record the number next to each selected option, and sum these values for the total score. There are three items on this scale, each of which has four options with values of 1, 2, 3, and 4; thus, you can have a score as high as 12 (3 x 4 = 12) or a score as low as 3 (3 x 1 = 3).

At the completion of this task, you will have three scores for each respondent. You will record the scores for satisfaction, stress, and support in Exhibit 7.10. For the first person, you will enter the scores in the first line, one score for life satisfaction, one score for stress, and one score for social support. The scores for the second person will be entered on the second line, and so forth. Be sure to record the scores in this fashion in order for you to properly execute the instructions on the statistical analysis of your data.

For the descriptive variables (age, race, and gender), you can simply compile the results by hand. When you have completed this recording, you simply compute the results for each variable. If you have access to statistical software such as SPSS, you can enter your data there.

EXHIBIT 7.10
SCORES FOR YOUR STUDY OF LIFE SATISFACTION

Person	Life Satisfaction Score	Stress Score	Social Support Score
1			
2			
3			
4			
5			
6			
7			
9			

(Continued)

EXHIBIT 7.10 (Continued)

Person	Life Satisfaction Score	Stress Score	Social Support Score
9			
10			
11			
12			
13			
14			
15			
16			
17			
18			
19			
20			
21			
22			
23			
24			
25			
26			
27			
28			
29			
30			
31			
32			
33			
34			

Step 4: Analyze Your Data Using an Internet Website

Now it is time to submit these scores to the computer for analysis using the Pearson correlation coefficient. Instructions for this part of the exercise are given in Exhibit 7.11 You will be engaging in two separate statistical analyses, one for the examination of the relationship

EXHIBIT 7.11

USING THE WEB FOR COMPUTING THE VALUE OF r FOR THE PEARSON CORRELATION

Use the following instructions to determine the value of r, which represents the Pearson correlation, and the value of p, which represents statistical significance.

Your first step is to access the website below.
www.vassarstats.net
Then, follow the following steps:

1. Select the option *Correlation & Regression*.

2. From the next set of options, select *Basic Linear Correlation and Regression*.

   a. Select *Direct-Entry Version*.

   b. You will see a box with the label, "Please enter the value of N (the number of paired bivariate values if X and Y)." In this box, you will enter the number of people in your study sample and click OK.

   c. Scroll down to Data Entry, and enter the scores on each of the two variables.

Enter the scores for one of the variables in the X column and the scores for the other variable in the Y column. Be sure to enter your data as you have presented it in Exhibit 7.10. This means that the scores on both variables for the first person are presented in the first line.

   d. When this is complete, click the *Calculate* option at the bottom of the table.

   e. You will see the value of r in the box beneath the letter r on the chart of various values. This is your correlation. When you report the correlation using the Pearson statistic, you will present it as "$r = .43$," "$r = .31$," or whatever.

   f. You will see the value of p in the same chart, next to the words "one-tailed."

Now repeat the above for the second correlation you will be computing.

---

between life satisfaction and stress and another for the examination of the relationship between life satisfaction and social support. In each case, you will be employing the Pearson correlation coefficient in the examination of the data. When you complete this part of the exercise, you will have both a correlation coefficient and a value for statistical significance (i.e., the value of p). The size of the correlation will reveal the strength of the relationship, while the value of p will reveal the level of statistical significance. If you have a p value less than .05, you can say that you have achieved statistical significance, which means

that your data cannot be reasonably explained by chance.

Step 5: Report Your Results

You will report your results with reference to a set of questions. You answered a set of questions about the 2017 study in the previous practice exercise. In this exercise, you will report on things that are different for your own study, namely, your sample and your data. The answers you gave to many of the questions in the previous exercise would be identical for your own study, so those questions will not be included in the list for you to report now.

Your job is to prepare a report that provides answers to each of the following questions:

1. Can you describe the study sample used in your study?

2. Can you describe your study population?

3. Can the results of your study be scientifically generalized to this population? Explain why or why not.

4. What was the first hypotheses that was tested in your study?

5. Did the data support this first hypothesis? Explain with regard to the facts.

6. What was the second hypothesis that was tested in your study?

7. Did the data support this second hypothesis? Explain with regard to the facts.

8. Did the results suggest that support did a better job of explaining life satisfaction than did stress? Explain with data.

9. What were your conclusions for this study?

10. Were your study results similar to those of the 2017 study? Explain.

Now you are prepared to design and conduct your own explanatory study. Congratulations!

CHAPTER REVIEW

Chapter Key Learnings

1. Among the special features of the explanatory study are (a) theory, (b) study hypothesis, and (c) inferential statistics. Theory guides the development of the study hypothesis, which is tested with the use of inferential statistics.

2. A study variable is something that varies in your study data. If all the persons in your study sample were students, you would not have the concept of student as a variable because everyone is the same on this concept.

3. Variables are measured at four levels, three of which are featured in this book. The nominal variable places you into

categories that have no order, such as gender or political party affiliation. The ordinal variable places you into categories that have an order, such as strongly disagree, disagree, undecided, agree, and strongly agree. You must know the level of measurement for your study variables to select a proper statistical test.

4. Descriptive statistics are used to describe variables, such as the frequency or the proportion. Inferential statistics are used to test study hypotheses. From the inferential statistic, you derive a value of p, which represents the number of times in 100 that your analyzed data would be expected to

occur by chance. The expression "$p < .05$" means that the data would occur by chance 5 times in 100. This is the normal standard in the social sciences for finding statistical significance.

5. The correlation coefficient is one statistic for examining the relationship between two variables to determine whether one of these variables may explain the other variable. If the correlation coefficient is negative, it will have a negative sign in front, and it will indicate that people who are higher on one of these variables will tend to be lower on the other one. If there is no negative sign in front of the correlation coefficient, you will have a positive relationship between the variables, which means that people who are higher on one of these variables tend to be higher on the other variable.

6. The study hypothesis is a statement that identifies the study variables being examined and the expected direction of the relationship between them. It should neither be stated as a question nor should it have an assertion of causation. You might say, for example, that your hypothesis is "There is a positive relationship between scores for self-esteem and school grades." However, you should not say, "Clients will improve on their self-esteem because of the school counseling services."

7. For you to say that your data supported your study hypothesis, you must have two pieces of data: (1) your data must go in the hypothesized direction and (2) your data must be statistically significant. If you fail to have either of these conditions, you must report that your data failed to support your study hypothesis.

8. You can generalize your study findings on a scientific basis if you have a random sample from the study population to which you wish to generalize your findings. You can generalize your findings on a logical basis if you have sufficient information on the characteristics of the sample and the population to logically argue that findings from your sample are likely to be repeated with studies of other samples drawn from the same population.

9. Reliability refers to the consistency of a measurement tool, while validity refers to its accuracy. One method for testing for reliability is the examination of the internal consistency of items on a scale. One method for examining the validity of a tool is to compare it with a published scale that has been designed to measure the same thing. If there is a strong positive correlation between the two scales, you have evidence of validity.

10. A theory is an attempt to explain. It is employed in explanatory research to establish the basis for a scientific study. It guides the articulation of the study hypothesis and assists in the identification of the relevant variables to be measured. A theory can be more or less formal, and it may or may not be published.

11. The structure of your data situation will guide the selection of a statistic for the testing of your hypothesis. For example, the Pearson correlation coefficient is appropriate if you are examining the relationship between two variables where each is measured at the interval level.

Chapter Discussion Questions

1. What is the key objective of Phase 1 (knowledge base) of explanatory research? In other words, what function does it plan in the explanatory research process?

2. What is the key issue that is addressed by the choice of a method of sampling? What kind of sample is superior in this regard?

3. In what phase of the explanatory research process do you articulate the study hypothesis? What is an example of a good statement of the study hypothesis?

4. Explain the difference between the positive empirical relationship and the negative empirical relationship.

5. What is the disadvantage of reading a report of an explanatory research study when the issues of reliability and validity are problematic (i.e., not reported or reported in a way that is not satisfactory)?

6. Explain what data structure means and how it is related to the choice of a statistic to test your study hypothesis in explanatory research.

7. What is the most important thing you should report in the conclusion section of your explanatory study?

8. With regard to the conclusion section of your report on your explanatory study, what should you do with your own opinions, assuming that these opinions are well-informed but not addressed by your data?

9. What conclusion should you draw if you find that the data went in the hypothesized direction but were not statistically significant?

Chapter Test

1. Which of the following is/are true about what we expect to find in our study?
   a. Persons who are higher on stressors will likely be higher on stress
   b. Persons who are higher on social support will likely be higher on stress
   c. Both of the above
   d. None of the above

2. Your literature review should help in what ways?
   a. Definition of concepts to be measured
   b. Understanding the theories or conceptual frameworks that help understand the thing being studied
   c. Articulation of the study hypotheses
   d. All of the above

3. Suppose we collected a random sample of all the social work students in our university for a study of stressors, stress, and social support. Which of the following would be true?
   a. We can scientifically generalize our findings to other people
   b. We can scientifically generalize our findings to all the social work students in our university
   c. Both of the above
   d. None of the above

4. Reliability and validity refer to what?
   a. The consistency of the means we use to measure study variables
   b. The accuracy of the means we use to measure study variables

c. Both of the above

d. None of the above

5. The selection of the study sample fits into what phase of research?

a. Development of the study purpose and knowledge base

b. Development of the study methods

c. Analysis of the data

d. Study conclusions

6. Suppose we find the following in our examination of the relationship between scores for stressors and scores for stress: $r = .34$; $p = .24$. Which of the following is true?

a. The data support the hypothesis about the relationship between stressors and stress

b. The data were found to be statistically significant

c. Both of the above

d. None of the above

7. In the above example ($r = .34$; $p = .24$), what conclusions should we draw?

a. We found that people with more stressors have more stress because we found a positive correlation between these two variables

b. We found that people with more stressors had less stress because we found a negative correlation between these two variables

c. We found that we can scientifically generalize our findings

d. We failed to find a relationship between stressors and stress

8. Which of the following would be examples of data structure?

a. We are examining the relationship between two variables where each is measured at the interval level

b. We have selected a convenience sample of social work students at our university

c. Both of the above

d. None of the above

9. The examination of statistical significance helps us address what theme?

a. Causation

b. Scientific generalization

c. Both of the above

d. None of the above

10. In what phase of the research process do we employ a statistical test?

a. Development of the study purpose and knowledge base

b. Development of the study methods

c. Analysis of the data

d. Study conclusions

11. Suppose that we select the members of our research class to collect data for our study of stress. Which of the following statements is/are true?

a. The members of our class would be the study population, rather than the study sample

b. The findings of our study could be scientifically generalized to all social work students at our university

c. Both of the above

d. None of the above

12. Which of these is a method of finding evidence with regard to the credibility (reliability or validity) of our measurement tools?

a. You test to see if there is a positive correlation between the odd-numbered items on our scale and the even-numbered items

b. You test to see if there is a positive correlation between scores on our tool and scores on a published scaled designed to measure the same thing as our scale

c. Both of the above

d. None of the above

13. For what kind of sample can you say that the results can be scientifically generalized to the study population?
   a. Convenience
   b. Hypothetical
   c. Random
   d. Seamless

14. Which of the following takes place in the data analysis phase of research?
   a. The determination is made of who will be in the study sample
   b. The basic research question is determined

   c. The hypothesis is tested
   d. The decision is made about the limitations of the study

15. You can say that your data supported your study hypothesis if . . .
   a. Your data were found to be in the hypothesized direction
   b. Your data were found to be statistically significant
   c. Both of the above
   d. None of the above

ANSWERS: 1 = a; 2 = d; 3 = b; 4 = c; 5 = b; 6 = d; 7 = d; 8 = a; 9 = d; 10 = c; 11 = d; 12 = c; 13 = c; 14 = c; 15 = c

Chapter Glossary

Explanatory research. Research that explains a variable by examining its relationship with another variable. If you wished to know if income explains self-esteem, you could conduct a study that examines the relationship between income and self-esteem.

Generalization of study results. An assertion that the results of the current study would likely be the same with another sample of people drawn from the same study population. If your hypothesis was supported by your study of students in your research class, would it likely be supported by another study of another class of students in the same program of the same university? That is the question for generalization.

Hypothesis for a research study. A specific statement predicting the results of the intended study. For example, you might have the hypothesis *Persons with higher self-esteem will have lower depression*. The hypothesis should identify the study variables and what is expected when the data are analyzed. It should *not* contain assertions of causation, such as, for example, *Clients will improve on depression because of the cognitive-behavioral therapy they will receive*.

Logical generalization of study results. The examination of the extent to which the results of a study can be generalized to persons in the study population on a logical basis, meaning that there is sufficient evidence of similarities between the study sample and the study population to convince people that the results of this study can be viewed as relevant to the study population. Logical generalization does not require a random sample.

Negative relationship. An empirical relationship between two variables in which higher values for one would tend to be associated with lower values on the other. For example, we would expect to find a negative relationship between school grades and depression. In other words, the higher your depression, the lower will be your grades.

Positive relationship. An empirical relationship between two variables in which higher values for one would tend to be associated with higher values on the other. For example, we would expect that age and income would have a positive relationship because older people are more likely to have higher salaries. In others words, the higher your age, the higher your income.

CHAPTER APPENDIX: QUESTIONNAIRE FOR STUDY OF LIFE SATISFACTION

You are asked to participate in a study that will be used for research exercises for social work students. You will be asked to answer a set of questions about yourself, your life satisfaction, your stress, and your perceptions of social support. Your participation is voluntary and anonymous. If you wish not to participate, you can turn in a blank form when they are collected. Do not place your name on this questionnaire so that your response will remain anonymous.

Part 1: Life Satisfaction

Examine each of the statements below about your life, and draw a circle around the phrase that indicates the level of your agreement with that statement. In other words, you will indicate, with each statement, if you (1) *strongly disagree*, (2) *disagree*, (3) *neither agree nor disagree*, (4) *agree*, or (5) *strongly agree*.

Statement	Level of Agreement				
In most ways, my life has been what I have wanted it to be.	(1) Strongly disagree	(2) Disagree	(3) Neither agree nor disagree	(4) Agree	(5) Strongly agree
The circumstances of my life have usually been excellent.	(1) Strongly disagree	(2) Disagree	(3) Neither agree nor disagree	(4) Agree	(5) Strongly agree
I am satisfied with what life has offered me.	(1) Strongly disagree	(2) Disagree	(3) Neither agree nor disagree	(4) Agree	(5) Strongly agree
So far, I have accomplished the important things I have wanted to accomplish in life.	(1) Strongly disagree	(2) Disagree	(3) Neither agree nor disagree	(4) Agree	(5) Strongly agree
If I could live my life over, I would change very little.	(1) Strongly disagree	(2) Disagree	(3) Neither agree nor disagree	(4) Agree	(5) Strongly agree

Part 2: Stress

Please review each of the following terms, and decide if it is a feeling you have experienced in the past few months *hardly ever*, *some of the time*, or a *great deal of the time*. Circle your response to each word.

Strained	(1) Hardly ever	(2) Some of the time	(3) A great deal of the time
Jolly	(3) Hardly ever	(2) Some of the time	(1) A great deal of the time
Edgy	(1) Hardly ever	(2) Some of the time	(3) A great deal of the time
Composed	(3) Hardly ever	(2) Some of the time	(1) A great deal of the time
Unglued	(1) Hardly ever	(2) Some of the time	(3) A great deal of the time
Satisfied	(3) Hardly ever	(2) Some of the time	(1) A great deal of the time

Pleased	(3) Hardly ever	(2) Some of the time	(1) A great deal of the time
Agitated	(1) Hardly ever	(2) Some of the time	(3) A great deal of the time
Shook-up	(1) Hardly ever	(2) Some of the time	(3) A great deal of the time
Joyful	(3) Hardly ever	(2) Some of the time	(1) A great deal of the time

Part 3: Social Support

Please indicate below your level of satisfaction with social support by responding to each item below.

(a) How satisfied are you with the extent of support you receive from friends?
___ (1) unsatisfied   (2) ___ undecided   ___ (3) satisfied   ___ (4) very satisfied

(b) How satisfied are you with the extent of support you receive from relatives?
___ (1) unsatisfied   (2) ___ undecided   ___ (3) satisfied   ___ (4) very satisfied

(c) How satisfied are you with the extent of support you receive from others (i.e., not friends or relatives)?
___ (1) unsatisfied   (2) ___ undecided   ___ (3) satisfied   ___ (4) very satisfied

Part 4: Yourself

Please answer the following questions about yourself by placing a check next to the option that describes you.

(1). What is your age? ___ below 30 years ___ 30 years or above

(2). What is your race? ___ White ___ African-American ___ Other

(3). What is your gender? ___ Male ___ Female

8

CONDUCTING RESEARCH THAT EVALUATES SERVICES

Carla provided individual therapy to eight children who had experienced posttraumatic stress disorder (PTSD) due to being the victims of trauma-like abuse or witnessing violence between parents. She employed trauma-focused cognitive–behavioral therapy (TF-CBT) because it had been found to be an evidence-based treatment for PTSD, in both children and adults. The model of TF-CBT is founded on the assumptions of cognitive–behavioral therapy (CBT), which emphasizes the examination of thoughts about life events to change the emotional response to the events. Trauma-focused cognitive-behavioral therapy (TF-CBT) is one form of CBT. This option was employed by Carla with her clients because they had all experienced a trauma. Among the components of the treatment used by Carla were psychoeducation, relaxation techniques, cognitive coping, and in vivo gradual exposure. The structure of this treatment was 8-hourly therapy sessions completed one per week for 8 weeks. Carla's credentials for being qualified for this job was the LCSW (Licensed Clinical Social Worker). She has been trained in the use of TF-CBT and has used it for a good number of clients in the past and believes that it is effective. The goal of this treatment for these eight clients was to achieve a life without the consequences of the traumas they had experienced. The objective was to reduce the symptoms of PTSD.

Carla measured client progress with the Child PTSD Symptom Scale. On this scale, the clients examined the symptoms of PTSD and indicated how much they were experiencing each symptom recently. Higher scores indicated a greater problem with PTSD. Scores on this scale can range from a low of 17 to a high of 51, with scores greater than 25 indicating a need for treatment and scores less than 17 indicating no need for treatment. This scale was administered to each client once before the treatment began and again at the end of the 8-week treatment period. Because Carla knew that these clients had experienced the symptoms of PTSD for many months, she believed that a comparison group research design was not needed. The one-group pretest–posttest design employed in her study was considered adequate because these clients were not expected to overcome the PTSD symptoms without treatment.

The mean pretest score for these eight clients on the Child PTSD Symptom Scale was 29.4, while the mean posttest score was 16.7. The differences between these sets of scores was found to be statistically significant. Carla concluded that her treatment had been effective.

INTRODUCTION

In this chapter, you will review the evaluation of social work interventions. There is a distinction you will see between a human service **program** and a human service intervention. The program is the broader thing to be measured, and the **intervention** is the more specific aspect that is the focus of evaluation. You can conduct a program evaluation of various aspects of the Child Welfare Program in your agency or the Adult Mental Health Program or you can evaluate a single intervention, such as the support group for abused women. Sometime interventions will be referred to as **services**. A broad program will normally have various services (interventions). This chapter reviews the evaluation of interventions, something that social work students and practitioners are more likely to be conducting. But first you will examine a few things about programs and interventions.

This chapter starts with an overview of the human service system, a concept most useful for the evaluation of a broad program. From this overview, you can put into perspective the evaluation of client outcome, the focus of this chapter. Then, you will review various aspects of how to evaluate an intervention, such as tutoring for 14 at-risk middle school students, therapy for eight women who have been abused, or parent training for 14 teenage mothers.

At the completion of this chapter, you will be able to do the following:

1. Describe the parts of the evaluation system with regard to input, process, output, and outcome

2. Identify the five major phases of evaluation research

3. Define and analyze the target behavior that is being treated

4. Review evidence with regard to interventions and target behaviors

5. Describe the intervention with regard to goal, objective, structure, model, and personnel

6. Select a research design that adequately addresses the critical threats to internal validity that should be of concern in a given situation

7. Select a tool for measuring client progress with appropriate attention to reliability and validity

8. Determine if the results of an evaluative study can be generalized from the study sample to a designated study population on a scientific basis and a logical basis

9. Compose an evaluative study hypothesis with attention to critical tips for doing so

10. Determine if a given set of data supported a given evaluative study hypothesis with attention to the two criteria for this endeavor

11. Determine if statistical significance or practical significance has been achieved for a given set of data for a given study

12. Prepare the study conclusions for a given evaluative research study

THE PARTS OF THE EVALUATION SYSTEM

As a reader of this book, you will likely be interested in knowing how successful a given human service has been. The application of the scientific analysis of data regarding client outcome would be expected to be among the questions of special interest. Has participation in your tutoring program had the effect of improving school grades? Have the homeless people who sought the help of your agency been more likely to find a home within 6 months than homeless people nationally? Are your clients less depressed after receiving your therapy than before receiving your therapy?

The issues for intervention research typically focus on one aspect of evaluative research—client outcome. The issue is whether clients are better off as a result of your intervention. There are other issues that are within the purview of program evaluative research. Among the questions that you might pose in program evaluation are the following:

1. Are our services reaching the target population?

2. Are we employing good standards of service?

3. Are we delivering services efficiently?

4. Are our clients satisfied?

5. Have our interventions improved client conditions?

All these are questions related to agency success in one way or another. Funding sources often ask for data on one or more of the above questions, with increasing emphasis on client outcome. If your tutoring program is supposed to be servicing at-risk middle school students, you need to demonstrate this through your descriptive statistics on the clients being served. This reveals the answer to Question 1 mentioned above. You might be called on to report the credentials of your service personnel to show that your services are being delivered by qualified people. This is one aspect of the standards of service that you will employ. Efficient delivery of service is measured by the amount of money your agency spends for each **unit of service**, such as a cost of $110 per hour of therapy. Client satisfaction is normally measured by simple surveys of clients. Data on this may also be expected by your funding source. And, of course, data on client outcome respond to the last question noted above. This will be the emphasis in this chapter. You may have noticed the two aspects of this question: (1) clients should have improved and (2) their improvement was caused by the service. You will address both these questions in this chapter.

All the above are ways by which success is measured in program evaluations. We are most often going to review success with regard to client outcome. But funding sources also want to know about the quality of services and the efficiency of service delivery. In this section of the chapter, you will review the elements of the service system as well as the depiction of programs and services.

Evaluating Input, Process, Output, and Outcome

One of the models for a service system shows some elements that are labeled **input** because they are energies that come into the system, and some are called **process** (i.e., services) because they refer to what happens to the inputs. **Output** is a term used to refer to the amount of service (output) provided, while **outcome** refers to the benefits that are derived by the processes that were employed. A client with need could be considered an input, while the nature of the service offered could be considered a process. Output would be the amount of service offered, while outcome would refer to the benefit to the client with regard to the need being addressed by the service. For example, a middle school student with poor grades (input) might receive tutoring service (process) in the form of 12 tutoring sessions (output) with the result that her or his grades were improved from an average of 63 to an average of 78 (outcome). Figure 8.1 shows a depiction of the service system.

The assessment of need typically takes the form of a descriptive type of study because the purpose is to describe need. To what extent, for example, is there a waiting list of clients who have asked for your service but have not yet been served? To what extent does your target population have people who qualify for your service because they have the characteristics of youth at-risk for delinquent behavior? These are descriptive inquiries into need.

The review of service characteristics is also an example of a descriptive study because the purpose is to describe the service. What are the credentials of the service providers? What is the average caseload of service staff? Have all clients been given the statement of the nature of the service and their rights as a client? In other words, you are examining the extent to which services have been provided according to plan. There may be a set of

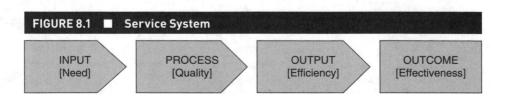

FIGURE 8.1 ■ Service System

INPUT [Need] → PROCESS [Quality] → OUTPUT [Efficiency] → OUTCOME [Effectiveness]

protocols that clarify the plan. To what extent were these protocols employed with the clients in the past 6 months? Sometimes funding sources provide audits of services to determine the extent to which service policies were executed.

The review of output is another example of a descriptive study that can be viewed as helping with the evaluation of service. This requires the quantification of services. The unit of service is the vehicle for this inquiry. There are a number of types of units of service that might be reviewed. The simplest one is a client served. If you served 368 clients in the past year, you have delivered 368 units of service if you have defined the unit of service in this way. If you are providing therapy sessions to clients, a therapy session provided to a single client could be your definition of a unit of service. If you are providing residential treatment, a day of service may be the unit of service.

You can use the units of service as one element of a review of efficiency. The other element is the cost. If you have provided service to 368 clients and your agency spent a total of $368,000 to provide this service, you can easily see that it cost $1,000 per client served. This is a measure of efficiency. If agencies of your type provide service at a cost of only $500 per client, you could be criticized for not being efficient. The measure of efficiency, of course, is not an indicator of outcome, so you might be achieving greater outcome even though you are operating less efficiently.

An evaluation of outcome, of course, requires a measure of benefit to the client. The key for this review is the outcome objective you have established for the service being offered. This could include improved grades in school, reduced anxiety, improved self-esteem, improved marital harmony, reduced health risks, and so forth.

In Practice Exercise A at the end of this chapter, you are asked to reflect on the various parts of the service system. You are called on to select one for a report. You may wish to review those questions now to get a better picture of the service system.

THE PHASES OF OUTCOME EVALUATION RESEARCH

In previous chapters, you have reviewed four major phases of research: (1) research purpose and knowledge base, (2) study methods, (3) data analysis, and (4) study conclusions. Evaluation research will be presented a little differently because of the critical role of the service that is being evaluated. Evaluative research begins with an examination of the nature of the **target behavior** that is being served. This is comparable with the articulation of the purpose and knowledge base. The second part is new. It is the presentation of information about the nature of the service that is being evaluated. If you prefer, you could consider this to be a part of the first phase of research as articulated previously, rather than a separate phase of research. The remaining phases of evaluative research are similar to that which has been presented—study methods, data analysis, and study conclusion.

Here is a very brief and condensed report of how this process may be viewed:

1. *Target behavior:* The target behavior being evaluated is chronic depression among persons who are within 1 year of experiencing divorce. Depression is a condition where individuals lose interest in life, are chronically feeling sad, and have difficulty in fully performing life activities such as dealing with work,

friends, and family. It is viewed as being partly caused by distorted thinking about life events. Divorced persons who become chronically depressed are different from divorced persons who become temporarily depressed. Chronic depression is depression that has existed for at least 6 months.

2. *Treatment:* The **goal** of **treatment** is to improve the client's adjustment to life after divorce, including work, relationships, and family life. The objective is to reduce depression. The model of treatment is CBT. The rationale for this choice is that this model focuses on distorted thinking, believed to be a cause for chronic depression. This treatment was delivered in hourly therapy sessions once weekly for 8 weeks. A credentialed therapist, who was a licensed clinical social worker, provided the therapy.

3. *Study methods:* The study sample consisted of 17 divorced persons recently treated at the Hampton County Family Service Association. The Beck Depression Inventory (BDI) was used to measure each client's depression once before the therapy began and once again at the end of the treatment period. Higher scores on this scale represent higher levels of depression. Scores on this scale that are greater than 30 indicate severe depression, whereas scores from 21 to 30 indicate moderate depression. This research design (one-group pretest–posttest) does not control for normal growth and development over time as the cause of the measured client growth as an alternative to the treatment as the cause. However, this explanation was not considered to be of special concern given the facts that (a) the depression of these clients had existed for more than 6 months without change and (b) the treatment period was only for 8 weeks. Therefore, significant change between the beginning and the end of the treatment period should logically be concluded as being the result of the treatment rather than the result of normal growth and development over time.

4. *Data analysis:* The pretest mean score on the BDI was 32.6, while the mean posttest score (at the end of treatment) was 22.4. This indicates that the average person went from a threshold for depression considered to be severe to one that is considered to be moderate. This indicates, in the opinion of the researchers, that practical (clinical) significance was achieved. These scores were analyzed statistically with the paired t test and found to be statistically significant ($t = 2.67$; $p < .01$). Thus, statistical significance was achieved. Because the data went in the hypothesized direction and were statistically significant, the data supported the study hypothesis (posttest scores on the depression scale will be less than the pretest scores).

5. *Study conclusions:* It was concluded that the recently divorced clients of this program of CBT achieved a reduction in depression that was of both statistical significance and practical significance. These findings cannot be scientifically generalized to the population of all divorced persons who are chronically depressed because this study did not employ a random sample of that population. These findings should give encouragement to therapists to employ CBT to chronically depressed persons who have recently been divorced.

In a full report of the research study, each of the aforementioned paragraphs would be elaborated on. This is just a synopsis to show the process of evaluative research from one phase to another.

You will notice that the target behavior section identified the behavior being treated and presented an analysis of its causes. This analysis is related to the choice of the intervention. The condition of depression was defined, so that methods for measuring client progress could be facilitated. The treatment was described sufficiently to be recognized so that the results could be interpreted with regard to what it was that was (or was not) found to be successful. The measure of client progress was identified as well as the research design. These contributions provide information to the reader regarding the credibility of measurement and the adequacy of the research design. Data were given on practical significance—the mean depression score of these clients changed from one threshold of depression to a lower one. Data were also given on statistical significance—the p value ($p < .01$) showed that these data cannot logically be explained by chance. The study conclusions were directly in line with the data results.

Phase 1: Target Behavior Examination

There are three major tasks in this phase of evaluative research: (1) to define the target behavior being treated sufficiently to guide the selection of a tool for measuring client progress, (2) to provide a logical justification for the selection of the service to be provided to the clients, and (3) to examine the evidence about what works in the treatment of this target behavior. This means that you define the behavior, you analyze it, and you seek evidence regarding the treatment of it. The later two are designed to provide guidance on the use of a service to achieve the outcome for the client. If you have evidence that CBT is effective in the treatment of depression, you have a basis for justifying the use of this model for your treatment of persons with depression. If you can link the causes of the behavior, or the special needs of those with this condition, with the nature of your intervention, you have a logical rationale for using your intervention for this target behavior. Treatments in the category of pseudoscience, discussed in Chapter 1, fail to be a source of justification for a treatment because it is not based on systematically collected scientific evidence of the effects of accompanying treatments for given target behaviors.

Target Behavior Definition

If you define stress as a certain type of psychological condition characterized in certain ways, you should find a tool that measures this psychological condition. You should not select a tool that measures life events that lead to stress, because you have not defined stress with regard to life events. Instead, you should measure stress with regard to the psychological condition you have defined.

Here are some examples of **target behavior definition**:

1. *Posttraumatic stress disorder*, according to the *Diagnostic and Statistical Manual of Mental Disorders, 5th edition* (*DSM-5*), evolves after an individual has experienced one or more traumatic events (American Psychiatric Association, 2013). The *DSM-5* defines posttraumatic symptoms within three specific dimensions: (1) reexperiencing, (2) avoidance, and (3) arousal. Reexperiencing

includes behaviors such as recurring memories, nightmares, dissociative episodes, and extreme physiological reactions to reminders of the traumatic event. Avoidance may include avoidance of memories, reminders, and thoughts. It can also include feelings related with the traumatic event. Arousal may be exhibited by behavioral disturbances, angry outbursts, hypervigilance, difficulty concentrating, and sleep problems (American Psychiatric Association, 2013).

2. *Obesity* is defined as a body mass index of 30 or greater and is calculated as weight in kilograms divided by the square of the height in meters.

3. *Adjustment disorder* is defined as a group of troublesome symptoms—such as stress, feeling sad or hopeless, and problematic physical symptoms—that can occur after a person has gone through a stressful life event.

4. *Classroom misbehaviors* refer to behaviors in the classroom that exhibit aggression, defiance of authority, or disruption of the learning of others.

5. *Anxiety* is excessive nervousness, worry, or fear, which may include feelings that things are unreal, and/or a sudden panic state. It often includes apprehension; feeling tense, stressed, or on edge; difficulty concentrating; racing thoughts; and unrealistic fears.

In each of the above definitions, there is guidance on how to select a tool for measuring client progress. When you examine alternatives for the measurement of your target behavior, you should review the definition to see that all aspects of the behavior that are included in your definition are included in your measurement tool.

Target Behavior Analysis

The purpose of **target behavior analysis** is to obtain guidance on the determination of the appropriate intervention for the clients. You can analyze target behavior with regard to causation, special needs, or both. If ignorance is the cause of the target behavior, training would be a logical intervention. If involvement with dysfunctional peers is the cause of drug abuse among youth, an intervention that changes the peer group for the client would make sense. In many situations, the analysis of special needs is better than the analysis of causation. For example, a mental disability may be due to a situation from birth, which cannot be changed. But clients with this condition have special needs. Your service should address these needs.

If your analysis of drug abuse for youth indicates that youthful drug offenders have good knowledge of the consequences of drug use, it would not make sense to provide training on the consequences of drug abuse as your service. That would not be logical. They understand the thing you have decided to train them on. Perhaps your service should address the causes of drug abuse in ways that might make a difference, such as intervening into the social life of the abuser, assuming that you have found out that many youthful drug abusers got into drug abuse because they stared socializing with others who were drug abusers. If you can get them to change their social group, you can have more hope that they will stop their use of drugs.

If the cause of poor parenting for an at-risk group is the lack of good parenting role models in the past, it would make sense for the treatment to include mentoring by parents who can display good parenting. If an outcome of a trauma is a feeling of being the only person who has experienced this trauma, leading to self-blame, it may be that a support group of people with similar experiences would help.

The nature of the problem is sometimes complex with regard to causation or need. Let's examine the theme of stressors, stress, and stress buffers as three concepts to be measured in your study. The theoretical model depicting causation indicated that stressors cause stress to get worse, while social support causes stress to get better. Thus, one intervention could be to reduce stressors, while another could be to increase social support.

Here are four examples of concise statements of target behavior analysis that have appeared in the research reports of social work students:

1. Children who have been exposed to sexual trauma caused by their caregivers are generally unable to reach normal developmental goals and have a high chance of falling behind in their emotional, social, and cognitive advancement. This inability to progress normally is related to dysfunctional thoughts about the trauma that was experienced. The needed treatment, therefore, is a service that combines opportunity to review the traumatic events in light of new ways of thinking about it and provides a supportive environment for the victim.

2. Individuals affected by severe obesity who are seeking bariatric surgery are more likely to suffer from depression or anxiety and to have lower self-esteem and overall quality of life than someone who is normal weight. Bariatric surgery results in highly significant improvement in psychosocial well-being for the majority of patients. However, there remain a few patients with undiagnosed preexisting psychological disorders and still others with overwhelming life stressors who have psychological difficulties. One of the problems for such persons is a feeling of being alone in the world; thus, the improvement of social connections is an important need. A social support group experience is one vehicle for the achievement of this outcome.

3. Drug addiction leads many to feel that there is no hope for recovery, and they must be addicted from now on. This condition is partly due to a lack of knowledge about the success of treatment options. What is needed, therefore, is education on these options and data about their success.

4. Persons who experience adjustment disorder have reacted to life stressors in ways that are more severe than normal, leading to a great deal of feelings of stress. What is needed, therefore, is an intervention that (a) removes stressors from the client's life and (b) improves social support, which reduces stress for those experiencing life stressors.

These concise statements, of course, were supported by a review of the literature and further information that supported the concise statement. They are presented here as examples that illustrate what is meant by target behavior analysis.

Review of Evidence

What works with your target behavior? That is the key question for the examination of **evidence**. As you encounter this task, let's see a definition of this concept. Evidence can be defined broadly as any information that is employed in determining action. However, we are examining evidence regarding outcome evaluation. In this regard, evidence is information collected from sources of a scientific nature that is viewed as credible by key actors in the human service system. The typical example is a research study of the effectiveness of tutoring in the improvement of the grades of at-risk middle school youth. This means that the intervention of tutoring was employed and that grade improvement was measured.

As you saw in the chapter on evidence-based practice, sources of evidence are not equal. Some studies measure outcome once before treatment and once again at the end of treatment, while a more complicated study would compare the gain of clients with the same for a comparison group of people who did not get the intervention. An even more sophisticated study would employ the traditional experimental design whereby a group of people are randomly assigned to be in a treatment group or a control group, with only the treatment group getting the intervention. The difference in measured growth between the two groups indicates the effect of treatment on the target behavior.

As you saw in the chapter on evidence-based practice, the review of a single study on evidence is a weak review. Several levels of evidence were presented in that chapter, including (a) the single article, (b) the traditional literature review, (c) the **meta-analysis**, and (d) the **systematic review**. These levels of evidence were presented in order of their level of scientific sophistication.

You are advised to start your review of evidence by finding systematic reviews. In some cases, the summary of that review is all that you will need. If you fail to find a systematic review, look for the meta-analysis. Failure to find a meta-analysis should lead you to examine traditional literature reviews of evidence for your target behavior and intervention. If there are no traditional literature reviews of evidence, you should find several individual studies. You should not stop your review because you found a study that gave you the results you were seeking. Remember the spirit of scientific inquiry! You should engage in a review of your own that is systematic in its procedures for finding evidence.

There are two key data sources for systematic reviews of human service research. One is the Campbell Collaboration (www.campbellcollaboration.org). It provides systematic reviews of various target behaviors and the treatments that have been studied.

Another source is the Cochrane Collaboration (www.cochrane.org). In one example, information on the treatment of PTSD was reviewed from the Cochrane Collaboration in June 2016. Some of the treatments were TF-CBT, EMDR (eye movement desensitization and reprogramming), and other treatments that were not trauma focused. Here are the author's conclusions:

> The evidence for each of the comparisons in this review was assessed as very low quality. This evidence showed that individual TFCBT and EMDR did better than waitlist/usual care in reducing clinician-assessed PTSD symptoms. There was evidence that individual TFCBT, EMDR and non-TFCBT are equally effective immediately posttreatment in the treatment of PTSD. There was some evidence that TFCBT and EMDR are superior to non-TFCBT between one to four months following treatment, and also that individual TFCBT, EMDR and non-TFCBT

are more effective than other therapies. There was evidence of greater drop-out in active treatment groups. Although a substantial number of studies were included in the review, the conclusions are compromised by methodological issues evident in some. Sample sizes were small, and it is apparent that many of the studies were underpowered. There were limited follow-up data, which compromises conclusions regarding the long-term effects of psychological treatment. (Bisson, Roberts, Andrew, Cooper, & Lewis, 2016)

These conclusions suggest that TF-CBT and EMDR are effective in the treatment of PTSD. Perhaps this is all we might want to know. This review also suggested that treatments specific to PTSD are more effective than no treatment or usual care. This includes TF-CBT and EMDR, both of which have a special focus on the trauma that has been experienced. The quality of the studies was viewed as poor, but we must realize that this source has high expectations regarding the quality of the research that was undertaken. Weak studies are better than no studies at all.

There are many Internet sources for evidence with regard to human service evaluations. Here is a small list:

Cochrane Collaboration: www.cochrane.org

Campbell Collaboration: www.campbellcollaboration.org

National Institute on Drug Abuse: www.nida.nih.gov

Substance Abuse and Mental Health Services Administration: www.samhsa.gov

American Psychological Association: www.apa.org

California Evidence-Based Clearinghouse for Child Welfare: www.cebc4cw.org

There are many more. When you access these websites, go to a place where you can find evidence and enter the key words you need to get what you want. For the APA website, you need to go to Division 12 for information on evidence.

In many situations in the human service, the search for evidence is not simple. For one, the service may not be easily classified to find the evidence. Consider, for example, the following description of the services of an inpatient treatment program: The intervention employed a family focus group, an activity group, a nurse and medication group, and individual therapy. In this situation, you need to know whether any of these individual services is evidence based, and you would report what you find.

Justifying Your Selection of an Intervention

Why did you select a certain service (treatment, intervention) to achieve the improvement of the client's target behavior? That question should be informed by your analysis of the causes of the target behavior, the needs of those who experience it, and the evidence that you found.

We have discussed ways by which you can justify your selection of a certain intervention on the basis of logic. This is done with an analysis of the nature of the target behavior you are treating and the logical connection of that behavior to the service being provided.

If knowledge is needed, training is a logical service. If the client has been negatively influenced by a peer group, some kind of intervention that would change the peer group could be a logical service.

We have also discussed how you can justify this selection on the basis of evidence. This can be a complicated task, but a simple approach is to find credible sources that provide lists of evidence-based practices. If you wish to publish your study, you will have a more complicated challenge than this. For the novice social work researcher, the avoidance of bogus treatments is a key concern. A bogus treatment is one that not only lacks evidence but also makes outlandish claims of success that seem to defy logic. If someone is asserting that a given treatment is successful for the treatment of all mental health disorders, and there is a lack of evidence to support this claim, you can be assured that you have an example of a bogus treatment. Finding credible sources that support a given treatment should deal with that concern.

The author once attended a presentation on equine-assisted therapy in 2017. The presenter was passionate about this treatment. This method of treatment was described along with a dramatic example of success. When you review a passionate presentation with a dramatic example, it is easy to fall into the trap of following a treatment that is not evidence based. When this presenter was asked about the evidence, a vague response indicated that there was evidence of effectiveness but no specifics were presented. After a review of the evidence, I concluded that equine-assisted therapy was not an evidence-based treatment. There was some evidence in its behalf, but the evidence taken as a whole was not supportive. This did not lead me to conclude that this treatment was harmful, or that it would never be found to be an evidence-based practice, but only that the current evidence on it was not positive. Given the number of treatments that are evidence based, it did not seem to me to be wise for a treatment to be used that failed this test. Evidence on treatments are relevant only to the policy issue of what treatments should be supported by agencies, insurance companies, and the government. Such evidence should not lead to the conclusion that this treatment does not ever work for anyone under any circumstances. You may have a treatment that works when you employ it for a given type of client, even if it is not evidence based. Under these circumstances, you should collect your own evidence on effectiveness. When you are seeking new treatments, you should examine those that are evidence based. And you should be sure you are adequately trained on the treatment that you employ.

Phase 2: Description of the Intervention

The description of the intervention (i.e., service or treatment) is not a phase of evaluation research that you have seen in the previous chapters because they dealt with studies that were not evaluating a service. In evaluation research, it is possibly the most important element of the report because the key question is whether a given service had the intended outcome. If you read an evaluation study, you will want to be clear on the intervention that is being evaluated.

The intervention is the composite of the activities that are provided to clients for the purpose of achieving a given outcome. Interventions (services) typically exist within a broad program delivered by the human service agency. We will describe services with regard to (a) broad goal, (b) specific outcome objective, (c) structure, (d) model, and (e) personnel. Each of these elements of the description of the intervention will be addressed in detail in this section of this chapter. Briefly, the goal is the long-range benefit to the client, while the outcome **objective** is a measured amount of progress toward the achievement of the goal. The structure of the service reveals what it looks like. The model is the theoretical or conceptual framework that connects the target behavior to the structure of the service and serves as a logical justification of it. The personnel of the service refers to the credentials of those who will deliver the service.

You have seen a review of evidence on what works in the previous section on target behavior analysis. You will, of course, be cognizant of this information when you describe your intervention, especially in the discussion of its model. You may or may not have specific evidence with regard to the specific intervention you are employing, but you are expected to connect your intervention to the evidence that is available regarding your target behavior. Perhaps you have evidence that tutoring normally works in the improvement of the school grades for your target population, but you may not have any evidence of the effectiveness of your specific form of tutoring. So you report what your evidence has revealed, and you examine how it connects to your specific form of tutoring. This means that you are using both evidence and logic to justify your selection of your intervention for the treatment of your specific target behavior.

Goal

The **goal** is the major benefit to the client and is more broad or long term than the outcome objective. Both, however, refer to client outcomes, not service processes. The goal of your adolescent parenting program may be to reduce the negative social consequences of adolescent parenting. Some of these consequences may be dropping out of school, poverty, child neglect, and/or poor parenting. The goal of the tutoring service for at-risk middle school students may be the completion of high school. The goal of your marital counseling service may be to achieve marital harmony. All these are statements of broad benefit to the client. The reason for stating the goal of the service is to indicate the connection between the service objective and the broader benefit. You will measure the achievement of your objective but you will not normally measure the achievement of your goal, partly because it will likely take you too much time to do the latter.

While the goal should be broad and long range, it should be specific enough to provide guidance. Take, for example, the phrase, "To improve the quality of life." What does quality of life mean? Couldn't you say that all services are designed to improve the quality of life in some way? This does not provide guidance on the nature of the long-term outcome in your specific treatment situation.

Objective

The **objective** is a measured amount of progress toward the achievement of the goal. If your goal is to achieve high school completion for at-risk middle school students, you may have an objective of improving grades. You will measure grades in your evaluation of this service, with the assumption that the improvement of grades is a measured amount of progress toward the achievement of high school completion.

The objective is the outcome you will measure in your evaluation study. When you state your objective, you should make sure that you have a measure of it. When you examine your measures, you should make sure that each is connected to an objective.

Each objective should be related to the goal. Here is a list of examples of goals and objectives that have appeared in evaluation research papers by graduate social work students:

1. The goal is to prevent PTSD from causing major problems and difficulties in life for children who have been sexually abused.

   • The objective is to reduce trauma symptoms in children who have experienced a potentially traumatic event.

2. The goal of the intervention is to prevent death by opiate overdose.

   • The objective of the intervention is to increase knowledge about Naloxone, an opiate overdose treatment.

3. The goal is to facilitate healthy grief, and prevent chronic depression, for those who have recently lost a close loved one.

   • The objective is to improve feelings of social support.

4. The goal of the intervention will be to help substance users stay drug free.

   • The outcome objective is to increase the amount of hope among substance abusers.

5. The goals of this service is to improve academic performance of participants.

   • The outcome objective is to improve classroom behavior.

In each of the above examples, the objective was measured to determine if the service had been successful. For the first one, symptoms of trauma were measured. For the second one, knowledge of Naloxone was measured, while the third example had a measure of feelings of social support. The fourth and fifth examples had measures of hope and classroom behaviors, respectively.

Structure

The **structure of the intervention** is a concrete statement that shows both the form and the intensity of the service being given. A group therapy service may be described as weekly 1-hour group sessions for a total of 8 weeks. A training service may be described as a single 3-hour training session, or weekly 1-hour training sessions, over a period of 6 weeks. A case management service may be described as a series of actions including assessment, referral, and counseling that are offered for the typical client for a period of 3 months. Each of these descriptions reveals the form of service (group therapy, training, case management) and the intensity of it, such as eight 1-hour sessions, a single 3-hour session, or a series of actions over a 3-month period of time.

Model

The **model of the intervention** is the framework that serves as the logical rationale for offering it in light of what is known about the dynamics of the target behavior being addressed. If improved knowledge is the need, education would make sense. Thus, you could label this the educational model if you like. In many instances, giving a label to a model is not necessary. You only need to show the connection of the knowledge about the behavior with the nature of the intervention. For example, if modeling of good behavior is the need, a mentor service would make sense. If dealing with a complexity of life challenges is the need, perhaps case management would make sense. If changes in peer groups is the need, then services that connect clients with different peer groups would make sense.

Some services are guided by a major model like the strengths perspective. This might mean that the strengths perspective is viewed as appropriate to all services that are offered by the agency. If that is the case, you could label your model the strengths perspective and briefly describe what this means.

Personnel

The **personnel of the intervention** refers to the credentials of the service providers? Are they persons with a college degree of any kind or persons with a social work degree? Are they licensed in some way (e.g., Licensed Clinical Social Worker)? This does not refer to the names of the staff members who deliver the service nor does it refer to the clients. It refers to the credentials that staff are required to have in order to be qualified to be a service provider.

In summary, the report on the evaluation of a service should describe the service with regard to the goal, the objective, the structure, the model, and the personnel of it. This part of the report will help readers know a lot about how to replicate this service in their own settings. They will also know what it is that was evaluated and shown to be successful or not.

Phase 3: Study Methods

The study methods reveal what data are to be collected from whom with regard to your study purpose. The three key themes are (1) sampling, (2) measurement, and (3) research design. The activities related to these tasks yield critical information for the reader in deciding the uses of your study report. Your method of selecting a study sample reveals the population to whom you can generalize your findings. The tools you employ show the reader whether your measurement was credible. And your research design will provide information on the extent to which one can conclude that the measured client growth was caused by your service rather than something else, such as normal growth over time.

The phase of research known as study methods has been presented in previous chapters as Phase 2 of the research process. In evaluative research, we insert the phase related to the description of the intervention as Phase 2 and shift study methods to the third phase in the process.

Random Sampling and Scientific Generalization

In the previous chapters, you have seen the following information about sampling:

1. The study sample is composed of all those persons from whom data were collected.

2. The study population is composed of the group of persons from whom a sample was selected.

3. If you employ a random sample, you can scientifically generalize your findings from your study sample to the population of persons from whom the sample was selected on a random basis.

4. If you do not employ a random sample, you can generalize your findings to a designated population on a logical basis if you have critical information on the similarities and differences between the members of the study sample and the members of the population.

5. Scientific generalization is superior to logical generalization.

We call generalization from a random sample as "scientific" generalization because with random sampling there is a scientific basis for measuring sampling error. What is **sampling error**? It is the difference in your data between the results you derive from your sample to the same for the study population. The data from your sample will not be identical to the same for the entire population. However, a random sample will yield data that are quite similar between the two groups even though not identical. It is similar enough to conclude that findings from the sample would normally be basically the same as what you would find if you measured your variables for the entire population. This conclusion is more true the larger your sample size. Sampling error is greater for small samples.

A **random sample** is a group of people selected from a study population where each person in the study population has an equal chance of being in the study sample. The students in your research class do not constitute a random sample of all students in your academic program, even though they each had the opportunity to sign up for this course but only some did so. This is not what equal opportunity means in random sampling. What it means is that the researcher drew a sample out of all in the study population on a random basis. The determinant of randomness is in the hands of the researcher, not the sample member.

Here is a challenge question for you: If you have 50 clients in your service program and you can collect outcome data on all 50 persons, should you include all 50 in your study sample or select a random sample of 25 clients from these 50 clients? The answer is that you should include all 50 clients in your study sample. The purpose of the sampling procedure is to be able to generalize your findings to a larger population. If you can include the entire population in your study, please do so. Data on the entire population are better than data from a random sample from that population. Data from the entire population have no sampling error, and they are larger than a sample.

How do you select a random sample? First, you obtain a list of all the names of people in your study population. Second, you select people for your sample on a random basis from the list of the entire population. You can select members randomly by employing a table of random numbers from a research text or just by going to the Internet for help. There are random number generators there.

There is no random sample option when you are evaluating the services for a single client. You have only one person in your sample. Generalization is not normally a major issue being addressed by such a study. Instead, you are evaluating whether a given service worked for this one client. Data from a single client do not lend themselves to the science of sampling.

In this section, we will discuss some specific things about sampling in the evaluative study, starting with the typical type of sample used by social work students—the convenience sample. You are more likely to find random samples in studies that are published.

Convenience Sampling and Logical Generalization

A **convenience sample** is a group of people who were selected for the study out of convenience. Social work students typically select clients with whom they are currently working. This might be a group of clients with the same treatment objective or a single client. Because this is not a random sample, the results of a study from this study sample cannot be scientifically generalized to a larger population of people.

So what can the social work student do? **Logical generalization** is a possibility. This means that you are generalizing on a logical basis rather than on a scientific one. If you have data on the study population, you can compare your study sample with that data to see if the sample seems to be similar to the population. Any major differences will lower the credibility of your logical generalization.

In one example of logical generalization, an inpatient treatment program for chronic alcoholics conducted a follow-up mailed survey for persons discharged from the service a year earlier. They used the addresses in their records but received only a 20% response rate (i.e., only 20% of the study population responded to the survey). The anonymous survey had questions about their use of alcohol and related behaviors. But they wondered if they could generalize their findings to all persons who had been sent a questionnaire. The 20% who responded was not a random sample. Their only option was logical generalization.

So what did they do? The surveys had questions about alcohol use history and family structure. The agency records of all persons sent a questionnaire had similar data. So they compared the sample (those who returned the surveys) with the population (all those who had been discharged 1 year before). The results in this case revealed that the sample was similar to the population on these variables, things that were thought to predict recovery. The staff concluded that the findings from the survey could be generalized to the population on a logical basis.

Using a Tested Instrument for Measuring Client Progress

Measurement refers to the tools used to measure each variable in your study. If you are examining the relationship between gender and income, you must have a way to measure gender and income for each person in your study sample.

In the previous chapters, you have learned the following about measurement:

1. When you conduct a research study, you must have tools to measure each of the variables in your study.

2. You will measure each variable in your study for each person in your study sample.

3. A variable must vary. If all the people in your study sample are men, you do not have data on the variable of gender, because it does not vary.

4. You can measure variables by a tool designed by yourself or one that has been published.

5. There are two general types of measurement: qualitative and quantitative. When you have qualitative measurement, your data are words. When you have quantitative measurement, your data are in the form of either categories (e.g., male or female for the variable of gender) or numbers (e.g., 34 for the variable of age or 21 for the score on the depression scale).

6. The key issue in measurement is credibility, which can be assessed with regard to reliability or validity.

7. Reliability in measurement refers to consistency.

8. Validity in measurement refers to accuracy.

9. Each variable is measured at one level. The levels form a hierarchy from nominal to ordinal, to interval, to ratio.

In this chapter, you will review concepts about measurement that are especially appropriate for evaluative research.

Alternatives for Data Collection

There are several options by which data can be collected. You might review agency records if outcome data are routinely collected and recorded. You might administer a questionnaire with measures of your variables for each individual in your study sample. You might collect data through an interview. In each case, the issue of credibility (reliability and validity) is relevant, but much easier to establish in some situations than others.

If you are lucky, you can simply gain access to agency records where outcome data are routinely recorded. If school grades are the measure of outcome, you will have an easy time collecting data and you might need to pay little attention to ways of testing for reliability and validity. But be sure you have a measure of client outcome, not client characteristics or amount of service delivered, or something like that. Review the situation to see if you have reason to believe that those who record the data for the agency records are doing so accurately.

Many social work researchers will need to administer a questionnaire to individual clients. The questionnaire typically will have scales that are designed to measure the target behaviors. If you have a published scale for measuring anxiety, you will typically have information on credibility (reliability, validity, or both), which you can report. If you have designed the measurement tool yourself, you have the issue of credibility to examine. In these situations, the minimum expectation you encounter is the reporting of **content validity** and **face validity**, each of which are discussed below in the section on reliability and validity.

Your first task is to see if you can find a published scale for measuring your study variable. The published scale is normally superior to a scale that you have developed yourself because it has been designed by an expert on the theme of the scale, and it normally has been tested for reliability and validity.

Most people will assume that grades are appropriate as a measure of school performance. A depression scale, however, is a different matter. There may be readers of your report who wish to know about tests for credibility for your depression scale. They want to know if there is evidence that this tool accurately measures depression. This evidence is a major advantage of using a published scale rather than one that you have developed yourself.

Another form of data collection is the interview. This is more likely to be the vehicle when you are measuring variables qualitatively (i.e., words rather than numbers). It might also be useful when you are measuring a client with a mental challenge who needs things to be explained in careful detail.

Reliability and Validity

The key issue in measurement is credibility. Do readers of your report have confidence that you have measured your study variables in a reasonable way? We have reviewed the issue of credibility with regard to the concepts of reliability (consistency) and validity (accuracy). We have seen that there are several ways to test for reliability. One is the administration of your tool to the same group of people at two points in time to see if the answers are consistent. A test for validity is to examine the correlation of scores on your tool with another tool designed to measure the same thing. You would expect a strong correlation between the scores on the two tests. There are many more tests for reliability and validity.

If you develop your own tool for measurement, you have to face the challenge of considering reliability and validity. At a minimum, you should test for face validity by asking a set of informed people to report whether they believe that your tool accurately measures what you intend for it to measure. If almost all say *Yes*, you can report this as your measure of face validity. You will review other ways of testing for reliability and validity in the chapter on measurement.

Finding a Measurement Tool

In this section, let's examine ways to develop or find a measurement tool. Your first step should be to examine existing tools to see if one is suitable for measuring your study variables. You can search the Internet for such tools. There are various sources from governmental websites that provide information on the nature of many tools for measuring target behaviors. You should first review the purpose of each tool that seems reasonable to see which one is designed to measure just what you wish to measure. You will likely find a copy of the tool through the Internet. You will find books with tools as well. Perhaps your library has many to choose from.

As you review published tools for measuring your variable, you should review several questions. One is the relevance of this scale to the variable you have defined. Another is the credibility of the tool for measuring what you want to measure. Finally, you need to understand the tool adequately to use scores on it to help with practical significance—the amount of change for clients that would be clinically noteworthy.

Here is a checklist of questions for selecting a measurement tool.

- Does this instrument clearly measure your variable as you have defined it?

- Is this tool appropriate for your clients? (Some scales have been developed for children and some for adults.)

- Is your instrument sensitive to the changes you can expect from your clients in the time period they will be measured? (You are more likely to see a change in knowledge from measuring clients before and after three training classes than to find significant change in anxiety with only three therapy sessions.)

- Does your tool have adequate credibility?

- Do you know how to score the instrument?

- Do you know what level of gain would constitute practical significance?

Your second step is to determine how to administer the tool to your clients. This entails making a copy of the tool along with an introduction to the respondent regarding how the information will be used. If you are employing a tool two different times and need to match each person's pretest score with his or her posttest score, you can employ a set of questions for the respondent that provide an anonymous identification number. Privacy, as you will recall, is one of the ethical themes in the use of human subjects in research. The questions might include things such as (a) What is the first letter of your father's middle name? (b) What is the number of letters in your mother's maiden name? (c) What is the last digit of your social security number? You put together the answers to each of these questions to form an identification number that the respondent will know but you do not know. Put the same questions both on the pretest and the posttest questionnaires.

Developing Your Own Tool for Measurement

There are times when the researcher needs to develop his or her special tool for measuring study variables. If you are employing a training program, you will often need to develop your own tool for measuring knowledge of the subject of the training. If your study variables are rather unique, the development of your own measurement tool may be warranted. However, you should always begin your quest for a tool by reviewing the literature to see if a suitable tool has been developed and tested. You do not want to reinvent the wheel. It is likely that any published scale will have been developed by an expert and tested for reliability and validity. Surely this is better than one you develop yourself! The first question, however, is whether that published tool measures what you need to measure. If you are trying to improve the parental skills of parents with an autistic child, a general parental skills tool may not be sufficient. Before you construct your own tool for measuring client progress, review the chapter in this book on measurement.

Research Designs and Causation

The research design specifies the procedures for the measurement of target behavior. You may measure a group of clients before and after the provision of an intervention and compare the two measurements to determine if the clients improved and if that improvement was statistically significant. This illustrates the **one-group pretest–posttest design**. Another design calls on you to measure a group of clients in the same way but compare the gain of the clients with another group of people who did not receive the intervention. In this situation, you are employing the **comparison group design**. There are designs for measuring the progress of a single client. If you are employing the **limited AB single-subject design**, you will measure a single client one time before treatment begins (perhaps the assessment interview) and several times throughout the treatment period (perhaps at the beginning of each treatment session). You cannot, however, measure a single client one time before treatment begins and one time at the end of treatment. That procedure does not constitute any recognized single-subject design because it fails to generate sufficient data to analyze statistically.

There are other designs that will be discussed in a later chapter. The above-mentioned three designs are often used by social work students who are called on to evaluate a service in their research courses. The first and second designs describe group designs, where one or more groups of people are measured to see if the service was effective. The last one is a single-subject design, where a single client is measured repeatedly over a period of time to determine if the service is working. These will be discussed in a later chapter.

The main reason you need to understand the research design employed in an evaluative study is because of the issue of whether the intervention was the cause of the client growth rather than something else, such as normal growth and development over time. If you use the one-group pretest–posttest design, you will have a measure of growth but will not have evidence that the treatment caused the growth. Maybe the clients were already on the path of recovery and have been making progress weekly. The amount of their growth during the treatment period may not be better than the pace of progress already underway.

On the other hand, suppose you compare the growth of your clients with the growth of a comparison group of people who did not receive the treatment. If you find that your clients did better, you will have evidence of causation. The growth of the comparison group should be a good gauge of the effect of normal growth over time. If your clients did better than this, you can assert that your treatment was the cause of the difference in growth between the two groups because you have controlled for the effects of normal growth over time.

When you make your decision about which research design to employ, you should consider the alternative causations of client growth. One, of course, is the effect of the treatment. But there are other alternatives. One is the effect of normal growth over time that was discussed earlier. Another possible cause is a change in the client's environment. These two causes of client improvement that is outside the effects of treatment are referred to as **threats to internal validity**. So clients may improve because of treatment or they may improve because of something else. The research design employed will help us decide which it is—the treatment or something else. More specifics regarding research designs and causation will be reviewed in a later chapter where you will see which design addresses which of the other causes of client growth.

If you have a good reason to believe that things other than the treatment will be the cause of your measured client gain, you should employ a research design that controls for these other effects. In many situations, you will conclude that it is unlikely that things other than the treatment will affect the target behavior. The issue here is not whether it is possible that something else will cause the measured client growth but whether it is *probable* that they will. If it is not probable, you do not need to worry about these alternatives, but you will report the limitations of your study in the conclusions section of your report, one of which may be the research design employed.

Ethics in the Use of Human Subjects in Research

In several previous chapters, you have seen information on key ethical issues in the use of human subjects in research. In evaluative studies, you will typically be asking clients to complete a questionnaire for your data. In this regard, you should be attentive to the issues of (a) privacy, (b) voluntary participation, (c) justice, and (d) potential harm. For the typical study, like the one illustrated in the research example given in the next section, you will only need to be attentive to the issues of voluntary participation and privacy, because your administration to a questionnaire to clients will not likely require special attention to the issues of justice and harm. You can attend to the issues of voluntary participation and privacy by having clients complete a questionnaire voluntarily and without their names on the instrument. However, if you need their names for research purposes (e.g., matching pretest and posttest scores), you can address the issue of privacy by keeping the questionnaires confidential.

Phase 4: Data Analysis

The key issue for data analysis in evaluative research is whether the data supported the study hypothesis. From previous instruction, you have learned that you must have data that are in the hypothesized direction and you must also have data that are statistically significant. The second key issue is whether the data are of practical significance. You have learned that you cannot easily make the case that you have practical significance if you do not have statistical significance. If your data can be explained by chance, how can you say they are of practical benefit in the support of the intervention that is being evaluated? What you have discovered is chance!

In this section, you will see a review of tips for constructing the study hypothesis. You will also be given further guidance on statistical analysis, especially for the evaluative study. And you will review some suggestions about practical significance.

Testing the Study Hypothesis

In the previous chapters, you have learned that the study hypothesis is an educated guess about the results you expect to find from your data analysis. You have been given examples like the following:

- Posttest scores for anxiety will be lower than pretest scores.

- Grades at the end of treatment will be higher than grades before the treatment began.

- The proportion of homeless clients who find a home within 6 months of service will be higher than the proportion of homeless people who find a home within 6 months on their own, according to national statistics.

Let's examine a few tips about writing the study hypothesis for the evaluation research study. Here are three such tips:

1. Your hypothesis should identify the client's target behavior that will be measured in your study (e.g., scores on the anxiety scale, grades in school, marital satisfaction scores, and getting a home.)

2. Your hypothesis should report what is expected (e.g., anxiety scores will go down, grades will go up, acts of aggression will go down).

3. Your hypothesis should not contain assertions of causation, for example, "Because of the tutoring service, clients grades will go up."

When you present your statement of hypothesis and your client data, another researcher should be able to test your study hypothesis, provided that he or she knows a statistical test that is appropriate. They will not have to ask you any further questions.

One more tip. Keep the statement of the hypothesis concise, like the ones mentioned above. You do not see unnecessary words that might be called *normal talk* among practitioners. For example, you did not see a statement such as, "Given the importance of anxiety to people who have recently been the victims of family violence, we expect that our clients will see their anxiety scores go down during the treatment they receive because our treatment addresses the causes of anxiety for victims of violence."

Your first step in testing your hypothesis is to submit your data to statistical analysis. With regard to the example about anxiety scores, you will need to determine if the posttest scores are lower than the pretest scores. If not, then you can conclude that your data failed to support your hypothesis. The issue of statistical significance is no longer relevant.

If your data fail to go in the hypothesized direction, you can report that your data failed to support your hypothesis. For example, if posttest scores are not better, you cannot say your data supported your hypothesis. If your data are in the hypothesized direction, you test for statistical significance. If your data go in the hypothesized direction but fail to achieve statistical significance, you must report that you data failed to support your hypothesis. On the other hand, if your data are in the hypothesized direction and are statistically significant, you can report that your data supported your study hypothesis.

You have been instructed that the value of p (converted to a whole number) represents the number of times in 100 that your data would occur by chance. The expression "$p < .05$" means that your data would occur by chance less than 5 times in 100. This is the normal standard in the social sciences for finding statistical support for your hypothesis. Always remember that you have two conditions for determining if you data supported your hypothesis: (1) the direction of the data and (2) statistical significance.

Practical Significance

Practical significance is a judgment about the extent to which the measured results are noteworthy. It is informed by knowledge of the nature of the target behavior that is being measured. You must first decide how much of a change is sufficient to be of practical significance. You might have the aid of information about various thresholds of functioning according to the scale that is being used. You might find, for example, that a score greater than 30 on your depression scale represents a severe level of depression, likely requiring hospitalization. You might learn that a score between 20 and 30 represents major depression and a need for therapy, whereas a score less than 20 represents no need for therapy. If your client moved to a lower threshold, you could claim this as evidence of practical significance.

You should become familiar with what a given score on your scale represents by examining the nature of your scale. If your scale consists of 10 things an abusing partner might do to a spouse and find that each of these items is significant, perhaps you could make the case that a change of only one point on this scale is of practical significance. On a different scale, you might make the case that a change of 25% constitutes practical significance by explaining what this level of change looks like in real life. What you cannot do, and assert an informed opinion, is to just say that it seems to you that this level of client gain is of practical significance. You have to offer a rationale.

You should decide on your standard for practical significance before you analyze your data. This decision should be independent of the actual data you have for the process to be objective. Remember that research is a process of discovery, not justification. If you know your data before you decide on your standard for practical significance, wouldn't this fact create a bias with regard to the selection of the standard?

Phase 5: Writing the Study Conclusions for the Evaluative Study

In the previous chapters, you have reviewed the following suggestions about the conclusions for your study:

- Your first task is to summarize your data with regard to your research question.

- Do not draw conclusions that outrun your data. Reserve your opinions that are not supported by the data for other venues.

- Discuss the limitations of your study, with a special reference to the kind of sample you employed, the manner in which you measured the variables, and the study design that was used.

- Discuss the implications of your findings for practice. How might practitioners make use of these results?

- In the explanatory or evaluative study, do not conclude that practical significance was found if your data were not statistically significant, given the fact that your data can be explained by chance.

Another thought about the last item mentioned above. If you believe that your data are of practical significance but fail to be statistically significant, you are very likely to have a small sample size. In this situation, you may declare your data not to be amenable to statistical analysis and conclude that another study should be conducted with a larger sample. You should not, however, conclude that your service was found to be effective in your study.

A few more general suggestions are in order. First, don't say you found "nothing" because your data failed to support your hypothesis. Failure to find support for your hypothesis is an important finding. Perhaps we should rethink the rationale for the hypothesis. Second, your conclusions should be tentative. You have not really found the final proof of anything. In fact, saying that you "proved" something is not in good form. Instead, you found, or failed to find, support for your hypothesis. This is more tentative than saying that you have proved something.

This chapter has discussed evaluative research, so your conclusions will be about your study that evaluated a service. This means that you will add the issue of practical significance to the themes you will address in your conclusions section. You need to provide a rationale for declaring that you did, or did not, find results that were of practical significance.

A consideration in the determination of practical significance is the extent of the resources that were employed by the service that is being evaluated. Suppose you found a 10% improvement in anxiety for a minimal service (e.g., weekly 1-hour therapy sessions for 3 weeks). Could these data support your claim for practical significance? Probably so, because the gain is minimal but so is the expenditure of resources. But now think of the same amount of gain for an extensive service such as mental health treatment given in a hospital for 30 days. Now, you would find it more difficult to convince others that you have practical significance.

RESEARCH EXAMPLE: ARE THE SERVICES OF THE NEW HORIZONS TREATMENT PROGRAM EFFECTIVE IN THE REDUCTION OF DEPRESSION FOR ADULT CLIENTS?

In this research example, you will review the entire process of evaluative research. This means that you will review (a) the development of the research question and knowledge base, (b) the selection of the research methods to be employed, (c) the analysis of the data, and (d) the drawing of conclusions. Each of the first two phases of the evaluative research process will be presented to you, but you will undertake the analysis of the data and the drawing of conclusions yourself.

A service within the New Horizons Treatment Program will serve as the example. Included in the services of this program is individual therapy for adults clients who are seeking services to reduce their depression. A group of clients provided this service constituted the study sample.

Phase 1: The Research Question and Knowledge Base for the New Horizons Study

The research question for this study is as follows: Is CBT offered by the New Horizons Treatment Program effective in the reduction of depression for adult clients? Because this is a research question for an evaluative study, it identified both the target behavior being treated and the treatment that was being evaluated. CBT was the model of therapy that was offered to the clients who were included in this evaluation study. The knowledge base examined for this study entailed the review of literature on the definition of depression, the causes of depression, and the results of studies of various treatments for depression. In particular, there was a focus on the evidence regarding the use of CBT in treatment.

What Is Depression?

You have probably discussed depression with others on many occasions, and you should have an idea of what it means. But your conception may be incomplete as a guide for an evaluation research study. For this reason, you would likely seek guidance from the literature. Tools that have been developed to measure depression will likely have a definition for this concept. The Internet will have multiple sources that you can use to find your definition. In the study reviewed here, depression was defined as follows:

> Depression is a feeling that can be depicted as sadness, worthlessness, and guilt. These feelings tend to be accompanied by a desire to be alone along with a loss of appetite, sleep, and general activity. Clinical depression is defined as a state of depression that has seriously interfered with normal human functioning for at least 6 months.

Depression as depicted above can be distinguished from normal feelings of sadness, which is short term and likely related to a stressful life event. As depicted above, depression accompanies a feeling of having given up on life in the normal sense. Ambition and hope are low, and the state of depression has been evident for a long period of time, like 6 months or more. A critical role for the definition of the target behavior is to provide guidance on the selection of a tool to measure it. You can examine the tool used to measure depression for the New Horizons study (identified in the section "Study Methods" of this report) to see if you believe that it does an adequate job of measuring depression from the definition given above.

Causes and Consequences of Depression

According to information from the National Institute of Mental Health, major depressive disorder (clinical depression) is a serious mood disorder that affects how a depressed person feels, thinks, and handles daily activities, such as sleeping, eating, and working. To be diagnosed with depression, these symptoms must be present for at least 2 weeks (National Institute of Mental Health, 2018). Among the risk factors (i.e., potential causes) of depression are (a) a family history of depression, (b) major life changes, (c) trauma, (d) stress, and (e) certain physical illnesses or medication (National Institute of Mental Health, 2018).

Among the treatments for depression is psychotherapy. According to the National Institute of Mental Health, there are several types of psychotherapy for the treatment of depression. Examples of evidence-based approaches include CBT, interpersonal therapy, and problem-solving therapy (National Institute of Mental Health, 2018).

What Works in the Treatment of Depression?

The next task is the review of the evidence regarding the treatment of depression. The federal government is one source of information on evidence-based practices for the treatment of various target behaviors. For example, the Substance Abuse and Mental Health Services Administration (samhsa.gov) lists both CBT and interpersonal therapy as being among the evidence-based practices for the treatment of depression (https://www.samhsa.gov/treatment/mental-disorders/depression#evidence-based).

Another source is the Society of Clinical Psychology, which lists the following evidence-based treatments for the treatment of depression: (a) CBT, (b) behavioral therapy, (c) problem-solving treatment, (d) interpersonal psychotherapy, (e) reminiscence therapy, and (f) cognitive bibliotherapy (https://www.div12.org/treatments)

These sources provide a number of treatments that are supported by evidence. Evidence-based practice is the theme of one of the other chapters in this book. The treatment employed in the treatment of depression at the New Horizons Treatment Program was CBT, one of the treatments listed in each of the above-mentioned sources.

Phase 2: Description of the New Horizons Treatment Program

You have reviewed how the intervention (or service) can be described comprehensively with regard to goal, objective, structure, model, and personnel. A major task in the report on the study of the New Horizons Treatment Program is the identification of the intervention with regard to these five concepts.

What should be the goal of treatment for the New Horizons Treatment Program? Should it be (a) to reduce depression, (b) to provide good quality services, (c) to enhance social and psychological functioning so as to improve self-sufficiency, or (d) none of the above? As you answer this question in the practice exercise, keep in mind the distinction between the goal and the objective, and keep in mind that they both focus on outcome rather than on process. What should be the objective? Is it one of the options mentioned above with regard to the goal statement? If not, what should be the statement of the objective of treatment?

The service of the New Horizons Treatment Program is a form of psychotherapy that is delivered in 1-hour sessions, once per week, for a period of 8 weeks. The therapy sessions are delivered at the agency.

The therapy model employed in this treatment is CBT. The Beck Institute is an entity that was developed by the founder of this model. According to the Beck Institute, CBT is a "time-sensitive, structured, present-oriented psychotherapy directed toward solving current problems and teaching clients skills to modify dysfunctional thinking and behavior" (Beck Institute, 2016). It is based on the cognitive model that suggests that the way in which we perceive situations is more closely connected to our behaviors than the situation itself (as viewed objectively). One important part of CBT is helping clients change their unhelpful thinking and behavior that lead to enduring improvement in their mood and functioning. A variety of cognitive and behavioral techniques are employed in CBT. It also employs problem-solving techniques as well as techniques from a variety of treatment models (Beck Institute, 2016). A key assumption of this model is that dysfunctional thinking causes psychological problems such as depression, so the treatment should address thinking patterns.

The staff who delivered this therapy at the New Horizons Treatment Program were licensed clinical social workers, each of whom have the LCSW credential and at least 2 years of clinical experience. These two qualifications are required by this agency for the position of therapist for this program.

Phase 3: Study Methods for the Evaluation of the New Horizons Treatment Program

The individuals from whom data were collected for this study consisted of the first 15 persons who sought treatment for depression from the New Horizons Treatment Program in the month of February 2017. These individuals were from the target population of persons treated by this agency who have reported to have been depressed at a level that interfered with their satisfaction with life for a minimum of 6 months. The New Horizons Treatment Program has provided the same treatment as revealed in this study to the same target population for the past 2 years to approximately 250 individuals.

The measurement tool was the revised version of the Beck Depression Inventory—II (BDI-II). In its current version, this scale is designed for individuals who are 13 years old and above. It is designed to measure depression and is composed of items relating to symptoms of depression (e.g., sadness, hopelessness, irritability), cognitions indicative of depression (e.g., feelings of guilt), as well as physical symptoms such as fatigue, weight loss, and lack of interest in normal activities of life such as sex. It has 21 questions about how the subject has been feeling in the past 2 weeks. Each question has a set of four possible responses, ranging in intensity. For example, the respondent is asked, on one item, to select one of the following four options with regard to the theme of sadness: 0 = *I do not feel sad*, 1 = *I feel sad*, 2 = *I am sad all the time and I can't snap out of it*, 3 = *I am so sad or unhappy that I can't stand it*. The individual gets 0 points for selecting the first option, 1 point for the second, 2 for the third, and 3 for the last option. This scale has been subjected to numerous studies of reliability and validity and has been shown to have passed the test in good form (see, e.g., Visser, Leentiens, Marinus, Stiggelbout, & van Hilten, 2006). There are several thresholds of functioning exhibited by scores on the BDI. Scores of 0 to 13 are considered minimal, while scores from 14 to 19 are considered mild. Treatment is not normally indicated for people at either of these levels. At the next level, scores from 20 to 28 are considered to be moderate depression, and scores of 29 and above are considered to be severe depression.

The research design employed in this study was the one-group pretest–posttest design. This means that all the 15 clients in this study were given the BDI before the treatment began and were given this same scale at the end of the treatment period. The difference in these two sets of scores were compared to test the study hypothesis.

Phase 4: Analysis of Data for the Evaluation of the New Horizons Treatment Program

The hypothesis for the study of the New Horizons Treatment Program was as follows: *Posttest scores on depression will be lower than pretest scores.* The pretest scores, posttest scores, and gain scores for each client are given in Exhibit 8.1. The statistic for testing this hypothesis will be the paired *t* test, because we have a set of matched scores for one group of people. You should remember that a statistical test will generate the value of *p*, which is considered statistically significant if its value is less than .05 (a *p* value of .05 means that these data would occur just by chance only 5 times in 100).

When you examine the data, you have two major questions to answer: (1) Are the data statistically significant? (2) Are the data of practical significance? The value of *p* is the key to statistical significance ($p < .05$). Practical significance is a matter of informed opinion. Is the client gain enough? Did it meet our expectations? On what basis do we answer these questions? It is not sufficient to say "I believe that practical significance was achieved?" Instead you could say "Practical significance was achieved because . . ." It will be the words after *because* that are critical. This is where you justify why you believe practical significance was achieved.

EXHIBIT 8.1

DEPRESSION SCORES FOR CLIENTS OF THE NEW HORIZONS TREATMENT PROGRAM

Client Number	Pretest Score	Posttest Score	Gain Score
1	31	28	3
2	34	30	4
3	30	20	10
4	28	28	0
5	41	30	11
6	26	25	1
7	31	25	6
8	38	28	10
9	35	22	13
10	45	33	12
11	41	30	11
12	30	30	0
13	31	31	0
14	38	31	7
15	44	28	16

What would, in your opinion, be a gain on the BDI that would be of practical significance in this study, given the extent of the treatment offered? Would it be a movement from one threshold to another in functioning (e.g., from severe depression to moderate depression)? Would it be a certain percentage of gain? What does one point of change mean, and how can this knowledge guide your determination of practical significance?

Phase 5: Study Conclusions for the Evaluation of the New Horizons Treatment Program

Study conclusions are based on the analysis of the data from the study. You have not seen that analysis because this task will be the first thing you do in the first practice exercise for this chapter. In the previous chapters, you have been given a set of tips about how to report your study conclusions. You have been instructed to summarize your findings on your research question and to be sure your conclusions do not outrun your data.

For example, you should not draw conclusions that are not supported by your data just because you believe these statements are true or have been supported by the literature. Your conclusions for an evaluative research study should be supported by your data.

You have been instructed to speak about the limitations of your study and the implications for practice. And you have reviewed the theme of practical significance, a topic that belongs in the conclusions section of the research report.

What follows are the two practice exercises for this chapter. In Practice Exercise 1, you will examine the data from the evaluation of the New Horizons Treatment Program, and you will provide a report on this study. In Practice Exercise 2, you will report what a familiar human service agency is doing with regard to the evaluation of input, process, and outcome.

Chapter Practice Exercises

Practice Exercise 1: Report on the New Horizons Treatment Program Evaluation

In this practice exercise, you will examine the data from the New Horizons Treatment Program and provide a report on key aspects of this evaluation study. You have been given information on this evaluation study with regard to (a) the articulation of the research question and knowledge base, (b) the research methods employed in the study, and (c) the intervention being evaluated. You have also been given the data from that evaluation study. Your tasks are to analyze the data that have been given, to draw conclusions for this study, and to report on all phases of this evaluation research study.

Competencies Demonstrated by Practice Exercise 1

1. The ability to use an Internet website to analyze data in an evaluative research study that includes matched scores from a single group of clients

2. The ability to report whether a set of analyzed data supported the study hypothesis with regard to both the direction of the data and statistical significance

3. The ability to draw appropriate conclusions from an analyzed set of data for an evaluative research study

4. The ability to report on all phases of evaluative research regarding (a) the research question and knowledge base, (b) the intervention being evaluated, (c) the study methods employed, (d) the analysis of data, and (e) the study conclusions

5. The ability to report on how ethical issues were addressed in an evaluative study

Activities for Practice Exercise 1

6. Review if the information on the evaluative research example (New Horizons Treatment Program) is sufficient to report (a) the research question and knowledge base, (b) the description of the intervention being evaluated, and (c) the study methods employed. In addition, review the data given in Exhibit 8.1.

7. Analyze the data in Exhibit 8.1 to determine if the study hypothesis was supported using the instructions from the chapter appendix on how to use an Internet website for this purpose.

8. Decide on the conclusions that should be drawn from the study of the New Horizons Treatment Program.

9. Provide a report on the evaluation of the New Horizons Treatment Program using the questions delineated in the instructions for your practice exercise report.

What You Will Report From Practice Exercise 1

Your task in your practice exercise report is to prepare answers to the questions given below.

A: Target Behavior

- What is the target behavior? What is your definition of it?

- What are some of the treatments that have been found to be effective in the treatment of this target behavior (include literature reference citations)? Is the treatment used by the New Horizons Treatment Program among the treatments found to be effective?

B: Intervention

- How would you describe the New Horizons Treatment Program with regard to goal, objective, structure, and personnel?

C: Study Methods

- What is the study population for the New Horizons Treatment Program evaluation? What is the study sample? Can you generalize your findings to this population on a scientific basis? Explain.

- What tool was used to measure the target behavior identified in the treatment objective? Name the tool and briefly describe it. Does this tool do an adequate job of measuring the target behavior (e.g., "Is it congruent with the target behavior definition?" "Has it passed any tests of reliability and validity?")?

- Do you believe that these 15 clients of the New Horizons Treatment Program would have achieved a noteworthy gain in depression scores if they had not had the intervention during the period of time of the treatment (8 weeks)? Explain.

- Does the research design employed in this study do an adequate job of addressing possible causes of client gain on the target behavior other than the intervention, such as normal growth over time? Explain. (*Note:* If there are no such causes that should be of special concern in this situation, you should say so in your answer.)

D: Data Analysis

- What was the hypothesis that was tested in the study of the New Horizons Treatment Program?

- What statistical test was employed to test the study hypothesis?

- Did the data support the hypothesis? Be sure to answer this question with specific data on the mean scores and the value of p.

E: Conclusions

Provide the first paragraph of your statement of conclusions. This includes only a summary of the study results and the basic conclusion that was warranted. You are not asked to discuss the implications of this study for practice or the strengths and limitations of the study methods employed.

Practice Exercise 2: Evaluating Various Aspects of Your Agency's Service System

In this exercise, you are called on to examine one aspect of a familiar service system, such as input, process, output, or outcome. The task is to report what is known from agency records regarding one of these aspects of system evaluation. You should select one of the following five questions to answer and provide a report.

1. What information does the agency have regarding the evaluation of input (need), and what does the agency do with this information?

    a. Is there a need assessment report that provides data on the extent to which the agency services are addressing the needs of the target population (e.g., abused children, alcoholics, homeless people, persons with eating disorders, mental health of military families, etc.)? These data should show a breakdown of client characteristics that show the extent to which the services are being delivered to this population.

    b. Does the agency have information on unmet needs, such as a waiting list of applicants for service or a report from the U.S. Census Bureau that shows how many people are in the target population for this agency as compared with the number that have been served.

2. What information does the agency have on the evaluation of service process, and what does the agency do with this information?

    a. Are there service protocols that show the agency's service policies with regard to the nature of the service being provided, such as clients being informed of their rights and clients receiving each of the various aspects of the service program (e.g., case management, counseling, and tutoring)? Are data reported on the extent to which these policies have been implemented?

    b. Does the agency monitor services to see to it that the approach of the agency to service is being delivered? For example,

if the agency reports that it provides strengths-based services, how does it demonstrate that this is happening with data?

    c. Does the agency report about standards of service regarding things such as the credentials of the service providers?

3. What information does the agency have on service output, and what does the agency do with this information?

    a. How does the agency define the unit of service for a given program? Is it a client served, a time unit (an hour of therapy), an episode of service (e.g., a child abuse investigation completed), or something else?

    b. Does the agency report the number of units of service that it provides?

    c. Does the agency report the cost per unit of service? If not, can you compute it by dividing the total cost of the program (e.g., $153,000) by the number of units of service delivered?

4. What information does the agency have on client outcome, and what does it do with this information?

    a. How does it define the outcome objective (e.g., to improve school grades, to reduce anxiety, to improve compliance with the medical treatment plan, etc.)?

    b. What data are collected on this outcome?

    c. What are the results?

5. Does the agency measure client satisfaction? If so, how does it do so (e.g., via a mailed survey conducted when the client is discharged, a suggestion box in the agency lobby, etc.)? What are the themes that are included in this information? What have been the results?

CHAPTER REVIEW

Chapter Key Learnings

1. The systems model can help illustrate the nature of evaluation research in a comprehensive fashion, including the assessment of need (input), the examination of service standards (process), the examination of service efficiency and quantity (output), and the evaluation of client outcome.

2. The normal phases of research include the knowledge base, the study methods, the analysis of data, and the drawing of conclusions. In evaluative research, another phase is included: the description of the intervention (service). Another special aspect of evaluation research is the essentiality of reporting on the research design in reference to the issue of causation.

3. The knowledge base for the evaluation study includes special attention to the definition and analysis of the target behavior being measured as well as the evidence on what works in its treatment. The definition provides special guidance for the measurement of the target behavior, while the analysis offers guidance on the justification of the chosen treatment.

4. There are good sources of evidence for what works in the treatment of various target behaviors, the systematic review of evidence being at the top of the list of scientific approaches to making decisions.

5. The selected intervention can be justified on the basis of evidence or logic or both. Evidence as a justification refers to scientific outcome studies that show that a treatment is evidence based for a given target behavior. Logical justification refers to the logical analysis of information. For example, if scientific studies reveal that persons who are depressed are more likely to exhibit dysfunctional thinking about life events, a treatment that addresses dysfunctional thinking would be logically justified.

6. The intervention should be described with regard to the goal, the objective, the structure, the model, and the personnel. These themes provide a comprehensive report on the nature of the intervention that is being evaluated.

7. The random sample provides the basis for scientific generalization of study findings. A convenience sample might be generalized on a logical basis if there is sufficient information that shows that the relevant characteristics of the study sample are similar to the characteristics of the study population.

8. There are times when the researcher is fortunate enough to have a measure of client outcome that is found in agency records such as school grades or disciplinary actions. But target behaviors that deal with social and psychological functioning require some attention to the science behind the scale to be employed. When you conduct an evaluative research that addresses such a variable, you should first seek a published scale for measuring client progress because it has been designed by experts and has typically been tested for reliability and validity. If an appropriate published scale cannot be located, you can develop your own tool for measurement of target behavior provided that you adhere to certain principles of survey measurement.

9. Among other issues in the selection of a means of measurement for psychosocial variables such as depression, marital harmony, and so on are the issues of reliability and validity. Reliability refers to the consistency of a measurement tool, which can be tested by giving the same group of people the tool at two points in time and checking the data for consistency. Validity refers to the accuracy of a tool and can be tested by computing the correlation between the designated tool and a published tool that measures the same thing. A positive correlation would be evidence of the validity of the designated tool.

10. Among the various research designs available for the evaluative researcher are the one-group pretest–posttest design, the comparison group design, and the limited AB single-subject design. A critical issue addressed by the selection of the research design is causation. Did the treatment cause the client's measured growth or was it caused by something else, like normal growth over time? The one-group pretest–posttest design does not address normal growth over time as the cause of the measured client growth because you only have a measure of whether the client improved, but this improvement might be due to normal growth over time. The comparison group design, however, does address this potential cause because the growth of the comparison group is a measure of the effect of normal growth over time. The

limited AB single-subject research design does not control for normal growth over time because you only have a measure of client growth but not a measure of the trends in the target behavior by the client over time.

11. The study hypothesis for an evaluative study identifies the target behavior being measured and the expected direction of the outcome. It should avoid assertions of causation or nonessential phrases. The hypothesis should be a simple statement such as, "Posttest scores for anxiety will be lower than pretest scores."

12. For your data to support your study hypothesis in evaluative research, you must find that the data showed client growth and the amount of growth was found to be statistically significant.

13. Practical significance in evaluative research is an informed opinion on the extent to which the study results were noteworthy. Is a 20% gain in client functioning good news or is it a disappointment? A study can have statistical significance without having practical significance; these are two different issues. Given the nature of a failure to find statistical significance, it would be difficult to argue that data that are not of statistical significance are, in fact, of practical significance.

14. Study conclusions in evaluative research should summarize the findings of the study and the implications of these results for social work practice or policy.

Chapter Discussion Questions

1. What is one of the major advantages of a careful definition of the client's target behavior in evaluative research? In other words, what other aspect of the research process is aided by a careful definition rather than a nebulous one?

2. What is one of the major advantages of a good target behavior analysis, where you examine the causes of the target behavior? In other words, what other aspect of the research process is aided by a good analysis?

3. Suppose that you searched for evidence regarding a social work practice and failed to find any research on this practice. How would this affect you?

4. Think of a study that you might do with a group of clients where you have a convenience sample? What makes this a convenience sample rather than a random one? To whom could you generalize your findings on a logical basis? Explain.

5. Think of a tool that you might design to measure client progress with this group of clients. This is not a tool that you selected from published tools but one that you will design yourself.

   a. What is your definition of the target behavior in this example?

   b. Present one item that would be on the scale you designed.

6. Can you have practical significance with your data if you do not have statistical significance? Explain.

7. When you are writing the conclusions section of your research report, what should you do with your own opinions? Should you present them in the same light as the results of your study, avoid presenting them, or something else?

Chapter Test

1. Which of the following are included in the evaluation of the service system?
   a. The efficiency of service delivered
   b. The needs of those in the target population
   c. The outcomes of services
   d. All of the above

2. Service standards refer to which of the following:
   a. Service input
   b. Service process
   c. Service output
   d. Service outcome

3. The best place to obtain guidance for the selection of a tool for measuring client progress would be
   a. The sampling procedure employed
   b. The analysis of the causes of the target behavior

   c. The definition of the target behavior to be treated.
   d. The analysis of client need

4. The sampling procedures employed in a study are helpful for which issue?
   a. The question of what caused the clients to improve
   b. The generalization of study results
   c. Whether chance is a good explanation for study results
   d. How to define the target behavior

5. The systematic review is a vehicle for
   a. Reviewing various methods of selecting a study sample
   b. Reviewing research designs
   c. Reviewing evidence
   d. Reviewing optional statistical tests

6. Which of the following would constitute appropriate statements of the structure of an intervention?
   a. Interpersonal therapy will be delivered in hourly sessions once per week for 6 weeks
   b. Interpersonal therapy is designed to reduce the anxiety of those who are the victims of violence
   c. Both of the above
   d. None of the above

7. Which of these statements would be the best statement for the outcome objective of the support group service for victims of rape?
   a. To reduce the social and psychological consequences of the experience of rape
   b. To improve feelings of social support
   c. To deliver support group services once per week for 5 weeks.
   d. To provide support group services using qualified personnel

8. You can examine test–retest reliability by
   a. Giving your measurement tool to the same group of people at two different points in time and examining the results to see if there is a good correlation between the scores for these two points in time
   b. Examining the average correlation among items on a measurement tool

c. Both of the above
d. None of the above

9. If you select a random sample of members of the Nebraska Chapter of the National Association of Social Workers, you can scientifically generalize your findings to what population?
   a. All social workers in the state of Nebraska
   b. All social workers in the nation
   c. All members of the Nebraska Chapter of the National Association of Social Workers
   d. None of the above

10. Does the one-group pretest–posttest research design control for normal growth and development as an alternative explanation of the study results?
    a. Yes, because it provides for two different measurements of the target behavior
    b. Yes, because it provides for a measurement of gain on the target behavior
    c. No, because it is not likely to generate results that are statistically significant
    d. No, because it does not measure trends in target behavior before treatment or have another mechanism for comparing client growth with normal growth over time

ANSWERS: 1 = d; 2 = b; 3 = c; 4 = b; 5 = c; 6 = a; 7 = b; 8 = a; 9 = c; 10 = d

Chapter Glossary

Comparison group design. A research design whereby the gain of a group of treated persons is compared with the gain of a group of non-treated persons.

Content validity. The extent to which the scale employed does a good job of including all aspects of the concept begin measured, with

special reference to the definition of the concept in the study report.

Convenience sample. A sample of people who were selected for the study out of convenience.

Evidence. Information collected from sources of a scientific nature that is viewed as credible by key actors in the human service system

Face validity. The extent to which key informants agree that the measurement tool does a good job of measuring the concept intended.

Goal. The major, long-term, benefit to the client of the intervention (service, treatment, etc.).

Input. The resources that are employed in the provision of the intervention.

Intervention. The composite of the activities that are provided to clients for the purpose of achieving a given outcome. This term is used in the same way as service and treatment in this book.

Limited AB single-subject design. A single-subject research design in which a single client is measured one time on the target behavior before treatment begins and several more times during the treatment period.

Logical generalization. Generalizing study findings from the sample to the population on a logical basis, based on information showing the similarities (and the differences) between people in the sample and people in the population.

Meta-analysis. An examination of the data from a group of published studies to determine a summary of the extent of the effect of a given treatment on a given target behavior.

Model of the intervention. The conceptual framework that serves as the logical rationale for offering the intervention in light of what is known about the dynamics of the target behavior being addressed.

Objective. A measured amount of progress toward the achievement of the goal. It is the thing that will be measured with regard to client outcome.

One-group pretest–posttest design. A research design in which one group of clients is measured before and after the intervention with regard to the objective of treatment.

Outcome. The benefit to the client.

Output. The amount of service that is provided, such as 254 hours of therapy.

Personnel of the intervention. The credentials of the service providers.

Practical significance. A judgment about the extent to which the measured results are noteworthy.

Process. That which happens to the clients in order to achieve the intended outcomes (i.e., the service).

Program. An organized set of services designed to achieve a social goal, such as reduction of child abuse, improvement of mental health, prevention of suicide, and/or improvement of family relations.

Random sample. A group of people selected from a study population on a random basis.

Sampling error. The difference in your data between the results from your sample and what would be the results if you had data from the entire population.

Services. A set of professional activities designed to achieve a specific objective for a given set of clients. This term is used in the same way as intervention and treatment in this book.

Structure of the intervention. A concrete statement that shows both the form and the intensity of the services being given.

Systematic review. A review of existing evidence about a problem or an intervention that includes all meta-analyses that have been found and usually includes studies that have not been published.

Target behavior. The behavior of the client that is being treated.

Target behavior analysis. The analysis of the client's behavior that is being treated.

Target behavior definition. The definition of the client's behavior that is being treated.

Threats to internal validity. Potential causes of the client's measured growth that are independent of the intervention, such as normal growth over time.

Treatment. What is done to the client in order to achieve the objectives. This term is used in same way as service and intervention in this book.

Unit of service. The concrete measure of the amount of a service, such as the number of hours of counseling provided or the number of child abuse investigations completed.

CHAPTER APPENDIX: STATISTICAL ANALYSIS OF THE DATA FOR THE NEW HORIZONS TREATMENT PROGRAM

This part of Practice Exercise 1 will provide you with guidance on the statistical analysis of the data given in Exhibit 8.1. You will use GraphPad for this purpose. Each step in this process is give below.

Step 1: Access GraphPad QuickCalcs by clicking on the following link:

https://www.graphpad.com/quickcalcs/

Step 2: Select *continuous data*.

Then click *continue*.

Step 3: Select *t test* to compare the two means.

Then click *continue*.

Step 4: You will be at the screen that says **Choose data entry format.**

1. Select *enter up to 50 rows.*

2. Enter your data in the two rows with the pretest score for the first client in the first column first row and the posttest score for the first client in the second column first row. Then, do the same for the second client and so forth. In other words, enter the data as you see it in Exhibit 8.1.

3. Select *paired t test*

4. Click *Calculate now*

Step 5: Review the results.

- One of the options is ***p* value and statistical significance**. This will give you the value of *p*.

- Another option is **intermediate values used in calculations**. Under this option, you will see the value of *t*.

- The means for Group 1 (pretest score) and Group 2 (posttest score) will be given on this page.

You should report the mean pretest score, the mean posttest score, the value of *t*, and the value of *p*. The values of *t* and *p* should be put in parenthesis following the reporting of the mean pretest and posttest scores.

CONDUCTING QUALITATIVE RESEARCH THAT EXPLORES THE UNKNOWN

John Powell (1984) was a social worker with an interest in the improvement of the process whereby older children are placed for adoption. His knowledge base for a study had shown that the decade of the 1970s had witnessed a major increase in the movement to place older and emotionally troubled children into adoptive care. These children had previously been left in foster care or children's institutions. What he could not find in the literature in the 1970s was knowledge about the experience of being adopted. What, he wondered, was it like to go through the process of being adopted when you were old enough to have ideas about the experience? More important, he wondered how a study of this experience could help with ideas for improving this experience. He decided that the lack of knowledge about this experience would suggest that he conduct an exploratory study using qualitative methods of measurement. He selected a qualitative method known as analytic induction as his means of inquiry. This method calls on the researcher to develop a set of tentative hypotheses from the knowledge base and to undergo a set of procedures for confirming, or adjusting, the hypothesis. In the protocol for analytic induction, the first person is studied in light of the hypothesis. If the case fits the hypothesis, it is classified as a case that supports it. If the case does not fit the hypothesis, the hypothesis is reformulated. Powell's study to recommendations that older children have more choice in the adoption experience and more careful preparation for it. In a nutshell, it seemed that the key observation was that the child be respected as an active participant in the process. Studies such as this one by Powell have led to major changes in the procedures used in the placement of older children for adoption in recent years.

INTRODUCTION

In this chapter, you will learn about qualitative research methods, which you will remember use data that are in the form of words rather than scores or categories. In a later chapter, you will engage in an exercise on qualitative data analysis. This chapter will examine various dimensions of qualitative research. After you review this chapter, you will be able to do the following:

1. Explain why qualitative measurement is particularly well suited to the exploratory research study

2. Identify what qualitative and quantitative research measurements have in common and what distinguishes them

3. Describe the key tasks of each phase of the qualitative research study

4. Identify the key characteristics of ethnography, grounded theory, and case study research as different approaches to qualitative research

5. Identify the key characteristics of the social survey, the interview, and the focus group as different data collection methods in qualitative research

6. Explain how content analysis and narrative analysis serve as data analysis methods in qualitative research

EXPLORATORY RESEARCH AND QUALITATIVE RESEARCH METHODS

A classic exploratory study was conducted by Elisabeth Kubler-Ross (1969), who interviewed people who were in the late stages of life. She examined the subject of death and dying. From these interviews, she developed the idea of the stages of death and dying. In other words, she noted a pattern consistent with a good number of people who were facing death, in which they started with a stage that she labeled *denial* and went on to a second stage, then a third, and so forth.

You may be familiar with the model of death and dying from Kubler-Ross (1969) because it is so famous and has been in the literature for a good number of decades. It has led to many studies and essays, and trainings for those who want to work with this population.

Kubler-Ross (1969) decided to conduct interviews with general questions and make notes, and she reviewed these notes to see what she had found. She decided on this qualitative study because there was little in the literature at that time (the 1960s) on how people approached this life event. So she did not have the means to construct a quantitative survey that put people in predetermined categories or gave them a score. Instead, she needed the flexibility of the qualitative approach to measurement. She let the study subjects tell their stories in their own words. Then she reviewed these words for meaning about how people approach death.

Another example of a qualitative study was that conducted by Powell (1984). His purpose was to gain new insight into the experience of being adopted. He decided to focus on the viewpoint of the child being adopted. He interviewed people who had been adopted at an age when they were old enough to remember the experience when they had become adults. He used a sample of such people from adoption agency records. From these interviews, he formulated a series of suggestions for practice, with an emphasis on the empowerment of the child in the experience.

Both of the above examples employed the interview as the vehicle for collecting qualitative data. But you will see from this chapter that there are a number of other vehicles for this endeavor. These include the focus group and the social survey.

You have examined types of research according to the purpose of the study. Descriptive research has the purpose of describing people, while explanatory research attempts to explain one variable by examining its relationship with other variables. Evaluative research has the purpose of evaluating services. Exploratory research endeavors to explore the unknown.

Because of the lack of clarity about the nature of knowledge for an exploratory research question, it tends to lend itself to qualitative research methods rather than quantitative methods of measurement. But by no means is the exploratory research study restricted to qualitative measurement. You could, for example, examine the relationships among a number of variables in your attempt to develop theories that may be further examined in explanatory research.

The exploratory study has the purpose of developing theories or describing phenomena in greater detail than is currently known or can be found in quantitative presentations. It is especially useful when you have limited knowledge about the research subject. Knowledge about the stages of death and dying is an example. Another is the 1984 study by John Powell, who wanted to know about the experience of going through the placement process in adoption. He could find little literature on this theme when he undertook his study in the 1970s. He decided to locate adults who had gone through this process as older children, old enough to remember what the experience was like. He interviewed them and analyzed his data and drew several conclusions that could be guides for practice.

If you wish to describe social processes, the exploratory study is what you will do. And you will need the flexibility of qualitative research methods for this endeavor. What if you wanted to describe the process of morale decline in individuals? How does one go from simple acts of delinquency (e.g., stealing something of small value) to a more serious act of crime (e.g., robbing a bank)? Some people move to higher levels of immorality, while others do not. Why? These questions would likely lead you to an exploratory study using qualitative methods of measurement if you could not find a suitable knowledge base from the literature that provided the necessary insight into the process of moral decline.

While quantitative research data either place study subjects into categories or give them a score, **qualitative research** data measure social phenomena with regard to words.

The answer to an open-ended question on a survey would be an example. The notes of the interviewer would be another. The text of newspaper articles on a given theme could be another example.

The task of data analysis is to make sense of these words by applying a protocol of qualitative data analysis to the words. In this chapter, you will review one model for content analysis developed by the author. In this exercise, you will see how certain answers to the question can be categorized and how the different categories have certain things in common that suggest that they be combined into broader categories. General themes for the categories will be constructed.

Qualitative research is more appropriate when the following conditions exist:

1. You are seeking to develop theories, hypotheses, or new conceptual frameworks of understanding rather than testing existing ones.

2. You are seeking an understanding of the subjective meaning of behaviors rather than their precise description.

3. The concepts of interest are not easily quantified.

4. There is relatively little that is known about the subject from the existing literature.

If the above conditions are to the contrary (i.e., you are seeking to test a theory rather than develop one), you will be guided toward quantitative measurement rather than qualitative. While the above situations will put you in the direction of seeking qualitative means of measurement, there is no concrete guide for making this decision. Two reasonable people in similar situations can disagree, especially if the evaluations of the above criteria are not entirely different.

In the first chapter, you reviewed a number of common sayings that relate to research. One of these is that you should not put the cart before the horse. In social research, this means you should not, for example, decide that you want to conduct a qualitative study before you examine the phenomenon under study with regard to the above criteria. Perhaps your situation will better lend itself to a quantitative means of measurement.

WHAT QUANTITATIVE AND QUALITATIVE APPROACHES TO RESEARCH HAVE IN COMMON

You have seen the differences between quantitative and qualitative research. Now let's look at the similarities. First, both approaches are based on the spirit of scientific inquiry. You have seen that science gives us a process of discovery, not justification. You do not engage in scientific research, whether qualitative or quantitative, for the purpose of proving your point. You do not engage in cherry-picking of data to support your preconceived ideas. Instead, you follow a method of inquiry that reduces the influence of your own biases in the pursuit of knowledge. An example is the systematic inquiry, which starts with decisions on what criteria make a published study fall into the category of included research. This is determined before the researcher knows the results of the study. If it fits according to the predetermined criteria for inclusion, you must include it in your report. You cannot ignore it because you do not like the results. The methods of the systematic inquiry were discussed in the chapter on evidence-based practice.

The second basis on which both qualitative and quantitative methods are similar is that both are founded on a knowledge base. You do not just think about things you would like to study and ignore what is already known. You do not want to reinvent the wheel. Instead, you examine the literature and other sources of knowledge to determine what is already known and how concepts have been defined and measured in other people's work.

Another way in which both are similar is that they employ a somewhat similar process for study. This process starts with a knowledge base, then moves to the determination of the methods of study (e.g., sampling and measurement), after which data are collected and analyzed. Finally, conclusions are drawn based on the analysis of the data.

A fourth manner whereby qualitative and quantitative approaches to research are similar is that each will be put forth with transparency of method, so that the reader of the report is in a position to critically analyze what means were used to draw the conclusions of the study. The method of quantitative research is more concrete, but both approaches require transparency. The qualitative researcher does not just say that he or she interviewed people and here are the conclusions. The researcher will report on the procedures that were used to apply the principles of scientific inquiry.

Finally, both qualitative and quantitative studies lead to conclusions that are consistent with the data. Suppose you engaged in a study about what causes drug abuse and found that knowledge about the damages of drug use on the body was not related to this usage but that peer relations were involved. You should draw conclusions about the importance of peer relations in treatment. But you would not draw a conclusion that knowledge of the effect of drugs on the body needs to be enhanced. You may have a reason to believe that this is true, but it if was not shown in your data, you should not offer it as a conclusion for this study.

THE PHASES OF EXPLORATORY RESEARCH EMPLOYING QUALITATIVE RESEARCH METHODS

In a previous chapter, you have seen several examples of the four major phases of the research process. You have been admonished to avoid putting the cart before the horse. The research process in all types of social work research has a fundamentally similar sequence. You start with a problem formulation, where the major research question is articulated, and the literature is reviewed concerning this question. Your next stage is the determination of the research methods to employ in order to find the answer to your question. In the third phase, you collect and analyze your data. Finally, you draw conclusions based on your data. This general process is relevant to both qualitative and quantitative studies. The key differences are in data collection and analysis.

In the problem formulation phase of exploratory research, you will present information on how you have defined the concepts and what you have found in the literature about your research theme. This is similar to the tasks of this phase for descriptive, explanatory, and evaluative research. The nature of the research question and knowledge base, however, tends to be a distinct feature of the exploratory research study. It examines themes where the knowledge base is weak and there is a need for more theory rather than the testing of existing theory.

Suppose you wanted to learn about the process of moral decline where one moves from one stage of morality to a lower level. You have decided to focus on the law as the basis for conceptualizing the idea of moral decline. You have decided that the greater the violation of the law, the lower one has gone with regard to morality.

One of your tasks would be the review of the literature. Suppose this endeavor revealed that there was much content on the stages of moral development but little information in the literature on the stages whereby one's morality declines from not breaking the law to breaking minor laws to breaking major laws. You have decided to conduct a study with the purpose of describing how one moves from one state of morality to a lower level. How one moves to a higher level is not the focus of your study.

Because you can find little knowledge on this question, you have decided that you will conduct an exploratory study. Because you do not have concepts that are easy to characterize in quantitative ways, you have decided that qualitative methods of measurement will be employed.

The second phase of qualitative research calls on you to select your study methods. In other words, what procedures or tools will you employ in your search for an answer to your general research question? Selecting a study sample is one of your key tasks. What levels of morality will be the ones that will be exhibited by those who are selected for your study? Perhaps you will select people for your sample who committed a lesser crime 10 years ago but have moved to a higher level than others have. You will examine what seem to be the reasons why some moved to a higher level but others did not.

You have decided that you will conduct interviews to collect your qualitative data. Thus, you will compose a questionnaire with mostly open-ended questions that ask interviewees about the process whereby they moved from one stage of morality to a lower one. This questionnaire will be based on what you have learned from the literature regarding influences on criminal behavior. You will compose notes from your interviews, and you will engage in the coding of the data. You will draw conclusions based on your analysis of your notes from these interviews.

The third phase of exploratory research entails the collection and analysis of data. Perhaps you will conduct your interviews, record these interviews, review the recordings of these interviews for themes (perhaps using levels of coding as a tool), and organize a report that seems to shed light on the general research question.

The final phase of the exploratory research study is the drawing of conclusions. You will review your data and decide how to describe the stages of moral decline for those convicted of a minor crime 10 years ago.

APPROACHES TO QUALITATIVE RESEARCH

Characterizing qualitative research into categories is a challenge. Publications of various kinds have a variety of labels for various approaches to this means of inquiry. One book on qualitative research has chapters on case studies, grounded theory, historical methods, biographical methods, and clinical research, among others (Denzin & Lincoln, 1994). Another book divides qualitative research into the categories of ethnographic methods, heuristic methods, grounded theory methods, narrative methods, discourse analysis, and clinical case evaluations. Unfortunately, there is a good deal of overlap among these approaches to qualitative research, rendering the task of classification problematic.

Three of these major types of qualitative research are ethnography, grounded theory, and case study. These three will be described in this chapter because they are widely used and should provide for a general understanding of the nature of qualitative inquiry. Ethnography is best suited in the description of a culture in some detail. Grounded theory is best suited for theory development because it starts with observations that are used to develop theory where such is lacking about a given theme. The case study approach is well suited to the comprehensive examination of a program because it normally combines qualitative and quantitative observation about a wide array of subjects with regard to a common case, the program being the case in this instance. The case studied, however, could be an organization, an event, or some other entity. When your focus is on social work practice, the program may make the most sense as the case being studied.

Ethnography

Ethnography refers to the study of a culture in its natural setting with the purpose of describing the way of life of a group. To conduct an ethnographic study, the researcher must gain entry into the field through various means that will help him or her gain acceptance. Questions are posed about the meaning of things to the culture. According to Fortune (1994), preconceived ideas and biases held by the researcher should be addressed so that they do not interfere with the interpretation of these meanings as held by the members of the culture.

The starting point for this form of research is the selection of the culture to study. This contrasts with the more common starting point for research, which tends to focus on a research question. Questions may emanate from the data that are collected and analyzed, but the question is not the start of the process.

The ethnographic researcher is advised to avoid entering the field of the culture with a restricted view based on prior experiences and learning. Getting in touch with such biases is a necessary step. For example, if a researcher entered the culture of second-generation Mexican Americans, it would be beneficial for this researcher to identify the characteristics of this culture and make a special attempt to avoid letting any preconceived ideas interfere with the information being examined in the study.

The ethnographic researcher immerses himself or herself in the culture being investigated through various activities that place the researcher at the heart of activities of this culture, such as the favorite grocery store or community center. The researcher interacts with people in the culture as they go about the activities of daily living. This is referred to as participant observation in qualitative research. Observations of the behaviors of members of the culture are recorded. Sometimes, interviews are conducted with a specified set of questions to be asked. Observations are recorded and organized by theme (e.g., family relations, religious activities, peer relations, etc.). Interactions among the themes may be analyzed so that some ideas about this culture can be articulated.

Grounded Theory

The purpose of **grounded theory** is to develop explanations, hypotheses, or theories that are grounded in observations of social behavior. While the literature will be of some assistance, it will not connect the researcher with well-developed theories. The idea of grounded theory research is to develop theories where they are lacking and to do so by observations of social behavior. So observations come before theory. Theory is derived from observations.

The methodology of grounded theory is somewhat more structured than that of ethnography, although some ethnographic researchers borrow from the methods of grounded theory.

Grounded theory is a methodology that entails the careful recording of observations or quotes from study subjects, the coding of this information in several stages of analysis, and the drawing of connections between themes that serve as the basis for the theory that is developed. One protocol for the coding of data into levels will be included later in this chapter. This is consistent with what a grounded theory researcher might do.

An illustration can be taken from the work of Belcher (1994), who studied the homeless in the city of Baltimore, Maryland. This study was conducted over a 3-month period, during which the researchers immersed themselves in the homeless community by familiarizing themselves with the providers of services to the homeless, focusing attention on a particular health care facility. A group of homeless people were identified for a series of informal interviews that took place in an environment familiar to the study subjects.

The grounded theory researchers employed an eight-step process for this study:

1. Open-ended questions were asked that emanated from the literature review.

2. Responses from these questions were recorded after each interview in a case file for each respondent.

3. The files were reviewed by using the constant comparative method, which included the comparison of files on responses over and over again until the researcher felt that all possible themes had emerged.

4. Themes were noted, and a second set of questions was developed.

5. These questions were posed to the same respondents in a second set of interviews.

6. The responses were recorded in the individual case files, and the constant comparative method was employed once again.

7. A set of working hypotheses was developed.

8. The working hypotheses were discussed with the respondents to test their accuracy.

An issue to be addressed, in both qualitative and quantitative research, is credibility as evidenced by both reliability and validity. This task is more concrete in quantitative research and often entails the examination of quantitative data. Credibility in qualitative research is addressed in a different way: To what extent can we depend on our analysis to be accurate? That is the central question for credibility.

For the qualitative research study by Belcher (1994), this basic issue was addressed in three ways: (1) prolonged engagement, (2) persistent observation, and (3) triangulation. The first strategy was achieved by the fact that the interviews took place over a 3-month period, which was sufficient for the researchers to obtain a meaningful entry into the lives of the study subjects. This would help them overcome the normal barriers to understanding the full meaning of behavior. Persistent observation, the second strategy, was achieved by the extensive, eight-step process of observation noted above. The third strategy was triangulation, the use of multiple sources of data. For example, if respondents in the study stated that they had been thrown out of a shelter, the researchers would verify this information from the shelter operators.

From this study, the phases of drift among the homeless were identified. The first phase is characterized by movement in and out of the homeless status as friends and relatives help with housing. In this phase, the homeless did not typically define themselves as homeless. They generally maintained good contacts with sources of support. After several months of homelessness, these people tended to drift into Phase 2, where their identity as a homeless person was not very strong but persistent problems such as substance abuse prevented them from getting out of the homeless status. In the third stage, these individuals came to accept themselves as being homeless and had lost hope for a different style of life. These individuals had typically been homeless for a year or more.

Cultural Competence and Grounded Theory

In their book on cross-cultural practice, Harper-Dorton and Lantz (2007) discuss naturalistic research (grounded theory) as the preferred method of understanding cross-cultural curative factors. They describe naturalistic research as a form of research that occurs in the environment that is being studied using flexible method to evaluate data. Connection with the social environment is the focus. From observations in the natural environment of the study population, the researcher is able to develop theories about life in the target population. This type of theory is grounded theory.

Naturalistic research was used to identify cross-cultural curative factors. According to Harper-Dorton and Lantz (2007), insight into these curative factors would be useful to the worker in developing culturally appropriate interventions with clients from different cultural backgrounds.

One of these curative factors is respect for the individual's worldview. Culture influences perspectives on religion, art, politics, and science. Your worldview will influence your answer to questions such as the following:

Who am I?

Where am I?

What's wrong?

What's the remedy?

According to Harper-Dorton and Lantz (2007), worldview respect refers to your respect for worldviews other than your own. This is the most important factor in gaining cultural competence as a social worker.

A second curative factor is hope. The more hope the client has for the effectiveness of the helping relationship, the more hope he or she will have for the success of the intervention. A third curative factor is practitioner attractiveness. This refers to the client's perception of the helper's ability to facilitate a good outcome. This factor is dependent on culture and worldview respect.

A fourth curative factor is control. "In Western helping practices, it is considered important that the client learn something from the helping intervention and that what has been learned be used after termination to prevent problems in the future" (Harper-Dorton & Lantz, 2007, p. 6). Psychoanalytic practitioners help the client use insight to gain control, while cognitive therapists help the client use different thinking patterns. In some cultures, people are taught to pray correctly or to engage in a certain ritual in accordance with a strict protocol. These accepted means of personal control are grounded in culture.

Analytic Induction

Analytic induction is a means of qualitative inquiry designed to generate knowledge that typically employs a structure of interviews where each interview has the potential of either supporting the initial perspective on the subject or refining it in some way (Hammersley, 2010). The process starts with a knowledge base that generates an observation (theory, hypothesis, etc.) on the study subject. Data collection often includes interviews of individuals who are informed parties. A process is undertaken where data are collected and the initial observation is supported by the interview or refined in some way. If the observation is as specific as a study hypothesis, this hypothesis is first established. The process can be used for both generating hypotheses and testing them (see Flick, 2006), but it seems best suited to the refinement of a hypothesis, as will be illustrated later. The comparison of cases is a part of this process, with attention to why a case is deviant. As the process continues, the tentative hypothesis is altered (see Smelser, 2001).

Analytic induction was the approach taken in a study of the recruitment experiences of programs designed to improve the use of walking as a regular exercise in the United Kingdom (Matthews et al., 2012). Two researchers conducted interviews with 28 managers of community-based programs for those who lived sedentary lives. The results indicated that some programs focused on health benefits but others did not have this focus. The selection of strategies for the recruitment of people into the walking programs varied with the ideas of the managers about "what works." Word of mouth was found to be the best recruiting strategy in the opinion of those interviewed. Those targeting younger participants, however, were found to make more use of social communication media. The basic conclusion was that effective walking programs required trained, strategic, labor-intensive word-of-mouth communication to be effective in the recruitment of disengaged sedentary communities.

A description of the methods of analytic induction employed in this particular study was offered as follows:

Data analysis adopted an approach using analytic induction. Such an approach, common to qualitative research, proceeds through the following series of steps [32]: (i) data are scanned to generate categories of phenomena, (ii) relationships between categories are sought, (iii) working typologies and summaries are written on the basis of the data examined, (iv) subsequent case analysis enables refinement and redefinition, and (v) negative and discrepant cases are deliberately sought to modify, enlarge or restrict the original explanation or theory. Using the Excel software package, the data were coded in the first instance by one researcher, followed by a cyclical pattern of thematic verification and revision during analysis with two other researchers. (Matthews et al., 2012)

In this section of the chapter, you will examine one protocol for the use of analytic induction that is simpler than the one described above. Powell (1984) employed this protocol in the investigation of the experience of going through the process of being adopted. For this protocol, you start your analytic induction process with a definition of the theme under study. Then, you develop a hypothetical explanation of these phenomena. This means that you will review the literature for guidance on the theme of your study. You then select a study sample and interview the study subjects one at a time. You examine your first case in light of your observation (hypothesis, theory, etc.) and decide if that case supports it. If so, you move on to another case. If not, you either revise your observation or define your sample to exclude cases of this type. This process continues until you have achieved saturation, a state where new cases are failing to change the hypothesis or alter the sample to which it applies. It is a matter of your judgment if saturation has been achieved; there are no concrete guides for this decision. If you have good reason to believe that continued review of cases is not likely to generate new information, you will decide that further investigation is not needed and the process is complete.

In the remainder of this section, you will go through these steps with a report on John Powell's study of the process of being adopted (1984). This researcher wanted to know what the experience was like for the child. Because many adopted children are too young to remember the experience, he decided to select adults who had been adopted when they were old enough to remember the experience.

Step 1: Definition of the Phenomenon to Be Explained

The phenomenon to be studied by Powell was the experience of being adopted as an older child. A major concern was the ability of the adopted person to reconcile (to restore to harmony) his or her family history with the change from birth family to adopted family. Another focus was how this reconciliation had influenced his or her life as an adult.

Step 2: Explanation of the Phenomenon

The theory of shared fate (Kirk, 1964) was the hypothetical guide for Powell. According to this theory, the acceptance of difference by both the child and the parents was an important determinant of how well the transition would work. Acceptance of difference facilitates understanding and closeness, whereas failure to accept difference is likely to lead to detachment and misunderstanding.

Another theoretical guide was the concept of arbitrariness. Is the adoption process arbitrary from the standpoint of the child? The better the child is prepared for the adoption experience and the more the child is allowed to participate in decisions about it, the better is the child's adjustment to the experience.

A third issue is identification. The older adopted child has the special challenge of adjusting to the transition from an identity as a biological child of the birth family to an identity as an adopted child in the new family. How is this handled? How is the past reconciled?

From these theoretical guidelines, Powell (1984) developed the following hypothetical statement: "When the adoptee's path is through greater acceptance of differentness, less arbitrariness by others, and more identification with the adoptive kin, then there will be greater reconciliation with the past" (p. 28).

Step 3: Selecting the Study Sample

The sample of adults who had been placed for adoption as an older child was selected from the records of a single adoption agency. From approximately 50 records of people who met the criteria for inclusion, 22 known addresses were secured, and 17 of these persons agreed to participate. The reasons for refusal to participate were described by Powell as varied, with some refusals based on convenience and others based on the painful memories of the experience. Each of these 17 persons was interviewed for this study.

Step 4: Determining the Interview Procedures

An interview guide was developed for the interviews to be undertaken. Among the 23 items on this guide were the following:

1. Background information

2. Memories of things such as events leading to the adoption

3. The first meeting with the adoptive parents

4. Childhood experiences in the adoptive home with siblings, the adoptive parents, and the extended adoptive family

5. Adult relationships with the adoptive family

6. The effects of the adoption experience on the present life

All the interviews were tape-recorded, with verbatim transcripts prepared for review. The names of the persons interviewed were not reported in the study. The participants were given descriptions that might be included in the report and an opportunity to delete statements they did not want to be reported.

Step 5: Conducting the Interviews

The first person interviewed was Mary A, age 21 years, who was married and living with her husband. She had experienced childhood trauma, abuse, and deprivation. Following her mother's death, she was placed for adoption at the age of 6 years. She recalls biting her adoptive father's arm in the transfer meeting and fighting to get out of the car on the route to the adoptive home. She reports rebelliousness and resentments during her adolescent years in the adoptive family, but she acknowledges that her lifestyle and values were shaped by her adoptive family and their close friends. She seemed to be living a happy life at the time of the interview.

When Powell reviewed this interview, he noted that a tentative pattern of trauma prior to adoption had left Mary feeling abandoned. She felt helpless and unprepared for adoption, but she developed a will to survive, with a tendency toward self-protection. So three themes emerged for Powell:

1. Early trauma and feelings of abandonment

2. Feeling helpless and unprepared for the adoption experience

3. Developing a tendency toward self-protection and self-reliance

The second person interviewed was Amy, age 28 years, who had been adopted at the age of 9 years. She was married, with a 3 year-old daughter. This interview suggested to Powell that the same pattern had been experienced as noted for Mary A. The third interview, however, did not fit this pattern. This was a person who had been adopted at the age of 3 years and had a very limited memory of the experience. This exception led to the redefinition of the phenomenon to include only those persons placed for adoption at the age of 6 years or older. At the completion of the interview process, the pattern emerged as early trauma, feelings of loss and helplessness, and the development of a tendency toward self-protection. Trust emerged as another theme.

Step 6: Data Analysis and Conclusions

An analysis of the interviews revealed several themes that, according to Powell, characterized the older children's adoption experience. One was the significance of the extended adoptive family, who had become important to the development of the adoptee. Another was an appreciation of adoption as an alternative for them in their circumstances. A third theme was interest in continuing with contacts with the birth family. A final theme was satisfaction with life as an adult.

Powell found that the interviewees were unanimous in reporting that the extended adoptive family treated them as part of the family. This was very helpful with their transition to the new life as a member of the adoptive family. In a few cases, the relationship with the extended adoptive family was better than that with the primary adoptive family.

There was a consensus among these people that the adoption experience had improved their lives. They were especially grateful for the educational and economic opportunities afforded by their adoptive parents. One person indicated that it is highly unlikely she would have gone to college if she had not been adopted.

The data revealed that 16 of the 17 individuals had reconnected with their birth families. These contacts, however, were more positive, and recurrent, with birth family siblings than with birth parents.

A final theme was life satisfaction. The tendency was for these individuals to express feelings of general happiness, even though some were looking forward to things in the future that could make things better. They often expressed their satisfaction with regard to vocations.

A model of older children's adoption was developed by Powell as a result of these interviews. Three themes were part of this model: choice, preparation, and participation. Here is how Powell summarized this model:

1. *More choice in adoption:* To be consulted and given a sense of choice in their new family; less arbitrariness in the selection process

2. *More preparation in adoption:* To be told in advance about adoptive plans; to given an opportunity to visit and move in at the adoptee's pace; to have follow-up support from agency social workers after placement

3. *More participation in adoption:* To be respected and listened to; to be given an opportunity to discuss the adoption with the adoptive parents; to be allowed to visit appropriate birth family members; to be able to keep in contact with biological siblings (Powell, 1984, p. 95)

The Case Study Method

When you wish to examine a single individual, a single event, or a single social setting (e.g., a single organization or a single community), the case study methodology would be appropriate. This approach is worthwhile when you wish to investigate your entity with sufficient intensity to obtain an in-depth understanding of it. The depth of understanding comes from an extensive array of information that can be a part of this type of study. You may use a number of data technologies such as life history, documents, oral histories, in-depth interviews, and participant observation (Berg, 2001, p. 225).

The **case study** is a way of investigating a theme by examining a set of procedures determined prior to the investigation. It is appropriate when the research question is about how or why. The case study is also appropriate when the focus is on a contemporary phenomenon within some real-life context. This method normally uses multiple sources of data, both quantitative and qualitative (Yin, 1984, 2014).

Yin (1984, p. 25) has noted several uses of the case study for the evaluation of programs. For example, you could examine the causal links in situations too complex for survey methods or experimental strategies. A second application is to use this approach to describe clearly the experiences of clients as they move from one stage of service to another, such as contemplation of service, access to service, receipt of service, and discharge. This evaluation could help you gain insight into how this process could be improved.

Basic Components of the Case Study Design

Here is a list of the components of the case study design according to Yin (1984):

1. A study's questions

2. Propositions (if any)

3. A unit of analysis

4. Logic linking data to propositions

5. Criteria for interpreting the findings

The first component is the study question. According to Yin (1984), the case study approach is better suited to questions of how and why rather than questions of who, what, or where. You might want to know about the effectiveness of your program's services. You might need to know which services have been most emphasized, the relationship between service emphasis and service outcome and so forth. You may want to know why certain clients achieve better outcomes than others. This may lead you to inquire into information on the characteristics of clients, the relationship between client characteristics and client outcome, the opinions of practitioners about clients who do best in treatment, and so forth.

A study **proposition** is a first attempt to develop a theory that explains some aspect of the theme under study. It provides guidance on the places where you need to go in order to find relevant information. For example, you may have little reason to measure whether your clients are left-handed or right-handed because it does not make sense that this variable influences client response to treatment. So you would not have a study proposition about being left-handed, but you might have one about the environmental stresses faced by clients.

The **unit of analysis** is the entity on which you will collect your data. The question is "How are you defining your case?" A case could be a single individual, an event, a program, or a community. If it is a single individual, you would collect all your data on this person. If you defined your unit of analysis as an event (e.g., an election), you would collect data on that event. If the unit of analysis is a program, you would collect a wide array of information that seems relevant to this program with regard to your study question.

Another component of the case study design is the logic that links information to propositions. In this endeavor, you need to think of the kinds of data that would support your propositions and, conversely, the types of data that would refute these propositions. You should derive these ideas before you collect your data. In other words, do not put the cart before the horse.

Desired Skills for the Case Study Researcher

The basic skills for the case study researcher listed by Yin (1984) are as follows:

1. Ask good questions.

2. Be a good listener.

3. Be adaptive and flexible.

4. Have a firm grasp on the issues being studied.

5. Be unbiased by preconceived notions.

According to Yin (1984), a major strength of the case study approach is its flexibility. What will be observed does not have to be determined completely ahead of the beginning of the time frame for the collection of data. You should be a good questioner and a good listener. You should be careful not to ignore information simply because it was not on the list of things to record.

Adaptability and flexibility are key components of a good case study research experience. You are admonished not only to go where the data lead but also to have a firm grasp of the issues being studied so you will better understand what you have observed. In addition, you should be unbiased by preconceived notions. A method of achieving this is to list your ideas about the thing you are evaluating prior to your study and continually ask yourself if there is evidence that these ideas are overly influencing the direction of your inquiry.

The Case Study Protocol

The **case study protocol** provides information on the procedures to be employed in the implementation of a case study. According to Yin (1984), the protocol should include the following:

1. An overview of the case study project (objectives, issues, auspices, etc.)

2. Field procedures

3. Sources of information

4. Case study questions, along with the possible sources of information for answering each question

5. A guide for the case study report

These steps show the nature of the system of investigation in the case study. As pointed out by Yin (1984),

> A quick glance at these topics will indicate why the protocol is so important. First, it reminds the investigator what the case study is about. Second, the preparation of the protocol forces an investigator to anticipate several problems, including how the case study reports might be completed. This means, for instance, that the audience for such reports will have to be identified, even before the case study has been conducted. Such forethought will help to avoid disastrous outcomes in the long run. (pp. 65–66)

The case study overview should contain background information on the project, the substantive issues being investigated, and the relevant readings about the issues. The description of the context is a part of this overview. What, for instance, is the general mission of the funding source, if this is a funded project? The field procedures need to emphasize the major tasks, including gaining access to key informants and information, having sufficient resources to get the job done, making a clear schedule for data collection, and being prepared for the unknown. The basic case study questions are unique in that they are posed to the investigator, not to the respondent. Respondents, however, will be asked to supply certain information. Questions will be pursued with various sources of information such as respondents, agency documents, or observations by the investigator. The case study is complex. Therefore, the development of a guide for the case study report is important. It will provide guidance throughout the process to the investigator because it will inform this individual of what is going to be required in the end.

Sources of Evidence in Case Studies

One of the advantages of the case study approach is the multiplicity of information that can be used. Six sources of evidence were noted by Yin (1984). The first of these is the document that is searched for information. This may include letters, memos, meeting minutes, and so forth. Archival records serve as a second source and are a form of document. However, the archival record is more formal and is regularly collected by the agency. Interviews serve as a third source of evidence. A fourth source is direct observation by the investigator of behaviors on display in various social contexts. Participant observation is the fifth source of evidence on Yin's list. This refers to the involvement of the investigator in the world of the study subjects whereby the investigator is present when natural things are occurring and can see firsthand what is happening. Physical artifacts serve as the sixth item on this list. A piece of art that reflects on the culture of the entity being studied is one example.

Principles of Data Analysis in Case Studies

Yin (1984) offered three principles of data collection:

1. Use multiple sources of evidence.

2. Create a case study database.

3. Maintain a chain of evidence.

Triangulation is a term relevant to the first principle noted above. This refers to the use of multiple sources of evidence. It is better fulfilled in case study research than most other approaches. When we get ideas from one source of information, can we be satisfied that we have learned what we need to learn in order to draw conclusions? No single source of evidence is sufficient to answer a question, according to the idea of triangulation. Because of the complexity of the information collected in a case study, a specific case study database is important. Otherwise, there will be information that is lost. A chain of evidence refers to the information that supports other information in a logical sequence. If one link in the chain is broken, we have reason to doubt the end result.

Utilization-Focused Evaluation

Utilization-focused evaluation is an approach that gives the key power in the research process to the intended users of the evaluation. In this approach, the research facilitator is a consultant, not a decision maker (Patton, 2008). The intended users decide on the topic of the research study, the methods to be used, the analysis of the data, and the conclusions to be drawn. They rely on research facilitators to provide consultation about things such as research methodology, statistical analysis of data, and other research issues that determine the strength of the study to be undertaken. For example, if the generalization of study findings is determined to be of special importance to the intended users, the research facilitators will inform the intended users about sampling methods that can best facilitate this purpose.

This approach can be contrasted with the typical research study where the research expert is in control. In those traditional studies, the research expert is in control of the total process, from deciding on the topic to drawing conclusions from the data analysis. The key advantage of the utilization-focused evaluation approach is the heightened likelihood that the results of the evaluation will be put to use. If the intended users are in control, the data will be meaningful. This type of study is not likely to be filed away and forgotten.

Utilization-focused evaluation can employ either qualitative or quantitative methods. The intended users decide if one or both of these approaches to measurement will be utilized. Thus, some utilization-focused studies can be classified as mixed-methods research. A mixed-methods approach is one that utilizes both qualitative and quantitative approaches.

The utilization-focused evaluation approach is organized and coordinated by the research facilitator, a person with expertise on research methodology and data analysis. It starts with the identification of stakeholders, persons who will benefit from the results of the study. The process moves to the identification of the intended users, the ones who will be in control. The intended use of the evaluation is the next theme, which is determined by the intended users. Then the intended users decide on the evaluation questions, followed by the determination of the means for collecting and analyzing data. Following the drawing of conclusions, the research facilitator helps the intended users to use the study results to improve some aspect of practice.

Step 1: Identifying Intended Users From the Identified Stakeholders

Intended users of the evaluation study are selected as key persons among the stakeholders. As the research facilitator, you could select the stakeholders—for example, the 36 social workers employed in the substance abuse treatment program of the Hampton Behavior Health Center. From this group, you might select eight intended users by finding ones to represent each of the four types of services being employed by this agency. You would need to select intended users who best represent the interests of the stakeholders. With a small number of stakeholders, there is no recommended quantitative method for doing so, such as selection at random. You would need to know something about the interests of the stakeholders and the leadership among these individuals.

Why did you select the 36 social workers of this program as your stakeholders? You could have selected the administrators and supervisors of the agency instead. Perhaps you have gotten to know this group of people sufficiently to know that they have a special set of concerns that seems to bind them together concerning a special need. This does not mean that you have selected a research question or research purpose for the intended study. Indeed, this would be contrary to the spirit and methods of utilization-focused evaluation. Instead, you have identified a common bond and concern that you are willing to help the group examine.

Step 2: Identifying the Intended Use of an Evaluation

Do your intended users wish to judge the worth of the services being provided, do they want to find ways to improve these services, or do they want to generate general knowledge? These are the three kinds of questions identified by Patton (2008) as typical for a utilization-focused evaluation. The answer to the first question will likely employ quantitative data, where outcomes are measured and compared with a set of expectations. The second question is likely to employ a qualitative method of measurement, where people (e.g., clients) are asked for their opinion on, for example, how best to improve the services being offered. The third question is just as likely to use qualitative means of measurement as quantitative ones.

A key set of questions focuses on the potential uses of the evaluation study. What decisions are likely to be influenced by the results of this study? For the identified stakeholders, it should be questions related to client service, where they have control, rather than questions related to how the agency will spend its money, something over which social workers on the front line often usually have little power. A second type of question deals with what is at stake and for whom. If the agency's executive has been putting pressure on the clinical staff about client outcome measurement, this would be a major influence on the nature of the study to be conducted. If there have been a rising number of client complaints about a given aspect of service, the clinical staff are likely to be concerned and to want to do something about it.

Step 3: Identifying the Evaluation Questions

The research facilitator will assist the intended users in determining the research questions to be pursued. This will typically require a dialogue in which the intended users are asked to develop broad questions and then narrow the scope into more specific ones that can be studied. A broad question might be "How can we improve our services?" and a more narrow one might be "What are the things we could do to improve the effectiveness of our intake system in screening in clients who are appropriate and screening out those who are not appropriate for our services?"

Step 4: Designing the Means for Collecting Data

The research methodology, as previously noted in this book, entails the determination of the study sample to be employed and the methods used for measurement. It might also include the determination of the research design, but this issue is more typical if you are employing quantitative measurement for the evaluation of client outcome. If your study is designed to obtain client opinions, you will need a sample of clients for your study. If you want opinions about how to improve services, you will need to determine if you can best employ open-ended questions (e.g., What is your advice about how we can best improve our services?) or closed-ended questions (e.g., How would you rate the services you received—excellent, good, fair, poor?)

Step 5: Collecting and Analyzing Data

The collection and analysis of data is another step in which the research facilitator and the intended users must interact. While data analysis is a technical endeavor, requiring research expertise, the intended users need to understand how the data are being analyzed and to agree that this method is satisfactory. The intended users must understand the data that were collected and analyzed. They might need to be schooled on the nature of the correlation coefficient or the steps used in the employment of the content analysis of the qualitative data that have been collected. In short, they must understand and have confidence that this set of data is what they need to find answers to the questions they have generated.

Step 6: Facilitating the Use of the Data

How will the results of the study influence action? Will the intended users make a report to the agency executive with specific recommendations, along with a willingness to take action to ensure the effective implementation of the recommendations? Will the intended users implement the changes themselves because they do not need the approval of others? If so, how will they implement these changes? Are they likely to experience resistance from others? If so, what are some strategies for preventing resistance or overcoming it? These are the questions to be pursued in this step of the process.

DATA COLLECTION IN QUALITATIVE RESEARCH

The survey as a method of data collection was discussed in a prior chapter, with special attention to the quantitative type of study. It is also one of the methods of data collection for the qualitative study. Perhaps the client satisfaction survey is the best example of the use of the survey in human service research. This survey can contain closed-ended questions useful for the quantitative study and open-ended questions for the qualitative study. A second type of data collection for the qualitative study is the interview. The focus group is a third alternative. A fourth approach is direct observation by the researcher. The examination of existing records can be viewed as a fifth type of data collection for qualitative research. This section of the chapter will focus on the first three alternatives.

The Interview as One Method of Data Collection

The **interview** is a personal encounter between persons in which one person (or persons) is seeking information from another person (or other persons). It can take place face-to-face or by phone. In this encounter, the interviewer asks questions and records the response of the interviewee. The interview is a purposive interaction. It goes beyond informal conversation. In it, different persons play different roles. The main purpose of the interview is for the interviewer to obtain information from the interviewee.

Interviews can be classified according to structure. A highly structured interview is one in which there is a precise set of questions that are to be asked in a given sequence, with established categories for responses, much like what you see on a mailed questionnaire. This type of interview employs an instrument that might be better characterized as quantitative rather than qualitative, so this type of interview is not the focus of this chapter.

There is also the highly unstructured interview, where little is determined ahead of time. In this type of interview, there are few questions to be posed, and of course, there are no predetermined categories for the responses. In this type of interview, the researcher poses a rather general question for response and lets the interviewee take it from there. This type of interview is not the focus of the present chapter. Instead, the focus of this chapter is the semistructured interview.

The Semistructured Interview

The **semistructured interview** is one with predetermined questions with an open-ended format, which are asked of all respondents in the same manner. Examples include the following:

1. What does stress mean to you?

2. How do you experience stress?

3. What are the three things you are most likely to do when you are under stress?

4. What do you find has been the best way to cope with stress?

Each of these questions would be asked of each respondent and would be asked in the same sequence.

With the semistructured interview, you should follow several guidelines:

1. Be aware of your own ideas or biases about the subject under study, and avoid revealing these predispositions to the person being interviewed.

2. Engage mechanisms to avoid allowing these predispositions to influence your observations.

3. Engage the interviewee in the validation of your notes by reporting what you heard in the interview and asking if it is correct.

4. Seek disconfirming evidence of your initial impressions to ensure that your biases have not influenced your observations.

5. Employ note-taking methods that place minimal burden on your memory, for example, recording your notes right after the interview takes place rather than a day later.

Phases of the Interview Process

Before you conduct the interview, you would have determined the interview subject and the sample of persons to be interviewed. There are several natural phases of the interview process. First, you must introduce yourself and the purpose of the interview. You obtain the permission of the study subject to ask questions and to report what you heard from the interviewee on an anonymous basis. In this phase, it is important that the purpose of the interview be stated but not any theories about the subject or anything else that might encourage a biased response from the study subject.

The second phase is the interview itself. You present the questions that have been selected prior to the interview, and you record what you have heard. In this phase, you are encouraged to report to the interviewee what you have heard and ask for feedback as a way of validating what you have recorded or changing it.

During the interview, you should ask the prepared questions with the same words and sequence for each of the persons who will be interviewed. You should consider beforehand how to define key terms so that you can use a uniform definition with your study subjects when needed.

In the interview, you should learn to engage in note-taking methods that place minimal burden on your memory. There is a lot of information that might be presented, so you should be sensitive to the fact that your long-term memory can be in error. For this reason, you should record brief notes during the interview and then expand these notes right after the interview is finished. What is recorded during the interview should give priority to the exact words used by the interviewee, especially if a particular set of words seems to capture the essence of an idea in the words of the interviewee.

The analysis of the results of the interview is the third phase of the process. You need to make sense of your notes. You do this by looking for themes that are common among the persons being interviewed. You will note the different terms that can be used to express the same theme; thus, you can combine statements that are different in wording but similar in meaning.

In the analysis of data in qualitative research, numbers often get ignored because we often associate numbers with quantitative research and words with qualitative research. But we count in qualitative research as well. We count things such as the number of references to a given theme or the number of study subjects who mentioned a given theme.

In a later chapter is an exercise on content analysis. This exercise will take you through an experience with the coding of statements at different levels. It will also take you through several other steps in the process of data analysis for qualitative research.

The Focus Group as a Data Collection Method

The **focus group** is a method of gathering qualitative data that entails a group meeting where a general question and specific questions are discussed and conclusions are drawn. There is a leader who is responsible for leading the group discussion, and there is a person who records the ideas that emanate from the discussion. The group meeting can be more or less structured depending on the context and the research issue. Most applications of the focus group can be characterized much like the semistructured interview because there normally is a clear focus for the questions, but there is a need for sufficient flexibility in the questions to obtain a full picture of the phenomenon under study. In fact, it is not easy to envision a situation in which the highly structured format would be used with a focus group.

An important distinction between the focus group meeting and the individual interview is the opportunity to observe the interactions among individuals with regard to the issue under investigation. The focus group meeting reveals how individuals take certain positions on a topic. The interaction among individuals in the group provides new insight on the topic and reveals insight into the dynamics of the group.

A typical focus group session consists of a small group of individuals responding to a set of questions delivered by a moderator who facilitates the discussion. According to Krueger (1994), the size of the group should be limited to a maximum of seven for complex questions.

There are several key elements to be considered when you employ the focus group for collecting qualitative data. First, the focus group should be focused on questions that are suitable for the semistructured interview. The ethnographic study attempts to describe a culture in some depth. This normally requires more flexibility than is present in the focus group experience. Broad questions are not suited to the focus group, such as the following:

1. What are the stages of moral regression for the young adult who is a repeat offender?

2. In general, how does the client experience our services?

These questions require a more flexible format than is typical for the focus group. Highly specific questions would also be inappropriate to the focus group experience, such as the following:

1. Do our clients like our new intake system better than the old one?

2. What proportion of our staff are satisfied with their jobs?

These questions are too specific for the focus group. They can be answered by structured interviews or a survey. Suppose, however, you wished to know certain things about your recently changed intake procedures for the admission of clients into service in your agency. You might ask a series of questions related to this experience, such as the following:

1. What was the first contact with the agency like for the client in the previous system?

2. What was the first contact with the agency like since the change?

3. How did the client feel after leaving the agency on the day of first contact prior to the change and after the change?

4. To what extent did the client feel well-informed about agency services prior to the change and after the change?

5. What recommendations does the client have about improving our intake system?

These questions could be posed to a group of clients or a group of staff who work with clients. Perhaps you can see from this information that the focus group is best suited to the situation where the moderator can think of a set of open-ended questions that will stimulate dialogue on a key issue being addressed.

A second element of a good experience is that the focus group members should be in a position to provide good information about the theme of the project. Some questions can be better answered by clients, some by staff, and some by others. Group members should feel comfortable offering ideas, and they should be given appropriate opportunities to do so. Most groups will have members who are more likely to talk than others. Sometimes they will dominate the discussion. So the moderator needs to address this issue by offering some structure to the group dialogue.

A third element to consider with the focus group is that the moderator must be a good listener. The role of the moderator is to listen rather than talk because this is a situation that calls on group members to supply information, rather than a situation in which the objective is for the leader to engage in persuasion. As noted by Berg (2001),

> Facilitators . . . must listen to what the subjects are saying. . . . It is important to have a schedule or agenda during the focus group; however, it should never be so inflexible that interesting topics that spontaneously arise during the group discussion are shortchanged or unnecessarily truncated. Because of the nature of group dynamics, it is possible that topics and issues not originally considered by the researcher as important surface as very important. (p. 124)

Opinions the moderator has about the questions under discussion should not be the source of discussion. It is the opinions of the group members that are being reviewed.

Another element of a good focus group experience is that the moderator should have the assistance of a note taker during the dialogue. The group moderator can and should make notes during the dialogue but will normally need the assistance of someone who can focus only on taking notes. The note taker should place major emphasis on direct quotes from participants. This will be less necessary if the group dialogue is taped and transcribed for analysis. If you have the luxury, you could have two note takers working with the moderator, who also takes notes. These three persons share notes as a method of validation.

The Survey as a Data Collection Method

A social **survey** is a purposeful inquiry into a subject for a designated sample of people by a researcher using a recording instrument, typically a questionnaire. The mailed survey is a typical example. A set of questions are posed on a questionnaire, and the respondent is asked to answer each question. The questions are designed to measure the themes of the study. If that survey has open-ended questions, you will have some data that are qualitative in nature.

An earlier chapter in this book provided many details about the nature of the social survey as a data collection method. Among the themes you encountered in that chapter was the interview as a mechanism for conducting a social survey. Tips for improving the interview was one of the subjects.

Because of the previous chapter on the social survey, you will not review these concepts in the present chapter. It is presented here as a reminder that the survey is a data collection method for qualitative research along with the interview and the focus group. There are, of course, several other mechanisms for data collection in qualitative research. These three are among those most prominently used.

DATA ANALYSIS IN QUALITATIVE RESEARCH

The nature of the data analysis in qualitative research varies with the type of research being undertaken. In all cases, there will be an analysis of words drawn from the data source. This may be the respondent's answers to open-ended questions on a survey, the notes of the interviewer, the notes of the focus group moderator, the notes of the participant observer, or some other variation based on the nature of the study and the type.

The form of the qualitative data can be segments of content, or it can be a story. The segment of content can be one sentence or one paragraph in response to an open-ended question. You can review segments of content through content analysis, one of the themes of this chapter. The story is displayed in a narrative that is composed of much more than a sentence or a paragraph, or even an entire page of content. A story is about what has been going on, rather than an opinion about a given subject. It is told in a sequence of observations, which can be analyzed for meaning. That meaning may lead to a theory about the nature of a life event or a culture. As a theory, it will focus on the causal link between happenings. Stories are reviewed through narrative analysis.

In the next section, you will review narrative analysis. In the section that follows the narrative analysis section, you will examine content analysis. The narrative is a story, told among people. The story may be about an experience of some kind that requires more than the examination of segments of content. **Content analysis** refers to the analysis of segments of content, such as suggestions on how to improve the curriculum of the social work program. As you can see, narrative analysis requires more qualitative data.

Narrative Analysis

One way in which to portray the narrative is that it is a story that is transmitted among people. It is more than a simple answer to a question. It typically reports a story that depicts some important reality to the reporter. It reveals themes and explanations. It is often the reporting of an important experience, such as having been adopted as an older child or experiencing treatment for cancer. **Narrative analysis** is the examination of narratives for meaning, deep description, or understanding.

Often a narrative analysis derives data from a semistructured interview rather than a social survey. It typically requires an interaction between the reporter and a participant, but in some cases, the story can be told through documents. When you examine a story, you look for sequences of events to portray a process, or you might look for connections between events to examine causation.

Manning and Cullum-Swan (1994) report that some studies contrast narratives as self-formulated stories with formal and externally formatted narratives in the form of something like a medical interview. They assert that neither approach adequately captures human information processing and sense making.

The basic distinction between a preformatted interaction with an instrument purpose, such as a medical or survey research interview, and a personal story, with its wandering, complex, sensate, and expressive forms, is a primary contrast in the literature on narratives. Whereas the life situation of the person, the embodied here-and-now reality, is looked at from the body's perspective, the medical interview looks at the body as an objective, functioning machine (Manning & Cullum-Swan, 1994).

The less structured the interaction between the interviewer and the interviewee, the more the report falls into the category of narrative analysis rather than content analysis. If a set of specific questions governs the interview, it is more likely that the data analysis method would be content analysis rather than narrative analysis.

It is not possible to report a set of concrete procedures for conducting a narrative analysis. This is more possible with content analysis. As noted by Manning and Cullum-Swan (1994),

If one defines narrative as a story with a beginning, middle, and end that reveals someone's experiences, narratives take many forms, are told in many different settings, before many audiences, and with varying degrees of connection to actual events or persons. Thus, themes, principal metaphors, definitions of narrative, defining structures of stories (beginning, middle, and end), and conclusions are often defined poetically and artistically and are quite context bound. (p. 465)

An advantage of the narrative analysis over the analysis of content is that the narrative will better portray the social context of the phenomenon you are analyzing. Context is critical to meaning; thus, the narrative will provide a more comprehensive picture of the study theme.

Content Analysis

Content analysis is a method for converting words into ideas that capture the essence of the words that were analyzed and lead to inferences about the reality of the theme under investigation. Suppose you ask 15 of your classmates to write down the most valuable part of their educational experience. You code each person's statements for themes and review those themes. From this analysis, you might conclude that relationships are more important than ideas in the educational experience.

Content analysis can be undertaken with any written form of communication: newspaper articles, public records, transcripts of interviews, and so forth. The basic task of content analysis is to reduce words to themes or concepts that have meaning in the observation of the phenomenon under study. The researcher, in content analysis, must take precautions to avoid the selective recording of information according to some of his or her opinions. All the information available should be objectively analyzed for relevance. Scientific research is a process of discovery, not justification.

Coding in Content Analysis

Coding of statements is an essential part of content analysis. Words that constitute the qualitative data in a study are examined for meaning, so that the essence of what was said is reduced to a more manageable length. What was said in a paragraph might be reduced to three words.

Let's look at an example. A survey was mailed to a sample of social workers with an MSW (Master of Social Work) degree where the respondents were asked to answer the following question: What is the most important advice you can give to those who are engaged in the planning of a new MSW program? The answers to this question were coded to derive the most important ideas from this survey. There were three levels of coding that transpired. The first level was simple: Each statement was reduced to a set of words or brief phrases that captured the essence of each idea or piece of advice. As reported by York (2009), one of the answers to this question was as follows:

I believe it is important to maintain the integrity of the profession by offering courses that will establish and enhance one's understanding of social work and its ethics. Also, many MSW students are nontraditional in terms of having already begun their careers and possibly having families. Therefore, it is important to include a certain degree of flexibility in the program by offering courses in the evening and weekends. (p. 153)

How would you code the above answer? You can recognize more than one idea, if appropriate. What word or phrase would you use to capture one of the ideas from this answer? Consider the first sentence. What about these options: *integrity of the social work profession*; *social work identity*; *emphasize an understanding of social work*; *ethics*? One could argue for each of these options. These are possible codes for that first sentence. They all refer to the nature of the social work profession. The last one is more specific. It refers to the ethics of the profession. So one might select one of the first three options and "ethics" as well. It could be argued, however, that ethics is an inherent part of professional integrity, so one might use only the words "professional integrity" as the code.

Then there are the other sentences in this statement that need to be coded. The second and third sentences are related to the theme of the special needs of the nontraditional student. The words "nontraditional student" and "flexible scheduling of courses" might be codes one could imagine. Or one could code it as "special needs of the nontraditional student." What do you think?

As you can see, there is no right or wrong set of words to use as the codes of a set of words that is being analyzed in content analysis. But if you had two coders who came up with codes that are not in the same conceptual realm, you would have a challenge regarding the credibility of the coding task. And you should be cognizant of the fact that your own opinions are not a part of the data being analyzed. You should not, for example, think of five special needs of the nontraditional student and list these as part of your data. The statement being coded only listed one special need—flexibility in class scheduling. After you draw conclusions from the data and you are thinking of how this study might influence your decisions, a discussion of the various special needs of the nontraditional student would be an appropriate topic. But this would be in the category of what you do with the results, not what the results actually said.

The study reported in York (2009) was used by a university to design a new MSW program. The results of the study led to the decision that clinical social work practice should be the major focus of the new program. This focus was clearly the one most mentioned by the employed MSW social workers as the recommended emphasis.

According to Miles and Huberman (1984),

a code is an abbreviation or symbol applied to a segment of words—most often a sentence or paragraph of transcribed field notes—in order to classify the words. Codes are categories. They usually derive from research questions, hypotheses, key concepts, or important themes. They are retrieval and organizing devices that allow the analyst to spot quickly, pull out, then cluster all the segments relating to the particular question, hypothesis, concept, or theme. (p. 56)

Several authors have discussed the idea of levels of coding. The first level is the one that sticks closely to the text, while higher levels of coding combine lower codes into higher conceptual meaning. In the study of advice for the development of a new MSW program, there were several ideas from the first level of coding that could be combined because they were in the category of the importance of field instruction. Therefore, the second level of coding simply had the words "field instruction' in it for all the first-level codes that provided advice about field instruction (internship).

Strauss (1987) describes three main types of coding in qualitative research: (1) open coding, (2) axial coding, and (3) selective coding. A discussion of these types of coding can be found in Neuman (1994). According to Neuman, open coding takes place in the researcher's initial passing through the data being examined. The objective of this type of coding is the identification of key concepts, which bind certain words together. Words such as *uptight* and *tense* might be coded as "stress." In this phase of coding, the researcher might write the word *stress* next to each line of data that contains words such as *uptight* or *tense*.

Axial coding takes place in a second review of the data. During this phase of coding, the researcher "asks about causes and consequences, conditions and interactions, strategies and processes" (Neuman, 1994, p. 408). Concepts can be divided into smaller divisions or enlarged into larger categories. Concepts can be organized into a sequence. Axial coding is what we call the second level of coding. At this second level, you combine first-level codes that have similarities (e.g., field instruction) and use a term that labels the concept under which all these first-level codes fall. If one person's first-level code said, "You should have a well-qualified field instructor" and a second person had the first-level code of "Field placement should offer meaningful work," you would have two first-level codes that focus on some aspect of field instruction. You might put both of these first-level codes in the second-level code of "the importance of field instruction."

Selective coding is the final phase of the coding process. In this phase, the researcher is looking selectively for cases that illustrate themes and makes comparisons and contrasts to identify further causal connections in the data or patterns that are broader than those identified in the previous phase. Neuman (1994) uses the example of a study of working-class life in the tavern, where marriage was noticed as a theme that emerged in much conversation. In the previous phases of coding, marriage was identified as a theme and was divided into major stages, such as engagement, weddings, extramarital affairs, and so forth. In the selective phase of coding, the focus turned to differences in the views of men and women. This analysis compared men and women on their ideas about each of these phases of marriage.

In this book, you will review these three types of coding as levels of coding. This means you will see the labels "first-level coding," "second-level coding," and "third-level coding" rather than the terms *open*, *axial*, and *selective*. This will be easier to remember, and they capture the essence of the differences between the types of coding. In a later chapter in this book, you will go through the experience of coding a set of qualitative data into levels of codes.

Analytic Comparison in Content Analysis

The work on logic by some of our early philosophers can be helpful in content analysis. Neuman (1994) discussed the method of agreement and the method of difference in logical inquiry and referred to this as **analytic comparison**. The method of agreement draws the researcher's attention to what is common across cases so that cause–effect relations can be examined. If several different cases have a common outcome (e.g., high stress), the researcher looks for other commonalities that might be candidates for the cause of the outcome. For example, let us suppose that our study of stress among graduate social work students revealed that each of our first four interviewees had a high level of stress and that they mentioned that they had an extra-long distance to drive from home to class. Each person has both high stress and a long commute to class.

This provides the beginnings of an exploration of the causal connection between commuting distance and stress. But what if we find that many of those with low stress also had a long commute? What do we do with this information? This is where the method of difference comes into play. With the method of difference, the researcher seeks information on cases with a different outcome from the initial cases and different causes. If four persons have high stress and a long commute and another four persons have low stress and a short commute, we have more evidence for hypothesizing a relationship between commuting and stress. However, if we find that persons with low stress are about as likely to have a long commute as persons with high stress, we have little evidence of a connection between these two variables.

Chapter Practice Exercise

An Experience With Coding in Content Analysis

In this exercise, you will use a preliminary content analysis to help in the design of a study of interest to yourself. Your study will employ qualitative data through a survey of open-ended questions to a sample of people. You will analyze the qualitative data for a small sample of people as a means of getting familiar with content analysis, as one mechanism of qualitative data analysis. In this exercise, you will engage in the four major phases of research.

Competencies Demonstrated by This Practice Exercise

1. The ability to design a basic qualitative research study that entails the content analysis of data from responses to a simple open-ended question

2. The ability to articulate a qualitative research question and collect basic qualitative data

3. The ability to engage in the content analysis of a simple set of qualitative data, including two levels of coding and the drawing of conclusions

Activities for This Practice Exercise

1. You will develop a research question that can be answered through a simple qualitative study that entails the collection and analysis of data from answers to an open-ended research question.

2. You will select a study sample and develop a questionnaire to be administered to these individuals where you will pose your single open-ended question.

3. You will engage in the coding of the answers to the open-ended question on the questionnaire.

4. You will draw conclusions about your research question.

The Phases of Your Research Process

You have reviewed four major phases of research in other chapters in this book. It begins with the articulation of the research question and ends with the conclusions that are drawn from the analyzed data. You will go through each of these phases in this section of the exercise. Then you will be given specific instructions on what you will report.

Phase 1: The Research Question and the Knowledge Base

Your research question is the beginning of this study process. This question is one that is of interest to you. It should be one that can be addressed by a study sample that is convenient to you. Normally, your research question would be informed by a specific knowledge base from the published literature. You are not expected to compose a knowledge base that informs the study of your question. This omission is designed to make this exercise manageable in the context of the time available for it.

Your research question might focus on what your fellow students would recommend in the way of improvements in your school's curriculum or what they believe are the characteristics of a good college teacher. Maybe you want to know what people do to improve their social support, reduce their levels of stress, or improve their life satisfaction. Maybe you want to know what has most hindered people's life satisfaction or improved it. Perhaps you could use tips about how to study for your research course, using the advice of your classmates.

There are any number of themes that could be the focus of your study. The process of research you will undertake will include the development of your basic research question, the composition of a set of open-ended questions for a questionnaire to collect qualitative data on your general research question, the selection of a sample of people for responses to your questionnaire, and the analysis of the data from their responses.

Phase 2: Study Methods

Your study methods will entail the selection of a study sample and the composition of a questionnaire to be administered to this study sample. As you have learned from previous chapters, sampling is a task that informs your decisions about the generalization of your study findings to people other than your study sample. If you select your fellow research students as your study sample, can you generalize your study findings to all social work students in your school, all social work students in your state, or all people in general? That is the question. You have seen that you can generalize on a scientific basis if you have a random sample and that logical generalization is based on comparisons of known data about your study sample and the study population.

The lessons you have learned about generalization of study findings have arisen from the methods employed in quantitative research rather than qualitative research. For this reason, we might see those lessons as more pertinent to quantitative research than to qualitative research. Thus, we will not address the theme of generalization of study findings in this practice exercise. It will be reserved for a later lesson.

Phase 3: Data Analysis

Your data analysis will entail the first two levels of coding in content analysis in relation to a single question asked to a small sample of people. In addition, this analysis will include the examination of the credibility of your coding by your effort to get another researcher to review your codes and give you feedback on their credibility.

This will not be a comprehensive experience in content analysis. Instead, it will help you become familiar with the experience of some aspects of content analysis. You will have a more advanced experience with this task in a later chapter on qualitative data analysis.

Your study sample should include at least 15 people, but you are advised to keep the number below 25 in order to keep the experience simple. You are expected to compose only one question for your questionnaire so that your data analysis experience will be manageable for this exercise. You might ask, "What are your recommendations for the improvement of the social work curriculum in this social work department?" Another choice you could make could lead you to ask, "What is the most important way in which your family has contributed to your life satisfaction?" Another example could lead to the following question: "In your opinion, how are good college teachers better than others?"

You will collect the responses to your questionnaire. Your next step is the first-level coding of the responses to your question. You might have more than one code for a given response because there may be more than one idea in a given answer. You will enter your data in Exhibit 9.1 by placing the respondent's comments in the first column and your code(s) for this statement in the second column. Following this procedure, you will examine your first-level codes and engage in second-level coding by combining first-level codes together when they have essential similarities.

Your next task is to share your Exhibits 9.1 and 9.2 with one or more fellow students and ask if they have any observations about your coding or if they have recommendations for how your coding might be improved. The other person should examine each first-level code in relation to the respondent's statement and report if he or she would have given the statement a code that was essentially similar to your code. This person will then examine the second-level codes in the same way. This will give you a brief experience with the assessment of the credibility of your coding of responses.

Phase 4: Study Conclusions

What conclusions can you draw from your coding of the respondent answers to your research question? The key place to look for conclusions is the second-level codes because these combined first-level codes into categories. If you examined the traits of a good college teacher, perhaps you will observe from your second level of coding that comments that referred to the relationships of teacher and student were more common than comments that referred to the level of knowledge possessed by the teacher. Perhaps a major theme was the extent to which the teacher was practical, gave special attention to individual students, or was a good lecturer.

What You Will Report From This Practice Exercise

You will provide a report on your study results by answering each of the following questions and attaching to your report your results for Exhibits 9.1 and 9.2.

1. Briefly explain the fundamental question that you were pursuing in your study? What is the question, and why are you interested in it?

2. How would you describe the study sample you employed in this exercise? For example, did you select the members of your research class or the members of your exercise club?

3. What specific question did you place on the questionnaire?

4. What were your second-level codes?

5. Did you have sufficient data to draw any tentative conclusions? If so, what were they?

6. Attach Exhibits 9.1 and 9.2 to this report.

EXHIBIT 9.1
FIRST-LEVELS CODES FOR YOUR QUALITATIVE DATA

Person #	Statement From This Person	Code
1		
2		
3		
4		
5		
6		
7		
8		
9		
10		

EXHIBIT 9.2
SECOND-LEVEL CODES FOR YOUR QUALITATIVE DATA

Second-Level Code	First-Level Codes That Fit This Second-Level Code	Number of First-Level Codes Here

CHAPTER REVIEW

Chapter Key Learnings

1. Because qualitative research is more flexible in measurement than quantitative research, it is especially well suited to the exploratory research study, which examines social phenomena that are not well known.

2. Qualitative and quantitative research processes have a number of things in common: They are both guided by the spirit of scientific inquiry, are founded on a knowledge base, pursue new knowledge through a systematic process, have transparency of method, and have conclusions that are based on the data analyzed.

3. The qualitative research process includes the review of a knowledge base, the articulation of study methods, the analysis of data, and the drawing of conclusions. Thus, it is fundamentally similar to the process for a quantitative study.

4. Ethnography refers to the study of a culture in its natural setting with the purpose of describing the way of life for a group. It is more likely to employ narrative analysis of qualitative data than content analysis.

5. The purpose of grounded theory is to develop explanations, hypotheses, or theories that are grounded in observations of social behavior. Thus, the observations (measurements) are undertaken before the form of the data is determined. In other words, this type of study does not present specific categories into which people should be placed before the data are collected and analyzed.

6. When you wish to examine a single individual, a single event, or a single social setting (e.g., a single organization or a single community) with sufficient intensity to obtain an in-depth understanding of it, the case study would be appropriate for your inquiry because of the extensive array of information that can be a part of this type of study.

7. The semistructured interview is one of the methods of data collection for the qualitative study. It entails a purposeful encounter between an interviewer and an interviewee that is guided by a set of open-ended questions that break down the general theme into subthemes.

8. The focus group is a method of gathering qualitative data that entails a group meeting where a general question and specific questions are discussed and conclusions are drawn. There is a leader who is responsible for leading the group discussion, and there is a person who records the ideas that emanate from the discussion.

9. Data analysis in qualitative research can take on many forms, two of which are narrative analysis, the review of stories, and content analysis, the review of segments of qualitative content.

Chapter Discussion Questions

1. Articulate an explanatory research question and an exploratory research question, and explain whether qualitative or quantitative research methods would be more appropriate for each.

2. With regard to the two research questions posed above, explain how they would be similar with respect to one of the bases on which both qualitative research and quantitative research are similar, and describe one basis on which they would be different.

3. What is one of the bases on which qualitative and quantitative research processes are different concerning the study methods employed?

4. With reference to the research questions you articulated in Question 1 above, which of the following would best suit the study of these questions: (a) ethnography, (b) grounded theory, (c) case study, or (d) something else?

5. With regard to the research questions posed in Question 1, what is the approach best suited to data collection: the interview, the focus group, the social survey, or something else?

6. Would your study (articulated in Question 1) be best suited to narrative analysis, content analysis, or something else?

Chapter Test

1. When you have qualitative data, you have
   a. Scores
   b. People in categories
   c. Words
   d. All of the above

2. Qualitative research is more appropriate when which of the following conditions exist?
   a. You are seeking to develop theories, hypotheses, or new conceptual frameworks of understanding, rather than testing existing ones
   b. You are seeking an understanding of the subjective meaning of behaviors rather than their precise description
   c. There is relatively little that is known about the subject from the existing literature
   d. All of the above

3. How are qualitative and quantitative research processes similar?

   a. They are both founded on the spirit of scientific inquiry
   b. They both typically start with the examination of a knowledge base
   c. They both base their conclusions on the data that were analyzed
   d. All of the above

4. Which of these phases of research is not included in a qualitative study?
   a. Examination of a knowledge base
   b. Development of study methods
   c. Analysis of data
   d. None of the above—all are included

5. If you collected your data by mailing a questionnaire to your study sample, what kind of mechanism would you be employing?
   a. An interview
   b. A focus group
   c. A survey
   d. None of the above

6. In qualitative research, a code is
   a. The number that you give to a category, such as male coded as "1" and female coded as "2" for gender
   b. A brief set of words (or a single word) that captures the essence of what is said in a statement
   c. A category of the statistic that will be used to test the hypothesis
   d. None of the above

7. In qualitative research, content analysis refers to
   a. The number of first-level codes for a given second-level code
   b. A set of procedures for the analysis of data that includes the development of codes for each set of text (e.g., the answer to an open-ended question on a survey)
   c. The examination of the content validity of the means used to measure the study variables
   d. The examination of the internal consistency of responses to a measurement tool that is designed to measure a study variable

8. Which of the following statements is/are true?
   a. Qualitative measurement is often employed with exploratory research

   because exploratory research is suitable for studies where little is known
   b. If you conducted an interview and examined your notes from that interview, you would be engaged in quantitative research
   c. Both of the above
   d. None of the above

9. In qualitative research, narrative analysis differs from content analysis in what way?
   a. It focuses on narratives in terms of the placement of people into categories or the provision of numbers
   b. It focuses on segments of content that are coded according to the essence of the meaning of the content
   c. Both of the above
   d. None of the above

10. In qualitative research, the assessment of credibility refers to
    a. The means used to select the study sample from the study population
    b. The means used to determine if one's coding of data is similar to that of other people who are coding the same data
    c. The means used to determine if further data should be analyzed
    d. None of the above

ANSWERS: 1 = c; 2 = d; 3 = d; 4 = d; 5 = c; 6 = b; 7 = b; 8 = a; 9 = d; 10 = b

Chapter Glossary

Analytic comparison. The application of the concepts of the method of agreement and the method of difference in logical inquiry.

Case study. An approach to research, using both qualitative and quantitative measurement,

that provides a comprehensive view of a single case, which might be an individual, an organization, a community, or an event.

Case study protocol. A set of guides on the procedures to be employed in the implementation of a case study, for example, field procedures, sources of information, case study questions, and so forth.

Coding. The use of a word or phrase to convey the meaning of a segment of content (e.g., sentence, paragraph, page) in content analysis.

Content analysis. A method for converting words into ideas that capture the essence of the words that were analyzed and lead to inferences about the reality of the theme under investigation.

Ethnography. A qualitative approach to research that refers to the study of a culture in its natural setting with the purpose of describing the way of life of a group.

Focus group. A method of gathering qualitative data that entails a group meeting, with a leader and a recorder, where specific questions are discussed, data are analyzed, and conclusions are drawn.

Grounded theory. An approach to qualitative research that develops explanations, hypotheses, or theories that are grounded in observations of social behavior.

Interview. A purposeful encounter among persons in which one person is seeking information from another person.

Narrative analysis. A depiction of some social reality, typically in the form of a story, that reveals themes and explanations through the analysis of qualitative data.

Proposition. A causal statement that is a part of a comprehensive theory.

Qualitative research. A form of research that uses words as the primary source of data, which distinguishes it from quantitative research, which measures variables by scores or by placing study subjects into predetermined categories.

Semistructured interview. An interview with a set of open-ended questions that are parts of a general research theme in a qualitative study.

Survey. A purposeful inquiry into a subject for a designated sample of people by a researcher using a recording instrument, typically a questionnaire.

Unit of analysis. The entity on which you will collect your data in a case study—for example, Mrs. Johnson, the Child Welfare Program for Hoover County, or the presidential election of 2016.

10

CONDUCTING PROGRAM EVALUATIONS

Janet is the chair of the program evaluation committee for a human service agency that provides an array of services related to mental health. Her committee has evaluated client need through a survey of current clients and has discovered the need for special day care for autistic children. It has reviewed a service audit from a funding source that revealed the standards employed by the agency to be consistent with expectations. In other words, this agency employs qualified staff who have reasonable size caseloads and executes service protocols appropriately. This committee has examined the agency's efficiency by comparing the cost per client served by their agency with that of three similar agencies in the community and found that all four agencies have similar costs per client served. The next task for the committee will be to compare the cost per counseling session for selected services at their agency with that of the other agencies. Because clients tend to vary on the amount of service used, this figure will be a better evaluation of efficiency than the former. The evaluation of client outcome is a major challenge the committee will face next. Much data are available on client characteristics and client satisfaction, but insufficient data are available on client outcome. The committee will institute a client outcome study by selecting several services at random and conduct outcome studies for these services. Most likely the research plan will entail the measurement of client outcomes such as anxiety, depression, PTSD (post-traumatic stress disorder), and persistent mental illness.

INTRODUCTION

All human services operate as a part of a human service program. You may be providing services to foster children under the Foster Care Program of a human service agency. This Foster Care Program may offer a variety of services for foster children. The Foster Care Program may be a part of the Child Welfare Program for this agency, which also hosts other general programs such as Adoptions or Family Counseling. When you see a program evaluation, you will see a wide variety of data on client services and client outcomes. On the other hand, when you evaluate a single intervention, you will typically collect outcome data for a single group you are serving or a single client. The main purpose of the evaluation of an intervention is to help the practitioner evaluate his or her practice in order to improve it. The evaluation of interventions might be a part of an overall program evaluation.

The purpose of the program evaluation is to assess how well the program is working in various ways. The chief purpose is to determine if the program is achieving the intended outcomes, such as improved school performance or improved mental health. Another purpose is to determine if the program is operating according to plans. For example, is it employing qualified personnel? Another purpose is to determine if the program is operating efficiently. If it costs other agencies in your county $100 per therapy session offered and your agency operates at a cost of $130 per session, your agency is not as efficient as the others. It may or may not be operating as effectively (regarding client outcome), but it is not operating as efficiently. Armed with information from program evaluations, your agency can find ways to make services better for the client, and it can achieve better accountability with funding sources.

In this chapter, you will examine various dimensions of program evaluations. On the completion of it, you will be equipped to examine some of these dimensions for a familiar human service agency. At a more specific level, you will be able to do the following:

1. Identify what your agency does with regard to program evaluation

2. List some of the uses of program evaluation

3. Suggest ways by which your agency can better evaluate its programs

4. Find evidence for programs such as the ones served by your agency

5. Discuss the characteristics of good human service programs

6. Identify the essential ingredients for the evaluation of client satisfaction, client need, service efficiency, service process, and client outcome

7. Apply the logic model to the characterization of critical aspects of your agency's program evaluation

8. Apply nominal group technique for the assessment of need

9. Explain the concept of treatment fidelity as an issue in program evaluation

WHAT DOES YOUR AGENCY DO TO EVALUATE PROGRAMS?

Does your agency report data about the services it offers, such as the number of clients served or the characteristics of its clients? Does it report the results of client satisfaction surveys, data on client outcomes, and/or information about adherence to service standards?

Why does it report these facts? Do funding sources need to know these things? Do administrators need to know? Do staff need this information? The results of program evaluations can assist in at least two ways: (1) to find ways to improve services and (2) to improve accountability. Everyone wants to improve services but few have major organizational responsibilities for accountability.

Have you engaged in discussions with others in a human service agency concerning the results of program evaluations? What did you learn? In what ways have you found the results of program evaluations to be beneficial. Can you identify improvements in services that came about as a result of evaluations? Can you identify ways by which your agency has benefited from evaluations in the improvement of accountability? Has it impressed the community or key funding sources?

What should your agency be doing with regard to program evaluation? What should it evaluate? Why should it evaluate this rather than something else? In other words, what good would come from this evaluation? What evidence would be credible for those who would be the audience for this kind of evaluation? These are some of the questions that you will examine in this chapter.

THE NATURE OF PROGRAM EVALUATIONS

What is a program? A **program** is an organized set of activities designed to achieve a particular goal or a set of objectives. The activities are interdependent in that they depend on one another for the achievement of the objectives. A program has an identity and specified resources. Programs within an agency or system can be conceptualized at various levels. You may be working with a group for abused women that you would conceptualize as an intervention that fails within the Women's Services Program for an agency. Your intervention might have the objective of improving the feelings of emotional support that these clients possess. All interventions in the Women's Services Program have a common goal of promoting the mental health and self-sufficiency of women in need. This program may fall under the Mental Health Program of the agency, where all services are related to the improvement of mental health. Thus, the overall goal is the same for all services within a given program.

A **program evaluation** is an effort to apply the principles of scientific inquiry to program decision making. For example, program managers need to know the character and incidence of the needs associated with target problems. They need to identify the characteristics of effective service so that programs can be designed well. In addition, they need to be able to justify their programs by demonstrating that they have been effective in meeting human needs.

ADVANTAGES OF PROGRAM EVALUATIONS

Can you imagine a human service agency that pays no attention to program evaluation at all? Their leaders would have no information on the number of clients served, the extent to which practitioners are qualified to provide agency services, the extent to which clients have gotten better as a result of agency services, or the aspects of service that seem most effective. In other words, they would have little information on how to make services better or how to convince funding sources to provide support. These agencies would not likely survive. And you would probably not be motivated to work there.

Not only can you better understand what works by reviewing data from your agency's program evaluations, but you can also review evidence from the evaluation of other similar programs to see what works best. In other words, you can get ideas both from your agency data and from publications on program evaluations. In Exhibit 10.1, you can see a brief summary of what has been learned by six systematic reviews of evidence related to various types of parent training programs. You can see, for example, that these programs have generally been found to be effective. You will also note that the evidence is much better for some outcomes than for others. Perhaps the results of these findings can stimulate a discussion among social workers about the use of parent training as a service.

EXHIBIT 10.1

A FEW THINGS LEARNED FROM SYSTEMATIC REVIEWS OF PARENT TRAINING PROGRAMS

Each of the following brief statements were constructed from the Campbell Policy Brief Number 1 (Effects of Parenting Programs) from the Campbell Collaboration. (www.campbellcollaboration.org). Here is an overview:

Parenting programs are provided to parents to enhance parents' knowledge, skills, and understanding and to improve both child and parent behavior and psychological outcomes. These programs are typically offered to parents over the course of 8 to 12 weeks, for about 1 to 2 hours each week. Among the techniques employed in these programs are discussion, role-play, watching video vignettes, and homework. These techniques can be offered one-to-one or in groups. The setting for these interventions are varied (hospitals, social work clinics, community centers, etc.). The Campbell Collaboration had published six systematic reviews at the time of this review. In general, these reviews provide unequivocal evidence to show that parenting programs are effective in improving some aspects of parents' psychosocial functioning in the short term. However, the results are varied as you will see below.

1. Programs for treating families with children who have experienced attention-deficit/hyperactivity disorder (ADHD) were found to be somewhat effective with relieving the stress of the parents and improving the general behavior of the children, but data on the improvement of ADHD-related behaviors of the children were inconclusive. Furthermore, the effects of these programs on school performance has not been well tested (Zwi, Jones, Thorgaard, York, & Dennis, 2012).

2. Programs for teenage parents were found to be effective in improving parent responsiveness to the child, parent–child interaction, and infant responsiveness to the mother in about half of a set of meta-analyses that were found, but the remaining meta-analyses were inconclusive (Barlow et al., 2011). Thus, teenage parenting programs were found to be promising, but further research is needed.

3. Group-based parenting programs for improving the emotional and behavioral adjustment of young children have shown modest evidence of their effectiveness, but the results are rather inconclusive. The evidence is insufficient to support any practice policies on this treatment. More research is needed.

4. The findings of a review of evidence on group-based parenting programs showed that they were effective in the improvement of the psychosocial well-being of parents (Barlow, Smailagic, Huband, Roloff, & Bennett, 2012).

5. A review of evidence on parent training programs for parents who are intellectually disabled was not conclusive. A few studies had promising results, but there was insufficient evidence overall to support practice policies on this theme (Coren, Hutchfield, Thomae, & Guystafsson, 2010).

6. Group-based parenting interventions were found to be effective and cost-effective for improving child conduct problems, parental mental health, and parenting skills in the short term (Furlong, McGilloway, Bywater, Hutchings, Donnelly, & Smith, 2012).

In the next section, you will review various types of program evaluations, some of which are related to need, some to service quality, some to service efficiency, and some to service outcome. The data from each of these forms of evaluation can assist with the two major outcomes of program evaluation: (1) improving services and (2) improving accountability.

CHARACTERISTICS OF GOOD PROGRAMS

What makes a program good? Have you received any notices to say that the staff of a given program are very satisfied with their jobs and have few client complaints? Have you witnessed programs that have received good publicity and seem to have a very good reputation? Have you noticed that some programs do not have enough staff, or have staff that do not seem well qualified for their jobs? Your answers to these questions can be useful in your discovery of what makes a good program.

Let's examine a few of these characteristics. First, good programs operate in a good service culture. This means that they have a clear philosophy of client service, which values client respect and client success. You may find slogans that illustrate this culture, such as "The client comes first" or "Respect is our first duty." To the extent that you find staff quoting these slogans, you will find a better program. But it does little good for slogans to only appear on the agency website but never to be spoken.

Second, good programs have a clear identity. The name of the program should be the first clue about identity. A good question is whether the public, especially those in need of the service, recognize the identity. It is easier to achieve good identity if a program deals with a target behavior such as substance abuse or child neglect. Programs with a vague identity have an uphill task of achieving community support.

A third characteristic of a good program is effective service. If a program is known for being effective, it will find greater community support. Program evaluation, of course, is the vehicle for documenting effectiveness. The more evidence you have to support your program, the better will be your accountability.

Royse, Thyer, and Padgett (2016) set forth a depiction of what should be if we all lived in the ideal world of program evaluation:

> In the best of all possible worlds, every human service program would be solidly established on the basis of scientifically credible evidence that had been previously published in peer-reviewed professional journals. That is, before the practitioners jumped into a social problem and started "helping," someone did a serious search and appraisal of the relevant evaluation studies that tested the usefulness of various methods of potential helping. If a careful search of the literature and critical review of the existing outcome studies found that one or more models of intervention had credible evidence of effectiveness, and these approaches were "testable" to the existing service providers, cost-effective, and ethical, contemporary standards of ethical practice would suggest that the service program be focused around these empirically supported services as opposed to interventions lacking a sufficient foundation in empirical research. (p. 10)

Stable funding is a fourth characteristic of a good program. Programs that rely exclusively on grants will be vulnerable to loss of funds, sometimes simply because the funding source has a policy of not continuing the funding of any given program over a long period of time. This requires the agency to be constantly on the prowl for other grant support.

FINDING EVIDENCE FOR HUMAN SERVICE PROGRAMS

You have reviewed the concept of evidence-based practice in a previous chapter. You saw that evidence-based practice entails the integration of research evidence with practitioner expertise and client preferences in the determination of the course of action for the services you will provide. Evidence, therefore, is one of the critical components of this type of practice, but it is not the only thing to consider. If you totally ignore evidence, however, you are not operating as an evidence-based practitioner.

In the pursuit of evidence, you are encouraged to start with the systematic review of evidence because it is the most sophisticated mechanism for this endeavor. If you fail to find adequate systematic reviews, you are encouraged to see if you can find a meta-analysis that answers your research question. In case of a failure to find adequate evidence in this regard, you could seek a traditional literature review that examines evidence. You have been encouraged not to stop with a report of a single study that shows that a given service will work for a given objective. You will avoid cherry-picking the evidence to find support for your intervention—this practice falls outside the boundary of the spirit of scientific inquiry.

Among the sources for finding systematic reviews are the Cochrane Collaboration (www.cochrane.org) and the Campbell Collaboration (www.campbellcollaboration.org).

On each of these sites you can enter the theme of your inquiry (e.g., eating disorders, posttraumatic stress disorder, autism) and get systematic reviews for your theme. In some cases, you will find that there is no systematic review for your theme. You have reviewed Exhibit 10.1 that revealed summaries of the findings of six systematic reviews of parent training programs. This provides some evidence of the contribution of systematic reviews of evidence in your practice decision-making process.

TYPES OF PROGRAM EVALUATIONS

What do we need to know about our programs in order to achieve the two critical benefits of good evaluation (improving services and improving accountability)? Do we need to know if our clients are satisfied? If the clients are not satisfied, they are not likely to continue using the service. Maybe dissatisfaction means our services are not effective. Do we need to know if our services are reaching the intended population (e.g., people with serious mental illness)? If not, we will be in trouble with our funding sources. Do we need to know if our services are being delivered according to good standards? If it becomes known that we are employing nonqualified therapists, we will be in trouble. Do we need to know if our services are efficient? If our cost per client served is much higher than what is normal, we will be subject to criticism, and potentially to the withdrawal of our funds. Do we need to know if our services are achieving the intended outcomes? If we have good evidence that our services are achieving the intended outcomes, we will have a good relationship with our funding sources and with the public.

Evaluation of Need

A **need** is a gap between what is and what should be. A **need assessment** is an attempt to identify the community's perceptions of gaps and to measure them. What one identifies as a need, another may not. What is generally recognized as a need in a given community may not be recognized in another community. What is recognized today as a need (or a social problem) may not have been recognized as such 50 years ago.

Needs originate from social problems, the latter being defined as an undesirable condition of the individual or the environment. We normally recognize unemployment as a problem. Society's goal regarding this problem is to reduce it as much as possible. The needs of the unemployed could entail skill development, enhanced motivation, increased self-confidence, improved knowledge about job openings, transportation, and so forth. Social problems and social needs serve as guides for program goals and objectives. The goal of an employment training program might be to reduce unemployment, or to place certain persons into jobs, while the objectives might be to improve job interviewing skills, job motivation, and/or knowledge of job openings.

You can find measures of need that are either quantitative or qualitative in nature. Quantitative measures generate data with regard to numbers or proportions. Qualitative measures generate ideas expressed as words.

Quantitative approaches to need assessment include the following:

1. The number of people on the program's waiting list for service

2. Agency data on the numbers of people served

3. Demographic reports from sources such as the U.S. Census

4. Social surveys that seek information from the community individuals about need

The first of these items is the most profound. It provides a very clear set of data on program need. Often, however, we have programs that serve all who apply, but we suspect there are many more people in the community with a need for it but who have not asked for the service. That's where the social survey can serve as a mechanism for documenting need. In addition, we can seek data from the census to show us how many people live in our community who have the characteristics of people who need our service.

Service statistics reveal the number of people served by each service. They sometimes reveal the characteristics of the clients. These statistics can reveal the extent that a program is serving the intended population. If a major goal is to serve people in poverty, the income information from service statistics can be useful.

The social survey is a mechanism for measuring a felt need that has not turned into a request for a service. Failure to request a service can result from a number of causes, including the fact that a person does not know that a given service exists. Another possible cause is that a needed service is not accessible to the potential client. In addition, a potential client may not believe that the service will be successful. Information from the survey can be used to address the reasons why people in need have not requested the service. The number of people with the need is another source of information that can be gained from a survey.

Demographic reports from sources such as the U.S. Census can be helpful for the documentation of potential need. If you have a preschool service for children, you would want to know how many families in your community have preschool-age children. Furthermore, you may want to know the number of such families who live under a certain level of income.

Among the qualitative approaches to needs assessment are public hearings, interviews of key informants, focus groups, and the nominal group technique (to be described in the next section). These approaches are better suited for identifying the nature of need and unearthing new needs than for precisely measuring needs, the latter being better served by quantitative methods.

One use of qualitative methods is the public hearing in which people are invited to say what they wish rather than respond to categories. Interviews with open-ended questions would constitute another example of qualitative measurement. The focus group is yet another example. These are small groups of people, usually made up of six to eight individuals, who participate in a structured discussion of a selected theme. That theme could be the unmet needs of senior citizens of Hinshaw County, the needs of the homeless in Cedar City, or the relative need for support, enhanced self-esteem, or legal assistance for abused wives.

Using Nominal Group Technique for Assessing Need

Nominal group technique (NGT) is a structured group method of decision making that is designed to maximize participation among a small group of key informants (Delbecq, Van de Ven, & Gustafson, 1975). The outcome of this tool is a prioritized list of ideas around a designated question. It is qualitative in nature because it begins with an open format for the generation of ideas. It is quite useful for identifying need and establishing priority among those needs.

The NGT entails the following steps:

1. The silent generation of ideas in writing by each participant

2. A round-robin recording of the participants' ideas

3. A serial discussion of each idea for clarification

4. A preliminary vote on items importance for each item

5. A discussion of the preliminary vote

6. A final vote on item importance

The greatest contributions to problem solving of NGT is that it promotes (a) equality of participation, (b) greater tolerance of nonconformity, and (c) a high level of task motivation. Persons who become engaged in an NGT meeting tend to come away with a heightened feeling of involvement and contribution to the outcome of the meeting. Thus, they tend to be more committed to follow-up efforts. This process also leads to a larger quantity and range of ideas for consideration.

Dominance of the discussion by a vocal few is minimized by the procedures of the NGT. Maximum participation is the key contribution of it. On the other hand, the NGT is a costly endeavor, especially for large groups, because the process is time-consuming and requires that large groups be divided into subgroups of five to nine members each for the NGT procedures. Thus, a group of 90 people would have to be divided into 10 groups of nine members, each of which, of course, would require the services of 10 group leaders skilled in the NGT procedures.

Preliminary Considerations in the Use of NGT

Your first task is to determine whether NGT is the appropriate tool for your purpose. The product of NGT will be a list of ideas in response to a key question such as "What are the most important unmet needs of the graduate social work students of this university?" If a comprehensive list already exists that you are confident will cover all important needs, you could simply give this list to key persons and ask for a ranking of priorities. The NGT procedures are designed both to generate new ideas and to rank them.

Another consideration is that the persons who participate must have knowledge about the question being posed. In the example above, social work students in this particular university would surely qualify. Furthermore, it must be feasible to divide the participants into groups of five to nine persons with a group leader for each. It is also essential that group leaders give thoughtful consideration to their unique role as facilitators of this process. They must be prepared to embrace the spirit of NGT. Finally, there should be a reasonable likelihood that the results will be taken seriously by those in key positions to make decisions about need.

In your preparation for the actual meeting, your first concern will be the meeting room.

It should be arranged with tables for each group, which can comfortably seat five to nine group members. There should be sufficient space among groups to prevent them from disturbing one another. You will need a flip chart for each group where ideas can be written and some tape to place each page on the wall for all to see. You will also need a set of 3 × 5 index cards for each participant to list their ideas in the first step in the process.

Six Steps in the NGT Process

The six steps in the NGT process were enumerated above. Perhaps this review illustrated the spirit of this technique and what it best contributes. Now, let's examine each of these steps in more detail.

In the first step, the group facilitator presents the question to be addressed and the time limit for the recording of brief ideas in writing (usually 5 minutes). The question is presented both verbally and in writing to ensure clarity. The level of abstraction is defined, but the facilitator avoids offering examples that may tend to lead group members in a narrow direction. For example, the question may ask about the chief problems of a given target population. The facilitator may go on to define "problem" as a condition, not a lack of a certain service. But the leader would want to avoid offering examples of problems to be identified by the participants. In this first step, it is important that one group member not be allowed to disturb another or attempt to influence their ideas. NGT leaders should model such behavior by working quietly themselves.

In the second step, the facilitator asks for one item from each member's list and records it on a flip chart, after which he or she asks for a second item from each member, and so on, until each member's list has been exhausted. Group members are encouraged to add items to their lists as this step progresses. It is important that the facilitator not allow group members to debate their ideas during this step. All members should be given equal opportunity to offer their ideas in their own words, but they should be encouraged to express them in brief phrases that can be realistically placed on a flip chart. Neither the group facilitator nor other members should suggest the wording for a member's idea unless it is entirely necessary.

In the third step, each idea is discussed in turn for purposes of clarification and to eliminate duplication. Items are not, however, debated. They are only clarified. They are not normally grouped into broad categories at this time. However, items that are very similar may be combined into one idea. You may consider the idea of grouping some items together if they are rather similar. But this step does not entail the grouping of 31 ideas into six general categories.

In Step 4, group members select five to nine items of most importance and rank them. (Everyone should select the same number of items.) The votes are tallied by assigning the highest value (e.g., 7 points) for a rank of 1, the second highest value for a rank of 2, and so forth. No points are given for items not included in the priority category (e.g., the top seven). These points are totaled for each item, and the results are presented to the group.

A certain degree of anonymity is important in this step. The facilitator could ask the group members to write their votes and pass them in. The range of votes should be displayed for each item to illuminate the group's variability and to facilitate a discussion of the preliminary vote.

Step 5 in the NGT process entails the discussion of the preliminary vote. The individuals reflect on the vote and share their ideas about it. Someone may point out that a given idea had dramatically different scores with several people giving it a very high score but most people not giving it a score at all. Perhaps this observation can generate ideas that may influence the final vote.

In the final step in the NGT process, participants give a second vote to the items on the list. The votes are computed and shared with the group members. This will entail the final list of ideas in priority order based on the scores.

Limitations of NGT

The NGT procedure is not useful for resolving conflict. The procedures are quite counter to this outcome. In fact, conflict is discouraged by the procedures. The outcome is designed to represent a consensus of the opinions of the participants. Another limitation is that the group should not have members who have inordinate power over the relevant decisions that are to be influenced by the ideas being presented. Furthermore, NGT is not useful for routine meetings and staff discussions.

Evaluation of Service Process

Service process refers to actions taken on behalf of the program in order to achieve the desired results. To achieve the goals of the program, staff with certain credentials are hired. These credentials are believed to be necessary for effective service. These persons are instructed to administer services as designed (process). This might include restricting services to clients who are eligible for the service according to established policies. The service process might include ensuring that each client is informed of his or her rights. It might include referrals of certain clients to certain other services. It might include ensuring that each client is served through an established protocol of services to ensure that important considerations are not overlooked, as, for example, a protocol for how the emergency room of the hospital will treat each victim of rape.

Monitoring variables such as those mentioned above serves as the focus of quality assurance efforts. The term **quality** is used in many ways by human service professionals. It could mean anything from whether the credentials of staff are appropriate (Are the staff qualified?) to whether the clients gained in their social functioning. According to Coulton (1991),

> quality is an elusive concept that implies value. A service that is of high quality has features that are valued by relevant individuals or groups. Quality assurance programs seek ways to objectify what are essentially subjective phenomena so they can be examined. (p. 253)

Coulton (1991) divides quality into three categories: (1) structure (or inputs), (2) process, and (3) outcome. Staff qualifications would fit into the first category, while service process fits into the second and client outcome into the third.

Quality assurance activities tend to focus on input and process variables, rather than on outcome. We often refer to these variables (input and process) as standards. Standards are developed because they are believed to lead to effective outcomes, but we should not lose sight of the fact that standards are not outcomes. The primary reason for the high degree of focus on standards is the lack of good information on client outcome and the difficulties in gathering such information.

A key question that can be best answered through qualitative methods is "What is it like being a client of this program?" If you were to follow a client through the entire process from calling the agency to being greeted by the receptionist, to being given the intake interview, to being given the central service, to being discharged, what kinds of insights could you gain about how to make the service better? Perhaps improvement is needed in the recruitment of clients, the intake procedures, the service design, and/or the termination of service and followup. These are the kinds of questions about service process that can be addressed by qualitative methods.

Evaluation of Efficiency

When we say that a service is delivered more efficiently, we normally are saying that we are getting more for the money. If the Hampton Family Counseling Center delivers family therapy at a cost of $115 per hour, we might say it is operating more efficiently than the Hampton Psychiatric Center that is delivering family therapy at a cost of $130 per hour. If the child abuse investigation program for the Parker County Department of Social Services (DSS) spent $200,000 this year and completed 200 child abuse investigations, you could say that the cost per child abuse investigation was $1,000 ($200,000/200 = $1,000). These figures, of course, would be based on the assumption that all of the $200,000 was devoted only to child abuse investigations. If the Walker County DSS was spending $1,400 per child abuse investigation, you could say that the Parker County DSS was operating its program more efficiently than the Walker County DSS.

In the above examples, costs were computed with regard to units of service delivered rather than client outcomes. The ultimate study of **efficiency** would be the computation of costs per client achievement or the benefits to the community. If you could compute the cost per child abuse incident prevented, or the cost per client rehabilitated, you would be in the best place to examine efficiency. However, this is not often feasible in human services; therefore, efficiency will be examined in this chapter with regard to units of service delivered.

To determine the cost per unit of service, you will need to engage in the following steps:

1. Define the unit of service

2. Compute the number of units of service that have been delivered by the program

3. Compute the total cost of the program, including both direct and indirect costs

4. Divide the total cost of the program by the number of units of service

Once you have computed the cost per unit of service, you need a reference point for comparison. Are you comparing this with the same figure for other agencies that offer the same program? Are you comparing it with the same figure for past years of service at your agency? Are you comparing it with the cost per unit of service that has been suggested by a reference group (e.g., funding source) as being acceptable? These are a few of your options.

Evaluation of Outcome

Outcome refers to the benefits of a program to the clients we serve. A few of the outcomes expected of human service programs are the reduction of unemployment for high-risk individuals, the improvement of mental health for the survivors of family violence, the reduction of the number of high school dropouts, and the prevention of child abuse. You have reviewed the evaluation of client outcome in many ways through various chapters in this book. You have learned about the role of target behavior definition in the selection of a means of measuring client progress. You have seen that a good analysis of the target behavior can be useful for selecting the appropriate intervention. You have reviewed evidence of what works. Methods for collecting and analyzing data have also been included in your learnings.

The focus for many of the chapters in this book has been on the evaluation of interventions for individuals and groups. The program evaluation includes these evaluations but often is broader when it comes to client outcomes. While a given intervention in a program may measure the outcome of improved feelings of social support for the victims of family violence, the outcome for the overall program may be the prevention of further acts of violence.

When you evaluate outcomes for a program, you need to have a view of why we have this program. Your view needs to be broad. What are the goals and objectives of the program? This requires a focus on the target behavior at a high level. You may find the goal of your program to be the improvement of health for those recently discharged from the cardiac unit of a hospital. One of the objectives may be the reduction of rehospitalizations. Collecting data on rehospitalizations would be one indicator of the achievement of that objective, which, in turn, represents a measured amount of progress toward the achievement of the goal. If your goal is to improve high school graduation rates, your objective may be to improve grades for at-risk students. You may analyze data on grades in the short run and graduation rates for the long term.

Evaluation of Client Satisfaction

Many human service agencies conduct surveys of clients where questions are posed about their level of satisfaction with various aspects of the services they have received. A critical question is whether the service met their needs. Are they better off because of the service? Also included on client satisfaction questionnaires are items that ask questions such as (a) Would you recommend this service to a friend in need? (b) Would you come back for the same service if you needed it? (c) Did you get the kind of service you needed? (d) Did the entire staff treat you with respect? In addition, there may be some aspects of the service that are unique and would generate a special kind of question.

Good client satisfaction data can be used for promotion and accountability. It is good to know if your clients are satisfied. If they are not satisfied, they will likely not continue in service. If they are dissatisfied, we should be concerned if our services are meeting client need, and our agency will likely get a bad reputation.

Client satisfaction data seem to be based on the assumption that client satisfaction is an indicator of client benefit. If clients are not satisfied, they probably did not benefit from the service. If they are satisfied, they probably achieved the outcomes they were seeking. While this seems to be a logical assumption, data on client satisfaction surveys raise serious questions about the validity of this assumption. The fact is that the overwhelming majority of the results of client satisfaction surveys show that clients are highly satisfied. Data on client outcomes, however, are not so uniformly positive.

We should acknowledge that client satisfaction is an opinion, not an indicator of client psychosocial functioning. You are measuring psychosocial functioning when you administer a scale for depression, anxiety, feelings of social support, or stress. We typically have one of these types of functioning that is the objective of our service. If we find growth on one of these types of functioning, we have evidence of the outcome of our services.

The key disadvantage of the client satisfaction survey is that the results tend to be highly positive with few exceptions. Royse et al. (2016) reviewed the available research and found that in almost every case the vast majority of respondents indicated satisfaction with services. They found out that it is typical for such a study to find that 80% to 90% of clients report satisfaction with services. The positive response seems uniform in that it has not been found to vary very much from one study to another where different types of services are being evaluated.

An issue to pose for client satisfaction is the validity of the data. Do these results accurately reflect the opinions of all the clients of the agency? One of the issues in this assessment is the response rate for the surveys, which tend to be quite low. So what do the nonrespondents think about the services? We do not know, but we can examine variables associated with response to see if some theories might be generated. Some of the information from Royse et al. (2016) suggests that clients who stay in service longer are more likely to respond to a client satisfaction survey. Perhaps those who respond are more satisfied than those who do not. Also, respondents tend to be more highly educated.

Some recommendations were offered by Royse et al. (2016) to improve the validity of client satisfaction surveys:

1. Employ a questionnaire with reliability and validity. There are many such tools available.

2. Include at least one open-ended question on the questionnaire. These items are more likely to generate both positive and negative data rather than just positive information.

3. Use the "ballot box" method of distributing the questionnaire. This is a method whereby the questionnaire is distributed to clients while they are at the agency receiving service. The clients are asked anonymously to place their completed questionnaires in a box in the waiting room. There are at least two options for this distribution: (1) select a day of the month for this endeavor rather than doing it every day and (2) ask the clients who have just completed service to complete the questionnaire. The ballot box method has the advantage of getting a much better response rate.

4. If you conduct the typical mailed survey to former clients, consider several suggestions for improving the response rate. For example, you can send out a reminder letter 10 days after sending the questionnaire. You might offer a gift certificate to encourage participation.

THE LOGIC MODEL AS A WAY OF PORTRAYING CRITICAL ASPECTS OF THE PROGRAM EVALUATION

The **logic model** is a means of illustrating the connections among assumptions, resources, activities, and outcomes for your program. It reveals the rationale for why your program is doing what is it doing. Perhaps your program is providing mentors for at-risk males who fail to have good male role models to guide their behaviors. Your program recognizes that one of the causes of delinquency among at-risk males is the absence of good male role models. The provision of these role models through mentoring services will have the potential effect of reducing the likelihood of delinquency among your clients. In these statements, you have explained what you plan to do and why. If you were submitting this information to the logic model, you would identify the types of clients being served, calculate the amount of service you will render, and measure the outcomes of your program.

There are several terms that are used in the presentation of the information for the logic model. First, there are the **inputs**, which identify what comes into the program system, such as clients and resources. The **activities** of the program constitute the second type of information displayed in the logic model. Activities reflect the things that are done to achieve the outcomes of the program. The activities normally take the form of what we call services. The third type of information contained in the logic model are the **outputs**, which reflect the units of service that are offered, such as counseling sessions, training sessions, or investigations completed. **Outcomes** are the fourth type of information provided by the logic model. This refers to the benefits to the clients.

In addition to the above, the logic model suggests that we identify the **assumptions** that provide the rationale for the services being provided. This part of the logic model addresses the same concerns as the portrayal of the model of the intervention in evaluation research. What are the theories about the nature of the target behavior that support the idea of doing what the program is doing to achieve the intended objectives? Is depression caused by distorted thinking about life events? If so, a therapy that addresses dysfunctional thinking would be warranted. Do some males engage in delinquency because they have not had good male role models? If so, a mentor service would be warranted. Do some persons have problems finding jobs because they lack knowledge of how to find a job and succeed in the job interview? If so, a training program would be appropriate.

A brief graphic depiction of the logic model can be seen in Exhibit 10.2. You see that assumptions are listed first. This is the logical foundation of the model being presented. Input is next followed by activities. Outputs follow activities, while the last item is the outcome. Each of these items are documented in the logic model for your program.

EXHIBIT 10.2
THE COMPONENTS OF THE LOGIC MODEL

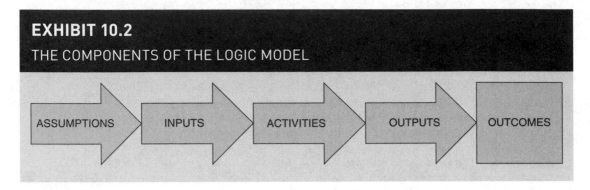

The Reach Program can be used as an example. This program serves people with developmental disabilities. Many of these individuals have failed to reach their full potential because of the limitations of their disabilities, the social opportunities afforded them, and the manner in which people react to this population. Each of the items in the logic model are presented for this program in Exhibit 10.3. In other documents presented with this program, more detail will be provided, such as the specific measures of outcome that will be used for each outcome identified.

EXHIBIT 10.3
LOGIC MODEL FOR THE REACH PROGRAM

Assumptions	Inputs	Activities (Services)	Outputs	Outcomes
Many persons with developmental disabilities have social skills lower than their potential due to limited exposure to others with similar social constraints. According to attribution theory, persons with limitations will be more likely to be motivated to improve if they witness such behavior of others with the same limitations.	Clients with developmental disabilities and low social skills. Trainers who are former trainees. Other staff to coordinate.	A series of training sessions on social skills, conducted in part by clients who have graduated from the training program	Ten 1-hour training sessions	Improved social skills

Many persons with developmental disabilities become over-reliant on others to do things that they can do themselves, and this condition reduces human autonomy and diminishes one's potential for positive self-esteem.	Clients with developmental disabilities and low social skills. Staff to coordinate. Resources for the activities.	Activities that promote autonomy, such as going to the grocery store alone	Five activity sessions	Improved self-esteem
Many persons with developmental disabilities have limited opportunity to engage in social activities, and it is apparent that experiences with social engagement builds social skills.	Clients with developmental disabilities and low social skills. Staff to coordinate activities.	Social activities (e.g., parties) with games that promote social engagement	Five parties	Improved social skills

SOME QUALITATIVE APPROACHES FOR PROGRAM EVALUATION

Most of the avenues we have discussed for program evaluation employ quantitative methods of measurement. There are many qualitative mechanisms for program evaluation. Some of these approaches use both qualitative and quantitative measurement. Among these approaches are the case study and the utilization-focused evaluation, each of which has been addressed in detail in the chapter on the use of qualitative research methods for exploratory research.

The case study method is appropriate when you wish to investigate a single individual, event, or social setting (e.g., a single organization) in sufficient intensity to obtain an in-depth understanding of how it operates or functions. This method can be applied to a program evaluation. In this instance, the case is defined as a given program. An advantage of the case study protocol is that it incorporates data that are both qualitative and quantitative. The case study was examined in detail in the chapter on the use of qualitative research methods in exploratory research.

Utilization-focused evaluation is a model of evaluation that focuses on the intended users of the results of the research study. In fact, it is the intended users who are in control. The evaluation expert is a consultant and facilitator. Developed by Patton (1997, 2008), it is designed to suggest ways in which program evaluation can make a difference. Too often, according to Patton, evaluation reports have been ignored. His suggestion is that evaluations will be put to use if they focus on the information needs of the key stakeholders. This approach was described in detail in the chapter on qualitative research methods for exploratory studies.

ISSUES IN PROGRAM EVALUATION

There are issues that you should review as you consider the task of completing a program evaluation. First, there is the issue of whether the program was implemented properly. Sometimes it is not. Another issue is the potential resistance of staff who feel threatened by the fact that their programs are under review, and the results may be disappointing. A third issue is whether the data were collected from a suitable sample. Often the clients who start the program being evaluated will drop out before sufficient data can be collected from them.

Treatment fidelity is the term that labels the first issue. You have reviewed the idea of the evaluation of service process. From this review, you noted the importance of having qualified staff to deliver the service. You also noted the importance of service standards about things such as the size of the caseload of the staff. If staff are overwhelmed by too many clients, they cannot be expected to deliver the service according to plan. If they are not qualified, they are not prepared to know how to properly implement the service. In the field of psychotherapy, we have licensure to testify to the issue of qualifications for the job. If you are not licensed to delivery psychotherapy, you are not allowed by law to offer this service in many states in our nation.

Special training is another consideration for the staff. Suppose your program is supposed to be delivering trauma-focused cognitive–behavioral therapy to victims of violence. What credentials should this program require of social workers employed in it? Should they be required to obtain a certain amount of training on this treatment method? If they are required to have such training, how many of them actually have received it? That would be a treatment fidelity question.

Treatment fidelity is sometimes ensured by the existence of service protocols. The treatment of rape victims at the emergency room of the hospital may have a list of items to be included in response to the client. For example, all clients must be notified of their rights and informed of an array of available services for follow-up. Also included would be procedures for collecting evidence. All these items are designed to ensure treatment fidelity.

Another issue regarding program evaluation is the resistance of staff who may feel threatened by the fact that their programs are under review. Maybe the results will not be good. Maybe the program will lose its funds and the staff will lose their jobs. Good communication about the purpose of the evaluation can help prevent this resistance. Another preventative strategy would be the involvement of the staff in decisions about the evaluation. The utilization-focused evaluation methods offer some ideas of how to do this.

A final issue is the adequacy of the size of the sample of people from whom data will be collected. If your data consists of all the clients of your agency, this is not normally a concern. There are usually plenty of people in this sample. But if you are engaged in the study of client outcome with a sample of your clients, you need to address the problem of client dropouts. Sometimes you have 15 clients who have volunteered to participate but half of this group drops out before sufficient data have been collected. There are two causes for concern in such a scenario. First, you would likely worry about the representativeness of the clients who remain active. If half the clients have dropped out, you ask yourself if the dropouts are different from those who stayed in treatment such that the results of the data from those who stay are not representative of those who dropped out. Another concern is that statistical analysis of data is hampered by having a small sample. The larger the sample, the more likely your data will be found to be statistically significant. The data from your sample of only six clients may show that clients had a gain in behavior, but this level of gain, with this small sample, may fail to be statistically significant. A preventative technique would be to start the study with a reasonable sample (e.g., 30 or more clients).

Chapter Practice Exercise

Practice Exercise 1: Reporting Your Agency's Program Evaluation Efforts

In this exercise, you will provide a brief report on various aspects of a familiar program in a familiar human service agency. This means that you will report on (a) the evaluation of need, (b) the evaluation of service process, and (c) the evaluation of client outcome.

You brief report will be on what your agency is doing in general. You might, for example, report that your agency does not engage in any systematic effort to assess need as far as you can see from your inquiry. On the other hand, you might report that the agency's evaluation committee reviews client intake data and service delivery data on a quarterly basis whereby they identify trends in service utilization. In the latter example, you might also report that this committee draws special attention to whether the number of clients being served has changed or whether the characteristics of clients (e.g., race, income, gender, age) has changed in recent quarters.

Competencies Demonstrated by Practice Exercise 1

1. The ability to distinguish among evaluation efforts that focus on (a) need, (b) process, (c) outcome, and (d) client satisfaction

2. The ability to identify evaluation efforts related to client need

3. The ability to identify evaluation efforts related to service process

4. The ability to identify evaluation efforts related to client outcome

5. The ability to assess evaluation efforts and suggest what improvements are most useful at the present time for a given program in a given human service agency

Activities for Practice Exercise 1

1. Select a human service program being delivered in a human service agency with which you are familiar.

2. Solicit information on what this agency does with regard to the evaluation of need for this program.

3. Find information about what this agency does with regard to the evaluation of service process for your selected program.

4. Solicit information about what this agency does with regard to the evaluation of client outcome.

5. Identify how this agency could improve its evaluation of one of the above aspects of program evaluation.

What You Will Report From Practice Exercise 1

1. The name of the program and the agency that is being reviewed

   Examples:

   a. The program is the Child Protective Services Program, and the agency is the Harper County Department of Social Services. This program investigates complaints of child abuse, reports to the court when it finds sufficient evidence for prosecution, and provides case management services to the families that it investigates. This may include the facilitation of the entry of the child into foster care.

   b. The Adult Mental Health Services Program of the Rockford Behavioral Health Services Center provides psychotherapy for adults suffering from various forms of mental health problems such as depression, anxiety, and posttraumatic stress disorder.

   c. The School Social Work Services Program for Harper Valley Middle School provides case management, individual counseling, and special projects such as tutoring for students who are having problems with school work and activities.

2. Report on what this agency does with regard to the evaluation of need for this program.

   Examples:

   a. This agency conducts an annual survey whereby citizens of selected high-risk neighborhoods are asked to identify their most important needs that are not currently being met, and the data from this survey are reviewed by the agency administrative team to decide on changes that need to be made by the agency.

   b. This agency collects data on service utilization patterns, but I could not find any actions that have been made as a result of this analysis. In fact, I could not find any meaningful efforts by any staff to analyze these data in a way that would be useful. It seems that these data are just put into a computer file and forgotten.

3. Report on what this agency does with regard to the evaluation of service process for your selected program.

   Example:

   a. This agency collects data on the average size caseload of social workers, whether the Rape Crisis Protocol is followed in each case, and the average time that cases are kept open. These data are analyzed by the agency executive who often uses this information to make changes in how services are offered.

4. Report on what this agency does with regard to the evaluation of client outcome.

   Examples:

   a. This agency collects much data on service process, but I could not find any meaningful efforts to analyze data on client outcome. It seems that the only data that matters are data related to service utilization. I could not find any examples whereby individual social workers had engaged in the evaluation of client outcome for the clients they were serving. I was not surprised at this finding because the agency does not encourage the evaluation of outcome.

   b. The funding source for this agency requires the reporting of data on the number of clients who find a job within 3 months of the beginning of service.

c. This program analyzes data on the school grades of their clients during the service period as compared with the grades these clients had received in the grading period before service was offered.

5. Briefly report your ideas on how this agency can improve one of the above aspects of program evaluation (i.e., need, process, or outcome).

Example:

a. This agency does not evaluate client outcome in any way. I suggest that this agency analyze data on major client outcomes such as improved grades in school, reduced incidences of school disciplinary actions on clients, and the improvement of the proportion of clients who are promoted from one grade to another. These data should be compared with the same data for the program clients in times prior to their receiving service.

Practice Exercise 2: Portraying Your Program Using the Logic Model

Your task is to use what you have learned about the logic model to portray the critical elements of your program. This means that you will report on assumptions, inputs, services, outputs, and outcomes in the same way as depicted in Exhibit 10.3. Your report will be in the form of a table like the one illustrated in this exhibit. In this exercise, you will demonstrate competence in the portrayal of your program evaluation system in the form of the logic model. This model of portrayal is usually helpful if you are preparing a grant proposal for the program. The activities entail the selection of the program to be depicted and the collection of information needed to complete the table for your report. In addition to the table, you will identify the program and agency portrayed in the table.

CHAPTER REVIEW

Chapter Key Learnings

1. Program evaluation is a vehicle for both improving services and achieving accountability because it examines the success of existing services and what explains the level of success.

2. A human service program is an organized set of activities designed to achieve a particular goal or a set of objectives and is normally delivered with regard to various services or interventions. A human service program

will normally have various interventions that are relevant to the general evaluation of the program. For example, the Dropout Prevention Program may include tutoring as a service within that program.

3. Programs can be evaluated with regard to client need (What needs are going unmet?), service process (Are we employing good standards of service?), service output (How much service are we delivering?), service outcome (How much are clients benefiting from our services?), and client satisfaction (Are our clients satisfied with the services they have been given?).

4. Systematic reviews of the evidence of programs can enlighten you with regard to what aspects of programs are most successful in achieving certain objectives. Perhaps your type of program has been found to be more effective with regard to certain objectives than others, and this knowledge can guide agency on how it can improve its services.

5. Good human service programs operate within a culture that focuses on client benefit, has a clearly recognized identity, delivers effective service, and has stable funding.

6. Nominal group technique is a structured group method of decision making that is designed to maximize participation among a small group of key informants. The outcome of this tool is a prioritized list of ideas around a designated question. It is qualitative in nature because it begins with an open format for the generation of ideas. It is quite useful for identifying need and establishing priority among those needs when a small group of key informants can provide the information

needed. A key advantage of NGT is that its structure equalizes participation among participants. It is not, however, a good mechanism for resolving conflict among people.

7. The term *quality* is most often associated with the evaluation of service process, but it means different things to different people, including the evaluation of outcome. In general, it is a term that means value. In human service evaluation, however, you are more likely to see this word associated with process-oriented themes such as service standards than outcome-oriented ideas like client benefit.

8. Efficiency refers to the extent of service that has been delivered for the money. It is normally evaluated with regard to the cost per unit of service. A unit of service refers to the output of a service and is defined in ways such as a day of day care, a 1-hour counseling session, or a child abuse investigation completed. The cost per unit of service is the vehicle for evaluating efficiency. If your agency is delivering its service units at a lower price than a comparable agency, your agency is operating more efficiently.

9. Outcome refers to the benefits of a program to the clients who are served. A few of the outcomes expected of human service programs are the reduction of unemployment for high-risk individuals, the improvement of mental health for the survivors of family violence, the reduction of the number of high school dropouts, and the prevention of child abuse.

10. The evaluation of client satisfaction can be used for promoting the agency in the community and suggesting ways by which

the agency's services can be improved. The result of client satisfaction surveys, however, is not a good way to evaluate client outcome because satisfaction surveys have tended to have results that are uniformly positive from one study to another, and the response rates to satisfactions surveys tend to be rather low.

11. The logic model is a means of illustrating the connections among assumptions, resources, activities, and outcomes for your program. It reveals the rationale for why your program is doing what it is doing. It is sometimes required for grant applications for services.

12. Treatment fidelity is an issue in program evaluation. It refers to the extent to which the intended program was implemented and focuses on things such as credentials of staff, service protocols, and service standards. If fidelity is not maintained in the program being evaluated, we do not know what was or was not effective once we analyze the data.

Chapter Discussion Questions

1. Give an example of how a program evaluation might help the agency find better ways to deliver services? What is an evaluation question that might lead to data that could help?

2. Illustrate how a given intervention can fall under a particular program, which can fall under a larger program. List each of these in order.

3. What is one recommendation you would make for a familiar human service organization with regard to one of the following: (a) the evaluation of need, (b) the evaluation of service process, (c) the evaluation of efficiency, (d) the evaluation of client outcome, or (e) the evaluation of client satisfaction? Illustrate your recommendation with the identification of one piece of data that would be a part of your recommendation.

4. Describe a familiar human service program with regard to whether or not the program has one of the following: (a) a culture that focuses on client benefit, (b) a clearly recognized identity, (c) evidence of effective service, or (d) stable funding.

5. What is a question you could pose to examine the efficiency of a human service program? This is a question that would generate data about efficiency.

6. Describe one thing your agency is doing with regard to the evaluation of client outcome.

7. What is one service standard that is used by your agency? Is there another standard that is not in place but should be?

8. What aspect of the logic model (assumptions, input, activities, output, or outcome) would be most difficult for you to report for your human service program? What aspect would be the easiest to report?

9. To what extent does your human service program have a problem with treatment fidelity?

Chapter Test

1. A program evaluation can be useful for
   a. Improving the program's services
   b. Improving accountability
   c. Both of the above
   d. None of the above

2. The efficiency of a program is typically evaluated with regard to
   a. The extent to which clients believe that the services were helpful
   b. The extent to which the lives of the clients improved
   c. The extent to which services are reaching the intended target population
   d. The cost per unit of service delivered

3. Which of the following statements is/are true?
   a. A major advantage of a systematic review of human service programs is that the review includes all relevant studies that could be found through a systematic search process
   b. The in-depth focus on only one study is normally considered better than a systematic review of evidence regarding a human service program
   c. Both of the above
   d. None of the above

4. Which of the following are characteristics of good human service programs?
   a. A culture that focuses more on efficiency than on client benefit
   b. Stable funding
   c. Both of the above
   d. None of the above

5. Which of the following employ small groups of key informants?
   a. Nominal group technique
   b. Focus group
   c. Both of the above
   d. None of the above

6. Which of the following statements is/are true?
   a. The results of client satisfaction surveys have been uniformly positive from one agency to another and from one type of service to another
   b. The participation rate for client satisfaction surveys has been uniformly high, such as between 80% and 90%
   c. Both of the above
   d. None of the above

7. Which of the following statements is/are true?
   a. The logic model is a means for illustrating the connections between inputs, activities, outputs, and outcomes for your program
   b. The logic model reveals the rationale for why your program is doing what it is doing
   c. The logic model is sometimes required for grant applications for services
   d. All of the above

8. If your program evaluation fails to demonstrate treatment fidelity,
   a. You will not know the nature of the program that was being evaluated
   b. You will not know if your clients were satisfied
   c. You will not know if your clients achieved a gain in the target behavior
   d. All of the above

ANSWERS: 1 = c; 2 = d; 3 = a; 4 = b; 5 = c; 6 = a; 7 = d; 8 = a

Chapter Glossary

Activities. Statements in the logic model that reveal the things done to achieve the outcomes of the program.

Assumptions. Statements in the logical model that reveal the rationale for a program by connecting target behaviors with service activities, such as the assumption of cognitive-behavioral therapy that depression is caused by dysfunctional thinking about life events, so that therapy should address dysfunctional thinking patterns.

Efficiency. The ratio of input to output normally measured with regard to the cost per unit of service delivered.

Inputs. The forces that enter the service system in the logic model, such as clients in need and service staff who will serve them.

Logic model. A means of illustrating the connections between assumptions, resources, activities, and outcomes for a program.

Need. A gap between what exists with regard to human services and what should exist, such as your agency has day care service for 1,200 children, and there are 1,600 children who need day care service.

Need assessment. An attempt to measure the community's gaps in need and resources.

Nominal group technique (NGT). A structured group method of decision making that is designed to maximize participation among a small group of key informants.

Outcomes. The benefits to clients from the services they received, such as the fact that a group of victims of trauma had a 40% improvement in anxiety during the course of treatment.

Outputs. The unit of service in a logic model, such as an hour of counseling.

Program. An organized set of activities designed to achieve a particular goal or a set of objectives, such as the Child Welfare Program of Henson County that has an array of services, all designed to improve the welfare of children.

Program evaluation. Systematic research activities aimed at the determination of how well a program is working with regard to meeting client need, providing good quality service, operating efficiently, and achieving client benefit.

Quality. A concept that implies value, which can be exemplified through mechanisms such as service standards or service outcomes.

Service process. The actions taken on behalf of a program to achieve the desired results, which is evaluated through mechanisms such as adherence to service standards.

Treatment fidelity. The extent to which a program is implemented according to plan, such as the extent to which its implementation is consistent with accepted standards of service.

CONDUCTING EACH PHASE OF SOCIAL WORK RESEARCH

This section of the book takes you from the beginning level of competence in conducting social work research to a higher level. There is a chapter in this section that provides detailed examination of each of the major phases of the research process. In the previous parts, you have encountered each of these phases and the fundamental tasks for each. In this part, you will examine each of them further. For example, you will encounter concepts such as theory, paradigm, and ideology in the chapter on the knowledge base for your study. You will examine various types of study samples in the chapter on sampling, such as the snowball sample. You will encounter concepts in measurement such as internal consistency as a means of testing the credibility of a measurement device. And you will see how a variety of research designs can be used to control for a variety of threats to internal validity

PART THREE

in the determination of whether it was the treatment, rather than something else, that should be credited with causing the measured client change.

You will examine and analyze data with regard to both quantitative data and qualitative data. The quantitative analysis may be more familiar to you because it deals with the statistical analysis of quantitative data. You will see how to select a statistic for your research study and how to put your data into an Internet website to see if statistical significance has been found. You will see that qualitative data refer to the analysis of words. In this regard, you will undertake a set of procedures for the content analysis of answers to an open-ended question from a social survey.

11

DEVELOPING YOUR KNOWLEDGE BASE AND INTERVENTION

Amy has a social work internship with a mental health agency that offers a treatment program for local high school students with mental health needs. She has noticed that anxiety is a major problem for a group of eight high school students in her caseload. She needs help with determining the method of treatment and the method of measuring client progress. Her review of the literature revealed that cognitive–behavioral therapy (CBT) was the treatment for anxiety that was most supported by evidence. She decided that a group therapy program for these eight clients would be appropriate. She was aware that there was a licensed therapist in her agency who would be willing to be the primary therapist of the group and was trained in CBT. Amy was currently taking a course on CBT, and she felt competent to assist the primary therapist with the group treatment experience. Her training had instructed her that CBT was designed to change the patterns of thinking or behavior that inhibit a client's ability to function in life. This treatment is based on the assumption that problems such as anxiety are caused by dysfunctional thinking about life events. By intervening in the client's thinking patterns, the therapist can help the client reduce anxiety. She also got some help from the literature in the selection of a means for measuring client progress. This started with a clear definition of anxiety that she used to seek a tool for measuring it. The literature guided her in finding the appropriate tool, the Beck Anxiety Inventory.

INTRODUCTION

This chapter will help you develop skill in the establishment of a knowledge base for a research study and to describe your intervention when you are engaging in evaluative research. In a number of previous chapters, you have reviewed some of the concepts relevant to these skills. Here are some of the things you have already learned from previous chapters in this book:

1. The knowledge base guides the framework for thinking. For example, stressors lead to stress, which can cause health problems, but it can be ameliorated by social support. So if you want to reduce stress, you can either enhance social supports or reduce stressors.

2. The knowledge base provides for good definitions of study variables, which can aid in the measurement of variables.

3. In evaluative research, the examination of causation can aid in the design of the intervention. If lack of knowledge is the cause of poor school performance, then tutoring would make sense as an intervention.

4. In descriptive research, the key theme for the knowledge base is the definition of study variables because the purpose of the study is to describe people or things with precision.

5. In explanatory research, a key theme for the knowledge base is the theory that guides the framework for conceptualization of study variables.

6. In exploratory research, a key theme for the knowledge base is the determination of whether qualitative or quantitative means of measurement is more appropriate.

7. The study hypothesis is a concise statement of the expected results of the data analysis—for example, posttest scores for depression will be lower than pretest scores.

8. A positive relationship between variables reveals that people who are higher on one of the two variables tend to be higher than others on the other variable.

9. A negative relationship between variables reveals that people who are higher on one of the variables tend to be lower than others on the other variable.

10. Causation refers to the influence of one variable on another, as evidenced by three realities: (1) there was found to be a relationship between the cause and the effect, (2) the effect is not well explained by variables other than the causal one, and (3) a change in the cause has been found to be followed by a change in the effect.

11. The goal of your intervention identifies the long-range benefit to clients, while the objective indicates a measured amount of progress toward the accomplishment of the goal. Thus, your goal may be to obtain employment, while your objective might be to learn how to prepare for the job interview and compose a good resume. Progress on the objective would be measured in an evaluative study.

12. The **structure of the intervention** is a concrete statement that shows both the form and the intensity of the services being given. A group therapy service may be described as weekly 1-hour group sessions for a total of 8 weeks.

13. The **model of the intervention** is the conceptual framework that serves as the logical rationale for offering it in light of what is known about the dynamics of the target behavior being addressed. Your model may be educational because your intervention is essentially a training experience designed to improve knowledge.

14. The **personnel of the intervention** refers to the credentials of the service providers.

In this chapter, you will see an elaboration of some of the above lessons along with a few new ones. Among the new learning outcomes, you will be able to do the following:

1. Articulate the role of the knowledge base for the research study

2. Describe the nature of theory, paradigm, and ideology in the building of the knowledge base for a research study

3. Clearly define terms in your research study, especially the concepts to be measured in your study

4. Organize content in your literature review

5. Discover the literature for your knowledge base

6. Prepare a well-organized literature review for your research study

7. Describe your intervention with regard to the goal, objectives, structure, model, and personnel

In keeping with the *learning-by-doing* theme of this book, you will undertake an exercise on the development of the knowledge base for your study. Furthermore, you will describe a familiar intervention with regard to the goal, objective, structure, model, and personnel.

PURPOSE AND KNOWLEDGE AS THE FOUNDATION FOR THE RESEARCH STUDY

In various examples in this book, you have seen that study examples started with a statement of study purpose and a knowledge base that guided various tasks in the research process. The purpose of the study example given in one of the previous chapters was to describe the human traits of a good work manager. The knowledge presented in that chapter suggested that many people favored male-stereotyped traits when they described the good manager. This, of course, would serve as a barrier to female advancement in the workplace. Women would have more difficulty getting a job as manager if this condition was prevalent. This knowledge led to the need to measure both male-stereotyped traits and female-stereotyped traits that were relevant to the characteristics of a work manager. It also required the selection of a study sample that was relevant. Because this theme is somewhat universal (e.g., it is believed that people in general are like this), the selection of a convenience sample was considered appropriate. Thus, the knowledge base helped in the development of the purpose of the study, the selection of a means of measurement, and the selection of a sample.

What the Knowledge Base Contributes

The knowledge base should do several things for you. First, it should provide for a conceptual framework into which your study purpose fits. For example, let's consider the relationships among the variables of stressors, stress, and social support. You might find the basis in the literature for the theory that stressors have a positive relationship with stress (the more stressors you have, the higher will be your stress) and that social support has a negative relationship with stress (the higher your support, the lower will be your stress). This could be your conceptual framework for conducting a study of these relationships by giving a sample of people a tool for measuring each of these three variables and examining their relationships.

Another contribution of the knowledge base is your development of definitions of your study variables. In your study, the concept of stressor might be defined as an event that can lead to stress, such as divorce or losing a job. Stress could be defined as a psychological state. This means that a tool to measure the variable of stressor should list life events, while a tool to measure stress should include words that describe a negative state of psychological tension.

The type of research to be undertaken will influence what should be included in the knowledge base. The knowledge base for an evaluation study should include a definition of the clients' target behavior as well as an analysis of it. The analysis can include variables that cause the target behavior or the social needs of people who experience it. Knowing the causes of the target behavior can guide the determination of the appropriate intervention. This information would not be relevant to a descriptive study because there is no intervention that is included in such a study. An explanatory study would be the one that most depended on a conceptual framework that depicts the expected relationships between the variables of interest because the intent is to express reality in some important way.

Here is a set of three key words that may help in your memory of what a knowledge base should do. The words are *what*, *why*, and *how*.

- WHAT is the problem you are addressing?
  - Is it stress? If so, how is stress being defined?
  - Is it child sexual abuse? If so, what behaviors falls within your definition of this concept?
- WHY are you investigating this problem?
  - Is it important?
  - Does it have a profound effect on those who experience it?

- ○ Is it increasing?

- ○ Does it cost society a lot of money to address it?

- HOW can you fix it or understand it better?

  - ○ What interventions can you call evidence based?

  - ○ Does CBT work better than psychodynamic therapy in the treatment of depression?

  - ○ Do the members of the Personnel Selection Committee express a preference for male-stereotyped traits in the description of a good work manager? If so, maybe this issue should be addressed before this committee reviews applicants for a vacant management position.

Theory, Paradigm, and Ideology

As you develop a knowledge base, you should be familiar with concepts such as theory, paradigm, and ideology because they influence the way in which you collect and examine knowledge. A **theory** is an attempt to explain. CBT attempts to explain problems such as depression by reference to the way in which that we think about life events. A **paradigm** is a framework that suggests where we look to find theories. The feminist paradigm suggests that fruitful theories come from an examination of gender in our society. Are males given more power? What are the differences in opportunity that are based on gender? An ideology, on the other hand, is a fundamental guide for decision making that reveals what we are likely to believe. A devout Christian is not going to entertain the idea that there is no God. This idea goes beyond the ideology that frames this person's basic view of life. A person with a conservative ideology is not going to entertain the idea that government is the solution to most of life's problems. A person with a liberal political ideology is more likely to look to the government as a solution.

A theory is an attempt to explain. Any attempt to explain can be viewed as a theory, and it does not have to be published. However, in this book, we will focus on published theories. CBT attempts to explain how people react to life events in their ways of thinking about them. Some patterns lead to problems in life, such as depression. Therefore, if therapy can help the depressed person think in a more healthy way, this person's depression will be lower.

When you are testing a theory, you need to measure essential concepts. In this way, you can test a theory. For example, you could test CBT by examining whether persons who are depressed are more likely than others to engage in dysfunctional thinking about life events. The theory would suggest that you would find a positive relationship between dysfunctional thinking and depression. In other words, the more you engage in dysfunctional thinking, the more depressed you will be. If a scientific study suggested that this is a false statement, we would have evidence against this theory.

The concept of theory will be examined here in more detail and will be compared with related concepts such as ideology and paradigm. Each is relevant to the review of the literature because these concepts are important for understanding it. A simple definition of theory was given above. There are more complicated definitions. For example, Rubin and Babbie (2014) define theory as "a systematic set of interrelated statements intended to explain some aspect of social life or enrich our sense of how people conduct and find meaning in their daily lives (p. 59). A definition from Wikipedia is, "A theory provides an explanatory framework for some observation, and from the assumptions of the explanation follows a number of possible hypotheses that can be tested" (https://en.wikipedia.org/wiki/Theory).

You might get confused by terms such as theory, paradigm, and ideology. So let's clarify. While a theory is an attempt to explain, a paradigm shows the person where to look for theories, and an ideology reveals the boundaries that frame the possibilities. Let's explain with definitions. Rubin and Babbie (2014) define a paradigm as "a fundamental model or scheme that organizes our observations and makes sense of them. Although it doesn't necessarily answer important questions, it can tell us where to look for the answers" (p. 53). A definition of paradigm from Wikipedia is as follows: "A distinct set of concepts or thought patterns, including theories, research methods, postulates, and standards for what constitutes legitimate contributions to a field" (https://en.wikipedia.org/wiki/Paradigm). So we could say that theories emerge from a paradigm.

An **ideology**, according to Rubin and Babbie (2014) is as follows:

> A closed system of beliefs and values that shape the understanding and behavior of those who believe in it. Its assumptions are fixed and strong and not open to questioning. To their believers, ideologies offer absolute certainty and is immune to contradictory evidence. (p. 53)

Thus, you might say that ideologies form the boundaries of what is a possible belief of an individual. Therefore, you will likely be frustrated if you try to change a person's ideology, but giving him or her a new theory may be easy, and introducing a new paradigm might be possible.

How can you put these concepts into practice in the development of a knowledge base for a research study? You can start with theories that you see or theories that we have constructed in your own mind. Is there good evidence with regard to these theories? Do these theories support certain interventions?

You can examine the paradigm within which your theory exists. Some psychotherapists embrace a psychodynamic paradigm, which focuses on our early life experiences and unresolved conflicts. Others embrace a behavioral paradigm, which focuses on the construction of behaviors that will ameliorate our disorders. Some focus on interpersonal relations or something else. A good summary of CBT as a paradigm shift in psychology is presented by Micallef-Trigona (2016). This historical overview showed how different ways of thinking (paradigms) dominated psychology throughout the past century.

THE LITERATURE REVIEW FOR A RESEARCH STUDY

You have much knowledge that you have gained from your life experiences and from many educational opportunities. The literature is a different source of knowledge. It shows you what others think with a focus on people considered to be experts on certain subjects. When you develop your knowledge base, you will need to find the literature, review the literature, and write your findings.

Finding the Literature

There are electronic databases on the Internet that can be used to find literature sources. These databases require that you enter the key words that depict the nature of your study theme. When these words are entered, a set of articles (books, newspapers, magazines) are displayed. If the list is too long, you can modify the list to be more specific with fewer sources for review.

In a previous chapter, you examined evidence-based practice, a model for using evidence in the determination of an intervention in practice. Underlying the process of evidence-based practice is both critical thinking and the spirit of scientific inquiry. These models of decision making place emphasis on the objective examination of information. That means you do not "cherry-pick" information that supports your opinion, ignoring those that are contrary to your opinion.

The spirit of these models of decision making suggests that you use procedures that reduce bias in your search for information. In the chapter on evidence-based practice, you saw a description of the meta-analysis approach in reviewing evidence as well as the systematic review. These approaches employ a procedure for reviewing studies that sets forth the procedures for doing so before the search begins. They avoid the cherry-picking of articles that supports a certain conclusion. If the article is within the boundaries set forth before the search began, it will be included in the review. The meta-analysis combines the results of various studies of the same intervention and behavior to determine the best estimate of the overall effect of this intervention on this behavior (e.g., the effectiveness of CBT in the treatment of depression). The systematic review may include various meta-analyses, and it is generally considered the best single source of evidence on a given treatment.

When you undertake your own version of a systematic review, one of the steps in your process is to determine how you will review the literature. You do this before you examine any relevant articles. One of your steps is to decide on the literature databases that you will review. You can examine how your library organizes these databases, and you will probably decide that the subjects of social work and psychology be included. Under these headings, you can find databases such as Social Work Abstracts, PsycINFO, or PsycARTICLES. You would decide on the databases you should include before you start your search.

Your next step is to determine the key words to employ in your search of articles. You would employ these words to generate articles for inclusion in your meta-analysis. You would decide on the types of articles to be included in your analysis—for example, the article must report on an evaluative study of the treatment of anxiety. You might decide to include in your review only evaluative studies that employ experimental research designs. There may be other requirements for inclusion in your review. Once you have completed your instructions on what to include, you would apply these instructions on the selection of articles.

While you will not find it necessary to employ such a complicated approach to the review of the literature for any given study you might undertake, it would be useful if you could describe the procedures you employed in the search of the literature that generated the sources that were included in your review. A good literature review would not be one that includes only articles you have already read, along with books on your bookshelf. A strong literature review would not be one that includes the articles you stumbled across as you examined the literature. In this weak approach to your literature review, you might start with a textbook in your possession, then review some of the articles in the reference list of that book, and then review a few more articles that were suggested by the sources in those articles. Instead, a good literature review would be a review that is systematically organized with the purpose of finding the literature you need for a good knowledge base. This means you start with the decision of the procedures you will employ in your search of literature.

Levels of Evidence

When you are reviewing evidence regarding an intervention in evaluative research, you can consider the relative merits of several types of sources. Evidence refers to scientific studies, not opinions of experts. The lowest type of evidence is the single research study that reports on one evaluation study. While this may be useful, it has the limitation of being only one source. You are unlikely to find a single study that tells you all you need to know. It is also vulnerable to being misused by people who wish to engage in cherry-picking of evidence in order to prove a point. If you have a colleague who has been arguing with you about what is most effective for a given practice objective, you should be wary of a single piece of evidence that this person shares with you. You should ask, "What do the other studies of this practice tell us?"

The second level of evidence is the traditional literature review of the evidence. This form of evidence is illustrated by the article that reports on a number of studies of a given practice issue and provides a summary of what this body of literature tells us. This form of evidence has the advantage of including a number of studies on a given theme rather than just one study. But we must consider the fact that the research literature varies a great deal on the conclusions that should be drawn from studies on a given theme; thus, the review of a single article can be rather misleading. The traditional literature review of the evidence takes us to a higher level.

While the traditional review of the research evidence has a major advantage over the single study, it can represent the biased review of the literature by the author of the article. It is certainly better to review an article that reports on a dozen research studies that show the effectiveness of a given intervention rather than do a single study on it. Now you have the evidence from a dozen articles rather than just one. This should be adequate to provide guidance for practice because this intervention has been shown to be effective by several research articles. But you may not be informed by such a review of the limitations of this intervention or whether it is better than other interventions. That agenda will be better served by the next level of evidence—the meta-analysis.

The **meta-analysis** is a tool that has emerged from the evidence-based practice movement in human service research. It is a technique for combining the results of a number of studies of a common theme. It is more than the author's summary of the evidence. It is a specific scientific technique for combining the results into a specific metric for drawing conclusions about the research question.

You saw a description of the meta-analysis in the chapter on evidence-based practice. A key contribution of this source is that it begins with the establishment of a protocol for searching the literature. This includes the selection of the electronic literature databases to review, the key words that will be used to search these databases for articles, and the criteria that will be used to select studies for the meta-analysis from all the articles that appear when the key words are used for the designated databases. Some meta-analyses, for example, include only studies that used a randomized control trial (the experimental design). A key advantage of this protocol is that it seriously cuts down on the filtering of information based on the researcher's bias.

An example of a meta-analysis was the report by Payne and Marcus (2008) on the effectiveness of group psychotherapy for older adult clients. Four electronic databases were selected: (1) PsycINFO, (2) Medline, (3) Academic Search Premier, and (4) Dissertations Abstracts. The search terms were *geriatric*, *older adult*, *elderly*, *aging*, and *gerontology*. These initial terms were combined with the terms *group psychotherapy*, *group therapy*, *group dynamics*, *psychotherapy*, and *support groups*. To be included, the studies had to have measurements of client gain and be testing group psychotherapy. A total of 44 studies were found in this search that together included 1,381 clients. The authors of this meta-analysis concluded that group psychotherapy was generally effective in the treatment of a variety of target behaviors. The effect sizes of the various studies included in this analysis ranged from .24 to .42, indicating a modest effect of group psychotherapy on the conditions being treated.

As you saw in the chapter on evidence-based practice, the **systematic review** employs a protocol for searching the evidence literature, which is a characteristic the systematic review has in common with the meta-analysis. The difference is that a systematic review may include one or more meta-analyses. So it is more comprehensive and sits at the top of the hill with regard to levels of evidence.

So what should the practitioner do? In the search for evidence, the systematic review is the first place to seek guidance. If you find little guidance there, you should consult the literature for meta-analyses. The next avenue will be the traditional literature review on evidence. Finally, if all else fails to generate sufficient evidence for your purposes, you can seek articles that report single studies that are of interest to your research question. You should seek this information by a systematic protocol for searching the literature and report this protocol in your paper. Do not yield to the temptation to cherry-pick the literature in order to support your preconceived conclusion.

Reviewing the Literature

After you have discovered the literature tor review, you should examine the abstract to see how pertinent the article is for your purpose. In some cases, you do not need to review anything else. In most cases, you need to also review the study conclusions, then seek some information from the article that provides more specifics. An article that is right on target for you will be reviewed in its entirety.

Here are some tips for reviewing individual articles:

1. Does the author seem to have a bias with regard to the research question? Sources of bias would be indicated by where the author has been in the past. Has he or she been an advocate for one point of view? Has he or she been a key author of a particular approach to the treatment you are examining?

2. Does the author reveal the methods used to review the literature? Was there a reasonable protocol for seeking articles? Was this protocol followed?

3. Were concepts clearly defined?

4. Were study methods clearly articulated? For example, was the sample selection procedure described sufficiently for you to determine how the results can be generalized? Was it clear that the tools used for measuring variables were sufficiently tested for reliability and validity? Did the study design adequately address the issue of whether the treatment was the cause of client gain (when it is an evaluation study)?

5. Did the results reveal information on both practical significance and statistical significance?

6. Were study conclusions congruent with the data analyzed?

The first tip directs your attention to the possible biases of the author of the article. You are not expected to know this about individual authors, but you may see some clues in the article itself. Have the authors quoted their own work, which has given some hints about the biases they may maintain? If they have consistently promoted one point of view, you should be sure to search for literature with a different point of view. Don't stop with the work of a single author.

Second, did the article report on the protocol for searching the literature? If so, did this protocol seem reasonable? If not, is there anything in the article that suggests a biased review of the literature.

Third, were concepts defined clearly enough that you have the guidance you need to understand what is being said or what was found in the study? Some research articles present study methods you may not understand and likely present statistical analysis techniques you do not understand. But you know what the value of p means, and if this information is presented clearly, you may have all you need from this article.

Fourth, were the study methods presented in a way that makes sense to you? You are not expected to understand all the nuances of the methods presented, but you should get enough knowledge about this from the article to understand the level of credibility of the findings, if this is a scientific study that is being reported.

Fifth, can you draw conclusions about both practical significance and statistical significance, in cases where you are reviewing articles that report the results of scientific studies? The value of p should be clearly articulated with regard to the research data being examined. The magnitude of the data should be presented sufficiently for you to determine your own opinion about practical significance. If you have the mean gain score, this would be sufficient. If you have the effect size, you should understand the information you need to determine practical significance.

Finally, you should see conclusions that are consistent with the data that were analyzed. It does not matter whether you agree with the conclusions. What matters is whether the conclusions are consistent with the data.

Justifying the Intervention in Evaluative Research

When you conduct evaluative research, you should provide a literature review that supports the selected intervention. There are generally two bases for justification: logical and empirical. **Logical justification** refers to the analysis of the nature of the behavior being treated and the nature of the intervention being employed. A support group intervention would make logical sense for those needing better feelings of social support.

A training program would make logical sense if the clients needed more knowledge (i.e., lack of knowledge has been found to be one of the causes of the troubled behavior). A type of therapy that was designed to change one's dysfunctional way of thinking about life events would make logical sense if it had been found that one of the causes of the behavior was dysfunctional thinking.

Scientific justification comes from studies of evidence on treatment of the target behavior by the selected intervention. Some treatments have been found to be effective in the treatment of certain behaviors in many scientific studies. In this regard, therefore, you will be seeking literature that provides evidence. Two important sources of evidence are the Cochrane Collaboration and the Campbell Collaboration. These are sources of systematic reviews of evidence. The systematic review sits at the top of the steps with regard to scientific sophistication as discussed in this chapter. You should start with the systematic review as you seek evidence.

The major question here is why this intervention got selected as the intervention to assist people who have this target behavior. We should not start our practice with a decision on what intervention will be used. Instead, we should focus on the nature of the target behavior and decide what makes sense, given our knowledge of the nature of the target behavior and certain interventions. Once we understand the target behavior, we are in a better position to select an intervention. Don't put the cart before the horse!

Preparing the Report of the Knowledge Base

Among the issues of the knowledge base report is the nature and the importance of the theme being addressed. This means you will clarify what is being studied and why. You should present this information at the beginning of the report, before you present conceptual frameworks and definitions of variables. See, for example, the following statements in a paper by Stevens (2015):

> When a child experiences a traumatic event such as witnessing an act of violence or physical/sexual abuse, biological parents (caregivers) also experience a myriad of emotions and subsequent parenting challenges. They must initially help their child to cope with what has happened and simultaneously deal with the secondary impact of the event/s themselves. Non-offending parents are also required to navigate protocols and directives from agencies they may have never dealt with previously including Law Enforcement, Child Advocacy Centers, and Child Protective Services to highlight only a few.

> Parents describe feeling overwhelmed by their lack of knowledge about what to expect and how to help their child recover. They frequently question previously used parenting approaches and strategies and can become ineffective or immobilized after a trauma has taken place. Secondary post-traumatic stress can also occur in caregivers and can be further exacerbated without appropriate information, supports, and intervention. In addition, parents are often unaware of the information that exists regarding post traumatic growth and resiliency skills that can be taught and promoted and which are particularly important to both children and themselves after a trauma. Without this kind of information and reduction in caregiver stress levels, parents are less able to offer effective parenting approaches and children's post traumatic symptoms can worsen or develop into PTSD.

The above introduction shows the reader the critical needs that emanate from the experience of being witness to child abuse. It also provides some clues about what should be the focus of the treatment that will be given. This would be followed by more specifics about the themes presented in these first two paragraphs.

Definitions of key concepts and variables are another part of the knowledge base that supports a literature review. In a previous chapter, you have seen a discussion of the definitions of the concepts of stress and stressor. A stressor was defined as a problematic event that can cause stress, while stress was defined as a problematic psychological state. The definition of the variables guides the measurement of it. A scale for measuring stressors would include life events, while a scale to measure stress would contain words that described a problematic state, such as tense, up-tight, troubled, and so forth.

If you are employing an evaluative study, you will need to analyze the target behavior being treated. Gordon-Garofalo and Rubin (2004) reported on the evaluation of psychoeducational group intervention for partners of persons with HIV or AIDS. A portion of their problem analysis is presented as follows:

> Stressors experienced by spousal and partner-caregivers include the series of opportunistic infections plaguing persons living with HIV disease and the subsequent caregiving tasks and feelings of fear and loss associated with each infection. Other stressors are the effect of social stigma, such as loss of social support and feelings of rejection, and the financial concerns associated with long term illness. . . .

> Dealing with the uncertainty that surrounds HIV infection and AIDS is a stressor common to family caregivers. . . . Fierson et al. (1987) found that the most prominent psychological stressors associated with HIV disease were fears of contagion, stigma, revelation of lifestyle, sense of helplessness, and grief. They note, however, that the most common stressors among families are the conflicts surrounding care and support provisions for the infected family member and responsibilities to other members of the family. (p. 14).

These authors went on to connect this analysis with the intervention to be evaluated:

> Client concerns in the health care arena generally calls for a psychoeducational approach because clients need both education about disease process and treatment and support in dealing with health care issues. Groups can be an effective way for social workers to fulfill these needs, providing a support network, opportunities for members to share problems that arise and possible solutions, and a forum for formal lectures on topics of mutual interest. (p. 15)

Here are a few suggestions on the presentation of the literature:

1. Establish the authority behind what you say.

2. Use a reference for statements of fact.

3. Don't send the reader on a fishing expedition to find your cited source. Give the reader the direct link to a given statement if it is on the Internet.

4. Don't be vague about what you learned from a source. Don't just say that a study was done on the evaluation of CBT on depression without saying what was found.

5. Be sure to keep it organized.

6. Stick to the knitting!

Let's examine each of the above suggestions. First, you must establish the authority behind what you say in a literature review. This mean you will give a reference citation when this is appropriate. If you have come across knowledge from the literature that was not familiar to yourself, you should cite it in the body of the text and list the information about the source in your reference list. If you directly quote the information from the literature source, you should put the words in quote marks if it is a small quote or indent the material if it is a large quote. Ask yourself at the end of each paragraph if you have given sufficient credit for ideas that were not your very own. Direct quotes should be limited. They should convey an idea in words that are better done by the author's words than your own.

Second, always provide a reference for statements of fact. If you say that unemployment has been going up in recent years, you must have a reference to support that statement of fact. I suggest that you avoid saying things such as, "It is well known that . . . ." Instead, you should either drop this phrase from your report or provide specific facts with a reference citation.

Third, don't send the reader on a fishing expedition when you give a reference citation to a web page. Be sure that the link you give takes the reader directly to the information you are discussing. Do not just give the reader the link to the home page of a website where the reader can find the relevant information by going through various pages from the website. Give the direct link to the specific information.

Fourth, provide substantive information from a source of the literature. Do not simply say that a study was done about the effectiveness of dialectical behavioral therapy in the treatment of borderline personality disorder. You should report what was found in the study. Was dialectical behavioral therapy effective according to the data?

Fifth, organize your literature according to themes, not reference sources. You should keep things in their place. A useful tool is to use headings of your themes to clarify your organization, especially if your literature review is more than a few pages. Developing an outline for your literature review is a good idea, because it will force on you a sound organization. A poorly organized presentation will be evident when you develop an outline.

Finally, you should stick to the knitting! Your literature review should devote most content to concepts and variables of key interest to your study. Don't give equal attention to variables that are not variables in your study. It is okay to mention ones as needed, but this should not be the major focus of the review. Also, do not make references to your study in the literature review. That will come later. This can sometimes be confusing because the reader may think that you are referring to a study from the literature but will not see a reference citation. Also, the literature review should provide the conceptual foundation for the study that you will describe later. If there is a need for a specific connection to the literature, you can offer that when you describe your study in the study methods section of the report. In other words, your literature review should be somewhat independent of your study design. You should complete the literature review first and then be guided by that knowledge as you prepare your study methods section of your paper.

DESCRIBING THE INTERVENTION OR PROGRAM

Your intervention (service) is the process used to achieve your objectives for your individual clients, while your program is a set of interventions (services) that have a common goal. Your intervention fits within a social program. Your therapy group for aggressive adolescents may be your intervention that fits within the School Social Work Program of Apple Valley Middle School.

You will describe your intervention with regard to five themes: (1) goal, (2) objective, (3) structure, (4) model, and (5) personnel. Each of these themes provides information to the reader of your evaluation study that facilitates replication by others. When you read an evaluation report, you want to understand the intervention that was evaluated. What conceptual model guided your therapy group for aggressive adolescents? How many sessions did you have? What are your credentials for conducting such an intervention? Armed with this information, you can better interpret the results of the evaluation study in terms that are meaningful to you.

Goals and Objectives for the Intervention or Program

Your intervention is designed to achieve certain outcomes for your clients. These outcomes can be stated in long-range terms (e.g., to achieve marital satisfaction) or short-range terms (e.g., to reduce the number of times there is a display of intense anger in disagreements). **Goals** are statements of long-range outcomes, whereas **objectives** are statements of measured amounts of progress toward goal achievement. Neither refers to the intervention to be provided; nor do they refer to the standards that will be maintained. They are focused on client outcomes, not service process.

Goals should provide guidance on the long-term intent of the intervention or program. There are several options you might consider with regard to the conceptual level of the statement. Let's suppose you are designing a program for adolescent mothers. The statement "to improve the quality of life" is too general to provide guidance. It could be used to describe any outcome because it is so general.

Look at this goal statement: to reduce the negative social consequences of adolescent parenting. This would work because it provides some guidance and focuses on the outcome. However, you might find some statements such as the following to be even more useful: (1) to reduce child neglect and abuse among children of adolescent mothers, (2) to reduce public dependency among adolescent mothers, and (3) to enhance self-sufficiency among adolescent mothers. The latter statements provide more specificity than the first one, but any would seem okay, depending on how much specificity is warranted in your situation.

You could provide even more specificity with statements such as the following: (1) to reduce the incidence of repeat pregnancies for adolescent mothers, (2) to prevent adolescent mothers from dropping out of school, (c) to enhance job entry skills for adolescent mothers, and (d) to enhance knowledge of appropriate parenting techniques for adolescent mothers. However, you might find it useful to refer to these statements as objectives of the program because each provides guidance on progress toward the goal. A key to this choice is that progress regarding the objectives should be measured in your study. You may or may not have data regarding progress toward the achievement of the goal, but you should have data on progress toward the achievement of each of the objectives.

Suppose you are going to offer a peer support group intervention to female victims of violence. The only measure of outcome included in the evaluation study of this program is the clients' scores on a life satisfaction scale. Given this situation, which of the following should be the statement of the outcome objective of this program?

1. To improve communication skills

2. To improve the management of anger

3. To improve life satisfaction

4. To develop peer support

5. All of the above

You should have noticed that Option 3 was the correct answer because this is the thing being measured in this study. The other things may be part of the focus of group discussions or counseling, but they are not being measured. If they are not being measured, they cannot be considered an objective of the intervention for the purpose of an evaluation research study.

Consider the Anger Management Program for Pendleton High School, which deals with students who have demonstrated problems with fighting and other consequences of poor anger management. Which of the following would be good statements of the goal of this program?

1. To provide good quality support services for students with anger problems

2. To increase the students' ability to manage and control their feelings of anger

3. To improve the students' knowledge of coping strategies for anger control

4. To enhance their quality of life

You should have recognized the first one as oriented toward service rather than outcome, so it is not the correct answer. You should have recognized the last one as too general. You must choose between Number 2 and Number 3. One of these is the goal, and the other is the objective. Improving a student's knowledge of coping strategies is a measured amount of progress toward the achievement of the goal of improved ability to cope with anger. Therefore, Number 2 is the better statement of the goal, while Number 3 is the better statement of an objective. This means that you would need to measure progress regarding knowledge of coping strategies.

When you have completed your articulation of the goal and the objective of your intervention, you will have identified the long-range benefit for clients and a measured amount of progress toward that long-term benefit. You will also know what will be measured. You will not, however, have identified service processes or standards.

Structure of the Intervention or Program

You will describe both the form and the intensity of your intervention. These are the two elements of the structure of your intervention. The form is what the intervention looks like. Is it counseling, training, tutoring, or something else? The intensity of the intervention or program refers to how much service is given. Will there be 8 counseling sessions, 12 training sessions, or 280 child abuse investigations?

Form of the Intervention or Program

Does your intervention entail a series of individual counseling sessions or group psychotherapy or training sessions? Does it include residential care? Is it more like talk therapy, play therapy, or something else? Is case management a part of the intervention? A good description of the structure of the intervention will facilitate replication by others. If you describe it very well, I will know how to implement the same thing in my practice.

A good description will also aid in the determination of the resources needed for the use of your intervention or program. Weekly therapy sessions for 6 weeks will cost less than residential care for 6 weeks. Group treatment is less expensive than individual therapy on a per case basis.

Intensity of the Intervention or Program

How much intervention are you giving? Are you offering individual therapy 1 hour a day once a week for 6 to 10 weeks? In this case, you could report that the clients typically receive 6 to 10 therapy sessions. If your service is 24-hour care, how many days are included in the typical service episode for the typical client? An inpatient treatment program for mental illness might typically be offered for a 20-day period. If your service is case management, you might provide a description of the typical service offered and report on the number of persons served.

Consider the Hopewell Behavioral Health Center's program for persons suffering from depression. This is an inpatient treatment program offered to clients typically for 2 to 3 weeks. The following is an excerpt selected to highlight the structure of this program:

1. Each subject attended one process group daily, Monday through Saturday, lasting approximately 1 hour.

2. Each subject attended two family focus meetings prior to their discharge from the unit. Each family focus meeting was for 1 hour.

3. Clients attended one activity group daily, lasting approximately 1 hour.

4. Clients met individually with their psychiatrist daily, Monday through Sunday, for at least 15 minutes to explore and discuss treatment and individual progress.

5. Subjects also attended 1-hour specialty groups three times a week.

6. Each client met with his or her therapist at least three times a week for an hour each session.

You can add the above hours to get an idea of the intensity of the program being offered to these clients. If you compared this array of services with that of another inpatient mental health treatment program, you may find the total number of professional hours of service to be rather different between the two. What if one offered 20 hours of professional service weekly, whereas another offered 50 hours? You would normally expect a better outcome for the one that offered more service and cost more? Thus, you need to know the intensity of the service to estimate the costs and expectations for outcome. When you analyze your data from an evaluation study, you will want to know if your data achieved practical significance. Was the measured gain noteworthy, given the context of the service? Perhaps you would view a mean gain of 10% to be of practical significance if your service is minimal and cost rather little, but perhaps you would expect a mean gain of 30% for a more expensive service.

Unit of Service

The unit of service is the tangible measure of the service you offered. It serves as a good indicator of the amount of service you provided. You might define your unit of service as a 1-hour therapy session. You could calculate the number of units of your service that you offered as an indicator of the intensity of the service you provided. Others might define their unit of service as (1) 8 hours of day care, (2) 24 hours of residential care, or (3) a child abuse investigation completed. In each case, you can see a tangible measure of the amount of service provided.

In some situations, you will find that the best indicator of the amount of service offered is a client served. This is especially relevant to case management, which entails a complex array of service activities. You would not want to be burdened with the task of computing the number of such activities offered to a given client. That would be a waste of time. Instead, you describe the array of services that are offered to clients and compute the number of clients served.

The unit of service is a measure of intensity that is especially relevant to the program evaluation than the evaluation of a single intervention. The issue of costs and efficiency is likely to be of special concern in the evaluation of the School Social Work Program, but it is not likely to draw your attention when you are offering a support group intervention to students who have recently had a parent die.

You may find the billable hour of service to be a useful way to define your unit of service. This is a definition given by funding sources and describes the way in which funding sources provide reimbursement for the service you are providing. If a billable hour is a 1-hour therapy session, you have the logical way to define your unit of service.

Model of the Intervention or Program

The model of the intervention is the theoretical or conceptual framework that illustrates the dynamics of the target behavior in such a way as to illustrate the essential connections between cause and effect or the special aspects of need being addressed by the intervention. Cognitive theory suggests that our problems are caused by distorted thinking of life events; thus, we should focus on how to rethink our events in order to get better. Training is based on an educational model, which suggests that more knowledge helps us improve.

Information about the model of the intervention also provides guidelines regarding aspects of treatment that have been found to be more effective. Sometimes, the practitioner has a well-defined theory that serves as the model. Cognitive theory is one example. Other times, there may be guidelines from the analysis of studies regarding the treatment of the given target behavior. One example is from the work of Royse, Toyer, Padgett, and Logan (2001) who summarized efforts to find best practices for family intervention programs:

> The conclusion was that there is no single best family intervention program. . . . However, several principles for best practices in family programs were identified. These included selecting programs that are: (a) comprehensive, (b) family-focused, (c) long-term, (d) of sufficient dosage to affect risk or protective factors, (e) tailored to target populations' needs and cultural traditions, (f) developmentally appropriate, (g) beginning as early in the family life cycle as possible, and (h) delivered by well-trained, effective trainers. (p. 110)

This information could be cited in the description of the model of your intervention if you incorporated each of the above elements into it.

The above description of family interventions is rather broad and provides guides for best practice. On a more specific level, Nathan and Gorman (2002) describe interpersonal and social rhythm therapy for the treatment of bipolar disorder as follows:

> IPSRT [interpersonal and social rhythm therapy] encourages patients to recognize the impact of interpersonal events on their social and circadian rhythms. There are two goals for IPSRT: (a) to help patients to understand and renegotiate the social context associated with mood disorder symptoms, and (b) to encourage patients to recognize the impact of interpersonal events on their social and circadian rhythms, and to regularize these rhythms in order to gain control over their mood cycling. In IPSRT patients are given the Social Rhythm Metric . . . , a daily self-report on which they record their sleep/wake times, levels of social stimulation, timing of daily routines (eating, exercise, work, etc.) and daily mood. By reviewing data from this assessment device, patients gradually see how changes in their mood states can occur as a function of variable daily routines, sleep/wake cycles, and patterns of interpersonal stimulation, and reciprocally how these factors are affected by their moods. In time, patients become motivated to regulate their rhythms and find balances among these factors as a means of stabilizing their moods. (p. 266)

There are many examples that illustrate the model of an intervention or program that provide a range of complexity. In each case, you will see the conceptual framework that illustrates how the intervention is guided conceptually. For example, the Foster Care Independent Living Program is designed to prepare older foster children for the transition to adulthood following foster care services. The model can be characterized as strengths based, where the client is viewed as the expert on his or her own needs. In this model, the agency encourages the youth's active participation in decision making. Because it is strengths based, it acknowledges that all youth have strengths. The optimal approach to treatment is to build on strengths rather than focus on weaknesses or problems. With this model, the agency treats the youth with respect, is supportive, and remains open to new information. It promotes the sharing of power and engenders partnership between the youth and the agency; the agency and its personnel refrain from taking the role of the expert. A technique of this approach is for the person in the helping role to ask the clients to identify how they overcame certain obstacles that have been put in their path, and how this same strength can be used for achieving their goals in various aspects of life.

Another example is illustrated by the Housing Department for Winslow County. This agency developed a program for those persons who have not yet learned or experienced how to be self-sufficient. The Self-Sufficiency Program was designed to help those who depend on government assistance for everyday necessities become self-sufficient and obtain home ownership. One of the assumptions underlying the model for this program is that many people fail to find self-sufficiency because they were never taught to be self-sufficient and have lacked good role models. This program provides training on credit, budgeting, parenting, and home ownership, and it encourages group interaction where self-sufficiency behavior can be demonstrated. Through credit counseling, the clients are told which debts to pay off first in order to raise their credit score. In the budgeting class, residents are shown how to manage their money. They bring in their check stubs and a list of their monthly expenses, and they are shown how to budget their money and pay their bills.

Personnel of the Intervention or Program

When you describe the personnel for your intervention, you will identify the credentials possessed by those who are delivering the service. You are not describing the particular characteristics of the individuals who provide it but the credentials they possess. What is required of your agency for persons to be qualified to do this job? Do they have to possess a certain college degree, be licensed in a certain way, or have completed a special training program? Are they required to possess a certain amount of experience of a certain kind? Among the items that might appear in a description of the personnel for a given intervention are the following:

1. The therapist for this intervention is a licensed clinical social worker who is required to have obtained special training in the use of CBT.

2. The social worker for this program is required to have at least a Bachelor of Social Work degree plus 1 year of professional experience in work with youth who have been adjudicated as delinquent. The Master of Social Work degree is preferred.

3. The personnel for the HOPE Program include all of the following: (1) a licensed clinical social worker (LCSW) or a licensed professional counselor (LPC), (2) a licensed clinical addiction specialist (LCAS), (3) a psychiatrist, and (4) a registered nurse (RN).

4. The staff who conduct the psychoeducational group for youth aging out of foster care must hold a college degree in social sciences with specific knowledge and experience working with this specific population. In addition, they must have local and state knowledge of available services for youth aging out of the foster care system.

PRELIMINARY INFORMATION FOR THE PRACTICE EXERCISES

This part of the chapter will include exercises in the construction of your own literature review and the description of your intervention (service). This exercise will assume that you will be conducting an evaluative study. This type of study has some special nuances that will guide how the literature review will be undertaken. It is assumed that social workers will be most interested in the evaluation of their practice rather than in the description of their clients (descriptive study) or the explanation of social phenomena (explanatory study).

In this section, you will see a synopsis of the tasks you need to understand in order to complete the practice exercise on the development of your knowledge base and the practice exercise on the description of your intervention. Following this section will be two practice exercises, one on the development of your knowledge base and another on the description of your intervention.

For each part of this experience, you will be given examples to follow; then you will be asked to complete the task yourself for your own study. This means, of course, that your first step is to determine the purpose of your own study. You purpose could be to evaluate the effectiveness of after-school tutoring on the grades of the middle school students in your special program. Your purpose might be to evaluate the effectiveness of your support group service for victims of physical abuse on the improvement of feelings of social support. Perhaps your purpose is to evaluate the extent to which your initial group treatment sessions with drug abusers have the effect of improving their motivation for long-term treatment.

In each of the above examples of purpose statements, you saw three pieces of information: (1) the target behavior that would be measured, (2) the treatment that was being offered, and (3) the target population that was being treated. This means that you will be offering a treatment (service), and you will be measuring your clients to see if the objective was achieved.

Your literature review will provide information that provides the justification for using your particular service to treat your client's particular behavior. If lack of knowledge of the dangers of using drugs is NOT the cause of drug abuse, it would not make sense to give training on the dangers of drugs as your essential service for the objective of reducing drug abuse. Training logically can be expected to improve knowledge. It is less likely to improve attitudes or behaviors. So one of the key tasks of your literature review is to present information that provides the logical connection between the nature of the behavior being treated and the nature of the treatment that is being used. Another task of your literature review is to present the empirical justification for the selection of the service (treatment) that is being offered. What is the evidence that suggests that this treatment will work?

Another contribution of the literature review will be conceptual clarity on what you will measure. This requires a definition of the target behavior being treated. Grades are easy to define and measure. But motivation for long-term treatment is a variable that is not so easy to define or measure. Depression and anxiety are other examples that are not easy to define or measure.

You will go through a process of (a) finding literature, (b) reviewing literature, and (c) writing a few segments of a literature review. Examples will be given along with guidelines for each step of the way.

Finding the Literature

Your first step in finding the literature is to determine the key words you will use when you examine an electronic literature database. These databases can be found in your library or an Internet source such as Google Scholar. When you access some of these databases, you can insert a set of words for the inquiry. One should be the target behavior, such as child abuse, poverty, unemployment, drug abuse, or eating disorders. The second word or phrase could be the service that is being considered. A third word or phrase could refer to treatment outcomes. If these words generate a list of 1,000 sources or only 2 sources, you will need to revise your set of words to either narrow the scope or expand it.

When you get a manageable number of sources, you should read the titles of these sources to see which ones are appropriate for your study and then examine the abstracts of these selected sources. This should generate a dozen or so items that are of special interest to your study. Now it is time to review these sources in some detail to get what you need to know.

Your review of the literature should provide information on how to define the target behavior being treated by your intervention and how to analyze it for causation or special needs of people. The definition will guide your choice of a method of measurement of client outcome.

The analysis of the target behavior will assist you in the justification of the choice of your intervention. For example, why will you use a support group service? Why will you provide case management? Why use CBT for your clients? You can see from the previous information that we will consider two bases for justification. You can examine both the target behavior and the intervention and present logical justification for the connection of the two. You can collect evidence that shows that your intervention has been effective. Or, of course, you can do both.

If you select the first path, you will need literature on the nature of the target behavior. What are the causes of this behavior? What are the special needs of people who have this target behavior? Perhaps you have learned that sexually abused children often experience unusual arousal, avoidance, and negative thoughts and moods. Then, you could ask yourself about treatments that address these conditions. When you find such a treatment, you have a link between the nature of the target behavior and the intervention.

You might go down a second path: finding evidence about treatments for your target behavior. Does trauma-focused cognitive–behavioral therapy (TF-CBT) seem to work in the treatment of children who have been sexually abused? Does it work better than some of the prominent alternative treatments? You are advised to seek evidence first from a systematic review of evidence and then move to the review of meta-analyses if your search of systematic reviews is not adequate.

Writing Your Review

A good review will begin with critical concepts and issues presented in the first paragraph. Consider, for example, the following first paragraph:

According to data from the U.S. Department of Health and Human Services, nearly one child in ten has been exposed to child sexual abuse, either as a victim or a witness (U.S. Department of Health and Human Services, 2007). A consequence of this exposure is the emergence of post-traumatic stress disorder (PTSD) for these children (Wamser-Nanney & Chesher, R. E., 2018). PTSD is a condition characterized by sleep disturbance, intrusive thoughts, depression, anxiety, and feelings of helplessness. Fortunately, there are treatments for PTSD that have been shown to be effective (Deblinger, Lippmann, & Steer, 1996).

This paragraph is a slight revision of a part of a paper by Hayson (2016). You can see from this first paragraph of a literature review that (a) the problem of exposure to sex abuse affects a lot of people in our nation, (b) abuse exposure leads to consequences we all would consider important, and (c) there is hope for a solution. Now you are ready to review more specific details about this situation.

One part of this literature review by Hayson (2016) was a definition of the behavior known as posttraumatic stress disorder. Here is that paragraph:

The *DSM-5* defines posttraumatic symptoms within three specific clusters: re-experiencing, avoidance, and arousal. Re-experiencing may include recurring memories, nightmares, dissociative episodes, and extreme physiological reactions to reminders of the traumatic event. Avoidance can include, avoidance of memories, reminders, thoughts, or feelings related with the traumatic event. Arousal may contain, behavioral disturbances, angry outburst, hypervigilance, difficulty concentrating, and sleep problems (American Psychiatric Association, 2013, p. 5).

The function of this definition is to guide the choice of a means of measuring it. Each of the behaviors and emotions in the definition should be included in the tool used to measure it.

Another task for Hayson (2014) is the analysis of the behavior in a way that would justify the selection of the intervention. As noted before, she has two bases for justification: logical and empirical. Logical justification refers to the analysis of the nature of the behavior being treated and the nature of the intervention being employed. A support group intervention would make logical sense for those needing better feelings of social support. A training program would make logical sense if the clients needed more knowledge (i.e., lack of knowledge has been found to be one of the causes of the troubled behavior). A type of therapy that was designed to change one's dysfunctional way of thinking about life events would make logical sense if it had been found that one of the causes of the behavior was dysfunctional thinking.

Empirical justification comes from studies of evidence with regard to the behavior and the intervention. Some treatments have been found to be effective in the treatment of certain behaviors in many scientific studies. In this regard, therefore, you will be seeking literature that provides evidence.

Hayson (2014) put her emphasis on empirical justification. This was a challenge because her selected treatment was relatively new. Her treatment was child and family traumatic stress intervention, which has many similarities to TF-CBT. She located a number of studies that found evidence of the effectiveness of TF-CBT. She was able to locate only one study that examined evidence for her specific treatment—child and family traumatic stress intervention. This study compared the outcomes of this intervention with a treatment that combined psychoeducation and supportive counseling. Her intervention was found to be more effective.

Let's take another example of how the literature review started and what was contained in it. Taverna (2016) undertook a study of the effectiveness of a support group on the outcomes of feelings of social support and depression for patients undergoing bariatric surgery for extreme obesity. Here is one of her first paragraphs from her literature review:

> Obesity has increased dramatically over the past 20 years, and it is currently at an all-time high (Centers for Disease Control and Prevention, 2016). A major public health problem involving both medical and quality-of-life issues, it is considered a worldwide health epidemic (Elkins, 2005). . . . Results from a national survey indicate that 64% of adults in the United States are overweight or obese, with approximately half of this group being obese and 5.7% being extremely obese (Centers for Disease Control and Prevention, 2016).
>
> Bariatric surgery is an operation that alters the stomach, intestines, or both and is among the most effective treatments for severe obesity (Shen et al, 2006). The surgeries are thought to lead to weight loss and improvements in related health conditions, such as type 2 diabetes, by reducing the size of the stomach.
>
> Individuals affected by severe obesity who are seeking bariatric surgery are more likely to suffer from depression or anxiety and to have lower self-esteem and overall quality of life than someone who is normal weight (Toussi, 2009). Bariatric surgery results in highly significant improvement in psychosocial well-being for the majority of patients. However, there remain a few patients with undiagnosed pre-existing psychological disorders and still others with overwhelming life stressors who commit suicide after bariatric surgery (Pontiroli, 2007, p. 7).

The nature of this experience, therefore, required a psychosocial treatment to reduce the chances of a poor psychological outcome. A support group experience was the chosen service. Taverna (2016) could find little empirical evidence of the effectiveness of support groups for people facing this surgery, so she was faced with a challenge. One of her sources reported that surgeons who conduct this procedure report that their patients have improved with a support group experience. This is rather weak evidence, but it was the most important source she could find with the limited time she had for the literature review.

What follows are the instructions for two practice exercises for this chapter. The first exercise calls on you to develop a basic review of the literature for an evaluative study you would like to conduct. The second exercise asks you to report on the goal, objective, structure, model, and personnel of the intervention (or service) that you will be evaluating in your proposed study.

Chapter Practice Exercises

Practice Exercise 1: Developing Your Knowledge Base

In Practice Exercise 1, you will report on your effort to secure a knowledge base for a study you would like to undertake in the evaluation of social work practice. The following information will show the competencies you will demonstrate in this exercise, the activities you will undertake, and the report you will provide.

Competencies Demonstrated by Practice Exercise 1

Here are the competencies you will demonstrate in your actions related to this practice exercise.

1. The ability to compose an evaluative research question that is appropriate for a research study that you will propose. This will include the identification of the target behavior, the target population, and the interventions that might serve as treatments.

2. The ability to secure an initial knowledge base for an evaluation study using an electronic database. An initial knowledge base is one that is adequate for the everyday practitioner to secure basic guidance for practice. It is not the extensive knowledge base required for publication of a study.

3. The ability to summarize a brief review of several articles that were found in your initial review of the literature employing an electronic database.

Activities for Practice Exercise 1

You will undertake the following activities for this exercise.

1. You will articulate your research question, including information on the intervention to be employed, the target behavior to be improved, and the target population of your study.

Example: Is strengths-based case management services effective in the reduction of school disciplinary problems for at-risk middle school students?

2. You will undertake a review of the literature with regard to your research question. This will entail the following: (a) the determination of the electronic literature databases to review, (b) the key words you will employ in your search for literature, (3) the strategy you will employ to retrieve a manageable number of relevant articles for your review, and (4) the application of these criteria in the finding of articles for your knowledge base. The strategy you might employ to reduce your extensive list of references to one that is manageable might include changing your key words for your search or deciding that you will review the titles of the first 50 entries on the list and stop your search if this review provides an adequate knowledge base.

Example: I searched for evidence regarding the use of both support groups and individual CBT in the treatment of postpartum depression. I consulted both the PsycINFO database and the PsycARTICLES database using the key words "postpartum depression" and "evidence." I restricted my search to words in the abstract of the references. One of these searches retrieved 79 references, and one retrieved 118 references. My strategy was to review the titles of the first half of these sources to see if I had an adequate search. I selected relevant articles and reviewed the abstracts of these articles. I reviewed further information in certain selected articles that were of high relevance. The result of this strategy was effective, because I found seven articles that were helpful, one of which was a systematic review.

3. You will provide a summary of your findings from your review of the literature.

Example: I learned the following regarding the use of either support groups or CBT in the treatment of postpartum depression: (1) telephone-based peer support reduced depression and improved feelings of social support for women with postpartum depression (Letourneau, Secco, Colpitts, Aldous, Stewart, & Dennis, 2015), (2) CBT was found to be effective with the reduction of depression in this population (Milgrom, Gemmill, Ericksen, Burrows, Buist, & Reece, 2015), (3) group treatment for postpartum depression was effective (Goodman & Santangelo, 2011), (4) both group therapy and interpersonal therapy were found to be effective in the improvement of the parenting ability of women with postpartum depression (Clark, Tluczek, & Wenzel, 2003), (5) women with higher social support during pregnancy were less likely to experience postpartum depression (Collins, Dunkel-Schetter, Lobel, & Scrimshaw, 1993) (6) spousal support prevents postpartum depression (Don & Mickelson, 2012); (7) social support prevents depression for postpartum mothers (Cutrona, 1989).

These references suggested that both CBT and support therapy are effective for those with postpartum depression. In my next step, I will review the Campbell Collaboration to see if I can find a systematic review of the outcomes of either CBT or support groups that are effective for postpartum women.

What You Will Report From Practice Exercise 1

You will report your information for each of the three items listed above.

1. Your research question

2. Your procedures for searching the literature

3. Your brief report on findings from the literature

Practice Exercise 2: Describing Your Intervention

In this exercise, you will identify the intervention that will be designed to treat the target behavior discussed in Practice Exercise 1. You will report five essential ingredients of the intervention that provide a comprehensive overview of it.

Competencies Demonstrated by Practice Exercise 2

There are five competencies that you will demonstrate in this practice exercise. The competencies correspond to the five essential ingredients in this endeavor.

1. The ability to articulate a goal of an intervention that depicts the long-range client benefit, rather than a measured amount of progress toward it (the purview of the treatment objective) or a focus on processes of service (e.g., standards of good service).

2. The ability to articulate an objective of the intervention that depicts a measured amount of progress toward the achievement of the goal of the intervention and indicates the concept that will be measured in the evaluation study.

3. The ability to describe the structure of the intervention that reveals both the form and intensity of it.

4. The ability to describe the model of the intervention that reveals the basis for the justification of the use of the specific intervention being used to treat the selected target behavior. This may reveal a connection between the causes of the target behavior and the actions of the intervention or the conceptual framework on which the intervention is based.

5. The ability to describe the personnel of the intervention with regard to the credentials of the staff who will provide the intervention. The issue here is what credentials are usually required in this agency for the staff who will provide this kind of intervention.

Activities for Practice Exercise 2

1. You will articulate the goal of the intervention your study will evaluate.

   Examples:
   a. To prevent at-risk middle school students from dropping out of school before they graduate
   b. To reduce the long-term social and psychological consequences of being a victim of family violence
   c. To promote self-sufficiency for youth who have graduated from foster care

2. You will articulate the objective of the intervention your study will evaluate.

   Examples:
   a. To improve the grades of at-risk middle school students
   b. To improve the anxiety of the victims of family violence
   c. To improve the daily living skills of youth who have recently graduated from foster care

3. You will describe the structure of the intervention your study will evaluate.

   Examples:
   a. Strengths-based tutoring services will be delivered in a series of 10 individual tutoring sessions of 1 hour each.
   b. Therapy will be delivered in 1-hour sessions once per week for 6 weeks.
   c. The daily living protocol service will be delivered in several forms of activities,

including individual 1-hour counseling sessions given once weekly for 12 weeks, a series of 1-hour training sessions given once per month for 6 months, and case management services which help the client obtain employment and living arrangements.

4. You will describe the model of the intervention your study will evaluate.

   Example: The rationale for tutoring is that individual training sessions will improve student grades for at-risk students because the clientele tend to be unable to make good use of educational classes for all students, most of whom are superior on the subject matter to the clients. Individual attention is necessary for the at-risk middle school students to obtain the understanding needed to improve grades. Improved grades are assumed to lead to a higher likelihood that one will graduate from high school.

5. You will describe the personnel of the intervention your study will evaluate.

   Example: The therapists who will provide this service are required to be licensed clinical social workers.

What You Will Report From Practice Exercise 2

For this exercise, you will report each of the following for the intervention that your proposed study will be evaluating:

1. Goal

2. Objective

3. Structure

4. Model

5. Personnel

CHAPTER REVIEW

Chapter Key Learnings

1. The knowledge base for the research study helps in the development of the purpose of the study, the definition of key terms, the selection of a means of measurement, and the selection of a study sample. In the evaluation study, the knowledge base also assists with the selection of a logical intervention in the treatment of the target behavior.

2. The knowledge base provides a conceptual framework by which the research study is guided. For example, the framework might show the expected relationships between the variables of stressors, stress, and health problems.

3. The knowledge base can help you better understand the answers to three key questions: (1) What is the problem I am studying? (2) Why am I studying this problem? (3) How can we fix the problem or better understand it with research?

4. An understanding of the concepts of theory, paradigm, and ideology can assist with various decisions as you undertake a research study. For example, a theory guides your determination of the hypothesis you will compose for the explanatory or evaluative study. A paradigm shows where to look for answers, while the ideology shows the natural boundaries of what might be understood by a given individual or a group.

5. There are electronic databases in libraries that can be used to find literature sources.

These databases require that you enter the key words that depict the nature of your study theme. When these words are entered, a set of articles (books, newspapers, magazines) are displayed. If the list is too long, you can modify the list to be more specific with fewer sources for review.

6. There are levels of evidence that depict the extent to which science is the basis for the information. The highest level is the systematic review, while the next level is the meta-analysis, each of which is guided by a protocol for the search that is determined before the search begins. Coming next is the traditional literature review followed by the single article that reports evidence.

7. When you review scientific evidence from the literature, you should be mindful of the extent to which the study followed the spirit of scientific inquiry and employed good study methods, such as a representative sample, valid methods of measuring study variables, appropriate consideration of the issue of causation, and appropriate analysis of the data.

8. In evaluation research, scientific justification of the choice of the intervention is addressed by the scientific evidence that suggests this intervention. Logical justification is revealed by the logical analysis of what is known about both the target behavior being treated and the various aspects of the intervention that is being employed.

9. When writing the knowledge base from the literature, you should be cognizant of (a) establishing the authority behind what you say, (b) providing an appropriate reference citation for statements of fact, (c) provide substantive information from each cited reference source, and (d) organize your review by themes, not sources.

10. Your intervention (or service) is the process used to achieve your objectives for your individual clients, whereas your program is a set of interventions (services) that have a common goal. Your intervention normally fits within a social program.

11. The key purpose of carefully describing your intervention is to provide the reader of your study report with information on the relevance of your study to the practice situation that may be most relevant to the reader. The comprehensive description of the intervention can also facilitate a replication of your study by others.

12. You should describe your intervention with regard to the following: (a) goal, (b) objective, (c) structure, (d) model, and (e) personnel.

Chapter Discussion Questions

1. Think of a research question you might pursue in a study. What would be the consequence of your conducting a study of this question without doing a review of the literature? What would such an endeavor lack?

2. Why do you want to study the subject you identified above?

3. Explain how one concept from the spirit of scientific inquiry or from critical thinking will affect your inquiry into the above-named subject for a research study.

4. Identify an example of one of the following: a theory, a paradigm, or an ideology. Which of these concepts is most likely to reduce critical thinking?

5. Explain how the hierarchy of evidence will influence your pursuit of knowledge for a study you would like to conduct. Where will you start? What will you do next? and so on.

6. Explain how you can justify an intervention you are employing (or have employed in the past) on a logical basis?

7. In what aspect of research will a careful definition of key variables be of most assistance: (a) helping you select a study sample, (b) helping you find a method of measuring your study variables, or (c) helping you select a research design? Explain.

8. In what aspect of evaluation research will a good analysis of the target behavior be of most assistance: (a) helping you select a study sample, (b) helping you find a method of measuring the target behavior, (c) helping you select a research design, or (d) helping you select an appropriate intervention? Explain.

9. When you offer a reference source from the Internet, what information do you need to supply to the reader? Is the general website

sufficient, or are you expected to provide the link to the specific source of the reference? Why?

10. Imagine that you have read an evaluation study where the report provided very little details about the nature of the intervention being evaluated. It did not specify the goal or the objectives being pursued. It did not provide details on the structure or the model. How would this failure affect your use of the results of this study?

Chapter Test

1. A theory is
   a. A framework that suggests where we look to find explanations
   b. An attempt to explain
   c. A closed system of beliefs and values that shape the understanding and behavior of those who believe in it
   d. All of the above

2. A paradigm is
   a. A framework that suggests where we look to find explanations
   b. An attempt to explain
   c. A closed system of beliefs and values that shape the understanding and behavior of those who believe in it
   d. All of the above

3. An ideology is
   a. A framework that suggests where we look to find explanations
   b. An attempt to explain
   c. A closed system of beliefs and values that shape the understanding and behavior of those who believe in it
   d. All of the above

4. The concept of feminism is best labeled a/an
   a. Theory
   b. Paradigm
   c. Ideology
   d. Practicum

5. A meta-analysis is
   a. An analysis of methods by which an intervention is going to be implemented along with the description of the various components of the intervention
   b. A method of literature synopsis that starts with a search protocol that clarifies which studies will be included in the analysis, along with combination of data from included studies, usually generating an effect size for all studies
   c. A statistical analysis of data from a single study that employed a hypothesis that has more than two variables
   d. The statistical analysis of data from two studies that employed a hypothesis that has two variables

6. Logical justification for the use of a given intervention for the treatment of a given target population is based mostly on
   a. Scientific evidence about the outcomes of interventions
   b. The idea of what makes sense from knowledge gained about the nature of the target behavior and the nature of a given intervention
   c. Statistical analysis of qualitative data in an exploratory study
   d. Empirical review of the agency manual

7. Which of these is considered the highest level of information for the justification of an intervention in the treatment of a target behavior?
   a. A systematic review of evidence
   b. A traditional literature review of evidence
   c. A single scientific study that collects evidence
   d. A meta-analysis of evidence

8. Which of the following should be addressed in a literature review?
   a. The question of what is the problem under investigation
   b. The question of why are we concerned about the problem under investigation
   c. The question of how we can fix the problem or understand it better
   d. All of the above

9. The main purpose for providing a comprehensive description of your intervention is
   a. To facilitate an understanding of how the literature supports your study conclusions
   b. To provide guidance on the replication of your intervention by others
   c. To initiate new research
   d. To facilitate the various elements of the research methodology such as sampling, measurement, and so forth

10. You have a support group intervention for the victims of family violence. You want them to have better options in life by seeing how others have handled this situation. You will measure their feelings of social support, a step of progress toward the search for decision options. Which of the following is a good statement of the goal of your support group intervention for victims of family violence rather than the objective of this intervention?
    a. To empower the victims of family violence to have good choices in life decisions
    b. To enhance the quality of life
    c. To improve the feelings of support of the victims of family violence
    d. To offer good quality services to the victims of family violence

11. Which of the following would be good descriptions of the structure of the support group services for victims of family violence?
    a. A series of services felt to be good for the victims of family violence
    b. A set of eight group sessions that each lasts about 1 hour
    c. Both of the above
    d. None of the above

12. Which of the following would be good descriptions of the personnel of the support group services for the victims of family violence?
    a. All of the victims of family violence who receive this service
    b. All of the staff of this agency
    c. Staff members who conduct the support group sessions are required to be licensed clinical social workers
    d. All of the above

13. The objective of a social work intervention should depict
    a. The long-term benefit the client will get from the intervention
    b. A measured amount of progress toward the goal of the intervention
    c. Exactly the same words as the statement of the goal of the intervention

d. All of the above depict the objective of a social work intervention

14. The model of a social work intervention should depict
   a. The standards of service that are demonstrated by the intervention that is offered

b. The rationale for using this particular intervention to treat this particular target behavior

c. The short-term outcomes of the intervention

d. The long-term outcomes of the intervention

ANSWERS: 1 = b; 2 = a; 3 = c; 4 = b; 5 = b; 6 = b; 7 = a; 8 = d; 9 = b; 10 = a; 11 = b; 12 = c; 13 = b; 14 = b

Chapter Glossary

Empirical justification. Justification for the selection of a particular intervention that is based on a review of evidence with regard to the behavior being treated and the intervention.

Goals. The long-range benefits to clients or society that provide guidance regarding the general intended outcome.

Ideology. A closed system of beliefs or values supported by fixed assumptions about the nature of human reality.

Logical justification. Justification for the selection of a particular intervention that is based on a logical analysis of the nature of the behavior being treated and the nature of the intervention being employed.

Meta-analysis. An investigation of a phenomenon through systematic procedures for searching the literature, including the designation of the nature of the sources that will be examined and the methods for examining them.

Model of the intervention. The conceptual framework that links the target behavior being treated with the intervention being employed.

Objectives. The measured amount of progress toward the achievement of the goal of the intervention.

Paradigm. A conceptual model that suggests where to look in order to better understand a social phenomenon.

Personnel of the intervention. The credentials of those who deliver the intervention that is being evaluated.

Structure of the intervention. The form and intensity of the intervention.

Systematic review. A systematic review of the literature, similar to the procedures of the meta-analysis that may include reports of meta-analyses as well as other sources, including sources that have not been published.

Theory. An attempt to explain, which provides a framework for the investigation of a theme.

12

DRAWING YOUR STUDY SAMPLE

Robert is a social worker who wishes to conduct an evaluation of the group therapy service he is providing to veterans who have experienced post-traumatic stress disorder (PTSD), a condition exemplified by anxiety in relation to being exposed to a threat of death, serious injury, or sexual violence. There are 12 clients in his therapy group. He wants to be able to conclude that his therapy service will be effective for veterans with PTSD who are being served by his agency but are not currently in his therapy group. In other words, he wishes to be able to generalize his study findings to those individuals. He has defined his study population as veterans with PTSD who are served by his agency. His study sample is the group of 12 clients he currently serves. He realizes that he does not have a random sample. That would require that he select his 12 clients at random from all clients being served by his agency who are experiencing PTSD. This group was not selected at random. They were assigned to him by his supervisor. Thus, he has a convenience sample. Because he does not have a random sample, he cannot generalize his findings on a scientific basis. He is considering whether he can generalize his findings on a logical basis, which refers to the relevant similarities and differences between the study sample and the study population. If he finds that the members of his group are similar to the study population, he can engage in logical general-ization, which is a matter of informed opinion. He considered the variables he should examine in this regard. He decided that there are four variables that determine one's likelihood of gaining from his treatment. He compared the members of his therapy group with the clients served by his agency who suffer from PTSD on each of these four variables and found that the two groups were similar on all variables. Therefore, he concluded that he could generalize his findings on a logical basis to the population of all clients served by his agency who have been diagnosed with PTSD. He recognized, however, that a random sample from this population would have been better. With that option, he could generalize his findings on a scientific basis.

INTRODUCTION

After you compose a knowledge base for your study, you encounter the tasks associated with your study methods. This includes the selection of a study sample, the measurement of study variables, and the selection of the study design. The better your research methods are, the more credibility you will have with the readers of your research report. If your study sample is one that is not relevant to certain readers, they will not find your results to be useful. If your measurement of variables is haphazard, the readers of your report will have little confidence in the relevance of your findings. If the research design in your evaluation study fails to control for normal growth over time as a potential cause of the change in the client's measured behavior, your argument for the intervention as the cause of client gain will be questioned. This chapter is devoted to the sampling task in the research process. The key issue for sampling is the generalization of the findings of your study. If you make the claim that you can generalize your findings from your sample to a designated population, you are asserting that a study similar to your own conducted with another sample of people from this same population would generate similar results.

When you undertake a study, you do so because you wish to generate information that you can use in the future. Maybe you want to conclude that the success of your recent evaluation of practice would be relevant to other clients at your agency who were not in your study. Maybe you want to know if your study is relevant to most people (in general) who exhibit the same target behavior as the clients in your study. In other words, you want to know if you can generalize your findings to people not in your study. You can generalize your findings to the extent that your study sample is representative of the population from which you drew your study sample.

The key to determining the wisdom of your generalization is the method you employed to select a study sample from your study population. If you have a random sample, you can generalize your findings to the study population on a scientific basis, because you have a scientific basis to estimate sampling error. If you do not have a random sample, you can employ logical generalization, which is based on informed opinion rather than on science. Logical generalization is more complex and less scientific, so the random sample is clearly the superior alternative.

In the previous chapters, you learned the following about sampling:

1. The **study sample** is the group of people from whom you collected data, and the study population is the larger group of people from whom you selected your sample.

2. Sampling deals with the key issue of generalization of findings. To generalize your findings means that you would expect similar results from another sample of people from the same population. Thus, you can conclude that your study findings are relevant to those in the study population, not just the study sample from whom you collected your data.

3. You can scientifically generalize your study findings to your study population if you selected your sample members at random from a list of those in the study population. This type of sample is superior to those that are not random samples.

4. **Scientific generalization** is based on the estimation of sampling error, which is the difference between the sample and the population.

5. When you do not have a random sample, you can generalize your findings on a logical basis if you have the data for the comparison of the sample and the population on relevant variables.

In this chapter, you will take your knowledge of sampling a major step forward. On completion of this chapter, you will be able to do the following:

1. Identify all the study populations that would be legitimate study populations, given the nature of a given study sample

2. Distinguish between random samples and nonrandom samples when given examples of each

3. Explain the basis for which you can generalize the findings of your study on a scientific basis if you employ a random sample

4. Explain the basis for which you can generalize the findings of your study on a logical basis if you employ a nonrandom sample

5. Describe various types of convenience samples and various types of random samples

6. Describe the steps in the process of selecting a study sample

7. Explain the concept of sampling error

THE STUDY SAMPLE AND THE STUDY POPULATION

A sample is a portion of something larger. In research, a sample consists of those persons from whom data were collected. The sample is selected from a designated study population. While your study sample is always those people who supply you with data, the study population can be defined in more than one way. The persons who are the current clients in your support group for victims of violent crime may be your study sample. You could define your study population in various ways, such as the following: (1) all the victims of crime who have been served by your support group service in the past year, (2) all the victims of crime who have been served by your support group service since this service began 6 years ago, or (3) all the victims of crime in the United States.

While you may define your study population in more than one way, you must define it so that everyone in your study sample is a member of that study population. This is true of all the examples given above of victims of crime. But it would not be true if you defined your study population as all women who have been the victims of a violent crime, assuming, of course, that there were men among the clients of your service. This definition would leave out the men who were being treated.

Let's look at an example of some of the ways in which one might define the study sample from York (2009). This example comes from a study of a treatment program for men who had been abusive to their wives. Here is the breakdown:

- 350 persons are estimated to be abusive husbands in the community of Parker Ridge.

  - Of these 350 persons, 143 men in Parker Ridge sought information about the program for abusive husbands.

    - Of these 143 men, 107 signed up for the program.

      - Of these 107 men, 81 started the program and completed the pretest measure of outcome.

        - Of these 81 men, 62 completed the program and took the posttest.

You can see several ways in which the study population could be defined in this example. You would not define it as the 62 men who completed the program and supplied the data for the study because this is your definition of the study sample. The study population is a larger group of people. Your study population could legitimately be defined as the 81 men who started the program, the 107 men who signed up, the 143 men who sought information, or the 350 men who are believed to be abusive husbands. You could go even further, but the further you go, the weaker would be your argument for logical generalization.

Several of these options, along with the study sample, are depicted in Figure 12.1 in the form of concentric circles. This figure demonstrates how each larger population contains all the persons in all smaller populations and each population also contains all the people in the study sample.

You should think of the population to whom you would like to generalize your findings. What kinds of people are of special concern to your study? Do you need to generate knowledge that is relevant to all men who abuse their spouses or just those who seek service?

Let's suppose you used the 23 students in your research class as the study sample for a study you would like to conduct. This means that each of these persons completed your questionnaire. A question that arises is, "How do I define my study population?" These 23 students are a part of the population of all social work research students in this semester in this school of social work ($n = 87$), and these people are a part of all

FIGURE 12.1 ■ Sample and Study Populations for the Treatment Program for Abusive Men

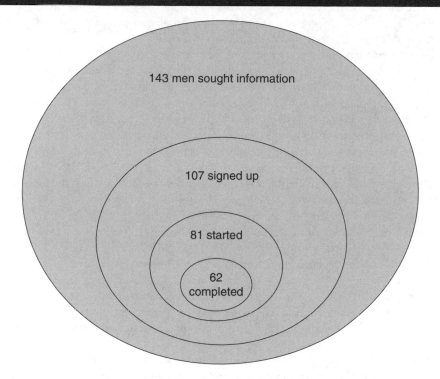

social work students in this school of social work ($n = 254$). All social work students in this school are a part of the population of all students in this university ($n = 18,724$). They are also a part of the population of all social work students in this state or all social work students in our nation.

GENERALIZATION OF STUDY RESULTS

The critical issue in sampling is the **generalization of study results**. To whom would you like to be able to generalize your findings? Generalizing results means you are estimating that the results you received from your study sample would likely be the same as the results that you would get from another sample from this study population. If you find that your special tutoring service for at-risk middle school students has been effective in the improvement of the grades of this target population, you also want to know if you should use this service with other at-risk middle school students. If you have used a good sampling procedure, you are on safe grounds to draw the conclusion that your service will be effective with other samples from this same population.

Generalization means to go higher. You technically cannot generalize your findings to your study sample. You have data on all those in your study sample, so you know for sure how these individuals responded to the tools used to measure the variables. Generalization means going to a larger group of people. So don't find yourself saying, "We can only generalize our findings to the study sample."

In the previous chapters, you have examined two bases for generalization: scientific and logical. You can engage in scientific generalization if you have a **random sample**. You can engage in **logical generalization** if you have a nonrandom sample. Logical generalization is an informed opinion. It is based on the comparison of known data from the sample with known data from the study population. If the proportions of people are similar in the two groups on the basis of age, gender, race, and income, you have some data that can support logical generalization, assuming that these four variables are important for your study. Scientific generalization is more recognized, and more credible, than logical generalization. In fact, you are likely to encounter only the concept of generalization in other works with the assumption that generalization is normally based on whether one has a random sample. You are not likely to see a reference to scientific generalization in other books on research methods. With logical generalization, it is not easy to know the relevant variables in a study that would lead you to a logical generalization of your findings. This is one of the bases that make scientific generalization better.

When you engage in generalization, you must be clear on your definition of the study population to whom you are generalizing. If you select a random sample of clients currently being served by your employment training program, you can scientifically generalize your findings to the population of clients currently being served, but not to a larger population.

You select a random sample by securing a list of the names of all the people in the designated study population and using a random sampling procedure for selecting your study sample. This procedure will be described later in this chapter. Do not make the mistake of asserting that you have a random sample due to the fact that everyone in the population had an opportunity to volunteer for the study. That is not a random sample. A random sample is the sample where you have selected the participants on a random basis.

We say that you can scientifically generalize your findings when you have a random sample because you have a scientific basis for estimating **sampling error**. We will not discuss how to do this in this book. That is for those who wish to publish articles where precise generalization is a serious need. We will take the simple path. But keep in mind that sample size is a basis for determining sampling error, so you are on somewhat weak ground if you refer to scientific generalization when you have a small sample.

When you do not have a random sample, logical generalization is an option. A theme to help is knowledge of the meaning of the concept of **sample selection bias**, which refers to things you know about the study sample and the study population that weaken your ability logically to generalize our findings. Sample selection bias is the bias introduced by the selection of individuals for a sample in such a way that the sample is not a random sample of the study population. Suppose that you select a sample of the students in your research class and find that 80% of these students are female and you find that 50% of all students in your university are females. If you wish to generalize your study findings to the entire university, do you have a sample selection bias? You have a sample that differs from the population regarding gender. This means you have a sample selection bias related to gender. When you decide if you can logically generalize your findings in this case, you need to know if gender is an important variable in your study. If studies have shown that men and women do not differ with regard to your key study variables (e.g., client outcome), you would not be as concerned with this sample selection bias as with other variables that have been found to be related.

Your generalization of findings refers to a given study sample and a designated study population. The example given about treatment for abusive men shows various ways to define the study population. Keep in mind that the further you get from the study sample, the weaker is your basis for logical generalization. It is more likely that you would find similarities between the 62 men who completed the treatment with the 81 who started it, than with the 350 men who are believed to be guilty of spouse abuse. It would be logical to assume that there are differences between abusive men who seek treatment and abusive men who do not. However, they are similar in the key characteristic of being guilty of spouse abuse. As you can see, engaging in logical generalization is neither easy nor very scientific. But it is likely to be the only basis for generalization when you undertake the evaluation of social work practice because you will not often have the opportunity to use a random sample from your study population.

Don't confuse your logical generalization of study findings with your logical justification of the intervention as discussed in a previous chapter. These are two distinct usages of the word logical. They are both based on logic but focus on different themes.

SAMPLING ERROR

When you select a study sample on a random basis from a study population, you are not sure how similar the sample is to the population. In other words, you are not sure how representative your study sample is to the study population. A representative sample is one that can be generalized. If your study sample and your study population were identical, you could engage in a perfect generalization of study results. This, of course, is not true in scientific research. You know that the sample and the population are different to some degree. The amount of that difference between the characteristics of the study sample and the study population is known as sampling error.

Because we have sampling error, we engage in an imperfect degree of generalization of study results, suggesting to others that we believe that the conclusions we drew from our study are basically similar to that which we would have found if we had included everyone in the study population in our study sample. Your sample data are not identical to your population data, but your basic conclusions from your sample data may be applied to your study population if you have small sampling error. In other words, you are asserting that the sample and the population are similar enough that the basic conclusions from your data can be generalized to your population. The degree of sampling error decides your confidence level in drawing conclusions about the generalization of your study results. With a high degree of sampling error, you would not be confident in this endeavor.

The concept of sampling error refers only to the random sample in this book. Random samples have the advantage of having a scientific method of estimating the sampling error. That is why we refer to the generalization of study results from random samples as scientific generalization.

The margin of error is a way of expressing the amount of sampling error in a given set of data. This concept is often used in survey results when the survey asked people for whom do they plan to cast their votes in the presidential election. If the data show that one candidate has 45% who favor him or her and the margin of error is 3 (i.e., ±3 percentage points), we can say that the percentage of people who favor this candidate is between 42% (45% – 3%) and 48% (45% + 3%). Often accompanying this report will be the fact that we can be 95% confident that the above is true.

Sampling error is influenced by sample size. The larger your sample, the lower is your sampling error. Therefore, you should be cautious in your generalization when you have a small sample. When you say that you can scientifically generalize your findings because you have a random sample, you will not necessarily be reporting on the extent of your sampling error. You might be leaving this issue open. But offer a word of caution if you have a small sample (e.g., less than 100).

Unfortunately, we do not have the ability to estimate sampling error on a scientific basis when we employ a nonrandom sample. With that type of sample, we must rely on informed opinion and hope that the reader believes that our analysis makes sense from a logical perspective.

SAMPLING ELEMENTS, SAMPLING FRAMES, AND SAMPLING INTERVALS

Before you examine the various types of samples and procedures for selecting one, there are three key concepts to be examined. These concepts are **sampling element**, **sampling frame**, and **sampling interval**. The sampling element is the person selected for the sample. If Jane Dewey is one person selected for your study sample, Jane would be an example of a sampling element. The sampling frame is the list of persons in the study population from which you select your sampling elements. If your study population is defined as all the clients currently served by your agency, your sampling frame would be this list of persons. For example, Jane Dewey, one of your sampling elements, would be one of the clients served by your agency, the sampling frame. Thus, your sampling elements are your study sample, and your sampling frame is your study population.

The sampling interval is the distance between sampling elements in your list of the study population (sampling frame). If you select one fourth of the clients of your agency as the proportion of people from your sampling frame that will be selected, your sampling interval is four. To determine your sampling interval, you should divide the number of your total study population (sampling frame) by the number of persons you wish to select for your sample. If your agency has 500 current clients and you wish to select a sample of 50, your sampling interval would be 10 (500/50 = 10).

Sampling error, as previously noted, is the difference between the sample and the population. Therefore, the difference between your sampling elements and your sampling frame is your sampling error.

For each set of procedures for selecting a study sample, you will be asked to define your sampling frame, and you will be instructed on how to select your sampling elements from that sampling frame.

RANDOM SAMPLES AND SCIENTIFIC GENERALIZATION

When you select the study subjects at random from a list of those in the study population, you have a random sample. You do not have a random sample simply because all those in the study population had an invitation to be in the study sample. You must select the sample on a random basis from the designated population. This means that everyone in your designated study population had an equal chance of being selected for your study sample. When you do this, you can scientifically generalize your study results to the study population from which you selected a random sample.

One of the things you will report is the rate of participation. If 67% of those who were sent a mailed questionnaire actually completed and returned it, you will report a 67% participation rate. This, of course, weakens the scientific generalization of your results, but it is suggested that you report this fact along with the random sampling procedures you employ and move on. When you engage in the evaluation of your practice with a group of clients, you will normally have a participation rate that is rather high, unless you had a good proportion of clients who dropped out of treatment. The dropout rate should be reported. In this book, we will not examine how to deal with the participation rate on a scientific basis when it comes time to engage in the generalization of results. That will be one of the many unknowns in your study that the reader of your report will deal with on an individual basis.

There are several types of random samples depending on the procedures used to select the people for your study. For each random sample you employ, each person in your designated study population must have an equal chance of being selected for your study sample. This means you have a list of all persons in the population, and you use some procedure for selecting the sample members on a random basis.

The first type is the **simple random sample**. This is a sample where each person in the population is selected on a random basis using a random selection procedure. Here are the steps:

1. Select your study population (sampling frame), and obtain a list of all persons in this population.

2. Determine the proportion of persons to be included in your study sample (your sampling elements).

3. Determine your sampling interval by dividing the number of people in your study population by the number of people in your study sample.

4. Assign a number to each person in the list of persons in the study population.

5. Select persons for the study sample by finding them at random from each sampling interval. For example, if your sampling interval is 10, you would enter the numbers 1 and 10 into the website below to find the first randomly selected person. This site is called "Math Goodies" and was found on the Internet in May 2017. If it is not in existence, you can find a similar one on the Internet.

http://www.mathgoodies.com/calculators/random_no_custom.html

On the first web page, you will see the following:

Enter a lower limit:

Enter an upper limit:

Random number:

The lower limit is the lowest number in your sampling interval. For your first interval, this number will be 1 (assuming you numbered the people in your study population starting with the number 1). If your sampling interval is 10, your upper limit for your first interval will be 10. Once you enter these two numbers, the computer will generate a number from 1 to 10 at random. This will be the number of the first person you select for your study sample. The lower limit for your second interval will be 11 and the upper limit will be 20. The lower limit for your third interval will be 21 and the upper limit will be 30. And this is the way you go until you have selected all the members of your study sample.

Another type of random sample is the **systematic random sample**. The first four steps in this procedure are the same as for the simple random sample. It is when you are selecting the persons for your sample that the procedures differ. With the systematic random sample, you select your first person from the first sampling interval at random. You can use the procedure described for the simple random sample for this step, or put a list of numbers from 1 to 10 in a hat and draw one out as your first number. Once you have the first number, you select the second number by adding the number of your sampling interval (e.g., 10) to the number that was first selected (e.g., number 3) to get the second person to be selected. If the first person selected was number 3 and your sampling interval is 10, the second person selected would be number 13. The third person selected would be number 23, the fourth would be number 33, and so forth.

There are a number of other random sampling procedures that you will encounter in published research, especially in descriptive research. But we will not discuss them because they are less likely to be useful for you when you undertake the kind of research typically conducted by social workers.

NONRANDOM SAMPLES AND LOGICAL GENERALIZATION

Most studies conducted by social work students or social work practitioners employ a sample of the clients currently served by the programs that employ them. This is not an example of a random sample because these individuals came to be in the sample from a procedure that does not entail the random selection of people for a study. That is why logical generalization is important in social work even though it is clearly weaker than scientific generalization.

The most prevalent type of sample is the **convenience sample**, which is simply a group of people who are in the study because they were convenient to the researcher. If you select the members of your research class for a study of opinion about the characteristics of a good work manager, you would have a convenience sample. You selected them because they were convenient to you. These individuals were not selected because they were experts in management. They were selected because they were convenient.

The **purposive sample** is one where the people have been selected for the study based on the characteristics of the population and the objective of the study. One could make the case that a typical evaluation study of one's own clients is a purposive sample because the purpose of the study is to determine if a service for this sample of people has been found to be effective. While your first question is whether this service was effective with these clients, your next question will be whether you can generalize your findings to other people, especially people who are likely to become clients in the future. You want to know if you should use this service again.

The label given to the sampling procedure is less important, however, than the question of what kind of generalization you can employ regarding your study results. If you only need to know how much gain was found for your current caseload of 17 clients, you need not worry about sampling and generalization. Your results are relevant to this group. But seldom do we stop there. We want to know whether we should employ this same treatment with a different group of people experiencing the same target behavior as our clients. So here we are back to generalization again. If we cannot generalize in any way, we have failed to generate useful knowledge for the future.

Another nonrandom sampling procedure will be discussed here. The **snowball sample** is a nonrandom sample that has been developed in stages, wherein a group of individuals of a certain type (e.g., homeless people) are sampled by asking the first stage of sampled people to identify others they know with the same characteristic (e.g., being homeless). So you start with the local homeless shelter and include these individuals in your study sample. Then you ask these individuals if they can identify other people who are homeless. Then you find that group and include them in your study. And you ask that group if they can identify other people who are homeless and include this third group in your study sample. You stop this process when you have a sample that seems reasonable in representing the people you wish to study.

Chapter Practice Exercises

Practice Exercise 1: Selecting a Random Sample for Your Study

In this exercise, you will be asked to report your plan for the selection of a random sample of people for a study you might undertake. You could select a 25% random sample of all the clients served by a particular program with which you are familiar. You might decide to select a 10% random sample of all the students at your university. Maybe you wish to conduct a survey of the 2,345 citizens of a certain community, and you wish to have 100 people in your survey.

You will not be asked to collect the names of all the people in your study population. You will need to have the number of people in your population and the number you wish to have in your study sample. Your task will be to report the steps that allow you to select the numbers assigned to all those from your study population who will be in your study sample.

1. Briefly describe the nature of the study you wish to undertake.

2. What is your definition of the study population?

3. How many people are in this population?

4. How many people do you wish to have in your study sample?

5. What is your sampling interval?

6. What method of random sampling will you employ: systematic random sampling or simple random sampling?

7. What is the number of each person who will be in your study sample? (e.g., if you have 1,000 people in your study population and plan to select 100 people for you sample using the systematic random sampling procedure, the number of the first person selected will be between 1 and 10. The second person would have a number between 11 and 20, and so forth.)

8. Can you generalize your study findings on a scientific basis? Explain.

Practice Exercise 2: Selecting a Snowball Sample

1. In this option, you will describe how you will select a sample of persons using snowball sampling methods. This entails the description of the nature of your study, the reason why snowball sampling would be appropriate, and the first group of people who will be asked to participate and to identify additional persons for your study.

2. Briefly describe the study you would like to undertake that could use snowball sampling.

3. Why is snowball sampling the appropriate method for selecting your study sample?

4. How would you describe the first group of people who will be asked to participate in your study?

5. What is the question you will pose to this group to get a second group of potential study participants?

6. Will you be able to generalize your study findings on a scientific basis? Explain.

7. If you do not believe that you will be able to generalize your findings on a scientific basis, what is the one thing you will do to facilitate your logical generalization of study results? For example, what is the one variable on which you will seek information about the study population that can be a basis of comparison with your study sample?

Practice Exercise 3: Logically Generalizing Your Findings From a Convenience Sample

Think of a research study you might undertake where a convenience sample will be the most likely type of sample you could select. Answer the following questions:

1. Briefly describe the study you would like to undertake that would employ a convenience sample.

2. What is your study sample?

3. What is your study population?

4. Why is the convenience sample the chosen type of sample for this study?

5. What variables are relevant to the question of the extent to which you can logically generalize your findings from your sample to this population? Explain why each one is relevant.

CHAPTER REVIEW

Chapter Key Learnings

1. While the study sample is always defined as the group of people who supplied data for your study, the study population can be defined in a number of ways, as long as everyone who is in the study sample is a member of the designated study population. The closer your definition of the study population is to the study sample, the better is your ability to generalize your study findings. For example, you would be on safer grounds to generalize the findings from your study of 12 persons in your addictions therapy group to the 78 clients seeking additional services from your agency than to all of the 217 clients who are seeking some kind of mental health service from your agency.

2. When you attempt to generalize your study findings to your designated study population, you are asserting that the results of a similar study of a different sample from this study population would lead to study conclusions that are similar to the conclusions you have drawn from your study data.

3. The selection of the sample determines the extent to which you can generalize your study findings from the study sample to the designated study population. The better your sampling procedures are, the better you are able to generalize your findings.

4. A random sample is one whereby every person in the designated study population had an equal chance of being selected to be in the study sample. A random sample is sometimes called a probability sample. An open invitation for people to participate in the study is not an example of a random sample because the individuals who volunteered were not selected at random from the designated study population.

5. When you have a random sample, you can generalize your study findings to the designated study population on a scientific basis because you have a scientific way of estimating sampling error.

6. When you have a nonrandom sample, you cannot generalize your findings on a scientific basis, but you can generalize your findings on a logical basis providing that you have a convincing array of data that compares the study sample with the designated study population.

7. Two of the various types of random samples are the simple random sample and the systematic random sample, each of which calls on the researcher to identify the sampling frame, and the sampling interval, and to select sampling elements on a random basis from that sampling frame.

8. Three of the types of nonrandom samples (nonprobability samples) are (1) the convenience sample, (2) the purposive sample, and (3) the snowball sample. Each of these types of samples calls on the researcher to identify the study population, the study sample, and the proportion of people from the study population who should be in the study sample.

9. Sampling error is the difference between the characteristics of the study sample and the characteristics of the study population. It serves as a basis for determining the extent to which the study results from the sample can be generalized to the study population.

Chapter Discussion Questions

1. Suppose that your friend who has not taken a research course asks you what it means to generalize the findings of a study. How would you answer?

2. Why is it that the sampling methods employed in your study determine the extent to which you can generalize your findings to persons who were not in your study? Why is it not that the chosen research design (e.g., one-group pretest–posttest design) is your best guide for generalizing your study findings?

3. Identify a nonrandom (nonprobability) study sample and its study population, and find some data on this study population that would be relevant to the comparison of your sample with your population when you wish to generalize your findings on a logical basis. For example, would gender be relevant? Why? Would ethnicity be relevant? Why?

4. Consider your perceptions about the generalization of study findings between a study that used a random sample and one that used a purposive sample. Does this difference mean anything to you? Explain.

5. Suppose you have decided to select a random sample of people from a designated study population. Identify the study population. Would you prefer to use the simple random sample procedure or the systematic random sampling procedure? Explain.

6. Before you started to read this book, what did you think about the advantages of the random sample over the nonrandom sample? What did you think were the advantages of the random sample?

7. Do you believe that logical generalization of study results makes any sense? In other words, is it useful? Would it make a difference in your interpretation of study results? Explain.

8. Identify an example of a convenience sample and a purposive sample for a set of studies you might undertake? Why is one called convenience and the other purposive?

Chapter Test

1. Which of these statements is/are true?
   a. The study sample consists of all those people who are in the target population from whom study participants were selected and data were collected
   b. The nature of your sample is the primary basis for generalizing your study results
   c. Both of the above
   d. None of the above

2. You can scientifically generalize your study findings if
   a. You have a nonrandom sample from the study population
   b. You have a random sample from the study population
   c. Both of the above
   d. None of the above

3. Which of the following statements is/are true?
   a. A random sample is one where the researcher selects study subjects on a random basis from a list of all those in the study population
   b. Logical generalization is based on knowledge that compares the study sample with the study population
   c. Both of the above
   d. None of the above

4. Which of the following is/are true?
   a. The systematic random sampling procedure is one of the procedures that supports the scientific generalization of study results
   b. A convenience sample is one that is chosen because the people in it are easily available
   c. Both of the above
   d. None of the above

5. Which of the following is/are true?
   a. The purposive sample is an example of a nonrandom sample
   b. The snowball sample is an example of a random sample
   c. Both of the above
   d. None of the above

6. The sampling interval is
   a. The persons who are selected to be in your study sample
   b. The list of persons in your study population from which your study sample will be selected
   c. The distance between sampling elements in your study sample
   d. The amount of difference between the characteristics of the study sample and the characteristics of the study population

7. The sampling frame is
   a. The persons who are selected to be in your study sample
   b. The list of persons in your study population from which your study sample will be selected
   c. The distance between sampling elements in your study sample
   d. The amount of difference between the characteristics of the study sample and the characteristics of the study population

8. Sampling error is
   a. The persons who are selected to be in your study sample
   b. The list of persons in your study population from which your study sample will be selected
   c. The distance between sampling elements in your study sample
   d. The amount of difference between the characteristics of the study sample and the characteristics of the study population

9. Generalization refers to
   a. The estimation that the results you received from your study sample would likely be about the same as results that would be achieved from another sample from this study population
   b. The distance between sampling elements in your study sample
   c. Both of the above
   d. None of the above

10. Which of the following statements is/are true?
    a. A snowball sample is a group of people selected for your study in stages whereby each group of people are asked to be a study subject in your study and to identify other similar people who could be asked to participate

b. You can scientifically generalize your findings to your study population when you have a random sample, because you have a scientific basis for estimating sampling error

c. Both of the above
d. None of the above

ANSWERS: 1 = c; 2 = b; 3 = c; 4 = c; 5 = a; 6 = c; 7 = b; 8 = d; 9 = a; 10 = c

Chapter Glossary

Convenience sample. A nonrandom study sample selected because it was easily available, such as the fellow students in your class.

Generalization of study results. The estimation that the results you received from your study sample would likely be about the same as the results that would be achieved from another sample from this study population. In other words, the conclusions you would draw from your study would be basically similar to the conclusions you would draw from a similar study of a different sample taken from the same population.

Logical generalization. Generalization of study results on the logical connection of the characteristics of the study sample and the study population.

Purposive sample. A nonrandom sample selected because of the special characteristics of these people that are of interest to the study. An example would be the selection of your current clients for an evaluative study or the selection of Hispanic people because you are studying something about this population.

Random sample. A study sample that was drawn from the study population on a random basis. This means each person in the study population had an equal chance of being selected for the study sample. It requires securing a list of persons in the population and selecting sample members from that list on a random basis.

Sample selection bias. Sample selection bias is the bias introduced by the selection of individuals for a sample in such a way that the sample is not representative of the study population. If you select persons for your study by asking for volunteers at your agency during the normal work day, you will have a bias that fails to represent clients who receive services in the evenings

Sampling element. The persons who are selected to be in your study sample

Sampling error. The amount of difference between the characteristics of the study sample and the characteristics of the study population. It can be estimated scientifically when you have a random sample and the necessary data.

Sampling frame. The list of persons in your study population from which your study sample will be selected.

Sampling interval. The distance between sampling elements in your study sample. If you select every fourth person for your sample using the systematic random sampling procedure, your sampling interval would be four.

Scientific generalization. Generalization of study results when you have a random sample, which provides you with a scientific basis for estimating sampling error.

Simple random sample. A study sample that has been selected by a procedure whereby the researcher obtains a list of members of the study population, decides on the sampling interval, and selects members from this list in a procedure that includes the drawing of numbers on a random basis.

Snowball sample. A nonrandom study sample selected in stages, wherein people selected in Stage 1 are asked to identify potential study subjects for Stage 2 of the selection procedure, and other stages are possible.

Study sample. In research, a study sample is the group of people from whom data were collected.

Systematic random sample. A sample that has been drawn from the list of the study population on a random basis, including the steps of deciding on the sampling interval, selecting the first person from the first sampling interval on a random basis, and selecting the next person who is one sampling interval beyond the first one, and so forth.

13

MEASURING YOUR STUDY VARIABLES

Allison conducts a support group for caregivers of elderly people in an agency where she is a social work intern. The objective of this intervention is to reduce caregiver burnout, because this phenomenon reduces the effectiveness of caregivers in the care of elderly clients. If the caregiving service does not work for an individual, a less appealing alternative will often be arranged. Allison noticed that the agency had not used any method of evaluating the outcome of this service, so she took on this task. She realized that she needed a good definition of the concept being measured before she sought a tool for this task. Burnout was defined as a state of physical, emotional, and mental exhaustion that may be accompanied by a change in attitude from positive and caring to negative and unconcerned. Allison sought a tool for measuring caregiver burden and found the Zarit Burden Interview Screen. After reviewing this tool, Allison found it to be consistent with her definition of caregiver burnout. She also discovered that this tool had passed several tasks of quality through the examination of reliability and validity. With this information, she concluded that she had the tool she needed for measuring outcomes for the caregiver support group. She suggested that this tool be given to the clients of the caregiver support group prior to beginning the support group experience and again after 6 months of attending the group.

INTRODUCTION

In a nutshell, the task facing Allison is the task that is addressed in this chapter: the measurement of study variables. Allison was conducting research on the outcomes of an intervention with a group of clients. This means that she was engaged in an evaluation study, rather than a descriptive, explanatory, or exploratory study. You might engage in an evaluative study where you are giving a group of clients a service, or you might evaluate the services for a single client. This chapter presents information on measurement that can be used both for groups and for single clients. However, there are some special challenges when you are dealing with a single client. Asking a single client to respond to an evaluation tool at the beginning of each counseling session is a different challenge from asking a group of clients to complete the questionnaire once before treatment begins and once again at the end of treatment. The tool for the single client should be less intrusive into the service experience, so it should be simple and not very time-consuming.

Allison's study was an evaluative study. Your study could be evaluative, but it could also be descriptive or explanatory. You might want to be able to describe the clients of your agency or examine the causes of client no-shows. In all types of studies, measurement is a necessity.

Measurement is one of the key elements of the study of methodology, two of the others being sampling and research design. Two major alternatives for measuring study variables will be addressed in this chapter: (1) finding a published measurement tool and (2) designing your own measurement tool. In this chapter, you will learn how to do the following:

1. Explain the nature of measurement, with emphasis on accuracy in measuring the concepts as they are defined

2. Describe the mechanisms for achieving measurement accuracy, with a focus on reducing measurement error by certain tests of the reliability and validity of measurement tools

3. Demonstrate how to find a measurement tool, with emphasis on tools for measuring client outcome in evaluative research

4. Construct a measurement tool when there is no published tool that will work for the measurement of the variable that has been defined

This knowledge will support your ability to apply what you have learned to the task of finding, or developing, a measurement tool for a study of interest to yourself. At the end of this chapter, there will be a practice exercise where you can demonstrate your skill.

WHY FRET OVER MEASUREMENT?

This chapter will help you determine how to measure each variable in your study. To accomplish this objective, the chapter will include a great number of concepts and checklists to ensure that your measurement is optimal. It will also focus on objectivity as a core principle, and it will encourage you to heighten the accuracy of the method you employ to measure variables.

For example, if you wanted to understand the level of the effectiveness of your alcoholism treatment program, you could ask the social workers working in this program to give their opinions about whether it is effective in reducing the problems associated with alcoholism. The social workers could either respond to a questionnaire in which they answer "Yes" or "No" when asked if the program is effective, or they could rate the program on a scale of 1 to 4, where 1 = *highly effective*, 2 = *mostly effective*, 3 = *somewhat effective*, and 4 = *not effective*.

However, this method would be highly vulnerable to subjectivity. The social workers who serve in this program would be expected to have a positive bias, as they do not want to engage in behaviors likely to lead to the elimination of a program that provides them their jobs.

Instead of asking the social workers, why not ask the clients to answer a very broad question, like the above example? This would be a step in the right direction because the clients are not protecting their jobs by being positive. However, this broad characterization of effectiveness would be vulnerable to the **social desirability bias**, whereby people are encouraged to give a socially desirable response; most of us have been encouraged throughout our lives to be positive.

If clients are asked about effectiveness, the nature of their responses should be broken down into categories of life where they are more likely to have differentiated responses and, thereby, be more objective and truthful. For example, clients could be asked about their interpersonal lives, their work lives, their home lives, and so forth. More specifically, they could be asked a series of questions designed to measure the extent to which they are depressed or suffering from the symptoms of posttraumatic stress disorder.

We could ask clients to give a statement about how well the treatment program has helped them. This could be very useful, especially in the improvement of services. However, a set of statements about client satisfaction would not be as useful as concrete data on, for example, the clients' scores on depression. The latter would be less vulnerable to the social desirability bias.

So effective measurement helps us get an objective picture of our research theme and avoid measuring a person's biases. Also, it helps us achieve credibility with others in the reporting of our results. If we reveal objective data, we are more likely to be heard.

THE NATURE OF MEASUREMENT IN SOCIAL WORK RESEARCH

Sometimes the social worker will have an easy measure of the study variable. This could include grades in school, the number of times a client fails to show up for an appointment, or whether a homeless person found a home. These researchers are lucky—they have a measure of outcome that gives little reason for concern.

But what if you need to measure something less concrete, like self-esteem, caregiver burden, or perceptions of social support? Now you have a challenge. You will need to define your variable carefully and seek a published tool for its measurement. If you cannot find one, you will need to construct one yourself.

In the previous chapters, you have witnessed the measurement of quite a few variables that were defined before they were measured. These variables included (a) the traits that describe the good work manager, (b) sex role stereotype about the characteristics of the good manager, (c) stress, (d) social support, and (e) depression. Therefore, you have had some experience with measurement. Now it is time for you seek more depth of understanding about this aspect of research.

In measurement, your critical issue is accuracy. Readers of your study results about marital satisfaction might have problems with your findings if your measure of marital satisfaction contained no items on extended-family relationships. They may believe that your measurement tool failed to be adequately comprehensive. Inaccurate measurement could also be a result of a tool that is difficult to understand; if your subject does not know what a question means, he or she is not going to answer the question accurately. Measurement accuracy will be discussed in this chapter by an examination of both reliability and validity, two means of reducing measurement error.

You have already seen the definitions of reliability (consistency) and validity (accuracy) in the previous chapters. Your foray into this subject started with the word *credibility*, which is used in everyday language and represents a general category into which both reliability and validity fall. Are your tools credible to the readers of your research report? If not, they will lack confidence in your results.

In a previous chapter, you saw descriptions of three levels of measurement: (1) nominal, (2) ordinal, and (3) interval. You need to know the level of measurement for your variables in order to select an appropriate statistic for finding the answer to your research question. For example, the various forms of the *t* test require that variables be measured at the interval level.

The lowest level of measurement is the nominal level. If your measure of a variable places study subjects into categories that have no order, you will have a nominal variable. An example of a nominal variable would be gender—males are neither higher nor lower than females. Another example would be political party affiliation. The second level of measurement is the ordinal level. If your measure of a variable puts people into categories that have an order, you have a variable measured at the ordinal level. An example of an ordinal-level variable would be an opinion statement with the response categories of *strongly agree*, *agree*, *disagree*, and *strongly disagree*. In this situation, there is an order among the possible responses, which go from lowest to highest. The highest level of measurement is the interval level. If you have measured your variable at the interval level, you have given it a score on a scale or some other measure that is numerical in nature, such as age measured in years (not categories of years).

These levels of measurement form a hierarchy. Nominal measurement is the lowest level, followed by ordinal, which is followed by interval. There is a fourth level of measurement, which is ratio. This level has not been given attention in this book because it has lesser importance for the social work researcher than the other levels of measurement.

STANDARDIZED TOOLS AND INDIVIDUALIZED TOOLS

Some measurement tools are standardized, and some are individualized. A standardized scale has a designated set of sentences and words that are used in the same way for each person who completes them. Examples include the Beck Depression Inventory and the Hare Self-Esteem Scale. You are more likely to see standardized tools used in published studies than individualized tools. You will see this form in examples of scales that are used in this chapter. The words on these scales are the same for each person who completes it.

However, there are times when you cannot find a standardized scale that measures what you want. This is when you seek, or develop, an individualized scale. You will then need to tailor the individualized scale for your individual client, so that the client will have his or her own unique scale. Some parts of the structure of your individualized scale may be common for more than one client, but the individual items for measurement are unique for each of them. For example, you will see a discussion of the Your Evaluation of Service (YES) scale in a later section of this chapter. When you employ this scale, you will ask the clients to describe, in their own words, the outcome objectives they want to achieve and to rate how well things have been going in the past week regarding each objective. One client may have the objective of "not shouting at my husband when he comes home late," while another might want to "stay calm when I discuss my son's school grades."

While each client will have unique objectives, the general form of the YES scale is the same for all clients. Each scale will have a 10-point rating system with 1 = *miserably* and 10 = *extremely well*. You will ask your client to rate each objective on this 10-point scale each time you seek an evaluation. For the single-client study, this may be done each week when you see the client for a treatment session.

MEASUREMENT ERROR

When you attempt to use human subjects to measure concepts such as anxiety, depression, and feelings of support, you should understand the concept of **measurement error**, which is the distance between the data you have and the truth about the concept you are trying to measure. Some tools for measuring depression will have less measurement error than others because they have been more carefully constructed and subjected to tests for reliability and validity. Measurement error tells you that your measurement tool is not perfect, but it does not have to be perfect; it simply has to be a credible way to measure your variable for your purposes. If you wish to publish your study results, you will pay careful attention to issues such as reliability and validity. However, if your study is designed to help you with decisions about client service, you will still be attentive to whether your measurement is credible but you may not feel the need to delve as deeply into the nuances of reliability and validity in the pursuit of perfection. Perhaps the pursuit of perfection is not cost-effective in this situation.

You have probably taken an exam in a class and been frustrated with your grade. On review of the items you answered incorrectly, you likely saw a question that you misread, leading you to make an error in your test even though you knew the concept that was being measured by that question. We can call this situation an example of measurement error. You knew more than your grade for this item on the test indicated. On the other hand, if you were very lucky with guessing the correct answer to questions you did not understand, this would also be a measurement error. In this situation, you would be the beneficiary of the error rather than the victim. Both are measurement errors because the grade for the test was not a perfect illustration of exactly what you knew about the subject of the exam.

Keep in mind that you will have some measurement error whenever you attempt to measure human variables. The question is not whether you have measurement error but whether it is an acceptable level of error. If the amount of measurement error is not acceptable, you have an inadequate tool for measuring your concept. If there were many examples of error in the research test you had in college, we might call this a bad test; it does not do a good job of measuring knowledge about the subject under study. There are various ways the professor can test for measurement error with regard to exams.

Sources of Measurement Error

A source of measurement error is the social desirability bias, which is a tendency to answer questions in accordance with what we believe is the socially desirable way rather than what we really believe. To avoid this bias, you should refrain from starting a questionnaire item with the words "Don't you believe that . . ." This phrase is suggesting what the subject should believe.

The social desirability bias is an example of systematic error in measurement. **Systematic error** occurs when the tool we use reflects inaccurate information in a consistent fashion. If a tool has a high potential for eliciting a social desirability bias, you will find a consistent pattern of socially desirable responses from research subjects. The wording of questions for a survey can encourage a biased response, as in the example above. Information given later in this chapter on constructing a measurement tool will help you avoid this mistake.

Another type of measurement error is known as **random error**. This type of error has no consistent pattern as in the case of systematic error. With systematic error, you might predict that your study's subjects will answer a given question in a given way because it is worded in a way that elicits a socially desirable response. With random error, however, you cannot predict the direction of the error. If, for example, you administered a questionnaire designed for adults to a group of third-grade students, you would likely get random errors; they would not understand the meaning of the questions, so they would just mark the tool in a random fashion.

Preventing Measurement Error

Among the methods for preventing measurement error are (a) preparing instruments that have items that are appropriately worded for the designated population and (b) using more than one method for measuring the same thing. The example of a tool for adults given to children illustrates the first method. You can employ the second error prevention method by using personal interviews of study subjects to measure your variable and comparing this result with that of a measurement tool designed to measure the same concept. If the two results are consistent, you have evidence of validity.

Two mechanisms for preventing measurement error are tests of reliability and validity. **Reliability** refers to the consistency of a measurement device, whereas **validity** refers to the accuracy of a measurement tool. A tool must be consistent to be accurate, but a consistent tool might not necessarily be accurate. In other words, a tool can be consistently inaccurate.

Reliability as One Means of Reducing Measurement Error

One method of testing for the reliability of a scale is known as **test–retest reliability**. Suppose the members of your research class took the Beck Depression Inventory today. Suppose further that the same students had taken this scale a week ago. Would you expect to see a positive correlation between their depression scores from a week ago and the scores of today? A positive correlation would mean that a person who scored higher than someone else on the first administration of the scale would tend to score higher than the other person on the second administration of it as well. A positive correlation between the two administrations of the scale would be evidence that this scale is consistent. We would then assume that someone who is clinically depressed today would have likely been clinically depressed a week ago and that someone who is not depressed today would likely not have been depressed a week ago. In that case, the clinically depressed person would score higher on the first administration of the scale, and this pattern would be repeated with a second administration of this scale, illustrating a positive correlation. So the answer to the above question is yes—you would expect to find a positive correlation between the two administrations of this scale. If you fail to get this result, you would conclude that you do not have evidence of the reliability of this scale. If a tool fails to be consistent, it is not reliable.

Another method of testing for reliability is testing the **internal consistency reliability** of the tool. This test examines whether the different items on the scale seem to be measuring the same thing. If the various items on the scale are measuring the same thing, different parts of the scale would have a positive correlation with one another. To test for internal consistency, you could compose a variable that contained only the even-numbered items on your scale and a second variable that contained only the odd-numbered items on the scale. You would expect a rather high correlation—.70 or higher—because each half of the scale is supposed to be measuring the same thing. If you failed to find a strong positive correlation, you would have reason to doubt the reliability of your tool and would need to reexamine whether the different items on this scale are measuring the same thing. A common tool for testing for internal consistency is Cronbach's alpha, the subject of Exhibit 13.1.

Validity as a Mechanism for Reducing Measurement Error

Validity refers to accuracy. Does the measurement tool accurately measure the concept as you defined it? To answer this question, you will need to revisit your definition of the variable when you engage in the examination of validity.

The weakest form of validity is **face validity**. This refers to whether the tool seems to be valid on the face of it, or on a surface level. In other words, if you give a tool to a group of knowledgeable people and ask them what it measures, they would consistently

EXHIBIT 13.1

USING CRONBACH'S ALPHA COEFFICIENT TO TEST FOR INTERNAL CONSISTENCY OF A SCALE

People who design published scales for the measurement of social variables often subject their scales to a test of internal consistency using a statistical measure known as **Cronbach's alpha**. This coefficient represents the analysis of all correlations of scale items with all the other scale items. The alpha coefficient combines them in a way that shows the strength of these combinations. In other words, Cronbach's alpha shows how well the various items on the scale seem to be measuring the same thing.

One of the scales for measuring social support has items such as the following: (a) "There are several people who I trust to help solve my problems" and (b) "If I needed help fixing an appliance or repairing my car, there is someone who would help me." The respondents are asked to select one of the following answers for each item on the scale: *definitely true* (3 points), *probably true* (2 points), *probably false* (1 point), or *definitely false* (0 points). Scores for social support are computed by summing the scores for each item on the scale. If you subjected this scale to a test of internal consistency, you would expect that scores for Item 1 on the scale would have a positive correlation with scores for Item 2 on the scale, Item 3 on the scale, and so forth. This pattern would suggest that the various items on the scale were measuring the same thing. If you failed to find this pattern, you would have reason to believe that the various items on the scale were not measuring the same thing,

so you would conclude that internal consistency was lacking. In other words, your analysis failed to show that the scale was reliable, which means that you lack evidence of its validity.

In the computation of the alpha coefficient, the correlation of Item 1 on the scale with Item 2 is computed. Then, the correlation of Item 1 with Item 3 is computed, and each possible correlation with each of the other items is computed. All these correlations are combined using a formula that determines the overall correlation level for the scale.

Coefficient alpha is one of the many options available in SPSS (Statistical Package for the Social Sciences), a statistical software. You enter the data for each item on the scale, treating each item on the scale as a separate variable. Then, you identify the individual variables to be included in the analysis of coefficient alpha, and SPSS will give you the value of alpha. Alpha values, just like correlation coefficients, can range from a low of 0 to a high of 1.0. A value of .70 or higher is considered sufficient as a determinant of internal consistency for a scale. If your coefficient is lower than .70, you can consider your tool to be lower than the normal standard, but this is a matter of opinion. A value of .50 also shows internal consistency, but it does not meet the accepted standard set forth by statisticians. A negative correlation, of course, would indicate that there is something seriously wrong with this scale.

refer to the concepts that you are attempting to measure. To test for face validity, you need a group of knowledgeable people and a procedure for asking their opinions on what the tool measures. It is best that you not tell them the name of the concept you are measuring, so you can avoid the social desirability bias—if they are your friends, they will want to please you. Instead, ask an open question about what key concept is measured by this tool. Report your findings, and the reader can decide if you have a credible tool.

A stronger type of validity is **criterion validity**. This refers to a test of whether the tool in question operates in the same way as another method of measuring the same concept. Suppose the members of your research class had been interviewed by a clinical social worker to determine if anyone in the class should be guided to treatment for depression. The entire class volunteered to be interviewed. The clinical social worker rated each person on a scale from 1 to 4 regarding the level of depression that was displayed in the opinion of the social worker. Level 1 indicated no depression at all, while Level 2 indicated some minor level of depression but not one that required treatment. Levels 3 and 4 were levels of depression that indicated that treatment would help, with Level 4 being the highest level of depression.

Now let us get to the issue of validity. A way to test the validity of the depression scale administered to this class would be to compute a correlation between the score for depression given by the scale and the rating of depression given by the social worker.

What should we find? Like the previous example, we would expect a positive correlation between these two variables: (1) the depression scale score and (2) the depression rating by the clinical social worker. This means that if John scored higher than Jane on the depression scale, he would be expected to also have been rated higher for depression by the clinical social worker. If this pattern among the participants holds up, you have reason to believe that your measurement tool has criterion validity.

Content validity is the final form of validity we will discuss. **Content validity** refers to the extent to which a measure includes all the dimensions of the variable being measured. For example, what are the dimensions of marital satisfaction? Would it include communication? How about agreement about child care practices? Would it include sexual satisfaction? What about satisfaction with finances or the amount of time the couple spends together? If you believe that marital satisfaction includes all of these dimensions, you would seek a marital satisfaction scale that included them all. If you found one that did not include finances or another key variable, you would continue your search.

There are other forms of validity and reliability that will likely be employed by those who design measurement tools. However, the task of this book is not to prepare you for the job of designing measurement tools for publication but, instead, to prepare you to construct your own tool and possibly employ some of the simple means of testing it for reliability and validity.

Can You Have Validity If You Do Not Have Reliability?

Can your measurement tool be reliable if it is not valid? Can it be valid if it is not reliable? Think about what each of these concepts means before you turn your attention to Figure 13.1. Reliability means consistency. Validity means accuracy. Can a tool be consistently inaccurate? Can it be accurate if it is not consistent? After considering these questions, take a look at Figure 13.1. This figure shows three targets on which you are testing three guns to see if they are reliable and valid. Target A has gunshots all over the target. Is this gun reliable? Is it valid? It appears to be neither. What about Target B? Is it reliable? All the shots landed in a very similar spot, so we would conclude that this gun is reliable. Is it valid? Is it failing to hit the bullseye? It has consistently failed to hit the bullseye, so you would conclude that it is not valid.

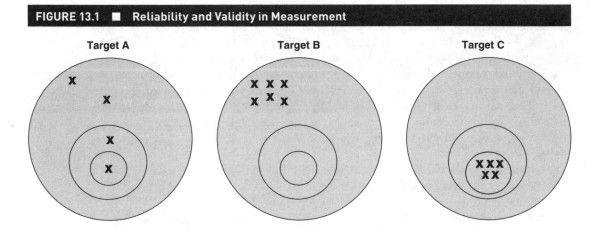

FIGURE 13.1 ■ Reliability and Validity in Measurement

Now, take a look at Target C. All the shots are in the center circle, where we were aiming our gun. We would conclude that this gun is not only reliable but also valid. These three figures illustrate that we can have reliability without validity, but we cannot have validity without reliability.

RELIABILITY AND VALIDITY IN QUALITATIVE MEASUREMENT

The previous sections were focused on quantitative measurement, where you measure variables by giving people a score or placing them into categories. The issues of reliability and validity are also relevant to qualitative measurement, where your data are words. When you conduct qualitative research, you will still be concerned with the consistency and accuracy of your measurement.

In qualitative research, reliability is the extent to which a set of meanings derived from several interpreters are sufficiently congruent. It refers to the degree to which different researchers performing similar observations in the field would generate similar interpretations (Franklin, Cody, & Ballan, 2010).

There are several methods for increasing reliability in qualitative research (Franklin et al., 2010). One method is the examination of the equivalence of responses to various forms of the same question. Perhaps you have two forms of a similar question that have different wording. You would examine whether the responses of the study subject were consistent for each version of the question. Another method for increasing reliability is the establishment of clear procedures for recording field notes. This prevents inconsistent recordings of observations on a theme. A third method for increasing reliability is cross-checking, a procedure whereby researchers use multiple team members to confirm their observations in the field. For example, one researcher might cross-check by comparing his or her enumerated codes with those of a fellow researcher.

Another method for improving reliability in qualitative research is being sure to stay close to the actual data (e.g., the actual words of the study subjects). For example, in first-level coding, the researcher should use the words given by the study subject rather than replacing them with similar words or phrases thought to be more pleasing.

The above methods focus on finding sufficient regularity in the methods used to examine qualitative data to ensure that results are reliable. As with quantitative data, we cannot have validity without reliability when you are measuring your variables qualitatively.

Validity in qualitative measurement focuses on the extent to which researchers see what they think they see (Franklin et al., 2010). If a researcher records that a study subject is expressing anger, is this true? Maybe this is the normal way in which the study subject expresses concern, not anger.

In qualitative research, credibility refers to the truthfulness of study findings (Guba, 1981). Therefore, credibility is essentially the same as validity. A key mechanism for establishing credibility is to test the study subjects' endorsement of the study findings. Do they agree with your observations? Another is to ensure that the amount of time researchers spend engaging with the study subjects is sufficient to seem credible to a reasonable person. A 10-minute interview would be viewed in this context very differently from regular contacts of significant duration over a period of 6 weeks. A third mechanism for establishing credibility is the search for negative information—data that contradict certain basic findings. If there is a meaningful effort in this direction and little negative information was discovered, you have enhanced the credibility of your qualitative findings.

SECURING THE TOOL FOR MEASURING YOUR STUDY VARIABLES

If you are engaged in evaluative research, you will seek (or design) a tool for measuring the target behavior. There are a great number of published tools for this purpose, so your first step would be to seek such a tool. One useful source is Corcoran and Fischer (2013), who have produced a two-volume set of books containing hundreds of scales. Each scale is revealed in its entirety, and information is supplied regarding the validity and reliability of each scale, along with how it should be scored.

If you are unable to find a suitable published tool, you will need to design your own. This is not an easy task. Those who have published scales are typically experts on both the content of the tool and the methods of testing for reliability and validity. If you are not such an expert, you will need the assistance of the second part of this section on securing a tool.

Tips for Finding a Measurement Tool

A key advantage of the published scale is that it was designed by an expert on the theme of the tool. This person has spent a lot of time with the various tasks one must undertake when designing such an instrument. Furthermore, the scale has normally been tested for reliability and validity. So if you can find a published scale to meet your needs, you should use it, trusting that it will provide the reliability and the validity you need. Some scales cost money to use, but there are a great number that do not. Keep looking until you find the right one.

There are several things you need to do before you seek a published measurement tool. First, you must be keenly aware of your definition of the concept that you are measuring. Second, you should examine the nature of the persons who will reply to the tool; for example, well-educated adults and children in the third grade should have different tools to respond to. Third, you should examine the constraints that you face, such as the amount of time you will have for your study participants to complete the questionnaire. A tool that takes 20 minutes to complete may not be practical if you only have 1 hour weekly with this client for therapy. A fourth consideration is what you plan to do with the results. If you plan to submit your data for publication, you will need to abide by a higher set of standards than if you plan to use the results for agency decision making.

Let's examine these considerations in more detail. You have seen from previous chapters that the key to the selection of the measurement tool is your definition of the variable to be measured. Let's suppose that you have defined the concept of stressor as an event in life that can lead to stress, such as divorce, being fired from a job, the death of a close family member, and so forth. Let's suppose further that you have defined stress as a psychological state exemplified by words such as *tense*, *nervous*, and *uptight* and you have defined the opposite of stress as indicated by words such as *relaxed*, *comfortable*, and so forth. When you seek a scale for measuring stress, would you be looking for one that asks for the extent to which the respondent has had experience of events such as divorce, the death of a friend, or being fired from a job? If you did, you would have a measure of the concept of stressor rather than stress.

If you wanted a tool for measuring knowledge, you would seek tests that look a lot like the tests you have seen in school. This might take the form of a multiple-choice test, or a true/false test. If you want to measure opinions, on the other hand, you would examine tools with items that have options such as (a) *strongly agree*, (b) *agree*, (c) *disagree*, and (d) *strongly disagree*. The measurement of mental health conditions such as depression or anxiety would likely take a different form. This type of measure may ask the respondent to indicate the extent to which he or she feels a certain way. Options might include (a) *I do not feel sad*, (b) *I feel sad a lot of the time*, and (c) *I feel sad so often I cannot stand it*.

You will need to find a measurement device that is appropriate for your study subjects. You should look at the tool for wording to see if there may be problems. Characteristics of the study sample such as age and ethnicity are considerations. Will the items on the scale make sense to them? Will the method for their responses be clear? You will likely find information accompanying the description of the scale that identifies the appropriate audience.

Will you face constraints regarding time? Some scales take 20 to 30 minutes to complete. If you are using a tool for a single client where you are measuring the client at the beginning of each weekly therapy session for 6 weeks, you will not likely consider a scale with 50 items to be appropriate because it will take up too much of the weekly therapy session time. Instead, you would want to use a very simple tool in this situation. Another option, the modification of a published scale, is discussed in the next section of this book.

The previously mentioned work by Corcoran and Fischer (2013) is highly useful because it is rather comprehensive and convenient. Entire scales are included, and they do not cost anything to use for research studies. A sample of scales from that work are listed in Exhibit 13.2, but it is not a comprehensive list; many other scales are also found in this work.

EXHIBIT 13.2

A SAMPLE OF THE SCALES IN THE WORK OF CORCORAN AND FISCHER (2013)

Alcoholism:
Michigan Alcoholism Screening Test (MAST)

Abuse:
Physical Abuse of Partner Scale

Anger:
State-Trait Anger Scale

Anxiety:
Clinical Anxiety Scale
Self-Rating Anxiety Scale
Stressful Situations Questionnaire

Assertiveness:
Assertiveness Scale for Adolescents
Children's Action Tendency Scale

Depression:
Depression Self-Rating Scale (Children)
Geriatric Depression Scale
Center for Epidemiologic Studies
Depression Mood Scale

Eating problems:
Bulimia Test
Compulsive Eating Scale
Eating Attitudes Scale

Family functioning:
Index of Family Relations
Family Awareness Scale

Guilt:
Perceived Guild Index

Health:
Coping Health Inventory for Parents
Hypochondriasis Scale for Institutional
Geriatric Patients
Illness Attitude Scale

Hope:
Hope Index

Loneliness:
Children's Loneliness Questionnaire
Revised UCLA Loneliness Scale

Marital relations:
Index of Marital Satisfaction

Obsessive-compulsive disorder:
Compulsiveness Inventory
Obsessive-Compulsive Scale

Parenting:
Adult-Adolescent Parenting Inventory
Parent–Child Relationship Survey

Peer relations:
Index of Peer Relations

Spouse abuse:
Index of Spouse Abuse

Posttraumatic stress:
Parent Report of Posttraumatic Symptoms
Impact of Event Scale

Problem solving:
Problem Solving Inventory

Satisfaction with life:
Life Satisfaction Index

Self-esteem:
Hare Self-Esteem Scale
Index of Self-Esteem

Social support:
Social Support Index

Stress:
Perceived Stress Scale

Using the Internet to Find a Measurement Tool

The Internet, of course, is a good source for finding a published scale. One option is to enter key words into an Internet search engine in order to find a tool. You will likely run into many results designed to get you to buy something, but if you push through those options, you should find something more in line with what you're looking for, like a book that contains the scale. Keep looking until you are successful.

What If the Published Scale Takes Too Long to Complete?

If an appropriate scale takes too long to complete, you can consider the option of taking a sample of items from this scale as your measurement tool. You should draw the items in a random fashion and report your procedures. In the opinion of this author, you should have a minimum of five items on your scale, and they should represent at least one third of the items on the original scale.

You will likely find that the administration of this modified scale and the administration of the entire scale would generate a rather high correlation, meaning that both versions of the scale are working in a very similar way, so the more extensive version is not necessary. You must, however, explain the nature of your modification in your report of your study. Furthermore, you cannot claim the reliability and validity reports that come with the full scale as the data for your modified scale. You should report both the information that accompanies the full scale and the fact that you have created a modified form of it.

Taking a portion of an existing scale for your own measurement will not work if you plan to publish your results. In that case, you will be expected to use the entire scale, the one with information on reliability and validity. Expectations about other aspects of the study will also be higher, such as the presentation of a knowledge base and the use of more sophisticated statistics. Getting published is a different ball game from doing a study for your agency or your research class.

EVALUATING MEASUREMENT TOOLS

Here are a few questions to ask yourself as you review possible measurement tools:

1. How well does this tool fit with my definition of the variable I am trying to measure?

    a. What does the author say it measures?

    b. What does it look like it measures?

    c. Is it close enough to my definition of the variable?

2. Will it work with my study sample? Will they understand the words or instructions?

3. Will it take too much time for my situation? If so, can it be shortened so that it will be appropriate?

4. Does it have reasonable reliability and validity?

   a. Start with face validity. Does it seem to you that it measures what you want to measure?

   b. Examine the information on reliability and validity. If it has passed the test of any form of reliability or validity (after you have examined it for face validity), you should have confidence that it will work for you, assuming that your study does not need to meet the standards for publication.

5. Do you understand how to administer it and compute the scores?

6. Is the tool sensitive enough to measure the kinds of changes you expect in situations where you are measuring gain?

Some scales are more complicated than others. You will often see scales with items that mean the opposite of what you want to measure, which necessitates the reverse scoring of certain items. For example, on the stress scale used in a previous chapter, you saw items that indicated stress and some that indicated the opposite. For those items that indicated stress, respondents were scored as 3 if they answered *most of the time*, 2 if they answered *often*, 1 if they answered *some of the time,* or 0 if they answered *seldom or never*. But for those items that indicated the opposite of stress, the response *most of the time* was given the lowest score. Other choices followed suit, so that the higher respondents score on this scale, the more they have indicated that they are stressed.

When you conduct evaluative research, you will measure client progress in some way. What level of progress can you expect to achieve given the nature of your intervention? You should select an outcome and a related measurement tool that is sensitive to change in this context. If your intervention is brief, you should be realistic about the level of measured change you can expect. You can expect knowledge to change in short periods of training, but depression is likely to require many treatment sessions for notable change to occur.

TIPS FOR DEVELOPING YOUR OWN MEASUREMENT TOOL

If your search for a published scale is not successful, your task will be to develop your own tool. This process starts with your definition of the variable you wish to measure. Does your definition mostly focus on knowledge, feelings, opinions, behaviors, or attitudes? The format for items on a measurement device should be consistent with the nature of the thing you are measuring. For example, if your objective is to improve the knowledge of teenage mothers on good parenting practices, you would likely use a test that looks a lot like what you have seen in school, with multiple-choice options. However, you would not measure knowledge by giving response options appropriate for opinions, like *strongly agree, agree, disagree*, and *strongly disagree*. These options are suitable for measuring opinions, not knowledge.

When you are constructing the items for your measurement tool, you should be attentive to a number of suggestions. Here is a set of suggestions from Grinnell and Unrau (2014):

1. Make questions clear.

2. Keep sensitive questions to a minimum.

3. Avoid socially desirable responses.

4. Use only relevant questions.

5. Use simple language.

6. Ask questions the respondents are qualified to answer.

7. Avoid double-barreled questions.

8. Avoid negative questions.

9. Keep questions short.

10. Use items that have options that are mutually exclusive.

11. Use items that have options that are exhaustive.

12. Pretest the instrument.

To achieve clarity, you should think of the different ways in which study subjects might interpret the question. For example, when you ask if the respondent has been feeling a certain way, do you mean presently or at any point in time? Also, be sure to avoid jargon or the use of acronyms. Keep sensitive questions to a minimum, and place them toward the end of the tool rather than at the beginning. This is especially important if you are asking about the respondent's past incidents of crime or unsafe behavior with others. You have recently reviewed the nature of the social desirability bias, so you know to avoid questions that might solicit such a response.

Many of the suggestions on this list are easy to understand, such as keeping questions simple, asking only relevant questions, and keeping questions short. However, you may not know what a **double-barreled question** is. These are questions that pose two separate opinions in one question while asking for an overall agreement or disagreement with the question. For example, you should not have a question like "Do you agree that the Supreme Court has made good decisions and can be trusted?" A person could agree with one part of the question (made good decisions) but disagree with the other (can be trusted). If you need both pieces of information, you should pose two questions here.

Another suggestion is to avoid negative questions. Here is an example of a negative phrase you should not put before your respondents: "The federal government should not give welfare benefits to people who were not born in the United States." Instead, find a way to make it positive, like "The Federal Government should give welfare benefits to all eligible people living here." You may have caught that the first statement actually had a double negative, with two instances of the word *not*, which is worse than a single negative.

Before you employ your tool in a study, you should pretest it by giving it to a sample group of people to see how they respond. You might give it to your fellow students or members of a social club. If possible, you should use it with people who are similar to the ones who will be in your study. Then ask the respondents to give you their evaluations of the tool. Look over the results for anything unexpected, like finding that every single person in your pretest sample answered a given question in exactly the same way, preventing this tool from measuring a variable (if all answers are the same, you do not have a measured variable).

Keep the questionnaire simple and short. Do not put items in the questionnaire that you do not have plans to use. It is easy to start developing a questionnaire with a multitude of questions about a person's characteristics, such as gender, age, race, and political party affiliation. Take time to ask yourself if you will be using this information in your study. Don't yield to the temptation of putting questions on a questionnaire because you are "just curious." The longer the questionnaire, the more likely potential respondents will fail to complete it.

The options for a question should be both mutually exclusive and exhaustive. If they are mutually exclusive, the options do not overlap; if they are exhaustive, they include all possible categories. Consider this question:

What is your age? __ 0–30 __ 30–40 __ 40–50 __ 50– 60?

You may have noticed that someone who is 30 years of age would have two different appropriate options, as would someone who is 40 or 50 years of age. This means that the options on this question are not mutually exclusive. You may have also noticed that there is no place for someone to indicate that they are 61 years of age or older. This means that the question fails to be exhaustive. If it is exhaustive, it will have a category for everyone.

COMPUTING THE SCORE FOR YOUR SCALE

You will find instructions for the computation of the score for your scale in the article that describes the scale. Usually, the instructions are not very difficult to understand. You will take each questionnaire and compute a score for each of the variables in your study. Each study subject will have a score for each variable that you measure at the interval level. Each item of the scale will have points assigned in order of the severity of the response, with higher scores normally representing a higher level of the condition you are measuring. For example, if you have higher self-esteem than John, you will receive a higher score than John on the Hare Self-Esteem Scale, because this scale gives higher scores for higher self-esteem. However, some scales operate in the opposite fashion, in that higher scores represent a lower level of the condition. Therefore, you should pay attention to this fact when you read the description of how to score the scale.

Your biggest challenge will likely be the reverse scoring of items. Items that are to be reverse scored are ones that are stated in a different direction from those items that will not be reversed. You can find an example of reverse scoring in the Hare Self-Esteem Scale. The instructions for this scale tell you to reverse score negatively worded items, where some items are positive and others are negative. An example of a positive statement is "I have at least as many friends as other people my age." An example of a negative statement is "I am not as popular as other people my age."

When an item is positive on this scale, you will assign the following scores:

1. A response of *strongly disagree* gets a score of 1.

2. A response of *disagree* gets a score of 2.

3. A response of *agree* gets a score of 3.

4. A response of *strongly agree* gets a score of 4.

However, when an item is negative, you will reverse the scores as follows:

1. A response of *strongly disagree* gets a score of 4.

2. A response of *disagree* gets a score of 3.

3. A response of *agree* gets a score of 2.

4. A response of *strongly agree* gets a score of 1.

You can see from the above instructions that in both cases the response indicating the highest level of self-esteem gets the highest score.

Always be sure to determine whether a higher score on your scale represents more of the target behavior or less. This is especially important when you are examining a correlation coefficient. If higher scores represent more negative conditions for your target behavior, you would normally expect to find a negative correlation between scores for this variable and other variables where higher scores represent positive behavior.

DESCRIBING YOUR MEASUREMENT TOOL

You will need to describe your measurement tool when you give your report about your research study. In this description, you need to clarify what higher scores represent. You also need to describe the nature of the items on the scale and define the variable that you are measuring. It is also helpful to include one or two items on the scale that give the reader a clearer idea of your measurement.

Typically, you will describe the phenomenon you are measuring along with your description of the scale. For example, you will see the following information on the Hare Self-Esteem Scale in the book by Corcoran and Fischer (2013).

- The Hare Self-Esteem Scale measures self-esteem in schoolchildren who are 10 years of age or older.

- The Hare Self-Esteem Scale is a 30-item instrument that consists of three subscales: (1) peer, (2) school, and (3) home. These dimensions of self-esteem represent the three main areas of interaction whereby a child develops a sense of self-worth.

- The Hare Self-Esteem Scale was tested on 248 students in the fifth and eighth grades, both boys and girls, and including both African Americans and Caucasians.

- The scoring entails the reverse scoring of negatively worded items and summing the scores using the following scores: a = 1, b = 2, c = 3, d = 4. Thus, higher scores represent higher self-esteem. Because there are 30 items on this scale, each of which can generate a score from 1 to 4, the total score for the scale can range from 30 to 120.

- This scale was tested for reliability using the test–retest method, where the correlation of the two scores was found to be .74. It was tested for validity through a comparison with two other scales designed to measure self-esteem, with the results indicating excellent validity.

- The primary reference for this scale is Hare (1985).

In some scales, you will see that the items are organized into categories that represent the dimensions of the scale. For the Hare Self-Esteem Scale, these dimensions include (a) peer self-esteem, (b) home self-esteem, and (c) school self-esteem. As you can probably guess, each of these categories represents self-esteem as viewed from each of these perspectives. It is possible that a child has higher self-esteem about peers than about the home or about school. If this is important to your study, you could calculate different scores for each of these dimensions of self-esteem.

Here is an example of one way to report on the Hare Self-Esteem Scale:

The Hare Self-Esteem Scale (Corcoran & Fischer, 2013) was employed to measure self-esteem for our study subjects. This scale measures self-esteem in children 10 years of age or above. It measures three dimensions of self-esteem: (1) peer self-esteem, (2) home self-esteem, and (3) school self-esteem. The items on this scale are consistent with the definition of self-esteem used in this study. For example, one of the peer self-esteem items is as follows: "I have at least as many friends as other people my age." An item on measuring home self-esteem is "My parents are proud of the kind of person I am." This scale has 30 items, each of which is scored on a 4-point scale with higher scores representing higher self-esteem. Scores can possibly range from 30 to 120. This scale has been subjected to tests of reliability and validity with positive results. For example, test–retest reliability for the scale was found to have a correlation of .74, while scores on this scale were found to have a correlation of .83 with scores on another scale of self-esteem.

DETERMINING PRACTICAL SIGNIFICANCE WITH YOUR MEASUREMENT METHOD

When you examine your data, you will address two issues: (1) statistical significance and (2) practical significance. As you have seen, statistical significance refers to the likelihood that your data can be explained by chance. If it can be explained by chance, you cannot conclude that your hypothesis was supported. The other issue is **practical significance**, which refers to whether the data had sufficient magnitude to be meaningful. You determine magnitude by examining the extent of the client gain, the extent of the difference between the groups being compared, or the strength of the correlation. Each of these items answers the question of *how much*. If your data are of practical significance, you would say that the difference was good enough to meet your expectations. However, practical significance is not relevant to the question of whether the data supported the study hypothesis—that is an issue addressed only by statistical significance and whether your data went in the hypothesized direction.

Once you have a measurement device for your study variable, you should examine it for indicators of magnitude. Is there a percentage that can guide this decision? Is a 30% gain for a group of clients good enough? Is there a threshold that can be useful? You might, for example, have a depression scale where the authors have decided that a certain range of scores represents a certain level of depression. You could consider each of these levels to be a different threshold of functioning. Perhaps you will decide that if your treated clients have moved from a low threshold to a higher one, you have achieved practical significance.

Another method of examining the tool for practical significance is to examine what the scores for the items mean. Suppose, for example, that you are measuring marital stability and you ask the client to check each of the following things they have experienced in the past 3 months: (a) being separated and getting back together, (b) having a fight that was physical, (c) having a fight that led to police action, (d) being evicted from the home, and (e) losing a job because of marital trouble. You can see that each item on this scale is noteworthy. The presence or absence of each of these things is quite important. You might therefore conclude that a change in score of 1 or 2 points is of practical significance.

SPECIAL CHALLENGES OF THE SINGLE-SUBJECT RESEARCH STUDY

With group research, you normally measure a group of clients once before service begins and again at the end of treatment. Another group option is to measure progress for your group of clients and use the same measure for a comparison group of people who did not receive the service. You would then compare the gains of each group to see if the treatment group did better than the comparison group. When you are conducting single-subject research, on the other hand, you will measure a single client repeatedly throughout the treatment period. You cannot measure a single client just once before treatment begins and again at the end of treatment and subject these two scores to statistical analysis, because you need several recordings of data for proper statistical analysis.

There are special challenges with the single-subject research study. The most prominent one is that you will likely not find it feasible to administer a complex published scale at the beginning of each treatment session if it takes 20 minutes to complete the scale. In fact, you might find that even a 10-minute time period is not feasible because it still takes too much of the time available for treatment.

So what do you do? The solution is to select a simple tool. If you cannot find a simple published scale, you can design your own tool. Another option is to select a small, **random sample** of items on a published scale to use as your tool—a scale that would normally take 10 minutes to complete might only take 3 minutes in its modified form.

Another challenge with the single-subject study is that you may find that your single client expresses an array of target behaviors, not just one. If depression is only one of five target behaviors that the client exhibits, measuring depression will give you only a small amount of outcome data.

INDIVIDUALIZED SCALES AS AN OPTION

Sometimes the published scales do not address the unique outcomes that a client needs to achieve. There are two options for meeting this challenge that you will review here: (1) the use of the Outcome Rating Scale (ORS) and (2) the use of the YES scale. Each of these is simple, and you can use them with any client. Neither option identifies a specific behavior to be evaluated. Instead, both give the client much flexibility in expressing their perceptions on how well things have gone in their lives. There is also the Session Rating Scale (SRS), which shows the client's perceptions of the conduct of the treatment sessions without reference to outcome.

The Outcome Rating Scale and the Session Rating Scale

The ORS measures the client's perceptions of how his or her life has been going individually (personal well-being), interpersonally (family, close relationships), socially (work, school, friendships), and overall (general sense of well-being) (Duncan & Miller, 2017). You ask the clients to look over the past week and rate how well they have been doing with regard to these four dimensions of life. You ask them to mark where they are on a line. The line has no anchor points showing what each place on the line represents; instead, it has a negative end and a positive end. Marks to the left represent negative feelings, while marks to the right represent positive ones. You compute the client's score based on the length of the line from the negative end to the place that the client has marked, using a ruler to compute the score for each measurement. You can submit your data to the authors of the SRS or the ORS (Miller, 2017). Otherwise, you can obtain a copy of the ORS or the SRS by simply entering the names of the scales into an Internet search engine—one of the results will provide you with a copy of the scale.

The SRS gives the client the opportunity to show how he or she feels about the treatment sessions. Clients are asked to mark a point on the same type of scale as the ORS, except that in this case each end of the line has an anchor point description. There are four categories on this scale:

1. Being heard, understood, and respected

2. Working on the things the client wanted to work on

3. The approach the therapist was taking

4. How the session went overall

Each end of the line for the client's rating mark is a statement related to one of the above, with a negative statement at one end (e.g., We did not work on or talk about what I wanted to work on or talk about) and a positive statement at the other end (e.g., We worked on and talked about what I wanted to work on and talk about).

You will see an elaboration of the ideas of the ORS and the SRS in Exhibit 13.3. Here, you can see a description of these scales in the words of the scales' authors. If you choose not to sign up for the service provided by these authors, you may find it difficult to score the client. In that case, perhaps you could develop your own version of the scale with numbers

EXHIBIT 13.3

THE SESSION RATING SCALE AS A MECHANISM FOR MONITORING THE THERAPEUTIC RELATIONSHIP

Miller, Duncan, Brown, Sparks, and Claud (2003) developed the SRS as a means for seeing how therapy sessions are progressing in the eyes of the client. The scale is completed by the client at the end of each therapy session. It does not focus on the outcome but on the nature of the session and how the client views it. This exhibit provides information from Duncan and Miller. References to the "alliance" in this work mean the relationship between the client and the therapist.

The following is a quote from this website: https://www.psychotherapy.net/article/therapy -effectiveness

Research shows repeatedly that clients' ratings of the alliance are far more predictive of improvement than the type of intervention or the therapist's ratings of the alliance. Recognizing these much-replicated findings, we developed the *Session Rating Scale* (SRS) as a brief clinical alternative to longer research-based alliance measures to encourage routine conversations with clients about the alliance. The SRS also contains four items. First, a relationship scale rates the meeting on a continuum from *"I did not feel heard, understood, and respected"* to *"I felt heard, understood, and respected."* Second is a goals and topics scale that rates the conversation on a continuum from *"We did not work on or talk about what I wanted to work on or talk about"* to *"We worked on or talked about what I wanted to work on or talk about."* Third is an approach or method scale (an indication of a match with the client's theory of change) requiring the client to rate the meeting on a continuum from *"The approach is not a good*

fit for me" to *"The approach is a good fit for me."* Finally, the fourth scale looks at how the client perceives the encounter in total along the continuum: *"There was something missing in the session today"* to *"Overall, today's session was right for me."*

The SRS simply translates what is known about the alliance into four visual analog scales, with instructions to place a mark on a line, where negative responses are depicted on the left and positive responses are indicated on the right. The SRS allows alliance feedback in real time so that problems may be addressed. Like the ORS, the instrument takes less than a minute to administer and score. The SRS is scored similarly as the ORS, by adding the total of the client's marks on the four 10-cm lines. The total score falls into three categories:

- SRS score between 0 and 34 reflects a poor alliance
- SRS score between 35 and 38 reflects a fair alliance
- SRS score between 39 and 40 reflects a good alliance

The SRS allows the implementation of the final lesson of the supershrinks: *seek, obtain, and maintain more consumer engagement.* Most clients drop out of therapy for one of two reasons: (1) either the therapy is not helping (hence monitoring outcome) or (2) there is an alliance problem—the clients are not engaged or turned on by the process. The most direct way to improve your effectiveness is simply to keep them engaged in therapy.

from 1 (negative end of each continuum) to 10 (positive end of the continuum.). Another option is to do what the authors do and measure the length of the line in centimeters.

One of the limitations of the SRS and the ORS is that they do not allow clients a great range of self-expression in describing the outcomes they seek. On these scales, each client is asked to rate how things are going with regard to the four dimensions specified on the scale, not in their own words. The YES scale, however, does use the words of the client.

The YES Scale

The YES scale asks the client to describe in his or her own words the outcomes being sought. These outcomes might include "feeling like getting up in the morning and going to work," "not yelling at my child when we talk about homework," or "attending all of the AA meetings." The clients list their desired outcomes and then rate their lives with regard to each outcome on a regular basis using a 10-point scale. The YES scale is presented in Exhibit 13.4.

EXHIBIT 13.4
THE YES SCALE

Your Evaluation of Service

This form is designed to receive your feedback on how well things are going for you with regard to the outcomes you would like to achieve from the service you are receiving. Your first task is to list the outcomes below:

Outcomes You Would Like to Achieve

1

2

3

4

5

Ask yourself how well things have gone for you (in the designated time period) with regard to each of the above outcomes. If things have gone miserably, you would circle Number 1. If things have gone only a little better than that, you would circle Number 2, and so forth, all the way up to a score of 10 if things have gone extremely well with regard to the designated outcome.

Objective 1	*Miserably* 1......2......3......4......5......6......7......8......9......10	*Extremely well*
Objective 2	*Miserably* 1......2......3......4......5......6......7......8......9......10	*Extremely well*
Objective 3	*Miserably* 1......2......3......4......5......6......7......8......9......10	*Extremely well*
Objective 4	*Miserably* 1......2......3......4......5......6......7......8......9......10	*Extremely well*
Objective 5	*Miserably* 1......2......3......4......5......6......7......8......9......10	*Extremely well*

Your first step in the use of the YES scale is to see if the client likes this idea. You will explain how the scale works and show the client a copy of it. Your second step, assuming that the client would like to use the scale, is to get the client to articulate his or her desired outcomes. You could also get the client to think of how to describe each end of the continuum. For example, if the outcome is to be more positive when talking with your son, the most negative end of the continuum might be that the client was very negative all the time, while the positive end might be that the client was never negative.

If the client is oriented to further development of the scale, you could ask for descriptions of the middle points on the scale as well. Middle points might indicate that the client was slightly more positive than negative or slightly more negative than positive.

Determining the time frame of each evaluation would be the third step in the process. If you are meeting with the client once a week, then the past week would be the logical time frame for the client's use of the scale. In other words, the client would reflect on how things have gone specifically in the past week when completing the scale.

Now the client is ready to use the scale at the beginning of each treatment session. He or she will complete the scale, and you may find the review of the scores from past weeks to be a useful point of discussion in a treatment session.

Chapter Practice Exercises

Practice Exercises on Measurement

You have seen that measurement in social work research refers to the selection of a means for measuring each of your study variables. The selection process requires an understanding of a number of concepts and resources, starting with your definition of the variable to be measured. Once you define your variable, you will first seek a published scale. If you cannot find a suitable scale, you will design your own tool for measurement. Next, before you analyze your data with your chosen measurement tool, you need to decide on what change in scores would represent practical significance (if you are using this scale for evaluative research).

In Practice Exercise 1, you will find a tool to measure the concept of alcoholism. You begin by securing a definition of this target behavior and finding a measurement tool that is consistent with this definition. You will then describe the selected tool in a manner suggested by the content of this chapter. You will also be asked to determine the amount of gain for clients on this tool that would be considered to be of practical significance after eight outpatient therapy sessions.

In Practice Exercise 2, you will select a tool for measuring client progress for a familiar intervention, preferably one with which you have had some experience. You will define the target behavior to be measured, secure a published scale for measuring it, and discuss what level of gain on this scale will constitute practical significance.

Practice Exercise 1: Finding a Tool to Measure Alcoholism

In this exercise, you will find a tool for measuring alcoholism. You will begin this process by developing a definition of this concept. Use the literature (and the Internet) for guidance on these tasks. Prepare a report that answers each of the following questions:

1. What is your definition of alcoholism?

2. Explain where you found guidance in the development of your definition. List the references that were helpful.

3. What measurement tool did you find for measuring alcoholism? How would you describe the structure of this tool? Give the source where you found this tool.

4. Explain where you found guidance in finding your measurement tool.

5. How much of a gain in pretest and posttest scores would you expect to find to conclude that practical significance has been achieved? Assume that the treatment has eight hour-long therapy sessions and four hour-long group therapy sessions. Identify the amount of gain (e.g., 8 points on the scale), along with the rationale for declaring that a certain amount of gain would constitute practical significance.

Practice Exercise 2: Finding a Tool for Measuring Your Clients' Progress

In this practice exercise, you will select a scale for measuring the progress of your clients on the objective being pursued. This exercise is only suitable for examples where you will be measuring some psychosocial variable such as depression, anxiety, or marital satisfaction. It is not appropriate if your target behavior can be measured by concrete agency records, such as school grades, whether the client showed up for an appointment, or whether the patient was readmitted to the hospital. It must be a scale that generates a score where the variable is measured at the interval level.

If your objective is to improve self-esteem, you will select a self-esteem scale. But if it is related to self-confidence, you would select a tool for measuring self-confidence, taking into consideration the differences between self-esteem and self-confidence. Your task, of course, will begin with your definition of the behavior to be measured.

You will prepare a report that answers the following questions:

1. What is the service you are evaluating?
   a. What is the objective of this service?
   b. What is the structure of this service?

2. What are the label and definition of the target behavior that is to be measured?

3. How would you describe the scale you will use to measure the target behavior?
   a. What is the name of the scale?
   b. How is the scale described in the literature with regard to what it measures and how?
   c. What are a few of the items on the scale?
   d. What is the range of scores that a person can get on this scale?
   e. Is there a set of suggested thresholds showing levels of the condition that is being measured (e.g., severe depression, mild depression, no depression)?
   f. What information is provided in the literature regarding the testing of the reliability or the validity of this scale?

4. What is the gain in functioning on your selected scale that would constitute practical significance? Explain.

CHAPTER REVIEW

Chapter Key Learnings

1. Effective measurement helps us get an objective picture of our variables and helps us achieve credibility with others in the reporting of our results. If you reveal objective data, you will be more likely to be heard.

2. Effective measurement requires attention to the reduction of measurement error, which is the distance between the data you have and the truth about the concept you are trying to measure. You reduce measurement error by demonstrating the reliability (consistency) and validity (accuracy) of the tools you are using for measurement.

3. You must understand the level of measurement of the variables in your study hypothesis to select an appropriate statistic for testing that hypothesis.

4. The chief mechanism for measurement in evaluation research is the standardized scale, where you give all study subjects the same instrument. Examples include the Beck Depression Inventory and the Hare Self-Esteem Scale.

5. You might use an individualized scale because you failed to find an appropriate standardized scale. Individualized scales are tailored for each client.

6. You evaluate the reliability and the validity of measurement tools in quantitative research by quantitative analysis of data regarding the tools you are using. These issues can be addressed in qualitative research by reviewing consistency among different observers and by having the study subjects review the results.

7. Finding a published scale for measuring your study variables is preferable to developing your own scale because the published scale has been developed by an expert on the concept being measured, who would have already tested the scale for reliability and validity.

8. Effective measurement requires a good definition of the study variable as well as congruence between the definition of the concept being measured and the tool that is measuring it.

9. When you need to develop your own scale, it can be helpful to review existing scales that measure concepts close to the one your scale will measure.

10. When you are developing your own measurement tool, you should be cognizant of the nature of the concepts you are measuring. For example, you will measure knowledge by test questions, you will measure opinions by items that ask about the degree of agreement one has about selected ideas, and you will measure psychological conditions with items that ask for the degree to which one has experienced certain feelings or thoughts.

11. In your description of your measurement tool, you will identify the name of the scale, give a careful definition of the concept being measured, provide information on the reliability and the validity of the tool, describe what the tool looks like, and report on how it is scored. There should be sufficient information from this description for the reader to assess the change in scores required for practical significance.

Chapter Discussion Questions

1. Under what circumstances would you likely use a standardized scale for measuring a study variable rather than an individualized one?

2. Under what circumstances would you likely use an individualized scale for measuring a study variable rather than a standardized one?

3. Describe the situation where the YES scale or the ORS would be most appropriate.

4. Explain why a scale can be reliable without being valid but a scale cannot be valid without being reliable.

5. Is Cronbach's alpha useful for the testing of reliability or validity? Explain.

6. Explain how your data might achieve statistical significant but not practical significance.

7. What is one tip for developing your own scale that you found helpful?

8. Review the description of the Hare Self-Esteem Scale under the section on describing your measurement tool. Did you find this description to be helpful? Do you have any suggestions about it?

Chapter Test

1. Which of the following is/are true?
   a. An example of measurement error is the distance between a person's score on a test (e.g., 80% correct) and the level of knowledge possessed by the person on the subject of the test (e.g., 90%)
   b. There are at least two types of measurement error—systematic error and random error
   c. Both of the above
   d. None of the above

2. Which of the following is/are true?
   a. Reliability refers to the accuracy of an instrument for measuring a study variable
   b. Validity refers to the consistency of an instrument for measuring a study variable
   c. Both of the above
   d. None of the above

3. Which of the following is/are true?
   a. A measurement tool can be reliable without being valid
   b. A measurement tool can be valid without being reliable
   c. Both of the above
   d. None of the above

4. Which of the following is/are true?
   a. Content validity refers to the extent to which a measurement tool is internally consistent
   b. Internal consistency can be evaluated with the employment of the alpha coefficient
   c. Both of the above
   d. None of the above

5. Which of the following is/are true?
   a. Because practical significance is a matter of opinion, the researcher does not need to explain why he or she came to the

conclusion that practical significance was achieved

b. Measurement tools should include items that elicit a socially desirable response

c. Both of the above

d. None of the above

6. What is the level of measurement of the following item on a questionnaire:

What is your gender? __ Male __ Female

a. Nominal

b. Ordinal

c. Interval

d. Consistent

7. When you compute a correlation between the score on your scale for measuring self-esteem with another scale designed to measure self-esteem, you would expect to find which of the following?

a. No correlation between the scores on the two scales

b. A positive correlation between the scores on the two scales

c. A negative correlation between the scores on the two scales

d. A curvilinear correlation between the scores on the two scales

8. Which of the following are advantages of using a published scale rather than developing your own scale to measure depression?

a. If it has been designed by an expert on depression

b. If it has typically been tested for reliability and validity

c. Both of the above

d. None of the above

9. What is the weakness of the following item on a questionnaire?

What is your age? __ 0–30 __ 30–40 __ 40–50

a. The options are not exhaustive

b. The options are not mutually exclusive

c. Both of the above

d. None of the above

10. Which of the following is *not* a thing you should do for a scale that you have designed yourself?

a. Keep sensitive questions to a minimum

b. Keep questions short

c. Pretest the scale

d. None of the above—that is, all should be done

ANSWERS: 1 = c; 2 = d; 3 = a; 4 = b; 5 = d; 6 = a; 7 = b; 8 = c; 9 = c; 10 = d

Chapter Glossary

Content validity. The extent to which a measurement tool includes all the dimensions of the defined variable.

Criterion validity. The extent to which a given scale achieves the same results as another method of measuring the same thing. If the ratings for depression among a group of clients by clinical social workers correlate positively with the scores given to these same people using your depression scale, you have evidence of criterion validity for your depression scale.

Cronbach's alpha. A coefficient that indicates the internal consistency of a scale by examining the correlations of different items with one another.

Double-barreled question. An item on a questionnaire that contains more than one issue but asks for only one answer.

Face validity. The extent to which a measurement tool appears to measure the intended variable in the opinion of knowledgeable people.

Internal consistency reliability. The extent to which a measurement tool contains items that are reasonably correlated with one another.

Measurement error. The distance between the reality of the variable under study and the value measured by an instrument designed to measure it.

Practical significance. The extent to which data results from a scientific study provide sufficient magnitude to be of practical utility. For example, you might ask, "Did the clients gain enough relief from their anxiety to suggest that the treatment was worthwhile, given its costs?"

Random error. Error in measurement that cannot be predicted.

Random sample. A study sample drawn from the study population on a random basis.

Reliability. The extent to which a measurement tool is consistent.

Social desirability bias. The tendency for some people to answer a question in a way that is socially desirable rather than saying what they really believe.

Systematic error. A form of measurement error that can be predicted, such as error based on the social desirability bias.

Test–retest reliability. The extent to which a measurement tool is consistent when applied to the same group of people at different times.

Validity. The extent to which a measurement tool is accurate.

14

SELECTING A RESEARCH DESIGN FOR A GROUP EVALUATION STUDY

Janet is a social worker employed by the Jump Ahead Program of Henderson County. This program is designed to help disadvantaged preschool children catch up with more advantaged children so that they are better prepared for kindergarten. The 38 four-year-old children in her program will enter kindergarten in 1 year. She will work with this group once per week for the year. The Jump Ahead Program includes a series of educational activities designed to improve readiness for kindergarten. One of the measures to be undertaken in the evaluation of this program is a test of reading readiness, which will be administered once at the beginning of the treatment year and once again at the end of this year of service. It is expected that reading readiness will be better at the end of the year because the Jump Ahead Program has exercises designed to improve it.

Janet faced the decision of what research design to employ for her study. She realized that she was engaged in a study that would employ a group research design rather than a single-subject design because she was going to measure client progress for 38 clients, not just one. She examined the issue of causation in her review of different research designs because she realized that some research designs do a better job of addressing causation than others. If she only measured her 38 clients before and after treatment, she will have no basis for asserting that these clients would not have gotten better on their own, without the help of the services of Jump Ahead. She would have a measure of their growth but would not have a scientific basis for asserting that it was the services of her program that should be given credit for this growth. Maybe they just grew over time in a normal way and did not need the special help of her program.

A critical question is whether her situation reveals a need for addressing other causes of client gain. Is it likely that a group of 4-year-old children will improve on their reading readiness in a 1-year period of time without the help of the Jump Ahead Program? Do children of this age normally improve their readiness for kindergarten in a year without special help? If so, Janet would need a research design that includes a comparison of her clients with a group of similar people who have not received the services of the Jump Ahead Program. The growth of the comparison group could be used as a measure of normal growth over time. If Janet compared the growth of her 38 clients with those in the comparison group, she would have a scientific basis for asserting that the difference between the improvement of her clients and the improvement of those in the comparison group was caused by the Jump Ahead program.

Janet decided that it is likely that 4-year-old children would improve in a year without special help. They experience many things in life over a year that could be of benefit to their reading readiness. They will observe people reading and will get ideas about where you start when you read something and that you read from left to right rather than from right to left. If her program lasted only a week, she would not need to be concerned with growth over time as a cause of client growth because this is such a short period of time that very little growth would be expected. So she decided that she needed to use the comparison group design for her study. She found a group of disadvantaged 4-year olds who do not have a special service like Jump Ahead, and she administered the reading readiness scale to that group at the beginning and at the end of the service year. She compared the growth of this comparison group with the growth of her clients. She found that her clients had better growth than the comparison group that was statistically significant.

INTRODUCTION

You will note that Janet had engaged in several tasks before she encountered the decision of what research design to employ. She had chosen her target behavior (kindergarten readiness), her program (Jump Ahead), her study sample (38 children currently served), and a measure of client progress (a scale to measure reading readiness). She selected her research design based on her analysis of the theme of **causation**. She chose a design that would include a comparison group because she believed that normal growth over time was a reasonable explanation for client gain on reading readiness when the time period was 1 year. She would expect that 4-year-olds would normally improve on this target behavior over a year without treatment. The growth measured for the comparison group would be a measure of the effect of normal development over time. Because her client group did better than the comparison group, she had evidence to support the conclusion that the program caused her client's gain, not normal growth over time.

The choice of a research design deals with the issue of causation in evaluative research. If your study employs a better research design than a study by someone else, you are in a better position to claim that it was your treatment that caused the measured client gain. Better research designs control for various alternative explanations for client growth such as normal growth over time, changes in the client's environment, and so forth. Your critical question is whether it was your services that caused the measured client growth.

Your **research design** identifies the structure whereby you will collect data and offer services. One such design calls on you to measure clients once before treatment begins and once after services have been offered and to measure client growth by comparing the two measurements. Another design requires a comparison group where growth is measured both for the group that did not receive your services and for the client group that did have the advantage of your treatment. In this situation, you compare the measured growth of the two groups. There are a number of additional designs that will be reviewed in this chapter. For each design, you will see the alternative explanations for client growth that are controlled by the structure of the design. The first task, however, is for you to decide on what alternative explanations for client growth would be expected in your situation. Often you will conclude that the short time period for your treatment suggests that alternative explanations are not likely to occur, so a simple design is appropriate for your research needs.

In this chapter, you will examine a number of **group research designs** along with a set of guides for selecting a design that meets your needs. In the next chapter, you will examine single-subject research designs for the evaluation of services for a single client. The various causes of client growth independent of treatment are known as **threats to internal validity**. You will examine a number of such threats with emphasis on two—(1) growth over time and (2) changes in the environment.

At the completion of this chapter, you will be able to do the following:

1. Explain the theme of causation in social work research, with particular attention to its importance in the selection of the research design for an evaluative study.

2. Distinguish between a group research design and a single-subject research design.

3. Describe the various threats to internal validity.

4. Identify which threats to internal validity should be of special concern in your specific evaluative study.

5. Describe various group research designs such as the one-group posttest-only design, the one-group pretest–posttest design, the comparison group design, the

alternative treatment design, the **basic experimental design**, the **posttest-only control group design**, and the Solomon four-group design.

6. Identify the threats to internal validity that are addressed by each group research design.

THE NATURE OF CAUSATION IN RESEARCH

A cause is something that determines the effect. We expect that our treatment determines the clients' improvement in the target behavior. But we also know that there are other potential causes. There are three bases for determining causality. To make a firm case for causation, you should be able to answer each of the following questions:

1. Is there a relationship between the cause and the effect?

2. Did a change in the cause precede a change in the effect?

3. Are there alternative causes that do a better job of explaining the effect?

You can answer the first question with the comparison group design whereby you are comparing the growth of the clients with the growth of those in the comparison group. You examine whether there is a relationship between being treated and obtaining growth on the target behavior. If there is a difference between the two groups that favors the treatment group, you have evidence of causality.

You could answer the second question by measuring the client's target behavior over a period of time before treatment begins and then measuring growth during the treatment period. This would test whether a change in the treatment (from not being treated to being treated) preceded a change in the target behavior. If the growth during the treatment period was superior to the growth during the pretreatment period, you would have evidence of causation. This condition is common for various single-subject research designs, addressed in the next chapter, but not with typical group designs. But you could engage in this activity as a test of causation. That procedure, however, will not be discussed further in this chapter.

The research design addresses the third question very clearly. If normal growth is believed to be an alternative cause of the target behavior, the comparison group design (and several of the other designs) will help you answer this third question.

THREATS TO INTERNAL VALIDITY

There are a number of alternative causes for client growth that we will refer to as threats to internal validity. You have seen illustrations of normal growth over time as one example. The term for this alternative cause is *maturation*. People normally grow over time on their own without treatment. Is this the cause of your clients' measured growth, rather than the treatment? That is the key question addressed by the research design that you employ.

Another threat is labeled history. This threat refers to changes in the client's environment, such as getting a job for an unemployed person, getting a divorce from an unhappy marriage, losing a job, or experiencing the death of a loved one. The environment can change the clients for the better or the worse. And these changes may be the cause of the client's gain, rather than the treatment.

Maturation and history are the two threats of most importance to the social worker or social work student because they are the ones most likely to occur and to be controlled by the choice of a research design. Additional threats to internal validity are described in Exhibit 14.1.

EXHIBIT 14.1
ADDITIONAL THREATS TO INTERNAL VALIDITY

Two threats to internal validity are discussed in the body of this text. Here are some additional ones.

Testing: This refers to the effects of the testing experience itself. Does the fact that I have been tested on my self-esteem in the past week affect the way I will respond to this same scale this week? Testing is especially important to consider for examinations of knowledge. I may remember the questions asked on the first exam and be better prepared to respond for that reason alone. Maybe I have had time to think about some of these questions and have realized my mistake on the previous test. The question here is whether my posttest grade is a reflection of my gain in knowledge about the subject of the training or a function of the fact that I remembered the questions from the first test. If it is the former, we have good evaluation data, but if it is the latter, we are in a situation where testing is a threat to internal validity.

Instrumentation: This refers to the validity of the measurement devices employed in the study. If these instruments are not valid measures of the dependent variable, you cannot conclude that the treatment was effective.

Statistical regression: Behaviors at the extreme among humans tend to move toward the mean on repeated measurements. In other words, they regress to the mean. For example, the client in your group who scored the lowest on your depression scale on the pretest is more likely to score higher the next time than would be the case of someone who scored at the mean. Likewise, a person who scored the highest would likely score lower the next time. In both cases, the extreme persons regressed to the mean. This regression is normal and not effected by your treatment. For this reason, it would not be wise for you to select only the clients with the worse scores on the pretest for your treatment. A certain amount of their gain can be assumed to be caused by their normal regression.

Selection bias: If your methods of selecting your study sample were biased in some way, you will have a selection bias. For example, if you selected only the most highly motivated clients for your study, you would have a motivational bias. If your study purpose is to test your treatment for highly motivated clients, you would be okay. You would need to report this in your conclusions. But if your purpose is to test your treatment with all your clients, you would have the weakness of a selection bias.

(Continued)

(Continued)

Reactive effect (placebo effect): Clients sometimes improve simply because they are being included in a study rather than the fact that the specific treatment protocol is effective in achieving progress. Clients may feel special because they are in a study, and this factor may influence their progress.

Mortality: Some clients drop out of treatment before it is complete and are removed from the study. Are these persons different from those who remained?

WHAT THREATS SHOULD BE OF SPECIAL CONCERN IN MY SITUATION?

The question that should begin your decision process is "What threats should be of special concern in my specific situation?" Traditional research literature does not usually address this question very well. This literature seems to assume that all threats are of special concern in all situations. But common sense will dictate otherwise. If you have a group of 15 chronic alcoholics in a 6-week treatment program, why would you be especially concerned that these clients would recover on their own without your treatment? In other words, why would you need to worry about **maturation as a threat to internal validity**? They have experienced problems with alcohol for several years and have not recovered or experienced major improvement. So why would they do this in the next 6 weeks in the absence of treatment. It just does not make sense. In other words, it does not seem logical.

What about **history as a threat to internal validity**? Would you have reason to expect that these clients would have a change in their environments over this 6-week period that would lead to their recovery? They have lived for years without the environment changing them. Why would you have reason to believe that they will have a major change in their environments in the next 6 weeks? Not much! Therefore, in this situation, you should not go out of your way to find a research design that controls for maturation or history as threats to internal validity. Instead, it would be better for you to use such a design, but you should not worry if this type of design is not feasible in your situation.

If a client's social history clearly suggests that she has been clinically depressed for a year without any noticeable change, you might conclude that there is no process of maturation underway with this client. If your treatment period is only 3 months, you may logically conclude that maturation is not a special concern. If, however, you provided parent training for adolescent mothers for a 6-month period, you might conclude that maturation is a special concern. You might conclude that new mothers normally learn lessons about parenting over a 6-month period without special training; thus, changes in parenting skill may be attributed to maturation rather than the treatment. In this situation, you would seek a research design that addresses maturation.

An advantage of this question is that you will often find that it is not feasible for you to use a certain design that addresses a certain threat to internal validity. If this threat should be of special concern but you do not control for it with your design, you will conclude that you have a major limitation in your research method for your study. If you do not need to be concerned with certain threats not controlled by your research design, you do not need to offer this observation.

When we speak of threats that might be of special concern, we are speaking of probabilities, not possibilities. It is, of course, possible that someone may spontaneously recover. You may know of such examples. It is possible that there will be a change in the environment that helps with recovery. But it is not the possibilities that should be our focus. The question is whether these things are probable. Is it likely that these things will happen? Also, it is not important that 1 person in a group of 12 clients had a certain experience that helped. It is important, however, if such an experience was typical of these 12 clients.

TWO GENERAL TYPES OF RESEARCH DESIGNS

There are two major categories of research designs for evaluative research: (1) group designs and (2) single-subject designs. With group designs, you are collecting data on the same variable for a group of clients who are receiving the same service. For example, you may measure self-esteem before treatment and again after treatment for all clients using the Hare Self-Esteem Scale.

With single-subject designs, you are collecting data repeatedly on a single subject. For example, you may measure school grades for your client for four grading periods prior to treatment and for six grading periods during the treatment period. In each type of study, you are using an array of data for statistical analysis. For that reason, there is no such thing as a single-subject design that only measures the single subject once before treatment begins and once at the end of treatment. Two scores as the total data are not adequate for statistical analysis of data. When you collect data for a group of clients before treatment begins and again at the end, you have multitude scores for analysis.

There is a variety of group designs for the evaluation of practice, and there is a variety of single-subject designs. Some group designs call for the measurement of target behavior only for a client group, and some designs have a comparison group. Some single-subject designs call for the repeated measurement of client target behavior before treatment begins, but one design requires only one pretreatment measurement. In all single-subject designs, you must measure client target behavior several times during the treatment period, preferably at least four times.

GROUP RESEARCH DESIGNS

Some texts divide research designs into the categories of preexperimental designs, quasi-experimental designs, and experimental designs. These general categories suggest the level of sophistication of the design in addressing threats to internal validity. The preexperimental design does not address any of the threats to internal validity, while the quasi-experimental design addresses them to some extent. The experimental design does the best job of addressing these threats through the random assignment of persons to treatment and control groups. One practical way to distinguish the quasi-experimental from the experimental designs is that the quasi-experimental group design will typically have a comparison group where the people in it were not assigned to their group status on a random basis, while the experimental design will have the control group that has been assigned on a random basis.

There are two practical questions answered by the research design. First, did the clients improve? Second, to what extent can you attribute the clients' measured growth to the treatment rather than something else? In other words, to what extent can you infer causality? If you only measure the one group of clients at the end of the treatment period, you do not have any evidence of client improvement. If you did not measure client growth, how can you assert that treatment was effective? However, there are some conditions that would suggest that posttest-only data can be used for evaluation, and these conditions will be discussed later.

In the next few sections, you will review the posttest-only research design, the one-group pretest–posttest design, the comparison group design, the basic experimental design, and the posttest-only control group design. In the descriptions of group designs, symbols will be used to designate a given design. The letter O will represent an observation (measurement of client conditions), while the letter X will represent a treatment. The letter R will represent a random assignment of persons to their group status. You can see these symbols in Exhibit 14.2 for the description of the basic experimental design and the one-group pretest–posttest design. In this exhibit, each line represents a group of people. The one-group pretest–posttest design has only one group, so there is nothing in the second line of the table describing it. For the basic experimental design, the first column

EXHIBIT 14.2
SYMBOLS FOR THE RESEARCH DESIGNS

The Basic Experimental Design

Group	Random Assignment of People to Group Status	Pretest Measurement	Treatment	Posttest Measurement
1	R	O_1	X	O_2
2	R	O_1		O_2

The One-Group Pretest–Posttest Design

Group	Random Assignment of People to Group Status	Pretest Measurement	Treatment	Posttest Measurement
1		O_1	X	O_2

shows the letter R for each line because each of the two groups are assigned to their group status on a random basis. You did not see the letter R for the one-group pretest–posttest design because it does not entail the random assignment of people to groups. The symbol O_1 represents a measurement at Time 1 (**pretest**), while the symbol O_2 reveals a **posttest** measurement. For the basic experimental design, you can see that the first group of people have the letter X in the treatment column, while the second group does not. This means that the first group got the treatment and the second group did not.

PREEXPERIMENTAL DESIGNS THAT FAIL TO ADDRESS THREATS TO INTERNAL VALIDITY

Two group research designs will be discussed that fail to address common threats to internal validity—the one-group posttest-only design and the one-group pretest–posttest design. The first of these not only fails to control for threats to internal validity but also fails to measure client growth, so it is the weakest design in our list. With this design, you must have a threshold for the comparison of posttest data. The second one measures client growth but has no mechanisms for controlling for threats to internal validity.

One-Group Posttest-Only Design

When you employ the one-group posttest-only design, you measure client behavior only one time—at the end of the treatment. The symbols for this design are given below.

X O

From these symbols, you can see that there is only one group, that this group does not have a pretest, but that it has a treatment (X) and a measurement (O) following treatment. You may have reason to believe that this is not much of a research design at all. There is no measurement of client growth. You would be correct.

If you have a threshold score for comparison, however, you will be moving toward a reasonable method of measurement but one that is weak nevertheless. Suppose that in the past year your agency has measured many groups of clients on anxiety using a given anxiety scale and found the mean pretest to range from 26.2 to 29.4 with the overall mean pretest for all clients being 28.1. You might employ the figure of 28.1 as your pretest mean and compare this mean with all the scores you have collected at posttest for your current group of clients. You will, of course, apply logic to this analysis. For example, you may have found in the past that a group of clients typically have a mean pretest score for anxiety of approximately 28 and a posttest mean score of about 17. Let us say that you fail to apply a pretest to your group but find a posttreatment mean score of 16.3. Suppose further that a mean score of 28 represents a noticeable amount of anxiety, while a mean of 16 shows much better behavior. And you have observed clinically that this group's demonstrated behavior on anxiety was typical of other groups at the pretest time and was also typical of these other groups at posttest time. As a result, you have data but you also have your clinical observations.

It would be much better, however, for you to collect pretest measurements for each of these clients as well as the posttest scores. In this way, you have data on growth for your specific group of clients. This method, of course, will have much better credibility in your report of your study. Persons representing grant-funding sources for your program will likely expect this form of measurement.

One-Group Pretest–Posttest Design

When you employ the **one-group pretest–posttest design**, you measure client behavior once before treatment begins, you administer a treatment, and you measure client behavior once at the end of treatment using the same device for measurement. The symbolic representation of this design was given in Exhibit 14.2.

Your measurement of client behavior before and after treatment can take many forms. Most likely you will measure client behavior using a scale. One's score on a self-esteem scale or a depression scale would be examples. You would compute a pretest score and a posttest score for each client and subject these data to statistical analysis to see if the mean posttest score is significantly better than the mean pretest score. There are other forms of measurement beside a scale. You could measure the days your client was absent from school during the pretest grading period and the posttest grading period. You could measure whether or not each client was employed at each time period.

With the one-group pretest–posttest design, you have a basis for measuring client progress. This is an advantage over the posttest-only design. With this design, however, you do not have a basis for addressing various threats to internal validity, so its claim to the depiction of causality is weak. For example, you do not have a basis for taking normal growth and development into consideration. You know your clients had a gain in functioning, but you do not know if that gain was due to the treatment or to normal growth over time.

QUASI-EXPERIMENTAL DESIGNS THAT ADDRESS CAUSATION MINIMALLY

None of the preexperimental research designs have a comparison group that could serve as a measure of normal growth over time. The quasi-experimental designs have this advantage. However, these designs do not have the provision of the random assignment of people to the two groups. This means that they address maturation as a threat to internal validity, but they do not do so in an optimal way.

In this section, you will review two quasi-experimental designs: (1) the alternative treatment design and (2) the comparison group design. With the alternative treatment design, you are comparing two or more groups of clients who had different treatments. You want to know which treatment was more effective. With the comparison group design, you have a group that receives your treatment and a group that does not receive your treatment. For both of these designs, you measure growth and compare this growth between the groups.

Alternative Treatment Design

With the alternative treatment design, you use different treatments for different groups of clients. With this design, you measure client gain for each person in each group to see if one group is superior to the other. For example, you might employ medication only for one group of clients and medication plus counseling for a second group of clients. The comparison of the level of gain for these two groups gives you a basis for determining the difference made by the addition of counseling. In another example, you might compare the academic achievement of students in two schools that employ different models of education to see if one model is better. Perhaps you will add a support group service to your existing counseling service for victims of violence and compare the gain for this group with the gain for a group that had only the counseling. With this design, you measure client behavior in the same way for all groups being compared.

With this design, you will first measure gain for each person in each group to see if it was significant. Was the mean posttest score higher than the mean pretest score for each group? Then, you will compare the gain scores for the two groups to see if one group did better. If one is better, you have information for future treatment of this target behavior. A disadvantage for this design is that you have no comparison group of people who had no treatment as a vehicle for estimating the effect of maturation. However, if one of your groups had a significantly better gain than the other, you might argue that the amount of gain for the inferior group is a combination of the effect of maturation and the effect of the treatment for that group. You can argue, therefore, that the superiority of the other group is based both on maturation and the effect of the treatment.

Comparison Group Design

In the **comparison group design (aka nonequivalent control group design)**, a treated group is compared with another group that did not receive the treatment. In the following designation, there are two groups of persons: one is receiving treatment and the other is not receiving treatment.

$$O_1 \quad X \quad O_2$$
$$O_1 \qquad\quad O_2$$

You will also notice the absence of the letter R for these two lines of information. This indicates the absence of the random assignment of people to the two groups.

With this design, you have the basis for measuring client progress and the basis for inferring causality to a limited degree. For example, maturation is addressed with this design because the comparison group should be a basis for estimating the amount of growth that people typically achieve in the absence of treatment.

You will measure gain for each group of people and compare this gain to see if the treatment group did better than the comparison group. Typically, this will entail the measurement of each person in each group at both the pretest time and the posttest time and computing the difference (i.e., gain). Persons from each group will be measured on the same tool. You will compare the gain scores for these two groups.

When you employ an experimental design, you will assign people to their group status on a random basis. This random assignment is believed to control for various threats to internal validity on an optimal basis because random assignment is believed to ensure that the two groups are similar. When you employ the comparison group, you do not have random assignment. Therefore, you could examine whether the two groups are comparable on the basis of important variables such as gender, ethnicity, age, and so forth. The more they are comparable, the better is your claim that your study addressed threats to internal validity. If you know of a basis in which the two groups are not comparable, you should report this fact and your claim for causality will be weakened.

According to Campbell and Stanley (1963), the comparison group design addresses several threats to internal validity, including maturation, history, **testing**, **instrumentation**, selection, and **mortality**. This design, however, does not address these threats as well as the experimental design because of the advantage of random assignment for the latter. Again, the greater the comparability between the two groups, the more similar the comparison group design is to the experimental design with regard to the argument that the measured gain in client functioning is due to the treatment rather than something else.

EXPERIMENTAL DESIGNS THAT ADDRESS THREATS OPTIMALLY

With experimental designs, you place people into groups on a random basis. This procedure is believed to address threats to internal validity on an optimal basis because the random procedure tends to ensure that there is equality between the people in the group being treated and those who are not being treated except that one group got the treatment and the other group did not. If getting treatment is the only difference between the two groups, you are in an optimal position to argue for causation. In other words, you are in a better position to argue that it was your treatment that caused the client's gain, not something like normal growth over time. It is possible that there is somebody in your treatment group who experienced spontaneous recovery and did not benefit from your treatment. However, it is likely that there will be an equal number of people in the control group who did the same; thus, this variable is controlled by the random assignment procedure.

There are a number of experimental research designs. You will review only two of them—(1) the basic experimental design and (2) the posttest-only control group design. These two designs are the ones you will most likely employ or see in research studies in the literature.

The Basic Experimental Design

The basic experimental design was illustrated graphically in Exhibit 14.2. When you employ this design, you have a group of people who you divide into two groups of people on a random basis. You give the treatment to one group (i.e., the treatment group) and you do not give the treatment to the second group (i.e., the control group). You measure the people in each group on the basis of your target behavior and you compare the two groups to see if the treatment group did better.

This design is often not feasible for the social work practitioner. You are more likely to see this design in published research than in the practice of a typical social worker. A critical issue here is ethicality. How can you deny people a treatment for the sake of research? Typically, you give services to all in need in accordance with some criterion (e.g., the date each person applied for service). There are, however, some situations where this random assignment is feasible and ethical. Suppose you have twice as many applicants for your service as you have the resources to serve. Maybe you could select one half of these people on a random basis and measure your target behavior for both groups but give the second group the service at a later date as you must do because of resources.

Posttest-Only Control Group Design

The posttest-only control group design has two groups of people, one that is randomly assigned to be in the group that gets treatment and one that is randomly assigned to the group that does not get treatment. In this way, it is similar to the basic experimental design. However, it is different in that there is not a pretest measurement of target behavior. It is graphically depicted as follows:

R   X   O

R   O

The random assignment of people to the two groups is believed to ensure that the two groups are similar at the pretest time; therefore, a pretest measurement is not essential. The difference in the posttest measurement of target behavior between the two groups should be a measure of the effect of treatment.

SUMMARY OF GROUP RESEARCH DESIGNS

A variety of research designs and threats to internal validity are depicted in Exhibit 14.3. This information was taken from Campbell and Stanley (1963). The plus sign is given where the design addresses the threat. The cell is blank if the design does not address the threat. If it is uncertain, the question mark sign is given in the cell.

You will see that the comparison group design addresses almost all these threats, and it looks like it is similar to the basic experimental design, but you should remember that the basic experimental design (and the posttest-only control group design) controls for the threats at a higher level of sophistication. So they are not as equal as they appear in Exhibit 14.3.

Exhibit 14.3 should be helpful when you have causation as a major issue to be addressed in your study or if you would like to have a good opportunity to publish your evaluation study.

EXHIBIT 14.3

THREATS TO INTERNAL VALIDITY ADDRESSED BY SELECTED RESEARCH DESIGNS[a]

Research Design	Maturation	History	Testing	Instrumentation	Regression	Selection	Mortality
One-group posttest only							
One-group pretest–posttest					?	+	+
Comparison group	+	+	+	+	?	+	+
Basic experimental	+	+	+	+	+	+	+
Posttest-only control group	+	+	+	+	+	+	+

a. For explanations and more information see Campbell and Stanley (1963).

Chapter Practice Exercises

In the two practice exercises in this chapter, you will determine what research design would be appropriate for a given situation. You will consider the issue of whether either maturation or history, as threats to internal validity, should be of special concern in each situation. If either of these are threats in the particular situation, you will identify a design that addresses these threats. If there are no threats of special concern, you will identify a design that seems most feasible. The first exercise provides descriptions of several proposed evaluation research studies and calls on you to identify a research design that is appropriate, given the themes of causation and feasibility.

In the second exercise, you will describe an evaluation study that you might undertake. With regard to this study, you will identify whether either maturation or history are threats to internal validity that should be of special concern in the selection of a research design. If either maturation or history are identified as being of special concern, you will identify a research design that would control for that threat. You will also offer your opinion about whether this design is likely to be feasible in your situation. If it is not feasible, you will indicate that this is a weakness of your study.

If neither maturation nor history are identified as being of special concern in your proposed study, you will identify a research design that is most feasible in this situation rather than the design that would be the very best design. In other words, you will identify an appropriate design, given the issues of both causation and feasibility.

You will keep in mind that whether a given threat (e.g., maturation) should be of special concern in a given situation is a matter of informed opinion. For this reason, you will be encouraged to discuss the situations in these exercises with others to see if there is agreement. Also, you will note that you must have a basis for your informed opinion. Why do you think maturation or history should or should not be of concern in this specific situation?

Competencies Demonstrated by These Practice Exercises

1. The ability to identify whether either maturation or history should be of special concern in a given evaluation research study, when given information on (a) the nature of the target behavior being treated, (b) the length of time the target behavior has existed, (c) the length of time of the intervention, and (d) whether the client situation suggests that the environment is likely to change in a way that would change the client's target behavior

2. The ability to provide a rationale for determining if either maturation or history should be of special concern in a given evaluation research study when given the information described in the previous objective

3. The ability to provide a rationale for determining if either maturation or history should be of special concern in a given evaluation research study

Activities for These Practice Exercises

1. Review each evaluation study description.

2. Identify whether either maturation or history should be of special concern in this specific situation, given the information provided on length of time of the behavior, length of time of the intervention, and information on likely changes in the client's environment.

3. Provide a rationale for the above decision. The issue here is what is probable not what is possible. All kinds of things are possible, but only some things are probable (i.e., likely to happen). Also, this question should be considered in light of what is likely to happen to the typical client, not what might happen to one or two clients in a group of 12.

4. If either maturation or history should be of special concern, you will do the following:
   a. Identify a research design that will control for this threat.
   b. Offer your opinion about whether this research is likely to be feasible in this situation.

5. If neither maturation nor history should be of special concern, you will identify a research design that is most feasible, not one that is the very best design that can be found. You will explain your decision. For example, the one-group pretest design is more likely to be feasible in most practice situations, but the basic experimental design is not likely to be feasible unless you are engaged in a study that is funded by a research grant. This exercise is designed for the evaluation of typical practice, not for the generation of knowledge to be published.

What You Will Report From These Practice Exercises

You will provide a report that follows the activities enumerated above. In other words, you will provide a report on each case. The name of the case will be the heading of each section (e.g., Case 1: Eight Biweekly Therapy Sessions for Adults With Generalized Anxiety Disorder). For each case, you will provide the following information:

1. In this situation, you will identify whether maturation should be of special concern and the rationale for this decision.

   Example: Maturation should be of special concern in this situation because . . .

2. In this situation, you will identify whether history should be of special concern and the rationale for this decision.

3. In this situation, you will identify the research design that would be most appropriate given the issues of causation and feasibility. If the needed design (e.g., one that controls for threats to internal validity that should be of special concern) is not feasible, you will identify the chosen research design as being a weakness of this study.

    Example 1: The one-group pretest–posttest research deign is appropriate because it is the most feasible design for this situation, and there is no special concern for either maturation or history in this situation.

Example 2: Maturation is a special concern in this situation. The comparison group design controls for this threat, but this design is not likely to be feasible in this situation because it is not practical for the social worker to find a comparison group of possible clients who will not be receiving the treatment. Because the one-group pretest–posttest design does not control for maturation, we must consider the research design to be a weakness of the research methods for this study.

Practice Exercise 1: Selecting an Appropriate Research Design in Specific Examples

In Exhibit 14.4, you will see brief descriptions of four possible evaluation studies. For each case, you will provide a report as noted above.

EXHIBIT 14.4
CASES FOR REVIEW

Case 1: Eight Biweekly Therapy Sessions for Adults With Generalized Anxiety Disorder

A group of 10 adults are being served by a community mental health center because they have been diagnosed with generalized anxiety disorder. This disorder comes on gradually over the life span but is more typical for those in childhood through middle age. When clients come to an agency for treatment, they have typically gotten to the point where the anxiety is interfering with normal life experiences and has been so for a period of time that is typically a year or more. The agency provides cognitive–behavioral therapy for these individuals on a biweekly basis for a total of eight sessions over a 16-week period of time. The envi-

ronments of these clients have been consistent for the past 2 years, and there are no anticipated changes in it in the coming months.

Case 2: Preparing Prekindergarten Children Through Educational Activities

The Henley Catch-Up Program offers a year-long program of educational services for at-risk 4-year-old children from low-income families to help them start kindergarten prepared to keep up with other children. The key outcome being measured is reading readiness. Many children in this environment fail to have the opportunities offered by parents of other children regarding lessons in how reading takes place and having the experience of being read to as a fun activity. The program provides a number of activities regarding how to read and provides some instruction in the letters of the alphabet. Reading readiness is measured at the beginning of the year and again at the end of the year. The environments of these clients have been consistent in the past 2 years, and it is not anticipated that these clients will experience major changes in their environments in the year of the service.

Case 3: Weekly Sessions for At-Risk Youth

A group of high school freshmen have been identified of being at risk for dropping out of school before graduation. These students have been identified as being at risk for dropping out of school because they have had low grades that do not appear to demonstrate their academic ability for a period of at least 1 year. They will be given a set of 45-minute weekly sessions for the entire school year. They will be measured on their self-confidence in completing school requirements both at the beginning of the school year and again at the end of the school year. The sessions are designed to improve both social and academic skills. They include lectures, group discussions, and group exercises. Many of the clients in this program will likely experience major changes in their

home environments because these environments have been chaotic in the past. They may move from one parent to another or be moved from a parent to a grandparent or other relatives.

Case 4: Six Months of Case Management Service to Prevent Rehospitalization

Adults with mental illness are often discharged from hospitals without adequate follow-up services resulting in their being admitted to the hospital again in a short period of time. A group of discharged patients have been identified as being at risk for premature rehospitalization because of their past histories of adherence to treatment plans, such as taking medications and living a safe life. Case management services have been introduced to this group for the purpose of preventing rehospitalization. Case management services include assistance with getting housing, food stamps, or financial assistance. A part of this service is educational in nature. The case manager gives some training in how to organize your life. A group of these patients will be measured on the number of rehospitalizations for the 6 months prior to service compared with the 6 months during the treatment period.

Practice Exercise 2: Selecting an Appropriate Research Design for Your Study

In this exercise, you are asked to identify a research design that would be feasible for your own study and would address threats to internal validity that should be of special concern for your specific situation. Remember that when you are considering things that might happen in your client's environment, you should focus on what is probable, not what is possible. All things are possible, but many things are not probable.

Prepare a brief report that addresses each of the following pieces of information. Be prepared to offer your report in a group discussion.

1. Briefly describe the target behavior being evaluated.

2. Identify if either maturation or history should be of special concern in your situation and explain why.

3. Identify a research design that would be most appropriate, given the issues of causation and feasibility.

CHAPTER REVIEW

Chapter Key Learnings

1. Your research design reveals the structure whereby data will be collected and services will be offered.

2. The function of the research design is to ensure that causation is adequately addressed in the research study. If a poor design is employed, you are in a weak position to argue that your intervention was the cause of your measured client growth, not something else like normal growth over time or changes in the clients' environment.

3. Group research designs entail the collection of data and the offering of service to one or more groups of people, whereas single-subject research designs reflect the measurement of a single entity (usually a single client) that is receiving a service.

4. A cause is something that determines the effect. We expect that our treatment determines the clients' behavior. But we know that there are other potential causes. There are three bases for determining causality—(1) empirical relationship, (2) time order, and (3) eliminating of alternative causes of the effect. We would expect to find a relationship between the cause and the effect (e.g., persons who have received our services will have better behavior than persons who have not received our services). We would also expect to be able to eliminate alternative causes of the effect (e.g., maturation will be controlled by the research design). Finally, we would expect to find that a change in the cause will be followed by a change in the effect, rather than the other way around.

5. Threats to internal validity are alternative causes of the effect (e.g., the client's target behavior). Maturation (changes due to normal growth over time) and history (changes in the client's environment) are two of the common threats to internal validity. Various research designs do a better or worse job of addressing each threat. For example, the basic experimental research design addresses various threats in an optional way, but we cannot say the same for the one-group pretest–posttest design.

6. A key task is the identification of the threats to internal validity that should be of special concern in your specific situation so that you can employ a research design that adequately addresses those threats. If there are no such threats, a simple design would be sufficient.

7. Influences on the threats to internal validity that should be of special concern include the length of time of the client's target behavior and the length of time between measurements of target behavior.

8. Preexperimental research designs fail to address threats to internal validity, while quasi-experimental designs address these threats at a basic level, and experimental designs address these threats optimally. The quasi-experimental designs tend to have a comparison group, while the experimental designs include the random assignment of people to the treatment group and the control group.

Chapter Discussion Questions

1. What are the three bases for determining causation? What is a question that would identify each of these three?

2. Consider the question of whether work performance causes work satisfaction or whether it is work satisfaction that causes work performance. How would you test for one of the three bases for causation with regard to this question? Be sure to identify the basis for causation that is illustrated by your study question.

3. What is the key thing that distinguishes a group research design from the single-subject research design? Which of these designs are you most likely to employ in the evaluation of your practice? Explain.

4. What is meant by maturation as a threat to internal validity? What is meant by history as a threat? Are either of these more likely than the other to be of special concern for you in the evaluation of your practice? Explain.

5. Why should we be concerned about threats to internal validity?

6. Identify the structure of each of these research designs: (a) the one-group pretest–posttest design, (b) the comparison group design, and (c) the posttest-only control group design.

7. Does the one-group pretest–posttest design address maturation as a threat to internal validity? Does it address history? Explain.

Chapter Test

1. The concept of threats to internal validity refers to
   a. Causation
   b. Generalization
   c. Chance
   d. Measurement error

2. Testing as a threat to internal validity refers to
   a. The effect of normal growth over time
   b. The effect of changes in the environment
   c. The tendency of extremes to regress to the mean
   d. The effect of the measurement experience

3. Which of the following designs provides for the measurement of client growth?
   a. The one-group posttest-only design
   b. The one-group pretest–posttest design
   c. Both of the above
   d. None of the above

4. Which of the following statements is/are true?
   a. Your best use of the one-group posttest-only design would be when you have a basis for estimating the clients' pretreatment condition on the target behavior
   b. The posttest-only design addresses maturation as a threat to internal validity
   c. Both of the above
   d. None of the above

5. Which of the following statements is/are true?
   a. The one-group pretest–posttest design addresses maturation as a threat to internal validity
   b. The comparison group design addresses maturation as a threat to internal validity
   c. Both of the above
   d. None of the above

6. Which of the following statements is/are true?
   a. The alternative treatment design compares the effectiveness of different interventions
   b. The alternative treatment design includes the measurement of client growth
   c. Both of the above
   d. None of the above

7. Which of the following designs does the best job overall of addressing threats to internal validity?
   a. The alternative treatment design
   b. The comparison group design
   c. The basic experimental design
   d. The one-group pretest–posttest design

8. Which of the following statements is/are true?
   a. The position advocated in this book suggests that we should focus our attention on identifying those threats to internal validity that should be of special concern in our specific situation, rather than all threats to internal validity regardless of their importance in our situation
   b. One of the bases for being especially concerned with maturation as a threat

   to internal validity is the amount of time between the pretest and the posttest measurement of target behavior
   c. Both of the above
   d. None of the above

9. The posttest-only control group design, which assigns people to the two groups on a random basis, addresses which of the following threats to internal validity?
   a. Maturation
   b. History
   c. Both of the above
   d. None of the above

10. What is the thing that all experimental research designs have in common that best distinguishes them from other designs?
    a. Random assignment of people to groups
    b. The use of random samples of people from larger populations
    c. The measurement of client gain using a validated scale
    d. The statistical analysis of data that controls for autocorrelation

ANSWERS: 1 = a; 2 = d; 3 = b; 4 = a; 5 = b; 6 = c; 7 = c; 8 = c; 9 = c; 10 = a

Chapter Glossary

Alternative treatment design. A research design in which different treatments are administered to two or more groups of clients and the progress of the groups is compared.

Basic experimental design. A research design where a group of people are randomly assigned to be in two groups, one that gets treatment and the other that does not. The two groups are compared regarding growth on the target behavior to see if the treatment group did better.

Causation. The effect of one variable on another, established by three conditions—(1) a relationship between the cause and the effect, (2) the ruling out of alternative causes of the effect, and (3) evidence that a change in the effect was preceded by a change in the cause.

Comparison group design (aka nonequivalent control group design). A research design in which the growth of a treated group is compared with the growth of a nontreated group on the same target behavior.

Group research designs. Research designs in which data are collected on target behavior for a group of clients, whether or not they are being given a group treatment.

History as a threat to internal validity. A change in the environment of clients that causes target behavior to change during the treatment period.

Instrumentation. The validity of the measurement devices employed in the study. If these instruments are not valid measures of the dependent variable, you cannot draw valid conclusions from your data.

Maturation as a threat to internal validity. The tendency of people to improve on their target behavior over time through normal development.

Mortality. The effect on study results based on the fact that some clients drop out of treatment.

One-group pretest–posttest design. A design whereby one group of persons are given a pretest of target behavior, followed by a treatment, followed by a posttest of target behavior.

Posttest. A measurement of the target behavior after the treatment has been completed.

Posttest-only control group design. A design whereby a group of people are randomly assigned into two groups, one that gets treatment and one that does not, and target behavior at the posttest time is compared between the two groups.

Pretest. A measurement of the target behavior before treatment begins.

Reactive effect (placebo effect). The effect on the target behavior during treatment of being given special attention by being selected for a study.

Research design. The protocol whereby target behavior is measured and treatment is administered.

Selection bias. A bias in your selection of study participants that hinders the validity of your research study, such as selecting only the most motivated clients for your study when you wish to generalize your findings to all your clients.

Testing. The effect on the target behavior of being measured on the study variables.

Threats to internal validity. A variable that may cause the target behavior to change during the treatment period that is independent of the treatment being offered.

SELECTING A RESEARCH DESIGN FOR A SINGLE CLIENT

Janet is a social worker who provides psychotherapy for individual adult clients who are suffering from mental health problems such as depression, anxiety, and posttraumatic stress disorder. She wishes to evaluate the outcome of her service with a single client being treated for depression using cognitive–behavioral therapy. She has a depression scale she can use to measure client progress. This client has been seriously depressed for more than a year and has not experienced any form of spontaneous recovery or serious improvement during this period. Janet expects to provide therapy for this client once per week for a 6-week period. She can measure this client in each session because she has found a short form of a depression scale that will take only a few minutes to complete. She realizes that there are several research designs for evaluating services for an individual client. One of these designs requires that you measure the client repeatedly over a period before treatment begins and continue to measure client behavior during the period when treatment is offered. This design is not feasible for Janet because she typically begins her treatment during the latter part of the first client session after the assessment part of that session is complete. She does not have contact with clients for several weeks before treatment begins so she cannot collect measurements repeatedly during several weeks of a baseline period. She reviews the issue of threats to internal validity. This client has been depressed for more than a year at a level that hampers her life. Janet does not believe that this client will achieve spontaneous recovery during the 6 weeks of the treatment period because she has had no such periods of recovery in the past year. She concludes that she does not need to be concerned with maturation as a threat to internal validity.

Janet has decided to measure depression for her client during that first session and use this as the baseline measure of target behavior. She will measure the client on depression at the beginning of each weekly treatment sessions over a 6-week period. She will compare the six treatment scores to the one baseline score to see if they are better. This means that she will employ the limited AB single-subject design. She knows of a statistical test that compares an array of scores with a single score and will use this to test her hypothesis.

Harper is a school social worker who is working with four middle school students. The objective of treatment is the improvement of school grades for these students. Because he has only four clients, he is concerned that this is not a large enough group to use a group research design, so a single-subject design seems more appropriate. Consequently, he will treat each of these four students as single subjects for the purpose of his evaluation study. The treatment lasts for a semester. Because the treatment lasts for an entire semester, Harper is a little concerned about the possibility of maturation or history as threats to internal validity. He is lucky because he has school records of grades for this student for the past four grading periods. He will use the numerical grade for this student during the past four grading periods as his baseline data and will compare these grades with those for the four grading periods during the treatment semester. Thus, he will be using a single-subject design known as the AB design. For each of his four students, he will measure the standard deviation of baseline recordings and will see if the mean of the treatment recordings is 2 standard deviations better than the mean of the baseline period. If he finds this to be true, he can conclude that his hypothesis was supported by his data.

INTRODUCTION

You are now familiar with the nature of the research design and how it helps you examine causation in evaluative research. If you have a superior research design, you are in a better position to assert that it was your intervention that caused the clients' measured growth rather than something like normal growth over time. You have also learned that there are two general types of research designs—group designs and single-subject designs. Chapter 14 addressed group designs. In this chapter, you will review single-subject designs.

Also familiar to you is the fact that you examine various threats to internal validity to see what research design you should employ. If you do not need to be especially concerned with any of the threats to internal validity, a **group research design** such as the one group pretest–posttest design will be appropriate. It measures client growth, and you are not concerned with growth over time in your particular situation. In this chapter, you will review this same theme with regard to the single-subject design. Some of these single-subject research designs address maturation and history as threats to internal validity and some do not.

At the completion of this chapter, you will be able to do the following:

1. Define the concepts of baseline period and treatment period in single-subject research studies

2. Identify how data are collected and interventions are administered in various single-subject research designs when given the symbols that characterize them (B, BC, AB, ABC, ABAB, etc.)

3. Identify which threats to internal validity should be of special concern in a variety of research situations

4. Identify which single-subject research designs address maturation as a threat to internal validity

5. Identify the steps in the employment of a single-subject research design

THE NATURE OF THE SINGLE-SUBJECT RESEARCH STUDY

When you employ a **single-subject research design**, you will measure a single client on the target behavior repeatedly over time. There are two types of periods: (1) the **baseline period** and (2) the **treatment period**. The baseline period is one in which client behavior is being measured but there is not a treatment being administered. During the baseline period, you can measure target behavior one time, but it is preferable for you to measure it several times. In the treatment period, you measure client behavior repeatedly while you are giving the treatment. You cannot measure client behavior only one time during the treatment period. There is not a single-subject research design whereby you measure a single client one time before treatment begins and one time at the end of treatment, as you do for the one-group pretest–posttest design. You need repeated treatment measurements with the single-subject design to analyze your data statistically.

You use the letter A to designate a baseline period, and you use other letters to signify a treatment period. If you have only one treatment, you will use the letter B to represent it. If you have more than one treatment, you will use other letters to designate each separate type of treatment.

When you employ the AB design, you collect data during the baseline period and one treatment period. If you administer a second type of treatment, you will refer to this as the ABC single-subject design with the letter C representing the second treatment offered to the client.

There are several steps in the employment of the single-subject research design:

1. Select a client for evaluation.

2. Select the objective of treatment and the tool to use in order to measure client progress.

3. Select the intervention.

4. Select the research design.

5. Measure client behavior during baseline and treatment periods in accordance with the protocol of the research design.

6. Analyze the measurements of client progress to determine (a) statistical significance and (b) practical significance.

7. Draw conclusions.

You have reviewed threats to internal validity in the previous chapter, including the question of what threats should be of special concern in your specific situation. If your client has been depressed for a year without improvement, it does not seem logical to expect this person to experience spontaneous recovery in the next 6 weeks, the period of your anticipated treatment. Therefore, you would not need to be especially concerned with finding a research design that controls for maturation. If it is feasible for you to employ a design that controls for threats, you should do so because you will be employing a design that is optimal.

SINGLE-SUBJECT DESIGNS THAT FAIL TO ADDRESS MATURATION OR HISTORY

Two of the single-subject research designs that address neither maturation nor history as threats to internal validity are the B design and the limited AB design. Neither of these designs address maturation (normal growth) as alternative explanations because in neither case are there sufficient data before treatment to establish a trend that can be projected into the treatment period.

The B Single-Subject Design

When you employ the **B single-subject design**, there are no baseline measurements but you have repeated measurements during the treatment period. This design is illustrated in Figure 15.1 where you can see scores for client behavior for each of the nine treatment sessions. The client's score for the first session was 23, while the

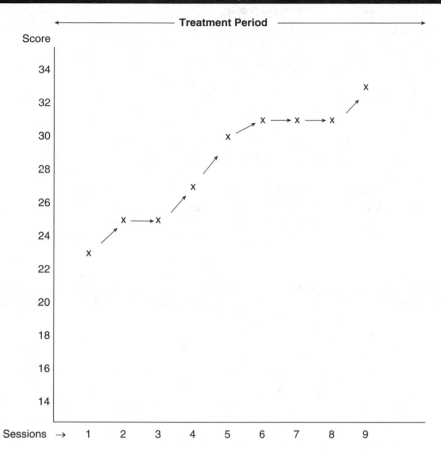

FIGURE 15.1 ■ The B Single-Subject Design

second session score was 25. The last score for this client (Session 9) was 32. The data question is whether these scores went up in a significant manner, both statistically and practically.

You employ this design when it is not feasible for you to measure client behavior before treatment starts. This design has the disadvantage of failing to have any pretreatment measurements of client behavior, so you have no basis on which to estimate what has been happening with the client before you started treatment. You will be measuring client progress, but you do not know if this amount of progress was already underway in the client's life. Therefore, it is clinically wise for you to examine this issue with the client. If you are convinced that the client has not recently experienced growth on the target behavior, you would have a limited basis for arguing that the treatment is the cause of the client's improvement during the treatment period.

The Limited AB Single-Subject Design

When you employ the **limited AB design**, you will measure client behavior one time during the baseline period and several times during the treatment period. You can use this design if your first session with the client is devoted to assessment rather than treatment and if you can measure client behavior during this session. You will consider your second client session to be the first treatment session. At the start of each treatment session, you will measure client behavior, and you will compare these treatment measurements with the one baseline score. This design is illustrated in Figure 15.2.

From Figure 15.2, you can see a baseline score of 17 followed by scores of 18, 20, 23, 24, and 26 during the five treatment sessions. This shows improvement. You can analyze these data statistically with the one-sample t test. This test compares an array of scores for treatment with the single baseline score to see if the treatment scores are significantly different. This helps you deal with the statistical significance question. To answer the practical significance question, you need to determine whether this array of treatment scores is better than the single baseline score at a level considered clinically noteworthy.

FIGURE 15.2 ■ The Limited AB Single-Subject Design

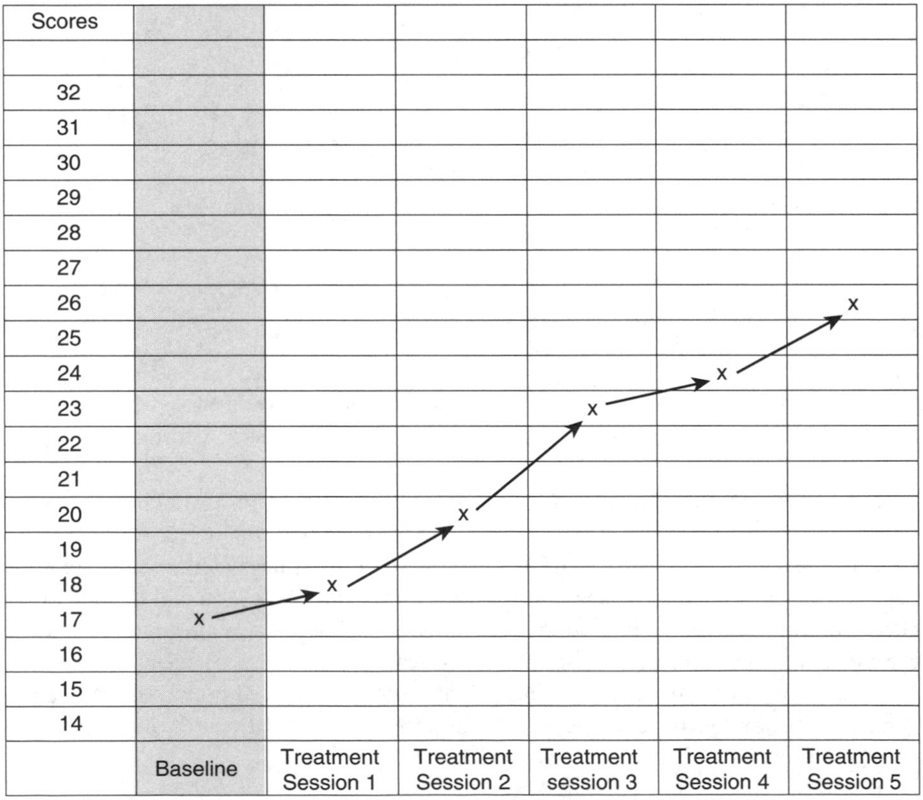

How much better is a score of 26 than a score of 17? The answer is a matter of informed opinion. You are informed by your knowledge of what is represented by scores on the tool you employ to measure client growth and what you can expect in the way of growth based on the structure of your intervention.

The limited AB design has an advantage over the B design because you can compare treatment recordings with the one baseline recording that came before the treatment began. You are not likely to see this design in other research texts not written by this author. It is one of the unique parts of the present text. It is included because it is often feasible for a social worker to measure a client one time before service begins, but the repeated measurement of pretreatment behavior, as required by the AB design, is often not feasible.

With this design, you have a measure of client growth but you do not have a design that controls for any of the threats to internal validity. You might find that the treatment scores are better, but you do not know if the client was already progressing at the level demonstrated by the scores depicted in Figure 15.2. Perhaps this client would have achieved this level of growth without treatment. For this reason, you are advised to ask the clients if they believe that their responses to the scale for the one baseline score were typical of responses they would likely have given a week ago, or the weeks preceding. If the client says that the baseline responses were typical of what would have been given in the past few weeks, you can feel safer in using the limited AB design. This answer, however, does not assure that your limited AB design is equivalent to using the AB design where measurements are taken several times during the baseline. In science, actual measurements are viewed as being superior to one's opinion about what a measurement might have looked like if it had been taken.

Each of these two designs (B and limited AB) also fails to address history as an alternative explanation for the client's growth because there is no accommodation for the effect of potential changes in the client's environment during the treatment period. Designs that introduce treatment, withdraw treatment, and reestablish treatment would address history because changes in the environment that influence target behavior are not likely to occur only during the treatment periods.

If you have two baseline recordings, you are advised to use the mean of these recordings as the one baseline score and employ the limited AB design. If you have three or more baseline recordings, you are advised to employ the AB single-subject design. The distinction is because the AB design should have sufficient baseline data to detect a trend, so that you can conclude that maturation has been controlled. Only two recordings are suspect as being sufficient for this purpose. If you are conservative, you might conclude that three recordings are not sufficient and set your standard at four.

The suggestion of using the limited AB design with only two baseline recordings is illustrated by a social worker who had two baseline recordings on a stress scale, which was being used to evaluate treatment for a woman with schizophrenia. On this stress scale, higher scores represented more stress, so the hypothesis was that the treatment scores would be lower than the baseline. The mean of these two baseline recordings (20 and 17) was 18.5, while the mean of the five treatment recordings (17, 14, 10, 6, and 8) was 11. When these data were subjected to statistical analysis with the one-sample t test, the treatment recordings were found to be significantly ($p < .05$) lower than the baseline mean.

SINGLE-SUBJECT DESIGNS THAT ADDRESS MATURATION

There are several single-subject designs that address maturation but not history. Among these are the AB design, the ABC design, and the BC design. Each of these designs has a baseline period sufficient to detect a trend (at least three measurements) and repeated measurement of target behavior during the treatment period.

The AB Single-Subject Design

When you employ the **AB single-subject design**, you measure target behavior several times during the baseline period and several times during the treatment period. You examine these measurements to see if the treatment data are superior to the baseline data. You have baseline data sufficient to detect a trend; thus, you have data that control for maturation as a threat to internal validity. If the client had some growth going on before treatment begins, this is taken into consideration when you examine the data. Thus, you have evidence that the improvement during the treatment period is due to the treatment rather than maturation. However, you do not have sufficient data to control for history as a threat to internal validity because you have only one baseline period.

You can see an illustration of the AB design in Figure 15.3. For this example, you can see baseline recordings for self-esteem of 14, 15, 15, and 13. Treatment recordings are 15, 17, 17, 19, and 23. On this scale, higher scores represent higher self-esteem; thus, the hypothesis is that the treatment scores will be higher than the baseline scores. When you employ the AB single-subject design, you can examine your data using the standard deviation approach, providing that your data are in the form of scores on a scale like that offered in Figure 15.3. If your treatment mean score is at least 2 standard deviations better than your baseline mean score, you have statistical significance. The mean baseline score for these data is 14.25, and the standard deviation of baseline scores is 0.957. If you double the standard deviation and add this figure to the mean of the baseline scores, you get a figure that is 2 standard deviations higher than the baseline data. That figure is 16.16; thus, the treatment mean must be at least 16.16 to be significantly better than the baseline. The mean for the treatment scores was 17.8, so statistical significance was achieved.

The ABC Single-Subject Design

When you employ the **ABC single-subject design**, you measure target behavior several times during a baseline period and several times during the first treatment period, much like you would do with the AB design. However, with the ABC design, you change the treatment and continue to measure client behavior several more times. You now have a baseline (period labeled A), the first treatment (labeled B), and a second treatment (labeled C). You compare the baseline with the first treatment to see if this treatment was better than the baseline (just like you do with the AB design); then you compare the data from the first treatment period with the second treatment period to see which one is better.

For example, you could be offering services to a kindergarten child with ADHD (attention-deficit/hyperactivity disorder), a condition whereby the child is hyperactive

FIGURE 15.3 ■ The AB Single-Subject Design

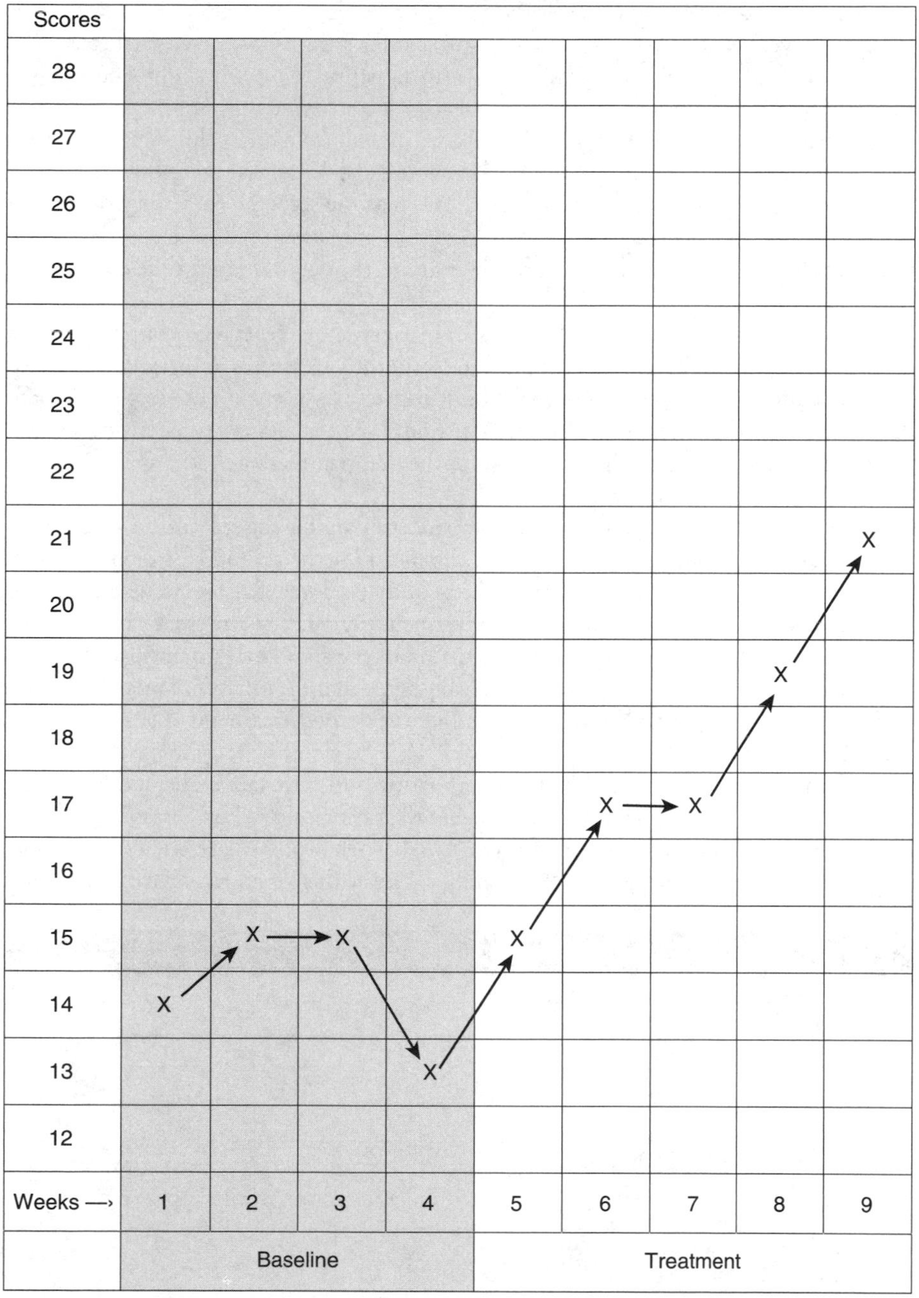

and has difficulty with attention. You are using exercises from a treatment program for this condition as your first treatment. You engage the child in these exercises for a period of 30 minutes each day. You review the school's data on daily conduct ratings for this client for 6 weeks before your treatment began and for 5 weeks from your first treatment. You find the daily conduct ratings for the treatment period to be only slightly better than those for the baseline period, so your first treatment is a little disappointing.

You are aware that children with ADHD are different from other children with regard to the stimulation of a certain part of the brain. You also learn that there is a medication that can help. You have decided to add medication as the second treatment. You will terminate your service that included the exercises and only offer medication as the second treatment for a period of 5 weeks before you examine the data. This example is illustrated in Figure 15.4.

As you can see from Figure 15.4, the mean number of incidents requiring disciplinary action was 6.16 in the baseline. It dropped to 4.8 in the first treatment period, which was a small change in the behavior. If you submitted these two sets of data to the standard deviation method of statistical analysis, you would see that statistical significance ($p <$ .05) was achieved. Thus, the data collected for the first treatment period was significantly lower than the data for the baseline.

With the ABC design, you can also compare the data for the second treatment with the data for the first one. You can see that the mean for the second treatment data was lower than the data for the first treatment period at a level that seems more noteworthy than the client's gain during the first treatment period. The difference between the mean of the first treatment period and the mean of the second treatment period is also statistically significant, and you would probably agree that the difference was of practical significance at a rather high level. It looks like the second treatment was much better than the first one.

The ABC design addresses maturation as a threat to internal validity because there is a baseline that reflects target behavior before treatment began. Furthermore, you have enough baseline recordings to record any trend in that behavior. This design, however, does not address history as a threat to internal validity because there is no second baseline period.

FIGURE 15.4 ■ The ABC Single-Subject Research Design

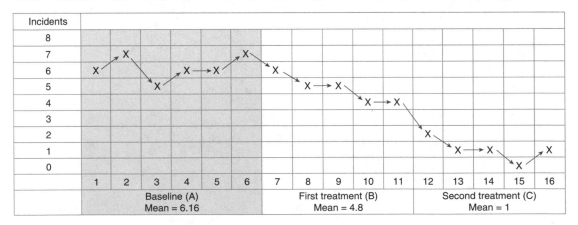

The BC Single-Subject Design

When you employ the **BC single-subject design**, you have no baseline measurements, but you have measurements during two different treatment periods using two different forms of treatment. This design is not illustrated here because you can simply examine Figure 15.3 and imagine that the first period is the B period (Treatment 1) and the second period is the C period (Treatment 2). You would examine the data for the BC design as you would with the AB design, but your research question is different. Now you want to know if the second treatment is better than the first one.

Because you have no baseline recordings, you do not have a clear measure of maturation. You could argue, however, that the BC design addresses maturation in that the recordings during the B phase reflect the combination of the effects of maturation and the first treatment. Therefore, if your C phase recordings are significantly better, you could argue that Treatment C is significantly better than the combination of maturation and Treatment B. However, recordings during a baseline period (when there is no treatment) would provide for the better argument of controlling for maturation.

SINGLE-SUBJECT DESIGNS THAT ADDRESS BOTH MATURATION AND HISTORY

According to Bloom, Fischer, and Orme (2003), there are several single-subject designs that meet the qualifications of being considered experimental designs. This means the issue *of* causation has been addressed rather fully. Most threats to internal validity have been addressed by these designs. Among the designs listed with this qualification are the ABA design, the ABAB design, and the BAB design (Bloom et al., 2003). A distinguishing feature of all these designs is that they have two baseline periods.

The ABA Single-Subject Design

When you employ the **ABA single-subject design**, you measure client behavior during a baseline period; then you measure this behavior during a treatment period; and then you withdraw treatment and continue to measure client behavior during a second baseline period. For each of these three measurement periods, you measure target behavior several times.

This design is illustrated in Figure 15.5. In this study, a caretaker for a patient with a serious health problem was provided with respite care whereby an attendant went to the home to care for the patient for an afternoon every other day. The client (i.e., the caretaker) was given a caretaker burden scale, which measures the feelings of being burdened by the caretaker responsibilities. Lower scores represented lower levels of burden, so the hypothesis was that caregiver burden scores would be lower during the treatment period. This scale was given each week during a baseline period and every week during the treatment period. The mean for the baseline was 18.16, while the standard deviation of these scores was 0.75. If you double this figure and subtract it from the baseline mean, you get a figure that is 2 standard deviations better than the baseline, and, of course, you

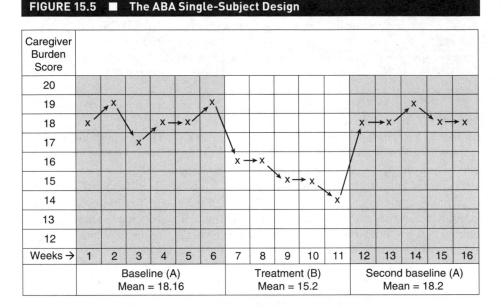

FIGURE 15.5 ■ The ABA Single-Subject Design

will have achieved statistical significance ($p < .05$). That statistically significant figure is 16.61. As you can see from Figure 15.5, the treatment mean was 15.2, which is lower than 16.61; thus, the hypothesis was supported.

The respite care service lost its funding at the end of the treatment period. Consequently, the respite care service was terminated. The researcher continued to measure the client's feelings of being burdened for 5 weeks following treatment. This was the second baseline period. As you can see from Figure 15.5, the caregiver's feelings of being burdened went back up during the second baseline. The mean of the second baseline was 18.2, nearly identical to the first baseline mean, and significantly higher than the mean for the treatment period. These data would suggest that the respite care service was the cause of the improved scores on caregiver burden. These scores were better in the one treatment period than in each of the two baseline periods.

The ABAB Single-Subject Design

When you employ the **ABAB single-subject design**, you first engage in the procedures of the AB design. Then you withdraw treatment but continue to measure target behavior during a second baseline period. This is followed by a second treatment period with continued measurement of target behavior. The two treatment periods employ the same treatment, so the label for each is B.

You can see an example of this design in Figure 15.6. Let us suppose that the caregiver respite service had been continued with funds already available to the agency so there is a second treatment period that is added. Now there are two baseline periods and two treatment periods that are alternated. You can see from Figure 15.6 that the caregiver burden scores in the second treatment period went down to the level of the scores for the

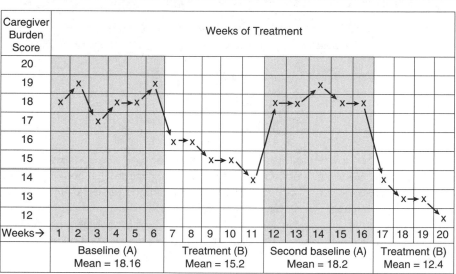

FIGURE 15.6   ■   The ABAB Single-Subject Design

first treatment period. Therefore, the treatment seems to be working, and you can assert that the improvement in caregiver burden was caused by the respite care service rather than maturation or history.

The statistical analysis of data takes three different forms. One of these forms is the comparison of the first A phase with the first B phase. The second form is the comparison of the first B phase with the second A phase, while the third form compares the second A phase with the second B phase. In each situation, you are determining the likelihood that differences between phases are due to chance.

With the ABAB design, you are in the optimal position to attribute the measured client gain to the intervention rather than something else. Maturation is addressed in the first half of this process (the first A and B phases), as was discussed in the section on the AB design. If you are concerned with the influence of changes in the client's environment, you can be comforted in the thought that the client is highly unlikely to have changes in the environment only during the two baseline periods and not during either of the two treatment periods. Therefore, we will assume that the ABAB design addresses history as a threat to internal validity in addition to maturation.

The BAB Single-Subject Design

With the BAB design, you start with a treatment and then withdraw treatment while continuing to measure client behavior, and then you administer the same treatment during a second treatment period. As with other designs, you measure target behavior repeatedly during each phase of the process. Because you have two baseline periods, you have evidence that the target behavior is caused by the treatment rather than maturation or history.

DATA ANALYSIS FOR SINGLE-SUBJECT RESEARCH

There are several major questions to pursue when you examine data for a single-subject design:

1. Are the data amenable to statistical analysis?

2. Are the data statistically significant?

3. Are the data of practical significance?

The pursuit of the first question focuses on the baseline data. Some baseline patterns suggest that the data should not be subjected to statistical analysis. The second question is one that has been dealt with in many parts of this book: Is the client improvement easily explained by chance? If so, you cannot take it seriously as an amount of growth you would expect to find in another study of similar clients. The third question has also been the subject of much discussion in this book. You want to know if the amount of client growth is clinically noteworthy.

Are the Data Amenable to Statistical Analysis?

When you measure client behavior during the baseline period, you expect to find data patterns that look like those displayed in Figure 15.3 and Figure 15.4. In other words, you would expect the baseline data to show a stable trend that is level. The scores do not vary a lot from one measurement to another.

There are several trends in baseline data, however, that suggest that you should not employ statistical analysis. You can engage in clinical analysis by reference to what you know about the client and what the client says, but these patterns suggest that you should avoid statistical analysis because the results will not be meaningful. These problematic baseline patterns include ones that are ambiguous, ones that are erratic, and ones that show a noteworthy amount of growth.

When you have sufficient baseline data to detect a trend with the AB design, you should examine it visually. This means you just put the data on a chart and look at it for information. You may find an **ambiguous baseline** trend such as that displayed in Figure 15.7. In this figure, you can see that the behavior has gone up in the first part of the baseline and has gone down in the second part. You should examine these scores clinically, not statistically. You need to make some sense of them during conversations with the client. However, you should not subject these data to statistical analysis using the normal statistics we use for single-subject analysis.

Another problematic baseline pattern is **erratic baseline**, such as that displayed in Figure 15.8. Here you can see data that move in a major way from one measure to another. These data are difficult to interpret. Why are they moving so erratically? Your response should be to avoid engaging in the statistical analysis of such data.

Are the Data Statistically Significant?

The key question for statistical analysis is whether the data in the treatment periods are better than the data for the baseline periods at a level that cannot be explained by

FIGURE 15.7   ■   An Ambiguous Baseline Trend

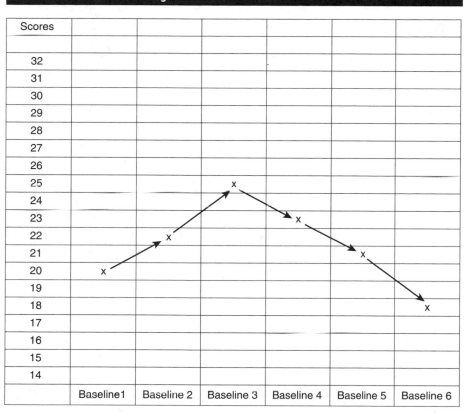

Scores						
32						
31						
30						
29						
28						
27						
26						
25			x			
24						
23				x		
22		x				
21					x	
20	x					
19						
18						x
17						
16						
15						
14						
	Baseline 1	Baseline 2	Baseline 3	Baseline 4	Baseline 5	Baseline 6

chance. Your fist question is whether the treatment data are better. The next question is whether this level of superiority can be explained by chance.

You will find various statistics that you can employ in the analysis of single-subject data. The standard deviation approach is one that has been illustrated. Other ones will be the subject of a later chapter on data analysis.

Here are the statistical analysis questions you will address with each of the single-subject designs discussed in this chapter:

1. *The B design:* Is the pattern of data during the treatment period significantly more positive than a horizontal line?

2. *The limited AB design:* Are the treatment scores better than the single baseline score?

3. *The AB design:* Are the treatment scores better than the baseline scores?

4. *The ABC design:* (1) Are the scores for the first treatment better than the baseline scores? (2) Are the scores for the second treatment better than the scores for the first treatment?

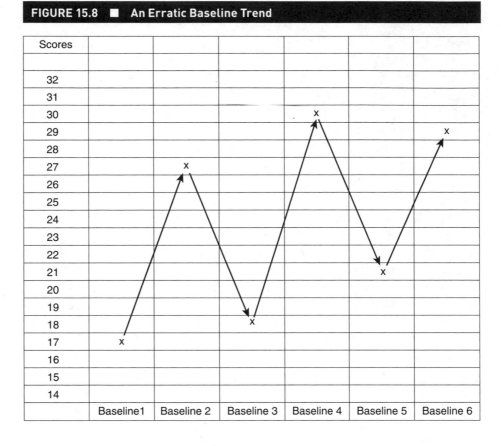

FIGURE 15.8 ■ An Erratic Baseline Trend

5. *The BC design:* Are the scores for the second treatment better than the scores for the first treatment?

6. *The ABA design:* Are the treatment scores better than the first set of baseline scores but not better than the second set of baseline scores?

7. *The ABAB design:* (1) Are the scores for the first treatment period better than the scores for the first baseline period but not better than the second baseline period? (2) Are the scores for the second treatment period better than the scores for the second baseline period?

8. *The BAB design:* (1) Are the scores for the first treatment period better than the scores for the first baseline period? (2) Are the scores for the treatment period better than the scores for the second baseline period?

Are the Data of Practical Significance?

You have reviewed the issue of practical significance many times in this book. For the single-subject study, the key question is whether the amount of measured gain for the client is noteworthy from a clinical standpoint. Did the client move beyond a given threshold of functioning (e.g., from severe depression to moderate depression)?

Did the client improve enough on the scale of measurement that the treatment was truly worthwhile? Is this level of gain exemplified by a 30% improvement, a 50% improvement, or what? To answer this question, you must achieve a certain amount of familiarity with the tool being used so that you can explain what a 30% improvement looks like. The meaning of a 5-point gain is quite different for a scale with a possible range of 50 points than one with a possible range of 20 points. For the first tool, a 5-point gain represents a 10% improvement, while a 5-point gain on the second tool represents a 25% improvement.

Limitations of the Single-Subject Research Design

While the single-subject design can help you evaluate your practice with a single client, you should be cognizant of several limitations of this approach to evaluation. Among these is the carryover effect from one treatment period to another period where the data are being collected. Another is the fact that you cannot generalize your findings from the data from a single client to other people, like you can when you employ a group design.

Carryover Effects From One Time Period to Another

When you offer a treatment to a single client, you are usually hopeful that the gains for the client will be continued after treatment is over. Perhaps the client's level of anxiety was consistently high during the baseline period and improved at a significant level during the 6 weeks of treatment. Would you expect the client to continue this growth after treatment is over? If so, it would not be wise to collect data during a second baseline period after treatment is over and interpret these measurements as being due to maturation. It may be because of the **carryover effects** of the treatment. This creates a problem for the single-subject designs that contain a second baseline period.

External Validity

External validity refers to the extent to which the results of your study can be generalized to populations who were not included in your study. You have only one study subject in single-subject research. This renders your ability to generalize rather problematic, even if you were to select your one client on a random basis. The science of random sampling is based on data from many people, not just one. With the single-subject study, you have data on your one client, so you know if this client improved. However, you are not in a position to generalize these findings. If you employed the same treatment for the same target behavior in five different single-subject design studies, you may be in a position to generalize on a logical basis, but not on a scientific basis.

Chapter Practice Exercises

There are two practice exercises for this chapter. In the first exercise, you will decide which single-subject research design would be most applicable for each of several practice situations. In the second exercise, you will present a case example in your practice and decide what single-subject research design would be most appropriate.

Your decision in both exercises will be based both on feasibility (i.e., What design would likely be feasible in this situation?) and appropriateness (i.e., Which design would control for threats to internal validity that should be of special importance in this situation?). In some cases, you may find a design that is appropriate but not feasible. Perhaps the AB single-subject design is appropriate because maturation is a threat to internal validity that should be of special concern, but it is not feasible for you to have an initial baseline set of measurements for this client. In this instance, you have a design that is not feasible but would be appropriate. What should you do? In most cases, it would be recommended that you employ a feasible design but have a discussion in the conclusions section of your paper that identifies the research design as a weakness of your study. After all, you are not likely to find any perfect research studies. All students have some limitations.

Competencies Demonstrated by These Practice Exercises

Here are the competencies you will demonstrate through your activities in the practice exercises in this chapter:

1. The ability to identify threats to internal validity that should be of special concern in a variety of practice situations

2. The ability to identify a single-subject research design that addresses threats to internal validity that should be of special concern in a variety of practice situations

3. The ability to determine if an appropriate research design is feasible in a given situation, with regard to the normal practical restraints of social work practice, in a variety of practice situations

4. The ability to select a single-subject research design for your practice, with reference to both feasibility and appropriateness

Activities for These Practice Exercises

In the first practice exercise, you will review a number of research practice situations where a single-subject research designs might be employed. In the second exercise, you will review your own practice situation where a single-subject research design might be warranted.

For each situation, you will do the following:

1. You will decide if maturation is a threat to internal validity that should be of special concern.

   Example 1: In this situation, a client who has been chronically depressed for the past year will be given therapy once per week for 8 weeks. Given the fact that this client's depression apparently has not gone down during the past year, it is unlikely that it will go down in the 8 weeks of the treatment if the client does not get an intervention designed to reduce depression. Therefore, maturation is not considered to be a threat to internal validity that should be of special concern in this situation.

   Example 2: This 4-year old child is behind other 4-year old children with regard to reading readiness fundamentals such as recognizing letters and understanding how reading takes place (e.g., sentences are read from left to right). He will undergo a year-long class experience designed to improve reading readiness. Because we would normally expect a 4-year-old child to improve on reading readiness over a year of time, we would find that maturation is a special threat to internal ability in this situation.

2. If maturation is not a special concern, you will identify a single-subject design that is feasible in this situation, given the normal practical constraints of social work practice research.

   Example: This client is in a support group that is designed to improve feelings of social support. She will be measured on a social support scale to determine outcome. Maturation is not considered to be of special importance in this situation. The limited AB single-subject design is a single-subject design that is feasible because the client will not be available to have social support measured repeatedly during a baseline period as would be the requirement for the AB single-subject design. The limited AB design does not address maturation as a threat to internal validity, but this threat is not considered to be of special importance. Therefore, the limited AB single-subject design is considered appropriate.

3. If maturation is a special concern, you will (a) identify a single-subject research design that would control for maturation and (b) decide if this design is feasible in this situation.

   Example: This 4-year old child will be given an intervention designed to improve reading readiness on a weekly basis for 1 year. Maturation is believed to be a special threat to internal validity. The AB single-subject design controls for maturation, so it will be one of the single-subject designs that would be appropriate. However, it is not feasible to measure this client's reading readiness several times before treatment begins; thus, the AB design will not be employed. The limited AB design will be used instead. The client will be measured one time before the service begins and once monthly during the year-long period of the intervention. Because the limited AB single-subject design does not control for maturation, the research design employed in this study will be discussed as a limitation of this study in the conclusions section of the report.

What You Will Report From These Practice Exercises

You will provide a report on the activities enumerated above. You will give a title to each

section of the report that identifies the particular research case (e.g., Situation Number 1: a child with autism). The following is the format for this report:

1. In this situation, you will identify whether maturation should be of special concern and the rationale for this decision.

2. In this situation, you will identify whether history should be of special concern and the rationale for this decision.

3. In this situation, you will identify the research design that would be most appropriate, given the issues of causation and feasibility.

   a. If neither of these threats is of special concern, you will identify the best design that is feasible.

   b. If either maturation or history is of special concern, you will identify a research design that would control for this particular threat. Then you will discuss whether this design is feasible, given the constraints you face in this situation. If the needed design (e.g., one that controls for threats that should be of special concern) is not feasible, you will identify the chosen research design as being a weakness of this study.

Practice Exercise 1: What Single-Subject Designs Should Be Employed Here?

In this exercise, you will review each of the following research situations and make a report as described above.

Situation 1: A Child With Autism

In this case, a 12-year-old child with autism spectrum disorder (ASD) will be treated in weekly 1-hour sessions for a period of 8 weeks. The treatment is a set of activities designed by a research institute that specializes in the study of this disorder. ASD is a lifelong developmental disorder characterized by neurological impairments, which manifest themselves in a variety of ways that most people would view as highly unusual. Among these manifestations are repetitive patterns of behavior that are not normal. Sometimes, individuals with ASD are hyposensitive to sensory stimuli. Among the characteristics of this population is difficulty with transitions in life from one task to another. This client has consistently demonstrated difficulty with transitions for many years prior to treatment. There are no expected changes in this client's environment during the period of the treatment. A scale will be administered at the beginning of each session whereby the child's parent will indicate the level of difficulty the child had with transitions during the past week. Scores can range from 0 to 9 on this scale. The parent will be asked to respond to this scale at the beginning of the first treatment session and at the beginning of each session throughout the treatment period.

Situation 2: A Depressed Man Who Was Recently Divorced

A 32-year-old man is suffering from depression following divorce from his wife 6 months ago from a marriage that has lasted for 5 years. He reports not to have been depressed until his wife told him that she was leaving, and that was 7 months ago. He also reports that his depression has not gotten better during the 7 months that have passed since his wife's announcement that she was going to leave him. He will be treated with cognitive–behavioral therapy on a biweekly basis for 16 weeks. Each treatment session will be 1 hour. His level of depression will be measured on a standard depression scale, which can be administered at the beginning of each therapy session. At the end of the first session where the client's situation was assessed, he was given a depression scale that can serve as a baseline because the treatment (cognitive–behavioral therapy) had not begun yet.

Situation 3: An At-Risk Middle School Student

A boy in middle school has been identified as being at-risk of dropping out of school. This risk was identified by his teachers because he exhibited low grades in school, grades that seemed lower than would be predicted by his level of intelligence. He has been referred to a special program of counseling and tutoring for at-risk youth. The outcome for this program will be the tracking of grades during the treatment semester and the semesters that preceded it.

Practice Exercise 2: What Single-Subject Design Should I Employ in My Study?

In this exercise, you will identify a situation where you will be evaluating practice with a single client. You will discuss whether maturation or history would be threats of special concern in this situation. You will also identify a single-subject research design that would be feasible in this situation. Then you will discuss whether your chosen single-subject research design addresses the threats to internal validity that are of special concern. You will first briefly describe the practice situation you are in. Then you will report each of the items listed in the report that is given in the activity description of the practice exercises. Part A of your report will be your summary of the situation. Part B of your report will entail your information as enumerated in the report description given for the practice exercises.

CHAPTER REVIEW

Chapter Key Learnings

1. The single-subject evaluation research study entails the collection and analysis of data on a single entity, usually a single client. Target behavior is measured repeatedly during baseline periods, where treatment is not offered, and periods where treatment is implemented. You examine the data from these periods to see if the treatment periods revealed behavior that is more positive.

2. The size and number of baseline periods determine the extent to which various threats to internal validity are addressed. If there are no baseline periods, or if the baseline only has one measurement, none of the threats to internal validity are controlled. If there is one baseline with sufficient measurements to detect a trend in the target behavior, maturation as a threat to internal validity is controlled. If there is more than one baseline period, both maturation and history are controlled.

3. Among the weaknesses of the single-subject research study are external validity and carryover effects from one phase of data collection to another. Because there is only one study subject, you cannot generalize your findings to other persons, even if you draw that single subject at random. When you withdraw treatment and continue to measure target behavior during a second baseline period, you must consider the possibility that the growth during the treatment period will continue because of the treatment. Thus, you might see continued growth during the second baseline period and interpret this to mean that maturation is causing this growth.

It is possible that you are viewing a carryover effect of the treatment.

4. Before selecting a single-subject research design, the social worker should analyze the case to determine if there are any threats to internal validity that should be of special concern in this particular situation. If there are no such concerns, you can select any of the single-subject designs. If there are distinguished threats, you should select a design that controls for this threat. If that is not feasible, you should discuss this fact as a major limitation of your evaluation study.

5. A single-subject design that is likely to be the most feasible for the social work practitioner is the limited AB design, where there is only one baseline measurement of the target behavior and several measurements during the treatment period. However, this design does not address any of the common threats to internal validity. Therefore, it is only appropriate when these threats are of little concern due to the circumstances in the particular case. Because of this weakness, you are not likely to see this design used in published research.

6. Before you examine your single-subject data statistically, you should review the baseline data to see if there are any bases for declaring the data not to be amenable to statistically analysis. Among these problems are the ambiguous baseline, the erratic baseline, and the baseline that shows that the client is already achieving noteworthy gains without treatment. In these situations, you should not subject your data to statistical analysis.

7. When you select a single-subject research design, you should be cognizant of the statistical question that will determine if your study hypothesis has been supported. For example, the statistical question in the use of the ABA design is whether the scores during the treatment period are better than the first baseline and whether they are not as good as the second baseline.

Chapter Discussion Questions

1. Why does statistical analysis for the single-subject design not allow for one measurement of client behavior before treatment and one measure of it at the end of treatment, like you would do with the one-group pretest–posttest design? In other words, why can you not apply statistical analysis in this situation?

2. How does the ABAB single-subject design control for history as a threat to internal validity while the AB design does not?

3. Suppose you want to evaluate the effectiveness of a model of treatment on the anxiety level of children recently the victims of abuse. For this evaluative study, you select your one client at random from the list of the 17 clients currently in your caseload. Can you scientifically generalize your findings from this study? If so, to what population can you scientifically generalize these findings? Can you generalize your findings on a logical basis? Explain.

4. Think of a single-subject evaluation study where the carryover effect is likely to occur. What does this fact mean about the single-subject research designs you might employ?

5. Do you believe that the limited AB single-subject research design is likely to be suitable for most evaluations you might undertake with a familiar client population? Explain.

6. Describe one situation where statistical analysis of single-subject data would not be appropriate.

7. The statistical analysis question for the B single-subject research design is as follows: Are the baseline recordings significantly different from a horizontal line. Why is this a statistical analysis question? In other words, why would you compare the treatment recordings with a horizontal line?

Chapter Test

1. Which of the following are single-subject research designs?
    a. The AB design
    b. The comparison group design
    c. The one-group pretest–posttest design
    d. All of the above

2. Which of the following designs controls for maturation as a threat to internal validity?
    a. The B design
    b. The AB design
    c. Both of the above
    d. None of the above

3. How many different types of treatments are in the ABAB design?
   a. One
   b. Two
   c. Three
   d. Four

4. Which of the following designs addresses both maturation and history as threats to internal validity?
   a. The ABA design
   b. The ABAB design
   c. Both of the above
   d. None of the above

5. Which of the following are limitations of the single-subject design?
   a. The carryover effect
   b. External validity
   c. Both of the above
   d. None of the above

6. In which of the following situations should you avoid the statistical analysis of data?
   a. When you have a baseline where the data are erratic (i.e., moving in extremes up and down)
   b. When you have a baseline that shows a noteworthy amount of client growth

c. Both of the above
d. None of the above

7. Which of the following statements is/are true?
   a. When you employ the AB single-subject design, you can scientifically generalize your findings to the study population from which you selected your client on a random basis
   b. If you believe that there will be a major carryover effect of your 6 weeks of therapy for your client, you should not employ the ABA single-subject design
   c. Both of the above
   d. None of the above

8. Which of the following is/are relevant to the AB single-subject design?
   a. There is one baseline period where data are collected repeatedly and one treatment period where data are collected repeatedly
   b. The statistical analysis question is as follows: Do the treatment data show superiority to the baseline data at a level that cannot be explained easily by chance?
   c. Both of the above
   d. None of the above

ANSWERS: 1 = a; 2 = b; 3 = a; 4 = c; 5 = c; 6 = c; 7 = b; 8 = c

Chapter Glossary

AB single-subject design. A research design in which a subject's target behavior is repeatedly measured during a baseline period and then is measured repeatedly during a period whereby treatment is offered.

ABA single-subject design. A research design where a single client's target behavior is

measured repeatedly during a baseline period, the measurements continue during a treatment period, and treatment is withdrawn but target behavior continues to be measured during the second baseline period.

ABAB single-subject design. A research design in which a single subject's target behavior is measured repeatedly during a baseline period, is given treatment and repeatedly measured during the first treatment period, is then measured repeatedly during a second baseline period where treatment has been withdrawn, and, finally, is measured repeatedly during a second treatment period where the same treatment is offered again.

ABC single-subject design. A research design in which a single subject is measured repeatedly during a baseline period, then is measured repeatedly during a period where treatment is implemented, and, finally, is measured repeatedly during a period where a second treatment is provided that is different from the first treatment that was offered.

Ambiguous baseline. A baseline where the scores are difficult to interpret because they are moving up and down in an inconsistent fashion, such as a trend that shows improvement in the first part of the baseline but deterioration in the second part.

B single-subject design. A research design in which the target behavior for a single client is repeatedly measured while a treatment is being administered but no baseline data are measured.

Baseline period. A period in single-subject research whereby the client is measured on the target behavior but no treatment is being provided.

BC single-subject design. A research design whereby a single client is measured on the target behavior during a treatment period, and is repeatedly measured on the same behavior during a period where a treatment is implemented that is different from the first treatment, but no baseline data are measured.

Carryover effects. The tendency of gains in a treatment period to continue without treatment possibly because the effect of the treatment is continuing; therefore single-subject designs that have a baseline following a treatment period should be undertaken with caution.

Erratic baseline. A set of baseline scores that fluctuate wildly from high to low and suggest that statistical analysis of data is not warranted.

External validity. The extent to which the results of a study can be generalized.

Group research design. A research design in which data are collected on the same target behavior for a group of clients who are being given treatment.

Limited AB design. A research design whereby a single client is measured on the target behavior one time before treatment begins and several times during the treatment period. If there are two baseline scores, the mean of these scores is used as the single baseline score.

Single-subject research design. A research design in which a single entity (usually a client) is measured repeatedly on the target behavior.

Treatment period. A period, in single-subject research, whereby the client is measured repeatedly while a treatment is being offered.

ANALYZING DATA AND DRAWING CONCLUSIONS

Sheldon is a social worker who has the task of preparing a report that describes the current clients of his agency as a part of a grant proposal. The relevant descriptive statistics he will report on the clients of the agency are the following:

1. The proportion of clients who are male and female
2. The proportion of clients in each category of race
3. The mean age
4. The mean income
5. The number of clients served in each category of service
6. The number of families who have a preschool-age child

Current client records can supply the data for each of these six characteristics. Sheldon will review all current client records for this information. He will use a data report sheet for each client and enter the data for each of the above characteristics on one sheet for the first client, then repeat this procedure for the second client, and so forth. Because there are 234 current clients, he will have 234 data sheets when he has completed this task. He will submit these data to the computer using statistical analysis software available to the agency. He will enter the data, obtain the results, and prepare the report. The descriptive statistics he will employ are identified in the category of data for each characteristic to be described. For example, the proportion is one example of a descriptive statistic. Sheldon will compute the proportion of clients who are male and female.

Dana is a social worker who wants to know what variables best explain client no-shows. She has identified three variables that she believes will be related to a client failing to show up for an appointment. Her review of the literature provided her with two additional variables to include. She will conduct a survey of clients who have failed to show up for an appointment more than once and clients who have not failed to keep an appointment at any time. She will compare each of these two groups on the basis of the five variables she has identified. Because each of these variables are measured as a dichotomy (i.e., there are only two categories), she has learned that she can use the chi-square statistic for her data analysis. This statistic will help her decide if any of these five variables are related to failing to show up for an appointment. On any of these variables if Dana finds that the proportion of clients who failed to show up for appointments is significantly higher than the other group, she will view this as evidence that this is one of the causes of failure to show up for an appointment. She may find that gender is a cause (e.g., males fail to show up at a higher rate than females), that being in poverty is a cause, or that one of the other variables reveals a possible cause. With this information, she can suggest efforts that the agency can implement to improve the appointment rates of clients.

Hanna is a social worker who plans to evaluate her practice with a depressed man who was recently divorced from his wife of 24 years. She has secured a depression scale and will measure this client once before treatment began and once before each of the six weekly treatment sessions. She will compare the six treatment recordings of depression with the one baseline recording using the one-sample t test, a statistic for determining if a set of scores (e.g., treatment scores) is significantly different from a single score (e.g., the one baseline score).

INTRODUCTION

The examples given for Sheldon, Dana, and Hanna represent three key ways in which we use data analysis in social work. Shelton engaged in data analysis to describe people using descriptive statistics. Dana engaged in data analysis to explain things using inferential statistics. Hanna used data analysis to evaluate service using inferential statistics.

We describe people by reference to frequencies, proportions, means, and so forth. If the core mission of your agency is to improve the lives of those in poverty, the discovery of a mean income for your clients that is above the official poverty level could be cause for concern.

We can use data to explain things by examining the relationship between variables. For example, in a previous chapter, you examined whether there was a relationship between stress and life satisfaction. You also examined whether social support was related to life satisfaction. One of the questions was whether the relationship between stress and life satisfaction was stronger than the relationship between social support and life satisfaction. Dana used data analysis to explain the primary causes of client no-shows. You can also use data to evaluate your services. Did your clients improve at a level that is not easily explained by chance?

We employ **inferential statistics** to examine data regarding explanatory studies. This means that we will be examining whether the relationship between variables is significant. We also employ inferential statistics for the analysis of data in evaluative studies: Was the amount of client gain statistically significant?

A number of concepts about data analysis were the subject of prior chapters in this book. For one thing, you examined the difference between quantitative data (numbers and categories) and qualitative data (words). You also learned how to use a website from the Internet to engage in the statistical analysis of data from a few simple studies. Here are additional learnings from these chapters:

1. Data analysis is the third major phase of social work research, coming after the development of the study question and the relevant knowledge base and the methods to be used to conduct the study. It precedes the conclusions phase of research.

2. Statistical significance refers to the extent to which data can be explained by chance, whereas practical significance is an educated opinion regarding whether the data results show a noteworthy outcome (e.g., a noteworthy gain for clients).

3. When you select a statistic, you need to know the level of measurement of your study variables (nominal, ordinal, interval, and ratio).

4. Statistics can help you describe people, explain things, or evaluate services. **Descriptive statistics** can be used to describe people. Inferential statistics can be employed to test the hypothesis in explanatory research and evaluative research.

5. You can employ websites from the Internet to analyze data statistically when you are engaged in simple studies.

6. One major use of data is to test your hypothesis. For your data to support your hypothesis, you must find that the data went both in the hypothesized direction and were statistically significant.

7. Your study conclusions must be consistent with your data analysis. They should also refrain from a focus on the author's opinions and should certainly not portray opinions as though they were supported by the data, unless this is true.

In this chapter, your journey to learn about data analysis will continue. The main contribution will be your enhanced ability to know how to analyze your own data. You will review the research process with an eye to the extent that the data analysis phase of research is connected to other phases of this process. You will examine several descriptive statistics (for descriptive research) and a few inferential statistics (for explanatory and evaluative research). At the end of this chapter, you will be able to do the following:

1. Describe the three key levels of measurement that are useful for finding a statistic

2. Identify descriptive statistics that you can use to describe variables based on their level of measurement

3. Identify the questions you must answer to select a statistic for testing your study hypothesis

4. Use a chart to select an inferential statistic for testing your hypothesis for explanatory research

5. Use a chart to select an inferential statistic for testing your hypothesis in evaluative research

6. Identify several guidelines for the presentation of your research report

7. Use an Internet site to analyze your data for selected situations in evaluative research

USING DESCRIPTIVE STATISTICS TO DESCRIBE PEOPLE

Your first task in a descriptive study is to determine the purpose of your study. The examples given at the beginning of this chapter illustrate three different purposes that were being pursued. Once Sheldon knew that he had to describe the clients of his agency for the grant proposal, he needed to identify the characteristics that he should describe. Was it important, for example, to describe the current clients regarding income? Many funding sources will want to know the income level of your clients because they focus on people who are in poverty. Do funding sources need information on how many of your clients are left handed? Probably not.

Before you can submit your data to analysis, you must have case-level data. This means that you have data on each study variable for each study subject. For example, you might have the age of each client, the income of each client, whether the client is male or female, and so forth.

When you engage in descriptive analysis of data, you will always have only one variable to analyze. You may have five different descriptive research questions, but in each case, you have one variable for analysis. For example, you might analyze the mean age of your clients in one analysis and the proportion of your clients who are male and female in another analysis. In each analysis, you have only one variable. This is different for the explanatory type of study where you are examining the relationship between two or more variables.

Levels of Measurement

Before you seek a statistic for your analysis, you must know the level of measurement of each variable in your study. Here is a summary of these levels described in prior chapters:

1. The variable measured at the **nominal level** places study subjects into categories that have no order, such as gender and race.

2. The variable measured at the **ordinal level** places people into categories that have an order, such as strongly agree, agree, undecided, disagree, and strongly disagree.

3. The variable measured at the **interval level** gives each study subject a number that has numerical value, in that the distance between each set of adjacent values (e.g., 4 and 5 or 17 and 18) is equal to the distance between any other set of adjacent values. Examples include age measured in years (not categories of years), height measured in inches, and scores on a depression scale.

Frequencies, Proportions, and the Median

Included in the descriptive statistics for variables measured at the nominal level are frequency and proportion. Frequency is the number of times a value occurs. If you have 29 males in your study for the variable of gender, the frequency for males as a category of gender is 29. In a report, you may see the letter n next to the frequency. For example, you may see the following: "The females ($n = 56$) substantially outnumbered the males ($n = 29$) in this study sample." The letter n indicates the frequency for each item being reported.

The **proportion** is the percentage of people in a category on a variable measured at the nominal level. If you have 40 males and 60 females in your study sample, you will have a total of 100 people in your sample, and the proportion of males is 40%. The 40% figure comes from dividing 40 by 100 and converting this to its whole number (i.e., 40/100 = .40 × 100 = 40).

You will often see frequencies displayed in a report in the form of a bar chart. This is the chart with columns (smoke stacks) revealing the frequency for each category. The category with the highest frequency, of course, would have the tallest column on the chart.

All the descriptive statistics appropriate for nominal variables are also appropriate for variables measured at the ordinal level because the ordinal level is higher than the nominal one. A descriptive statistic for the variable measured at the ordinal level, but not the nominal level, is the median. The **median** is the middle value when all values are organized from the lowest to the highest. Suppose, for example, you have the following ages presented for the nine clients in your study: 23, 19, 28, 33, 17, 19, 44, 15, and 55 years. If you organize these ages in chronological order, you will have these ages organized as 15, 17, 19, 19, 23, 28, 33, 44, and 55 years. Please note that the age of 19 years is listed twice because two clients had this age. The median age is 23 years because you have four people whose ages fall beneath this age and four people whose ages come above it.

Mode, Mean, Range, and Standard Deviation

For variables measured at the interval level, you can add the mode, the mean, the range, and the standard deviation to your list of descriptive statistics. Because the interval level is higher than either the ordinal or the nominal levels, all the descriptive statistics appropriate for nominal or ordinal levels are appropriate for the interval level.

The **mode** is the value that occurred most often in an array of data. For example, the ages given above had two people who were 19 years of age, but no other age had more than one person; therefore, the mode for this sample of people would be 19 years. The **mean** is the average of all values. For example, the mean for the ages of 15, 17, 19, 19, 23, 28, 33, 44, and 55 years would be 28.11. To compute the mean, you add up all the scores and divide this sum by the number of scores you have.

The range is the distance between the highest and the lowest scores in an array of data. The range for the ages given above is 40 years because the lowest age is 15 years, the highest age is 55 years, and the difference in these values is 40 years (55–15 = 40).

The **standard deviation** is a measure of variance that is employed in many statistical tests. It is perhaps easier to understand the concept of standard deviation by reference to the average deviation because the latter is more simple and also measures variance. The average deviation is the average amount that each person in your study deviates from the mean of all people on a selected variable (measured at the interval level). The standard deviation is not computed in the same way as the average deviation and will have a value that is usually a little different from the average deviation. But the average deviation tells us how much variance you have found on the variable in focus, which is what the standard deviation will tell you.

USING INFERENTIAL STATISTIC TO TEST YOUR HYPOTHESIS IN EXPLANATORY RESEARCH

When you engage in explanatory research, you are examining the relationships between variables because you believe that one explains another. You will articulate a study hypothesis, measure study variables, and subject your data to inferential statistical analysis.

In a previous chapter, you engaged in a study where you examined the relationship between social support and life satisfaction. You measured each of these two variables using scales. You examined the relationship between these variables using a statistic known as the Pearson correlation coefficient. This analysis showed whether social support is related to life satisfaction. In other words, you examined whether people with more support tend to have higher life satisfaction. You also examined whether stress was related to life satisfaction. In addition, by comparing the strength of the correlation coefficient, you could see if one of these variables did a better job than the other of explaining life satisfaction. For each of these analyses, you were directed to an Internet website where you entered your data and got the value of the correlation coefficient and the value of p, so you could see both the direction of the relationship (did you find a positive correlation or a negative one?) and whether the data were statistically significant.

When you seek a statistic to test your hypothesis in explanatory research, you will need the answers to each of the following questions:

1. How many variables are in my analysis?

2. At what level is each variable measured?

3. Which variable is the dependent variable, and which is the **independent variable**?

4. Are the data drawn from independent samples?

You will examine each of these questions in the information that follows. These answers will reveal the structure of your data, which will guide you to a proper statistic for your research hypothesis. Testing your hypothesis in an evaluative study will be the subject of the next section. While the evaluative study is an explanatory study in nature, it has some special features that require special treatment.

QUESTIONS YOU MUST ANSWER TO FIND YOUR STATISTIC IN EXPLANATORY RESEARCH

There are several questions you must answer to select a statistic for the testing of your explanatory study hypothesis. To some degree, these questions are appropriate for evaluative research hypotheses as well, but the evaluative research study will be the subject of the section that follows this one on explanatory research. For the explanatory research hypothesis, the questions you must answer to find an appropriate statistic are as follows:

1. How many variables are there in the hypothesis?

2. At what level is each variable measured?

3. Are the data independent?

The answers to each of these three question will guide the determination of the structure of the data, which will guide the identification of a statistic that will be appropriate for the study hypothesis. This section is only appropriate for study hypotheses where there are two variables. When you undertake the analysis of hypotheses with three or more variables, you will have another question added to the inquiry.

How Many Variables Are in the Analysis?

When you engage in explanatory data analysis, you will always have at least two variables. Here is an exercise for you. Each of the following questions may identify one variable or more than one. For each of the following questions, determine how many variables are there in each question:

1. What is the average salary of those in this study sample?

2. Are salaries different for males and for females in social work?

3. Are males more likely than females to be employed in management positions in social work agencies?

4. Is gender related to salary when position level is taken into consideration?

How many variables are there in the first question? There is only one, salary. This is a descriptive question that attempts to describe people with regard to mean salary. You will only have data on salary for this question. How about Question 2? You have two variables—salary as one variable and gender is the second variable (the concepts of male and female are categories of the variable of gender). You have two variables for Question 3—gender and management position. What about Question 4? We have gender, salary, and position level. This means we have three variables.

At What Level Is Each Variable Measured?

In this chapter, you have seen a summary of various levels of measurement. You must know the level of measurement when you seek a statistic. An important consideration in the selection of a statistic in some cases is whether the variable is measured as a dichotomy. A dichotomous variable is one that divides people into only two groups, like the traditional way to classify gender. A nominal variable may be dichotomous or have more than two categories. There are some statistical measures that are appropriate only for dichotomous variables.

Which Variable Is Dependent, and Which Is Independent?

For explanatory research questions with three or more variables, you need to know which variable is the dependent variable and which ones are the independent variables. The **dependent variable** is the one that is believed to be dependent on the other variable. The other variables are known as the independent variables. In other words, the independent variables are believed to be the cause of the dependent variable.

Suppose you know that males report higher salaries than females and that males are more likely to be found in management positions. Therefore, you expect to find a relationship between gender and salary and between gender and being in a management position. You wonder if management position fully explains the relationship between gender and salary. In other words, do males receive higher salaries only because they are in higher positions on the organizational chart? Now, you have three variables to examine: (1) gender, (2) salary, and (3) management position. In this case, you will have to know that salary is the dependent variable because you are examining whether it is dependent on gender and management position. This means that both gender and position are independent variables.

Are the Data Independent?

You can classify data into the categories of paired and independent. Paired data are when you have pretest and posttest scores for one group of people—that is, you have two sets of scores from one group of people that are matched. In most other situations in the examination of data for social work, you will have independent data.

This means that you have data from two groups of people, not matched scores for a single group.

What Is the Structure of Your Data?

The structure of your data combines the information given above. For example, your structure may indicate that you are examining the relationship between two variables where each is measured as a dichotomy. Maybe you are examining the relationship between one variable measured at the nominal level and one measured at the interval level where the nominal variable has more than two categories. An appropriate statistic is displayed in the next exhibit for seven different data structures. Each one of these statistics is explained in the section that follows this exhibit.

FINDING YOUR STATISTIC IN EXPLANATORY RESEARCH

You can use Exhibit 16.1 to find an appropriate statistic for testing your hypothesis if your data structure falls into one of the seven categories given.

EXHIBIT 16.1
SELECTED STATISTICS FOR TESTING THE EXPLANATORY RESEARCH HYPOTHESIS THAT HAS TWO VARIABLES

Situation	Data Structure	Statistic
1	Relationship between two dichotomous variables	Chi-square for large samples; Fisher exact test for small samples
2	Relationship between two nominal variables	Chi-square
3	One dichotomous variable and one interval variable	Independent *t* test
4	One nominal variable with more than two categories and one interval variable	**Analysis of variance**
5	Relationship between two interval variables (scores)	Pearson correlation coefficient
6	Relationship between two ordinal variables	Spearman rank–order correlation coefficient
7	Relationship between one dependent variable measured at the interval level (e.g., scores) and more than two independent variables that are also measured at the interval level	**Multiple regression analysis**

INTERPRETING DATA IN EXPLANATORY RESEARCH

When you are reviewing a research report from an explanatory research study, you will review the data. You may see data in a table that shows the relationship between two variables measured at the nominal level. You will need to interpret what is meant by the data. Did they support the study hypothesis? You will do the same for measures of relationships between variables measured at the interval level, such as the correlation coefficient. In this section, you will see how to interpret data in each of these two situations.

Interpreting Data in Tables

You might see data in an explanatory research study that portrays information on the relationship between two variables where each is measured at the nominal level. From Exhibit 16.2, you can see data on the relationship between gender and failing to show up for appointments. You may want to know if gender is related to failing to show up. The data in Exhibit 16.2 show that 19 men failed to show up and 23 women did the same. The key figure, however, is the proportion of men and women who failed to show up. You will note that there are more women than men in this set of data. When you examine the percentages, you will see that 27% of the men had a no-show in the time period of the study and only 17% of the females had the same behavior. This shows that males were more likely to fail to show up for an appointment. Before you draw any conclusions, of course, you need to examine the statistical significance. In the case of the data in Exhibit 16.2, the **chi-square** statistic is appropriate. When these data were subjected to this statistical test, they were found to be not significant at the .05 level. If we accept .05 as the standard, we have to conclude that we failed to find a relationship between gender and failing to show for appointments.

Interpreting Correlations

A correlation depicts the strength of the relationship between two variables where each is measured at the ordinal or the interval level. A **correlation coefficient** can range

EXHIBIT 16.2
GENDER AND FAILING TO SHOW FOR APPOINTMENTS

Failed to Show Up	Male	Female	Total
Yes	19 (27%)	23 (17%)	42
No	51 (73%)	111 (83%)	162
Total	70 (100%)	134 (100%)	204

from 0, which represents no relationship at all, to 1.0, which represents a perfect relationship. The higher the correlation coefficient, the stronger is the relationship between the two variables.

The correlation can be positive or negative. You would normally expect a positive correlation between self-esteem and grades in school because you would expect that those who have higher self-esteem will have higher grades. However, you would normally expect to find a negative relationship between scores for depression and grades in school because you would expect that those who are higher on depression would be lower on grades. When you see a negative correlation depicted, it will have the negative sign in front of the correlation coefficient (e.g., $r = -.34$).

A perfect relationship would indicate that one of these variables fully explains the other variable. If you found a correlation of 1.0 between grades on the first exam in a research course with grades on the second exam, you would know that if Paula had a higher grade than Jane in the first exam, she will have a higher grade in the second exam. Grades on the first exam fully explains grades on the second exam. You do not need to know anything else if your task is to predict the grade of a person who took these two exams. This perfect relationship is depicted in Exhibit 16.3.

As you can see in Exhibit 16.3, each person who had a higher grade than someone else on Exam 1 had a higher grade than this person on Exam 2. This is a positive relationship. If it had been a negative relationship, you would see the slope of the line as the opposite of the above. It would slant in a straight line from top to bottom rather than from bottom to top as illustrated in Exhibit 16.3.

EXHIBIT 16.3
PERFECT RELATIONSHIP BETWEEN GRADES FOR EXAMS 1 AND 2

Grade Exam 1								
95								Jeremy
90							Ester	
85						Charlotte		
80					Paula			
75				Jane				
70			Kelly					
65		Barb						
60	John							
Grade Exam 2 →	60	65	70	75	80	85	90	95

Note: $r = 1.0$.

When you examine the relationship between two interval variables, you will employ the Pearson correlation coefficient. This is usually depicted with the lowercase r with a negative sign in front if the correlation is negative or no sign in front if the correlation is positive. For the data in Exhibit 16.3, you will see $r = 1.0$ rather than $r = -1.0$, because it was a positive relationship rather than a negative one. If you see a correlation depicting a relationship between two variables measured at the ordinal level, you will use the Spearman correlation coefficient. The meaning of the values of the coefficient are the same as when you use the Pearson correlation.

When you examine the correlation coefficient, you will review the value of p to determine if you have statistical significance. If your data are explained by chance, you cannot conclude that you have found a relationship between the variables.

The correlation coefficient shows you the strength of the relationship between two variables. The higher the value of the coefficient, the stronger is the relationship between the variables. Suppose that you found a strong relationship between hours of tutoring and grades in school (e.g., $r = .71$) and a weak relationship between self-esteem and grades in school (e.g., $r = .31$). Would this point you in the direction of putting more focus on hours of tutoring? I would think so.

Interpreting the Value of *t*

The t test is employed in many situations in explanatory research. You will see more of this when you examine evaluative research. The value of t is used to find the value of p, but it is not a depiction of the strength of the relationship like the correlation coefficient. In other words, you would not examine the value of t between two studies to decide which one showed the strongest relationship. The higher value of t will point to a lower value of p but not to the strength of the relationship. You are expected to report the value of t, but you would not be advised to spend time reviewing what a given value of t means.

Interpreting Effect Size

Effect size is a measure of the strength of a relationship that is represented as standard deviations. If your clients achieved a gain between pretest and posttest that is equal to one standard deviation in the pretest scores, you will have an effect size of 1.0. A key advantage of the effect size is that it facilitates the comparison of data from different studies using different instruments to measure the same variable. Suppose you used the Beck Depression Inventory to measure depression and found that clients achieve an average of 14.3 points on this scale and that this represents 1 standard deviation of pretest scores. Suppose further that someone else used a different depression scale and the average gain for this study was 16.7 but the effect size for the other study was 0.45, which is smaller than your effect size of 1.0. You win! Why? Because you have the greater effective size. Comparing the mean gain for the two studies gets you into the apples and oranges situation. These scales do not have the same number of points, so a gain of 14.3 is not the same for the two measures.

Effect size is often reported in evaluative research, especially in the meta-analysis whereby data from various studies are combined into one overall effect size for a given outcome for a given treatment. This facilitates the comparison of treatments.

USING INFERENTIAL STATISTICS TO TEST YOUR HYPOTHESIS WHEN YOU ARE EVALUATING PRACTICE

When you test your hypothesis in evaluative research, you will have data on your clients' target behavior as portrayed in the statement of your treatment objective and study hypothesis. Your hypothesis will reveal what you expect to find if your intervention is shown to be effective. Here are some examples:

1. Posttest scores for depression will be lower than pretest scores.

2. In the treatment period, the proportion of clients who achieve recovery will be higher than the proportion of comparison group persons who achieve recovery.

3. The gain in scores on the parenting quiz will be higher for those in the treatment group than those in the comparison group.

4. The scores for anxiety during the treatment period for the single client will be higher than the one score that was taken during the baseline.

For the first hypothesis above, you are using the one-group pretest–posttest research design. You will have a pretest score and a posttest score for each of your clients in your study. If you collect data in such a way that the pretest score for each client can be matched with his or her posttest score, you have matched data. If you did not collect data in such a way as to match pretest scores with posttest scores, you will compute the mean of the pretest scores and compare this one score with all the posttest scores. These two situations call for different statistical tests.

For the second hypothesis, you are employing the comparison group design where you have data on whether or not each client achieved recovery, and you have the same data for each person in the comparison group (who did not have the intervention). So each person (in the treatment group and the comparison group) is classified as YES or NO for the variable of recovery.

The third hypothesis demonstrates the comparison group design where the target behavior is measured as a score (interval level). You will measure each person in each group two times, once before the treatment period and again at the end of the treatment period. You will then compute a gain score for each person in each of the two groups by taking the difference between these scores, with higher scores representing a higher level of gain.

The fourth hypothesis reveals the limited AB single-subject design where you are measuring client progress by scores. You have measured the client one time before treatment began (the baseline period), and you have measured this client several times (preferably at least five times) during the treatment period.

Using a Guide to Find Your Statistic for Evaluative Research

In each of the above illustrations, you could see the structure of the data. When you know the structure of the data, you can use the guide in Exhibit 16.4 to find the statistic for your specific situation. That exhibit includes statistics for data, which are measured either as a score or as a dichotomy (only two categories). If you have a target behavior that is measured at the ordinal level, you can decide either to treat the variable as an interval or to find a guide elsewhere. Treating an ordinal variable as though it is measured at the interval level is more relevant to the academician than the practitioner, because this error is considered to be minor from the standpoint of the evaluation of everyday practice.

The guide in Exhibit 16.4 portrays five situations (numbered in the first column) for statistical analysis. The second column shows the research design employed. The third column reveals the measurement, which will be either scores or a dichotomy. The dichotomy option means that you have all persons measured into one of two categories, like recovered or not recovered. The fourth column portrays the data structure, while the fifth column indicates the statistic that is appropriate for that data structure.

The one-group pretest–posttest design fits the first two of these five situations enumerated in Exhibit 16.4. Situation 1 is when you are comparing a set of matched scores. This means that you can match each client's pretest score with his or her posttest score. If you cannot do this, you will need to refer to Situation 2, where you will compute the mean pretest score for all clients and you will compare this with all the posttest scores for

EXHIBIT 16.4
QUICK GUIDE FOR SELECTED STATISTICS FOR EVALUATIVE RESEARCH

Situation	Research Design	Measurement	Data Structure	Statistic
1	One-group pretest–posttest	Matched scores	You are comparing the matched pretest and posttest scores of one group of people.	Paired t test
2	One-group pretest–posttest	Scores not matched	You are comparing the mean pretest score with all the posttest scores for one group of people.	One-sample t test
3	Comparison group	Scores	You are comparing the gain scores of a treatment group and a comparison group.	Independent t test
4	Limited AB single-subject design	Scores	You are examining whether the mean of several treatment period scores is better than a single baseline score for a single client.	One-sample t test
5	AB single-subject design	Scores	You are comparing a set of baseline scores with a set of treatment scores for a single client.	Standard deviation

the group. As you will see from the exhibit, the paired *t* test is an appropriate statistic for Situation 1, while the **one-sample *t* test** is appropriate for Situation 2.

From Exhibit 16.4, you can see that Situation 3 refers to the use of the comparison group design. This situation is for those who are comparing the mean gain scores of a treatment group with a comparison group. In this case, each person in each group will be measured at pretest time and posttest time and a gain score will be computed for each person. Each of the gain scores for each person in each group will be compared with the use of the **independent *t* test**. This test will show you if the difference in the mean gain scores of these two groups is statistically significant.

In Situation 4, you are employing the limited AB single-subject design, and you have measured client progress with regard to a score. This means that you have one baseline score (before treatment started) and you have several treatment scores that will be compared with this one baseline recording. The one-sample *t* test will work for you in this situation.

Situation 5 portrays the AB single-subject design, where you have a set of baseline scores (3 or more) and a set of treatment scores to be compared. You employ the standard deviation approach in this situation. This means that you first compute the standard deviation of the baseline scores, then you double this value and add it to the mean of the baseline scores and compare it to the mean of the treatment scores. If the mean of the treatment scores is better than this figure, you have treatment scores that are better than the baseline scores at a level that is statistically significant ($p < .05$).

Reporting Your Results for Evaluative Research

In your report of the testing of your hypothesis using inferential statistics, you should provide information that can be used to determine both practical significance and statistical significance. For practical significance, you might report the correlation coefficient, the difference between the means of two groups, or the difference between the mean treatment score for a single client and the baseline score(s). In each of these situations, you can decide if your opinion suggests that the data are clinically noteworthy. For statistical significance, of course, you will report the value of p or its designation (e.g., $p < .05$).

When you review research reports, you will see the results of the study presented according to the statistic that was employed. Here is an array of examples of how you would report your results for each of the five situations included in Exhibit 16.4.

1. The mean pretest score for anxiety for these 17 clients was 24.5, while the mean posttest score was 17.1, revealing that these clients' level of anxiety went down. These data were subjected to statistical analysis with the paired *t* test and were found to support the hypothesis ($n = 17$; $t = 2.21$; $p < .05$).

2. The mean pretest score for depression for these 11 clients was 29.6, while the mean posttest score was 24.4, showing that depression went down for these clients. The posttest scores were not matched with the pretest scores, so the 11 posttest scores were compared with the mean of the pretest score with the one-sample *t* test. The data were not statistically significant. Therefore, the data did not support the hypothesis ($n = 11$; $t = 1.21$; $p > .05$).

3. The gain scores for each person in the treatment group were compared with the gain scores of those in the comparison group using the independent t test. The gain scores for social support for the treatment group was 7.1, while the gain scores for the comparison group was 1.8. This difference in gain scores between the two groups was found to be statistically significant ($n = 19$; $t = 2.6$; $p < .05$); therefore, the hypothesis was supported by the data.

4. The client's baseline score for self-esteem was 14.3, while the mean of the treatment scores was 22.6, showing that the self-esteem of this client improved. These data were subjected to the one-sample t test and were found to support the hypothesis ($t = 2.4$; $p < .05$).

5. The mean of the four baseline scores for this client on depression was 32.4, while the mean of the five treatment scores was 23.6, suggesting that the client's level of depression went down. The difference between the treatment scores and the baseline scores was found to be statistically significant ($t = 2.3$; $p < .05$).

PRESENTING YOUR STUDY CONCLUSIONS

You have reviewed a number of suggestions on how to present your study conclusions. Here is an elaboration of the main points covered in previous chapters.

First, summarize your data with regard to your research question at the beginning of the conclusions section of your report. For example, you might say something such as the following:

> The question examined in this study was whether gender was related to failure to show up for a therapy appointment in the Mental Health Program. Some prior research suggested that we would find males more likely to engage in this behavior. Our data failed to show a difference between males and females with regard to the variable of failure to keep a therapy appointment.

Second, do not draw conclusions that outrun your data. Reserve your opinions that are not supported by the data for other venues. Your opinion may be very wise, but it should not be the focus of your conclusions section. Suppose you find that support from the boyfriend is positively correlated with the self-esteem of the pregnant teenager but support from the mother is not correlated with it. You may have a dozen reasons to believe that mother support is related to self-esteem of teenagers, but you cannot draw this conclusion in this study because that is not what you found.

Third, do not draw a conclusion that suggests that your hypothesis was supported by your data if the data failed to achieve statistical significance. This can be very tempting when your data go in the hypothesized direction (e.g., your clients' posttest scores were better than their pretest scores). Failure to achieve statistical significance should lead to conclusions that you failed to find a relationship between X and Y or that your clients failed to show improvement.

Fourth, discuss the limitations of your study, with special reference to the kind of sample you employed, the manner in which you measured variables, and the study design that was used. A sample that was not drawn at random is more limited with regard to the population to which the findings of the study can be generalized. You cannot scientifically generalize your findings in this situation. However, you can use knowledge that compares the sample with your designated population as support for the logical generalization of your findings.

The methods you employed to measure your study variables is another possible weakness. Did you make optimal choices with regard to measurement? There are many ways by which you could have chosen to measure variables. A third source of potential limitation of your study lies in the study design you employed, especially for the evaluative study. Did your research design address the threats to internal validity that should have been of special concern in your situation?

Fifth, discuss the implications of your findings for practice. How might practitioners make use of these results? Your findings may suggest that your agency offer office hours at night, send out reminders of when appointments are drawing near, or put more emphasis on a certain perspective for treatment.

Finally, you have been reminded several times that the scientist is cautious in drawing conclusions. A single study should not be presented as profound in its implications. We should continue to conduct scientific studies because each one tends to add more relevant information for our conclusions. As we build evidence, we can be more and more confident of our conclusions. But a single study should be presented as tentative evidence.

Chapter Practice Exercise

In this exercise, you will conduct the statistical analysis of data for several research studies. You will review each case where you will see a description of the variables being measured and the data from the hypothetical study. For each of these three cases, you will (a) compose the study hypothesis, (b) select the appropriate statistic for the testing of the hypothesis, (c) use an Internet website to analyze your data, and (d) report your results.

Competencies Demonstrated by This Practice Exercise

1. The ability to compose an appropriate study hypothesis when given a description of what was measured and whether higher scores represent gain or loss

2. The ability to find an appropriate statistical test for testing a given hypothesis when the structure of the data situation is described

3. The ability to employ an Internet website for the testing of an evaluative study hypothesis when given the data and the instructions for using this website for this situation

4. The ability to appropriately report the results of the testing of an evaluative research hypothesis

Activities for This Practice Exercise

1. For each case situation, you will review the information given in the description. You will use this case as your guide for each of the steps that follow.

2. Compose the study hypothesis.

   Example: Posttest scores for anxiety will be lower than pretest scores.

3. Select the statistic using the table from Exhibit 16.4.

   Example: We have a set of matched pretest and posttest scores drawn from a single group of people. In Exhibit 16.4, we can see that the paired *t* test is appropriate for this situation.

4. Use the instructions in the Chapter Appendix to analyze the data using the Internet.

   Example: You will find the appropriate set of instructions in the chapter appendix for using the Internet website. You will gain access to the Internet website and enter the data from the practice situation description using the instructions given in this appendix.

5. Report the results.

   Example: Twelve clients were given the Hare Self-Esteem Scale once before treatment began and once again at the end of the treatment period. On this scale, higher scores represented higher self-esteem. The following hypothesis was tested: Posttest scores for self-esteem will be higher than pretest scores. The mean pretest score for self-esteem for this group of clients was 17.4, while the mean posttest score was 23.2. These data were analyzed with the paired *t* test, which revealed that the posttest scores were significantly higher than the pretest scores ($n = 12$; $t = 3.1$; $p < .05$). Thus, the data were found to support the study hypothesis.

What You Will Report From This Practice Exercise

Your report will follow the format given above in the activity section titled "Report the Results." This means that you will report (a) what was measured in this study, (b) the number of clients measured, (c) the hypothesis that was tested, (d) the data showing the results of the data analysis, and (e) whether the data supported the hypothesis.

Research Cases You Will Analyze

Case A: The Improvement of Depression

You measured a set of eight clients on the Beck Depression Inventory. This scale gives higher scores for higher levels of depression. You measured these clients before treatment began and at the end of treatment. You were not able to match each persons' pretest score with his or her posttest score. The mean for the pretest scores was 17. The individual posttest scores for these eight clients are given below:

21   19   31   28   22   21   19   22

Case B: Improving Grades for At-Risk Youth

You have measured a set of clients who received your special tutoring service for at-risk middle school students and you want to compare the gain in grades for this group and for a group of at-risk middle school students who are on your waiting list for the same service. You measured each person in each of these two groups regarding the numerical average of the grades they received in the grading period before the tutoring was offered and the grades they received at the end of the tutoring period. The pretest grade average was subtracted from the posttest grade average to ascertain the gain for each student. The data are given in Exhibit 16.5.

EXHIBIT 16.5
NUMERICAL GAIN SCORES FOR GRADES

Treatment Group	Comparison Group
11	0
6	12
21	7
14	3
11	0
6	3
8	5
14	2

Case C: Improving the Self-Esteem of a Client

You have a single client being treated for low self-esteem. You have measured this client on the Hare Self-Esteem Scale one time before treatment began and again at the beginning of each of six counseling sessions. You wish to compare the six measurements of self-esteem with the single score before treatment began to see if the treatment scores are significantly better. On this scale, higher scores represent higher self-esteem. The baseline score was 17. The treatment scores, chronologically organized, were as follows: 21, 19, 22, 23, 26, and 23.

CHAPTER REVIEW

Chapter Key Learnings

1. Among the descriptive statistics for variables measured at the nominal level are frequency and proportion. For variables measured at the ordinal level, you can use the previous ones in addition to the median. Interval variables can be described with regard to all the above plus the mean, the mode, and the standard deviation.

2. To select a statistic to test your explanatory research hypothesis, you need to be able to identify the number of variables in your hypothesis, the level of measurement of each variable, which variable is the dependent variable and which one is the independent variable, and whether the data are matched or independent.

3. Matched data are indicated by two sets of scores from the same people where each person's score on one of these measurements can be matched with his or her score on the other one. The pretest and posttest measurement of a group of clients on depression is one example. Data that are not matched are considered independent. The typical example is the comparison of the scores of two groups of people. Different statistical tests are used for matched data and independent data.

4. The independent variable is the one believed to be the cause of the dependent variable. For example, it may be believed that gender is one of the causes of salary. This means that gender is the independent variable, and salary is the dependent variable.

5. To test your hypothesis in evaluative research, you need to know the structure of the data, including reference to the level of measurement and the research design employed. One of these many structures is the comparison of a single baseline score for a single client with a set of treatment scores for this client.

6. When you review data in a table where both variables are nominal, you should compare the percentage of people in two categories of one of these two variables with regard to the other variable. For example, you might find that 45% of your male clients have achieved some improvement during the process of treatment, while 65% of females have done so. These data would suggest that gender is related to recovery, but you would submit these data to statistical analysis before drawing this conclusion.

7. For your data to support your study hypothesis, you must have two things: (1) the data must go in the hypothesized direction and (2) the data must be statistically significant.

8. A correlation depicts the strength of the relationship between two variables where each is measured at the ordinal or the interval levels. A correlation coefficient can range from 0, which represents no relationship at all, to 1.0, which represents a perfect relationship. The correlation can be positive or negative. You would normally expect a positive correlation between self-esteem and grades in school because you would expect that those who have higher self-esteem will have higher grades. However, you would normally expect to find a negative relationship between scores for depression and grades in school because you would expect that those who are higher on depression will be lower on grades. When you see a negative correlation depicted, it will have the negative sign in front of the correlation coefficient (e.g., $r = -.34$). If the reported correlation coefficient does not have the negative sign, it will represent a positive correlation.

9. In your report of the testing of your hypothesis using inferential statistics, you should provide information that can be used to determine both practical significance (e.g., the difference in gain scores between the treatment group and the comparison group) and statistical significance (e.g., the value of p).

10. There are Internet sites that will compute a number of statistics for you, including most of the data structures you are likely to employ in the evaluation of your practice.

11. The conclusions section of your research report should start with a summary of your data with regard to the major research question examined. Your conclusions section should be congruent with your data and not go beyond it. In addition, you should report on the limitations of your study in this section of your report.

Chapter Discussion Questions

1. Among the graphic ways in which a variable may be described are the pie chart and the bar chart. The pie chart is a circle (a pie) that is divided according to the proportions of persons who fall into certain categories. Each of these categories would have a slice of the pie in the chart. A bar chart is a chart with columns that look like smoke stacks where each bar represents the number of people who fall into the relevant category. When each category is displayed, you can see how each category compares with the other categories with regard to size. Would a pie chart or a bar chart be a better way to display data for the following four categories of race: (1) White, (2) African American, (3) Hispanic or Latino, and (4) Other. Explain your answer.

2. What would be the better way to display data on one's level of agreement with a certain statement, with the categories of (a) strongly agree, (b) agree, (c) undecided, (d) disagree, and (e) strongly disagree. Would it be the pie chart or the bar chart?

3. Compose a study hypothesis and describe the method of measuring the study variables. What is your answer to each of the following questions? (1) How many variables are in the hypothesis? (2) At what level is each variable measured? (3) Which variable is dependent, and which is independent? (4) Are the data matched or independent?

4. Name and describe the three levels of measurement that we have discussed (this does not include the ratio level). Which level is the lowest and which is the highest? Why is this latter question important? Can you compute a mean score for the variable of race? Why or why not?

5. Review the data in Exhibit 16.2. When you examine these data, is it better to compare the frequencies for each gender or the proportions? Why?

6. Suppose that you gave a self-esteem scale to a group of at-risk adolescents before you began your support group intervention and you gave them this same scale at the end of the intervention period (8 weeks later). On your scale, higher scores represent higher self-esteem. You found your pretest mean score to be 15.6 and your posttest mean score to be 19.7 ($p > .05$). Did your data support your hypothesis? Explain.

7. How should you begin your conclusions statement for your research report? In this section of your report, what should be the role of your professional opinion about the answer to your research question?

Chapter Test

1. The frequency for a variable can be reported for variables measured at what level?
   a. Nominal
   b. Ordinal
   c. Interval
   d. All of the above

2. The mean can be reported for a variable measured at what level?
   a. Nominal
   b. Ordinal
   c. Interval
   d. All of the above

3. Consider the following hypothesis: Males will report higher salaries than females when position level is controlled. How many variables are there in this analysis?
   a. One
   b. Two
   c. Three
   d. Four

4. Consider the following hypothesis: Males will report higher salaries than females when position level is controlled. What variable is the dependent variable in this hypothesis?
   a. Client
   b. Salary
   c. Position level
   d. Gender

5. Consider this situation: You will measure your single client's progress during treatment with the Beck Depression Inventory, which gives higher scores for higher levels of depression. You will measure this one client one time during the baseline period and five times during the treatment period. Which of the following statistics would be appropriate for testing your hypothesis?
   a. The chi-square statistic, which tells us whether there is a significant relationship between two variables where each is measured at the nominal level
   b. The independent t test, which examines the scores of two groups of people
   c. The paired t test, which examines a set of matched scores for one group of people
   d. The one-sample t test, which compares a set of scores with a single score

6. What do you need to find in order to report that your data supported your hypothesis?
   a. The data were in the hypothesized direction
   b. The data were statistically significant
   c. Both of the above
   d. None of the above

7. You should begin your statement of conclusions with
   a. A summary of your findings with regard to the research question
   b. Your educated opinions about the research question
   c. What you have found in your literature review about your research question
   d. The implications of your findings for social work

8. Which of the following is/are true about the correlation coefficient?
   a. It reveals the strength of the relationship between two variables
   b. It can be used to examine the relationship between two variables measured at the interval level
   c. Both of the above
   d. None of the above

9. Which of the following statements is/are true?
   a. You would normally expect to find a negative correlation between grades in school and scores for anxiety when higher scores for anxiety represent higher anxiety
   b. You would normally expect to find a positive relationship between grades in school and scores for depression when higher scores for depression represent higher depression
   c. Both of the above
   d. None of the above

10. Descriptive statistics are used for which of the following reasons:
   a. The examination of the relationship between two variables where each is measured at the nominal level
   b. The characterization of the study subjects on individual variables
   c. The examination of the relationship between two variables where each is measured at the interval level
   d. All of the above

ANSWERS: 1 = d; 2 = c; 3 = c; 4 = b; 5 = d; 6 = c; 7 = a; 8 = c; 9 = a; 10 = b

Chapter Glossary

Analysis of variance. A collection of statistics for examining variance among groups, the one used in this book being the analysis of variance where you are examining the relationship between an independent variable measured at the nominal level and two or more dependent variables variable measured at the interval level.

Chi-square. A statistic for determining if there is a significant relationship between two variables where each variable is measured at the nominal level.

Correlation coefficient. A measure of the strength of the relationship between two variables measured at either the ordinal or the interval levels. The specific correlation coefficient for variables measured at the ordinal level is the Spearman correlation coefficient. The specific correlation coefficient for variables measured at the interval level is the Pearson correlation coefficient.

Dependent variable. The variable in a relationship that is believed to be caused by the other variable, which is known as the independent variable.

Descriptive statistics. Statistics used to describe individual variables, such as the mean age of a group of people or the proportion of people in a group who are female.

Effect size. A measure of the strength of a relationship that is represented as a standard deviation. An effect size of 1.0 means that the difference between two groups being compared for treatment outcome would show that the typical scores of one group represented 1 standard deviation of scores better than the other group.

Independent *t* test. A statistic for determining if there is a significant relationship between the scores of two groups of people (e.g., gains scores of the treatment group and gain scores of the comparison group).

Independent variable. The variable that is believed to be the cause of the dependent variable.

Inferential statistics. Statistics used to test the hypothesis in explanatory and evaluative research.

Interval level. A level of measurement where people are assigned a number with traditional numerical value like age measured in years or scores on an anxiety scale. Traditional numerical value means that the distance between two intervals (e.g., the ages of 23 and 24 years) in one adjacent set is identical to the distance between another adjacent set (e.g., the ages of 34 and 35 years).

Mean. The average of a variable measured at the interval level, which is computed by adding up the scores and dividing by the number of scores.

Median. The midpoint value in an array of data that have been organized in numerical sequence from the lowest value to the highest value. The median for the ages of 17, 23, 29, 30, and 31 years would be the age of 29 years because this is the age of the middle person in this sequence.

Mode. The value that occurs the most in an array of data. If there are three people with the age of 41 years in your sample and there is no other age with more than two people, you would have the age of 41 years as the mode.

Multiple regression analysis. A statistic for examining how well certain independent variables predict a dependent variable.

Nominal level. A level of measurement where people are placed into categories that have no order. Examples include gender, political party affiliation, and the category of the service your clients are receiving.

One-sample *t* test. A statistic for determining if there is a significant relationship between two interval variables where one variable is a single score (e.g., a single baseline score) and the other variable has several scores (e.g., four treatment scores).

Ordinal level. A level of measurement where people are placed into categories with an order, such as strongly agree, agree, disagree, and strongly disagree.

Proportion. The percentage of people in a category.

Standard deviation. A measure of variance used in many statistical tests. It shows how much each individual in a sample varies from the mean of the sample, so if the standard deviation of females is lower than the standard deviation of males, you can say that the males vary more from one another than do the females.

CHAPTER APPENDIX: INSTRUCTIONS FOR USING AN INTERNET WEBSITE TO ANALYZE DATA

The material that follows in this appendix entails the use of Internet sites for the statistical analysis of data for evaluative studies. You can use it to analyze the data given in the cases for data analysis from the practice exercise for this chapter.

You will see step-by-step instructions for analyzing your data. In some of these instructions, you will be advised to accept the default setting with regard to one of the steps in the process. This means that you do not do anything for this step. You will just accept what has already been selected for you by the computer program. You can, of course, change this specification, but you are asked not to do so if you have been instructed to accept the default specification.

Before you employ the instructions in this appendix, you should have your data from the research case you are examining. This might be a set of pretest and posttest scores for a group of clients or a set of baseline and treatment scores for a single client. There are five sets of instructions, one for each of the following data structures:

1. You have the matched pretest and posttest scores of one group of clients (Situation 1).

2. You have the mean pretest score for a group of clients, which you will compare with each of the posttest scores for each member of the group. This means that you have computed the mean of the pretest scores for this group, and you have the posttest score for each person in this group (Situation 2).

3. You have the pretest and posttest scores for each person in the treatment group and each person in a comparison group. You will compute the gain scores for each person and compare these gain scores between the two groups (Situation 3).

4. You are treating one client, and you have a single baseline score and several scores taken during the treatment period (Situation 4).

5. You are treating one client, and you have a set of baseline scores and a set of treatment scores for this client (Situation 5).

Situation 1: Using the Paired *t* Test to Compare the Matched Pretest and Posttest Scores for one Group of Clients

In this procedure, you have matched pretest and posttest scores for a single group of people. You should first calculate the mean pretest and the mean posttest and determine if the mean posttest is better than the mean pretest. If this is not true, you stop your journey here. You already know that your data failed to support your study hypothesis.

If your posttest mean is better than your pretest mean, you will continue with the following steps. You will have a pretest score and a matched posttest score for each client in your study. For example, you will know both the pretest score and the posttest score for the first client. You will have the same scores for the second client, and so forth. If you were not able to match the pretest and the posttest scores for each client, you will not use this statistical test.

Access the following web address:

http://graphpad.com/quickcalcs/contMenu/

Here are the steps to be followed in using this website:

1. Accept the default specification for Item 1 (**Choose data entry format**)—"Enter up to 50 rows."

2. Enter data for each person in your group for the pretest score (Group 1) and the posttest score (Group 2).

3. Select **paired t test**.

4. Select the option **Calculate now**.

5. Review the results.

P value and statistical significance:

Two-tailed P value equals _____ [This will show the value of p]

Intermediate values used in calculations:

t = _____ [This shows the value of t that should be reported]

Group   Group One   Group Two

Note: See the means for each group to see if the posttest score, which is Group 2, is better than the pretest score, which is Group 1.

Situation 2: Using the One-Sample *t* Test to Compare the Mean Pretest Score of a Group With the Posttest Scores for Each Member of This Group

In this situation, you have pretest and posttest scores for a single group of people, but you are not able to match each person's pretest scores with his or her posttest scores. You calculate the mean of the pretest and the mean of the posttest to see if the posttest scores are better. If not, you stop this journey and conclude that your data failed to support your study hypothesis. If your posttest mean is better than your pretest mean, you will continue your journey of statistical analysis. Below are the steps for this application.

Compose the data for the analysis. You will have a pretest mean and you will also have a posttest score for each person.

Access the following web address:

http://graphpad.com/quickcalcs/

1. The first thing you will see on the screen is the heading **Choose the kind of calculator you want to use**.

    a. You will see a default specification of *Categorical data*. You will change this to *Continuous data* by clicking on this option.

    b. You will then select *Continue* at the bottom of the page.

2. On the next page, you will see the heading **Analyze continuous data**.

    a. You will see the default specification of *t test to compare two means*.

    b. You will change this to *One sample t test* by selecting this option.

    c. You will then select *Continue* at the bottom of the page.

3. On the next page, you will see the heading **One sample t test**. There are several steps on this page.

    a. *Choose data entry format:* You will leave this at the default specification "Enter up to 50 rows" unless you have more than 50 clients in your data. If you have more than 50, select the next option.

    b. *Enter data:* In this step, you enter your posttest scores for each of your clients.

    c. *Specify hypothesis mean value:* You will see the numbers 0, 1, and 100, and a box to enter another option. In this box, you enter the mean of your pretest scores.

    d. View the results: Select *Calculate now*.

    e. *One-sample t-test results:* This page will give you the results.

Here is one example of the output from this page.

P value and statistical significance:

The two-tailed P values equals 0.65

By conventional criteria, this difference is considered to be not statistically significant.

Confidence interval:

The hypothetical mean is 30.00

The actual mean is 33.00

The difference between these two values is 3.00

The 95% confidence interval of this difference:

From 21.84 to 27.84.

Intermediate values used in calculations:

t = 0.5196

df = 2

standard error of difference =5.774

Here are some explanations.

- **The p value (two tailed) is given in the first instruction.** This tells you if the difference between the posttest scores and the mean pretest score is statistically significant.

- **The hypothetical mean is the mean pretest score you gave.**

- **The actual mean is the mean of the posttest scores.**

- **The t value should be reported.** It is normally reported in parenthesis with the small letter t (t = 0.5196).

Situation 3: Using the Independent t Test to Compare the Gain Scores of a Treatment Group With the Gain Scores of a Comparison Group

You will have a pretest score for each person in each group, and you will have a posttest score for each person, and you will use these scores to compute a gain score for each person. If higher scores are better, you will subtract the pretest score from the posttest score to compute the gain score. If higher scores are worse, you will subtract the posttest score from the pretest score to compute the gain score. Compose the data for the analysis with the following information: Gain score for each person in the treatment group. Gain scores for each person in the comparison group.

Access the following web address:

http://graphpad.com/quickcalcs/contMenu/

Here are the instructions for each step in using GraphPad.

1. Accept the default specification for Item 1 (**Choose data entry format**)—"Enter up to 50 rows."

2. Enter gain scores for each person in each of the two groups (Group 1 and Group 2).

3. Accept default specification for Step 3 (**unpaired t test**).

4. Select the option *Calculate now*.

5. You should focus your attention on the following items in the results.

P value and statistical significance:

The Two-tailed P value equals _____ [This will show the value of *p*]

Intermediate values used in calculations

t = _____ [This shows the value of *t* that should be reported]

Group   Group One   Group Two

Note: See the means for each group to see if the treatment group did better.

Situation 4: Using the One-Sample *t* Test to Compare a Set of Treatment Scores With the One Baseline Score for a Single Client

The instructions for the use of the one-sample *t* test for the limited single-subject evaluative research design is the same as that for Situation 2 above, except that the single baseline score is the same as the mean pretest score, and each treatment score is like the posttest scores from that application. In other words, you enter your single baseline score when you see the instruction **Specify hypothesis mean value**, and you will enter your treatment scores under the heading **Enter data**.

Situation 5: Using the Standard Deviation for Comparing a Set of Treatment Scores With a Set of Baseline Scores for a Single Client

When you are employing the AB single-subject design, you have a set of baseline scores and a set of treatment scores for a single client. You can employ the standard deviation to test your hypothesis. If your treatment scores are two standard deviations better than your baseline scores, you can conclude that your data supported your hypothesis ($p < .05$). Your first task, of course, is to determine if the treatment mean is better than the baseline mean. If so, you continue your statistical analysis journey.

You compute the mean and standard deviation of your baseline scores. You double your standard deviation of baseline scores, and add this to the mean of the baseline scores. You compute the mean of your treatment scores, and compare it with the figure that is 2 standard deviations better than the baseline mean. If it is better, you can conclude that your data supported your hypothesis ($p < .05$).

Use the following steps for calculating the standard deviation of your baseline scores.

1. 1. Access graphpad by clicking below.

http://graphpad.com/quickcalcs/contMenu/

2. You will see **Analyze continuous data** as the first heading.

   a. The default will be *t test to compare two means*. You will change this to *Descriptive statistics and confidence interval of a mean* by clicking on the circle next to this option.

   b. Click *Continue* at the bottom of the screen.

3. You will see the heading **Choose data entry format**. Leave this at the default specification of *enter up to 50 rows* unless you have more than 50 client scores to analyze.

   c. **Enter data.** Enter each of your baseline scores.

   d. Click *Calculate now*.

4. You will see the results. The first is the *mean for the baseline*. The second is labeled *SD*. This is your standard deviation.

17

ANALYZING QUALITATIVE DATA

Hopkins, Clegg, and Stackhouse (2016) were aware that a good deal of research had determined that youthful offenders have low language ability. However, they found that there was little information in the literature about the perceptions of young offenders about their literacy ability and their communication interactions with others. This lack of information suggested to them that they should conduct a qualitative study rather than a quantitative one. Consequently, these researchers conducted a qualitative study using semistructured interviews with 26 adolescents in a youth offender service. They also conducted two focus group sessions with these youth.

They posed questions with these study subjects about their level of satisfaction with their communication ability, with a focus on their communication interactions with others. Quotes from the respondents were organized into themes. The credibility of the authors' presentation of themes was tested by a procedure where a group of students in a language course were trained on how to review such quotes and were asked to give their analysis of the same data. There was a high degree of agreement between the researchers and this group of students, thereby supporting the credibility of the researchers' coding of the comments of the study subjects.

The results suggest that these adolescents were dissatisfied with their communication abilities. They expressed the opinion that they had difficulty understanding others, lacked support and respect from others, and were often in situations of dispute with authority figures. They avoided using positive communication as a problem-solving device. The authors noted that one of the practice implications of this qualitative study was a need for training these

youth in interactive communication and the value of using positive communication in solving problems with others.

INTRODUCTION

In previous chapters, you have seen that qualitative research differs from quantitative research in several ways. It is better for you to employ qualitative research methods, for example, when the available knowledge of your research theme is sparse. This leaves you with uncertainty about the identity of the key variables to include in your study. One of the distinctions between qualitative research and quantitative research is the form of the data. In qualitative research, you will collect and analyze words from a study sample. In quantitative research, you will collect and analyze data where study subjects have been either given a number (e.g., age or score on a scale) or placed into a predetermined category on each study variable (e.g., male and female). This chapter is about how qualitative data are analyzed.

In previous chapters, you were also introduced to the nature of qualitative research. You have seen how qualitative research and quantitative research are similar and how they are different. You have seen various forms of qualitative research that include ethnography, grounded theory, and case studies. You have also reviewed two protocols for qualitative research: analytic induction and utilization-focused evaluation. Each of these protocols was described with regard to specific steps in the research process. This chapter focuses on the analysis of qualitative data. In a prior chapter, you were introduced to two types of data analysis: **content analysis** and **narrative analysis**. Content analysis refers to the analysis of qualitative content by the coding of data at different levels, leading to conclusions about the research question. In narrative analysis, you examine the story being told by the study participants. It is content analysis that will be a major focus of the practice exercise in this chapter because it can be employed in many different types of qualitative research.

You will review examples of narrative analysis and a summary of what they have in common. You will also examine one protocol for content analysis, using an example of simple answers given to an open-ended question about the experience of being a graduate social work student.

In an example that serves as the focus of the practice exercise for this chapter, you will employ content analysis as the method of **qualitative data analysis**. Your data will be the responses of a group of social work graduate students to a set of questions about the experience of being in a graduate social work educational program. You will analyze this set of qualitative data using a protocol for content analysis, and you will draw conclusions from the data.

AN OVERVIEW OF QUALITATIVE DATA ANALYSIS

There are many forms of qualitative data. You may review the content of answers to an open-ended question on a survey, or you may review your own notes from an interview. Perhaps you will review photographic images that appear in television commercials and record your observations of the meaning of certain themes, such as the way in which men and women are portrayed differently. Maybe you will observe the behavior of people on a busy street and take notes on the nature of what you see. In each case, you will have words to analyze. From these words, you will draw meaning. You will do so according to a specific structure. You will not, for example, walk across your college campus for the purpose of observing the different behaviors of males and females and simply write a summary of what you observed. Instead, you will take notes, and you will review these notes using a structure such as the one outlined in this book for **coding** in content analysis. In other words, there is a method to qualitative data analysis.

Qualitative data analysis has evolved through many decades of development in the field of qualitative research. When you analyze qualitative data, you go from the specific words examined to the meaning they have for the subject of your study.

> In conventional qualitative methodology, therefore, data frequently are construed as mute, brute, passive, simple, and concrete. These portrayals contrast with the more complex or abstract entities that data will help generate, such as meaning, information, knowledge, evidence, concepts, or argument. Data thus are always insufficient; something must always be done to them to render the fit for human consumption. (Koro-Ljungberg, MacLure, & Ulmer, 2018, p. 463)

Perhaps you can envision a progression from a set of words to the categorization of words with regard to higher concepts, to the drawing of conclusions about the meaning of the totality of the data analyzed. That is the journey that will be discussed in this chapter.

Two forms of qualitative data analysis will be examined here: narrative analysis and content analysis. As noted before, a narrative can be viewed as a story, so narrative analysis is the discovery of the meaning of stories people tell about their life experiences. Content analysis is the review of specific content in a series of steps regarding the coding of the content at various levels, which leads to conclusions about the research question. You may find a narrative study that employs some variation of content analysis as part of the analysis of the data. The key to the narrative study is that data are collected on stories, not on simple answers to simple questions given in a social survey.

NARRATIVE ANALYSIS

Narrative has been defined as a distinct form of discourse that shapes the ordering of past experience through retrospective meaning making. It is a way of understanding actions and ordering social experience into a meaningful whole (Chase, 2018, p. 547). In other words, it is a method of inquiry that reveals meaning through reflections on the past—with emphasis on the relationships of social events—that reflect the totality of a theme. We can better understand the whole if we can view a series of stories told by people's life experiences.

Narratives can be told through stories about certain life experiences, such as being a cancer patient in our health system or the experience of residing in a homeless shelter. It can be told through efforts to determine the identity of institutions or the philosophy of a given agency. When the narrative study is complete, you should have a comprehensive view of the study subject.

There is no single protocol for the employment of narrative analysis in qualitative research. Instead, this form of analysis borrows from parts of protocols that may be found in research that does not necessarily employ narrative analysis. The best way to portray this form of analysis is through examples. You will review three such examples: (1) a study of organizational narratives that lead to self-reinforcing mechanisms, (2) a study of the lives of women who had been the victims of child maltreatment, and (3) a study of the impact of homelessness and shelter life on family relationships.

Case 1: A Review of Organizational Dynamics

Our first example is a study of organizational dynamics, with emphasis on blind spots and organizational inertia (Geiger & Antonacopoulou, 2009). Here is the abstract to that study:

> This article aims to demonstrate how narratives have the potential to bring about organizational inertia by creating self-reinforcing mechanisms and blind spots. Drawing on extensive interview data from a U.K. bio-manufacturing company, the empirical analysis shows how such narratives emerge by constructing a web of related, self-reinforcing narratives reflecting a consistent theme. The analysis demonstrates how the dominant (success) narrative remains vivid despite the existence of deviating narratives and severe crisis. In particular, the empirical findings illustrate how narratives construct a self-sustaining frame of reference, preventing the organization from questioning the principles underlying its past success. The discussion explains how narratives create self-reinforcing mechanisms and blind spots. It contributes to our understanding of the role of narratives in organizational change efforts and illustrates the way such self-reinforcing blind spots become a potential source of organizational inertia and path-dependence. (p. 411)

The study undertaken was designed to build on insights regarding the way in which organizational narratives influence and construct organizational dynamics. This examination can assist you in understanding the coexistence of stability and change in the organization.

The organization that served as the arena for this study was a small bio-manufacturing organization in the United Kingdom. It had recently sought to become a bigger player in the biopharmaceutical sector. At the time of the study, the organization was facing a major financial crisis. It had lost key clients and the support of venture capitalists, on whom it relied for financial investment. It was time for considering new directions. A key theme of the study was how narratives shape the dynamics of the organization. Consequently, the special challenge faced by this company provided a good opportunity for this focus.

This study, conducted in 2006 and 2007, employed a range of data collection methods. The primary method was the semistructured interview, along with focus groups. The first phase of the data collection process entailed discussions with senior management about the broad strategic issues that the organization was facing. The second phase included narrative interviews with 38 employees, four clients, and one external consultant. The use of the term *narrative* to describe the interview means that these employees were given the opportunity to tell their stories based on their experiences in the organization. These 38 employees represented 10% of the workforce of this organization and were selected to represent various aspects of it.

Each person was asked the following questions, typical of a semistructured interview:

1. Can you please tell us your personal story within Bio-Mule (the hypothetical name of the organization)?

2. What specific events, people, and practices shaped the identity of the organization and its position in relation to its competitors?

3. What were/are—from your perspective—the key success factors today and in the past?

4. Have they changed?

5. What was your experience of the transition into an independent organization? What is currently critical? (Geiger & Antonacopoulou, 2009, p. 417)

During these interviews, the interviewers frequently asked, "What happened next?" This was done to keep the storytelling process uninterrupted. Interviews were conducted face-to-face by two members of the research team and typically lasted 60 to 90 minutes. All interviews were tape-recorded and transcribed verbatim.

The first step in the analysis of the data was open coding of each transcript to identify common themes. Individual stories were aggregated into a storytelling episode by the identification of the recurrent repetition of a common theme. In other words, a second level of coding was undertaken. As part of this higher-level coding, the particular period of time of the story was noted. The researchers met to compare their coding of data from the interviews in order to identify major themes. Following this phase, the researchers held a feedback meeting with the participants to get feedback on the authenticity of their observations.

A key finding from this study was the emphasis on the concept of customer intimacy. It was mentioned by many participants in this study. One senior manager described this phenomenon as follows:

What makes us distinct is a combination of people and technology. Our people who work closely with the customer make the real difference, which is hard to sell. A key aspect of our work is customer intimacy. There is no single formula. Every customer is different and has to be treated according to its needs. . . . We are open with the customer and have customer contacts at all levels and all functions. (Geiger & Antonacopoulou, 2009, p. 422)

Thus, working closely with the customer and recognizing the uniqueness of each one were two themes that were derived from this one quote and from the comments of others.

Customer intimacy was not only a philosophy advocated by top management, but it was also a theme in the everyday work of the employees. This was one of the aspects of the view expressed by many as the uniqueness of this organization. Furthermore, the examination of information about the history of this organization suggested that customer intimacy was a major distinction from the beginning.

However, customer intimacy was also viewed as having a role in the organization's crisis. As one participant put it, the customer does not understand the necessities of licensing and efficiency and so forth, but these are important determinants of success. In other words, you can go too far in making sure that each customer is fully satisfied. A review of the narratives of the study participants led to conclusions about the role of self-reinforcing philosophies that may prevent innovation. If everyone embraces customer intimacy in the extreme, the organization is not fully prepared for crises and the development of innovative ways to achieve success.

Case 2: A Review of Resilience Among Women Who Had Suffered Child Maltreatment

Another example of narrative research was a study of the life stories of women who had suffered child maltreatment. Here is the abstract for the report:

The purpose of this feminist interpretive study was to portray the experience of women thriving after childhood maltreatment (CM) through personal narratives. An interdisciplinary team conducted multiple in-depth interviews of 44 women survivors of CM who identified themselves as successful and doing well. The interviews focused on "what worked" and "what did not" with the aim of exploring aftereffects of CM; strengths and strategies; interactions helpful in overcoming abuse; and related sociopolitical contexts. Narrative analyses revealed a distinct, dynamic process of becoming resolute characterized by six dimensions that were not sequential steps but characteristics, actions, and interactions. This study offers a new understanding of the experience of women gaining solid footing in their lives, the peace of knowing the abuse is over, and power to move in an upward trajectory. (Hall et al., 2009, p. 375)

The long-term goal of this study was the development of evidence-based interventions to improve the mental health of survivors of child maltreatment. Among the specific aims were (a) to discover patterns in the lives of female victims of child maltreatment, (b) to identify self-protective strategies that could improve health, (c) to describe the patterns of interactions between victims and others, and (4) to identify the social dimensions of work and relationships with others that were viewed as effective by these victims.

The sample was selected both by means of a newspaper article and through recruitment by the researchers. About 70% of the participants responded to a newspaper article where the study was described as focusing on what was helpful for survivors of child maltreatment in becoming successful in life.

The choice of specific parts of the research methods was guided by the intent of using research on the narratives to discover patterns that cut across the various life stories of this population, leading to improvements in the way in which society responds to child maltreatment and victims develop mechanisms for resilience.

A set of female psychiatric nurses conducted 2-hour interviews that were digitally recorded for analysis. The questions that were posed were neither given in a specific sequence nor asked in identical fashion. Instead, the interviewers had a general guide of questions that asked participants to reflect on their lives in various ways, including the effects of their child maltreatment experience on their lives.

The research team consisted of four PhD-prepared nurse faculty, a research psychologist, a psychiatrist, two psychiatric nurse practitioners, two doctoral research assistants, and doctoral students. These individuals reviewed the transcripts of each interview and held meetings for dialogue, which was structured in various ways (too complex to report here). The mean age of these 44 women was 46, a majority of whom were well educated. A majority of these women were Caucasian, while 24% were African American. Nearly all of these women had experienced depression and had been given treatment for it.

After the discovery of several themes in the patterns noted, the team decided that the word *resoluteness* was the best overall characterization of how these women coped with their abuse and entered adult life in a way they could pursue success. The term *resolute* was defined as separating conditions into their parts and clearing away doubts. It also entails the settling of things conclusively and transforming the circumstances into a different reality. Being resolute means being firm, determined, and unwavering. It was witnessed in this study as having at least six dimensions:

1. *Determined decisiveness:* Having the willingness and energy for challenge and change. One of the women said, "I am learning to captain my own ship."

2. *Counterframing:* The realization that the world of abuse was limited to one aspect of life; therefore, there were possibilities of escape from abuse.

3. *Facing down death:* Overcoming the fear of abuse, which could have led to death. This was empowering to the individual and led a few to have physical confrontations with their abusers.

4. *Redefining abusers and families of origin:* Participants redefined abusers as "very sick," "alcoholic," "criminals," or "rapists" as a way to disempower them. They maintained strict boundaries with their abusers and their accomplices in adulthood.

5. *Quest for learning:* Participants searched for meaning through books and movies and relationships with key individuals.

6. *Moving beyond:* A line was drawn in the life story: That was then, this is now. Now is different in important ways. I have redefined myself. My life is different.

Many of these participants had undertaken therapy, but for about half of them, the therapy was not viewed positively. However, about one third had very positive therapy experiences. The researchers summarized the therapy experiences as follows:

Listening, acceptance and belief were paramount characteristics in the person of the therapist for some, but not all. The most egregious behavior of a therapist was to disbelieve the woman's story of abuse. Participants appreciated the therapist "Being with and allowing for" versus breaking through their defenses. Premature delving into particulars of the abuse or push to confront was not helpful. (Hall et al., 2009, p. 382)

From this study, it is evident that resilience is a key to recovery from child maltreatment. The women who were participants in this study had worked toward a life of success through a list of mechanisms that they discovered mostly by their own initiatives. Others had played a role in their recovery, but mostly it looks like resilience is the key to this process.

The focus of this study was on success, so we learn a lot less about victims who have not done well in life. It appears that therapy was highly successful for only about one in three of these women who had sought it. The credentials of the therapists were not reported, but it is obvious from the standpoint of the author of this book that social work training is focused on the positive characteristics of therapy noted above.

Case 3: The Impact of Homelessness and Shelter Life on Family Relationships

Lindsey (1998) conducted a narrative analysis of data from interviews of mothers who had lived in homeless shelters with their children but had successfully found regular housing for at least 6 months. Here is the abstract of that study:

> This study explored mothers' perceptions of how homelessness and shelter life affected family relationships. Participants reported increased closeness and heightened quality and quantity of interaction with their children, but a disruption in their roles as disciplinarians and providers/caretakers. Factors which mothers perceived to affect relationships were shelter conditions (rules and interactions with staff and residents), the mother's emotional state, and the child's emotional state, temperament, and behavior. Implications for practice are suggested. (p. 243)

Two phases of this study were undertaken: one for participants from nonurban communities in the state of Georgia and the second from urban communities in North Carolina. The size of the sample was rather small due to the employment of saturation (referred to as "redundancy" by the authors), which closed the recruitment of participants when new interviews were failing to generate new ideas. This method will be illustrated in the practice exercise on content analysis given later in this chapter.

In this study, qualitative data were collected from the interviews of 17 mothers who met the qualifications of having lived in a homeless shelter with at least one child and maintained regular housing for at least 6 months. The interviews were transcribed and coded at two levels. The first level of coding (open coding) was designed to capture the essence of each idea presented by the participants. The second level of coding generated categories into which the first level of coding could be placed and based on which general themes could be identified. Following the second level of coding, each transcript was reanalyzed to ensure that data had not been lost. Then, exemplars were sought for each category to illustrate its meaning. Finally, Ethnograph, a computer software package, was used to further code interview segments and organize the data according to conceptual categories and subcategories.

A number of suggestions were given by the author of this study for those who work with homeless shelters. First, it was suggested that mothers be given as much authority and control as possible over daily matters regarding bedtimes, bath times, and eating arrangements. Often agencies develop rules that make the life of the shelter employees easier but are not functional for the mothers. The primacy of the client should be maintained in such matters. Second, shelters should develop ways to show mothers how to use noncorporal methods of discipline. These mothers were not happy with the rule against corporal punishment, but did not seem to have alternatives, so they would sometimes violate this rule. Third, staff should undertake a review of their typical interactions with mothers in this situation so as to better engage in practices that support family relations. Fourth, rules that prevent boys of a certain age from being allowed to live in the shelter should be abandoned. This rule is dysfunctional for family life.

Reflections on Narrative Analysis

This review of examples of narrative analysis of qualitative data was designed to illustrate the kinds of methods used when the researcher is examining stories as the mechanism for gaining understanding of the theme of interest. You saw that one of the procedures employed was content analysis of interviews. So you can see that content analysis and narrative analysis are not totally separate entities. The key distinction is that narrative analysis is a review of stories, whereas content analysis is a review of qualitative data that are not normally seen as a story.

What you saw in each example is data collection through interviews that took a minimum of 1 hour. These interviews were guided by questions that solicited a discussion rather than simple answers. You also saw that the qualitative data for each interview were transcribed and these transcriptions were subjected to some form of coding, usually in more than one level. More than one researcher engaged in this coding procedure, with opportunities for analysis through engaged discussions by the researchers. Therefore, you saw that narrative analysis is more than just observing things and telling others what you believe you saw in some general sense. It entails a careful set of data analysis procedures.

Content Analysis

Content analysis entails a set of procedures where you reduce a number of statements from study subjects into themes that lead to conclusions about the nature of the research theme. One of the themes identified by Hopkins et al. (2016) in the study of youth offenders was the avoidance of positive communication techniques as a problem-solving method. This theme emerged from the content analysis of statements made by these youth. This observation led to a conclusion that training was needed with this target population on the methods and benefits of positive communication.

In this chapter, you will have an experience of content analysis using a protocol developed by the author. This protocol includes the following:

1. The bracketing of your own ideas about the major research question being pursued, so that you can review the extent to which your own biases are interfering with critical analysis of the content that is being provided by the study subjects

2. First-level coding of the content of the qualitative data

3. The assessment of the credibility of these first-level codes

4. Second-level coding of the first-level codes into themes and the assessment of the credibility of these codes

5. Enumeration of the second-level codes (themes)

6. **Saturation assessment**

7. Conclusions

Each of these themes will be discussed in detail in the next part of this chapter.

Bracketing

You have used brackets in your writing. You use brackets to set apart certain kinds of content from others in your sentences. In qualitative research, you engage in **bracketing** to set apart your ideas on the theme of your study from the ideas that come from your study participants (Tufford & Newman, 2012). The function of this procedure is for you to heighten your self-awareness in order to engage in exercises in which you review your analysis of the data that come from your study subjects in light of your own ideas about the study theme. Your analysis should not be influenced by your ideas on the study theme. Instead, you should be a reporter of what your study subjects have said.

A group of graduate social work students of mine once engaged in interviews of fellow students with regard to sources of social support. One group of three interviewers reviewed the comments of the five social work students whom they interviewed and found that religion was expressed as a source of support by two of them. There was another source of support, family, that was identified by three of these students. However, the three students conducting the interviews reported that religion was a source of support for all three of them; therefore, they concluded that religion was the top source of support in their study.

What was their error? They put themselves into the data. Instead of reporting that two of the five students mentioned religion and three of these students identified family as a source of support, they included themselves in the data and drew a conclusion that religion was a greater source of support than family.

Bracketing is more subtle than the example described above. It entails the description of your own ideas about the theme of the study so you can be cognizant of the potential interference of your ideas in the analysis of what is being said. For this book, the procedure of bracketing will simply entail the recording of your ideas and encouragement to review that list again as you code the data from your study subjects.

Bracketing is a greater source of concern when the volume of content that is being coded is greater. If you were coding a set of essays on a theme, you would be more vulnerable to the influence of bias than would be the case if you were coding a set of sentences. In a practice exercise in this chapter, you will be coding a set of statements that are typically only a few sentences each. Bracketing, therefore, should be of less concern. However, you should engage in this part of the exercise as a precaution and as an opportunity to have the experience of bracketing in content analysis.

Given the fact that the practice exercise in the next section deals with the personal experiences of the respondents, the bracketing part of content analysis will not be a part of the protocol employed in that exercise. If the question had dealt with public policy or school policies, a bracketing step would have been warranted.

First-Level Coding

A code in qualitative research is a segment of words that reduces text from many words to a few and captures the essence of what is being said in the text. Suppose that you asked the following question on a survey: "How would you describe your approach to getting your child to do what he or she needs to do?" Suppose further that one parent in the survey wrote the following:

I believe that you need to let your child know the rules and that you should be prepared to offer punishment in the form of spankings if the rules are broken. In other words, I would say that if you spare the rod, you will spoil the child.

How would you code this response? You might say simply "believes in corporal punishment." If you did this, you would have reduced the words from 48 to 4 and would have captured the essence of the message.

When asked to give an opinion about what is most important about the experience of being a social work student, a subject may prepare two paragraphs that summarize the importance of having a good field internship. The words "importance of field" or something similar may be used as the code for two paragraphs of content from the study subject.

In a previous chapter, you saw some definitions of different levels of coding. The first level is the code that captures the essence of a given set of words expressed by the study subject. The second-level code is a method of taking first-level codes and developing themes that show the similarities of the first-level codes. In other words, it is a way to group the first-level codes. In a study of what is important about the social work education experience, you may find study subjects mentioning various aspects of the field internship experience. One person may mention the importance of having a good field instructor. Another may mention the importance of having good opportunities to work with certain types of clients. Someone else may mention the field agency. The common theme for these would be the importance of the field internship experience. The importance of the field internship, therefore, would be one of your second-level codes.

A study was undertaken by a school of social work regarding the advice of persons with an MSW (Master of Social Work) degree on how to design a good MSW program. There was an open-ended question at the end of a survey that asked respondents to give their advice about this. Here are a few answers:

Very selective criteria for enrollment

Emphasis on clinical techniques in classroom settings via role-playing, case scenarios, videotapes

In-depth education on three theories as opposed to a brief overview of many

Your job as the researcher is to select a word or a phrase that captures the essence of what is being said in this statement. You will probably find that there are at least three themes. Each of these three quotes from the same person addressed different ideas. For the first statement, you might put "selective enrollment" as the code. There are other words that would be appropriate as the code as long as you stay as close as possible to the words of the study subject. You would not, for example, say something like "Keep out the dummies from admission." You did not see these words from the study subject. There was no reference to the word *dummies*. Instead, "selective criteria for enrollment" were the words employed. In this case, you have not reduced the number of words very much, but this is okay in a situation where the respondent has already been concise in expression. In fact, if you had simply coded this first expression with all the words of the respondent, it would be okay. Only five words were employed by the study subject, and this is not too many words for a code.

What would you do with the second statement? How about using "clinical techniques in class" as the code? What about the third statement? How about "in-depth education on selected theories"? As you think of how you might code the statements, you will see that there is some room for using different words to convey the same message.

Credibility Assessment

You can test how well you did with the first-level coding by engaging in a **credibility assessment** exercise where you compare your codes with those of another researcher who is reviewing the same content. You compare each of your codes with that of the other researcher and decide if the codes are essentially the same. Being the same does not necessarily mean the exact words. There are more than one word that can be used to convey a message. The issue is whether the meanings of the two codes (your code and the other researcher's code) are fundamentally the same.

What proportion of your codes were similar to those of the other researcher? If you have produced 36 codes and 31 were the same as the codes of the other person, you would have a level of agreement of 86% (31/36 = 0.86, or 86%). This would be good news. There are no clear criteria for what is a good level of agreement, but you would probably agree that a level of agreement that is less than 50% would be bad news. In such a case, you might chose to find a second and a third research partner, as a check on the possibility that your first partner is not doing so well. If you fail to find agreement between yourself and the other researchers, you need to review the idea of coding and try again to see if you have improved.

Second-Level Coding

When you engage in second-level coding, you place your first-level codes into categories. Consider the survey of social workers who were asked for their advice regarding the development of a new graduate social work program. Suppose that you coded the first three persons as follows:

Person 1:   1.1: Long field placements

Person 2:   2.1: Teach theory

2.2: Appropriate field placement

2.3: Strong supervision

Person 3:   3.1: Heighten recognition of MSW degree

3.2: Improve pay of those with MSW

Suppose further that you have composed a second-level code that you name "field instruction." You have placed first-level codes of 1.1, 2.1, and 2.3 into this second-level code. Your data suggest that there were three statements about field instruction that were offered by two people in the study. You also have one statement about teaching theory. This idea will not be included among the second-level codes unless it is duplicated by another person. "Improving the profession" may have been your second-level code for Statements 3.1 and 3.2, but because these two codes are about the same thing from only one person, it would not be included in the second-level codes unless duplicated by another study subject.

Your will report from the above data that you had three codes with the theme of field instruction and two codes with the theme of improving the profession. You can count both the number of statements made and the number of people who stated them. This task deals with enumeration, the next concept to be examined.

Enumeration

Enumeration simply refers to the counting of things. You have already been notified that you will count how many comments were made by study subjects with regard to a given theme. Did more respondents mention field instruction than classroom instruction? Was clinical practice emphasized over community practice? Was theory emphasized more than techniques? These are the questions that might be answered in a survey seeking the advice of social workers on how to design a good MSW program.

Your enumeration will not only result in the articulation of various themes but also show the extent to which the people in the survey expressed the theme. You can report both the number of comments on a given theme and the number of people who expressed something with regard to the particular theme.

Saturation Assessment

Saturation refers to being in a state where nothing more needs to be reviewed (Fusch & Ness, 2015). It means that you are full. Maybe you cannot eat anything else after a really big Thanksgiving dinner. So what does this have to do with content analysis? It deals with the stage when your data seem to be generating no more new ideas. Suppose your first 20 respondents to a survey mentioned field instruction, clinical practice, and accessibility and your second set of 20 statements listed the same three themes with nothing added. You have achieved saturation. When you achieve saturation, you have less reason to continue your review of data. However, if your second set of comments yielded a number of new ideas, you would continue your review of data. This continuance might entail another survey of additional respondents, or it might entail the review of more client records if this is your source of data.

Conclusions

Your conclusions will be drawn from your analysis of your qualitative data. If you found more people mentioning the importance of field instruction that anything else, you would report this. If clinical practice was mentioned more often than community practice, you would report this as well. And you would simply follow your data in a way that summarizes them. Perhaps your final review of the data suggests one broad theme, such as whether the idea is more about the similarities of the respondents than their differences.

Chapter Practice Exercise

What Was Most Meaningful About This MSW Program?

In this exercise, you will go through the process discussed above using a set of qualitative data taken from a survey. In the spring of 2017, a school of social work was engaged in the evaluation of its MSW program. One part of that evaluation was a survey conducted of graduate students who were scheduled to complete their MSW degree programs in 2 months. The respondents were asked the following question: "What is the most important thing you have gained from your experience with the MSW program?" The data for this practice exercise came from those who responded to the survey from two classes of students. They represented about one half of the students who were at the midpoint of their last semester of matriculation in this MSW program.

In this practice exercise, you will review the answers to this question through one protocol for content analysis that was described in the previous section. The questions posed on this survey were qualitative in nature because this school wanted to get feedback that was not circumscribed by previous notions of what students like or do not like. Having a lot of ideas about this issue would be necessary for the researchers to conduct a survey using questions that generated quantitative data.

The first set of content analysis procedures you will undertake will be with the 12 students in the first class. The procedures you will undertake include the following: (a) the first-level coding of the answers from the first class of students, (b) the assessment of the credibility of your first-level codes for this first segment of data, (c) the second level coding of your first-level codes. Next, you will undertake the same procedures for the answers to the question from the second class of students. In other words, you will examine the answers to the central question from the second class of 11 respondents to the survey. Then, you will undertake an examination of saturation to see if there is a need for the collection of additional data from the study population. The step of bracketing has been left out because the question posed to the study respondents was regarding one of their experiences (completing the work for the MSW degree), which those who are reading this book have not likely experienced. In this situation, it may be difficult for the readers of this book to imagine their own opinions about this experience.

Competencies Demonstrated by This Practice Exercise

1. The ability to engage in first-level coding of simple answers to an open-ended survey question

2. The ability to engage in the credibility assessment of one's first-level codes

3. The ability to engage in the second-level coding of simple answers to an open-ended survey question

4. The ability to engage in saturation assessment of codes from two segments of responses to an open-ended question

5. The ability to draw appropriate conclusions from a content analysis of a set of qualitative data

Activities for This Practice Exercise

1. First-level coding of the responses to an open-ended question from a survey given to Class A

2. Credibility assessment of data from the first-level codes for Class A

3. Second-level coding of the responses to an open-ended question from the survey for Class A

4. First-level coding of the responses from Class B

5. Second-level coding of the responses from Class B

6. Saturation assessment of the second-level codes for Class A and Class B, with conclusions about whether there should be further collection of data

7. Drawing conclusions for the study

What You Will Report From This Practice Exercise

Your report for this exercise will include the following:

1. Your first-level coding of the comments from Class A (Exhibit 17.1), which are offered by you in Exhibit 17.2

2. Your credibility report from your comparison of your first-level codes offered in Exhibit 17.2 with the codes of the same data of another researcher

3. Your second-level coding of the data from Class A, which are offered by you in Exhibit 17.3

4. Your first-level coding of the answers given by Class B (Exhibit 17.4), which are offered by you in Exhibit 17.5

5. Your second-level coding of the answers given by Class B, which are offered by you in Exhibit 17.6

6. Your saturation assessment report

7. Your study conclusions

In other words, your report will entail Exhibit 17.2, your credibility report; Exhibit 17.3; Exhibit 17.4, Exhibit 17.5; Exhibit 17.6, your saturation assessment; and your study conclusions. The next section will take you step-by-step through the data analysis process.

Analysis of Qualitative Data From the 2017 Study of a Graduate Social Work Program

In this section, you will find the qualitative data that were acquired from the answers of two sets of MSW students to the question "What is the most important thing you have gained from your experience with the MSW program?" You will conduct an analysis of these data and offer your report.

Step 1: First-Level Coding of Data for Class A

In Exhibit 17.1, you will see the answers given to the first survey question by the 12 students from Class A. Your task in this part of the exercise is to develop first-level codes for each statement. You will enter your codes in Exhibit 17.2. If you have more than one code for person A-1, you will separate it from the others by giving the number of the code in parentheses, such as (1), (2), and so forth. If you need to refer to a given code in a report, you can designate, for example, the first code for the first student as A-1(1), while the second code for the third person would be A-3(2).

EXHIBIT 17.1
ANSWERS TO QUESTION 1 FROM CLASS A

Student Number	Question 1: What Is the Most Important Thing You Have Gained From Your Experience in the MSW Program?
A-1	Empathy and passion for working with individuals with substance use disorders Clinical skills, ethics, and therapy modalities.
A-2	Most important is the quality of my experience—quality in relationships within CHHS (College of Health and Human Services), quality of useful class lectures and materials, quality of community resources and connections, quality of hands-on practice through quality field placements, quality of various speakers/ideas that CHHS has brought to campus.
A-3	Personally and professionally to advocate for myself as well as my clients Participating in education opportunities within the community was very important as if allowed me to gain better understanding of what was presented in class and apply it in the field and validate what I was learning.
A-4	The most important thing I have gained from the MSW program is practice experience integrated with coursework. I have had the opportunity to use my field placement experience as a base to write exploratory papers and potential research examples on. Having practice coursework curious for information to stick much better as I can directly apply it as I learn it, and I can bring back questions from my field experience.
A-5	A lot of modalities and ways to approach a situation, as well as life-applicable professional knowledge (billing, etc.). I personally function better when I have an array of perspectives and a tool belt of methods that I can tailor to client needs. Professors have both a plethora of information on all this and life experience to illustrate them.
A-6	The internship is by far the most useful learning tool in the MSW program. I have really enjoyed the entire field experience. You are able to directly apply all the concepts, frameworks, and therapy modalities in real-world situations. It helps to reinforce the validity of what you are learning with real clients. It's the most crucial part of this program.
A-7	I think that students should be required to go to counseling themselves or at least given the option. It is something that I have sought out and paid for on my own, but I think it would help us better talk to the struggle clients have, to be open and vulnerable with us. I also think we have a responsibility to grow as people if we are asking others to do that. I can't see any reason why it isn't an option and I think, like field supervision, it should be a requirement. I also think that a number of students who are drawn to this field have themselves not dealt with personal issues that are certain to affect their work. Field supervision is not enough to address these personal issues.
A-8	The most important thing I have gained from my experience with the MSW program is a greater sense of understanding of myself in the context of being a social worker. Before this program, I knew I was a naturally caring person and social work "called" to me in a way, but with this program, I have been able to fine-tune those natural abilities in a way to better myself as not just a social worker but as a person in general.

A-9	I believe that the most important thing I have gained from my MSW program experience is a strong sense of self in context to my purpose for entering the program. I don't mean to say that the knowledge I have gained is not important, it is, rather that is would not be as useful if I was unable to develop what I think is an improved and solid sense of self in the 2 years I have been in this program.
A-10	The clinical practice courses and experience.
A-11	The importance of meeting clients where they are with becoming more accepting and understanding of others I have been able to become more self-aware of myself and my own capacity to be a changing agent. My future work will focus on *rehabilitation*, not habilitation. Acknowledging that clients are resilient and have their own strengths which should always be brought to the surface in the social work field.
A-12	Learning the different models of practice to use when working with a client.

EXHIBIT 17.2
YOUR FIRST-LEVEL CODES FOR CLASS A

Student Number	Your Codes (Separated by Numbers for Each Code, e.g., (1), (2), etc.)
A-1	
A-2	
A-3	
A-4	
A-5	
A-6	
A-7	
A-8	
A-9	
A-10	
A-11	
A-12	

Step 2: Credibility Assessment for the First-Level Codes of Data From Class A

In this part of the exercise, you will examine the credibility of your coding of the answers to the first question posed to Class A, as indicated in Exhibit 17.2. You will find a fellow researcher who has done the coding of the responses in Exhibit 17.1 and presented his or her data in Exhibit 17.2. In other words, you will compare your Exhibit 17.2 with the Exhibit 17.2 of the other researcher. You will compare each of your codes in this exhibit with the same by the other researcher and determine whether your code is congruent with that of the other researcher. For codes to be congruent, they do not have to have exactly the same words, but they must have the same meaning. For example, the code "field placement" may be viewed as congruent with the words "field internship." The word "clinical" may be viewed as congruent with the words "direct practice."

You will compute your coefficient of congruence by computing the number of your codes and the number of codes that are congruent with the other person, and by dividing the number of congruent codes by the total number of your codes. Here is an example:

1.   My total number of codes is 23.

2.   The number of my codes that were congruent with those of the other researcher is 19.

3.   My coefficient of congruence (Item 2 above divided by Item 1) is 0.826, or 0.83 rounded off (19/23 = 0.826). In other words, I have an 83% level of congruence.

Your credibility report will provide the above data (Items 1–3) regarding your coding of the data given in Exhibit 17.2. This report will not include a number of items that would be included in a comprehensive examination of congruence. That report would entail the examination of congruence for all of your different data analyses, including the second-level coding for Class A and the coding of data for Class B. This part of the exercise is designed to give you an experience in credibility assessment so you will know how to engage in it on a more comprehensive level when you undertake your own qualitative data analysis that is comprehensive.

Step 3: Second-Level Coding for Class A

In your second-level codes, you find the common denominator between two or more of your first-level codes. You group first-level codes according to commonalities. If there is a first-level code that is not similar to a code for another study subject, this code will be left off the list of second-level codes.

Your second-level code report will entail the completion of Exhibit 17.3. In the first column, you enter your second-level codes. In the second column, you enter all the first-level codes that fall within the purview of a second-level code. In the third column, you enter the number of first-level codes that are identified in the middle column.

You now have your first-level codes and second-level codes for the data for the first class. Your next set of steps is to repeat the previous procedures for the data on the first research question for Class B.

EXHIBIT 17.3
SECOND-LEVEL CODES FOR CLASS A

Second-Level Codes (Enter the Words of the Codes)	First-Level Codes That Fit This Second-Level Code (Enter the Words of the Code, Not the Code Number or the Entire Set of Words of the Study Participant.)	Number of First-Level Codes

Step 4: First-Level Coding for Class B

In this step, you repeat the procedures for first-level coding for the first class using the data from the second class. The students in Class B answered the same question as the students in Class A. The data for Class B are given in Exhibit 17.4 and the first-level codes in Exhibit 17.5.

EXHIBIT 17.4
STATEMENTS FROM CLASS B

Student	What Is the Most Important Thing You Have Gained From Your Experience in the MSW Program?
B-1	I think that the most important part of the program is the field internship. It taught me more than I could learn from any class, and being able to process these experiences in field class was also helpful.
B-2	The most important thing I've learned is how to be present with people in the moment and how to just be mindful of others. All of the therapeutic techniques can be acquired and are definitely helpful. But having that foundation to build on helps me to know I'm actually helping people with the problems they want fixed. Knowing how to be mindful helps other things fall into place to have the most success possible.
B-3	Knowledge about different diagnosis and treatment approaches.
B-4	I have learned that the way each individual sees a problem, person, event (based on their experiences, relationships, etc.) impacts their actions, perceived solutions, etc. In the same line, we bring meaning to the things and construct our experiences based on our point of view and experiences. It is important for us as social workers to recognize this.
B-5	My field placement has been by far the most valuable part of this program. Without the experience and skills learned there, I would feel very unprepared.
B-6	I cannot name just one thing, but I have gained greater self-awareness, a toolkit of professional skills, and a social work network. Professor investment in student success and my internship have been my favorite aspects.

(Continued)

EXHIBIT 17.4   (Continued)

Student	What Is the Most Important Thing You Have Gained From Your Experience in the MSW Program?
B-7	The most important thing I have gained in this MSW program is clinical knowledge to help me in my future career. I have gained so much material I will be able to use for the rest of my life—life books, journals, and clinical terms grid. I feel that I now have the skills to be more open and accepting. I thought I was open-minded before, but the MSW program has definitely helped me to be more genuine, open-minded, and a better listener. My internship has also helped me understand how to put what I learned in the MSW program to use in the real/working world.
B-8	The most important thing that I have gained from my experience is effective clinical skills and the confidence to employ these skills. I feel that my experience has taught me a wide array of social skills, including the confidence to be silent sometimes during my clinical work. I have opened up to the being more directed towards new experiences, and I notice that I enjoy challenges more, with less social anxiety.
B-9	The ability to further assess and research clinical interventions while accounting for a person-in-the-environment perspective. All addition to this, I feel I have gained strength-based tools that further establish rapport and support the social work values of human relationships.
B-10	It is hard to nail down a single most important thing that I have learned since I feel I have gained so many things in my professional and personal life experiences. I have developed relationships with individuals who share the idea for empowering clients and helping access the tools within themselves to become the best individuals they can be. I have learned vulnerability and relationships change things. It helps us realize our human-ness and how connected we all really are, I think that is really important.
B-11	Clinical experience with treatment modalities. I had no experience prior to this program, and learning about how to do therapy is what I came here for; and among other things, it's what I got. If anything, I would've liked more of that even in the theory classes—how to apply social theories in clinical practice.

EXHIBIT 17.5
YOUR FIRST-LEVEL CODES FOR CLASS B

Student Number	Your Codes (Separated by Numbers for Each Code, e.g., (1), (2), etc.)
B-1	
B-2	
B-3	
B-4	
B-5	

B-6	
B-7	
B-8	
B-9	
B-10	
B-11	

Step 5: Second-Level Coding of Data From Class B

You repeat your procedures for Step 2 except that you are reviewing the data for Class B rather than Class A. In other words, you find the common denominator between your first-level codes and group them accordingly.

Your second-level code report will entail the completion of Exhibit 17.6. In the first column, you enter your second-level codes. In the second column, you enter all the first-level codes that fall within the purview of a second-level code. In the third column, you enter the number of first-level codes that are identified in the middle column.

You now have your first-level codes and second-level codes for the data for Class B to add to your study of the data from the first class. Your next set of steps will entail the examination of whether you have achieved saturation when you compare what you have learned from Class A and what you have learned from Class B.

EXHIBIT 17.6
SECOND-LEVEL CODES FOR CLASS B

Second-Level Codes (Enter the Words of the Codes)	First-Level Codes That Fit This Second-Level Code (Enter the Words of the Code, Not the Code Number or the Entire Set of Words of the Study Participant)	Number of First-Level Codes

Step 6: Saturation Assessment

Saturation means that something is full. If you have given all the water your lawn can take without flooding, you might say that you have saturated your lawn with water. If you have reviewed several segments of qualitative data on a given theme and have found that the most recent segment of data did not yield any useful additional information, you can say that you have achieved saturation. This means that it is not essential for you to continue your search of similar data in order to obtain a comprehensive picture. You apparently already have that.

You have two sets of second-level codes of information regarding what was most meaningful about the experience of graduate social work education for two groups of students. These 23 students were in two sections of a research course that was taken in the last semester of a four-semester MSW program. There are additional sections of this class at this university, so you would want to know if you should continue your study by collecting and analyzing data from the other sections of this course.

You have rather limited data, so you would not normally expect to find evidence of saturation in this particular instance. However, you will engage in a brief experience with saturation to determine if you need to seek similar data from the additional classes of students. In a nutshell, if you find that the information gained from the second class of students did not add useful knowledge to your inquiry, you will conclude that you have achieved saturation and you will not feel the need to continue your collection of data. If your second class provided useful information, you will decide to continue your collection and analysis of data. You do not have these additional data for this exercise, but you will know that you have not achieved saturation and what that means to your study.

Your task is to compare the second-level codes for Class A (Exhibit 17.3) and Class B (Exhibit 17.6) to see how much new information was generated from the data from Class B. You can complete Exhibit 17.7 as your guide. In this exhibit, you will present the second-level codes for the data from the first class in the first column. In the second column, you will enter either Yes or No to designate whether the code is similar to the one from the second class. In the third column, you will enter the new codes you got from Class B. It is the last column that is the most instrumental in your saturation assessment. To what extent does this column provide meaningful information?

There is no technical recommendation that provides precise guidance for you in this assessment. You simply review the information and draw a conclusion based on it. You will not likely find that saturation has been achieved, given the limited amount of data at your disposal, but you will have undertaken a saturation assessment of qualitative data, so you now know how to do that.

EXHIBIT 17.7
SATURATION ASSESSMENT

Second-Level Codes, Class A	Was This Code Similar to the One for Class B? (Yes or No)	New Codes Added by Class B

Step 7: Conclusions

You will draw basic conclusions about what was found in your coding of qualitative data. You may report the second-level codes with the number of people who offered them. You may review these second-level codes as a whole and see what major themes were found. As you review these major themes, you may note an overall observation about the nature of the things found to be most meaningful to students. For example, you may find a tendency in these students to identify the helpfulness of people as a major overall theme, or you may find a tendency in these students to identify a type of learning that was most meaningful. On the other hand, you may not find a major observation to bind these students together.

CHAPTER REVIEW

Chapter Key Learnings

1. Qualitative data analysis entails the translation of words into meaning, with two major alternatives being the review of stories through narrative analysis and the review of specific content through content analysis.

2. Narrative analysis typically entails the collection of qualitative data through extensive interviews of study subjects, the transcription of interview content, the coding of data from the transcripts at more than one level by a research team, and an extensive dialogue by researchers that leads to major observations about what was said in the interviews. These dialogues also lead to major conclusions.

3. Content analysis typically includes the collection of qualitative data through surveys or existing documents, the bracketing of researcher bias, the coding of data in more than one level, the assessment of the credibility of content codes, the review of whether saturation has been achieved, and the drawing of conclusions about the theme of the study.

4. Bracketing entails the recognition of the researcher's biases regarding, or general orientation to, the theme of the study, to reduce the extent to which researcher bias influences the data analysis.

5. The first level of coding (sometimes called open coding) is exhibited by a word or a phrase that captures the essence of the meaning of a statement, contained typically in a sentence or a paragraph. It is a way of reducing the number of words to be examined so that messages can be more efficiently reviewed.

6. A second-level code is a category that incorporates more than one first-level code. When you review the number of first-level codes in a given second-level code, you can see the emphasis that study subjects have placed on the themes that are revealed in the content.

7. Credibility assessment in qualitative data analysis entails the comparison of codes, of the same content, by different researchers to determine the congruence of perceptions. Poor congruence challenges the credibility of the coding of data.

8. Saturation refers to the extent to which current data have sufficiently revealed meaning so that further collection of data is not warranted. It is examined by reviewing segments of qualitative data to see if new segments generate new observations.

Chapter Discussion Questions

1. Think of a research question that is better answered through stories (narrative analysis) than through simple content assessment. Why is this question better examined through narrative analysis?

2. What is a research question that might be answered by a review of agency documents, such as client records? Should this be a narrative analysis or a content analysis? Explain.

3. What is an open-ended research question you could pose to your fellow students that would be appropriate for content analysis? Identify two of the steps you might undertake in the content analysis of the data you would collect from this question.

4. With regard to the above question, what is one or more of your own opinions about the open-ended question that might influence your review of the data? What is the category of this step in the research process?

5. Explain how you would examine the credibility of your coding of responses to the above open-ended question.

6. What is an advantage that qualitative research has over quantitative research? In your opinion, does qualitative research have equal value to quantitative research in the minds of the leaders of social work, such as agency directors, social work association officers, writers of articles in social work journals, and so forth?

7. Which of the following aspects of qualitative data analysis would be the most challenging for you to undertake: bracketing, first-level coding, second-level coding, credibility assessment, or saturation assessment? Why?

Chapter Test

1. Qualitative data, unlike quantitative data, take what form?
   a. The placement of study subjects into predetermined categories that have no order (e.g., male and female)
   b. The provision of a number that has numerical meaning (e.g., age measured in years)
   c. The placement of study subjects into categories that are ordered (e.g., *strongly agree*, *agree*, *disagree*, *strongly disagree*)
   d. None of the above

2. Which of the following statements is/are true about qualitative data analysis?
   a. The purpose of coding is to reduce the number of words examined so as to improve the efficiency of the analysis
   b. Narrative analysis entails the examination of stories
   c. Both of the above
   d. None of the above

3. Narrative studies typically include which of the following?
   a. The interviewing of study subjects
   b. The coding of content
   c. A dialogue among researchers about the nature of the meaning of content
   d. All of the above

4. Second-level coding of content entails the following:
   a. The final conclusion about the theme under investigation
   b. The categorization of first-level codes
   c. A word or a phrase that captures the essence of what was said by the study subject
   d. None of the above

5. Saturation has been achieved in qualitative data analysis when
   a. There is a need for the examination of more data on the study subject
   b. The second-level codes have been enumerated
   c. Both of the above
   d. None of the above

6. Which of the following is/are true about qualitative data analysis?
   a. When you have demonstrated credibility in data analysis, you have found congruence in the coding of content by different researchers
   b. You engage in bracketing to improve the saturation of content
   c. Both of the above
   d. None of the above

7. Bracketing in qualitative data analysis entails
   a. The review of new segments of data because your review of existing data continues to reveal a good deal of new information
   b. The recognition by researchers of their own biases regarding the study subject
   c. The examination of congruence between different research studies of the same content
   d. The enumeration of the number of first-level codes that are contained in a given second-level code

8. Which of the following statements is/are true about qualitative data analysis?
   a. You decide on the categories into which your qualitative data will be placed before you examine the qualitative data. For example, you might have categories such as clarity of expectations, quality of

instruction, and the importance of field instruction, into which to place answers to the open-ended question to social work students about what was most important in their learning experiences

b. Open coding (aka first-level coding) refers to the word or phrase that captures the

essence of the meaning of a set of content from a segment of the answers to a question that was given to study subjects (e.g., a sentence, a paragraph, etc.)

c. Both of the above

d. None of the above

ANSWERS: 1 = d; 2 = c; 3 = d; 4 = b; 5 = d; 6 = a; 7 = b; 8 = b

Chapter Glossary

Bracketing. The identification of researcher biases regarding the theme of study so as to reduce the effect of these biases on qualitative data analysis.

Coding. A mechanism in qualitative data analysis that identifies themes that show the meaning of the words of the respondents. First-level coding captures the essence of a brief segment of qualitative data, while second-level coding entails the categorization of first-level codes.

Content analysis. The examination of qualitative data through a set of procedures that are designed to reveal meaning for various quantities of data.

Credibility assessment. A procedure in qualitative data analysis where the codes of one researcher are compared with the codes of another researcher with regard to the same data to determine if there is sufficient

congruence between the codes to trust the coding as legitimate.

Enumeration. The counting of first-level codes in second-level coding to determine the weight of each concept in qualitative data analysis.

Narrative analysis. The examination of stories through a set of procedures designed to reveal meaning through reflections on the past, with emphasis on the relationships of social events that reflect the totality of a theme.

Qualitative data analysis. The examination of words spoken, or written, with regard to a research purpose to gain the meaning of the theme under investigation.

Saturation assessment. The examination of segments of qualitative data to determine if enough new information is being acquired in order to indicate that further collection of data is warranted.

GLOSSARY

AB single-subject design. A research design in which a subject's target behavior is measured repeatedly during a baseline period and then is measured repeatedly during a period whereby treatment is offered.

ABA single-subject design. A research design where a single client's target behavior is measured repeatedly during a baseline period, the measurements continue during a treatment period, and treatment is withdrawn but target behavior continues to be measured during the second baseline period.

ABAB single-subject design. A research design in which a single subject's target behavior is measured repeatedly during a baseline period, is given a treatment and measured repeatedly during the first treatment period, is then measured repeatedly during a second baseline period where treatment has been withdrawn, and, finally, is measured repeatedly during a second treatment period where the same treatment is offered again.

ABC single-subject design. A research design in which a single subject is measured repeatedly during a baseline period, then is measured repeatedly during a period where treatment is implemented, and, finally, is measured repeatedly during a period where a second treatment is provided that is different from the first treatment that was offered.

Activities: Things done to accomplish the outcomes according to the logic model

Alternative treatment research design. A research design in which different treatments are administered to two or more groups of clients and the progress of the two groups is compared.

Ambiguous baseline. A baseline where the scores are difficult to interpret because they are moving up and down in an inconsistent fashion, such as a trend that shows improvement in the first part of the baseline but deterioration in the second part.

Analysis of variance. A statistic for determining if there is a significant relationship between two variables, where one is measured at the nominal level (with three or more categories) and one is measured at the interval level.

Analytic comparison. The application of the concepts of the method of agreement and the method of difference in logical inquiry.

Assumptions (in the logic model). Statements that reveal the rationale of a program by connecting target behaviors with service activities, such as the assumption of cognitive–behavioral therapy that depression is caused by dysfunctional thinking about life events, so that therapy should address dysfunctional thinking patterns.

B single-subject design. A research design in which the target behavior for a single client is measured repeatedly while a treatment is being administered but no baseline data are measured.

Baseline period. A period in single-subject research whereby the client is measured on the target behavior but no treatment is being provided.

Basic experimental research design. A research design where a group of people are randomly assigned to be in two groups, one that gets treatment and one that does not. The two groups are compared regarding growth on the target behavior to see if the treatment group did better.

BC single-subject design. A research design whereby a single client is measured on the target behavior during a treatment period, and is measured repeatedly on the same behavior during a period where a treatment is implemented that is different from the first treatment, but no baseline data are measured.

Beneficence. The ethical principle that requires that we minimize harm and maximize benefits when engaging in the use of human subjects in research.

Bona fide treatment. A well-recognized treatment that is based on sound psychological principles.

Bracketing. The identification of researcher biases on the theme of study so as to reduce the effect of these biases on qualitative data analysis.

Carryover effects. The tendency of gains in a treatment period to continue without treatment possibly because the effect of the treatment is continuing; therefore, single-subject designs that have a baseline following a treatment period should be undertaken with caution.

Case study. An approach to research, using both qualitative and quantitative measurement, that provides a comprehensive view of a single case, which might be an individual, an organization, a community, or an event.

Case study protocol. A set of guides on the procedures to be employed in the implementation of a case study, including, for example, field procedures, sources of information, case study questions, and so forth.

Causation. The effect of one variable on another, established by three conditions—a relationship between the cause and the effect, the ruling out of alternative causes of the effect, and evidence that a change in the effect was preceded by a change in the cause.

Chance. A possibility that is not predicted.

Cherry picking. The selective reporting of facts that support a given assertion along with the intentional failure to report facts that refute the assertion.

Chi-square. A statistic for determining if there is a significant relationship between two variables where each variable is measured at the nominal level.

Coding. The use of a word or a phrase to convey the meaning of a segment of content (e.g., sentence, paragraph, page) in content analysis.

Common factors in treatment outcomes. Those variables that affect treatment outcome and are common to all bona fide treatments, such as the quality of the therapeutic relationship between the practitioners and the client.

Comparison group design (aka, nonequivalent control group design). A research design in which the growth of a treated group is compared with the growth of a nontreated group on the same target behavior.

Confidentiality (for research subjects). The practice of not reporting the identity of an individual who participated in a research study along with the information derived from that individual.

Content analysis. A method for converting words into ideas that capture the essence of the words that were analyzed and lead to inferences about the reality of the theme under investigation.

Content validity. The extent to which a measurement tool includes all the dimensions of the defined variable.

Convenience sample. A nonrandom study sample selected because it was easily available, such as the fellow students in your class.

Correlation coefficient. A measure of the strength of the relationship between two variables measured at either the ordinal or interval level. The specific correlation coefficient for the variables measured at the ordinal level is the Spearman correlation coefficient. The specific correlation coefficient for the variables measured at the interval level is the Pearson correlation coefficient.

Credibility assessment. A procedure in qualitative data analysis whereby the codes of one researcher are compared with the same of another researcher with regard to the same data to determine if there is sufficient congruence between the codes to trust the coding as legitimate.

Criterion validity. The extent to which a given scale achieves the same results as another method of measuring the same thing. If the ratings for depression in a group of clients by clinical social workers correlate positively with the scores given to these same people using your depression scale, you have evidence of criterion validity for your depression scale.

Critical thinking. Disciplined thinking that favors rationality, open-mindedness, systematically analyzed evidence, and a tendency to require an idea (theory, proposal, opinion, etc.) to be effectively subjected to criticism.

Cronbach's alpha. A coefficient that indicates the internal consistency of a scale by examining the correlations of different items with one another.

Cultural competence. Knowledge, values, and skills that recognize the influence of culture with regard to practice.

Dependent variable. The variable in a relationship that is believed to be caused by the other variable, which is known as the independent variable.

Descriptive research. Research that has the purpose of describing people (or things).

Descriptive statistics. Statistics used to describe individual variables, such as the mean age of a group of people or the proportion of people in a group who are female.

Dodo bird verdict. The assertion that all bona fide treatments are equal in achieving client outcome.

Double-barreled question. An item on a questionnaire that contains more than one issue but asks for only one answer.

Effect size. A measure of the strength of a relationship that is represented as standard deviation. An effect size of 1.0 means that the difference between two groups being compared for treatment outcome would show that the typical scores of one group represented one standard deviation of scores better than the other group.

Efficiency. The ratio of input to output normally measured with regard to the cost per unit of service delivered.

Empirical justification for the intervention. Justification for the selection of a particular intervention that is based on a review of evidence with regard to the behavior being treated and the intervention.

Enumeration. The counting of first-level codes in second-level coding to determine the weight of each concept in qualitative data analysis.

Erratic baseline. A set of baseline scores that fluctuate wildly from high to low and suggest that statistical analysis of data is not warranted.

Ethics. Rules of behavior based on moral values.

Ethnography. A qualitative approach to research that refers to the study of a culture in its natural setting with the purpose of describing the way of life for a group.

Evaluative research. Research that has the purpose of determining the success of an intervention or a program.

Evidence. Data that have been systematically collected and analyzed according to the principles and practices of scientific inquiry.

Evidence-based intervention (or program). An intervention or a program that has credible evidence in support of it for a particular target behavior.

Evidence-based practice. Practice that employs the judicious use of the best available evidence, along with considerations of client preferences and therapist expertise, in making practice decisions.

Explanatory research. Research that has the purpose of explaining things by examining the relationship between two variables where one is believed to be the cause of the other.

Exploratory research. Research that has the purpose of examining things that are not yet well known.

External validity. The extent to which the results of a study can be generalized.

Face validity. The extent to which a measurement tool appears to measure the intended variable in the opinion of knowledgeable people.

Face-to-face interview survey. A survey conducted face-to-face between the researcher and the respondent.

Face-to-face self-administered questionnaire. A questionnaire completed by the study respondent when face-to-face with the researcher.

False dichotomy. Asserting a claim based on the faulty assumption that there are only two alternatives when there are more.

Focus group. A method of gathering qualitative data that entails a group meeting, with a leader and a recorder, where specific questions are discussed, data are analyzed, and conclusions are drawn.

Frequency. The incidence of something, such as the number of females and the number of males in a study sample.

Generalization of study results. The estimation that the results you received from your study sample would likely be about the same as the results that would be achieved from another sample from this study population. In other words, the conclusions you would draw from your study would be basically similar to the conclusions you would draw from a similar study of a different sample taken from the same population.

Goal. The major, long-term benefit to the client of the intervention, service, or program.

Grounded theory. An approach to qualitative research that develops explanations, hypotheses, or theories that are grounded in observations of social behavior.

Group research design. A research design in which data are collected on the same target behavior for a group of clients who are being given the same treatment.

History as a threat to internal validity. A change in the environment of clients that causes target behavior to change during the treatment period.

Hypothesis for a research study. A specific statement predicting the results of the intended study. For example, you might have the hypothesis, "Persons with higher self-esteem will have lower depression." The hypothesis should identify the study variables and what is expected when the data are analyzed.

Ideology. A closed system of beliefs or values supported by fixed assumptions about the nature of human reality.

Independent *t* test. A statistic for determining if there is a significant relationship between the scores of two groups of people (e.g., gains scores of the treatment group and gain scores of the comparison group).

Independent variable. The variable that another variable depends on (the variable that causes another variable to be the way it is). If salary depends on gender, then gender would be the independent variable.

Inferential statistics. Statistics used to test the hypothesis in explanatory and evaluative research.

Informed consent. The practice of assuring that study subjects have given their consent and they were clearly informed about the risks.

Input. The resources that are employed in the provision of the intervention.

Inputs (in the logic model). The forces that enter the service system, such as clients in need and service staff who will serve them.

Institutional review board. A body of people whose job is to review proposals for conducting research with the objective of protecting human subjects in research from harm, invasion of privacy, or coercion.

Instrumentation as a threat to internal validity. The validity of the measurement devices employed in the study. If these instruments are not valid measures of the dependent variable, you cannot draw valid conclusions from your data.

Internal consistency reliability. The extent to which items on a scale are reasonably correlated with one another, and, therefore, seem to be measuring the same thing.

Interval level of measurement. A level of measurement where people are assigned a number with traditional numerical value such as age measured in years or scores on an anxiety scale. Traditional numerical value means that the distance between two intervals (e.g., the ages of 23 and 24) in one adjacent set is identical to the distance between another adjacent set (e.g., the ages of 34 and 35).

Intervention. The composite of the activities that are provided to clients for the purpose of achieving a given outcome. The same thing as the service or the treatment.

Intervention evaluation. The assessment of the success of a social work intervention (service) for an individual or a group of clients with a common treatment objective.

Interview in qualitative research. A purposeful encounter between persons in which one person is seeking information from another person.

Justice. An ethical principle that requires us to design research that does not unduly target its risks to certain groups of people and fails to treat different types of people equably or fairly.

Level of measurement. The hierarchy of measurement that has four levels from low to high. Three of these levels are nominal, ordinal, and interval, in that order. The ratio level is not discussed in this book because it is not useful to the examples used. Level of measurement is related to the proper statistic to employ in the examination of your data.

Limited AB single-subject design. A research design whereby a single client is measured on the target behavior one time before treatment begins and several times during the treatment period. If there are two baseline scores, the mean of these scores is used as the single baseline score.

Logic model. A means of illustrating the connections between assumptions, resources, activities, and outcomes for a program.

Logical generalization of study results. The examination of the extent to which the results of a study can be generalized to persons in the study population on a logical basis, meaning that there is sufficient evidence of similarities between the study sample and the study population to convince people that the results of this study can be viewed as relevant to the study population. Logical generalization does not require a random sample.

Logical justification for the intervention. Justification for the selection of a particular intervention that is based on a logical analysis of the nature of the behavior being treated and the nature of the intervention being employed.

Mailed survey. A form of the self-administered survey that is completed by the study subject but is not administered face-to-face.

Maturation as a threat to internal validity. The tendency of people to improve on their target behavior over time through normal development.

Mean. The average of a variable measured at the interval level, which is computed by adding up the scores and dividing by the number of scores.

Measurement error. The distance between the reality of the variable under study and the value that was measured by an instrument designed to measure it.

Median. The midpoint value in an array of data that has been organized in numerical sequence from the lowest value to the highest. The median for the ages of 17, 23, 29, 30, and 31 would be the age of 29 because this is the age of the middle person in this sequence.

Meta-analysis. A review of the evidence on a selected theme using a specific protocol for searching the literature and combining the results of all selected results into a common metric, the effect size.

Mode. The most frequent value for a variable. If you had the ages of 21, 23, 23, 24, and 28, your mode would be 23 because there are two of these ages and no other age is repeated.

Model of the intervention. The conceptual framework that serves as the logical rationale for offering the intervention in light of what is known about the dynamics of the target behavior being addressed.

Mortality as a threat to internal validity. The effect on study results based on the fact that some clients drop out of treatment.

Multiple regression analysis. A statistic for determining if there is a significant relationship between one dependent variable, measured at the interval level, and more than one independent variable, all measured at the interval level.

Narrative analysis. A depiction of some social reality, typically in the form of a story, that reveals themes and explanations through the analysis of qualitative data.

Need. A gap between what exists with regard to human services and what should exist—for example, your agency has day care service for 1,200 children and there are 1,600 children who need day care service.

Need assessment. An attempt to measure the community's gaps in need and resources.

Negative relationship. An empirical relationship between two variables in which higher values for one would tend to be associated with lower values for the other. For example, we would expect to find a negative relationship between school grades and depression. In other words, the higher your depression, the lower will be your grades.

Nominal group technique (NGT). A structured group method of decision making that is designed to maximize participation among a small group of key informants.

Nominal level of measurement. A level of measurement where people are placed into categories that have no order. Examples include gender, political party affiliation, and the category of the service your clients are receiving.

Objective. A measured amount of progress toward the achievement of the goal. It is the thing that will be measured with regard to client outcome.

One-group pretest–posttest design. A research design in which one group of clients is measured before and after the intervention with regard to the objective of treatment.

One-group pretest–posttest research design. A design whereby one group of persons are given a pretest of target behavior, followed by a treatment, which is followed by a posttest of target behavior.

One-sample *t* test. A statistic for determining if there is a significant relationship between two interval variables where one variable has a single score (e.g., a single baseline score) and the other variable has several scores (e.g., four treatment scores).

Online survey. A survey where the questionnaire is sent to respondents through the Internet.

Ordinal level of measurement. A level of measurement where people are placed into categories with an order, such as *strongly agree*, *agree*, *disagree*, and *strongly disagree*.

Outcome. The benefits to clients from the services they received—for example, the fact that a group of trauma victims had a 40% improvement in anxiety during the course of treatment.

Output. The amount of service that is provided, such as 254 hours of therapy.

Outputs (in the logic model). The unit of service, such as an hour of counseling.

Paradigm. A conceptual model that suggests where to look in order to better understand a social phenomenon.

Personnel of the intervention. The credentials of those who deliver the intervention that is being evaluated.

Phone interview survey. A type of social survey conducted through a phone call where the respondent answers a set of questions given from a questionnaire administered by the researcher.

Population. The people from whom your study sample was drawn.

Positive relationship. An empirical relationship between two variables in which higher values for one would tend to be associated with higher values for the other. For example, we would expect that age and income would have a positive relationship because older people are more likely to have higher salaries. In others words, the higher your age, the higher your income.

Posttest. A measurement of the target behavior after the treatment has been completed.

Posttest-only control group design. A design whereby a group of people are randomly assigned into two groups, one that gets treatment and one that does not, and target behavior at the posttest time is compared between the two groups.

Practical significance. A judgment about the extent to which the measured results are noteworthy.

Pretest. A measurement of the target behavior before treatment begins.

Privacy. Our ability to control access to information about ourselves.

Process. That which happens to the clients to achieve the intended outcomes (i.e., the service).

Program. An organized set of services designed to achieve a social goal, such as reduction of child abuse, improvement of mental health, prevention of suicide, or improvement of family relations.

Program evaluation. Systematic research activities aimed at the determination of how well a program is working with regard to meeting client need, providing good quality service, operating efficiently, and achieving client benefit.

Proportion. The percentage of people in a category.

Proposition. A causal statement that is a part of a comprehensive theory.

Pseudoscience. A process that relies on methods that are not scientific but is portrayed in a manner that seems scientific.

Purposive sample. A nonrandom sample selected because of special characteristics of these people that are of interest to the study. An example would be the selection of your current clients for an evaluative study or the selection of Hispanic people because you are studying something about this population.

Qualitative data analysis. The examination of words spoken, or written, with regard to a research purpose to gain meaning of the theme under investigation.

Qualitative measurement. Research that measures concepts with words rather than numbers or predetermined categories.

Qualitative research. A form of research that uses words as the primary source of data, which distinguishes it from quantitative research, which measures variables by scores or by placing study subjects into predetermined categories.

Quality. A concept that implies value, which can be exemplified through mechanisms such as service standards or service outcomes.

Quantitative measurement. Research that measures concepts numerically (e.g., age or score on the depression scale) or by predetermined categories (e.g., gender, race, etc.).

Random error. Error in measurement that cannot be predicted.

Random sample. A group of people selected from a study population on a random basis.

Reactive effect (placebo effect) as a threat to internal validity. The effect on the target behavior during treatment of being given special attention by being selected for a study.

Reliability. The extent to which a measurement tool is consistent.

Research design. The protocol whereby target behavior is measured and treatment is administered.

Respect. An ethical principle that deals with autonomy and self-determination, so that potential research subjects are allowed to choose for themselves the risk they will undertake.

Sample. The people from whom you collect your data for your study.

Sample selection bias. The bias introduced by the selection of individuals for a sample in such a way that the sample is not representative of the study population. If you select persons for your study by asking for volunteers at your agency during the normal work day, you will have a bias that fails to represent clients who receive services in the evenings.

Sampling element. The persons who are selected to be in your study sample.

Sampling error. The amount of difference between the characteristics of the study sample and the characteristics of the study population. It can be estimated scientifically when you have a random sample and the necessary data.

Sampling frame. The list of persons in your study population from which your study sample will be selected.

Sampling interval. The distance between sampling elements in your study sample. If you select every fourth person for your sample using the systematic random sampling procedure, your sampling interval would be four.

Saturation assessment. The examination of segments of qualitative data to determine if enough new information is being acquired in order to indicate that further collection of data is warranted. If the second segment of data does not produce new information, you have achieved saturation and do not need to examine a third set of data.

Science. A process that relies on a carefully articulated question; the systematic, and objective, collection of data on an objective basis; the analysis of data; and the drawing of conclusions consistent with the data.

Scientific generalization. Generalization of study results when you have a random sample, which provides you with a scientific basis for estimating sampling error.

Selection bias as a threat to internal validity. A bias in your selection of study participants that hinders the validity of your research study—for example, selecting only the most motivated clients for your study when you wish to generalize your findings to all your clients.

Semistructured interview. An interview where the researcher provides a set of focused open-ended questions to the interviewee.

Service process. The actions taken on behalf of a program to achieve the desired results, which are evaluated through mechanisms such as adherence to service standards.

Services. A set of professional activities designed to achieve a specific objective for a given set of clients. This term is the same as intervention and treatment in this book.

Simple random sample. A study sample that has been selected by a procedure whereby the researcher obtains a list of members of the study population, decides on the sampling interval, and selects members from this list in a procedure that includes the drawing of numbers on a random basis.

Single research study of evidence. An evaluative study of a specific sample of people (e.g., women with postpartum depression), who have been given a certain treatment (e.g., cognitive–behavioral therapy) and have been administered a certain method of measurement (e.g., the Beck Depression Scale) that measures success.

Single-subject research design. A research design in which a single entity (usually a client) is measured repeatedly on the target behavior.

Snowball sample. A nonrandom study sample selected in stages whereby people selected in Stage 1 are asked to identify potential study subjects for Stage 2 of the selection procedure, and other stages are possible.

Social desirability bias. A tendency for some people to answer a question in a way that is socially desirable rather than saying what they really believe.

Social scientist. Someone who applies the principles and methods of science to learn more about social phenomena.

Social survey. A purposeful inquiry into a social subject for a designated sample of people by a researcher using a recording instrument, typically a questionnaire.

Spirit of scientific inquiry. An atmosphere that adheres to the principles of science.

Standard deviation. A measure of variance used in many statistical tests. It shows how much each individual in a sample varies from the mean of the sample, so if the standard deviation of females is lower than the standard deviation of males, you can say that the males vary more from one another than do the females.

Statistical significance. A finding that suggests that chance is not a good explanation of these data results.

Statistical test. A mathematical formula that determines the likelihood that a set of data would occur by (or be explained by) chance.

Structure of the intervention. A concrete statement that shows both the form and the intensity of the services being given.

Study sample. In research, a study sample is the group of people from whom data were collected.

Survey. A purposeful inquiry into a subject for a designated sample of people by a researcher using a recording instrument, typically a questionnaire.

SurveyMonkey. A software program on the Internet that can be used to conduct an online survey.

Systematic error. A form of measurement error that can be predicted, such as error based on the social desirability bias.

Systematic random sample. A sample that has been drawn from the list of the study population on a random basis including the steps of deciding on the sampling interval, selecting the first person from the first sampling interval on a random basis, and selecting the next person who is one sampling interval beyond the first one, and so forth.

Systematic review. A comprehensive review of evidence designed to sum up the best available research on a research question, through a rigorous protocol for the collection and analysis of results.

Target behavior. The behavior of the client that is being treated.

Target behavior analysis. The analysis of the client's behavior that is being treated.

Target behavior definition. The definition of the client's behavior that is being treated.

Testing as a threat to internal validity. The effect on the target behavior of being measured on the study variables.

Test–retest reliability. The extent to which a measurement tool is consistent when applied to the same group of people at different times.

Theory. An attempt to explain, usually by portraying the relationships between concepts.

Threats to internal validity. Potential causes of the client's measured growth that are independent of the intervention, such as normal growth over time.

Traditional literature review. A review of selected articles of evidence that have been secured by the authors of the work, where the protocol for the selection of articles for review is not enumerated.

Treatment. What is done to the client to achieve the objectives. This term is the same as service and intervention in this book.

Treatment fidelity. The extent to which a program is implemented according to plan—for example, the extent to which its implementation is consistent with accepted standards of service.

Treatment period. A period, in single-subject research, whereby the client is measured repeatedly while a treatment is being offered.

Unit of analysis. The entity on which you will collect your data in a case study—for example, Mrs. Johnson, the Child Welfare Program for Hoover County, or the presidential election of 2016.

Unit of service. The concrete measure of the amount of a service—for example, the number of hours of counseling provided or the number of child abuse investigations completed.

Validity. The extent to which a measurement tool is accurate.

Voluntary participation in research. Avoiding the coercion of people to participate in a research study, so that each participant engages in the research study on a voluntary basis.

Vulnerable population. A group of people who are vulnerable to feeling pressured to participate in a research study because of their social status, such as being in prison, living in a public housing project, or being a member of a minority group.

REFERENCES

American Psychiatric Association. (2013). *Diagnostic and statistical manual of mental disorders* (5th ed.). Washington, DC: Author.

Barker, R. L. (2003). *The social work dictionary.* Washington, DC: National Association of Social Workers Press.

Barlow, J., Smailagic, N., Bennett, C., Huband, N., Jones, H., & Coren, E. (2011). Individual and group-based parenting programmes for improving psychosocial outcomes for teenage parents and their children. *Campbell Systematic Reviews,* (3), CD002964. doi:10.1002/14651858.CD002964.pub2

Barlow, J., Smailagic, N., Huband, N., Roloff, V., & Bennett, C. (2012). Group-based parent training programmes for improving parental psychosocial health. *Campbell Systematic Reviews.* doi:10.4073/csr.2005.3

Beck Institute. (2016). *What is cognitive behavior therapy?* Retrieved from https://www.beckinstitute.org/get-informed/what-is-cognitive-therapy

Belcher, J. R. (1994). Understanding the process of social drift among the homeless: A qualitative analysis. In E. Sherman & W. J. Reid (Eds.), *Qualitative research in social work* (pp. 126–134). New York, NY: Columbia University Press.

Berg, B. L. (2001). *Qualitative research methods for the social sciences* (3rd ed.). Boston, MA: Allyn & Bacon.

Bisson, J., Roberts, N. P., Andrew, M., Cooper, R., & Lewis, C. (2016). Psychological therapies for chronic post-traumatic stress disorder (PTSD) in adults. *Cochrane Collaboration.* Retrieved from http://www.cochrane.org/CD003388/DEPRESSN_psychological-therapies-chronic-post-traumatic-stress-disorder-ptsd-adults

Bloom, M., Fischer, J., & Orme, J. G. (2003). *Evaluating practice* (4th ed.). Boston, MA: Allyn & Bacon.

Brenner, O. C., & Bromer, J. A. (1981). Sex-role stereotypes and leaders' behavior as measured by the agreement scale for leadership behavior. *Psychological Reports, 48,* 960–962.

Broverman, I. K., Vogel, S. R., Broverman, D. M., Clarkson, F. E., & Rosenkrantz, P. S. (1972). Sex-role stereotypes: A current appraisal. *Journal of Social Issues, 28*(2), 59–78.

Brown, J. L., MacDonald, R., & Mitchell, R. (2015). Are people who participate in cultural activities more satisfied with life? *Social Indicators Research, 122*(1), 135–146.

Burger, K., & Robin, S. (2017). The role of perceived stress and self-efficacy in young people's life satisfaction: A longitudinal study. *Journal of Youth and Adolescence, 46*(1), 78–90.

Byrnes, G., & Kelly, I. W. (1992). Crisis calls and lunar cycle: A twenty year review. *Psychological Reports, 71,* 779–785.

California Evidence-Based Clearinghouse for Child Welfare. (n.d.). *List of programs.* Retrieved from http://www.cebc4cw.org/search/by-program-name

Campbell, D. T., & Stanley, J. C. (1963). *Experimental and quasi-experimental designs for research.* Boston, MA: Houghton Mifflin.

Centers for Disease Control and Prevention. (2014). *Practice strategies for culturally competent evaluation.* Atlanta, GA: Author. Retrieved from https://www.cdc.gov/dhdsp/docs/cultural_competence_guide.pdf

Centers for Disease Control and Prevention. (2016). *Overweight and obesity.* Retrieved from http://www.cdc.gov/obesity/data/index.html

Chase, S. E. (2018). Narrative inquiry: Toward theoretical and methodological maturity. In N. K. Denzin & Y. S. Lincoln (Eds.), *The Sage handbook of qualitative research* (pp. 546–560). Los Angeles, CA: Sage.

Clark, R., Tluczek, A., & Wenzel, A. (2003). Psychotherapy for postpartum depression: A preliminary report. *American Journal of Orthopsychiatry, 73*(4), 441–454.

Clifford, S. (n.d.). *Tipsheet: Qualitative interviews.* Durham, NC: Duke Initiative on Survey Methodology. Retrieved from https://dism.ssri.duke.edu/sites/dism.ssri.duke.edu/files/pdfs/Tipsheet-Qualitative_Interviews.pdf

Cohen, S., & Hoberman, H. (1983). Positive events and social supports as buffers of life changes. *Journal of Applied Social Psychology, 13,* 19–25.

Collaborative Institutional Training Initiative. (n.d.). *Research ethics and compliance training.* Lake Success, NY: Biomedical Research Alliance of New York. Retrieved from http://www.citiprogram.org

Collins, N. L., Dunkel-Schetter, C., Lobel, M., & Scrimshaw, S. C. (1993). Social support in pregnancy: Psychosocial correlates of birth outcomes and postpartum depression. *Journal of Personality and Social Psychology, 65*(6), 1243–1258.

Corcoran, K., & Fischer, J. (1987). *Measures for clinical practice.* New York, NY: Free Press.

Corcoran, K., & Fischer, J. (2013). *Measures for clinical practice* (5th ed.). New York, NY: Free Press.

Coren, E., Hutchfield, J., Thomae, M., & Gustafsson, C. (2010). Parent training support for intellectually disabled parents: A systematic review. *Campbell Systematic Reviews,* (3). doi:10.4073/csr.2010.3

Coulton, C. J. (1991). Developing and implementing quality assurance programs. In Edwards, R. L., & Yankey, J. A. (Eds.), *Skills for effective human services management* (pp. 251–266). Washington, DC: National Association of Social Workers Press.

Cusack, K., Jonas, D. E., Forneris, C. A., Wines, C., Sonis, J., Middleton, J. C., & Gaynes, B. N. (2016). Psychological treatment for adults with posttraumatic stress disorder: A systematic review and meta-analysis. *Clinical Psychology Review, 43,* 128–141. doi:10.1016/j.cpr.2015.10.003

Cutrona, C. E. (1989). Ratings of social support by adolescents and adult informants: Degree of correspondence and predictors of depressive symptoms. *Journal of Personality and Social Psychology, 57*(4), 723–730.

Day, D. R., & Stogdill, R. M. (1972). Leader behavior of male and female supervisors: A comparative study. *Personnel Psychology, 25,* 353–360.

Deblinger, E., Lippmann, J., & Steer, R. (1996). Sexually abused children suffering posttraumatic stress symptoms: Initial treatment outcome findings. *Child Maltreatment, 1,* 310–321.

Delbecq, A. L., Van de Ven, A. H., & Gustafson, D. H. (1975). *Group techniques for program planning.* Glenview, IL: Scott Foresman.

Dennis, C. L., & Hodnett, E. D. (2007). Psychosocial and psychological interventions for treating postpartum depression. *Cochrane Database of Systematic Reviews,* (4), CD006166. doi:10.1002/14651858.CD006116.pub2

Denzin, N. K., & Lincoln, Y. (Eds.). (1994). *Handbook of qualitative research.* Thousand Oaks, CA: Sage.

Diener, E., Emmons, R. A., Larsen, R. J., & Griffin, S. (1985). The satisfaction with life scale. *Journal of Personality Assessment, 49,* 71–75.

Don, B. P., & Mickelson, K. O. (2012). Paternal postpartum depression: The role of maternal postpartum depression, spousal support, and relationship satisfaction. *Couple and Family Psychology: Research and Practice, 1*(4), 323–334.

Duncan, B., & Miller, S. (2017). *When I'm good, I'm very good, but when I'm bad I'm better: A new mantra for psychotherapists.* Retrieved from https://www.psychotherapy.net/article/therapy-effectiveness

Durm, M. W., Terry, C. L., & Hammonds, C. R. (1986). Lunar phase and acting out behavior. *Psychological Reports, 59,* 987–990.

Ehlers, A., Bison, J., Clark, D. M., Creamer, M., Pilling, S., Richards, D., . . . Yule, W. (2010). Do all psychological treatments really work the same in posttraumatic stress disorder? *Clinical Psychology Review, 30,* 269–276.

Elkins, G. (2005). Noncompliance with behavioral recommendations following bariatric surgery. *Obesity Surgery, 15*(4), 546–551.

Elliot, R., Bohart, A. C., Watson, J. C., & Greenberg, L. S. (2011). Empathy. *Psychotherapy, 48*(1), 43–49.

Farber, B. A., & Doolin, E. M. (2011). Positive regard and affirmation. In J. C. Norcross (Ed.), *Psychotherapy relationships that work: Evidence-based responsiveness* (2nd ed., pp. 168–186). New York, NY: Oxford University Press.

Fierson, R., Lippman, S. B., & Johnson, J. (1987). Psychological Stress on the Family. *Psychosomatics, 28,* 65-68.

Festinger, T. B., & Bounds, R. L. (1977). Sex-role stereotyping: A research note. *Social Work, 22,* 314–315.

Flick, U. (2006). Analytic induction. In V. Jupp (Ed.), *The Sage dictionary of social research methods.* Thousand Oaks, CA: Sage. Retrieved from http://srmo.sagepub.com/view/the-sage-dictionary-of-social-research-methods/n4.xml

Flynn, M. (1991). Critical comment on Hicks-Causey and Potter, "Effect of the full moon on a sample of developmentally delayed, institutionally delayed women." *Perceptual and Motor Skills, 73*(3 Pt 1), 963–968.

Fortune, A. E. (1994). Commentary: Ethnography in social work. In E. Sherman & W. J. Reid (Eds.), *Qualitative research in social work* (pp. 63–67). New York, NY: Columbia University Press.

Franklin, C. S., Cody, P. A., & Ballan, M. (2010). Reliability and validity in qualitative research. In B. A. Thyer (Ed.), *The handbook of social work research methods* (pp. 355–374). Thousand Oaks, CA: Sage.

Furlong, M., McGilloway, S., Bywater, T., Hutchings, J., Donnelly, M., & Smith, S. (2012). Behavioural and cognitive–behavioural group-based parenting programmes for early-onset conduct problems in children aged 3 to 12 years. *Campbell Systematic Reviews, 2012, 9*(1).

Fusch, P. I., & Ness, L. R. (2015). Are we there yet? Data saturation in qualitative research. *The Qualitative Report, 20*(9), 1408–1416.

Gambrill, E. (2015). Foreword. In B. A. Thyer, & M. G. Pignotti (Eds.), *Science and pseudoscience in social work practice* (pp. vii–xxii). New York, NY: Springer.

Geiger, D., & Antonacopoulou, E. (2009). Narratives and organizational dynamics: Exploring blind spots and organizational inertia. *Journal of Applied Behavioral Science, 45*(3), 411–438.

Goodman, J. H., & Santangelo, G. (2011). Group treatment for postpartum depression. *Archives of Women's Mental Health, 14*(4), 277–293.

Gordon-Garofalo, V. L, & Rubin, A. (2004). Evaluation of a psychoeducational group for seronegative partners and spouses of person with HIV/AIDS. *Research on Social Work Practice, 14,* 14–26.

Grinnell, R. M., & Unrau, Y. A. (2014). *Social work research and evaluation* (10th ed.). Oxford, England: Oxford University Press.

Guba, E. G. (1981). Criteria for assessing the trustworthiness of naturalistic inquiries. *Educational Communication and Technology Journal, 29*(2), 75–91.

Hall, D. M. (2009). Social work education and personal characteristic predictors of cultural competence in MSW Students. *University of Maryland Baltimore County, Dissertation Abstracts International, 69*(7), 2877.

Hall, J. M., Roman, M. W., Thomas, S. P., Travis, C. B., Powell, J., Tennison, C. R., . . . McArthur, P. M. (2009). Thriving as becoming resolute in narratives of women surviving child maltreatment. *American Journal of Orthopsychiatry, 79*(3), 375–386.

Hammersley, M. (2010). A historical and comparative note on the relationship between analytic induction and grounded theorizing. *Forum: Qualitative Social Research, 11*(2). Retrieved from http://www.qualitative-research.net/index.php/fqs/article/view/1400/2994

Hare, B. R. (1985). *The HARE general and area specific (school, peer, and home) self-esteem scale.* Unpublished manuscript, Department of Sociology, Stony Brook University, The State University of New York, Stony Brook, NY.

Harper-Dorton, K. V., & Lantz, J. E. (2007). *Crosscultural practice: Social work with diverse populations.* Chicago, IL: Lyceum Books.

Harris, L. H., & Lucas, M. E. (1976). Sex-role stereotyping. *Social Work, 21,* 390–395.

Hayson, A. (2016). *Evaluating CFTSI and its effects on posttraumatic symptoms in sexually abused children.* Unpublished paper presented in a course in the School of Social Work, University of North Carolina Wilmington, Wilmington.

Hicks-Casey, W. E., & Potter, D. R. (1991). Effect of the full moon of a sample of developmentally delayed institutionalized women. *Perceptual and Motor Skills, 72,* 1375–1380.

Hopkins, T., Clegg, J., & Stackhouse, J. (2016). Youthful offenders' perspectives on their literacy and communication skills. *International Journal of Language and Communication Disorders, 51*(1), 95–109.

Horvath, A. O., Del Re, A. C., Fluckinger, C., & Symonds, D. (2011). Alliance in individual psychotherapy. In J. C. Norcross (Ed.), *Psychotherapy relationships that work: Evidence-based responsiveness* (2nd ed., pp. 25–69). New York, NY: Oxford University Press.

Howard, K. I., Krause, M. S., Saunders, S. M., & Kopta, S. M. (1997). Trials and tribulations in the meta-analysis of treatment differences: Comment on Wampold et al. (1997). *Psychological Bulletin, 122*(3), 221–225.

Institutional Review Board for Health Sciences Research, University of Virginia. (2017). *Additional categories of vulnerable subjects.* Retrieved from http://www.virginia.edu/vpr/irb/hsr/vulnerable_other.html#minorities

Johnson, H. (2012). *Ten tips to improve your online surveys* [Web log post]. Retrieved from https:www.surveymonkey.com/blog/2012/04/13/10-online-survey-tips

Kirk, D. H. (1964). *Shared fate.* New York, NY: Free Press.

Kirmayer, L. J. (2012). Rethinking cultural competence. *Transcultural Psychiatry, 49*(2), 149–164.

Koro-Ljungberg, M., MacLure, M., & Ulmer, J. (2018). D...a...t...a... Data++, Data, and some problematics. In N. K. Kenzin & Y. Lincoln (Eds)., *The Sage handbook of qualitative research* (5th ed., pp. 462–483). Thousand Oaks, CA: Sage.

Krueger, R. A. (1994). *Focus groups: A practical guide or applied research* (2nd ed.). Thousand Oaks, CA: Sage.

Kubler-Ross, E. (1969). *On death and dying.* New York, NY: Simon & Schuster.

Larsen, D. L., Atkisson, C. C., Hargreaves, W. A., & Nguyen, T. D. (1979). Assessment of client/patient satisfaction: Development of a general scale. *Evaluation and Program Planning, 2,* 197–207.

Letourneau, N., Secco, L., Colpitts, J., Aldous, S., Stewart, M., & Dennis, C. (2015). Quasi-experimental evaluation of a telephone-based peer support intervention for maternal depression. *Journal of Advanced Nursing, 71*(7), 1587–1599.

Lewis, A. D., Huebner, E. S., Malone, P. S., &Valios, R. F. (2011). Life satisfaction and engagement in adolescence. *Journal of Youth Adolescence, 40*(3), 249–262.

Lindsey, E. W. (1998). The impact of homelessness and shelter life on family relationships. *Family Relations, 47,* 243–252.

Manning, P. K., & Cullum-Swan, B. (1994). Narrative, content, and semiotic analysis. In N. K. Denzin & Y. S. Lincoln (Eds.), *Handbook of qualitative research* (pp. 463–477). Thousand Oaks, CA: Sage.

Massengill, D., & DiMarco, N. (1979). Sex-role stereotypes and requisite managerial characteristics: A current replication. *Sex Roles, 5,* 561–570.

Matthew, V. M., Lindsay, J., Shanmjganatan, N., & Eapen, V. (1991). Attempted suicide and the lunar cycle. *Psychological Reports, 68,* 927–930.

Matthews, A., Brennan, M. A., Kelly, P., McAdam, C., Mutrie, N., & Foster, C. (2012). Don't wait for them to come to you, you go to them: A qualitative study of recruitment approaches in community based walking programmes in the UK. *BMC Public Health, 12,* 635. doi:10.1186/1471-2458-12-635

Micallef-Trigona, B. (2016). The origins of cognitive behavioral therapy. *PsychCentral.* Retrieved from http://psychcentral.com/lib/the-origins-of-cognitive-behavioral-therapy/

Miles, M. B., & Huberman, A. M. (1984). *Qualitative data analysis.* Thousand Oaks, CA: Sage.

Miley, A. (2016). *Study of the effectiveness of a caregiver support group in reducing caregiver* burden. Unpublished paper presented to a graduate social work research class, University of North Carolina Wilmington, Wilmington.

Milgrom, J., Gemmill, A. W., Ericksen, J., Burrows, G., Buist, A., & Reece, J. (2015). Treatment of postnatal depression with cognitive behavioural therapy, sertraline, and combinative therapy: A randomized control trial. *Australian and New Zealand Journal of Psychiatry, 49*(3), 236–245.

Miller, S. D. (2017). *Performance metrics*. Retrieved from http://www.scottdmiller.com/performance-metrics

Miller, S. D., Duncan, B. L., Brown, J., Sparks, J. A., & Claud, C. A. (2003). The outcome rating scale: A preliminary study of the reliability, validity, and feasibility of a brief analog measure. *Journal of Brief Therapy, 2*(2), 91–100. Retrieved from https://pdfs.semanticscholar.org/a39c/ba5afb4f00fcd4af26df-1937d9acaa448d21.pdf

Nathan, P. E., & Gorman, J. M. (2002). *A guide to treatments that work*. New York, NY: Oxford University Press.

National Association of Social Workers. (2005). NASW *standards for clinical social work in social work practice*. Washington, DC: Author. Retrieved from https://www.socialworkers.org/LinkClick.aspx?fileticket=YOg4qdefLBE%3D&portalid=0

National Association of Social Workers. (2016). *Code of ethics*. Washington, DC: Author. Retrieved from https://www.socialworkers.org/About/Ethics/Code-of-Ethics

National Institute of Mental Health. (2018). *Depression*. Retrieved from https://www.nimh.nih.gov/health/topics/depression/index.shtml

National Institutes of Health. (n.d.). *Research involving human subjects*. Retrieved from https://humansubjects.nih.gov/walkthrough-investigator#tabpanel11

Neuman, W. L. (1994). *Social research methods* (2nd ed.). Boston, MA: Allyn & Bacon.

Osborn, R. N., & Vicars, W. M. (1976). Sex-role stereotypes: An artifact in leader behavior and subordinate satisfaction analysis. *Academy of Management Journal, 19*, 439–449.

Oude Luttikuis, H., Baur, L., Jansen, H., Shrewsbury, V. A., O'Malley, C., Stolk, R. P., & Summerbell, C. D. (2009). Interventions for treating obesity in children. *Cochrane Database of Systematic Reviews, (1)*, CD001872. doi:10.1002/14651858.CD001872.pub2

Patton, M. Q. (1997). *Utilization-focused evaluation*. Thousand Oaks, CA: Sage.

Patton, M. Q. (2008). *Utilization-focused evaluation* (4th ed.). Thousand Oaks, CA: Sage.

Paul, R., & Elder, L. (2004). *The miniature guide to critical thinking*. Tomales, CA: The Foundation for Critical Thinking. Retrieved from https://www.criticalthinking.org/files/Concepts_Tools.pdf

Payne, K. T., & Marcus, D. K. (2008). The efficacy of group psychotherapy for older adult clients: A meta-analysis. *Group Dynamics: Theory, Research and Practice, 12*(4), 268–278.

Petrosino, A. P., Turpin-Petrosino, C., Hollis-Peel, M., & Lavenberg, J. G. (2013). "Scared Straight" and other juvenile awareness programs for preventing juvenile delinquency. *Cochrane Database of Systematic Reviews*, (4), CD002796. doi:10.1002/14651858.CD002796.pub2

Pontiroli, A. E. (2007). Post-surgery adherence to scheduled visits and compliance predict outcome of bariatric restrictive surgery in morbidly obese patients. *Obesity Surgery, 17*(11), 1492–1497.

Powell, G. N., Butterfield, A., & Mainiero. L. A. (1981). Sex-role and identity and sex as predictors of leadership style. *Psychological Reports, 49*, 829–830.

Powell, J. Y. (1984). *Adults who were adopted as older children* (Unpublished doctoral dissertation). University of North Carolina Greensboro, Greensboro.

Proctor, C. L., Linley, P. A., & Maltbe, J. (2009). Youth life satisfaction: A review of the literature. *Journal of Happiness Studies, 10*, 583–630.

Reamer, F. G. (2010). Ethical issues in social work research. In B. Thyer (Ed.), *The handbook of social work research methods* (pp. 564–578). Thousand Oaks, CA: Sage.

Research Ethics & Compliance. (2018). *Informed consent guidelines & templates*. Retrieved from http://research-compliance.umich.edu/informed-consent-guidelines

Richardson, A. (2016). *An evaluative study of the effectiveness of cognitive behavioral therapy on the reduction of anxiety for adolescents*. Unpublished paper submitted for a research course, University of North Carolina Wilmington, Wilmington.

Roberts, C. (2016). *Evaluating the effectiveness of TRP in reducing PTSD symptoms in veterans*. Unpublished paper submitted for a research course, University of North Carolina Wilmington, Wilmington.

Rosen, B., & Jerdee, T. (1978). Perceived sex differences in managerially relevant characteristics. *Sex Roles, 4*, 837–843.

Rosenbach, W. F., Dailey, R. C., & Morgan, C. P. (1979). Perceptions of job characteristics and affective work outcomes for women and men. *Sex Roles, 5*, 267–277.

Rosenkrantz, P., Vogel, S., Bee, H., Broverman, I., & Broverman, D. M. (1968). Sex-role stereotypes and self-concepts in college students. *Journal of Consulting and Clinical Psychology, 32*(3), 287–295.

Rotten, J., & Kelly, I. W. (1985). Much ado about the full moon: A meta-analysis of lunar-lunacy research. *Psychological Bulletin, 97*(2), 286–306.

Royse, D., Thyer, B. A., & Padgett, D. K. (2016). *Program evaluation: An introduction to an evidence-based approach* (6th ed.). Boston, MA: Cengage Learning.

Royse, D., Toyer, B. A., Padgett, D. K., & Logan, K. (2001). *Program evaluation: An introduction.* Belmont, CA: Brooks/Cole.

Rubin, A., & Babbie, E. R. (2014). *Research methods for social work.* Belmont, CA: Brooks/Cole.

Sackett, D. L., Straus, S. E., Richardson, W. S., Rosenberg, W., & Hayes, R. B. (2000). *Evidence-based medicine: How to practice and teach EBM* (2nd ed.). New York, NY: Churchill Living.

Schein, V. E. (1973). The relationship between sex-role stereotypes and requisite management characteristics. *Journal of Applied Psychology, 57*, 95–100.

Schein, V. E. (1975). Relationship between sex-role stereotypes and requisite management characteristics among female managers. *Journal of Applied Psychology, 60*, 340–344.

Science Council. (n.d.). *Our definition of science.* Retrieved from http://sciencecouncil.org/about-us/our-definition-of-science

Shen, R., Dugay, G., Rajaram, H., Cabrera, J., & Siegel, P. (2004). Impact of patient follow-up on weight loss after bariatric surgery. *Obesity Surgery, April*(4), 514–519.

Siev, J., & Chambless, D. L. (2007). Specificity of treatment effects: Cognitive therapy and relaxation for generalized anxiety and panic disorders. *Journal of Consulting and Clinical Psychology, 75*, 513–522.

Siev, J., & Chambless, D. L. (2009). The dodo bird, treatment technique, and disseminating empirically supported treatments. *The Behavior Therapist, 32*, 69–75.

Smelser, N. J. (2001). Analytic induction. In N. J. Smelser & P. B. Baltes (Eds.), *International encyclopedia of the social and behavioral sciences.* Retrieved from http://www.sscnet.ucla.edu/soc/faculty/katz/pubs/Analytic_Induction.pdf

Stevens, D. (2015). *Parenting after trauma: The effects of a new biological caregiver psychoeducational group program on parental stress levels and trauma knowledge.* Unpublished paper presented for a research course, University of North Carolina Wilmington, Wilmington.

Strauss, A. (1987). *Qualitative analysis for social scientists.* New York, NY: Cambridge University Press.

Svartberg, M., Tore, C., & Stiles, T. C. (1991). Comparative effects of short-term psychotherapy: A meta-analysis. *Journal of Consulting and Clinical Psychology, 59*(5), 704–714.

Taverna, C. (2016). *An evaluative study on the effects of support groups on the long-term outcomes in bariatric surgery patients.* Unpublished paper presented in a course at the University of North Carolina Wilmington, Wilmington.

Thyer, B. A., & Pignotti, M. G. (2015). *Science and pseudoscience in social work practice.* New York, NY: Springer.

Tolin, D. F. (2010). Is cognitive–behavioral therapy more effective than other therapies? A meta-analytic review. *Clinical Psychology Review, 30*, 710–720.

Totty, L. M., Rothery, M. A., & Grinnell, R. M. (1996). *Qualitative research for social workers.* Boston, MA: Allyn & Bacon.

Toussi, R. (2009). Pre- and post-surgery behavioral compliance, patient health and post bariatric surgical weight loss. *Obesity, 17*(5), 996–1002.

Tryon, G. S., & Winograd, G. (2011). Goal consensus and collaboration. In J. C. Norcross (Ed.), *Psychotherapy relationships that work: Evidence-based responsiveness* (2nd ed., pp. 153–167). New York, NY: Oxford University Press.

Tufford, L., & Newman, P. (2012). Bracketing in qualitative research. *Qualitative Social Work, 11,* 80–96.

University of Southern California Libraries Research Guides. (n.d.). *Organizing your social science research paper: Qualitative methods.* Retrieved from http://libguides.usc.edu/writingguide/qualitative

U.S. Department of Health and Human Services, Administration for Children and Families, Administration on Children, Youth and Families Children's Bureau. (2007). *Child maltreatment 2005.* Washington, DC: Government Printing Office. Retrieved from https://www.acf.hhs.gov/sites/default/files/cb/cm05.pdf

U.S. Department of Health and Human Services, Centers for Disease Control and Prevention. (2010). *Increasing questionnaire response rates* (Evaluation briefs, No 21). Retrieved from https://www.cdc.gov/healthyyouth/evaluation/pdf/brief21.pdf

Visser, M., Leentiens, A. F., Marinus, J., Stiggelbout, A. M., & van Hilten, J. J. (2006). Reliability and validity of the Beck Depression Inventory in patients with Parkinson's disease. *Journal of Movement Disorders, 21*(5), 668–672.

Wampold, B. E. (2001). *The great psychotherapy debate: Model, methods, and findings.* Mahwah, NJ: Lawrence Erlbaum.

Wampold, B. E., & Imel, Z. E. (2015). *The great psychotherapy debate* (2nd ed.). New York, NY: Routledge.

Wamser-Nanney, R., Chesher, R. E. (2018). Trauma characteristics and sleep impairment among trauma-exposed children. *Child Neglect and Abuse, 76,* 469-479.

Watson, D., O'Hara, M. W., & Stuart, S. (2008). Hierarchical structures of affect and psychopathology and their implications for the classification of emotional disorders. *Anxiety and Depression,* 25, 282–288.

Wilson, K., Mottram, P. G., & Vassilas, C. (2008). Psychotherapeutic treatments for older depressed people. *Cochrane Database of Systematic Reviews,* (1), CD004853. doi:10.1002/14651858.CD004853.pub2

Yin, R. K. (1984). *Case study research: Design and methods.* Beverly Hills, CA: Sage.

Yin, R. K. (2014). *Case study research: Design and methods* (5th ed.). Thousand Oaks, CA: Sage.

York, R. O. (1997). *Building basic competencies in social work research.* Boston, MA: Allyn & Bacon.

York, R. O. (2009). *Evaluating social work practice.* Boston, MA: Pearson.

York, R. O. (2015). Review of *The Great Psychotherapy Debate,* 2nd ed. *Research on Social Work Practice, 25*(5), 635–636.

York, R. O. (1987). Sex-role stereotypes about social work administration. *Journal of Sociology and Social Welfare, 14*(3), 87–104.

York, R. O., Henley, H. C., & Gamble, D. N. (1985). *Strategies for reducing barriers to female advancement in social work administration.* Paper presented at the Annual Program Meeting, Council on Social Work Education, Washington, DC.

York, R. O., Henley, H. C., & Gamble, D. N. (1987). Sexual discrimination in social work: Is it salary or advancement? *Social Work, 32*(4), 336–340.

Zwi, M., Jones, H., Thorgaard, C., York, A., & Dennis, J. A. (2012). Parent training interventions for attention deficit hyperactivity disorder. *Campbell Systematic Review,* (12), CD003018. doi:10.1002/14651858.CD003018.pub3

INDEX